T0390986

CULTURAL TRANSMISSION

Cultural Transmission discusses psychological, developmental, social, and methodological research on how cultural information is socially transmitted from one
generation to the next within families. Studying processes of cultural transmission
may help analyze the continuity or change of cultures, including those that have to
cope with migration or the collapse of a political system. An evolutionary perspective is elaborated in the first part of the book; the second part takes a cross-cultural
perspective by presenting international research on development and intergenerational relations in the family; and the third part provides intracultural analyses
of mechanisms and methodological aspects of cultural transmission. Consisting of contributions by experts in the field, this state-of-the-art source book is
intended for anyone with interests in cultural maintenance and change – especially
researchers and teachers in disciplines such as psychology, social and behavioral
sciences, and education – and for applied professionals in culture management
and family counseling, as well as professionals involved with migrants.

Ute Schönpflug teaches at Free University of Berlin's Department of Psychology
and is an adjunct member of the Institute of Cognitive Science at the University of
Colorado. She is also Associate Editor of the *Journal of Cross-Cultural Psychology*
and author and co-author of several textbooks on psychology.

CULTURE AND PSYCHOLOGY

Series Editor
David Matsumoto, *San Francisco State University*

As an increasing number of social scientists come to recognize the pervasive influence of culture on individual human behavior, it has become imperative for culture to be included as an important variable in all aspects of psychological research, theory, and practice. Culture and Psychology is an evolving series of works that brings the study of culture and psychology into a single, unified concept.

Ute Schönpflug, *Cultural Transmission*

Evert van de Vliert, *Climate, Affluence, and Culture*

Cultural Transmission

PSYCHOLOGICAL, DEVELOPMENTAL, SOCIAL, AND METHODOLOGICAL ASPECTS

Edited by

Ute Schönpflug
Free University of Berlin

CAMBRIDGE UNIVERSITY PRESS

CAMBRIDGE UNIVERSITY PRESS
Cambridge, New York, Melbourne, Madrid, Cape Town, Singapore,
São Paulo, Delhi, Dubai, Tokyo, Mexico City

Cambridge University Press
The Edinburgh Building, Cambridge CB2 8RU, UK

Published in the United States of America by Cambridge University Press, New York

www.cambridge.org
Information on this title: www.cambridge.org/9780521880435

© Cambridge University Press 2009

First published 2009

A catalogue record for this publication is available from the British Library

Library of Congress Cataloguing in Publication Data

Cultural transmission : psychological, developmental, social, and methodological aspects /
edited by Ute Schönpflug.
    p. cm. - (Culture and psychology)
Includes index.
ISBN 978-0-521-88043-5 (hardback) - ISBN 978-0-521-70657-5 (pbk.)   1. Socialization.
2. Ethnopsychology.   3. Cognition and culture.   4. Learning - Social aspects.   5. Learning,
Psychology of.   I. Schönpflug, Ute, 1940-   II. Title.   III. Series.
GN510.C83   2008
303.3'2-dc22   2008029336

ISBN 978-0-521-88043-5 Hardback
ISBN 978-0-521-70657-5 Paperback

CONTENTS

Foreword   *page* xi
  David Matsumoto

Contributors   xv

1. Introduction to Cultural Transmission: Psychological,
   Developmental, Social, and Methodological Aspects   1

2. Theory and Research in Cultural Transmission:
   A Short History   9
   Ute Schönpflug

PART ONE: EVOLUTIONARY PERSPECTIVE

3. Cultural Transmission: A View from Chimpanzees and
   Human Infants   33
   Michael Tomasello

4. Transmission, Self-Organization, and the Emergence
   of Language: A Dynamic Systems Point of View   48
   Paul van Geert

5. Relationship-Specific Intergenerational Family Ties:
   An Evolutionary Approach to the Structure of
   Cultural Transmission   70
   Harald A. Euler, Sabine Hoier, and Percy A. Rohde

PART TWO: CROSS-CULTURAL PERSPECTIVE

6. An Ecocultural Perspective on Cultural Transmission:
   The Family across Cultures   95
   John W. Berry and James Georgas

7. Intergenerational Relations and Cultural Transmission   126
   Gisela Trommsdorff

8. Intergenerational Transmission, Social Capital,
   and Interethnic Contact in Immigrant Families   161
   Bernhard Nauck

9. Developmental Processes Related to Intergenerational
   Transmission of Culture: Growing Up with Two Cultures   185
   Amado M. Padilla

10. The Transmission Process: Mechanisms and Contexts   212
    Ute Schönpflug and Ludwig Bilz

11. Accounting for Parent–Child Value Congruence:
    Theoretical Considerations and Empirical Evidence   240
    Ariel Knafo and Shalom H. Schwartz

12. Culture, Migration, and Family-Value Socialization:
    A Theoretical Model and Empirical Investigation with
    Russian-Immigrant Youth in Israel   269
    Ariel Knafo, Avi Assor, Shalom H. Schwartz, and Limor David

13. Immigrant Parents' Age Expectations for the
    Development of Their Adolescent Offspring:
    Transmission Effects and Changes after Immigration   297
    Eva Schmitt-Rodermund and Rainer K. Silbereisen

PART THREE: INTRACULTURAL VARIATIONS

14. Intergenerational Transmission of Moral Capital across
    the Family Life Course   317
    Merril Silverstein and Stephen J. Conroy

15. Similarity of Life Goals in the Family: A Three-Generation Study   338
    Alexander Grob, Wibke Weisheit, and Veronica Gomez

16. The Intergenerational Transmission of Xenophobia and
    Rightism in East Germany   370
    Bernd Six, Kristina Geppert, and Ute Schönpflug

17. Intergenerational Transmission of Violence   391
    Haci-Halil Uslucan and Urs Fuhrer

18. "Don't Trust Anyone over 25": Youth Centrism,
    Intergenerational Transmission of Political Orientations,
    and Cultural Change   419
    *Tom F. M. ter Bogt, Wim M. J. Meeus, Quinten A. W. Raaijmakers,
    Frits van Wel, and Wilma A. M. Vollebergh*

19. Value Transmission and *Zeitgeist* Revisited 441
    Klaus Boehnke, Andreas Hadjar, and Dirk Baier

20. Epilogue: Toward a Model of Cultural Transmission 460
    Ute Schönpflug

Index 479

FOREWORD

Although cross-cultural studies in psychology have existed for more than 100 years, it has only been in the past decade or two that contemporary, mainstream psychology has embraced the importance of culture as a significant influence on psychological processes. In the past two decades, we have gained much knowledge and improved our understanding of the nature, contents, and functions of culture as a macrosocial variable and of its relationship to behavior on the individual level. At a time when more and more of psychology is looking inward and at the micro-level building blocks of behavior in neurons, neurochemicals, and brain processes, the study of culture and its relationship with psychology is refreshing as it looks outward, beyond the individual, into groups and contexts to find frameworks and platforms for understanding human behavior.

This work is still in process, however, and one of the major problems that psychologists doing work involving cultures face entails how to link individual-level human behavior with cultural-level phenomena. Indeed, the field is still plagued by studies dominated by quasi-experimental designs, in which differences are observed across supposed cultural groups and researchers interpret the source of these differences as cultural with little or no empirical justification (Matsumoto & Yoo, 2006). In fact, many researchers go beyond making these ecological fallacies (Campbell, 1961) and even attribute causal mechanisms to culture from such data, interpreting that culture "caused" the differences observed or that their data highlighted "cultural influences on" psychological processes. (Matsumoto and Yoo [2006] called these kinds of mistaken attributions "cultural attribution fallacies.")

It is in this important gap in our theoretical conceptualizations and empirical approaches that work on cultural transmission makes a strong contribution. Examining the ways in which the contents of culture – explicit and implicit, objective and subjective – are transmitted to members of a cultural group, studies of cultural transmission ultimately aim to forge those linkages between culture as a macro-level, social construct and individual-level psychological processes that many researchers take for granted or blatantly ignore. By understanding those linkages, cultural-transmission researchers are able to highlight how the contents of culture are translated and communicated, highlighting the close bonds that are formed between individuals and the societies and cultures in which they live.

This edited book, *Cultural Transmission: Psychological, Developmental, Social, and Methodological Aspects*, is the first volume published in the series titled "Psychology and Culture." The focus of this series is the impact of culture on a wide variety of psychological processes. This book highlights the major contributions that this effort has made to date. Schönpflug has assembled the world's foremost researchers in the area of cultural transmission, each of whom has brought to bear the state-of-the-art thinking and research in his or her respective area. Collectively, this volume amasses the amazing amount of work that has been accomplished in the field and highlights many of the significant contributions to our understanding of this important topic to date. This work describes the contents and processes of culture as a uniquely human product; the direction in which transmission occurs – vertically, horizontally, and obliquely; and its manifold ways of spreading out. Because of this work, we can discard primitive notions of cultural transmission as being primarily vertical and unidirectional (e.g., parent to child) and understand transmission as occurring within families, peers, and institutions – and going in both directions.

The work in this volume also shows that cultural transmission is selective: not all of the contents of culture are transmitted to all cultural members. This important concept provides the basis for understanding individual differences as well as cultural fluidity, both clearly important topics in the study of culture and psychology. The work emphasizes not only what is being transmitted but also how and why – that is, allowing for survival mechanisms and ways of being to "rachet up" in each successive generation, ensuring not only the survival of the human species but also its flourishing.

By presenting the major contributions that this work on cultural transmission has made to psychology in recent years, the volume also takes a thorough, objective look at what is missing – the gaps in our knowledge – and the limitations in current research approaches to transmission. The final chapter provides readers with a road map of the future, one that should forge new ways to understand transmission as well as new ways to study it.

In my opinion, no serious student of culture and its relationship with psychological processes should be without a strong, solid foundation in understanding the nature of cultural transmission, because this is precisely the work that allows us to make those precious links between culture and psychology. Without those links, our understanding of the relationship between culture and psychology is doomed to be confined by the inherent limitations of doing research without incorporating cultural-context variables (Poortinga, 1990) or understanding the nature, processes, and mechanisms of cultural transmission. This volume should be read by all serious students of culture.

David Matsumoto
San Francisco, CA, USA
July 2008

REFERENCES

Campbell, D. T. (1961). The mutual methodological relevance of anthropology and psychology. In F. L. Hsu (Ed.), *Psychological anthropology* (pp. 333–352). Homewood, IL: Dorsey.

Matsumoto, D., & Yoo, S. H. (2006). Toward a new generation of cross-cultural research. *Perspectives on Psychological Science, 1*(3), 234–250.

Poortinga, Y. H. (1990). Towards a conceptualization of culture for psychology? *Cross-Cultural Psychology Bulletin, 24,* 2–10.

CONTRIBUTORS

AVI ASSOR is Associate Professor and head of the educational psychology program at Ben Gurion University (Israel). His research focuses on processes affecting children's autonomous internalization of values endorsed by parents and educators. He is also involved in the development and assessment of school reforms based mainly on self-determination theory.

DIRK BAIER is currently Research Associate at the Criminological Research Institute in Hannover (Germany), where he organizes a large youth survey on violence. His main interests are in deviance, right-wing extremism, and youth sociology.

JOHN W. BERRY is Professor Emeritus of Psychology at Queen's University (Canada). He obtained his Ph.D. at the University of Edinburgh (Scotland) and has received honorary doctorates from the University of Athens (Greece) and Université de Genève (Switzerland). He has published more than 30 books in the areas of cross-cultural, social, and cognitive psychology. His main research interests are in the areas of acculturation and intercultural relationships, with an emphasis on applications to immigration, educational, and health policy.

LUDWIG BILZ is Assistant Professor at the Faculty of Educational Science of the Technical University of Dresden (Germany). His research interests are in health psychology and educational psychology.

KLAUS BOEHNKE is Professor of Social Science Methodology at the International University, Bremen (Germany). He is the current Secretary General of the International Association for Cross-Cultural Psychology. His research interests are youth research and methodology. He also actively pursues activities in peace psychology.

STEPHEN J. CONROY is currently Associate Professor of Economics at the University of San Diego (United States). He also completed a National Institute on Aging postdoctoral research traineeship in gerontology. His multidisciplinary research has appeared in a variety of well-known venues.

LIMOR DAVID was a student at the Open University (Israel). Her research focuses on cross-cultural psychological aspects of migration. She is now engaged in educational activities.

HARALD A. EULER received his Ph.D. from Washington State University. Since 1974, he has been Professor of Psychology at the University of Kassel (Germany). His current research interests include the evolutionary psychology of family relations, children, and women from nontraditional families.

URS FUHRER is Professor of Developmental and Educational Psychology at the Otto-von-Guericke-University, Magdeburg (Germany). His main research focuses on the relationship between parenting and child development within the family and cultural context. In addition, his research involves mediational theories of mind, with a special interest in identity formation.

JAMES GEORGAS is Emeritus Professor of Psychology at the University of Athens (Greece). He is President of the International Association for Cross-Cultural Psychology and a member of the executive boards of several international psychological associations. His current research interests are in family across cultures, theory and methodology in cross-cultural research, construction of psychometric tests, and attitudes and values.

KRISTINA GEPPERT received her M.A. in psychology from Martin Luther University, Halle-Wittenberg (Germany). Her interests are in workplace, organizational, and educational psychology.

VERONICA GOMEZ is a Ph.D. student in personality and developmental psychology at the University of Basel (Switzerland). Her research interests involve self-regulation across the life span with a focus on cohort-specific personality processes and subjective well-being across cultures.

ALEXANDER GROB is trained in developmental and clinical psychology. Since 2005, he has been Professor of Personality and Developmental Psychology at the University of Basel (Switzerland). His research interests focus on transgenerational processes in the family and personality development across the life span, as well as structure and antecedents of life events.

ANDREAS HADJAR is research associate in an internationally comparative project on dominance ideologies among youth and lecturer at the Department of Sociology of Chemnitz University of Technology (Germany), where he also received his Ph.D. in sociology in 2003. His research interests encompass a broad range of topics in political sociology, family sociology, and sociology of education.

SABINE HOIER received her M.A. in biology and sociology from the University of Kassel (Germany) and is now Assistant Professor at the same university. Her research interests include human sperm competition, family relations, children, and women from nontraditional families.

ARIEL KNAFO is Assistant Professor of Psychology at The Hebrew University of Jerusalem (Israel). He completed his Ph.D. in intergenerational value transmission at The Hebrew University of Jerusalem. His research projects focus on adolescents' values and behaviors (e.g., aggression and substance abuse) and on the influence of genetics and the environment on the development of prosocial behavior and values in adults and children.

WIM M. J. MEEUS is Professor of Adolescent Psychology at Utrecht University (the Netherlands). He has published on adolescent moral development, political attitudes, and missing-data treatment.

BERNHARD NAUCK is Professor of Sociology at Chemnitz University of Technology (Germany). His main areas of interest are family population, life course, and migration, with special emphasis on cross-cultural comparisons. He is the author of some of the reports for the German government regarding the situation of families and migrants in Germany.

AMADO M. PADILLA is currently Professor of Educational Psychology at Stanford University and a Fellow of the American Psychological Association (United States). He has published extensively on ethnic identity, acculturation, bilingualism, and education of immigrant students. He is the founding editor of the *Hispanic Journal of Behavioral Sciences*.

QUINTEN A. W. RAAIJMAKERS is Senior Researcher at Utrecht University (the Netherlands). He has published on adolescent moral development, political attitudes, and missing-data treatment.

PERCY A. ROHDE received his Ph.D. in biology from the University of Kassel (Germany). He published in the field of sexual selection and parental care in birds and has more recently turned to human evolutionary psychology. His research interests include sexual selection, family relations, and parental care.

EVA SCHMITT-RODERMUND is Director of the Division for Academic and Student Affairs at the University of Jena (Germany). Her research interests concern human development across the life span, with an emphasis on adolescence. Her main research interests focus on the acculturation of immigrants and career development.

UTE SCHÖNPFLUG was Professor of Developmental Psychology at Martin Luther University, Halle-Wittenberg (Germany), until 2002. She is an adjunct member of the Institute of Cognitive Science in Boulder, Colorado (United States) and teaches at Free University of Berlin (Germany). Her research interests are in the areas of cultural transmission, bilingual language development, and text processing.

SHALOM H. SCHWARTZ is Emeritus Professor of the Leon and Clara Snyderman Chair of Psychology at The Hebrew University of Jerusalem (Israel). He started his academic career in the United States. Since 1979, he has taught in Israel, where his research interests have included helping behavior, intergroup conflict, and basic human values. He coordinates an international project in more than 60 countries that is studying the antecedents and consequences of individual differences in value priorities and the relations of cultural dimensions of values to societal policies and characteristics.

RAINER K. SILBEREISEN is Professor and Chair of Developmental Psychology at the University of Jena (Germany) and Adjunct Professor of Human Development and Family Studies at Pennsylvania State University (United States). He is Director of the Center for Applied Developmental Science in Jena. His research is mainly on behavioral development across the life span, with emphasis on cross-national differences and the role of social change.

MERRIL SILVERSTEIN is Professor of Gerontology and Sociology at the University of Southern California (United States). His research focuses on aging within the context of family life, including such issues as intergenerational transfers and transmission, grandparenting, migration, and public policy toward caregiving families. He currently serves as Principal Investigator of the Longitudinal Study of Generations and Mental Health. International projects include a study of aging families in rural China.

BERND SIX is Professor of Social and Organizational Psychology at Martin Luther University in Halle-Wittenberg (Germany). His research interests in social psychology involve the relationship of attitudes and behaviors, conditional analysis of organ donation in Germany and Japan, stereotypes and prejudices targeting minorities, differences between groups of foreigners, and East–West differences in Germany.

TOM F. M. TER BOGT is Professor of Pop Music and Popular Culture at the University of Amsterdam (the Netherlands). He has published on Protestant work ethic, leisure time, substance use, pop music, and popular culture. He produced a television series on the history of youth culture in the Netherlands.

MICHAEL TOMASELLO taught at Emory University and worked at the Yerkes Primate Center in the United States for several years. He is now Codirector of the Max Planck Institute for Evolutionary Anthropology in Leipzig (Germany). His research interests focus on the processes of social cognition, social learning, and communication in human children and great apes.

GISELA TROMMSDORFF is Professor of Developmental Psychology and Cross-Cultural Psychology at the University of Konstanz (Germany). Among her many international positions in scientific organizations, she holds the position of vice president of the German-Japanese Society for Social Sciences. Her main interests involve child–parent relationships, values of children, development of emotions, prosocial behavior, and control orientations.

HACI-HALIL USLUCAN is Assistant Professor in the Department of Developmental and Educational Psychology at Otto-von-Guericke-University, Magdeburg (Germany). His main research focuses on juvenile violence, acculturation problems of migrants, and child–parent relationships in cultural contexts. He teaches developmental psychology, educational psychology, and applied cultural psychology.

PAUL VAN GEERT is Professor of Developmental Psychology at the University of Groningen (the Netherlands) and former Fellow of the Center of Advanced Studies in the Behavioral Sciences. His main interest lies in the application of dynamic systems thinking to modeling and studying development. Originally working in the field of early language development, he has recently extended his interest to a dynamic approach of social development and learning in childhood and adolescence.

FRITS VAN WEL is Senior Researcher at Utrecht University (the Netherlands). His publications are in the field of culture, care, and welfare, in general, and parent centrism and adolescent media use, in particular.

WILMA A. M. VOLLEBERGH is Professor of Pedagogy at the University of Nijmegen (the Netherlands) and Director of the research program on developmental psychopathology at the Trimbos Institute, the Netherlands Institute on Mental Health and Addiction. She has published on political attitudes and adolescent mental health.

WIBKE WEISHEIT completed her Ph.D. at the Department of Personality Psychology, Individual Differences and Assessment at the University of Bern (Switzerland). Her research interests focus on transgenerational processes in the family, especially with respect to life goals, subjective well-being, and personality traits, as well as on personality development across the life span.

1

Introduction to Cultural Transmission: Psychological, Developmental, Social, and Methodological Aspects

UTE SCHÖNPFLUG

Every view of life that becomes extinct, every culture that disappears, diminishes a possibility of life.
(Octavio Paz, 1978, Nobel Prize winner)

INTRODUCTION

The topic of cultural transmission – according to its current meaning of a transfer process carrying cultural information from one generation to the next, and from one group to the next – has received increasing interest in many disciplines. This volume attempts to impart perspectives on cultural transmission, what is known and – more important for future research – which issues still have to be clarified. The topic has been elaborated and refined in various academic contexts in Europe and the United States. This first chapter provides an outline of the history of prominent issues of cultural transmission. This chapter and the following contributions may serve as sources for the various perspectives outlined in the literature.

This volume is based on a special issue of the *Journal of Cross-Cultural Psychology* published in 2001. Some of the authors were already included in the special issue, and all of those asked agreed to elaborate on their contributions for chapters of this edited book. All contributors felt that the topic called for more theory, more data, and more stringent interpretations. However, other contributions also were included to extend the range of perspectives and the range of countries with their particular cultural variations. More specific, the extensions were oriented toward providing more contents, more contexts, and more mechanisms of transmission, as well as including the full range of the life span of the transmitters and the transmittees, with additional situational and dispositional characteristics of both.

This volume focuses on the contributions of psychologists and social scientists. Three contributions from multidisciplinary evolutionary psychologists whose interests extend to evolutionary biology and anthropology (Tomasello, this volume) and to sociological and psychological issues (Euler, Hoier, & Rohde; van Geert, this volume) convey insights to the many links of cultural transmission with biological evolutionary theory and its roots therein. Other contributions demonstrate that it is useful to forgo the analysis of historical roots and focus instead on issues of cultural transmission from a social scientific or psychological perspective (see Part II). Even when the research is located within one culture, we are able to gain insight to a specific mechanism or content of transmission, or the role of a specific characteristic of either the transmitter or the transmittee (see Part III).

Cultural transmission is a universal process. We need to know, however, whether the mechanisms and contents involved in the process are also universal. We need to know whether the function of cultural transmission to maintain culture over time and space may be fulfilled by the contents and mechanisms identified. We hope the information provided is transmitted to students, readers, researchers, and theorists and leads to more research and theorizing. The contributors hope that the impact of their insight to the cultural transmission process helps all involved to acquire better judgment and more adequate measures to intensify cultural transmission when and where it is wanted and to constrain it when and where it is not desirable. Control of cultural transmission in societies and in terms of their politics can already be observed now, but another major aim of this volume is to deepen and extend insight to the benefits and the dangers involved in such control.

1.0. CULTURAL TRANSMISSION: A MULTIDISCIPLINARY RESEARCH FIELD

Cultural persistence is essentially a question of transmission, the passing on of information from individual to individual or from groups to other groups. Theoretical conceptualizations of cultural transmission come from various disciplines. The roots of thinking about cultural transmission as opposed to genetic transmission are located in biology. The biologists Cavalli-Sforza and Feldman (1981) wrote a seminal paper on the specific phenomena related to cultural as opposed to biological transmission. The term *cultural* may apply to traits that are acquired by any process of nongenetic transmission, be it by imprinting, conditioning, observation, imitation, or as a result of direct teaching. Cavalli-Sforza and Feldman pointed out that genetic transmission may not be the only source for parent–offspring biological similarity. Social orientations, skills, and accumulated knowledge are also similar in parent–offspring dyads and – as far as today's scientific insights hold – are not tied to genes. Hence, other mechanisms of transmission must be found to explain this kind of social or psychological similarity between successive generations.

What may be unique to mankind is the capacity to transmit knowledge explicitly to other individuals in space and time by means of such devices as deliberate teaching through shaping the behavior of other individuals (see Tomasello, this volume). Various human behaviors seem to rely on just such explicit social-learning processes and, in fact, many behavioral acquisitions simply would not be possible without them.

Cultural anthropology generally assumes a commonsense pretheoretical view of the acquisition of culture, which Boyer (1994) calls the theory of "exhaustive cultural transmission." This conception of cultural acquisition is cognitive. The main point is that people brought up in a culture are given a ready-made conceptual scheme, which is absorbed (as it were) in a mysterious, *passive* way that is never described. Cultural anthropologists tend to think that the way in which children gradually acquire adult cultural competence, in most cognitive domains, is mainly driven by experience. Van Geert (this volume) demonstrates that language transmission may constitute such a case. However, Boyer contradicts this conception of cultural acquisition, arguing that cultural representations are underdetermined by cultural transmission because they are implicit, incomplete, and inconsistent (see also Knafo & Schwartz, this volume). It may be concluded that not all cultural information is transmittable or is transmitted and that individuals work with the same implicit assumptions because they are equipped with the same intuitive principles emerging from their general inferential capacities. In this case, cultural transmission simply provides explicit cues, which are likely to trigger in most subjects roughly similar spontaneous inferences.

Boyd and Richerson (1985) understand culture as the transmission of knowledge, values, and other factors that influence behavior from one generation to the next. Some findings suggest that vertical (i.e., parent–offspring) as opposed to horizontal (i.e., peer) transmission serves the function of spreading less primitive cultural units and that horizontally transmitted traits are advantageous in rapidly changing, spatially heterogeneous environments. Evolutionary intergenerational thinking extends this notion by looking at investments in progeny over more than one subsequent generation. These vertical investments of, for instance, grandparents to grandchildren (Euler, Hoier, & Rohde, this volume) must further slow down the pace of cultural change via transmission.

Parent–offspring transmission does not necessarily corroborate adaptation to variable environments. The capacity for cultural transmission probably has complex effects on the rate of genetic evolution. More recently, sociobiological and anthropological approaches (Cronk, 1995; Tooby & Cosmides, 1991) have been integrated. Culture may lead not only to direct genetic assimilation, which has only just begun to be understood, but may also increase the likelihood of group selection, which is also regarded as a mechanism of genetic assimilation. Cronk distinguishes "transmitted" culture from other aspects of culture: The transmitted culture refers to the spreading of mental representations from one person to the next. Other aspects of culture might be innovations that emerge in one epoch or generation and are forgotten in the next.

The limits of cultural transmission involve ethnocultural variability, which, like biological variability, promotes and sustains ways of life. Insofar as we insist on homogeneity, we are closing off ourselves from options and alternatives that are needed. Adaptive evolution requires variability because variability requires and creates the differences necessary for adaptation to changing environmental demands. The "unenlightened society" continues to insist on "cultural homogeneity" and strict reproductive transmission; in so doing, it fosters its own demise. The "enlightened society" acknowledges and promotes "diversity" and, in this way, encourages its own survival.

Sociologists look at transmission issues from a cultural-capital point of view. Brinton (1988) suggested that education and family comprise a conjoint system of human development. She sees this system as having a social-institutional dimension and a familial dimension of exchanges and investments. Bourdieu's (1984) notion of cultural capital suggested a general description of what is transmitted. In many contexts, families and schools work in concert to ensure the educational advantages of some groups, whereas the disadvantaged position of other groups remains. A conjoint system of cultural-capital transmission requires us to consider the complex relationships among families, school types, educational experiences, and educational outcomes (Persell, Catsambis, & Cookson, 1992).

Nauck (this volume) emphasizes that the transmission of cultural capital is a special process when it takes place in a culture-contact situation. In addition, sociological analyses point out that the separation of intergenerational transmission results from societal changes in the same content area is usually neglected (Boehnke, Hadjar, & Baier, this volume). Parent and offspring similarity is influenced to a certain extent by the *zeitgeist* of the historical epoch in which they are living, as well as by transmission processes.

This volume arises from the conviction that cross-cultural psychology may contribute to theory and empirical evidence in the domain of cultural transmission. The psychological contributions to this volume are predominantly concerned with mechanisms that affect the extent and selectivity of transmission (e.g., the "transmission belts"; see Schönpflug & Bilz, this volume; see also Six, Geppert, & Schönpflug, this volume) and the mediation through parental goal-setting.

2.0. THE CARRIERS OF TRANSMISSION

Different social systems or cultures weigh various possible transmitters or models in the transmission process differentially: mother, father, teacher, and peers differ in their importance for the cultural transmission of certain behaviors or traits. Homogeneity of transmitters with reference to the transmitted contents ensures the greatest transmission effects. Knafo and Schwartz (this volume) show that the similarity between generations of migrants is less than that in families of the receiving society, due to perceived inconsistencies and uncertainty of orientation of the transmitting parents. Ter Bogt, Meeus, Raaijsmakers, van Wel, and Vollebergh (this volume) demonstrate that the recipient of the transmission, the offspring generation, has a potent selective filter, enhancing transmission from the parent generation, which is non–youth centrist or adult-oriented. Different cultural contexts also allow for either one or more than one model for copying. An issue still to be studied is the choice of a model when cultural context does not constrain the number of models. This is certainly the case for horizontal (i.e., peer) and oblique (i.e., teacher/mentor) transmission and less so for vertical (i.e., parent–offspring) transmission.

3.0. THE CONTENTS OF TRANSMISSION

All important theoretical approaches of cultural transmission (Boyd & Richerson, 1985; Cavalli-Sforza & Feldman, 1981) state evidence that the three "channels" or directions of transmission transport different transmission contents: *Vertical transmission* includes factors such as personality traits, cognitive development, attitudes, attainments, educational and occupational status, patterns of upward/downward mobility, sex-role conceptions, sexual activity, attitudes toward feminism, political beliefs and activities, religious beliefs, dietary habits, legal and illegal drug abuse, phobias, self-esteem, and language and linguistic usage. *Horizontally* and *obliquely* transmitted traits include attitudes; career and social mobility; aspirations; sex role and sexual behavior; adolescent behavior; aggressive behavior; altruistic behavior; morals; social values; conformity; language and dialect; technological innovations; clothing fashions; consumer behavior; and children's games, rituals, stories, and rhymes. As may be seen from these lists, many traits are transmitted either way. Other traits follow a dual-inheritance model: *Genetically* and *culturally* transmitted traits include handedness, cerebral dominance, intelligence, and possibly religious and political beliefs (Laland, 1993). The contributions in this volume focus mainly on values as a central content of transmission (Cavalli-Sforza, 1993; see also Knafo & Schwartz; Knafo, Assor, Schwartz, & David; and Boehnke, Hadjar, & Baier, this volume).

4.0. THE MECHANISM OF THE TRANSMISSION PROCESS

The first considerations in the process of transmission lead us to postulate that it is a two-stage process: The first stage is awareness of the information to be transmitted, and the second is acceptance of it. The two stages are only distinguishable when there is a choice to accept or not to accept. A further complication that strengthens the confounding of awareness and acceptance is the possible existence of spontaneous tendencies or drives to teach and thus impart knowledge. Kuczynski, Marshall, and Schell (1997) suggested externalization attempts on the side of the transmitter and internalization on the side of the receiver as two main component mechanisms of the transmission process. In the transmission process, both the teaching and the learning may be deeply motivated. Which parameters determine the transmission dynamics? Which transmission belts are most effective with given carriers, contents, and contexts of transmission? Do different social-learning mechanisms have different transmission dynamics? Answers to these questions, like our understanding of the transmission process, are still rudimentary. In this volume, the chapters by Berry and Georgas; Knafo and Schwartz; Knafo, Assor, Schwartz, and David; Nauck; Schönpflug and Bilz; Six, Geppert, and Schönpflug; Trommsdorff; and Uslucan and Fuhrer contribute essential new answers to these fundamental questions.

5.0. DEVELOPMENTAL PERSPECTIVE ON TRANSMISSION

The effects of transmission mechanisms may be confounded with developmental phenomena – namely, the existence of biologically founded "critical periods" – such as are known, for example, in the learning of the pronunciation of a language. However, there probably exists a host of other age-dependent sensitivities in acquiring specific behaviors or cognitions via transmission.

Conversely, the mode of transmission may be age-specific because of normative developmental transitions in the sociocultural context: Obligatory full-day schooling, for instance, implies that children are among their peers for several hours during the day. This is a favorable condition for horizontal transmission and emerging youth centrism counteracting vertical parent–offspring transmission. Cross-cultural studies may be especially useful in exhibiting the variation of such life-cycle phenomena. Tomasello (this volume) looks at the ontogeny of human cultural learning and compares it to primate social learning. Human children grow up in a cultural niche but need to have cognitive skills to utilize the preexisting cultural resources. Typically, these social skills begin to develop at the end of the first year of life, if Tomasello's criteria for cultural transmission are accepted. Silverstein and Conroy (this volume) take on a life-span view: Parents build early in the family life cycle a "support bank" – that is, a latent reserve of social capital by investing time, labor, and money in their children. This social capital is later drawn on in the form of social support from children when the parents develop age-related dependencies.

This volume shows diverse approaches to the study of cultural transmission. The various aspects presented contribute more to a complex theoretical model of transmission rather than being able to communicate final and perfectly consistent results. The chapters presented herein, however, reflect promising routes to further research. As with any edited volume, each chapter in this book is a coherent whole in its own right, such that it is not necessary to read the chapters in any specific order. Nevertheless, they do focus on somewhat different questions and it makes sense to combine them loosely together according to some broad organizational structure of three sections.

Part I is a collection of three studies and analyses that owe much to classical evolutionary theory and biology, as presented in the introductory chapter on the history of research and theorizing in the domain of cultural transmission.

Part II includes cross-cultural perspectives on cultural transmission, with all of the contributions focusing on vertical, intergenerational transmission in various cultural and national groups. Among them are immigrant populations with a special situation for cultural transmission because the culture transmitted is not the culture of the macrosocietal context. Part III emphasizes the importance of intracultural variations, including the comparison of the transmission between third and second generations and second and first generations. Nevertheless, smaller scale regional variations within one culture are also mentioned. The final two chapters deal with a crucial methodological issue inherent in all transmission research: In addition to the effect of the transmitter on the transmittee, a third factor – identified here as the *zeitgeist* – may influence both roles in the transmission process, thereby accounting for some part of the similarity between transmitter and transmittee. In the most extreme case, the similarity approaches a zero level when the *zeitgeist* factor is introduced into the analyses. The last chapter presents some afterthoughts that may be helpful in defining a valid model of cultural transmission, along with many allusions to issues that remain unresolved and that would be worthwhile to pursue in future research.

This book presents a set of theories, ideas, and research findings that reveals in detail the ways in which psychological processes influence the elements that constitute cultures. With a topic this large, no single volume can be entirely comprehensive; the tradeoff between breadth and depth is inevitable. Moreover, this volume is an attempt to balance the two, supported by the availability of qualified research, theories – and contributors.

REFERENCES

Bourdieu, P. (1984). *Distinction: A social critique of the judgment of taste.* Cambridge, MA: Harvard University Press.

Boyd, R., & Richerson, P. J. (1985). *Culture and the evolutionary process.* Chicago: University of Chicago Press.

Boyer, P. (1994). Cognitive constraints on cultural representations: Natural ontologies and religious ideas. In L. A. Hirschfeld & S. A. Gelma (Eds.), *Mapping the mind: Domain specificity in cognition and culture* (pp. 391–411). New York: Cambridge University Press.

Brinton, M. C. (1988). The social-institutional bases of gender stratification: Japan as an illustrative case. *American Journal of Sociology, 94,* 300–334.

Cavalli-Sforza, L. L. (1993). How are values transmitted? In M. Hechter, L. Nadd, & R. E. Michail (Eds.), *The origins of values* (pp. 305–315), Part III: *Biological perspectives.* New York: Aldine de Gruyter.

Cavalli-Sforza, L. L., & Feldman, M. W. (1981). *Cultural transmission and evolution: A quantitative approach.* Princeton, NJ: Princeton University Press.

Cronk, L. (1995). Is there a role for culture in human behavioral ecology? *Ethology and Sociobiology, 16,* 181–205.

Kuczynski, L., Marshall, S., & Schell, K. (1997). Value socialization in a bidirectional context. In L. Kuczynski & J. E. Grusec (Eds.), *Parenting and children's internalisation of values* (pp. 23–50). New York: John Wiley.

Laland, K. N. (1993). The mathematical modelling of human culture and its implications for psychology and the human sciences. *British Journal of Psychology, 84,* 145–169.

Paz, O. (1978). *The labyrinth of solitude.* New York: Grove Press.

Persell, C. H., Catsambis, S., & Cookson, P. W. (1992). Family background, school type, and college attendance: A conjoint system of cultural-capital transmission. *Journal of Research on Adolescence, 2*(1), 1–23.

Tooby, J., & Cosmides, L. (1991). The psychological foundations of culture. In J. Berkow & J. Tooby (Eds.), *The adapted mind: Evolutionary psychology and the generation of culture* (pp. 19–136). Oxford: Oxford University Press.

2

Theory and Research in Cultural Transmission: A Short History

UTE SCHÖNPFLUG

INTRODUCTION

Transmission may be understood as the deliberate or unintended transfer of information from a transmitter to a transmittee. The concept of *cultural transmission*, however, indicates the transmission of culture or cultural elements that are widely distributed: social orientations (e.g., values), skills (e.g., reading and writing), knowledge (e.g., the healing power of certain herbs), and behaviors (e.g., the exchange of rings in a wedding ceremony). The scope of this distribution defines the boundaries of the respective culture. The research traditions presented herein reveal that theorists have generally thought of cultural transmission as a process of replication of whatever is transmitted in another individual or in other groups. However, as pointed out by Reynolds (1981) (see also Henrich & Boyd, 2002), the replication has its limits. This debate is elaborated on throughout this chapter.

The transmission of culture is a necessary process to maintain culture; thus, it has always taken place, from ancient to newly developed cultures. In traditional, slowly changing societies, the transmission of culture is a common undertaking of the older generation applied to the younger generation. The mechanisms involved in the cultural transmission of either slowly or rapidly changing societies form the basis of various theories that have been developed in the history of transmission research.

The history of cultural transmission theories and research is characterized by interdisciplinary contributions. This chapter traces the origins and ramifications of theoretical approaches and looks at empirical evidence and counterevidence. Neither the literature cited nor even the many publications consulted in the course of compiling this chapter exhaustively cover the history of cultural psychology. The short history of cultural transmission presented here attempts to structure the contributions to theory and research over a span of 150 years.

1.0. EARLY THOUGHTS AND STUDIES ON CULTURAL TRANSMISSION

1.1. Neo-Lamarckism and the Inheritance of Acquired Traits

The roots of thinking on cultural transmission as opposed to genetic transmission are anchored in evolutionary biology and philosophy. Influenced by the controversial Lamarckian philosophy, which postulates the inheritance of acquired physical "characters" (de Lamarck, 1809), the zoological study of generations of diverse species showing individual environmentally induced organic changes revealed generally negative results: According to contemporaneous observations, environmental induction may not directly affect the living protoplasm or genes.

Decades after Darwin's influential writings, the transmission of environmental effects became a topic of discussion in 1913 in the *Philosophical Transactions of the Royal Society* (Agar & Kerr, 1913; Kerr, 1913). These biologists claimed that environmental conditions might affect the organism – in particular, the gonad of the F1 generation (i.e., parents). The developing gonad, with its affected protoplasm, develops into a new individual of the F2 generation (i.e., offspring), carrying changed soma. New metabolic substances in the F1 organism are passed on to the organism of the newly developing individual, which consequently shows the same variation as the parent, albeit removed from the inducing environment in question. These substances might be of such a nature as to stimulate the formation of antibodies, thus causing a reaction in a later generation.

In 1908, Hartog reviewed the controversial ideas of his time but claimed that even Darwin stressed the "Lamarckian factor" (Hartog, 1908). According to Hartog, his contemporary biologists believed in the genetic transmission of acquired mental traits. They used this mechanism to explain the phenomenon of "innate instincts." Spencer (1893a, 1893b) sparked a controversy regarding this issue together with the rigid (later) anti-Lamarckian biologist Weismann (Hartog, 1893). Hartog himself rejected the complex theory of Weismann and revealed himself to be a neo-Lamarckian.

Early thinking within the constraints of the knowledge of biology of the late 19th and early 20th centuries was rather ideological and not based on extensive empirical evidence. However, the usefulness of these early contributions for later theoretical developments becomes evident as the approaches of subsequent epochs are presented. Through these contributions, the issue of nongenetic or cultural transmission was born, which did not die out due to lack of interest.

1.2. Social Inheritance

The discussion regarding the plausibility of the Lamarckian hypothesis instigated thinking about *nongenetic* or *social inheritance*, terms that were sometimes used instead of *transmission*. These concepts not only indicated that there is another path of transmission in addition to genetic transmission but also extended the discourse to nonorganic features. The psychologist Thorndike elaborated on this idea, expressing his thoughts about the inheritance of mental traits, especially intelligence, and the interaction of education and predisposition to intellectual performance (Thorndike, 1903). By reporting decreasing twin correlations with age, he demonstrated that the environment seemed to have a growing influence on academic performance. However, the term *transmission* was not used.

Clapp (1894), a predecessor of Thorndike, complained about "the inadequacy of the transmission of learning" in the educational system of the eastern United States. He claimed that educational institutions should transmit to the student not only what has to be learned (i.e., necessary knowledge) but also the necessity of the individual's own creative and independent thinking and how to learn by one's own initiative. According to his view, German universities were already more advanced in this direction.

The sociologically inclined British philosopher, English, wrote a note on "social inheritance," or traditions that were passed on to the next generation and depended on the mother's family (English, 1919). English believed that the mother had a greater influence on the child than other socializing agents. A previous study on the same topic also focused on the role of social inheritance for "spiritual development" (Branford, 1913).

The term *social inheritance* emerged from the close relationship of early thinking on cultural transmission with genetics and evolutionary theory. Later, the term appeared only occasionally in biological and sociological writing (Diekmann & Jann, 2004); instead, the term *cultural transmission* was selected to express issues concerning the complementary relationship between genetic and cultural transmission.

2.0. THE SECOND PERIOD: 1950s, 1960s, AND 1970s

2.1. The Role of the Family in the Transmission Process

In this second period, social psychology gained a certain reputation with the writings of Allport (1954), who contended that children's identification with their parents moderates the intergenerational transmission of prejudice. His study used the basic methodological approach that is still common in the research domain of transmission: Parental and children's prejudice was measured to assess similarity, and the child's identification with the parents was introduced as a moderator variable. A classic result emerged: High-identifying children showed the greatest similarity with their parents. This type of thinking still prevails today in social psychological and developmental research on cultural transmission.

Rosen (1964) conducted an interview study 10 years later on value transmission and family structure between mothers and sons (8–14 years, $M = 11$ years). The value similarity between mothers and their sons was enhanced through early autonomy training and love-oriented techniques. Social class was found to be an influential factor, with greater value similarity in high-socioeconomic status

(SES) families compared to low-SES families, and the relationship between SES and value similarity remained valid even when the age of the child on receiving autonomy training was controlled. Family size was also discovered to be a decisive factor in creating value similarity. In small families, emotional closeness and interactional intensity is assumed to be greater because the parental hopes and expectations focus on the only child or the only two children of the family. In large families, the parents focus less on the emotions of the individual children. The presence of another sibling might act as an alternative love object, and other models could reduce the influence of the parent. In small (i.e., one or two children) and medium-sized families (i.e., three or four children), value similarity was higher than in families with more than four children, although the differences were not statistically significant. The relationship between age of independence mastery and family size was curvilinear: Small and large families trained for later mastery of independence more than medium-sized families. Unlike later studies (Cavalli-Sforza, Feldman, Chen, & Dornbusch, 1982; Schönpflug, 2001; Six, Geppert, & Schönpflug, this volume), Rosen (1964) found a greater value similarity between mothers and children who were the only males or firstborn sons. A further effect was also found: The mother's age differentiated between high- and low-value similarity in terms of its interaction with social class. In high- and medium-SES families, the age of the mother was not related to the value similarity between mother and son, whereas in lower-class families, value similarity was lower in families with younger mothers (up to 39 years) as compared to older mothers. Low SES coupled with high-value similarity in mother–son dyads tended to involve older mothers. In view of the finding that older mothers tend to use more positive emotional parenting strategies (also if they have a low-SES background), this age effect of mothers appears plausible. Indeed, this effect of the mother's age on the value similarity between mother and child was also found in Schönpflug and Bilz's studies (this volume), who used a regression analysis to estimate transmission coefficients.

In another interview study, Borke (1967) studied a three-generation upper-middle-class family, conducting interviews and observing interactions. The four variables that appeared to be significant for the transmission of parental interacting and relating patterns were ordinal position, husband–wife selection, cultural impact, and conscious and unconscious motives of individual members of the family.

In this second historical period, the social psychological studies based on the family were complemented by early macrosocial studies and analyses. They are presented selectively, merely to convey an impression of the various paths taken by approaches to cultural transmission.

2.2. The Role of the Social System in Intergenerational Attitude Change

Processes of institutionalization in a given society might provide adequate explanations of cultural persistence or continuity. Zucker (1977) argued that internalization, self-reward, or other intervening processes need not be present to ensure cultural persistence because social knowledge, once institutionalized, exists as a fact, as part of the objective reality, and can be transmitted directly on that basis. For highly institutionalized acts, it is sufficient for one person simply to tell another that this is how things are done – for instance, in a discussion group in which raising one's hand signals the desire to take one's turn. Individuals are motivated to comply because their actions and those of others in the system would otherwise not be understood. The fundamental process is one in which the moral of not interrupting becomes factual: When the social facts are not well established, their transmission is problematic and may well depend on a moral response to a specific situation. However, when social facts are well established, the moral character becomes less significant. Zucker (1977) identified three processes necessary for cultural persistence: (1) *transmission* from one generation to the next must occur, with the degree of generational uniformity directly related to the degree of institutionalization; (2) once transmission has taken place, *maintenance of the culture* must occur, with the degree of maintenance directly related to the degree of *institutionalization*; and (3) once maintenance has occurred, *cultural resistance* depends on the resistance to change, with the degree of resistance directly related to the degree of institutionalization. Like Jacobs and Campbell (1961) in previous experiments, Zucker (1977) simulated transmission over generations by introducing new naïve subjects to a Sherif-type conformity situation involving judgments of the autokinetic light effect (Sherif, 1967), exposing them to group pressure to comply with an arbitrary norm. Subjects were led to believe that conformity with an experienced subject was expected in situations of simulated institutions like "organizational context" and "office." Transmission was positively influenced through the manipulated organizational-context condition and even more so in a manipulated office condition, leading the subjects to believe that they were influenced by a greater number of people belonging to the two kinds of institutions. In this study, the transmission coefficient indicates the relationship between perceived light movement of a successive "generation" as predicted by the perceived light movement of the previous generation. During the three generations tested, the transmission coefficient was approximately .43 for personal influence, .88 for the organizational context, and .94 for the office condition. The maintenance of culturally transmitted arbitrary norms was also higher under the two institutionalization conditions. Furthermore, the resistance to change was higher under the institutionalization condition than under the personal-influence condition.

Long before Harris (1998) wrote her book on the influence of siblings and peers on children's development, Mead (1940) put forward her social analysis regarding the importance of children's companions for transmitting cultural standards. In addition, the school takes on a leading role in transmitting the potential for desirable social change – a role assumed by the family in predemocratic social systems.

Comparing vertical and horizontal transmission, Rettig (1966) investigated the change of moral attitudes (i.e., religion and affluence) in two types of Israeli communities: kibbutz and moshav. The study covered three generations. In the kibbutz – despite its greater cohesion in the community – the kinship system carrying vertical transmission was replaced by a horizontal age-group system for the transmission of attitudes. Nevertheless, in two areas, intergenerational changes were greater in the kibbutz: religious family life and affluence.

Kohn's insight to social class and parental values triggered a lengthy series of studies on the socializing impact of social structure on values (Kohn, 1959). The main idea was that members of the same social class show a resemblance in their values and middle- and lower-social-class parents show different value profiles: Lower-class parents emphasize conformity values, whereas middle-class parents socialize their children to achieve self-determination. According to Kohn's subsequent research, the specific value structures of social classes are mediated by work experiences: The lower educational level of lower-class parents was associated with less self-determination in the workplace. These work experiences, in turn, were transferred to parenting styles of emphasizing conformity. The higher educational level of the middle to upper class qualified them for jobs with greater self-determination. Only in a later study did Kohn (1983) explicitly address the issue of the transmission of values. In another study, he also recognized the utility of cross-national comparisons (Kohn, Slomczynski, & Schoenbach, 1986).

From a more sociological point of view, various forces within the family or society can be distinguished from more interpersonal dyadic mechanisms. They also contribute to the existence of interpersonal relationships in the field of child-rearing practices. In this context, Bengtson and Troll (1978) introduced the concept of family solidarity as the sum of expectations, activities, feelings, and functions that are shared by different members of the family. According to Bengtson and Troll, solidarity exists not only among members of one generation but also, even more strongly, among members of different generations within a process of social and biological duplication. Dimensions of this solidarity that are aimed at sharing meanings, values, beliefs, and orientations with regard to parenting play a role in the transmission of parenting attitudes to the next generation.

The transmission of skills has been a central issue in the field of cultural anthropology dating back to early studies. It is generally presented using the label of "cultural learning." Landy (1959) was one of the first to use the term *cultural transmission* in this context, looking at children's learning of ways to produce cultural artifacts in a rural Puerto Rican village. As is the case with more recent studies (see the following section), this early study aimed only at describing what is transmitted, who the transmitter is, and to whom it is transmitted. A theoretically oriented analysis of the transmission process was and, indeed, continues to be beyond the scope of such studies.

3.0. THE THIRD PERIOD: 1980s TO THE PRESENT

3.1. Cultural Transmission: Biology Contributes Again

After discovering analogies between genetic and cultural processes, biologists used population genetic models as the basis for analogous models of cultural transmission, cultural evolution, and gene-culture coevolution. The problems they addressed are of fundamental interest to psychology and the human sciences in general. Do our genes restrict and delineate the nature of our culture? Is there a genetic basis underlying cross-cultural or gender differences in terms of beliefs and values? How does culture change? Many biologists argue that culture is itself subject to an evolutionary process, with cultural variants being generated, selected, and socially transmitted (for a review, see Durham, 1990).

Lumsden and Wilson's (1981) gene-culture coevolution model specifies the numerous steps involved in moving from genes to culture and back to genes again. More specifically, they defined a unit of culture, the *culturegen*, as "a relatively homogeneous set of artifacts, behaviors or mentifacts" (p. 27). *Mentifacts* can be understood as equivalent to cultural mental representations or cultural schemata. In gene-culture transactions, individuals choose between culturegens; they periodically reassess this choice, influenced by the epigenetic rules and the pattern of culturegen usage in the population. The rates at which individuals adopt alternative culturegens are determined by the product of the *innate* (i.e., genetic) *bias function* and an updated *assimilation* (e.g., copy others) *bias function*. Lumsden and Wilson attach importance to an "exponential trend watcher" model, which refers to a simple regularity: As more people adopt one culturegen, the probability of others switching to it increases exponentially. If people are strongly inclined to follow what others around them are doing, then small initial differences in switching propensity can be dramatically magnified at the level of the group.

New impulses to the study of cultural transmission arose with the adoption of the original theme of nongenetic inheritance. Cavalli-Sforza and Feldman (1981) and Cavalli-Sforza, Feldman, Chen, and Dornbusch (1982), who came from the field of biostatistics, had in mind the development of a quantitative theory of cultural evolution when they focused on cultural transmission as a critical mechanism that allows the prediction of variation between and within populations over time and space. In their 1982 article, Cavalli-Sforza et al. defined cultural transmission as "the process of acquisition of behaviors, attitudes or technologies through imprinting conditioning, imitation, active teaching and learning or combinations of these" (p. 19). They provided prospects for analyzing vertical (i.e., parent–offspring) and horizontal (i.e., conjugal partners and offspring–peers) transmission and claimed that "no statistical measure of association can indicate bona fide causation (transmission). Yet if an individual, at the end of a period of socialization and education resembles its mentors, some process of transmission (conscious or subconscious) must have been going on" (p. 26). The measure of similarity between transmitter and transmittee suggested is bivariate correlation or partial correlation. The authors found strong vertical transmission for political attitudes and religion along with "forms of entertainment and sports, superstitions and beliefs, and customs and habits" (p. 26). Mother and father are differentially efficient transmitters with regard to various transmission content areas. However, among all of the content areas looked at in this study, there was no evidence of an interaction between the two parental transmission components. Instead, the authors found an analogy for the genetic law of the dominant-recessive inheritance in the social-transmission domain: If both parents hold strong social attitudes, they will most likely have offspring with strong attitudes. If both hold weak attitudes, it is highly probable that they will have offspring with weak attitudes. If one of the parents holds strong beliefs and the other weak, then the variant of the mother will be found more frequently in the offspring generation, irrespective of its intensity. Cavalli-Sforza et al. (1982) even suggested some age periods in ontogenesis in which individuals might be more sensitive to the reception of cultural transmission. These considerations, together with the fact that the mode of cultural transmission is presumably also culturally transmitted, suggest that variations between and within populations could be strongly influenced by specific epochal effects.

In a simple model of evolution in a spatially varying environment, Boyd and Richerson (1985, 1996) showed that a tendency to acquire the most common behavior exhibited in a society was adaptive because such a tendency increased the probability of acquiring adaptive beliefs and values. Henrich and Boyd (1998) studied the evolution of this type of *conformist transmission* in a more general model, in which environments vary in both time and space. The analysis of this model indicated that conformist transmission was facilitated under a very broad range of conditions, which were, in fact, broader than those that favor a substantial reliance on social learning. The authors believe that imitation and conformism are the two basic mechanisms through which transmission operates successfully. Boyd and Richerson (1996) and Tomasello, Krüger, and Ratner (1993) argued that the human ability to acquire novel behaviors by observation constitutes the reason why human cultural change is cumulative.

The two mechanisms of imitation and conformism do not imply cultural transmission but rather are forms of individual social learning. Boyd and Richerson (1985) conceptualized cultural transmission as the product of a series of analytically separable cognitive-learning processes, or *transmission biases*; in this context, learning refers to both passive (e.g., observational learning, imitation) and active (e.g., teaching processes) transmission. Because it is highly unlikely that evolution produced a generalized problem-solving capacity, it makes sense to postulate a complex set of learning mechanisms, or transmission biases, that allows humans to effectively and efficiently acquire beliefs, ideas, and behaviors from the immense amount of confusing and often contradictory information presented by the external world. Evolutionary considerations suggest that our cognitive abilities consist of learning rules that preferentially select and evaluate sensory data from prescribed subsets of externally produced information. These learning mechanisms provide rules of thumb that bias humans toward acquiring certain beliefs and behaviors without exhaustively examining and processing the vast amount of available social and environmental information.

In the literature on cultural transmission within the context of cultural evolutionary thinking, *conformist transmission* implies that individuals possess the propensity to preferentially adopt the cultural traits that are most frequent in the population. The most frequent trait is most likely the most adaptive one. *Unbiased transmission* refers not only to the copying of any individual but also to the model of the parents, who do not always offer adaptive traits in their transmission attempts. If the transmission is unbiased, the variation of the trait in the next generation will be approximately the same. If the transmission is biased or conformist, it will result in higher frequencies of the adaptive trait in the next generation. Conformist transmission creates a directional force that tends to establish and maintain cultural norms. It acts to increase the accuracy of social learning by providing individuals with a guide to accessing the more adaptive variant of behavior.

Another form of biased transmission is the *prestige-biased oblique transmission* (Henrich, 2001; Rogers, 1962/1995), according to which opinion leadership determines transmission: Innovations are accepted by a given population if they have been previously accepted by opinion leaders, but they are rejected by the population if more conservative opinion leaders do not accept them. Rogers underlined the mechanism of prestige-biased transmission by describing the example of Dutch farmers. Small farmers adopted the farming methods of prestigious large-scale farmers in their local region even when such practices were clearly inappropriate for the particular application the adopters had in mind.

Henrich (2001) pointed out that if "early adopters" or "innovators" are involved, transmission is enhanced by their greater social networks and higher social status, more money, more cosmopolitan contacts, and greater exposure to mass media outlets as compared to late adopters. If the adopters are poor and of low status, nobody will copy them, meaning that the trait tends not to be diffused.

Detailed ethological studies of learning and teaching behaviors constitute fairly recent research innovations. Lumsden (1984) addressed an issue introduced by Trivers (1974) referring to parent–offspring conflict among humans and pongids. The main focus of their contribution was juvenile rebellion against parental value transmission. Despite the importance of enculturation and social learning of the young in all human societies and in a large number of animal societies, parent–offspring conflict across enculturation is not well understood, even though it is fundamental for understanding the biological basis of culture and its transmission.

Lumsden's (1984) conflict model of transmission starts with the premise that a basic understanding of cultural norms, values, roles, and lore is achieved by the offspring. The parent might have the opportunity to teach things that are of greater value to the parent than to the offspring, thus engendering costly acts of conflict with the offspring. When taken together, the cost to the parents of teaching or preparing learning situations is likely to increase as a function of offspring age and the amount of cultural information already learned. In line with the cost-benefit analysis of social-cultural learning, Kamela and Nakanishi (2002) hypothesize that the acquisition of knowledge and skills in a temporarily unstable environment only allows for uncertain expectations about the utility of the learned skills or behavior in the future. Individual learning is costly because the knowledge and skills acquired might soon be outdated. Individuals who skip the information search and free-ride on other members' search efforts coexist at a stable ratio. This type of "producer–scrounger" structure qualifies the effectiveness of social-cultural learning, particularly in terms of a "conformity bias," by using social information. Evidence for these considerations was provided by a simulation study and experiment in which participants were found to be more likely to choose the most frequent trait (i.e., they showed the conformity bias) when individual learning or information search costs were high.

At some point, the costs to the parent of enculturating the offspring with specific types and amounts of information may exceed the benefits provided. When the costs are equal to or greater than the benefits, a conflict constellation arises. The parent might cease transmission efforts, either completely or regarding a specific topic. However, this does not mean that the offspring does not favor the elicitation of cultural transmission behaviors from the parent.

An additional factor of the cost-benefit model of parental transmission efforts is the number of offspring toward whom the transmission efforts have to be directed. The more children parents have, the smaller the share of transmission efforts each offspring receives. The situation might arise that the offspring prefers more transmission efforts than the parents are able or willing to grant.

When the verbal lore shifts from knowledge and skills to the inculcation of values and attitudes, formal learning settings assume more of the dimensions of the classic parent–offspring conflict. Parents might use cultural transmission to teach and equip offspring with value systems that are beneficial to the parents rather than the offspring. Insofar as epigenetic rules provide offspring with genetic programming that resists values in favor of individuals other than themselves, the groundwork is laid for a novel conflict in which socializers try to provide learners with information that they do not wish to assimilate.

Tomasello (1990) claimed that not all social learning in animals might be due to cultural transmission, as suggested by other authors (see Tomasello, this volume). Indeed, he was reluctant to acknowledge social transmission in primates at all. The migration of an individual or subpopulation showing a particular behavior to another group that does not show that particular behavior would require horizontal transmission for its dissemination. Horizontal-transmission behavior is highly unlikely among pongids (Tomasello, Davis-Dasilva, Camak, & Evans, 1987). The potential peer model does not show the behavior slowly and repeat it deliberately until the observing animal has learned it. In this regard, the burden of transmission must shift to adult–child vertical transmission. In addition, young animals seem to be more willing to learn than older individuals. The mechanism of learning is *emulation* – that is, reaching the same goal through varied forms of behavior rather than exact imitation. These varied forms of behavior, however, have to be learned individually. Tomasello (1990) concluded the presentation of his evidence by affirming that in no case has cultural transmission been observed in the form of true deliberate teaching and true imitative learning among primates in the wild. In a target article, Tomasello, Krüger, and Ratner (1993) presented a refined theory of human *cultural learning*: Cultural learning is identified with those instances of social learning in which intersubjectivity or perspective-taking plays a vital role, both in the original learning process and in the resulting cognitive product. Cultural learning manifests itself in three forms during human ontogeny: imitative learning, instructed learning, and collaborative learning – in that order. Evidence is provided that this progression arises from the developmental ordering of the underlying social-cognitive concepts and processes involved. Imitative learning relies on the concept of intentional agent and involves simple perspective-taking. Instructed learning relies on the concept of mental agent and involves alternating/coordinated perspective-taking (i.e., intersubjectivity). Collaborative learning relies on a concept of reflective agent and involves integrated perspective-taking (i.e., reflective intersubjectivity). A comparison of normal children, autistic children, and wild and enculturated chimpanzees provided further evidence for these correlations between social cognition and cultural learning. Cultural learning is a uniquely human form of social learning that allows for a fidelity of transmission of behaviors and information among conspecifics that is not possible in other forms of social learning, thereby providing the psychological basis for cultural evolution.

In line with Tomasello et al.'s (1987) conclusion, Sherry and Galef (1984) presented results of an experiment with birds (i.e., *paridae*) involving the opening of milk bottles. They established a baseline of spontaneous bottle-opening in five pretraining periods. The birds that did not spontaneously open bottles were either assigned to a tutored training condition (in which a trained conspecific opened bottles), an open-tub training condition (in which a preopened bottle contained food), or a control condition with no elicitation attempts. In the testing phase, both the tutored and the open-tub conditions revealed an equal number of bottle-openings; in the control condition, none was observed. The clear implication of the data is that the interpretation of the spread of milk-bottle-opening as an unequivocal instance of imitative learning by free-living birds is not justified. It may be more appropriate to regard this – and possibly other instances of cultural transmission of learned behavior observed in nature – as due in part to changes in the environment produced by those individuals introducing novel behaviors into a population.

Furthermore, a longitudinal study on signals for social functions revealed considerable intra-individual instability and little inter-individual consistency. The process responsible for the few signals common to part of the animals was due to conventionalization after individual learning took place under conditions of common social experiences. Tomasello et al. (1993) concluded their argument by stating that for species whose ontogeny depends heavily on learning, behavioral continuity across generations may be maintained in any number of ways: for example, environmental shaping, social learning, and cultural transmission. The principal argument is that despite the minimal importance of cultural learning (i.e., instructed learning and imitation) in chimpanzee ontogeny, this species achieves some of the same results through more general learning processes – namely, *emulation* in their acquisition of tool use and *conventionalization* in their acquisition of communicatory signals. Whereas the social environment plays an absolutely indispensable role in both of these learning processes, they both also rely heavily on individual learning and cognition, especially reasoning processes about the causal relations involved in object manipulation and interaction. These processes are the same for human children, but children also employ imitation and are explicitly instructed. Chimpanzees have culture in a very different sense than do humans. Much of the continuity across generations in tool use and communication is due to the continuity of learning experiences available to the individuals – which "shape" individual learning. Little of the learning comes from observing and reproducing the behavior of conspecifics, which in the current account is a defining feature of cultural transmission. Each generation has to struggle to reach the skill level of their progenitors. In human societies, the more faithful transmission effected by intentional instruction and imitation preserves useful behavioral adaptations more faithfully across generations (Bullock, 1987; Parker, 1985) and it does this even in the face of changing environments (Boyd & Richerson, 1985) – something that individual learning and environmental shaping cannot do.

Two American zoologists, Helfman and Schultz (1984), published a study on what they believed to be *social transmission* of behavioral traditions in coral reef fish. They defined a tradition as subpopulation-specific social behavior patterns across age classes or generations. Information necessary to maintain traditions may be acquired through genetic inheritance or may be transmitted socially via learning from other, usually older, individuals. Social transmission permits the rapid acquisition of advantageous behavioral traits and is intimately related to the evolution of sociality. Helfman and Schultz claimed to be the first to have shown that low-level vertebrates learn their routes when swimming in schools with resident (i.e., knowledgeable) fish by imitation because thereafter – when swimming without them – they show a learning effect of the behaviors of the resident (i.e., expert) fish. Helfman and Schultz suggested that aggregation is an adaptive social response common to many taxa and serving many functions: In fish, it may serve the function of adaptation to predation.

The newest theoretically relevant animal research is reported by White, Gros-Louis, King, Papakhian, and West (2007) involving young cowbirds. Depending on the subpopulation and the intensity and type of social interaction between the learning bird and other potential models of the learning bird, the birds revealed courtship and male-male competitive behavior depending on the social groups' interactive patterns even if they had not observed the behavior patterns they came to replicate. The kind of interactive experiences seemed to induce the construction of behaviors similar to the adult males' behavior in their first year.

Contributions to cultural transmission in other disciplinary fields presented in the following sections show that they borrowed heavily from the theoretical approaches developed in biology. The summary of important reflections tracing back to biology and evolutionary theory reveals that human cultural transmission has the unique feature of deliberate teaching of the transmitter aimed at the reproduction of behaviors, attitudes, or skills in the transmittee. The challenging task for cross-cultural studies of cultural transmission is to find evidence for the universality of this uniquely human quality of cultural transmission.

3.2. Contributions from the Social Sciences and Anthropology

The increasing interest in work and family issues led to the question of how the workplace shapes an adult's family sphere. The sociologist Kohn (1983) chose this question as the focus of his research and theorizing. This line of thinking was continued by Parcel and Menaghan (1994) throughout the 1990s. From their studies with U.S. national samples, they concluded that parental work experience, especially the occupational complexity of parents' jobs – and particularly that of the mother – play a decisive role in the development of the child.

A more recent study in Great Britain by the Dutch authors Taris, Semin, and Bok (1998) also found a dominant effect of the mother on the child's value of sexual permissiveness. The authors considered two moderator effects: SES and quality of family interaction. Their main finding was that with weaker familial interaction, the impact of SES on the child's attitude toward sexual permissiveness increased. Thus, a direct transmission from parent to child is given only when the interaction reaches an intermediate to high level.

According to Vermulst, de Brock, and van Zutphen (1991), transmission is not a rigid process. Representatives of a macrolevel point of view have repeatedly stated that generations are not fixed, unchangeable entities. The dynamics of the sociocultural and historical context in which generations follow one another provides the conditions under which every generation distinguishes itself from former and future generations by a number of specific and characteristic qualities (Dunham & Bengtson, 1986). These distinctive characteristics also have effects on parenting and its resulting determinants. Whereas the psychological perspective tends to suggest that the transmission of parenting might be more or less of an absolute quality, the sociological perspective tends to emphasize the uniqueness of each generation; as a consequence, parenting and its determinants across generations will change. There are many indications in the literature that absolute transmission of parental characteristics is not to be expected but is rather a *relative transmission*. Relative transmission means that parental characteristics are transmitted to some extent to their offspring; however, under the influence of social-cultural and historical conditions, overall shifts in the intensity of some characteristics will also be observed. In other words, correlations will still be observed between parents and children relative to several characteristics but, at the same time, there may be differences between the levels of parents' and children's characteristics (e.g., in terms of mean values preferred). However, mean-level differences in attitudes or values (or attitude shifts) between generations cannot be clearly interpreted: They could be due to transmission or to a lack of transmission. Furthermore, Vermulst et al. (1991) suggest a plausible explanation for findings that show a decisive role of mothers in the transmission process: Mothers are more involved than fathers in the parenting process and are therefore the dominant transmitters when it comes to analyzing the transmission of parenting practices. It appears that mothers play an important role in the transmission of social and material disadvantages and, above all, in the transmission of personality characteristics (e.g., inadequate coping skills) (Elder, Downey, & Cross, 1986). It is possible that the influence of the mother or father depends on the child's age. Only longitudinal data would enable an appropriate analysis in this regard.

In the 1970s, the sociologists Bengtson and Troll (1978) provided arguments demonstrating that transmission is not a one-way street: We have to assume *retroactive transmission* from child to parent as well. Transmission may be characterized as a transactional process in which the parent impacts the child and the child influences the parent in return.

The anthropologist Hewlett and the biologist Cavalli-Sforza (1986) claimed that anthropological studies of cultural transmission stressed the inculcation of attitudes, values, and personality traits rather than details of the transmission of practical skills and knowledge. Details about the transmission of knowledge in terms of artifact production and foraging activities are rare (for a notable exception, see Ruddle & Chesterfield, 1977). Apart from the vertical parent–offspring transmission, which is closest to genetic transmission, Hewlett and Cavalli-Sforza looked at horizontal transmission among peers, which is closest to the phenomenon of contagion. In addition, they found many-to-one transmission or social transmission, but they did not observe one-to-many transmission – although communication is highly efficient in this way and if acceptance follows communication, cultural change may be very rapid. Many-to-one transmission is most efficient when the many transmitters act in concert so that the influence is reciprocally reinforced. Consequently, change in the frequency of a trait over time and space should be slow and variation within and across populations low.

This conformity mode of transmission tends to generate the highest uniformity within the group. The authors' research aim was to determine quantitatively who transmits which traits to whom. Only then can the dominant models of transmission for certain traits be identified. Based on the skills and knowledge examined, they concluded that horizontal transmission is fastest when contacts with the transmitter and acceptance by transmittees are frequent. Because both authors acknowledged the changing plasticity with age, they sampled adults, adolescents, and children to compare the spread of a trait. In their studies of Aka pygmies, they found extreme vertical gender-specific transmission of skills from mother to daughter and from father to son. This mode of transmission guarantees division of labor over generations in a society. The age-specific transmission analyses revealed that in this society, during late childhood (i.e., about 10 years of age), girls and boys know all of the essential skills and these skills do not change significantly in adolescence and adulthood. Because enculturation of pygmy children is early, a habit fixation at an early age molds the children so that later changes are less likely than in other societies. By far, the dominant mode of transmission (i.e., 80% of all traits investigated) was the vertical parent–child transmission. More detailed analyses of the quantitative variation of each mode of transmission of either knowledge or skill (e.g., length of time known, quality of skill performance) revealed greater variation. The second and third most frequent and yet rare types of transmission are many-to-one and horizontal transfer of knowledge and skills. If a many-to-one transfer occurs, it leads to a conservative spread of a trait or transmission due to conformity among the members of a population. If horizontal or peer transmission occurs, it leads to a rapid spread of a trait.

According to their most recent anthropological considerations, Norenzayan and Atran (2004) claim that it is clear that cultural transmission has two components: cognitive and emotional. The cognitive part in the transmission process is constituted by the contents of the transmission: beliefs and folk tales as well as myths. The authors review evidence that cultural beliefs exploit the same operations based on intuitive ontologies and domain-specific theories of physics, biology, and mind. The emotional component comes into play with nonnatural beliefs such as religion. Religion is rooted in the fear of death. The authors assume that emotionally toned contents have a greater chance of being transmitted, just as they have a higher probability of being remembered. This greater chance of being transmitted might be derived from emotionality, but it might *also* be due to the fact that unnatural beliefs such as religion, superstitions, and myths contain minimally counterintuitive concepts. Consequently, they are easily remembered and transmitted. Thus, certain concepts seem to have a *transmission advantage*. Those that are omitted during transmission have special attributes such as deviating slightly from ontological insights without being bizarre or fully intuitive, as experiments by Barret and Nyhof (2001) showed.

The emotional component was demonstrated in an anthropological study in Lithuania with a large sample of almost 2,000 families from all over the country encompassing mother, father, and the oldest school-aged child. Parental motivation for transmission is taken for granted. However, the author observed that parents train their children to achieve independence, thus loosening their bonds with the child and reducing the transmission efforts as the child develops toward autonomy (Ustinova, 1988).

The sociologist Mark (2002) adds a new theoretical approach to identifying potential mechanisms. He noticed that prior exposure to a particular behavior that is subject to cultural transmission seemed to be the effective mechanism. Disproportionate prior exposure to the behavior to be transmitted is the mechanism through which transmission works. This principle works in a positive and a negative direction: If cooperation is the previously predominantly experienced behavior, then transmission of cooperation is highly likely. If the previously dominant behavior is exploitative, then exploitative behavior is transmitted. This mechanism resembles conformist transmission – as described previously in the biological section: The transmission is best accepted when normative traits are involved. In unbiased transmission, the normative context plays a major role because individual transmitters are not as successful (if at all) if they transmit traits that are counternormative.

3.3. A Contribution from Economics

A study by the National Bureau of Economic Research at Harvard University (Curie, 2002) collected evidence for the intergenerational transmission of human capital in the form of higher education (see Nauck, this volume). More highly educated women were more likely to have more highly educated daughters. This relationship was mediated by higher health orientation of educated women, leading to healthier children whose path into higher education was therefore smoother. Mothers with a higher level of education apply more sophisticated parenting methods, and their elevated intelligence level is transferred in part genetically to the child. Because educated women live in environments with a good opportunity structure for education (e.g., schools, colleges), many factors may function as transmission belts to establish similarity in education between mother and daughter. Increasing the opportunities for education in poorer neighborhoods could therefore increase women's educational attainment in the offspring generation. Curie's public health data analyses revealed transmission results augmented by opportunity structure.

3.4. The Contributions of Psychology and Educational Science

The developmental psychologist van Ijzendoorn (1992) defined intergenerational transmission of parenting as the process through which, purposely or unintentionally, an earlier generation psychologically influences the parenting attitudes and behavior of the next generation. Van Ijzendoorn suggested that research on intergenerational transmission of parenting should involve at least three generations: grandparents, parents, and children. A direct influence of grandparents on children is usually estimated as low. Grandparenting in Western societies is reduced because the families' living arrangements generally exclude the grandparent generation. When researchers speak of the grandparents as "socializing the socializer," this concept refers to the transmission of grandparent to parent, not to direct grandparental influence on the child. In fact, van Ijzendoorn limits the concept of intergenerational transmission of parenting to the investigation of (dis-)continuities between different generations (i.e., grandparents, parents, and children) in terms of attitudes and behavior displayed at about the same chronological or social age. This limitation proves to be necessary to avoid confusing our theme with grandparenting or child-rearing in general and with grandparental support of the parents more specifically.

The belief that parents matter in their children's development is well ensconced in the field of developmental psychology and well documented from a variety of research approaches employing different outcome variables. Increasingly, however, the attention of developmental psychologists is being drawn to discerning the antecedents of these relevant parental behaviors. Considerations regarding the role of parenting that the parents themselves received as children and the extent to which they employ the same type of parenting are increasingly characterizing research in the area of developmental psychology.

Developmental psychology also provided another important contribution when van Ijzendoorn (1995) introduced the concept of *transmission gap* to account for variation in the transmission of attachment or parenting styles. Individual differences in temperament and personality condition the transmission process. Fox (1995) proposed that the most likely characteristics might be reactivity and affective bias. The idea of a transmission gap might also be an important contribution for the general notion of a generation gap.

Most transmission attempts seem to aim at cultural continuity. The impact of either a continuous or discontinuous cultural context was analyzed in Putallaz et al.'s (1998) more recent overview of the impact of cultural continuity on the social development of children. The authors addressed efforts made by psychologists to explore the consequences of cultural continuity in three subsequent generations in five research areas of social development: (1) child abuse, (2) attachment status, (3) parenting and child-rearing behavior in humans and (4) in nonhuman primates, and (5) in peer and sibling relationships. Their various meta-analyses provided some general insight to mechanisms of transmission: The main conclusion is that the transmission of attachment is conditioned in early individual differences in temperament or personality interacting with the environment.

The literature regarding patterns of human enculturation (e.g., Cole, Gay, Glick, & Sharp, 1971; Mead, 1928, 1930) indicates that there are, universally, periods of each individual life history (typically, childhood and adolescence) in which culture learning is emphasized and constitutes a predominant activity – reflected, for example, in exploratory and observational learning behavior, imitation of adult roles, parental efforts of training and inculcation of norms and values, rites of passage, and initiation into elite groups. The time spent learning important aspects of a given culture (as opposed to other activities), and efforts devoted by parents to transmit them, tapers off as adolescence and early adulthood proceeds and the individual becomes familiar with the prevailing norms, social rules, roles, and lore. In older studies, children were viewed mainly as passive participants in enculturation, the observers of culture and receivers of training regimens delivered by the society. In more recent approaches, their active role is emphasized (e.g., Kuczynski, Marshall, & Schell, 1997).

Tallman, Gray, Kullberg, and Henderson (1999) follow up on the question of which kind of transmission is responsible for the sad fact that children of divorced parents carry a higher risk of divorce in their adult life. However, parental conflicts without divorce also affect offspring's harmonious relationships. They defined a commonly used three-phase individual model of transmission: Family experiences in one generation contribute to key individual personality characteristics, and these characteristics in turn affect the quality of the marital relationship in the next generation (Caspi & Elder, 1988). Starting from this initial model, they point out that the model ignores some important steps in the transition process and thus fails to account for three critical factors: (1) it does not reflect the individual's potential to learn and change over the life course; (2) it does not consider the consequences of the changing contexts involved in moving from the parents' family to a family of one's own; and (3) it does not consider the learning opportunities that occur as spouses interact with one another. As a consequence, they developed a five-step transmission model. The couple-level theoretical approach taken in this study is, so far, unique among studies dealing with vertical intergenerational transmission.

The many facets of cultural transmission, its mechanisms, and its functions reflect the scientific *zeitgeist* of several epochs. The study of cultural transmission will bring insight to what causes continuity and discontinuity of culture over generations. It will answer the question of how the emergence, maintenance, and change of culture may be conceptualized in future research. It may also help in the important tasks of modern societies to manage and control culture.

REFERENCES

Agar, W. E., & Kerr, G. (1913). The transmission of environmental effects from parent to offspring in simocephalus vetulus. *Philosophical Transactions of the Royal Society of London, B, 203*, 319–350.

Allport, G. (1954). *The nature of prejudice.* New York: Addison-Wesley.

Barret, J. L., & Nyhof, M. A. (2001). Spreading nonnatural concepts: The role of intuitive conceptual structures in memory and transmission of cultural materials. *Journal of Cognition and Culture, 1*, 69–100.

Bengtson, V. L., & Troll, L. (1978). Youth and their parents: Feedback and intergenerational influence in socialization. In M. R. Lerner & G. B. Spanier (Eds.), *Child influences on marital and family interaction: A life span development* (pp. 215–240). New York: Academic Press.

Borke, H. (1967). A family over three generations: The transmission of interacting and relating patterns. *Journal of Marriage and Family, 29*, 638–655.

Boyd, R., & Richerson, P. J. (1985). *Culture and the evolutionary process*. Chicago: University of Chicago Press.

Boyd, R., & Richerson, P. J. (1996). Why culture is common, but cultural evolution is rare. *Proceedings of the British Academy, 88*, 77–93.

Branford, V. (1913). *St. Columba: A study of social inheritance and spiritual development*. Edinburgh: Geddes & Co.

Bullock, D. (1987). Socializing the theory of intelligence. In M. Chapman & R. Dixon (Eds.), *Meaning and the growth of mind: Wittgenstein's significance for developmental psychology* (pp. 187–218). New York: Springer Verlag.

Caspi, A., & Elder, G. H. (1988). Emergent family patterns: The intergenerational construction of problem behavior and relationships. In R. A. Hinde & J. Stevenson-Hinde (Eds.), *Relationship within families: Mutual influences* (pp. 218–240). Oxford: Clarendon Press.

Cavalli-Sforza, L. L., & Feldman, M. W. (1981). *Cultural transmission and evolution: A quantitative approach*. Princeton, NJ: Princeton University Press.

Cavalli-Sforza, L. L., Feldman, M. W., Chen, K. H., & Dornbusch, S. M. (1982). Theory and observation in cultural transmission. *Science, 218*, 19–27.

Clapp, H. L. (1894). The inadequacy of the transmission of learning. *Education, 15*, 1–9.

Cole, M., Gay, J., Glick, J., & Sharp, D. (1971). *The cultural context of learning and thinking*. New York: Basic Books.

Curie, J. (2002). Mother's education and the intergenerational transmission of human capital: Evidence from college openings and longitudinal data. *Working Paper 9360 of the National Bureau of Economic Research*. Cambridge, MA.

de Lamarck, J. (1809). *Zoologische Philosophie* (Philosophie zoologique). Leipzig: Körner.

Diekmann, A., & Jann, B. (Eds.) (2004). *Modelle sozialer Evolution* [Models of social evolution]. Wiesbaden: DTV.

Dunham, C. C., & Bengtson, V. L. (1986). Conceptual and theoretical perspectives on generational relations. In N. Datan, A. L. Green, & H. W. Reese (Eds.), *Lifespan developmental psychology: Intergenerational relations* (pp. 1–28). Hillsdale, NJ: Erlbaum.

Durham, W. H. (1990). Advances in evolutionary culture theory. *Annual Review of Anthropology, 19*, 187–210.

Elder, G. H., Jr., Downey, G., & Cross, C. E. (1986). Family ties and life changes: Hard times and hard choices in women's lives since the 1930s. In N. Datan, A. L. Greene, & H. W. Reese (Eds.), *Life-span developmental psychology: Intergenerational relations* (pp. 151–183). Hillsdale, NJ: Erlbaum.

English, H. B. (1919). A note on social inheritance. *Psychological Bulletin, 16*, 393–394.

Fox, N. A. (1995). On the way we were: Adult memories about attachment experiences and their role in determining parent–infant relationships: A commentary on van Ijzendoorn (1995). *Psychological Bulletin, 117*, 404–410.

Harris, J. R. (1998). *The nurture assumption*. New York: The Free Press.

Hartog, M. (1893). The Spencer–Weismann controversy. *Contemporary Review, 64*, 50–59.

Hartog, M. (1908). The transmission of acquired characters. *Contemporary Review, 94*, 307–317.

Helfman, G. S., & Schultz, E. T. (1984). Social transmission of behavioral traditions in a coral reef fish. *Animal Behaviour, 32*, 379–394.

Henrich, J. (2001). Cultural transmission and the diffusion of innovations: Adoption dynamics indicate that biased cultural transmission is the predominant force in behavioral change. *American Anthropology, 103*, 992–1013.

Henrich, J., & Boyd, R. (1998). The evolution of conformist transmission and the emergence of between-group differences. *Evolution and Human Behavior, 19*, 215–241.

Henrich, J., & Boyd, R. (2002). On modeling cognition and culture: Why cultural evolution does not require replication of representation. *Journal of Cognition and Culture, 2.2*, 87–112.

Hewlett, B. S., & Cavalli-Sforza, L. L. (1986). Cultural transmission among Aka pygmies. *American Anthropologist, 88*, 922–934.

Jacobs, R. C., & Campbell, D. T. (1961). The perpetuation of an arbitrary tradition through successive generations of a laboratory microculture. *Journal of Abnormal and Social Psychology, 62*, 649–658.

Kamela, T., & Nakanishi, D. (2002). Cost-benefit analysis of social/cultural learning. *Evolution and Human Behavior, 23*, 373–393.

Kerr, G. (1913). Transmission of environmental effects. *Philosophical Transactions of the Royal Society, B, 203*, 319–350.

Kohn, M. L. (1959). Social class and parent–child relationship. *American Journal of Sociology, 64*, 337–351.

Kohn, M. L. (1983). On the transmission of values in the family: A preliminary formulation. *Research in the Sociology of Education and Socialization, 4*, 3–12.

Kohn, M. L., Slomczynski, K. M., & Schoenbach, C. (1986). Social stratification and the transmission of values in the family: A cross-national assessment. *Sociological Forum, 1*, 73–102.

Kuczynski, L., Marshall, S., & Schell, K. (1997). Value socialization in a bidirectional context. In J. E. Grusec & L. Kuczynski (Eds.), *Parenting and children's internalization of values: A handbook of contemporary theory* (pp. 23–50). New York: John Wiley & Sons.

Landy, D. (1959). *Tropical childhood: Cultural transmission and learning in a rural Puerto Rican village*. Chapel Hill, NC: University of North Carolina Press.

Lumsden, C. J. (1984). Parent–offspring conflict over the transmission of culture. *Ethology and Sociobiology, 5*, 111–136.

Lumsden, C. J., & Wilson, E. O. (1981). *Genes, Mind and Culture*. Cambridge, MA: Harvard University Press.

Mark, N. P. (2002). Cultural transmission, disproportionate prior exposure, and the evolution of cooperation. *American Sociological Review, 67*, 323–344.

Mead, M. (1928). *Coming of age in Samoa*. New York: W. Morrow.

Mead, M. (1930). *Growing up in New Guinea*. New York: Blue Ribbon Books.

Mead, M. (1940). Social change and cultural surrogates. *Journal of Educational Sociology, 14,* 92–104.

Norenzayan, A., & Atran, S. (2004). Cognitive and emotional processes in the cultural transmission of natural and nonnatural beliefs. In M. Schaller & C. S. Crandall (Eds.), *Psychological foundations of culture* (pp. 149–169). Mahwah, NJ: Lawrence Erlbaum Associates.

Parcel, T. L., & Menaghan, E. G. (1994). *Parents' jobs and children's lives.* New York: Aldine de Gruyter.

Parker, S. (1985). A social-technological model for the evolution of language. *Current Anthropology, 26,* 617–639.

Putallaz, M., Constanzo, P. R., Grimes, C. L., & Sherman, D. M. (1998). Intergenerational continuities and their influences on children's social development. *Social Development, 7,* 389–427.

Rettig, S. (1966). Relation of social systems to intergenerational changes in moral attitudes. *Journal of Personality and Social Psychology, 4,* 409–414.

Reynolds, P. C. (1981). *On the evolution of behavior: The argument from animals to man.* Berkeley, CA: University of California Press.

Rogers, E. M. (1962/1995). *Diffusion of innovations.* First and fourth editions. New York: Free Press.

Rosen, B. C. (1964). Family structure and value transmission. *Merrill-Palmer Quarterly, 10,* 59–76.

Ruddle, K., & Chesterfield, R. (1977). *Education for traditional food procurement in the Orinoco Delta.* Berkeley, CA: University of California Press.

Schönpflug, U. (2001). Intergenerational transmission of values: The role of transmission belts. *Journal of Cross-Cultural Psychology, 32,* 174–185.

Sherif, M. (1967). *Social interaction: Process or product.* Chicago: Aldine.

Sherry, D. F., & Galef, B. G. (1984). Cultural transmission without imitation: Milk-bottle opening by birds. *Animal Behaviour, 32,* 937–938.

Spencer, H. (1893a). The inadequacy of natural selection. I. *Contemporary Review, 63,* 153–166.

Spencer, H. (1893b). The inadequacy of natural selection. II. *Contemporary Review, 63,* 439–456.

Tallman, I., Gray, L. N., Kullberg, V., & Henderson, D. (1999). The intergenerational transmission of marital conflict: Testing a model. *Social Psychology Quarterly, 62,* 219–239.

Taris, R. W., Semin, G. R., & Bok, I. A. (1998). The effect of quality of family interaction and intergenerational transmission of values on sexual permissiveness. *Journal of Genetic Psychology, 159,* 237–250.

Thorndike, E. L. (1903). The inheritance of mental traits. In E. L. Thorndike (Ed.), *Educational Psychology* (pp. 47–65). New York: Lemcke & Buechner.

Tomasello, M. (1990). Cultural transmission in the tool use and communicatory signaling of chimpanzees? In S. T. Parker & K. R. Gibson (Eds.), *"Language" and intelligence in monkeys and apes: Comparative developmental perspectives* (pp. 274–311). New York: Cambridge University Press.

Tomasello, M., Davis-Dasilva, M., Camak, L., & Evans, E. (1987). Observational learning of tool use by young chimpanzees. *Human Evolution, 2,* 175–183.

Tomasello, M., Krüger, A. C., & Ratner, H. H. (1993). Cultural learning. *Behavior and Brain Sciences, 16*, 495–552.

Trivers, R. L. (1974). Parent–offspring conflict. *American Zoologist, 14*, 249–264.

Ustinova, M. Y. (1988). *Intergenerational transmission of ethnocultural traditions: The example of the peoples of the Soviet Baltic Republics.* Moscow: NAUKA Central Department of Oriental Literature.

van Ijzendoorn, M. H. (1992). Intergenerational transmission of parenting: A review of studies in nonclinical populations. *Developmental Review, 12*, 76–99.

van Ijzendoorn, M. H. (1995). On the way we are: On temperament, attachment, and the transmission gap: A rejoinder to Fox (1995). *Psychological Bulletin, 117*, 411–415.

Vermulst, A. A., de Brock, A. J. L. L., & van Zutphen, R. A. H. (1991). The transmission of parenting across generations. In P. K. Smith (Ed.), *The psychology of grandparenthood: An international perspective* (pp. 100–122). London and New York: Routledge.

White, D. J., Gros-Louis, J., King, A. P., Papakhian, M. A., & West, M. J. (2007). Constructing culture in cowbirds. *Journal of Comparative Psychology, 121*, 113–122.

Zucker, L. G. (1977). The role of institutionalization in cultural persistence. *American Sociological Review, 42*, 726–743.

PART ONE

EVOLUTIONARY PERSPECTIVE

3

Cultural Transmission: A View from Chimpanzees and Human Infants

MICHAEL TOMASELLO

INTRODUCTION

Primates are highly social beings. They begin their lives clinging to their mother and nursing, and they spend their next few months, or even years, still in proximity to her. Adult primates live in close-knit social groups, for the most part, in which members individually recognize one another and form various types of long-term social relationships (Tomasello & Call, 1994, 1997). As primates, human beings follow this same pattern, of course, but they also have unique forms of sociality that may be characterized as "ultrasocial" or, in more common parlance, "cultural" (Tomasello, Krüger, & Ratner, 1993). The forms of sociality that are mostly clearly unique to human beings emerge in their ontogeny at approximately 9 months of age – what I have called the 9-month social-cognitive revolution (Tomasello, 1995). This is the age at which infants typically begin to engage in the kinds of joint-attentional interactions in which they master the use of cultural artifacts, including tools and language, and become fully active participants in all types of cultural rituals, scripts, and games. In this chapter, my goals are to (1) characterize the primate and human forms of sociality and cultural transmission, and (2) characterize in more detail the ontogeny of human cultural propensities.

1.0. PRIMATE CULTURE

The most often-cited case of nonhuman primate culture is that of Japanese macaque potato-washing (Kawai, 1965). In 1953, an 18-month-old female named Imo was observed to take pieces of sweet potato, given to her and the rest of the troop by researchers, and wash the sand off of them in nearby water (at first a stream and then the ocean). About 3 months after she began to wash her potatoes, the practice was observed in Imo's mother and two of her playmates (and then their mothers). During the next 2 years, seven other youngsters also began to wash potatoes, and within 3 years of Imo's first potato-washing, about

40% of the troop was doing the same. The fact that it was Imo's close associates who learned the behavior first, and their associates directly after, was thought to be significant in suggesting that the means of propagation of this behavior was some form of imitation in which one individual actually copied the behavior of another.

The interpretation of these observations in terms of culture and imitation has two main problems, however. The first problem is that potato-washing is much less unusual a behavior for monkeys than was originally thought. Brushing sand off food turns out to be something that many monkeys do naturally; indeed, this had been observed in the Koshima monkeys prior to the emergence of washing. It is thus not surprising that potato-washing was also observed in four other troops of human-provisioned Japanese macaques soon after the Koshima observations (Kawai, 1965) – implying at least four individuals who learned on their own. Also, in captivity, individuals of other monkey species learn quite rapidly on their own to wash their food when provided with sandy fruits and bowls of water (Visalberghi & Fragaszy, 1990). The second problem has to do with the pattern of the spread of potato-washing behavior within the group. The fact is that the spread of the behavior was relatively slow, with an average time of more than 2 years for acquisition by members of the group who learned it (Galef, 1992). Moreover, the rate of spread did not increase as the number of users increased. If the mechanism of transmission were imitation, an increase in the rate of propagation would be expected as more demonstrators became available for observation over time. In contrast, if processes of individual learning were at work, a slower and steadier rate of spread would be expected – which, in fact, was observed. The fact that Imo's friends and relatives were first to learn the behavior may be due to friends and relatives staying close to one another; Imo's friends likely went near the water more often during feeding than other group members, increasing their chances for individual discovery.

The other most widely cited case of animal culture concerns chimpanzees. For example, there are a number of population-specific tool-use traditions that have been documented for different chimpanzee communities – for example, termite-fishing, ant-fishing, ant-dipping, nut-cracking, and leaf-sponging (Whiten et al., 1999). Some of these population differences are due to the local ecologies of different groups of chimpanzees – individuals of each group learn to solve the problems presented by their local environment using the resources available in that environment. However, experimental studies have shown that there is more to it than this: Chimpanzees can learn from observing others using tools. What they learn, however, is less than what might be expected. What they learn are the effects on the environment that can be produced with a particular tool; they do not actually learn to copy another chimpanzee's behavioral strategies. For example, in one study, chimpanzees were presented with a rake-like tool and an out-of-reach object. The tool could be used in either of two ways, leading to the same end result of obtaining the object. One group of chimpanzees observed one method of tool use and another group observed the other method. The result was that chimpanzees used the same method or methods to obtain the object no matter which demonstration they observed (called *emulation learning*). When human children were given this same task, they much more often imitatively learned the precise technique demonstrated for them (Tomasello, 1996). Studies of chimpanzee gestural communication have found similar results. Young chimpanzees ritualize signals with group mates over repeated encounters; they do not learn the signals of group mates via imitation (Tomasello et al., 1997).

Chimpanzees and other nonhuman animals may thus engage in some forms of cultural transmission – defined broadly as the nongenetic transfer of information – but they do not do this by means of imitative learning if it is defined more narrowly as the reproduction of another individual's actual behavioral strategy to achieving a goal. In contrast, human beings learn from conspecifics by perceiving their goals and then attempting to reproduce the strategy that the other person uses in attempting to achieve that goal – truly cultural learning, as opposed to merely social learning (Tomasello et al., 1993). This small difference in learning process leads to a huge difference in cultural evolution; namely, it leads to cumulative cultural evolution in which the culture produces artifacts – both material artifacts such as tools and symbolic artifacts such as language and Arabic numerals – that accumulate modifications over historical time. Thus, one person invents something, other persons learn it and then modify and improve it, and then this new and improved version is learned by a new generation – and so on across generations. Imitative learning is a key to this process because it enables individuals to acquire the use of artifacts and other practices of their social groups relatively faithfully, which then serves as a kind of ratchet – that is, keeping the practice in place in the social group (perhaps for many generations) until some creative innovation comes along. In using these artifacts to mediate their interactions with the world, human children thus grow up in the accumulated wisdom of their entire social group, past and present.

It may be objected that there are a number of convincing observations of chimpanzee imitation in the literature and, indeed, there are a few. It is interesting, however, that basically all of the clear cases in the exhaustive review of Whiten and Ham (1992) concern chimpanzees that have had extensive human contact. In many cases, this has taken the form of intentional instruction involving human encouragement of behavior and attention, and even direct reinforcement for imitation for many months (e.g., 7 months of training in the case of Hayes and Hayes [1952] and 4 months of training in the case of Whiten and Custance [1996]). This raises the possibility that imitative learning skills may be influenced or even enabled by certain kinds of social interaction during early ontogeny.

This point of view is confirmed in a study by Tomasello, Savage-Rumbaugh, and Krüger (1993), which compared the imitative learning abilities of mother-reared captive chimpanzees, enculturated chimpanzees (raised like human children and exposed to a language-like system of communication), and 2-year-old human children. The subjects were shown 24 different and novel actions on objects, and their behavior on each trial was scored as to whether they successfully reproduced (1) the end result of the demonstrated action, and/or (2) the behavioral means used by the demonstrator. The major result was that the mother-reared chimpanzees rarely reproduced both the end and means of the novel actions (i.e., imitatively learned them). In contrast, the enculturated chimpanzees and the human children imitatively learned the novel actions much more frequently, and they did not differ from one another in this learning. Interesting corroboration for this latter finding is the fact that earlier in their ontogeny, these same enculturated chimpanzees seemed to learn many of the human-like symbols by means of imitative learning (Savage-Rumbaugh, 1990).

These observations raise the interesting possibility that a human-like socio-cultural environment is an essential component in the development of human-like social-cognitive and imitative learning skills no matter the species. That is, a sociocultural environment is essential not only for chimpanzees but also for human beings: in all likelihood, a human child raised in an environment lacking intentional interactions and other cultural characteristics would also not develop human-like skills of imitative learning. Therefore, the idea is that the learning skills that chimpanzees develop in the wild in the absence of human interaction (i.e., skills involving individual learning supplemented by emulation learning and ritualization) are sufficient to create and maintain their species-typical cultural activities, but they are not sufficient to create and maintain human-like cultural activities displaying the ratchet effect or cumulative cultural evolution. The fact that chimpanzees and other great apes raised from an early age and for many years in human-like cultural environments may develop some aspects of human social cognition and cultural learning demonstrates the power of cultural processes in ontogeny in a particularly dramatic way – although it is obvious that these processes do not turn chimpanzees into humans capable of creating their own culture from scratch.

2.0. HUMAN CULTURE

2.1. A Comparative Perspective

We may conclude, then, that whereas chimpanzees clearly create and maintain social traditions broadly defined, these traditions likely rest on different processes of social cognition and social learning than the cultural traditions of human beings. In some cases, this difference of process may not lead to any concrete differences of outcome in social organization, information transmission, or cognition. In other cases, however, a crucial difference emerges, which manifests itself in processes of cultural evolution – that is, processes by which a cultural tradition changes over time within a population.

Some human cultural traditions change over time in ways that seem to be adaptive and, moreover, that seem to accumulate modifications made by different individuals over time in the direction of greater complexity such that a wider range of functions is encompassed – what may be called "cumulative cultural evolution" or the "ratchet effect" (Tomasello et al., 1993). For example, the way that human beings have used objects as hammers has evolved significantly over the course of human history. This is evidenced in the artifactual record by various hammer-like tools that gradually widened their functional sphere as they were modified repeatedly to meet novel exigencies, evolving from simple stones, to composite tools composed of a stone tied to a stick, to various types of modern metal hammers and even mechanical hammers (some with nail-removing functions as well) (Basalla, 1988). Although we do not have such a detailed artifactual record, it is presumably the case that some cultural conventions and rituals (e.g., human languages and religious rituals) have become more complex over time as well, as they were modified to meet novel communicative and social needs. This process may be more characteristic of some human cultures or types of activities than others, but all cultures would seem to have at least some artifacts produced by the ratchet effect. However, there do not seem to be any behaviors of other animal species, including chimpanzees, that show cumulative cultural evolution (Boesch & Tomasello, 1998).

Tomasello et al. (1993) argued that cumulative cultural evolution depends on imitative learning – and perhaps active instruction on the part of adults – and cannot be brought about by means of "weaker" forms of social learning such as local enhancement, emulation learning, ontogenetic ritualization, or any form of individual learning. The argument is that cumulative cultural evolution depends on two processes – innovation and imitation (possibly supplemented by instruction) – that must take place in a dialectical process over time such that one step in the process enables the next. Thus, if an individual chimpanzee invented a more efficient way of fishing for termites by using a stick in a novel way that induced more termites to crawl onto it, youngsters who learned to fish via emulation from this individual would not reproduce this precise variant because they would not be focused on the innovator's behavioral techniques. They would use their own method of fishing to induce more termites onto the stick, and any other individuals watching them would use their own method as well, and so the novel strategy would simply die out with the inventor. (This is precisely the hypothesis of Kummer and Goodall [1985], who believe that many acts of creative intelligence on the part of nonhuman primates go unobserved by humans because they are not faithfully preserved in the group.) Conversely, if observers were capable of imitative learning, they might adopt the innovator's new strategic variant for termite fishing more or less faithfully. This new behavior would then put them into a new cognitive space, so to speak, in which they could think about the task and how to solve it in something like the manner of the innovator (standing in her "cognitive shoes"). All of the individuals who have done this are then in a position, possibly, to invent other variants that build on the initial one – which then others might adopt faithfully or even build on as well. The metaphor of the ratchet in this context is meant to capture the fact that imitative learning (with or without active instruction) provides the kind of faithful transmission that is necessary to hold the novel variant in place in the group so as to provide a platform for further innovations – with the innovations themselves varying in the degree to which they are individual or social/cooperative.[1]

In general, then, human cultural traditions may be most readily distinguished from chimpanzee social traditions – as well as the few other instances of culture observed in other primate species – precisely by the fact that they accumulate modifications over time; that is, they have cultural "histories." They accumulate modifications and have histories because the cultural-learning processes that support them are especially powerful: They are supported by the uniquely human cognitive adaptation for understanding others as intentional beings like the self – which creates forms of social learning that act as a ratchet by faithfully preserving newly innovated strategies in the social group until there is another innovation to replace them. We can see the relationship between these social-cognitive and cultural-learning skills most clearly in early human ontogeny.

2.2. The Ontogeny of Human Cultural Learning

Human children grow up in the ontogenetic niche of their culture that, in a very real sense, exists before they are born (Krüger & Tomasello, 1996). However, children also need to have social-cognitive skills if they are to exploit the pre-existing cultural resources in a species-typical manner (Vygotsky, 1978). These skills cannot be simply presupposed, as is often the case in cultural psychology.

---

[1] I should acknowledge at this point that things may not be quite as black and white as I have made them out to be. In a very interesting paper entitled "Why culture is common, but cultural evolution is rare," Boyd and Richerson (1996) hypothesize that humans and other primates both engage in the same kinds of social and imitative learning, but there may be a quantitative difference. Thus, chimpanzees may have some imitative learning abilities, but they may display them less consistently than humans or in a narrower range of contexts than humans – or it may even be that only some chimpanzee individuals have these skills. Boyd and Richerson argue that a rarity of key social-learning processes could make cultural evolution of the cumulative type impossible. The basic problem would be that there is too much slippage in the ratchet as, for example, one individual might imitatively learn another's innovation but then no other individuals could imitate her, or the individuals who did attempt to imitate her would do so only very poorly. Thus, the basic argument is that there is a quantitative difference in social-learning skills that leads to a qualitative difference in the historical trajectories of the resulting cultural traditions. In either case, however – whether the difference in human and ape social-learning skills is more qualitative and absolute or more quantitative and relative – the effect is that human beings currently have the social-cognitive and cultural-learning skills to create, as a species, some unique cognitive products based on cumulative cultural evolution.

This point is clearly demonstrated by the unfortunate case of children with autism, the majority of whom lack the social-cognitive skills necessary to participate fully in or to appropriate the artifacts and social practices characteristic of those around them (Baron-Cohen, 1993; Hobson, 1993). For typically developing children, the ontogeny of social-cognitive skills begins at the end of the first year of life.

2.2.1. *Joint Attention*

Six-month-old infants interact dyadically with objects, grasping and manipulating them, and they interact dyadically with other people, expressing emotions back-and-forth in a turn-taking sequence. However, at approximately 9 to 12 months of age, infants begin to engage in interactions that are triadic in the sense that they involve the referential triangle of child, adult, and an outside entity to which they share attention. Thus, infants at this age begin to flexibly and reliably look where adults are looking (i.e., gaze following), use adults as social reference points (i.e., social referencing), and act on objects in the way adults are acting on them (i.e., imitative learning) – in short, to "tune in" to the attention and behavior of adults toward outside entities. At this same age, infants also begin to use communicative gestures to direct adult attention and behavior to outside entities in which they are interested – in short, to get the adult to tune in to them. In many cases, several of these behaviors come together as the infant interacts with an adult in a relatively extended bout of joint engagement with an object (Bakeman & Adamson, 1984). Most often, the term *joint attention* is used to characterize this whole complex of triadic social skills and interactions (Moore & Dunham, 1995), and it represents something of a revolution in the way infants relate to their world.

Infants begin to engage in joint-attentional interactions when they begin to understand other persons as intentional agents like the self (Tomasello, 1995). Intentional agents are animate beings with the power to control their spontaneous behavior – but they are more than that. Intentional agents also have goals and make active choices among behavioral means for attaining those goals. Importantly, intentional agents also make active choices about what they pay attention to in pursuing those goals (see Gibson and Rader [1979] for the argument that attention is intentional perception). All of the specific joint-attentional behaviors in which infants follow, direct, or share adult attention and behavior are not separate activities or cognitive domains; they are simply different behavioral manifestations of this same underlying understanding of other persons as intentional agents. Strong support for this view comes from a study by Carpenter, Nagell, and Tomasello (1998), who followed a group of infants longitudinally from 9 to 15 months of age and found that for any individual child, these skills emerged together as a group, with predictable orderings among individual skills.

2.2.2. *Imitative Learning*

The social-cognitive revolution at 1 year of age sets the stage for the infants' second year of life, in which they begin to imitatively learn the use of all kinds of tools, artifacts, and symbols. For example, in a study by Meltzoff (1988), 14-month-old children observed an adult bend at the waist and touch his head to a panel, thus turning on a light. The children followed suit. Toddlers engaged in this somewhat unusual and awkward behavior, even though it would have been easier and more natural for them simply to push the panel with their hand. One interpretation of this behavior is that these children understood that (1) the adult had the goal of illuminating the light and then chose one means for doing so, from among other possible means; and (2) if they had the same goal, they could choose the same means. Cultural learning of this type thus relies fundamentally on children's tendency to identify with adults and on their ability to distinguish in the actions of others the underlying goal and the different means that might be used to achieve it. This interpretation is supported by a later finding of Meltzoff (1995) that 18-month-old children also imitatively learn actions that adults intend to perform, even if they are unsuccessful in doing so. Similarly, Carpenter, Akhtar, and Tomasello (1998) found that 16-month-old toddlers will imitatively learn from a complex behavioral sequence only those behaviors that appear intentional, ignoring those that appear accidental. Young children do not just mimic the limb movements of other persons, they also attempt to reproduce other persons' intended actions in the world.

Although it is not obvious at first glance, something like this same imitative learning process must happen if children are to learn the symbolic conventions of their native language. Although it is often assumed that young children acquire language when adults stop what they are doing, hold up objects, and name the objects for them, this is empirically not the case. Linguistics lessons such as these are (1) characteristic of only some parents in some cultures, and (2) not characteristic of any parents in any culture for words other than concrete nouns and some actions; that is, no one names for children acts of "giving" or prepositional relationships such as "on" or "for." In general, for the majority of their language, children must find a way to learn a new word in the ongoing flow of social interaction, sometimes from speech not even addressed to them (Brown, 2000). In some experiments, something of this process was captured as children learn words in situations in which the adult is not specifically intending that they learn a word, the referent is not perceptually available when the word is said, and there are multiple potential referents in the situation that the child must choose among based on various kinds of adult social-pragmatic cues. For example:

> In the context of a finding game, an adult announced her intentions to "find the toma" and then searched in a row of buckets all containing novel objects. Sometimes she found it in the first bucket searched, smiling and handing the object to the child. Sometimes, however, she had to search longer, rejecting unwanted

objects by scowling at them and replacing them in their bucket until she found the one she wanted (again, indicated by a smile and termination of the search). Children learned the new word for the object the adult intended to find regardless of whether or how many objects were rejected during the search process (Tomasello & Barton, 1994).

Also in the context of a finding game, an adult had the child find four different objects in four different hiding places, one of which was a distinctive toy barn. Once the child had learned which objects went with which places, the adult announced her intention to "find the gazzer." She then went to the toy barn, but it turned out to be "locked." She thus frowned at the barn and then proceeded to another hiding place, saying, "Let's see what else we can find" (taking out an object with a smile). Later, children demonstrated that they had learned "gazzer" for the object they knew the experimenter wanted in the barn – even though they never saw the object after they heard the new word, and even though the adult had frowned at the barn and smiled at a distracter object (Akhtar & Tomasello, 1996; Tomasello, Strosberg, & Akhtar, 1996).

An adult announced her intention to "dax Mickey Mouse" and then proceeded to perform one action accidentally and another intentionally (or sometimes in reverse order). Children learned the word for the intentional, not the accidental, action regardless of which came first in the sequence (Tomasello & Barton, 1994).

Tomasello et al. (1993) called this kind of imitative learning *cultural learning* because the children are not just learning things *from* other persons, they are also learning things *through* them – in the sense that they must know something of the adult's perspective on a situation to learn the active use of this same intentional act. The adult in the previous scenarios is not just moving and picking up objects randomly, she is *searching* for an object and the child must know this to make enough sense of her behavior to connect the new word to the adult's intended referent. The main theoretical point is that an organism can engage in cultural learning of this type only when it understands others as intentional agents like the self who have a perspective on the world that can be followed into, directed, and shared. Indeed, a strong argument can be made that children can only understand a symbolic convention in the first place if they understand their communicative partner as an intentional agent with whom one may share attention – because a linguistic symbol is nothing other than a marker for an intersubjectively shared understanding of a situation (Tomasello, 1999). As a point of comparison, children with autism do not understand other persons as intentional agents – or they do so to only an imperfect degree – and so they are very poor at the imitative learning of intentional actions in general (Smith & Bryson, 1994). Only half of them ever learn any language at all, and those who do learn some language are poor in word-learning situations such as those described previously (Baron-Cohen, Baldwin, & Crowson, 1997).

2.2.3. *Cognitive Representation*

It is important to also emphasize that when children learn linguistic symbols, what they are learning is a whole panoply of ways to manipulate the attention of other persons, sometimes on a single entity, based on such things as follows:

- generality (*thing, furniture, chair, desk chair*)
- perspective (*chase-flee, buy-sell, come-go, borrow-lend*)
- function (*father, lawyer, man, American; coast, shore, beach*)

There are many other perspectives that arise in grammatical combinations of various sorts (e.g., *She smashed the vase* versus *The vase was smashed*). Consequently, as children internalize a linguistic symbol – as they learn the human perspective embodied in that symbol – they cognitively represent not just the perceptual or motoric aspects of a situation, they also cognitively represent one way – among other ways of which they are also aware – that the current situation may be attentionally construed by "us," the users of the symbol. The perspectival nature of linguistic symbols thus represents a clear break with straightforward perceptual or sensory-motor cognitive representations; indeed, this perspectivity is what gives linguistic symbols their awesome cognitive power (Tomasello, 1999). It even allows children to learn linguistic means for conceptualizing objects as actions (e.g., *He porched the newspaper*), actions as objects (e.g., *Skiing is fun*), and many other metaphorical construals of things (e.g., *Love is a journey*).

3.0. FROM THE SOCIAL TO THE CULTURAL

To summarize, human beings share the majority of their cognitive skills and knowledge with other primates – including both the sensory-motor world of objects in their spatial, temporal, categorical, and quantitative relations and the social world of behaving conspecifics in their dominance and affiliative relationships. All primate species use their skills and knowledge to formulate creative and insightful strategies when problems arise in either the physical or social domain. However, humans have cognitive skills in addition to those shared with other members of the order: Human beings possess a species-unique cognitive adaptation that is in many ways an especially powerful cognitive adaptation because it changes in fundamental ways the *process* of cognitive evolution.

This adaptation arose at some specific point in human evolution, perhaps fairly recently, presumably based on some genetic and natural-selection events. This adaptation consists of the ability and tendency of individuals to identify with conspecifics in ways that enable them to understand them as intentional agents like the self, possessing their own intentions and attention, and eventually to understand them as mental agents like the self, possessing their own desires and beliefs. This new mode of understanding other persons radically changed the nature of all types of social interactions, including social learning, so that a unique form of cultural evolution began to take place over historical time as multiple generations of developing children learned various things from their forebears and then modified them in a way that led to an accumulation of these modifications – most typically as embodied in some material or symbolic artifact. The ratchet effect thus produced radically changed the nature of the ontogenetic niche in which human children develop ontogenetically so that, in effect, modern children encounter and interact with their physical and social world almost totally through the mediating lenses of preexisting cultural artifacts, which embody something of the inventors' and users' intentional relationships to the world when using them. Developing children are thus growing up in the midst of the best tools and symbols their forebears have invented for negotiating the rigors of their physical and social world. Moreover, as children internalize these tools and symbols – as they learn to use them through basic processes of cultural learning – they create in the process powerful new forms of cognitive representation based in the intentional and mental perspectives of other persons.

Thus, this understanding of how a single human cognitive adaptation could account for all of the many differences in the human and nonhuman primate cognition is that this single adaptation makes possible an evolutionarily new set of processes (i.e., processes of sociogenesis) that have done much of the actual work – and on a much faster time scale than biological evolution. Perhaps this single novelty changed the way that human beings interacted with one another, and with much effort over much historical time, these new ways of interacting transformed such basic primate phenomena as communication, dominance, exchange, and exploration into the human cultural institutions of language, government, money, and science – without any additional genetic events. The transformations in the different domains of human activity as a result of this new adaptation were not necessarily instantaneous. For example, human beings were already communicating with one another in complex ways when they began to understand one another as intentional agents. Therefore, it took some time, perhaps many generations, for this new understanding of others to make itself felt and thus for symbolic forms of communication to emerge. The same would hold true of the other domains of activity – such as various forms of cooperation and social learning – as this new kind of social understanding gradually enabled new kinds of social interactions and artifacts. Figure 3.1 presents an oversimplified and certainly nonexhaustive list of domains of human activity and how they might have been transformed by the uniquely human adaptation of social cognition as it worked itself into the social interactive process over many generations of human history.

	Social Domain	Cultural Domain
Communication	SIGNALS	SYMBOLS (intersubjective, perspectival)
Gaze of Others	GAZE FOLLOW	JOINT ATTENTION (intersubjectivity)
Social Learning	EMULATION, RITUALIZATION	CULTURAL LEARNING (reproducing intentional acts)
Cooperation	COORDINATION	COLLABORATION (role-taking)
Teaching	FACILITATION	INSTRUCTION (mental states of others)
Object Manipulation	TOOLS	ARTIFACTS (intentional affordances)

Figure 3.1. Some different domains of social activity transformed over historical time into domains of cultural activity by the uniquely human way of understanding conspecifics.

4.0. CONCLUSION

It is difficult to simultaneously keep one's eye on similarities and differences, but that is what we must do if we are to understand human culture in its evolutionary context. Human culture emerged evolutionarily from primate social organization, which forms its foundation. Primate social organization includes the recognition of individuals, the forming of long-term social relationships, and many complex cooperative and competitive activities. Differences between groups of primates within the same species demonstrate that there is much flexibility in primate cognition and learning and that much information may be passed along socially in primate groups.

However, human cultures pass along information in a different way and therefore result in different kinds of social (i.e., cultural) organizations. Because human beings understand one another in special ways – that is, because human beings have certain species-specific social-cognitive skills – they engage in various forms of cultural learning and instruction. This leads to a species-unique pattern of cumulative cultural evolution, characterized most dramatically by the creation of artifacts with histories such as languages and other social institutions. Human children then grow up in the midst of the accumulated cultural products of their culture and, given that they have the requisite social-cognitive skills, this allows them to benefit – in a way not possible in other species – from the accumulated knowledge and skills of all the previous individuals in their culture, past and present. It is these cultural processes, more than anything else, that make human cognition and social organization so dazzlingly complex.

REFERENCES

Akhtar, N., & Tomasello, M. (1996). Two-year-olds learn words for absent objects and actions. *British Journal of Developmental Psychology, 14,* 79–93.

Bakeman, R., & Adamson, L. (1984). Coordinating attention to people and objects in mother–infant and peer–infant interactions. *Child Development, 55,* 1278–1289.

Baron-Cohen, S. (1993). From attention-goal psychology to belief-desire psychology: The development of a theory of mind and its dysfunction. In S. Baron-Cohen, H. Tager-Flusberg, & D. J. Cohen (Eds.), *Understanding other minds: Perspectives from autism* (pp. 211–245). New York: Oxford University Press.

Baron-Cohen, S., Baldwin, D., & Crowson, M. (1997). Do children with autism use the speaker's direction of gaze to crack the code of language? *Child Development, 68,* 48–57.

Basalla, G. (1988). *The evolution of technology.* Cambridge, UK: Cambridge University Press.

Boesch, C., & Tomasello, M. (1998). Chimpanzee and human culture. *Contemporary Anthropology, 39,* 591–604.

Boyd, R., & Richerson, P. (1996). Why culture is common but cultural evolution is rare. *Proceedings of the British Academy, 88,* 77–93.

Brown, P. (2000). The conversational context for language acquisition: A Tzeltal (Mayan) case study. In M. Bowerman & S. Levinson (Eds.), *Language acquisition and conceptual development* (pp. 133–154). Cambridge, UK: Cambridge University Press.

Carpenter, M., Akhtar, N., & Tomasello, M. (1998). Sixteen-month-old infants differentially imitate intentional and accidental actions. *Infant Behavior and Development, 21,* 315–330.

Carpenter, M., Nagell, K., & Tomasello, M. (1998). Social cognition, joint attention, and communicative competence from 9 to 15 months of age. *Monographs of the Society for Research in Child Development, 63*(255), 1–174.

Galef, B. (1992). The question of animal culture. *Human Nature, 3,* 157–178.

Gibson, E., & Rader, N. (1979). Attention: The perceiver as performer. In G. Hale & M. Lewis (Eds.), *Attention and cognitive development* (pp. 6–36). New York: Plenum Press.

Hayes, K. J., & Hayes, C. (1952). Imitation in a home-raised chimpanzee. *Journal of Comparative Psychology, 45,* 450–459.

Hobson, P. (1993). *Autism and the development of mind.* Hillsdale, NJ: Erlbaum.

Kawai, M. (1965). Newly acquired precultural behavior of the natural troop of Japanese monkeys on Koshima Islet. *Primates, 6,* 1–30.

Krüger, A., & Tomasello, M. (1996). Cultural learning and learning culture. In D. Olson (Ed.), *Handbook of education and human development: New models of teaching, learning, and schooling* (pp. 169–187). Oxford, UK: Blackwell.

Kummer, H., & Goodall, J. (1985). Conditions of innovative behavior in primates. *Philosophical Transactions of the Royal Society of London, 308,* 203–214.

Meltzoff, A. (1988). Infant imitation after a one-week delay: Long-term memory for novel acts and multiple stimuli. *Developmental Psychology, 24,* 470–476.

Meltzoff, A. (1995). Understanding the intentions of others: Reenactment of intended acts by 18-month-old children. *Developmental Psychology, 31,* 838–850.

Moore, C., & Dunham, P. (1995). *Joint attention: Its origins and role in development.* Hillsdale, NJ: Erlbaum.

Savage-Rumbaugh, S. (1990). Language as a cause-effect communication system. *Philosophical Psychology, 3,* 55–76.

Smith, I. M., & Bryson, S. E. (1994). Imitation and action in autism: A critical review. *Psychological Bulletin, 116,* 259–273.

Tomasello, M. (1995). Joint attention as social cognition. In C. Moore & P. Dunham (Eds.), *Joint attention: Its origins and role in development* (pp. 103–130). Hillsdale, NJ: Lawrence Erlbaum.

Tomasello, M. (1996). Do apes ape? In C. Heyes & B. Galef (Eds.), *Social learning in animals: The roots of culture* (pp. 319–346). New York: Academic Press.

Tomasello, M. (1999). *The cultural origins of human cognition.* Cambridge, MA: Harvard University Press.

Tomasello, M., & Barton, M. (1994). Learning words in non-ostensive contexts. *Developmental Psychology, 30,* 639–650.

Tomasello, M., & Call, J. (1994). Social cognition of monkeys and apes. *Yearbook of Physical Anthropology, 37,* 273–305.

Tomasello, M., & Call, J. (1997). *Primate cognition.* New York: Oxford University Press.

Tomasello, M., Call, J., Warren, J., Frost, T., Carpenter, M., & Nagell, K. (1997). The ontogeny of chimpanzee gestural signals: A comparison across groups and generations. *Evolution of Communication, 1,* 223–253.

Tomasello, M., Krüger, A., & Ratner, H. (1993). Cultural learning. *Behavioral and Brain Sciences, 16,* 495–552.

Tomasello, M., Savage-Rumbaugh, S., & Krüger, A. (1993). Imitative learning of actions on objects by children, chimpanzees, and enculturated chimpanzees. *Child Development, 64,* 1688–1705.

Tomasello, M., Strosberg, R., & Akhtar, N. (1996). Eighteen-month-old children learn words in non-ostensive contexts. *Journal of Child Language, 23,* 157–176.

Visalberghi, E., & Fragaszy, D. M. (1990). Food-washing behaviour in tufted capuchin monkeys, *Cebus apella,* and crab-eating macaques, *Macaca fascicularis. Animal Behaviour, 40,* 829–836.

Vygotsky, L. (1978). *Mind in society: The development of higher psychological processes* (M. Cole, Ed.). Cambridge, MA: Harvard University Press.

Whiten, A., & Custance, D. (1996). Studies of imitation in chimpanzees and children. In C. Heyes & B. Galef (Eds.), *Social learning in animals: The roots of culture* (pp. 78–111). New York: Academic Press.

Whiten, A., Goodall, J., McGrew, W., Nishida, T., Reynolds, V., Sugiyama, Y., Tutin, C., Wrangham, R., & Boesch, C. (1999). Cultures in chimpanzees. *Nature, 399,* 682–685.

Whiten, A., & Ham, R. (1992). On the nature and evolution of imitation in the animal kingdom: Reappraisal of a century of research. In P. J. B. Slater, J. S. Rosenblatt, C. Beer, & M. Milinsky (Eds.), *Advances in the study of behavior* (pp. 239–283). New York: Academic Press.

4

Transmission, Self-Organization, and the Emergence of Language: A Dynamic Systems Point of View

PAUL VAN GEERT

INTRODUCTION

Language is a human capacity that is typically transmitted from one generation to another (one speaks about one's mother tongue, for instance). However, what does transmission mean in this regard? The concept of transmission is well defined in fields like physics or the mathematical theory of information, where it relates to deep principles of the organization of matter, such as entropy. To what extent do we understand transmission if language is concerned? How does it relate to claims about language as an innate capacity? How does intergenerational transmission relate to the emergence or evolution of language over many generations? This chapter discusses these questions from the point of view of dynamic systems theory, which provides a general approach to understanding processes of change and emergence.

1.0. A TALE OF HEAT AND ORDER...

Since the early 1990s, developmental psychologists have been exploring a new approach to describing, explaining, and understanding developmental processes – namely, dynamic systems theory (Thelen & Smith, 1994, 1998; van Geert, 1994, 2003). Dynamic systems theory offers a natural and intuitive approach to such processes. It emphasizes the actual development as it takes place in real time. It explicitly accounts for each step in the process as the direct outcome of the preceding step. It focuses on mutual interactions between variables – that is, forces or components that affect one another. A major feature of dynamic systems thinking is its emphasis on the ubiquitousness of self-organization (Lewis & Granic, 1999). Self-organization refers to the spontaneous creation of order, structure, complexity, or information in a system, mostly under highly specific conditions that do not contain the structures or contents that will emerge through the self-organizational process. The notion of order is crucial here and will lead us on a journey that covers some basic axioms of scientific thinking.

1.1. The Timeline of Order

If I throw a box of plastic letters on the ground, the final position of the letters is accidental; that is, I have not specified explicitly where every single letter should land. The position of the letters does not show any order – that is, a specific association between various kinds of letters; it would be greatly surprising if the letters that fell on the ground spontaneously formed the sentence, *The quick brown fox jumps over the lazy dog*, or some other type of message. If any salient association occurs in the pile of letters, it is most likely due to the fact that the letters started out that way – for instance, because the vowels and consonants lay together in the box of letters. In this sense, whatever order there is after I throw the letters on the ground was most likely present before. Moreover, whatever order is left after the throwing is less than the order present beforehand. However, in the unlikely case that some sort of Harry Potter scenario occurred, and the letters that at first lay crisscross on the ground began to move toward each other and spontaneously assembled themselves into a meaningful message, we would probably not believe our eyes and would think somebody was playing tricks on us.

1.1.1. *Entropy*

In nature, there are myriad processes in which order spontaneously decreases. A cup of coffee cools down and a house becomes messy if not properly cleaned. It is this inevitable breakdown of order that came to be of interest to theoretical physicists working in the heyday of capitalism and the industrial revolution (see Prigogine and Stengers [1984] for a discussion on the context of self-organizing systems). When confronted with the steam engine, those physicists discovered basic laws about the nature of energy. They discovered that on the whole, energy does not disappear, but rather it becomes less useful (the actual reasoning is more complicated, but this nevertheless is the central point). Ironically speaking, if you are a 19th-century capitalist, you do not want energy to become less useful: You want to keep your wealth and, even better, you want to increase it. Thus, although the first law of thermodynamics – because it was thermodynamics that resulted from the investigations of the physicists of those days – tells you that energy on the whole will be conserved, the second law tells you that if you leave things on their own, there will be a spontaneous decay of order and wealth and, ultimately, everybody and everything will end up just as rich – or as poor – as anybody else. This inevitable decay of order is also called the *increase of entropy*, which is a measure of the amount of disorder in a system. Thus, in short, entropic systems are systems characterized by the spontaneous loss of order (e.g., energy or structure).

1.1.2. *Transmission*

It was also in the same historical era that scientists became interested in the formal understanding and analysis of transmission. This interest entailed a fundamental definition of *work*, which was basically the practical impetus behind the interest in thermodynamics. In the Newtonian tradition, work relates to the energy invested in applying a force over a distance. This is fine if you have an oven that burns coal and produces a lot of heat, but you need to transmit that heat to make steam, and transmit the steam to make a movement, and transmit the movement to do something, such as weaving cotton or producing artificial dyes to color the fabric. We have just seen that in the process of transmission, heat and energy is inevitably lost. However, technology helps solve this problem, in that it helps to limit the loss as much as possible and make the transmission of heat and energy as efficient as possible.

Meanwhile, in those early days when the ovens burned and the steam engines rolled, the phenomenon of self-organization was all around – as it always had been – although it did not get along very well with the entropic machines that augmented the wealth of the entrepreneurs. Self-organization was demonstrated by the growth of seeds into plants, the growth of organisms in general, the increase in technological skills over generations, the emergence of the masses rising up, and the foundation of socialist and other political parties.

It is interesting that when information became a major commodity, around the middle of the 20th century, the basic ideas of thermodynamics were exported to the realm of information (Pierce, 1961). Shannon's mathematical theory of information has much in common with the theories that describe energy, energy transmission, and entropy (Shannon, 1948). The theory deals with the transmission of information over a distance, from one receiver to another. Information is similar to order and structure: If information is transmitted, it spontaneously loses some of its order and structure. The technology of information transmission helps one to transmit information as efficiently as possible – that is, with the least possible loss of information for the smallest possible cost. However, in a system that transmits information between a sender and a receiver, the best possible state – if at all achievable – is that of an entirely conserved message. It never occurs that in the process of transmission or storage, the message spontaneously increases the amount of useful information it contains; it does not spontaneously increase its order and structure. (This is not an entirely true statement – it is just that the probability of such a spontaneous increase occurring is extremely small, given that the order it must increase is already very complex.) At the time Shannon published his mathematical theory of communication (in reality, 1 year earlier), Ashby (1947) published a short article in which he introduced the term *self-organization*. His major point was that self-organization is possible in what he called "an absolute system" or "machine." This idea linked the paradigm of mechanistic explanation to the realm of complex biological and psychological phenomena, such as children developing and increasing in mental complexity and order; spontaneously constructing basic concepts such as space and number; and spontaneously constructing the grammar of their mother tongue as they go through the classic stages of babbling, one-word phrases, the two-word stage, and so on.

1.2. Transmission and Developmental Theory

At this point, however, our story grinds to a halt. In the 1950s, there were not that many scholars who saw development in children – cognitive or linguistic – as an example of self-organization (i.e., the spontaneous increase of order, structure, and knowledge in a child's mind). An obvious but somewhat isolated defender of this position was the Swiss Piaget, whose theories were rooted in a European philosophical tradition that was already obsolete at that time and that focused on the spontaneous tendency of living things to become ever better and more complex (Piaget, 1975). There was another defender, but his work lay buried in Soviet Russian archives, deemed politically incorrect by the officials and largely unknown in the West. This defender was Vygotsky (1978, 1987), who had pointed out the fact that the development of an individual is a link in the historical chain of culture and civilization. Every new generation incorporates the means and tools developed by previous generations and, in turn, contributes to the further enhancement and extension of those tools. Thus, there is spontaneous increase in information: It is the work of society, through its historical development, incorporated in the growth, education, and development of its members (van der Veer & Valsiner, 1991; van Geert, 1994).

However, the major point of view at that time was that development – of knowledge, skills, language, and so forth – was a product of learning and that learning was an aspect of transmission. Children learned their mother tongue in the sense that they incorporated the information about that language given to them. Child-rearing, education, and schooling comprised the technology by which the process of knowledge transmission proceeded as efficiently as possible, with the least possible loss of information (although it is likely that the elder generation, as it always has done, must have complained about the fact that the younger generation knew increasingly less and was increasingly less educated, thus invoking a [not very serious] educational analog of the entropic principle). The theories of learning, which were among the new scientific insights developed in the first half of the 20th century, tried to unravel the process of transmission from the perspective of the receiver. How does the receiver incorporate the information given such that it becomes stored and maintained, with as little loss and deformation as possible?

There is, unfortunately, a basic flaw with the view that sees development and learning from the standpoint of transmission, as expressed, for instance, in the mathematical theory of communication and backed up by the laws of thermodynamics. The flaw is easy to find: If order can, at best, remain the same and, in practice, deteriorates, then recurrent transmission – which is what happens in any historical society – must inevitably lead from the more complex to the lesser, from knowledge to ignorance. This, of course, is not what we see happening around us. Perhaps the scholars who favored the approach of learning and transmission were not capable of making the link between what they daily observed in reality and what some fundamental axioms of physics prescribed to happen. However, if their theories entailed transmission, they were forced to obey the laws that governed such transmission, and these laws did not leave room for the natural observation that things become more mature and complex as they grow and that people make and invent new things that others had not yet invented.

1.3. Chomsky and the Issue of Language Transmission

The scholar who was to find the basic flaw, the dangerous tear in the fabric, was Chomsky. The discovery occurred in the late 1950s and concerned a particularly radical version of the transmission theory of language – namely, Skinner's theory of operant learning as applied to verbal behavior (Chomsky, 1959; Skinner, 1957). Although he did not state it in these terms, Chomsky's reasoning was basically this: Every mature user of language knows things – that is, has information about language that is not transmitted in the learning sense of the word. This information concerns general properties of grammar, and Chomsky argued that it could not be incorporated in the channel(s) through which language was transmitted. To state it in information-theoretical terms, these channels had insufficient bandwidth to convey the message in question, and there exists no technical solution to the problem of how to convey it anyway. (The argument is better known under the term *poverty of the stimulus*, with the connotation that there exists no technological way to make it sufficiently rich.) Yet, the information is there, in the mind of the speaker. So, how did it get there?

To solve this problem, there are at least three logical possibilities. The first is that Chomsky was wrong, in that the information in question was transmitted anyway, perhaps by some complicated means that was not yet understood in the 1950s. The second possibility is that this information was already there before the language was transmitted; that is, the information is innate. The third possibility is that it was neither transmitted nor already there: It emerged spontaneously, as a consequence of the transmission of those aspects of language that were transmittable. For various reasons, the third possibility was not a possibility at that time (the 1960s, say) and if it was seen as one, then it was of the same order as possibilities that referred to magic, divine interference, or fairy tales (note, however, Ashby's 1947 proof of the possibility of self-organization in machines). When Chomsky and allies such as Fodor (1975) had their "official" discussion with Piaget, the notion of spontaneous emergence was explicitly shoved aside as implausible (Piatelli-Palmarini, 1980). This obvious disbelief must have surprised the old man Piaget, who sympathized with Chomsky's view that something as complex as language cannot be transmitted and, therefore, cannot be learned (de Graaf, 1999). In fact, Fodor had already explicitly denied the possibility for a system to become more complex out of itself, without the potential of higher complexity being present in the system in advance. Fodor thus rejected Piaget's developmental theory of increasing complexity of cognitive structure (Fodor, 1975).

The point at issue here is the number of plausible logical possibilities to answer Chomsky's criticism of the transmission theory of language. The number of plausible answers was set at two: Something is either transmitted or it is already there. At present, we would set it at three: the possibility that something is either transmitted, or is already there, or spontaneously emerges through a process of self-organization.

The point emphasized here is that there are, in fact, not really three but indeed two possibilities, but they differ from the two possibilities distinguished in the 1960s and 1970s. One is based on the notion of transmission and obeys the entropic principle (i.e., the spontaneous decrease of order). It entails the actual transmission (i.e., the environmentalist teaching and learning) solution as well as the innateness solution. The innateness solution also implies that a complex structure does not emerge by itself and that it must be transmitted from a source or sender – genes, in this particular case – to a receiver, the brain, the language user, or whatever. The implicit idea is again that the arrow of time is the arrow of entropy; that is, it inevitably points from more structure to less (or, at best, to conservation of structure if the technology of transmission is good enough). Conversely, the basic idea of complex dynamic systems is that for many natural (i.e., biological, cultural, social, psychological) contexts, the arrow of time points in the opposite direction – namely, from less to more structure, order, or information. Let it be clear that the latter solution does not run against any basic law of thermodynamics: The increase in order proceeds at the cost of energy consumption and, therefore, ultimately favors the increase of entropy anyway (Greene, 2005; Prigogine & Stengers, 1984).

At this point, we have arrived at a fundamental question, which is whether the "entropic" model of transmission applies at all to the realm of biological, cultural, social, or psychological entities. It is undeniable that – for instance, in the development of children – transmission plays a crucial role. Much of what we call development is indeed the transmission and appropriation of skills, knowledge, habits, and so forth, a transmission that occurs from more to less mature persons. Conversely, I think it is equally undeniable that much of what we call development is indeed a process of spontaneous emergence, or self-organization of forms that is not prescribed or directly guided by instruction. Thus, is human development – to continue with this example – a mixture of transmission and self-organization: some things being transmitted, others spontaneously emerging? I think the answer is that understanding a developmental system, such as a child growing up in a cultural environment, requires a unification of the notions of transmission and self-organization into a synthetic theory (van Geert, 1989, 1998).

Let me begin by explaining why a process of transmission as described under the classic theory of entropic communication (implying spontaneous loss of order and increase of noise) is not applicable to living systems.

2.0. A SYNTHESIS OF TRANSMISSION AND SELF-ORGANIZATION: THE CASE OF LANGUAGE EVOLUTION AND LANGUAGE ACQUISITION

2.1. Principles of Information Transmission

Shannon's (1948) mathematical theory of communication, which forms our "standard" model of transmission, relates information to probability. Consider, for instance, an imaginary sender and receiver, each equipped with a "mind" consisting of a piece of paper with eight photographs of European heads of state and thus capable of eight possible "mental states," each specifying a particular photograph. In this case, the sender's and receiver's internal states are highly structured. However, it suffices that the sender and receiver are connected by a very narrow channel of three bits. With these 3 bits, 2^3 messages can be formed, and this suffices to determine which of the 8 photographs is "meant" (Aleksander, 2002). It is clear that the bandwidth of the channel greatly underdetermines the information given (i.e., the photographs). Sender and receiver contain a massive amount of information (i.e., photographs) but their uncertainty is only 1/8. Thus, to understand the process of information transmission, one needs to know the structure of sender and receiver to determine the content or meaning of the transmitted message (by meaning, we simply understand that which the receiver "does" with the message, which in this case is to select one of eight photographs). Not only does this example demonstrate that messages commonly underdetermine the complexity of the associated meanings, it also illustrates some other properties that become more interesting in the context of developmental processes. To begin with, the system shows a clear bias with regard to the information given. If the three-bit channel were replaced by a four-bit channel, all information exceeding the three bits needed to identify the photograph at issue would be treated as noise and, in fact, not be attended to.

Assume that the internal structure is now expanded to 16 instead of 8 photographs. There exist various possibilities to solve the communication problem that has arisen here. One possibility would be to increase the bandwidth of the channel so that it can now transmit four bits. Another solution would be to change the system's internal structure by dividing the 16 pictures into 4 quadrants of 4 pictures each. Once this has been done, the bandwidth of the channel can be reduced to two bits and the messages expanded to two submessages:

One specifies the quadrant and the other specifies the picture in the quadrant. From an evolutionary point of view, a "mutation" of this kind, in the direction of a compositional internal structure, could easily lead to a compositional language that requires only a two-bit channel (Brighton, 2002). This example shows that there are important principles behind the organization and meaning of messages that are independent of how complex the system of messages, senders, and receivers is. One principle is the connection between form and meaning, exemplified by the connection between the syntax of the message (i.e., two ordered submessages in our example) and its meaning (i.e., the internal state corresponding with the message). Another principle is that the receiver is, by definition, biased toward the structure of the information and that the bias changes as the receiver's structure changes. Yet another principle is that nonlinearity can be a basic property from the start, such as when the increase in internal structure gives rise to a decrease in required bandwidth and the emergence of compositional structure.

2.2. Information Transmission as an Iterative Process

Meanwhile, the mathematical theory of communication confines itself to a simple system of sender–channel–receiver. The basic process consists of a message transmitted by a sender via a channel, which is received by a receiver. The channel carries the message and is subject to noise. As far as the latter is concerned, it is easy to make a distinction between noise that emerges from an external source and noise that emerges from the internal source. The standard option is that noise emerges externally: The channel leaks information or is subject to an accidental invasion of information. This is the type of noise that forms the subject of engineering or statistical efforts: how to shield the channel from incoming or outgoing noise, how to filter the real signal from the noise imposed. However, we just had an example of noise that emerges because of internal constraints: For a system consisting of 8 possible states, a 4-bit channel contains 1 bit too many; this bit is – by definition – noise, irrespective of how meaningful this noise would be for a system consisting of 16 states, for instance. (The fourth bit could be used to make the information more redundant and thus more reliable, but that possibility does not affect the principle.)

In dynamic systems theory, conversely, systems are described in the form of iterative (also called recursive) processes. An iterative process takes an "input" to produce an "output" and then takes this "output" as its next "input" to produce another output, and so on.

The mathematical definition of *dynamic(al) system* is "a means of describing how one state develops into another state over the course of time" (Weisstein, 1999, p. 501). Thus, if x_t is a specification of a "state" at time t, a dynamic model takes the following form:

$$x_{t+1} = f(x_t) \qquad [1]$$

For example, x_{t+1} can represent the size of a population at time $t + 1$, which is a function of the population's size at time t. It can be the next message in a chain of messages, in which each message is a function of the message that precedes it. More precisely, an iterative process of information transmission sends a message to a receiver, who receives the message and then sends a transformation of *that* message to another receiver, and so on. Mostly, technical transmission systems can be described in the form of confined, noniterative systems; this is the application that was implicitly referred to in Shannon's theory. A television program, for instance, is broadcast to my home and shown on my television. Where the program originates and what I, the viewer, do with it is of no concern to the technical problem of transmission. If I were to make a video copy of that program, give it to another person who makes a video copy that he then gives to another person, and so on, I would witness a good example of the fact that in those recopied messages, entropy increases in the form of increasing noise and deterioration of quality.

Biological transmission systems comply with the iterative model, which makes all the difference. For instance, a parent organism transmits its DNA to its offspring, which then acts as a parent organism to transmit the DNA to its offspring, and so forth. This iterative (or recursive) process takes place many times and in that process, the message – and, in this case, by definition, also the sender and receiver – undergoes radical transformations. It was Darwin's (1836) major insight that such a process can lead to an increase in complexity, in the sense of a differentiation of biological species. (Note that adaptation does not automatically entail an increase in "average" complexity; see Gould, 1996.) For many of Darwin's contemporaries, this idea was difficult to accept because they strongly believed in a world that was created in the beginning and transmitted its forms and properties unchanged. It is not unlikely that had Mendel's (1993, originally published in 1865) research on genetic transmission been widely known at that time, Darwin's case would have been considerably more difficult to defend because Mendel's research basically uncovered the mechanism of genetic transmission of discrete properties, not of spontaneous increase in complexity (Marantz-Henig, 2000). The problem with these discrete packages of information is guaranteeing that they do not deteriorate over time, like the copied and recopied videotapes of the preceding example.

Under the entropic model, in the end, the transformation cannot be but a deterioration, a decrease of information and structure. Such entropic processes, if they occur, die out – to use a metaphor from the biological realm. Thus, there are two possibilities for iterative (or recursive) transmission processes: (1) they remain invariant for some time, if the technology of transmission (biological or otherwise) is good enough to conserve the information; or (2) they are, in fact, nonentropic processes, which lead to differentiation of structure or information, increase of structure, and so forth. That is, given the vulnerability of entropic transmission processes, every transmission process with a long enough history must be a process that has major features of self-organization (i.e., spontaneous generation of order and structure).

2.3. Scenarios for Iterative Information Transmission

2.3.1. *Scenario 1*

Biological systems involved in a cultural, historical process are a good example of iterative (or recursive) processes of information transmission. Organisms have a limited life span and must be replaced through processes of biological reproduction. A biological organism *in statu nascendi* is a structure of incredible complexity. Let us continue to use the overly simplified system with its eight messages and eight meanings (i.e., internally stored photographs) as an example of an information-processing system. Assume that this system enters into a process in which it receives information from a previous generation of systems and then passes the information to the next generation of systems. We have seen that even in this extremely simplified example, receivers are not just simple containers. It is the structure of the receiver that determines the information given. Thus, receiving information brings about an internal, causal process in the system (which, at its limit, might be extremely simple). In the example, we saw how eight bits of information select one of the information-rich photographs represented in the imaginary receiver. If, in this case, the biological structure is seen as the eight pictures, the cultural information is the simple message about which of the eight pictures to choose. It is conceivable that in this kind of system, the meaning of the messages – that is, the mapping of a symbol onto an internally stored photograph – can be learned. It is also conceivable that over the generations, the photograph-symbol mappings fluctuate or change (e.g., a symbol "1" once mapped onto photograph 1 is now associated with photograph 2, and photograph 1 becomes associated with symbol "2"). Because the mappings belong to what we can term the system's culture (i.e., it is not part of the system's biology), they provide an example of cultural change over a fixed biological structure. (In the simulation studies discussed later, this is roughly the level of simplification at which issues such as learning, culture, and genetic transmission are simplified. Although such simplifications seemingly reduce reality to a toy world, they can be of considerable help in making difficult problems manageable for further understanding.)

If iterated many times (i.e., over many generations), the system will at best remain stable; that is, the information content will at best be conserved over the iterations. Given the difference in complexity between the internal system and the simple message, it is conceivable that such a system could survive for quite some time – at least as far as the transmission aspect of "cultural" information is concerned. However, given the omnipresence of noise, it is more likely that in a system like this, the entropy increases; that is, the biological structure, which is complex, gets lost over the generations and, therefore, the message transmission also becomes impoverished and finally dwindles. The questions, of course, are where the highly complex internal structure comes from and how and where it originated; however, that does not need to be of concern here. The internal structure and the messages are separate realms that are mapped onto each other during the course of a system's "life span" but that are not causally intertwined.

In this unrealistic example, we already have a number of ingredients that are similar to those found in real language and language development. There is form and meaning, syntax, eventual nonlinearity in the mapping, a distinction between biology and culture – there are even cultural change and history. However, there is no causal interaction between the messages and the internal structure of the system.

In short, the first scenario of iterated message transmission is that there exists some complex internal structure that arose basically by accident, that provides for an opportunity of message-structure mapping, and that is subject to entropy – that is, to spontaneous loss of structure if not otherwise counterbalanced (e.g., by a robust genetic transmission system that conserves the structure over generations). This scenario is similar to Chomsky's notion of Universal Grammar as a nonadaptationist, biologically emergent property (Chomsky, 1972). The motive behind discussing this scenario is not to criticize this idea (see Pinker and Bloom [1990] for a thorough discussion of the nonadaptationist view); rather, the point is to show that it arises quite naturally if a fundamentally transmission-oriented view is applied to an iterative process (e.g., intergenerational transmission of language). In the next section, I show that the bifurcation between the "message" and the internal structure is incompatible with the notion of iterating systems (i.e., "historical" or evolutionary systems).

2.3.2. Scenario 2

The alternative scenario is based on the notion that a message of whatever kind amounts to some sort of physical process that causes its receiver to change in some way – more precisely, to change as a causal function of the combination of the structure of the message with the structure of the receiver itself. Because in an iterative process of transmission the message must depend on, among other things, the structure of the sender (and the structure of the channel, but that is not at stake here), and because the sender is, by definition, also a receiver, the message sent by the receiver is now a function of how that receiver was changed by the message transmitted earlier. (This is similar to Ashby's [1947] original reasoning with regard to the emergence of self-organization.) The notion of change can incorporate basically anything, from a transient change to a fundamental alteration of the internal structure.

Let us specify this chain in the form of a series of simple equations. First, a message M is some function of the structure of a sender/receiver system, SR, as follows:

$$M_t = f_a(SR_t) \qquad [2]$$

where t is an indication of a moment in time and f_a is an indication of the function. That is, a message is determined by what a sender can send and what a receiver can receive.

In line with our theoretical speculations, we assume that the message is a causal condition that affects the structure of SR (the sender/receiver organism); thus:

$$SR_{t+1} = f_b(SR_t, M_t) \qquad [3]$$

where SR_{t+1} is a specification of the structure of the sender/receiver at time $t+1$.

Thus, the message at $t+1$ is specified as a function of the altered structure of the sender/receiver, as follows:

$$M_{t+1} = f_a(SR_{t+1}) = f_a(f_b(SR_t, M_t)) \qquad [4]$$

At $t+2$, it is specified as follows:

$$M_{t+2} = f_a(SR_{t+2}) = f_a(SR_{t+1}, f_a(f_b(SR_t, M_t)) \qquad [5]$$

and so on. In this iterative process, the message is transforming the internal structure of the sender/receiver and the structure of the sender/receiver is transforming the message.

Iterative processes often tend to move toward an attractor state, which is a state in which the next iteration is similar to the preceding one. This definition applies to a point attractor, which is the standard case discussed herein; more complex attractor states are possible (Mitchener & Nowak, 2004).

Thus, the transmission system has reached a point attractor state if

$$f_b(SR_t, M_t) = SR_t \qquad [6]$$

and, thus, if

$$SR_{t+1} = SR_t \qquad [7]$$

and

$$M_{t+1} = M_t \qquad [8]$$

What these equations mean is that, first, an iterative transmission system has reached a point attractor (i.e., stability) if (1) the transformation caused by the message sent results in a reproduction (or conservation) of the structure necessary to send this message, and (2) the messages are now identical in terms of their underlying structure and causal functions.

If we apply these equations to explain the life span of a single transmission system, we find the following process. First, the initial structure of the sender/receiver is a product of biological transmission (e.g., genetic transmission, embryogenesis). We know that this initial structure must be different from the final state structure, which, to a certain extent, is the result of the chain of messages that the mature system received during its lifetime. These messages are cultural in the sense that they are not the product of the biological transmission system. Assuming that a message is a causal event, the consequence of which depends on its own properties and the properties of the system that receives it, we can conclude that a message sent by a "mature" sender/receiver (that is in the attractor or equilibrium state) must have a different effect on the immature sender/receiver than it has on the mature one. In the mature system, the effect of the message is to maintain the mature system's structure (remember that we are dealing with an extremely simplified system). In the immature sender/receiver, the message causes a process of transformation of the sender/receiver structure, in which case we say that the immature sender/receiver "learns," or "acquires" something, or "develops." If it does not cause such a transformational process, we have no way to explain where the mature sender/receiver originated any-way, unless we assume that maturity arises through merely biological processes, which are represented in the following way:

$$SR_{t+n} = f_g(SR_{t+n-1}) = f_g(SR_{t+n-2}) = \cdots \qquad [9]$$

The following assumptions hold: First, the immature sender/receiver sends its "immature" messages, M^i, just as the mature sender/receiver sends its mature ones – that is, messages of (stable) type M^m. Both types of messages are received by the immature sender (e.g., most of the language that productive children hear is the language that they produce themselves; see Elbers's output-as-input argu-ment [Elbers, 1995, 1997]). Thus, the transformation of the internal structure of the immature sender/receiver (SR^i) is a function of its existing structure and of the mature (M^m) and immature messages (M^i):

$$SR^i_{t+1} = f_b(SR^i_t, M^i_t, M^m_t) \qquad [10]$$

$$M^i_{t+1} = f_a(SR^i_t) \qquad [11]$$

or by substituting for the *SR* term:

$$M^i_{t+1} = f_a(f_b(SR^i_{t-1}, M^i_{t-1}, M^m_{t-1})) \qquad [12]$$

Let us assume that this iterative process leads to a mature system, which pro-duces mature messages (whatever that might mean). We know in this particular case (because it was our starting assumption) that this iterative process must lead to a point attractor as defined previously, with the additional specification that

$$M^i_t = M^m_t \qquad [13]$$

That is, the messages produced by the (formerly initial, immature) struc-ture are now structurally equivalent to those produced by the "mature" sender/receiver structure. In that case, we say that the organism has "acquired" or, better, "appropriated" the knowledge needed for the transmission of a par-ticular type of message.

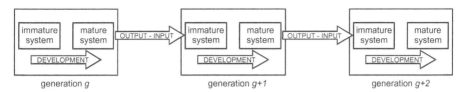

Figure 4.1. Iterative structure of transmission.

Note that in this model, there is a distinction between the "internal structure," named *SR*, and cultural artifacts, which in this highly simplified case consist only of the messages produced. This "culture" not only consists of the mature cultural artifacts (the mature messages) but also of the artifacts (i.e., the messages) produced by the immature system itself. Thus, the generator structure – that is, the structure that generates messages – is a combination of internal components and external (cultural) components. There are no a priori requirements about which aspect is more important. The combination of choice is the combination of components that succeeds in producing the type of messages that will alter the structure in such a way that an equilibrium state is achieved. Stated differently, there are no a priori reasons why an iterative system like this would not exploit all available possibilities to arrive at its stable state. A system that exploits all possibilities has more chances of arriving at its goal than a system that, for some reason or another, exploits only a subset (e.g., only the internal resources, or the cultural resources, or a limited number of internal-cultural combinations).

In the previous model, the iterations refer to the steps in the exchange of messages and the transformation of the structure during a system's lifetime – that is, from its immature to its mature state. There is a second iterative structure that is closely related to the first – namely, the iterative structure of successive generations of systems (i.e., the parent–child/parent–child/parent structure) (see Figure 4.1).

In this iterative structure, each iterative step represents a "life span" of an individual language-learning-and-producing system, which takes the language output of the former generation as its input and generates a language output that will be the input for the next generation. (When evaluating statements like the preceding one, it is absolutely necessary that they should be understood as formal descriptions referring to the simplified system, not as factual descriptions.) If this long-term structure is evolutionarily stable, as it is called – that is, if it succeeds in linking a long series of such generations while maintaining or gradually transforming its structure – its strategies will be compatible with those employed in the short-term iterative cycle, that of the individual system's life span.

In the next section, I discuss what such general reflections on iterative transmission and transformation systems can teach us about the properties of language evolution and language acquisition.

2.4. The Evolution and Acquisition of Language

The first question is whether the formal, iterative model described in the preceding section provides a valid formalization of the class of probable event histories of both language evolution and language acquisition. There is now extensive evidence from computational and simulation studies to support the claim that these iterative models combining the time scale of inter- and intra-generational change indeed provide plausible formal models of both language evolution and language acquisition (Christiansen & Dale, 2003; Christiansen & Kirby, 2003; Nowak & Komarova, 2001; Nowak, Komarova, & Niyogi, 2002). The computational simulation models discussed in these overviews can all be subsumed under the class of dynamic systems models because they all involve a particular specification of the basic iterative equation of a dynamic system, as described by equation 1. Smith, Kirby, and Brighton (2003) explicitly call their model the Iterated Learning Model. They regard the iterative nature of the transmission of language from one generation to the next as the motor behind evolutionary and ontogenetic transformations of the structure of language (Brighton, 2002; Kirby, 2002; Kirby, Smith, & Brighton, 2004). An important feature of these models is the close dynamic interaction they propose among learning, culture, and biological evolution. Over the course of language evolution, these three components transform each other in a process generally known as *coevolution*. In that sense, human biology is deeply transformed by human culture and vice versa. For instance, the biological preadaptation for language acquisition – in whatever form specified – is the result of a dynamic systems process occurring over the intergenerational (i.e., evolutionary and historical) and intragenerational (i.e., ontogenetic) time scales. In this respect, the dynamic-systems approach can help explain – in principle – how language structure emerged through self-organization over the course of generations (Kello, 2004; Niyogi & Berwick, 2001).

   In the context of this chapter's main theme – transmission and self-organization from a dynamic systems point of view – I discuss the following topics. First, how does the iterated-process framework relate to the issues of transmission and language learning? Second, to what extent is language learning based on a genetically transmitted language-learning condition? Third, how does the transmission from genes to behavior – and eventually back – function?

2.4.1. *Iterated Processes, Transmission, and Language Learning*
Some forms of rule-governed behavior can be taught by means of simple transmission processes. For instance, one can tell – that is, transmit to – another person the rules of chess or checkers. This type of simple transmission learning does not apply to language acquisition. In the case of language, the notion of learning refers to a process of inductive inference (Nowak et al., 2002). There is now consensus about the fact that with regard to language, such a type of

learning must be biased. That is, in an iterated-process framework, unbiased learning, if any exists, is soon replaced by biased learning. (Note, however, that as explained in the section on the principles of information transmission, "bias" is, in fact, the default option.) Biased learning means that there are constraints that precede learning and result in selective attention for particular types of information, restriction of the hypothesis space, and so forth. Given the framework presented in equations 2 through 10, the bias must change as the learning process progresses, in that learning has a direct effect on the nature of the constraints that guide further learning. The conjecture of iterated-process models that learning must be biased and that the bias changes as learning proceeds is consistent with an influential model of language acquisition: the *coalition* (i.e., emergentist) *model* (Hirsh-Pasek, Golinkoff, & Hollich, 1999; Hollich, Hirsh-Pasek, & Golinkoff, 2000). The primacy of learning bias is also emphasized in another class of language-acquisition models – namely, the statistical learning models based on the parameters and principles approach (Nowak et al., 2002; Yang, 2004). The authors of the coalition model explicitly place it in the context of dynamic systems theory. An important point in this model is that children use multiple input sources for language acquisition – for example, semantics, syntax, prosody – and that the importance or weight of these sources changes in time, as a consequence of the acquisition process itself. The fact that language acquisition makes use of multiple sources is consistent with yet another consequence of the evolutionary, iterated-process models. They predict that evolutionary, iterated processes will recruit any possible available resource if it enhances the survival value of the phenomenon at issue. Stated differently, a process of language learning that is able to use multiple resources soon outperforms competitive processes that rely on more specific and limited resources. Thus, from an evolutionary viewpoint, language-acquisition processes relying on complex, multiple inputs are more likely than those relying on highly specific and, thus, vulnerable resources.

Moreover, the iterative-process models discussed previously view the process of language evolution not only as a process of adaptation of the learning process to the structure of language but also as a process of adaptation of the structure of language to the process of learning. Hence, the linguistic structure that is selected through the evolutionary process is that type of structure that is most easily learnable, and the most easily learnable structure is the structure that employs a greater diversity of resources.

2.4.2. *To What Extent Do the Iterated Processes Rely on Biology?*

The view on learning as inductive inferencing does not in itself clearly constrain the actual forms of learning or inference. One particular group of authors has built evolutionary models of language by combining principles of evolutionary game theory with the principles and parameters framework (Nowak et al., 2002; Nowak & Komarova, 2001; Nowak, Komarova, & Niyogi, 2001). Although the authors do not take a representationalist stand in the discussion on the nature of Universal Grammar, they do contend that it corresponds with a constraint on the set of possible learnable grammars and that learning the grammar is to select the right grammar from the set. Universal Grammar itself is the result of an evolutionary process in a population of language users. Universal Grammar, defined as the innate component necessary for language acquisition (Nowak & Komarova, 2001), is transmitted from one generation to the other. The question, of course, is whether the components necessary for language acquisition, if defined as a set of constraints on learning, can be confined to the biological realm. Researchers working in the context of the Iterated Learning Model have a broader view and contend that the constraints on learning are distributed over the system. They uniquely reside neither in the biological component nor in the cultural component. Current functionalist theories of language acquisition comply with this view, in that they anchor the acquisition of language into a variety of factors, including nonlinguistic cognitive precursors, social knowledge and interaction, specific adaptations of the language addressed to children (i.e., "Motherese"), and so forth (MacWhinney, 1998; Seidenberg & McDonald, 1999; Tomasello, 2003).

The notion of distributed causes is at the heart of dynamic systems. Distributed causes have the advantage that individuals can differ among each other in terms of the exact composition of the distributed causal structure and that, within the distributed set, compensatory relationships are possible if one or another resource aspect is occasionally less well developed at the start. All this guarantees a robust starting point for development. However, for distributed causes to be effective, they must also be dynamical. For instance, they must self-organize into patterns of causes and conditions that are themselves altered by the developmental processes they bring about (Thelen & Smith, 1994).

The dynamic nature of the constraints for language learning is illustrated by a particular evolutionary phenomenon – namely, the transformation of cultural constraints into biological constraints and vice versa. An example of such a dynamic process is the evolutionary emergence of compositionality of language (e.g., syntactic structure and recursiveness). In a mathematical and simulation study, Brighton (2002) showed that compositionality is a linguistic property that emerges through evolution as a consequence of cultural transmission of that language, given that such transmission has to reckon with the kind of limitations that are known under the term *poverty of the stimulus*. Hence, it is not because of compositionality that the problem of the poverty of the stimulus emerges; in an evolutionary context, it can easily be the other way around.

Another example of the dynamic nature of the constraints on an evolutionary time scale is the Baldwin effect, which implies that an adaptation that has survival value and has to be learned during the lifetime of an individual tends to become part of the genetic composition of individuals over evolutionary time. The explanation is that any mutation or biological change that facilitates the learning of the adaptive trait tends to become conserved in the genome because the trait at issue has survival value (the mechanisms are none other than the neo-Darwinian mutation and fitness mechanisms). The Baldwin effect can be used to explain how a Universal Grammar or a set of principles and parameters can become innate, not because the grammar or the principles and parameters themselves have survival value but rather because the language that is governed by such principles has survival value and the learning has a certain cost (Deacon, 1997; Pinker & Bloom, 1990). The Baldwin effect provides an example of a transmission from *culture* (in the broadest sense of the word) to *nature*. However, if the relevant environment is not sufficiently static, the resulting Baldwin effect is far less specific. For instance, if there is intergenerational fluctuation in the structure of the language, the Baldwin effect results in a genetic consolidation of a general learning mechanism, not of a set of language-specific rules (Munroe & Cangelosi, 2002). Stated differently, the outcome of the Baldwin effect in the case of language evolution depends on what is most survival-effective under a specific evolutionary set of circumstances and is not in itself confined to giving rise to a highly specific set of learning constraints, in the form of a Universal Grammar.

A final point of discussion relates to the dynamic nature of the language-learning constraints on the ontogenetic time scale. According to current functionalist approaches to language acquisition, the language-learning constraints are distributed across many domains and levels, including biological, cognitive, social, and cultural aspects (MacWhinney, 1998; Seidenberg & MacDonald, 1999; Tomasello, 2003). The distributed nature of these constraints does not withhold them from being highly organized. However, this organization comes about as a consequence of self-organization, in the way described by dynamic-systems theories (Hirsh-Pasek, Tucker, & Golinkoff, 1996; Hirsh-Pasek, Golinkoff, & Hollich, 1999; Hollich, Hirsh-Pasek, & Golinkoff, 2000). Assume for purposes of the argument that part of this structure of constraints is formed by specific rules similar to the set of principles and parameters as described by Chomsky (Yang, 2004). Because these rules are constraints on learning, they cannot be learned themselves (i.e., inductively inferred from the linguistic information given). In the introductory chapters, we have seen that classical transmission theory is based on two options: A content is either transmitted through learning or transmitted through a biological, genetic process. Thus, if the rule-based constraints are not learned, they must be innate. However, we have also seen that the two options, in fact, are organized differently: One option is transmission (by learning or by genetic transmission) and the other option is self-organization. Given the right conditions, complex structures can emerge through self-organization. In that case, the conditions that give rise to the self-organization need not in any way contain the content or structure that arises through the self-organization. If this reasoning is applied to the (assumed) rule-based learning constraints, it suggests that such rule-based structures (e.g., the principles and parameters framework) can emerge through self-organization during the development of an individual child. More precisely, there exist no objections of principle about why some sort of principle and parameters structure (if one is needed) could not emerge on the ontogenetic time scale. If such a structure is necessary for language acquisition, it must either emerge on the time scale of evolution (the current belief) or on the time scale of ontogenesis (an equivalent possibility); the third possibility is, of course, a combination of both. The fact that it (probably) took many generations to establish such a structure in evolution is not in itself an argument against the claim that such a structure can also self-organize on a considerably shorter time scale – that of the individual's life. The mechanisms that establish a principles and parameters structure, whatever its exact nature, on the level of the genome are different from those that operate on the level of individual development. A process that takes millennia on the biological time scale can possibly take years or months on the developmental time scale. A good example of this inequality of rates of change is the historical change of cultures and technologies. Cultural changes far outpace the evolutionary processes that would be needed to anchor the cultural skills into the genome; in fact, it is likely that many innovations that occur on the cultural level simply cannot be transmitted to the biological level (see Downing [2004] for a discussion on the limitations and conditions of the Baldwin effect). The point here is not that such highly specific constraints for language acquisition, such as the principles and parameters structure, are necessary. Neither do I contend that if they were necessary, they must emerge, through self-organization, on the time scale of individual development. The point is only that if such constraints are believed to emerge by self-organization on the evolutionary time level, there is no reason to reject the possibility that they can also emerge by self-organization on the level of individual development. If the highly specific structure of constraints emerges in individual development, it is likely that it will be a highly transient structure that is transformed as language acquisition proceeds. That is, it should not be viewed as some sort of organ with which the subject is equipped and that will serve the subject for the rest of its life. The basis for the argument is that transmission – through either learning or genetic biological processes – is not the only mechanism for establishing highly specific content in individuals. Emergence through self-organization is another such possibility, which needs to be further investigated.

CONCLUSION

The aim of this chapter is to discuss in general a number of theoretical notions that are fundamental to our understanding of the process of language acquisition and language evolution. These notions refer to transmission, iterative processes, and self-organization. The Chomskyan view on language acquisition – and some of the more recent views, for that matter – was based on an implicitly "entropic" notion of transmission, premised on the thesis that transmitted information can at best retain its structure and that replication processes cannot be based on the spontaneous construction of a new structure. A distinction is made between transmission through learning and transmission through genetic replication; that which cannot be accomplished by one must be accomplished by the other. Dynamic-systems theory makes a distinction between transmission and self-organization. Under the right conditions, replicative structures can spontaneously emerge through self-organization. The process of language acquisition is likely to require a close collaboration between various forms of both transmission and self-organization. Dynamic-systems theory emphasizes the iterative nature of processes, on the time scales of both language evolution and language development. Iterative processes can have surprisingly creative effects, shaping both the structure that produces the language and the language produced. Formal and theoretical accounts of the dynamic, iterative nature of evolutionary and developmental processes, including simulation studies, can help direct the empirical search process for a deeper understanding of the interplay between language evolution and language acquisition.

REFERENCES

Aleksander, I. (2002). Understanding information, bit by bit: Shannon's equations. In G. Farmelo (Ed.), *It must be beautiful: Great equations of modern science* (pp. 213–230). London and New York: Granta Books.

Ashby, W. R. (1947). Principles of the self-organizing dynamic system. *Journal of General Psychology, 37*, 125–128.

Brighton, H. (2002). Compositional syntax from cultural transmission. *Artificial Life, 8*, 25–54.

Chomsky, N. (1959). Review of *Verbal Behavior* by B. F. Skinner. *Language, 35*, 26–58.

Chomsky, N. (1972). *Language and mind*. New York: Harcourt, Brace Jovanovich.

Christiansen, M. H., & Dale, R. (2003). Language evolution and change. In M. A. Arbib (Ed.), *Handbook of brain theory and neural networks* (2nd ed.) (pp. 604–606). Cambridge, MA: MIT Press.

Christiansen, M. H., & Kirby, S. (2003). Language evolution: Consensus and controversies. *Trends in Cognitive Sciences, 7*, 300–307.

Darwin, C. (1836). *On the origin of species by means of natural selection*. New York: Modern Library.

de Graaf, J. W. (1999). *Relating new to old: A classical controversy in developmental psychology*. Groningen: Doctoral Dissertation.

Deacon, T. (1997). *The symbolic species: The co-evolution of language and the human brain*. London: Allen Lane/The Penguin Press.

Downing, K. L. (2004). Development and the Baldwin effect. *Artificial Life, 10*, 39–63.

Elbers, L. (1995). Production as a source of input for analysis: Evidence from the developmental course of a word-blend. *Journal of Child Language, 22*, 47–71.

Elbers, L. (1997). Output as input: A constructivist hypothesis in language acquisition. *Archives de Psychologie, 65*, 131–140.

Fodor, J. A. (1975). *Language of thought.* New York: Crowell.

Gould, S. J. (1996). *Full house: The spread of excellence from Plato to Darwin.* New York: Three Rivers Press.

Greene, B. (2005). *The fabric of the cosmos.* New York: Vintage Books.

Hirsh-Pasek, K., Golinkoff, R. M., & Hollich, G. (1999). Trends and transitions in language development: Looking for the missing piece. *Developmental Neuropsychology, 16,* 139–162.

Hirsh-Pasek, K., Tucker, M., & Golinkoff, R. M. (1996). Dynamic systems theory: Reinterpreting "prosodic bootstrapping" and its role in language acquisition. In J. L. Morgan & K. Demuth (Eds.), *Signal to syntax: Bootstrapping from speech to grammar in early acquisition* (pp. 449–466). Hillsdale, NJ: Lawrence Erlbaum Associates.

Hollich, G. J., Hirsh-Pasek, K., & Golinkoff, R. M. (2000). Breaking the language barrier: An emergentist coalition model for the origins of word learning. *Monographs of the Society for Research in Child Development, 65,* v–123.

Kello, C. T. (2004). Characterizing the evolutionary dynamics of language. *Trends in Cognitive Sciences, 8,* 392–394.

Kirby, S. (2002). Natural language from artificial life. *Artificial Life, 8,* 185–215.

Kirby, S., Smith, K., & Brighton, H. (2004). From UG to universals: Linguistic adaptation through iterated learning. *Studies in Language, 28,* 587–607.

Lewis, M. D., & Granic, I. (1999). Who put the self in self-organization? A clarification of terms and concepts for developmental psychopathology. *Development and Psychopathology, 11,* 365–374.

MacWhinney, B. (1998). Models of the emergence of language. *Annual Review of Psychology, 49,* 199–227.

Marantz-Henig, R. (2000). *The monk in the garden. Lost and found: Genius of Gregor Mendel.* New York: Houghton Mifflin.

Mendel, G. (1993). *Experiments on plant hybrids (1865).* New Brunswick, NJ: Rutgers University Press.

Mitchener, W. G., & Nowak, M. A. (2004). Chaos and language. *Proceedings of the Royal Society of London: Biological Sciences, 251*(1540), 701–704.

Munroe, S., & Cangelosi, A. (2002). Learning and the evolution of language: The role of cultural variation and learning costs in the Baldwin effect. *Artificial Life, 8,* 311–339.

Niyogi, P., & Berwick, R. C. (2001). A dynamical systems model for language change. *Complex Systems, 11*(3), 161–204.

Nowak, M. A., & Komarova, N. L. (2001).Towards an evolutionary theory of language. *Trends in Cognitive Sciences, 5*(7), 288–295.

Nowak, M. A., Komarova, N. L., & Niyogi, P. (2001). Evolution of Universal Grammar. *Science, 291,* 114–118.

Nowak, M. A., Komarova, N. L., & Niyogi, P. (2002). Computational and evolutionary aspects of language. *Nature, 417,* 611–617.

Piaget, J. (1975). *L'Equilibration des structures cognitives: Problème central du développement.* Paris: Presses Universitaires de France.

Piatelli-Palmarini, M. (1980). *Language and learning.* London: Routledge.

Pierce, J. R. (1961). *Symbols, signals and noise.* New York: Harper.

Pinker, S., & Bloom, P. (1990). Natural language and natural selection. *Behavioral and Brain Sciences, 13,* 707–784.

Prigogine, I., & Stengers, I. (1984). *Order out of chaos.* Boulder, CO: New Science Press.

Seidenberg, M. S., & MacDonald, M. C. (1999). A probabilistic constraints approach to language acquisition and processing. *Cognitive Science, 23*, 569–588.

Shannon, C. E. (1948). A mathematical theory of communication. *The Bell System Technical Journal, 27*, 379–423 and 623–656, July and October 1948. Retrieved from http://cm.bell-labs.com/cm/ms/what/shannonday/shannon1948.pdf.

Skinner, B. F. (1957). *Verbal behavior.* New York: Appleton-Century-Crofts.

Smith, K., Kirby, S., & Brighton, H. (2003). Iterated learning: A framework for the emergence of language. *Artificial Life, 9*, 371–386.

Thelen, E., & Smith, L. B. (1994). *A dynamic systems approach to the development of cognition and action.* Cambridge, MA: Bradford Books/MIT Press.

Thelen, E., & Smith, L. B. (1998). Dynamic systems theories. In W. Damon & R. Lerner (Eds.), *Handbook of Child Psychology* (pp. 563–634). New York: Wiley.

Tomasello, M. (2003). *Constructing a language: A usage-based theory of language acquisition.* Cambridge, MA: Harvard University Press.

van der Veer, R., & Valsiner, J. (1991). *Understanding Vygotsky: A quest for synthesis.* Oxford: Blackwell.

van Geert, P. (1989). Psychological development: Organized self-organization. In G. Dalenoort (Ed.), *The paradigm of self-organization* (pp. 146–166). New York: Gordon and Breach.

van Geert, P. (1994). Vygotskian dynamics of development. *Human Development, 37*, 346–365.

van Geert, P. (1998). A dynamic systems model of basic developmental mechanisms: Piaget, Vygotsky and beyond. *Psychological Review, 105*, 634–677.

van Geert, P. (2003). Dynamic systems approaches and modeling of developmental processes. In J. Valsiner & K. J. Conolly (Eds.), *Handbook of developmental psychology* (pp. 640–672). London: Sage.

Vygotsky, L. S. (1978). *Mind in society: The development of higher mental processes.* Cambridge: Harvard University Press.

Vygotsky, L. S. (1987). Thinking and speech. In R. W. Rieber & A. S. Carton (Eds.), *The collected works of L. S. Vygotsky: Vol. I. Problems of general psychology* (pp. 37–285). New York: Plenum.

Weisstein, E. W. (1999). *CRC concise encyclopedia of mathematics.* Boca Raton, FL: Chapman & Hall/CRC.

Yang, C. D. (2004). Universal Grammar, statistics or both? *Trends in Cognitive Sciences, 8*, 451–456.

5

Relationship-Specific Intergenerational Family Ties: An Evolutionary Approach to the Structure of Cultural Transmission

HARALD A. EULER, SABINE HOIER, AND PERCY A. ROHDE

INTRODUCTION

Cultural transmission encompasses those processes that transmit and modify beliefs, attitudes, and values in a population. To understand these processes, it might not be satisfactory merely to know how the existing structures of cultural transmission give rise to cultural change. Rather, we also need to understand *why* cultural transmission has the structures that it shows (Boyd & Richerson, 1985; Richerson & Boyd, 2003). Evolutionary theories of human behavior are indispensable for finding satisfactory answers to this "why" question. Such theories address the question of why the human mind (or that of other animals) holds the particular design features that it does, as opposed to other, nonexistent yet conceivable ones (Pinker, 1997; Tooby & Cosmides, 1992). Because culture is a product of the mind, mind features can explain cultural phenomena to some extent (Dawkins, 1982; Miller, 2000), including cultural transmission. Evolutionary theories may facilitate understanding by guiding us to see the relevant aspects of natural phenomena or, as Socrates suggested and Plato wrote, to "carve nature at its joints" (Gangestad & Snyder, 1985, p. 317). Such guidance may help to steer us away from suboptimal concepts like those inspired by changing *zeitgeist* or individual predilections. With it, we avoid becoming entangled in an overabundance of unconnected middle-level theories, a state that characterizes several disciplines of human behavior and impedes scientific progress. The newly emerging science of evolutionary psychology integrates concepts and findings from diverse disciplines such as behavioral ecology, genetics, cognitive sciences, and sociology (Barret, Dunbar, & Lycett, 2002; Bridgeman, 2003; Buss, 2004; Cartwright, 2000; Gaulin & McBurney, 2001; Tooby & Cosmides, 1992).

1.0. INVESTMENT IN PROGENY

A variety of a person's features can be transmitted socially from one generation to the next within the family. In this chapter, we address two interrelated aspects of intergenerational dyads, which can be considered conducive to all or most social (i.e., nongenetic) vertical transmissions: (1) investment in progeny, and (2) emotional closeness of intergenerational dyads. Investment in progeny can express itself in many ways, such as time invested, acceptance of risks, emotional and material costs, feelings of obligation, and grief intensity on the death of a descendant. In noneconomic terms, it is the extent of solicitude. We show here that investment in progeny and emotional closeness of intergenerational dyads are highly and robustly structured. Furthermore, this structure is simple and to a considerable extent accounted for by a few basic reproductively relevant variables, which, in principle, apply to all species with biparental care. Because investment and emotional closeness are instrumental – albeit not sufficient – conditions for social transmission, we argue that intergenerational social transmission in families is similarly structured. After all, the adoption of cultural norms and values presupposes specific motivations and requires interpersonal contact, both of which depend on interpersonal closeness and investment.

Researchers from various disciplines have repeatedly noted that kinship systems have an obvious leaning toward the maternal side of the family. This asymmetry is reflected in various measures, whether social interactions, feelings of closeness and obligations (Rossi & Rossi, 1990), or importance of family ties (Salmon & Daly, 1996). In summary, women are the kin keepers. Most apparent is the asymmetry in parental care: In general, mothers care for their offspring more than fathers do (reviewed in Geary, 1998), and it is not even always clear just how much of the fathering is due to paternal efforts and how much is attributable to mating efforts (Anderson, Kaplan, Lam, & Lancaster, 1999; Anderson, Kaplan, & Lancaster, 1999a; Hawkes, 1991; Marlowe, 1999).

The proximate causes for lower paternal than maternal investment in humans do not seem to reside in men's lower ability to care for infants or in fathers' absence (Geary, 1998) but rather in a lower threshold of mothers to respond to an infant's needs and the ensuing development of the infant's preference for the breast-feeding caretaker (Hrdy, 1999). Minor initial gender differences thus develop into marked gender differences, exaggerated and solidified by social norms and customs. The ultimate causes of why the maternal threshold in responding to an infant's needs is lower than the paternal threshold can be found in sex differences pertaining to relative costs and benefits of parental investment (Trivers, 1972). The minimum investment required for producing offspring is higher for female mammals than for males, mainly due to gestation and lactation. As a result, the potential reproductive rate is lower for females than for males (Clutton-Brock & Vincent, 1991).

During our ancestral past, human females had to find an optimal mate and invest in offspring to reproduce successfully. Men could do the same; however, in contrast to women, they could also improve their reproductive outcome by maximizing the number of mates. The mating-opportunity costs of parenting (Alcock, 1998) are therefore higher for males than for females because time and energy spent in parenting cannot be invested in finding additional mates. These sex-specific reproductive strategies led to corresponding sex-dimorphic psychological adaptations such as preferences, desires, and motivations, which are still present today, despite the introduction of contraceptives, baby bottles, supermarkets, pediatricians, and maternity leave (Geary, 1998; Mealey, 2000).

A second possible ultimate cause of the lower paternal than maternal willingness to invest in offspring is paternity uncertainty. Because ancestral women sometimes engaged in extra-pair copulations (Baker & Bellis, 1995; Birkhead, 2000), the men recurrently encountered the risk of investing in another male's offspring, which led to male adaptations such as partner surveillance, male forms of jealousy, and the sexual double standard across cultures (Buss, 2003). Accordingly, paternal investment has been shown to correlate with paternity confidence across cultures (Gaulin & Schlegel, 1980) and among human males (Anderson, Kaplan, & Lancaster, 1999b).

Both of these ultimate causes – sex-specific reproductive strategy and paternity uncertainty – contribute to the clear matrilateral bias in human family structures. We now demonstrate how asymmetry between the sexes is evident not just in human but also in other intergenerational investment – namely, grandparental investment (Euler & Weitzel, 1996), grandparent–parent relations (Euler, Hoier, & Rohde, 2001, extended with new data), and aunts and uncles (Hoier, Euler, & Hänze, 2000). An in-depth presentation of the ramifications of sex-specific parental investment for cultural transmission would require a chapter of its own and is not undertaken here.

2.0. GRANDPARENTAL SOLICITUDE

In social species, reproductive endeavor is not restricted to mating and parenting. Alexander (1987) regards lifetimes as being composed of efforts (i.e., caloric expenditure and risk-taking), which can be differentiated into somatic effort and reproductive efforts. Somatic effort (e.g., eating, health care, growing, learning, cultivating relationships with nonkin) amasses resources whereas reproductive efforts reduce them. In addition to mating and parenting, reproductive effort can be carried on as extraparental nepotistic effort – that is, the investment in descendants with whom one shares a high proportion of alleles. These are mainly the young relatives, who in Italy are called *nipote* – namely, grandchildren, nephews, and nieces.

By assisting their adult son or daughter in his or her parental effort, grandparents can continue to contribute to their own genetic-inclusive fitness. Because the average amount of parental care differs between the genders (Geary, 1998), grandparents differentiate according to whether it is a daughter's or a son's parental effort that is to be assisted. At the proximate level, and as perceived by the recipient of grandparental help, a mother needs more assistance in direct childcare than a father does. Therefore, Euler and Weitzel (1996) predicted that maternal grandparents care more for their grandchildren than paternal grand-parents do, in terms of both implicit meanings of the verb *care*.

A second factor that may account for discriminative grandparental care is paternity uncertainty. Because two generations of descendants are involved in grandparental solicitude, grandparents have a double possible parental uncer-tainty. The most uncertain grandparent is the paternal grandfather, who can be certain neither of his own nor of his son's paternity. The absolutely certain grandparent is the maternal grandmother, who is certain of both her own and her daughter's maternity. In comparison, the paternal grandmother and the maternal grandfather have intermediate levels of grandparental uncertainty.

If the two factors – assistance in sex-specific reproductive strategy and pater-nity uncertainty – are combined, we obtain an ordered prediction regarding discriminative grandparental investment. From the grandchild's perspective, the mother of the mother presumably invests the most and the father of the father the least. Although both have one link of paternal uncertainty, the maternal grandfather is expected to invest more than the paternal grandmother because the former is helping a daughter and the latter a son.

Euler and Weitzel (1996) examined grandparental solicitude as perceived retrospectively by adult grandchildren, on the assumption that ratings of care by recipients are a better indicator of grandparental solicitude than ratings given by grandparents themselves because norms of impartiality prevent grand-parents from making self-descriptive statements about favored grandchildren. Participants (720 male, 1,125 female, 12 unspecified; ages 16 to 80 years) were asked on a 7-point rating scale how much each grandparent had cared for them (*gekümmert*) up to the age of 7 years, from 1 (not at all) to 7 (very much). The German verb *kümmern* has both a behavioral and a cognitive-emotional meaning: (1) to care for, to look after; and (2) to be emotionally and/or cog-nitively concerned about. From the total sample of 1,857 respondents, only those 603 cases were selected for the analysis whose four (i.e., putative) genetic grandparents were all still alive when a participant was 7 years old.

The results confirmed the authors' prediction regarding the discriminative-ness of grandparental solicitude. The maternal grandmother was rated as hav-ing been the most caring ($M = 5.16$), followed by the maternal grandfather ($M = 4.52$), the paternal grandmother ($M = 4.09$), and the paternal grandfather ($M = 3.70$). Maternal grandparents were significantly more caring than paternal grandparents, and grandmothers were significantly more so than grandfathers. The effect sizes, given as the partial η^2 (Tabachnik & Fidell, 1996), which denotes the variance attributable to the effect of interest divided by this variance plus error variance, were .11 for the lineage effect (maternal versus paternal) and .17 for the effect of gender of grandparent. The two effects together account for a sizable proportion of the variance.

Of special interest is the finding that the maternal grandfather cared more than the paternal grandmother. If grandparental caregiving were solely determined by a social role and childcare traditionally ascribed to women, then grandmothers should provide more care than grandfathers. Accordingly, this argument should apply particularly to the older grandchildren in the sample, whose grandparents were presumably more influenced by traditional gender roles than those of the younger participants. However, the difference was in the opposite direction – indeed, significantly so – and was even more pronounced for older participants (i.e., 40 years or older) compared to younger participants.

The grandchild's gender mattered little. Female grandchildren rated their grandparental solicitude just slightly higher than male grandchildren (partial $\eta^2 = .01$, $p = .046$). This might be explained by a rater effect – namely, the higher family sentiment of women compared to men (Salmon & Daly, 1996) – rather than a sex-specific allocation of grandparental solicitude. As expected, residential proximity had a large influence on grandparental care; however, because the four grandparents did not differ in mean residential distances, this factor was of no importance. Unexpectedly, neither age of grandparent nor availability of any other grandparents had a significant effect on the solicitude of the grandparent. In the total sample, grandparental care was unaffected by whether one, two, or three other grandparents were alive. Discriminative grandparental solicitude was a robust phenomenon under various conditions, with one exception. When comparing separated (i.e., divorced and estranged) with nonseparated grandparents, separated grandfathers showed significantly less solicitude than grandfathers still living with their spouse (i.e., the grandmother of the child in question). This reduction was most pronounced in separated paternal grandfathers, whose solicitude dropped to a low mean of 1.77. The same decrease was not observed in widowed grandfathers. The low level of care provided by separated grandfathers may be taken as evidence that grandpaternal care, like paternal care (Hawkes, 1991), is to a considerable extent a postmating effort directed at their spouses.

This same pattern of discriminative grandparental solicitude has been found in comparable studies in various countries – namely, the United States (DeKay, 1995), France (Steinbach & Henke, 1998), Sweden (Å. Nilsonne, personal communication, July 2002), England (R. Banse, personal communication, February 2004), and Greece (Pashos, 2000). The pattern of grandparental solicitude among urban Greeks was essentially the same as in the other studies cited; however, it differed among rural Greeks, especially for male respondents, who rated the care given by paternal grandparents higher than that given by maternal grandparents. This paternal bias is only partially explained by prevailing patrilocality in rural Greece and a possible reduced paternity discrepancy. Rather, patrilinearity with preferred investment in paternal grandchildren, especially paternal grandsons, is the explanation that best fits Pashos's (2000) data from rural Greek grandparents.

Various studies that investigated aspects of grandparental investment other than grandchild-rated solicitude confirmed the general pattern of discriminative grandparental investment: perception of closeness to (Fischer, 1983) and time spent with grandchildren (Smith, 1988); interaction frequencies (Eisenberg, 1988; Hartshorne & Manaster, 1982; Hoffman, 1978/1979; Salmon, 1999); perceived emotional closeness to grandparents (Eisenberg, 1988; Hoffman, 1978/1979; Kennedy, 1990; Matthews & Sprey, 1985; Rossi & Rossi, 1990; Russell & Wells, 1987); naming favorite grandparents (Kahana & Kahana, 1970; Steinbach & Henke, 1998); gifts received from grandparents (DeKay, 1995); grandparental mourning after a grandchild's death (Littlefield & Rushton, 1986); and adoption of grandchildren (Daly & Wilson, 1980; Berger & Schiefenhoevel, 1994).

We previously argued that sex-specific reproductive strategy and paternity uncertainty explain discriminative grandparental caregiving. Rossi and Rossi (1990) put forward another reason for the grandparents' preference to invest more in their daughters' children than in their sons' children. With the sharp rise in divorce rates and custody typically being vested in the hands of mothers, investment in daughters' children assures steadier and less risky relations than investment in sons' children. If this risk difference holds, then the solicitude difference between maternal and paternal grandparents should vary with divorce rates across countries and cohorts – that is, it should be higher in the American sample (DeKay, 1995) than in the German (Euler & Weitzel, 1996) or French (Steinbach & Henke, 1998) samples – and higher among the younger grandparents in the German sample than among the older grandparents. However, none of those predictions is supported by the available data.

Another variable that influences grandparental caregiving, in addition to the two main reproductive variables considered so far, was detected by Salmon (1999), who found that grandparents have significantly less contact with grandchildren of their middleborn daughters or sons than with grandchildren of firstborn and lastborn children, a finding explained by the fact that middleborns show less attachment to their parents than do firstborns or lastborns (Rohde et al., 2003; Salmon & Daly, 1998). Salmon (1999) asked Canadian students about the frequency of visits and found large effects: Visits with both maternal and paternal grandparents were approximately twice as frequent for grandchildren of firstborn and lastborn parents than for grandchildren of middleborn parents. We replicated this study using our own procedure in a sample of 464 female and 172 male students – that is, asking about the amount of grandparental solicitude received in childhood – and found the same, albeit very small, effects. For all eight possible comparisons (i.e., parent middleborn versus parent firstborn and parent middleborn versus parent lastborn, both for each of the four grandparents; subsample sizes between $N = 73$ and $N = 229$; functional birth rank – i.e., requiring an age difference of successively ranked siblings of no more than 7 years), solicitude was lower for grandchildren of middleborn mothers or fathers than for grandchildren of firstborn parents in all four comparisons. In three of the comparisons, solicitude was lower for grandchildren of middleborn than for grandchildren of lastborn mothers or fathers. Thus, the hypothesis was numerically confirmed for seven of eight comparisons, one of which turned

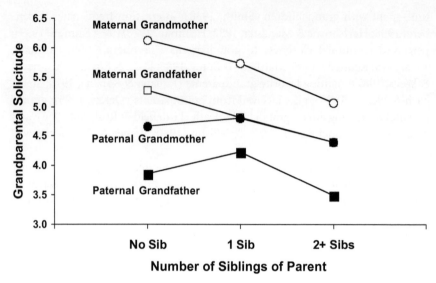

Figure 5.1. Grandparental solicitude as a function of kind of grandparent and number of siblings of parent.

out to be significant (i.e., the maternal grandmother cared more for grandchildren of lastborn daughters than for grandchildren of middleborn daughters). The median effect size for all eight comparisons, however, was a mere $d = .11$. Apparently, there is indeed some effect of parental birth order, but it is doubtful whether the effect is as sizeable as suggested in the Salmon (1999) study.

While we were investigating potential parental-birth-rank effects of grandparental solicitude, we serendipitously came across another effect of grandparental care unknown thus far. We examined the amount of grandparental care as a function of the number of siblings a parent has and expected a straight solicitude-diffusion effect. The more children a grandparent couple has, the more grandchildren there are on average and, therefore, the less solicitude is available for each grandchild. As we assessed grandparental solicitude through ratings of adult grandchildren, we expected the ratings from grandchildren to be lower the more siblings the parent has or had. This solicitude diffusion effect is clearly seen in Figure 5.1 but, unexpectedly, only for the maternal grandparents (i.e., open data points in Figure 5.1). Here, the solicitude ratings are highest for grandparents who have only a daughter, lower for grandparents if the daughter has only one brother or sister, and lowest if the daughter has more than one sibling. As expected, the curve is lower for the maternal grandfather than for the maternal grandmother. For the paternal grandparents, however, this solicitude-diffusion effect is countered by some other effect. It is surprising that paternal grandparents care *less* for the children of their son if that son is the only child and care more for the son's children if the son has a sibling. It makes no difference whether this sibling is a brother or a sister. In our first sample, we considered this unusual finding to be a chance effect, but it arose consistently in the two successive samples collected in the following 2 years. In a sample of 1,112 participants, which yielded valid and complete entries for 840 participants, we obtained the expected significant main effects for lineage (i.e., matriline versus patriline), grandparent gender, and number of siblings of parent, but we also found a significant interaction between lineage by number of siblings of parent ($F[2, 840] = 3.23$, df $= 2$, $p = .04$). Because there was no significant higher order interaction between this interaction and gender of grandparent, we pooled the data for both grandparental genders, which lowered the p-value for the interaction ($F[2, 1010] = 4.39$, df $= 2$, $p = .013$). Whatever unknown effect is reducing the care for grandchildren if the son is an only child or increasing the care for grandchildren if the son has a sibling, or both, it must be strong enough to counter the solicitude-diffusion effect. Therefore, a fair significance test for this only-child-son effect should correct for the solicitude-diffusion effect. When we did this by taking as the null hypothesis not a horizontal line but rather the decline in the maternal solicitude ratings, we found that paternal grandparents cared significantly more for grandchildren from only-child sons than for grandchildren from sons with a sibling ($t = 3.28$, df $= 456$, $p = .001$, $d = .34$).

How can this small but clearly real effect be accounted for theoretically? When a counterintuitive finding is examined post hoc, explanations are usually quickly at hand and are indeed sometimes in abundance. The search for explanations in this case could be focused on whether we knew if the effect to be expounded came about because grandparents *decreased* their solicitude if their son was an only child or *increased* their solicitude if their son had a sibling but only one, or both. However, our current data are insufficient to answer this question. Of several possible solutions that we considered, there are two for which we have some data. (1) The Sibling Equity Hypothesis would entail the following argument: If the son has a sister, then the sister's children receive more grandparental care than her brother's children and, to counter this effect, grandparents ensure that the son's children are not disadvantaged. If the son has more siblings, the effect becomes diluted. The explanation assumes that the effect of increased grandparental solicitude for offspring of sons with one sibling is due to increased solicitude for those cases in which the son has a sister and can thus be easily tested. If the son has a sister, grandmaternal solicitude is rated at 4.75 and grandpaternal solicitude at 4.53; if the son has a brother, the values are 4.64 and 4.20, respectively. The differences are in the expected direction but not significant. (2) The Mother-in-Law/Daughter-in-Law Conflict Hypothesis draws on the observation that this relationship is generally the most problematic in-law relationship (see the following section), whereas the relationship with the son-in-law is considerably better. If the son has a sister, there is a daughter as the family female to allow for grandparental solicitude transmission to grandchildren. If the son has a brother, there is a choice of daughters-in-law, and the grandparents are less prone to attribute relationship problems to the personality of the granddaughters but rather to the relationship constellation. If, however, the son is an only child, there is only one female in the next generation and that is a daughter-in-law. Grandparental abstention might then help to alleviate the problem. A variant of this hypothesis would be to reason that in the case of an only male child, grandparents are impelled to support their son more in his potential strategy to maximize mates rather than in his strategy to be a good father (see the following section). This goal can be achieved by rejecting the daughter-in-law. In any case, this hypothesis predicts that the relationships to the daughters-in-law are worse if the son is an only child than if he has one or more siblings. The evidence for this hypothesis is ambivalent. The relationship between mother-in-law and daughter-in-law is indeed worse if the son is an only child compared to sons with one or several siblings ($M = 3.79$, $N = 111$ versus $M = 4.29$, $N = 799$; $t = 2.98$, $p = .003$; relationship rated on a 7-point scale with $1 =$ very bad relationship, $7 =$ very good relationship). However, for fathers-in-law, the difference is not significant ($M = 4.34$ versus $M = 4.44$). For mothers-in-law, the significance of the difference is mostly due to relatively good relationships with the daughters-in-law in those cases in which the son has more than one sibling.

A third possible explanation is not primarily an evolutionary one but resorts instead to son-and-heir. In the last century, German parents still preferred the first child to be a son rather than a daughter, and the decision to have a second child was made more often if the first child was a girl. Perhaps grandparents tend to become overly possessive of grandchildren from an only-child son, with counter-reactions by the daughter-in-law and consequent alienation.

Because the reduced investment of grandparents with an only child is clearly restricted to children of sons, the idea is suggested that the reason might be found in some gender-related asymmetry. Reproductive strategies are asymmetric and, from an evolutionary viewpoint, this asymmetry is reflected in a pervasive pattern of consequent asymmetries, one of which is the difference in relationship quality between parents-in-law and sons-in-law on the one hand and daughters-in-law on the other. This asymmetry is investigated in the next section.

Effective investment in progeny requires an ability to recognize kin in paternal descendants. Therefore, it can be predicted that fathers rely more on child resemblance for their investment than mothers (Porter, 1987). Indeed, mothers and their relatives seem to comment and even insist on resemblance to the father more often than to the mother, seemingly to ascertain his paternity and thus promote his willingness to invest in the infant (Daly & Wilson, 1982; McLain, Setters, Moulton, & Pratt, 2000; Regalski & Gaulin, 1993). Results on whether infants actually resemble more the father or the mother are conflicting (Brédart & French, 1999; Christenfeld & Hill, 1995; McLain et al., 2000), probably due to methodological differences. Most recent findings suggest that infants vary in their parental resemblance, with some looking more like their father, some more like their mother, and some like both parents (Bressan & Grassi, 2004). It might be in the reproductive interest of a father to sire infants that do not resemble him too much or else his children sired in another woman's extra-pair copulation might be too easily detected as illegitimate. Correspondingly, it is in the best genetic interest of mothers to decrease their mates' paternity uncertainty and thereby promote paternal investment (Bressan, 2002).

Euler and Weitzel (1996) found that in retrospect, the participants rated their physical and behavioral resemblance to their father during childhood higher than the resemblance to their mother. However, resemblance to paternal grandparents was not rated higher than resemblance to maternal grandparents, and resemblance to grandfathers was not rated higher than to grandmothers. What did come to light, however, was a correlation between resemblance and grandparental solicitude, which tended to systematically vary with the number of links of paternity uncertainty. For the maternal grandmother (i.e., no link of paternity uncertainty), the correlation was $r = .37$; for the maternal grandfather and the paternal grandmother (i.e., one link each), the correlations were $r = .39$ and $r = .42$, respectively; and for the paternal grandfather (i.e., two links), the correlation was $r = .47$ ($N = 458$ for each coefficient). Apparently, the higher the general paternity uncertainty is, the greater the extent to which grandparental solicitude is made dependent on resemblance to the grandchild.

3.0. RELATIONSHIPS BETWEEN GRANDPARENTS AND PARENTS

The relationships between grandparents and grandchildren have been shown to be systematically structured by a few reproductively relevant variables (Euler & Weitzel, 1996). A comparable structure can be expected to reveal itself in the relationships between grandparents and parents. If grandparental investment is to be transmitted to grandchildren, then parents are usually the mediators. Grandparental investment is thus facilitated by good relationships between parents and grandparents and obstructed by poor relationships.

With four grandparents and two parents, there are eight different grandparent–parent dyads, four of which are in-law dyads. Among the in-laws, the mother-in-law seems to play a salient role. In many cultures, she is the target of scorn and derision in jokes and songs. The relationship between the mother-in-law and the daughter-in-law is a source of particularly intense conflict (Duvall, 1954). Why, though, is the image of the mother-in-law so negative? The most popular explanation, nourished by psychoanalytic theory, is rivalry between the two over the son's/husband's love and attention. This is a proximate explanation, which requires an ultimate explanation – namely, of why such a rivalry arises in the first place and why there is no corresponding rivalry between the father-in-law and son-in-law over the daughter/wife. Even if rivalry between the father-in-law and son-in-law does exist, it is not invoked to explain long-lasting in-law relationships.

Evolutionary psychological theory might provide a more satisfactory answer. First, a key reproductive variable that differentiates the eight grandparent–parent dyads is consanguinity. The son or daughter is genetically closer than his or her spouse; therefore, the four parent–child dyads are expected to be more positive relationships than the four in-law dyads. Second, parental support of the adult child's reproductive strategy is another factor to consider. It is in the reproductive interest of grandparents to support their adult child in his or her sex-specific reproductive strategy. An adult daughter – more restricted than a son to the reproductive strategy of parental care – is best aided by her parents within the context of a good parent–daughter relationship. A poor parent–son relationship is comparatively less detrimental for a son's opportunistic reproductive strategy of maximizing mates. Therefore, grandparents can be expected to have generally better relationships with daughters than with sons. Third, due to uncertainty of paternity, a better relationship is predicted between mother and children than between father and children. These two latter factors – daughter support and paternity uncertainty – yield predictions about the differential quality of the four relationships between grandparents and their adult children. The best relationship is expected to exist between the grandmother and her adult daughter, the worst of the four relationships is expected between the grandfather and his adult son. Depending on the relative strengths of the two factors mentioned (i.e., daughter support and paternity uncertainty), the grandfather–daughter or the grandmother–son relationship is expected to be the second best relationship.

Let us now examine in-law relationships. How do evolutionary considerations differentiate these four dyads? The factor of daughter support again plays a role here. A daughter needs a more stable partner support in her childcare than a son needs in his strategy of maximizing mates. A daughter is best aided by her parents if they welcome and relate well to the husband she has chosen. A son, insofar as he is inclined toward polygyny, is comparatively less impeded by a poor relationship between his wife and his parents. Rejection of their son's partner may even be strategically appropriate and unconsciously in the grandparents' own reproductive interest. Therefore, the relationship with the son-in-law is expected to be better than the relationship with the daughter-in-law. Again, considering paternity uncertainty as a factor, the mother-in-law is expected to have a better relationship than the father-in-law to the spouse of the adult child. (However, as we realized later and as explained herein, we must again consider an asymmetry between the genders.)

Taken together, these considerations predict a relatively good relationship between the mother-in-law and the son-in-law and a relatively poor relationship between the father-in-law and the daughter-in-law, with the other dyads – again, depending on the relative strengths of both factors – somewhere in between. However, folklore and perhaps our own experiences object to this. Is it not the relationship between the mother-in-law and the daughter-in-law that is said to be the most problematic of the eight relationships?

From a sample of 2,319 participants, we obtained a rating on a 7-point scale of how good each one of their eight grandparent–parent relationships was

Table 5.1. *Predictions regarding grandparent–parent relationships and results*

Grandparent–Parent Dyad	Predictions on the Basis of			Relationship Rating	
	Consanguinity	Daughter Support	Paternity Uncertainty	M	SD
Mother/Daughter	+	+	+	5.49	1.56
Father/Daughter	+	+	−	5.16	1.67
Mother/Son	+	−	+	5.03	1.56
Father/Son	+	−	−	4.71	1.64
Mother-in-law/Son-in-law	−	+	+	4.45	1.61
Father-in-law/Son-in-law	−	+	−	4.35	1.65
Mother-in-law/Daughter-in-law	−	−	+*	3.75	1.76
Father-in-law/Daughter-in-law	−	−	−*	4.03	1.71

Note: Plus or minus sign denotes better or worse relationship predicted; $N = 962$.
* See text (p. 83) for reinterpretation of direction of effect.

when the participants were children (1 = very bad relationship, 7 = very good relationship). The participants (888 male, 1,426 female, 11 unspecified) were between 12 and 67 years old, with a median age of 21 years and 11 months. Of those participants, 962 provided complete ratings (337 males, 619 females, 6 unspecified; ages 16 to 62 years, median age 21 years and 7 months) – that is, a rating for all eight grandparent–parent dyads.

Table 5.1 shows the predictions on the basis of consanguinity, daughter support, and paternity uncertainty, as well as the means and standard deviations of the relationship ratings. The plus or minus sign denotes whether the column condition leads to a prediction of a better or a worse relationship for that particular grandparent–parent dyad relative to the other dyads. A MANOVA showed a large significant main effect for consanguinity ($F(1,961) = 788.55$, $p < .001$, partial $\eta^2 = .45$). Relationships between grandparents and their own sons or daughters were rated as better than relationships with spouses of sons or daughters. Gender of the parent yielded a significant main effect ($F(1,961) = 99.12$, $p < .001$, partial $\eta^2 = .09$). Relationships with daughters and their husbands were better than with sons and their wives. Gender of the grandparent also yielded a significant main effect ($F(1,961) = 15.32$, $p < .001$, partial $\eta^2 = .02$). Relationships between grandmothers and parents were better than between grandfathers and parents. Same-sex grandparent–parent dyads were rated as having had slightly better relationships than cross-sex dyads, as shown by the Sex of Parent by Sex of Grandparent interaction ($F(1,961) = 9.12$, $p = .003$, partial $\eta^2 = .01$). The sex of the participant (i.e., grandchild) showed no effect.

How well do siblings agree with one another in their retrospective ratings of their grandparent–parent relationships during their childhood? We additionally obtained ratings from the siblings of the participants and calculated – for the families with two children ($N = 87$) – the intraclass correlations within sibling pairs. The average correlation over all eight grandparent–parent dyads was $r = .64$. This correlation varied negatively with the age difference of the sibling pair, which can be expected because the quality of relationships can vary with time and because the age gap between siblings is one determinant of a child's family niche (Sulloway, 1996). There is considerable agreement between siblings regarding the quality of grandparent–parent relations.

Two other studies that investigated the various parent–child relationships delivered comparable results. Rossi and Rossi (1990) found that affinal kin (i.e., those acquired through marriage or remarriage) evoke lower feelings of obligation than do consanguineal kin in comparable positions, and sons-in-law evoke higher feelings of obligation than daughters-in-law. The bond between mothers and children was stronger than between fathers and children and was strongest between mothers and daughters and weakest between fathers and sons. Szydlik (1995) obtained results that on one point differed from those presented previously. When adults were asked how close their relationship was to their various relatives, including their parents and their children but not their in-laws, he found that mothers and daughters had the closest of the four parent–child relationships (i.e., the percentage of respondents answering "close" or "very close") and fathers and sons had the least close relationship, as was also found by the authors and by Rossi and Rossi (1990). However, the relationship between mother and son was, on average, somewhat better than that between father and daughter. Whether this difference is due to differences in the samples, survey questions, or data presentation cannot be answered here.

The three reproductive determinants listed in Table 5.1 predicted the poorest relationship for the father-in-law/daughter-in-law dyad and the second poorest for the mother-in-law/daughter-in-law dyad. However, it is the latter relationship that is actually the worst. The mean difference between the two dyads is significant ($t(1,961) = 4.772, p < .001$), as are all adjacent mean differences in Table 5.1, with the exception of that between father/daughter and mother/son ($t(1,961) = 1.850, p = .065$). This reversal of the bottom two dyads, not predicted by our original reproductive conditions but suggested by folklore, is also reflected in a significant Consanguinity by Sex of Grandparent interaction (MANOVA, $F(1,961) = 124.98, p < .001$, partial $\eta^2 = .12$). Daughters-in-law are clearly less of a problem for grandfathers than for grandmothers. Can this finding be explained, at least post hoc?

The father-in-law/daughter-in-law relationship is, in one respect, a special relationship. This dyad has a direct reproductive potential, which no other grandparent–parent dyad has; that is, it involves two unrelated reproductive individuals of both genders with the man usually being older than the woman. The other seven dyads are mismatches with respect to direct reproduction because of incest barriers, same gender, or age relation in the case of mother-in-law/son-in-law. We hypothesize in hindsight that the reproductive potential of the father-in-law/daughter-in-law dyad contributes to a positive relationship. If this hypothesis were valid, the goodness (i.e., quality) of this relationship should covary with the mate value of the daughter-in-law.

The hypothesis was tested in a subsample of 370 participants (232 female, 138 male), in which the mate value was a composite score of the z-transformed 7-point ratings of the mother's and the father's physical attractiveness, intelligence, chances of finding another mate, prudence, job prospects, agreeableness/warmth, and self-confidence (the last for the father only) during the participant's childhood. Because mate value also depends on age, especially for females (Symons, 1979), each parent's age at the time of the participant's birth was also recorded. However, the results did not support our hypothesis that the reproductive potential of the father-in-law/daughter-in-law dyad causes the relationship between a daughter-in-law and her father-in-law to be better than that between a daughter-in-law and her mother-in-law. Grandparents cherish high mate value in both their descendants and their descendants' mates. This makes evolutionary sense because the affiliate kin will become part of the parents' genetic lineage.

The riddle of the comparatively good father-in-law/daughter-in-law relationship was solved, or so we believe, by our colleague Paola Bressan (personal communication, May 2003), who brought to our attention an obvious – indeed, embarrassing – error in our theoretical deductions. The last two relationships in Table 5.1, those to the daughter-in-law, differ in one important aspect from the other six relationships: Whereas the other six relationships, from mother/daughter to father-in-law/son-in-law, are receptive, supportive relationships, the last two are rejective relationships. Parental certainty is not a primary factor but rather a secondary one: If the relationship is a supportive one, as is usually the case among close relatives, paternity uncertainty detracts from emotional closeness and all kin supports that it entails. If, however, the relationship is repudiative, as we indicated previously for the relationship to the daughter-in-law, paternity uncertainty *detracts from the rejection*. The father-in-law, being generally less certain about his paternity than his spouse is about her maternity, has comparatively fewer reasons to reject his daughter-in-law than his spouse does. Therefore, the corresponding plus and minus signs in Table 5.1 (marked with an asterisk) should actually be reversed.

4.0. INVESTMENTS OF AUNTS AND UNCLES

Evolutionary theory predicts differential investment of consanguineal aunts and uncles. Due to paternity uncertainty and sex-specific reproductive strategy, matrilateral aunts and uncles can be expected to show more concern for their nieces and nephews than patrilateral aunts and uncles, and aunts show more concern than uncles. Of all four types of consanguineal aunts and uncles, matrilateral aunts are expected to be the most caring and patrilateral uncles the least caring. These hypotheses were tested in a sample of 302 participants (109 male, 193 female; ages 19 to 40 years) whose genetic parents were cohabiting (Hoier et al., 2000). Those participants who had either both matrilateral and patrilateral uncles or both types of aunts were asked whether the matrilateral or the patrilateral uncle or aunt showed more concern for the participant's welfare. A significant matrilateral bias was revealed with respect to both aunts and uncles: Matrilateral aunts and uncles were chosen more often as showing more concern than their patrilateral equivalents.

The participants rated each aunt's and uncle's level of concern on a 7-point scale. Repeated measures ANCOVA, corrected for the relative's age and residential distance to the participant, again showed a significant matrilateral effect (i.e., a greater investment in descendants of a sister than in those of a brother) and a significant gender effect (i.e., more care by aunts than by uncles). Finally, the interaction between the two effects was significant: The matrilateral bias was greater in aunts than in uncles. Studies from the United States (Gaulin, McBurney, & Brakeman-Wartell, 1997; McBurney, Simon, Gaulin, & Geliebter, 2001; Rossi & Rossi, 1990) provided the same results, with the exception that there was no interaction effect. This difference could be due to a floor effect in the German data: German uncles were rated as showing considerably less concern than American uncles (Gaulin et al., 1997).

5.0. DISCUSSION

We have shown that investment in progeny and emotional closeness of cross-generation dyads is highly structured. This structure is only modestly affected by circumstances that do not tap into reproductive conditions (Rossi & Rossi, 1990). The predictor variables addressed in our research account for a sizable share of the variance in the quality of intergenerational relationships. Nepotistic investment was sex-specific with respect to the investor and the linking kinsperson for distant kin but less so with respect to the gender of the beneficiary.

We looked at intergenerational nepotistic investment and relationships from an evolutionary perspective. From this angle, it can be asked for what purpose a phenotypic trait – in this case, a relationship-specific investment – was designed. The answer to such a question does not conflict with proximate explanations. For example, Rossi and Rossi (1990) correctly note that the pervasive matrilateral bias in family relationships (i.e., the fact that women are kin keepers) is due to the close mother–daughter bond. We were not satisfied with this explanation and asked *why* the mother–daughter bond is so close.

If cultural norms and values are familially transmitted, then the transmission belts – that is, the conditions or factors that enhance transmission (Schönpflug, 2001) – can be expected to be structured like the intergenerational investment patterns, notwithstanding the possibility that social transmission structures also may vary with transmission content. Giving technical advice, providing financial resources, and teaching technical skills might be areas in which male kinspersons are more involved than in emotional investment. However, reproductive conditions are nonetheless equally relevant for various transmission contents, as can be seen in the transmission structures of wills, in which the decisions regarding who inherits how much have been shown to be strongly influenced by genetic closeness and other factors that affect genetic replication (Bossong, 2001; Judge, 1995; Smith, Kish, & Crawford, 1987).

This chapter was not written to illuminate the "how" question – that is, the processes of cultural transmission. Its purpose was not merely to empirically demonstrate that the various familial relationships do indeed differ in measures of solicitude and closeness. Rather, the aim was also to explain why this is the case in the first place. We believe that this and other studies of kin relationships guided by an evolutionary perspective can contribute to providing an understanding of the processes of cultural transmission within the family. Although it has long been suggested that the affectional ties between the cultural model and the recipient influence the ease and reliability of transmission, a finely structured theoretical framework to explain *why* some family relationships are more affectionate than others is only now emerging with the introduction of evolutionary concepts to social psychology. Daly, Salmon, and Wilson (1997) argued that from an evolutionary perspective, the qualities of the various kin relationships are expected to be highly specific. We agree with this and suggest that this specificity of relationships contributes to the shaping of transmission pathways.

Theorists seem to agree that cultural transmission, or "cultural adoption" (Tooby & Cosmides, 1992), involves learning by observation. However, imitation is highly selective, as is readily revealed in a situation of high cultural variability. It would indeed be surprising if this selectivity in the choice of models and traits were not influenced by the quality of the relationship between recipient and model.

Cultural transmission is an interesting problem only inasmuch as it implies the possibility of failed transmission. Cultural traits can get lost because they either are not adopted or are actively exchanged for newly introduced traits. Only when there is competition among several cultural traits to be adopted by the next generation will the significance of specific kin relationships and other possible transmission pathways be revealed. The question of intergenerational cultural transmission, therefore, has to be posed in the following way: Which structures and processes determine whether a cultural trait is being conservatively passed along from one generation to the next? Which structures and processes, conversely, promote cultural change?

There are reasons to question the assumption that familial social transmission of norms and values is the sole or most important process of cultural transmission. On the one hand, repeated findings in the field of behavioral genetics (Plomin, DeFries, McClearn, & Rutter, 1997; Rowe; 1994; Tesser, 1993) point to genetic transmission, which – due to conventional genetics-insensitive socialization research designs – has frequently been erroneously interpreted as social transmission. Harris (1995, 1998), on the other hand, points to the peer group and not the parents as the main agent responsible for social transmission of norms and values. It makes good evolutionary sense that children should extract as much investment as possible from their family of origin, especially in their first years of life, while also adopting the culture of their own generation within which they will encounter most of their potential competitors, allies, and mates. The empirical evidence for the presumed superior role of peer-group influence provided by Harris, however, is restricted largely to language acquisition and is otherwise more anecdotal than systematic.

The transmission pathways between parents and children are the most frequently studied, although it has been suggested that the significance of parents as models is overestimated (Harris, 1995; Plomin, Ashbury, & Dunn, 2001). With respect to our own studies, it is interesting to note that the quality of the parent–child relationship correlates positively with the child's acceptance of his or her parents as cultural models (Hood, Spilka, Hunsberger, & Gorsuch, 1996). We suggest that the results from our own participants' ranking of their relationships with grandparents, parents-in-law, and aunts and uncles imply that future research will find a similar ranking pattern when the same family members are studied as potential cultural models.

A similar prediction can be made with respect to the specific family niche of the focal child recipient. Several studies have shown that university students' closeness to their parents is influenced by birth order (Kennedy, 1989; Kidwell, 1981; Rohde et al., 2003; Salmon & Daly, 1998), which is considered the strongest proxy of a child's family niche (Sulloway, 1996). Firstborns were the birth rank who most often named their parents as the persons to whom they felt closest, followed by lastborns and, finally, middleborns. Not only does the quality of family relationships determine cultural adoption when we act *within* these relationships; to some degree, these relationships may also mold the personality in such a way that they influence the choice of model *outside* the family, at least in some realms, even if the influence of birth order outside of the family of origin appears not to be strong or at least not pervasive (Pinker, 2002). Sulloway (1996) provided impressive evidence for the paramount importance that family relationships have played in scientific and other cultural revolutions in Western history. The author interpreted his findings within the general evolutionary framework of parent–offspring conflict (Trivers, 1974), which is driven by sibling competition for parental care. Sulloway's results (1996, 2001) serve as a warning that the study of intrafamilial cultural transmission should not be restricted merely to different model–recipient dyads. In the long run, we ought to identify the individual family niche in a network of relationships that seems to shape the recipient's personality and thereby his or her inclination to adopt, reject, or actively exchange a cultural trait for a new one.

REFERENCES

Alcock, J. (1998). *Animal behavior: An evolutionary approach* (6th ed.). Sunderland, MA: Sinauer.

Alexander, R. D. (1987). *The biology of moral systems.* New York: Aldine de Gruyter.

Anderson, K. G., Kaplan, H., Lam, D., & Lancaster, J. B. (1999). Paternal care by genetic fathers and stepfathers I: Reports by Xhosa high school students. *Evolution and Human Behavior, 20,* 433–451.

Anderson, K. G., Kaplan, H., & Lancaster, J. B. (1999a). Paternal care by genetic fathers and stepfathers I: Reports from Albuquerque men. *Evolution and Human Behavior, 20,* 405–431.

Anderson, K. G., Kaplan, H., & Lancaster, J. B. (1999b). *Paternity confidence and fitness outcomes: Abortion, divorce, and paternal investment.* Paper presented at The Annual Meeting of the Human Behavior Evolution Society, June 2–6, Salt Lake City, UT.

Baker, R. R., & Bellis, M. A. (1995). *Human sperm competition. Copulation, masturbation and infidelity.* London, England: Chapman & Hall.

Barrett, L., Dunbar, R., & Lycett, J. (2002). *Human evolutionary psychology.* Princeton, NJ: Princeton University Press.

Berger, C., & Schiefenhoevel, W. (1994, October). *Adoption in Tauwema, Tobriand-Inseln.* Poster presented at the Congress "Anthropologie Heute" of the Gesellschaft für Anthropologie. Humboldt-University at Berlin und University of Potsdam, Germany.

Birkhead, T. (2000). *Promiscuity: An evolutionary history of sperm competition.* Cambridge, MA: Harvard University Press.

Bossong, B. (2001). Gender and age differences in inheritance patterns: Why men leave more to their spouses and women more to their children. An experimental analysis. *Human Nature, 12,* 107–122.

Boyd, R., & Richerson, P. J. (1985). *Culture and the evolutionary process.* Chicago, IL: University of Chicago Press.

Brédart, S., & French, R. M. (1999). Do babies resemble their fathers more than their mothers? A failure to replicate Christenfeld and Hill (1995). *Evolution and Human Behavior, 20,* 129–135.

Bressan, P. (2002). Why babies look like their daddies: Paternity uncertainty and the evolution of self-deception in evaluating family resemblance. *Acta Ethologica, 4,* 113–118.

Bressan, P., & Grassi, M. (2004). Parental resemblance in one-year-olds and the Gaussian curve. *Evolution and Human Behavior, 25,* 133–141.

Bridgeman, B. (2003). *Psychology and evolution: The origins of mind.* Thousand Oaks, CA: Sage Publications.

Buss, D. M. (2003). *The evolution of desire: Strategies of human mating* (2nd ed.). New York: Basic Books.

Buss, D. M. (2004). *Evolutionary psychology: The new science of mind* (2nd ed.). Boston, MA: Pearson Education, Inc.

Cartwright, J. (2000). *Evolution and human behavior: Darwinian perspectives on human nature.* Cambridge, MA: MIT Press.

Christenfeld, N. J. S., & Hill, E. A. (1995). Whose baby are you? *Nature, 378,* 669.

Clutton-Brock, T. H., & Vincent, A. J. C. (1991). Sexual selection and the potential reproductive rates of males and females. *Nature, 351,* 58–60.

Daly, M., Salmon, C., & Wilson, M. (1997). Kinship: The conceptual hole in psychological studies of social cognition and close relationships. In J. A. Simpson & D. T. Kenrick (Eds.), *Evolutionary social psychology* (pp. 265–296). Mahwah, NJ: Erlbaum.

Daly, M., & Wilson, M. (1980). Discriminative parental solicitude: A biological perspective. *Journal of Marriage and the Family, 42,* 277–288.

Daly, M., & Wilson, M. (1982). Whom are newborn babies said to resemble. *Ethology and Sociobiology, 3,* 69–78.

Dawkins, R. (1982). *The extended phenotype: The long reach of the gene.* Oxford, England: Oxford University Press.

DeKay, W. T. (1995, July). *Grandparent investment and the uncertainty of kinship.* Paper presented at the Seventh Annual Meeting of the Human Behavior and Evolution Society, Santa Barbara, CA.

Duvall, E. M. (1954). *In-laws: Pro & con.* New York: Association Press.

Eisenberg, A. R. (1988). Grandchildrens' perspectives on relationships with grandparents: The influence of gender across generations. *Sex Roles, 19,* 205–217.

Euler, H. A., Hoier, S., & Rohde, P. A. (2001). Relationship-specific closeness of intergenerational family ties: Findings from evolutionary psychology and implications for models of cultural transmission. *Journal of Cross-Cultural Psychology, 32,* 163–174.

Euler, H. A., & Weitzel, B. (1996). Discriminative grandparental solicitude as reproductive strategy. *Human Nature, 7,* 39–59.

Fischer, L. R. (1983). Transition to grandmotherhood. *International Journal of Aging and Human Development, 16,* 67–78.

Gangestad, S., & Snyder, M. (1985). "To carve nature at its joints": On the existence of discrete classes in personality. *Psychological Review, 92,* 317–349.

Gaulin, S. J. C., & McBurney, D. H. (2001). *Psychology: An evolutionary approach.* Upper Saddle River, NJ: Prentice-Hall, Inc.

Gaulin, S. J. C., McBurney, D. H., & Brakeman-Wartell, S. L. (1997). Matrilateral biases in the investment of aunts and uncles. *Human Nature, 8,* 139–151.

Gaulin, S. J. C., & Schlegel, A. (1980). Paternal confidence and paternal investment: A cross-cultural test of a sociobiological hypothesis. *Ethology and Sociobiology, 1,* 301–309.

Geary, D. C. (1998). *Male, female: The evolution of human sex differences.* Washington, DC: American Psychological Association.

Harris, J. R. (1995). Where is the child's environment? *Psychological Review, 102,* 458–489.

Harris, J. R. (1998). *The nurture assumption: Why children turn out the way they do.* New York: The Free Press.

Hartshorne, T. S., & Manaster, G. L. (1982). The relationship with grandparents: Contact, importance, role conceptions. *International Journal of Aging and Human Development 15,* 233–245.

Hawkes, K. (1991). Showing off: Tests of another hypothesis about men's foraging goals. *Ethology and Sociobiology, 11,* 29–54.

Hoffman, E. (1978/1979). Young adults' relations with their grandparents: An exploratory study. *International Journal of Aging and Human Development, 10,* 299–310.

Hoier, S., Euler, H. A., & Hänze, M. (2000). Diskriminative verwandtschaftliche Fürsorge von Onkeln und Tanten: Eine evolutionspsychologische Analyse [Discriminative solicitude of aunts and uncles: An evolutionary analysis]. *Zeitschrift für Differentielle und Diagnostische Psychologie, 22*, 206–215.

Hood, R. W., Jr., Spilka, B., Hunsberger, B., & Gorsuch, R. (1996). *The psychology of religion: An empirical approach* (2nd ed.). New York: Guilford Press.

Hrdy, S. B. (1999). *Mother nature: Natural selection and the female of the species.* London, England: Chatto & Windus.

Judge, D. S. (1995). American legacies and the variable life histories of women and men. *Human Nature, 6*, 291–323.

Kahana, B., & Kahana, E. (1970). Grandparenthood from the perspective of the developing grandchild. *Developmental Psychology 3*, 98–105.

Kennedy, G. E. (1989). Middleborns' perception of family relationships. *Psychological Reports, 64*, 755–760.

Kennedy, G. E. (1990). College students' expectations of grandparent and grandchild role behaviors. *The Gerontologist, 30*, 43–48.

Kidwell, J. S. (1981). Number of siblings, sibling spacing, sex, and birth order: Their effects on perceived parent–adolescent relationships. *Journal of Marriage and the Family, 43*, 315–332.

Littlefield, C. H., & Rushton, J. P. (1986). When a child dies: The sociobiology of bereavement. *Journal of Personality and Social Psychology, 51*, 797–802.

Marlowe, F. (1999). Showoffs or providers? The parenting effort of Hadza men. *Evolution and Human Behavior, 20*, 391–404.

Matthews, S. H., & Sprey, J. (1985). Adolescents' relationships with grandparents: An empirical contribution to conceptual clarification. *Journal of Gerontology, 40*, 621–626.

McBurney, D., Simon, J., Gaulin, S. J. C., & Geliebter, A. (2001). Matrilateral biases in the investment of aunts and uncles: Replication in a population presumed to have high paternity certainty. *Human Nature, 13*, 391–402.

McLain, D. K., Setters, D., Moulton, M. P., & Pratt, A. E. (2000). Ascription of resemblance of newborns by parents and nonrelatives. *Evolution and Human Behavior, 21*, 11–23.

Mealey, L. (2000). *Sex differences: Development and evolutionary strategies.* San Diego, CA: Academic Press.

Miller, G. F. (2000). *The mating mind: How sexual choice shaped the evolution of human nature.* New York: Doubleday.

Pashos, A. (2000). Does paternal uncertainty explain discriminative grandparental solicitude? A cross-cultural study in Greece and Germany. *Evolution and Human Behavior, 21*, 97–109.

Pinker, S. (1997). *How the mind works.* New York: W. W. Norton & Company.

Pinker, S. (2002). *The blank slate: The modern denial of human nature.* New York: Penguin Putnam, Inc.

Plomin, R., Ashbury, K., & Dunn, J. (2001). Why are children in the same family so different? Nonshared environment a decade later. *Canadian Journal of Psychiatry, 46*, 225–233.

Plomin, R., DeFries, J. C., McClearn, G. E., & Rutter, M. (1997). *Behavioral genetics* (3rd ed.). New York: W. H. Freeman.

Porter, R. (1987). Kin recognition: Functions and mediating mechanisms. In C. B. Crawford, M. S. Smith, & D. Krebs (Eds.), *Sociobiology and psychology: Ideas, issues and applications* (pp. 175–203). Hillsdale, NJ: Lawrence Erlbaum.

Regalski, J. M., & Gaulin, S. J. C. (1993). Whom are Mexican infants said to resemble? Monitoring and fostering paternal confidence in the Yucatan. *Ethology and Sociobiology, 14,* 97–113.

Richerson, P., & Boyd, R. (2003). *The nature of cultures.* Chicago, IL: University of Chicago Press.

Rohde, P. A., Atzwanger, K., Butovskaya, M., Lampert, A., Mysterud, I., Sanchez-Andres, A., et al. (2003). Perceived parental favoritism, closeness to kin, and the rebel of the family: The effects of birth order and sex. *Evolution and Human Behavior, 24,* 261–276.

Rossi, A. S., & Rossi, P. H. (1990). *Of human bonding: Parent–child relations across the life course.* New York: Aldine de Gruyter.

Rowe, D. C. (1994). *The limits of family influence.* New York: Guilford Press.

Russell, R. J. H., & Wells, P. A. (1987). Estimating paternity confidence. *Ethology and Sociobiology, 8,* 215–220.

Salmon, C. A. (1999). On the impact of sex and birth order on contact with kin. *Human Nature, 10,* 183–197.

Salmon, C. A., & Daly, M. (1996). On the importance of kin relations to Canadian women and men. *Ethology and Sociobiology, 17,* 289–297.

Salmon, C. A., & Daly, M. (1998). Birth order and familial sentiment: Middleborns are different. *Evolution and Human Behavior, 19,* 299–312.

Schönpflug, U. (2001). Intergenerational transmission of values: The role of transmission belts. *Journal of Cross-Cultural Psychology, 32,* 174–185.

Smith, M. S. (1988). Research in developmental sociobiology: Parenting and family behavior. In K. B. MacDonald (Ed.), *Sociobiological perspectives on human development* (pp. 271–292). New York: Springer.

Smith, M. S., Kish, B. J., & Crawford, C. B. (1987). Inheritance of wealth as human kin investment. *Ethology and Sociobiology, 8,* 171–181.

Steinbach, I., & Henke, W. (1998). Grosselterninvestment: Eine empirische interkulturelle Vergleichsstudie [Grandparental investment: An empirical cross-cultural comparative study]. *Anthropologie, 36,* 293–301.

Sulloway, F. (1996). *Born to rebel: Birth order, family dynamics, and creative lives.* New York: Pantheon.

Sulloway, F. (2001). Birth order, sibling competition, and human behavior. In H. R. Holcomb III (Ed.), *Conceptual challenges in evolutionary psychology: Innovative research strategies* (Vol. 27, pp. 39–83). Dodrecht, Netherlands: Kluwer Academic Publishers.

Symons, D. (1979). *The evolution of human sexuality.* New York: Oxford University Press.

Szydlik, M. (1995). Die Enge der Beziehung zwischen erwachsenen Kindern und ihren Eltern – und umgekehrt [The closeness of relationship between adult children and their parents – and vice versa]. *Zeitschrift für Soziologie, 24,* 75–94.

Tabachnik, B. G., & Fidell, L. S. (1996). *Using multivariate statistics* (3rd ed.). New York: HarperCollins.

Tesser, A. (1993). The importance of heritability in psychological research: The case of attitudes. *Psychological Review, 93,* 129–143.

Tooby, J., & Cosmides, L. (1992). The psychological foundations of culture. In J. H. Barkow, L. Cosmides, & J. Tooby (Eds.), *The adapted mind* (pp. 19–136). New York: Oxford University Press.

Trivers, R. L. (1972). Parental investment and sexual selection. In B. Campbell (Ed.), *Sexual selection and the descent of man 1871–1971* (pp. 136–179). Chicago, IL: Aldine.

Trivers, R. L. *(1974)*. Parent–offspring conflict. *American Zoologist, 14*, 249–264.

PART TWO

CROSS-CULTURAL PERSPECTIVE

6

An Ecocultural Perspective on Cultural Transmission:
The Family across Cultures

JOHN W. BERRY AND JAMES GEORGAS

INTRODUCTION

Cross-cultural psychology attempts to understand how human behavior is shaped by the cultural context in which it developed. One approach to understanding this relationship is by examining the ecological and cultural settings in which individuals live and the patterns of behavior that emerge in them (Berry, 1976). To explain how a group's culture becomes incorporated in individual behavior, some form of linkage between them needs to be postulated. This connection is to be found in the process of cultural transmission (Cavalli-Sforza & Feldman, 1981), which is seen as the main link among groups of people (i.e., cultures, communities, and families) and the development of individuals (including their overt behaviors and the inferred characteristics that underlie their behavior). Within this process of cultural transmission, three subprocesses have been distinguished: *enculturation, socialization,* and *acculturation* (Berry, Poortinga, & Segall, 2002). The first is a general enfolding of the developing individual by one's cultural group, often without specific instruction; the second also takes place within a person's own cultural group but is usually accomplished by way of deliberate shaping (i.e., child-rearing practices) and formal instruction (i.e., education); however, the third results from cultural influences arriving from outside a person's own culture, typically involving both enfolding as for enculturation (e.g., by mass telemedia) and deliberate changing as for socialization (e.g., by formal schooling).

For all three forms of cultural transmission, another set of distinctions is necessary. Vertical, horizontal, and oblique transmission derive from cultural influence from three sources: respectively from one's parents, from one's peers, and from social institutions. In addition to these occurring within one's own society, these three forms of transmission may arrive from sources outside one's own culture, creating a double cultural transmission (Berry, 2007; Berry & Cavalli-Sforza, 1986). In our view, a valid understanding of how individual behavior comes to be present in individuals requires the examination of all three forms of cultural transmission and from all three sources. A complete study in cross-cultural psychology thus requires not only the comparative examination of systematic relationships between cultural and psychological phenomena, but also of the processes of cultural transmission in all its forms, in order to determine how these relationships came to be established.

1.0. AN ECOCULTURAL PERSPECTIVE

An important theme in cultural anthropology is that cultural variations may be understood as adaptations to differing ecological settings or contexts (Boyd & Richerson, 1983). This line of thinking, known as *cultural ecology* or *ecological anthropology*, has a long history in the discipline (Feldman, 1975). Its roots go back to Forde's classic analysis (1934) of relationships between physical habitat and societal features in Africa and Kroeber's early demonstration (1939) that cultural areas and natural areas covary in Aboriginal North America. Unlike earlier simplistic assertions by the school of *environmental determinism* (Huntington, 1945), the ecological school of thought has ranged from *possibilism* (in which the environment provides opportunities and sets some constraints or limits on the range of possible cultural forms that may emerge) to an emphasis on *resource utilization* (in which active and interactive relationships between human populations and their habitat are analyzed).

Of particular interest to psychologists is the notion of the cognized environment, which refers to selected features of the environment that are of greatest relevance to a population's subsistence. With this notion, ecological thinking moved simultaneously away from any links to earlier deterministic views and toward the more psychological idea of individuals actively perceiving, appraising, and changing their environments.

The earlier ecological approaches tended to view cultures as relatively stable (even permanent) adaptations (as a state), largely ignoring adaptation (as a process) or adaptability (as a system characteristic) of cultural populations (Bennett, 1976). However, it is clear that cultures evolve over time, sometimes in response to changing ecological circumstances and sometimes due to contact with other cultures. This fact has required the addition of a more dynamic conception of ecological adaptation as a continuous as well as an interactive process among ecological, cultural, and psychological variables. It is from the most recent position that we approach the topic. It is a view that is consistent with more recent general changes in anthropology, away from a "museum" orientation to culture (collecting and organizing static artifacts) to one that emphasizes cultures as constantly changing and being concerned with creation, metamorphosis, and re-creation.

Over the years, ecological thinking has influenced not only anthropology but also psychology. The fields of ecological and environmental psychology have become fully elaborated (Werner, Brown, & Altman, 1997) with substantial theoretical and empirical foundations. In essence, individual human behavior

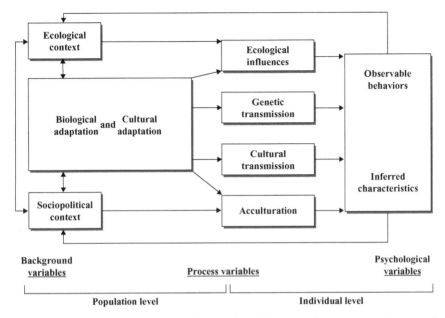

Figure 6.1. The Ecocultural Framework.

has come to be seen in its natural setting or habitat, both in terms of its develop-ment and its contemporary display. The parallel development of cross-cultural psychology (Berry et al., 1997) has also "naturalized" the study of human behav-ior and its development. In this field, individual behavior is accounted for to a large extent by considering the role of cultural influences on it. Ecological as well as cultural influences are considered as operating in tandem – hence, the use of the term *ecocultural approach* (Berry, 1976; Sam & Berry, 2006).

The current version of the Ecocultural Framework (Figure 6.1) proposes to account for human psychological diversity (both individual and group simi-larities and differences) by considering two fundamental sources of influence, *ecological* and *sociopolitical*, and two features of human populations that are adapted to them, *cultural* and *biological* characteristics. These population vari-ables are transmitted to individuals by various transmission variables such as enculturation, socialization, acculturation, and genetic transmission. The first three are considered forms of cultural transmission, whereas the fourth is bio-logical. Our understanding of cultural transmission has been greatly advanced by work on culture learning (Tomasello, Krüger, & Ratner, 1993) and on the process and outcomes of acculturation (Chun, Balls-Organista, & Marin, 2003). The latter form has come to the fore as a result of the dramatic increase in intercultural contact and change.

To summarize, the Ecocultural Framework considers human diversity (both cultural and psychological) to be a set of collective and individual adaptations to context. Within this general perspective, it views cultures as evolving adaptations to ecological and sociopolitical influences, and it views individual psychological characteristics in a population as adaptive to their cultural context. It also views (group) culture and (individual) behavior as distinct phenomena at their own levels that need to be examined independently (see the following discussion).

Within psychology, research on ecological and environmental psychology has sought to specify the links between ecological context and individual human development and behavior. Cross-cultural psychology tends to view cultures (both one's own and others with which one is in contact) as differential contexts for development and to view behavior as adaptive to these different contexts.

The ecocultural approach offers a "value-neutral" framework for describing or interpreting similarities and differences in human behavior across cultures (Berry, 1994b). As adaptive to context, psychological phenomena can be understood "in their own terms" (as the anthropologist Malinowski [2001] insisted), and external evaluations can usually be avoided. This is a critical point because it allows for the conceptualization, assessment, and interpretation of both culture and behavior in nonethnocentric ways. It explicitly rejects the idea that some cultures or behaviors are more advanced or more developed than others (Berry, Dasen, & Witkin, 1983). Any argument about cultural or behavioral differences being ordered hierarchically requires the adoption of some absolute (usually external) standard – but who is so bold, or so wise, to assert and verify such a standard?

The second main input in the Ecocultural Framework is the sociopolitical context, which brings about contact among cultures so that individuals have to adapt to more than one context. In situations of culture contact and acculturation, psychological phenomena can be viewed as attempts to deal simultaneously with two (sometimes inconsistent, sometimes conflicting) cultural contexts (Berry, 2003). Of course, these intercultural settings need to be approached with the same nonethnocentric perspective as all cross-cultural settings (Berry, 1985).

Initially, the link among ecology, culture, and behavior was elaborated into a framework to predict differential development of some perceptual and cognitive abilities among hunting- and agriculture-based peoples (Berry, 1966). The first step was to propose that the *ecological demands* for survival that were placed on hunting peoples were for a high level of these perceptual-cognitive abilities, in contrast with peoples employing other (particularly agricultural) subsistence strategies. Second, it was proposed that *cultural aids* (e.g., socialization practices, linguistic differentiation of spatial information, and the use of arts and crafts) would promote the development of these abilities. As predicted, empirical studies of Inuit (then called Eskimo) in the Canadian Arctic and Temne (in Sierra Leone) revealed marked differences in those abilities. Further studies were carried out and, during the course of this empirical work, the ideas became further elaborated into an Ecocultural Framework. In each case, a consideration of ecological, sociopolitical, and cultural features of the group were taken as a basis for predicting differential psychological outcomes in a variety of domains. For example, differential degrees of reliance on hunting (Berry, 1967, 1979), variations in social stratification ranging from "loose" to "tight" (Pelto, 1968), and in child socialization practices ranging from emphases on "assertion" to "compliance" (Barry, Child, & Bacon, 1959) were used to predict variations in the development of these functional abilities. These cultural features are closely linked to the structure and functions of the family, as discussed later in this chapter.

Further work on perceptual and cognitive abilities, aligned in part to the theory of psychological differentiation, particularly the cognitive style of field dependence – field independence (Witkin & Berry, 1975) – resulted in three volumes reporting results of studies in the Arctic, Africa, Australia, New Guinea, and India (Berry, 1976, Berry et al., 1986; Mishra, Sinha, & Berry, 1996). The Ecocultural Framework has also been used to understand sources of variation in perceptual-cognitive development (Dasen, 1975; Mishra, Dasen, & Niraula, 2003; Nsamenang, 1992). This developmental focus necessarily implicates the structure and function of the family.

Although most use of the Ecocultural Framework has been in the study of perception and cognition, it equally applies to the exploration of social behavior. For example, studies of social conformity (Berry, 1967, 1979) showed that greater conformity to a suggested group norm is likely to occur in cultures that are structurally tight (i.e., with high norm obligation). The relationship is robust, whether examined at the level of individuals or by using the group's mean score as the variable related to ecology (for a review, see Bond & Smith, 1996). A further example shows how ecocultural indicators are related to the currently popular concepts of "individualism" and "collectivism" (Berry, 1994a). It is suggested that individualism may be related to the differentiation (i.e., structural complexity) dimensions of society, with greater differentiation being predictive of greater personal individualism. However, collectivism is proposed to be related more to the integration (i.e., structural tightness) dimension, with greater integration predictive of greater collectivism. It is further suggested that when individualism and collectivism are found to be at opposite ends of one value dimension, it is because data are usually obtained in societies (i.e., industrial urban) where the two cultural dimensions (i.e., differentiation and integration) are strongly distinguished; if data were to be collected over a broader range, in other types of societies (e.g., hunting or agricultural) where the two dimensions coincide, then this value opposition or incompatibility may not be observed.

Other work has further extended this interest in social aspects of behavior (Georgas & Berry, 1995; Georgas, van de Vijver, & Berry, 2004). The first study sought to discover ecological and social indicators that might allow societies to be clustered according to their similarities and differences on six dimensions: ecology, education, economy, mass communications, population, and religion. The second study further examined ecosocial indicators across societies and then sought evidence of their relationships with a number of psychological variables (e.g., values and subjective well-being). Results showed that many of the indicators came together to form a single economic dimension, termed *affluence*, and this was distinct from the variable of *religion* in the pattern of relationships with the psychological variables. Specifically, across cultures, a high placement on affluence (along with Protestant religion) was associated with more emphasis on individualism, utilitarianism, and personal well-being. In contrast, for other religions, together with low affluence, there was an emphasis on power, loyalty, and hierarchy values.

2.0. THE ROLE OF THE FAMILY

As a cultural institution, family may be seen as adaptive to ecocultural context and as a vehicle for cultural transmission (Berry, 1976; Georgas, 1988). The family thus occupies a central place in the ecocultural approach, serving to link background contexts to individual behavioral development. It is well established that features of family and marriage are closely related to ecocultural features of a society, especially to settlement pattern, role differentiation, and social strat-ification. These relationships were already noted in a public lecture by Tylor (1871), who proposed that nomadic societies (mainly hunting- and gathering-based peoples) tended to have nuclear families and monogamous marriages, in contrast to sedentary societies (mainly agricultural peoples), who tended to have extended families and polygamous marriages. Tylor suggested that these family and marriage types allowed for efficient economic functioning in their respec-tive habitats: hunters operate best in small units, with symbiotic relationships between two spouses and their direct offspring, whereas agriculturalists require larger working units, facilitated by multiple spouses and a larger network of kin and offspring.

Since these early observations, many empirical studies have demonstrated their validity and have expanded the network of relationships. For example, role differentiation (i.e., the number of specialized tasks that are distinguished within the society) and social stratification (i.e., the hierarchical arrangement among these roles, leading to variations in status) are now important elements of these complex patterns.

The ecology element of the Ecocultural Framework proposes that human organisms interact with their physical environments in ways that seek to satisfy their needs. Because of variations in environmental features (e.g., temperature, rainfall, and soil quality), variations in economic possibilities will emerge that may satisfy those needs.

A well-established dimension of varying economic pursuits is that of an exploitive subsistence pattern (Murdock, 1969, pp. 130–131), in which pre-industrial societies were classified as gathering, hunting, pastoral, fishing, and varieties of agriculture. Two demographic patterns vary as a function of these economic patterns. For Murdock, settlement patterns may be classified as fully nomadic, seminomadic, semisedentary, and fully sedentary; the size of local population units may be arranged from small camps or settlements up to large towns. Both settlement pattern and population unit size are empirically related to exploitive pattern (Murdock, 1969), with hunting and gathering societies being predominantly nomadic or seminomadic with small population units, and agricultural and pastoral societies being predominantly sedentary or semisedentary, with much larger population units.

In summary, evidence for the ecology element of the framework shows that the knowledge of physical environmental features in which a population lives allows prediction of the economic possibilities (i.e., exploitive pattern and food accumulation), which in turn allows prediction of the demographic distribution (i.e., settlement patterns and size of population units). The relationships are all probabilistic rather than deterministic; nevertheless, they are extant and are of sufficient strength to make predictions from ecological factors to the cultural adaptation element of the Ecocultural Framework.

Although we espouse a definition of culture that includes functional adaptation to ecology, it stands to reason that numerous aspects of culture could be considered. One of these is social stratification, which can be related to the number of elements in the ecological component. For example, Nimkoff and Middleton (1960) divided societies into categories of "great" or "little" social stratification and into four exploitive patterns. They found that the majority (76%) of the societies classed as "agriculture present" are also classed as "highly stratified," whereas among the societies classed as "hunting or gathering," most (78%) were in the "low-stratification" category.

With respect to cultural transmission, as discussed previously, a distinction is commonly made between enculturation and socialization. Both these forms of cultural transmission have been proposed to be adaptive to ecological context. As outlined in detail herein, Barry, Child, and Bacon (1959) were able to demonstrate a clear relationship between type of ecological exploitive pattern and the way socialization takes place: Training of children for responsibility and obedience appeared more often in agricultural and pastoral societies, whereas training for achievement, self-reliance, and independence was more frequent in hunting and gathering societies. Thus, we have evidence that an exploitive subsistence pattern is a reasonably good predictor of socialization emphases.

In summary, we may label a broad ecological dimension running from hunting and gathering to agricultural interactions with the environment. Associated with the latter end of the dimension are a sedentary lifestyle, high population density, high sociocultural stratification, polygamy, extended families, and socialization emphases on compliance. Associated with the former end of the dimension are a nomadic lifestyle, low population density, low stratification, monogamy, nuclear families, and socialization practices that emphasize assertion. Societies that range along this ecological dimension vary concomitantly on these other ecological and cultural variables (Berry, 1976).

When this ecological dimension is extended to include contemporary industrial and postindustrial societies, a curvilinear pattern becomes apparent (Berry, 1994a, 2001). With the increasing high density of cities, we observe a reduction in pressures toward compliance as a result of loss of community cohesion and the anonymity afforded by the large cities. There is also a reduction in the frequency of extended families and a parallel increase in proportion of nuclear families, which is accompanied by a further reduction in pressures toward compliance.

Beyond the ecological context, the sociopolitical context has played an important role in shaping both cultural and transmission features of the Ecocultural Framework. In particular, the colonization of Asia by Indian and Chinese societies and of Africa and the Americas by European societies brought about societal changes that altered cultural patterns, including family arrangements and emphases in cultural transmission. Colonization introduced new religions and forms of education, particularly formal schooling, in most of those societies. The telemedia continue to promote change from outside by portraying alternative lifestyles and consumer goods. Its impact has led to an apparent increase in nuclear families and monogamous marriages in previously polygamous societies with extended families. Associated changes, such as delayed marriage, fewer children, and increased divorce rates, have also been assigned to acculturative influences, mainly emanating from contemporary Western domination of people in the "Majority World." Changes in cultural transmission have also been postulated, including increased pressures toward assertion and a decline in compliance during socialization.

3.0. CULTURAL TRANSMISSION

The concept of cultural transmission was introduced by Cavalli-Sforza and Feldman (1981) to parallel the notion of biological transmission, in which – through genetic mechanisms (see Figure 6.1) – certain features of a population are perpetuated over time across generations. By analogy, using various forms of cultural transmission, a cultural group can perpetuate its behavioral features among subsequent generations employing teaching and learning mechanisms. To illustrate the three forms of cultural transmission (i.e., vertical, horizontal, and oblique), Figure 6.2 (from Berry & Cavalli-Sforza, 1986) displays them for both one's own society and for those coming from outside one's own society. Cultural transmission from parents to their offspring was termed *vertical transmission* by Cavalli-Sforza and Feldman because it involves the descent of cultural characteristics from one generation to the next. However, whereas vertical descent is the only possible form of biological transmission, in the two other forms of cultural transmission (i.e., *horizontal* and *oblique*) there is no role for biology.

In vertical transmission, parents transmit cultural values, skills, beliefs, motives, and so on to their offspring. In this case, it is difficult to distinguish between cultural and biological transmission because one typically learns from

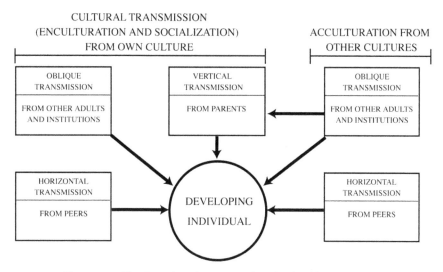

Figure 6.2. The Ecocultural Framework and cultural transmission.

the very people who were responsible for one's conception; that is, biological parents and cultural parents are the same. In horizontal cultural transmission, one learns from one's peers (in primary and secondary groups) during the course of development from birth to adulthood; here, there is no confounding between biological and cultural transmission, with the exception of learning from siblings. In the case of oblique cultural transmission, one learns from other adults (including members of one's extended family) and institutions (including community organizations and formal schooling). When the process takes place entirely within one's own or primary culture, then *enculturation* and *socialization* are the appropriate terms (see the left side of Figure 6.2). However, when the process derives from contact with another or secondary culture, the term *acculturation* is employed (see the right side of Figure 6.2), which refers to the form of transmission experienced by an individual resulting from contact with and influence from persons and institutions belonging to cultures other than one's own (Berry, 2007).

Although these forms of cultural transmission are shown in Figure 6.2 with arrows flowing toward the developing individual, reciprocal influences are known to be important, particularly so among peers but also in parent–child relationships. Thus, double-headed arrows, representing interaction and mutual influence, would more accurately represent what occurs during cultural transmission and acculturation.

4.0. ENCULTURATION AND SOCIALIZATION

The concept of *enculturation* was developed within the discipline of cultural anthropology and was first defined and used by Herskovits (1949). As the term suggests, there is an encompassing or surrounding of the individual by one's culture; the individual acquires, by learning, what the culture deems to be necessary. There is not necessarily anything deliberate or didactic about this process; often, there is learning without specific teaching. The process of enculturation involves parents and other adults and peers in a network of influences on the individual, all of which can limit, shape, and direct the developing individual. The end result (if enculturation is successful) is a person who is competent in the culture, including its language, rituals, values, and so on.

The concept of *socialization* was developed in the disciplines of sociology and social psychology to refer to the process of deliberate shaping – by way of tutelage – of the individual. It is generally employed in cross-cultural psychology in the same way. When vertical, horizontal, or oblique cultural transmission involves deliberate teaching from within one's group, then we are dealing with the process of socialization; resocialization occurs when the deliberate influences come later in one's life, often from outside one's own culture. The net result of both enculturation and socialization is the development of behavioral similarities within cultures and behavioral differences between cultures. They are thus the crucial cultural mechanisms that produce the distribution of similarities and differences in psychological characteristics at the individual level.

The concept of acculturation comes from anthropology and refers to cultural and psychological change brought about by contact with other peoples belonging to different cultures and exhibiting different behaviors (see the lower path in Figure 6.1 and the right-hand side of Figure 6.2). For example, many groups in India and Africa became acculturated to aspects of British lifestyle during the Empire (i.e., changing their social structure, economic, and other institutions), and many individuals changed their own behaviors (e.g., their religion, language, and dress). In a sense then, acculturation is a second or later form of enculturation and socialization, and it can take place over the whole of one's life-span development, not just during childhood. It involves relearning (including some specific resocialization) and can create both new problems and new opportunities for the individual (Berry, 2003; Berry & Sam, 1997; Camilleri & Malewska-Peyre, 1997).

As discussed in the next section, these processes occur in a larger ecological and cultural context: The forms (or style) and the content (what) of transmission are generally viewed as adaptive to the ecocultural setting and are functional in that they ensure that the developing individual acquires the behavioral repertoire necessary to live successfully in that setting. It is for this reason that cultural transmission is placed in such a central position in the Ecocultural Framework (see Figure 6.1).

The process of cultural transmission does not lead to replication of successive generations; it falls somewhere between an exact transmission (with hardly any differences between parents and offspring) and a complete failure of transmission (with offspring who are unlike their parents). Where it usually falls is closer to the full transmission end rather than to the nontransmission end of this spectrum. Functionally, either extreme may be problematic for a society; exact transmission would not allow for novelty and change – hence, the ability to respond to new situations – whereas failure of transmission would not permit coordinated action between generations (Boyd & Richerson, 1985).

5.0. CROSS-CULTURAL STUDIES OF CULTURAL TRANSMISSION

Studies of how a society characteristically raises its children have been reported in the literature for more than a century. Many of the reports have been accumulated in an archive mainly composed of ethnographic reports known as the Human Relations Area Files. One approach to the study of cultural transmission is to employ the files to discover the major dimensions of variation in these practices as they are used around the world. This approach provides a broad overview and allows us to examine cultural transmission (earlier called child-rearing practices) in the context of other ecological and cultural variables also included in the archives. We are thus able to examine how enculturation and socialization fit into or are adaptive to other features of the group's circumstances.

Studies of cultural transmission employing ethnographic archives are termed *holocultural*. Because they examine materials from cultures the whole world over, they offer the possibility of discovering commonalities in the process of cultural transmission. For example, Barry, Child, and Bacon (1959) were able to (1) identify some common dimensions of child training; (2) place societies at various positions on these dimensions; (3) show some characteristic differences between training for boys and girls; and (4) relate all of these to features of ecological and cultural variation (e.g., economy and social structure) – thereby placing socialization in a broader context. Barry, Child, and Bacon (1959) identified six of the common dimensions: (1) obedience training (i.e., the degree to which children are trained to obey adults); (2) responsibility training (i.e., the degree to which children are trained to take on responsibility for subsistence or household tasks); (3) nurturance training (i.e., the degree to which children are trained to care for and help younger siblings and other dependent people); (4) achievement training (i.e., the degree to which children are trained to strive toward standards of excellence in performance); (5) self-reliance training (i.e., the degree to which children are trained to take care of themselves and to be independent of assistance from others in supplying their needs or wants); and (6) general independence training (i.e., the degree to which children are trained toward freedom from control, domination, and supervision).

Barry, Child, and Bacon (1959) considered whether these six dimensions were independent of each other or were related in some systematic way across cultures. Their analyses showed that five of the six dimensions tended to form two clusters. One cluster, termed *pressure toward compliance*, combined training for responsibility and obedience; training for nurturance was only marginally part of this cluster. The other cluster, termed *pressure toward assertion*, combined training for achievement, self-reliance, and independence. These two clusters were negatively related. Thus, a single dimension was created along which societies were placed, ranging from compliance training at one end and assertion training at the other end. The six initial dimensions were thus reduced to a single dimension. Variations in cultural transmission along this dimension have also been described as from "narrow" to "broad" socialization (Arnett, 1995). Narrow socialization (cf. compliance) is characterized by obedience and conformity and is thought to lead to a restricted range of individual differences, whereas broad socialization (cf. assertion) is characterized by the promotion of independence and self-expression and is thought to lead to a broad range of individual differences.

Barry and colleagues questioned whether variations in practices could be adaptations to ecological context. They asked, "Why does a particular society select child training practices that will tend to produce a particular kind of typical personality? Is it because this kind of typical personality is functional for the adult life of the society, and training methods which will produce it are thus also functional?" (Barry, Child, & Bacon, 1959, p. 51). They began their search for an answer to these questions by examining one of the most basic functions in a society: the economic relationship between a population and its ecosystem. For each society, the economic mode of subsistence was rated on dimensions of gathering, hunting, fishing, pastoralism, and agriculture. In the view of Barry, Child, and Bacon (1959, p. 52), with a dependence on pastoralism (i.e., raising animals for milk and meat), "future food supply seems to be best assured by faithful adherence to routines designed to maintain the good health of the herd." At the opposite extreme is hunting and gathering. Where "each day's food comes from that day's catch, variations in the energy and skill exerted in food-getting lead to immediate reward or punishment. . . . If the change is a good one, it may lead to immediate reward" (p. 52). Agricultural- and fishing-based societies are thought to be between these two extremes.

On the basis of these observations, they argued that in pastoral and agricultural societies (which are high in "food accumulation"), people should tend to be relatively "conscientious, compliant and conservative," while in hunting and gathering societies (which are low in "food accumulation"), people should be relatively "individualistic, assertive and venturesome" (p. 53). Assuming that societies train their children for these appropriate adult behaviors, Barry, Child, and Bacon (1959) predicted a relationship between type of subsistence economy and child-rearing practices.

To assess the argument that child-training practices are adaptive to subsistence economy, they were compared in a sample of 104 societies with the degree of food accumulation (defined in terms of exploitive patterns). Before examining these relationships, it is useful to note that other cultural elements (e.g., social stratification and political integration) and ecological elements in addition to subsistence economic practices (e.g., population concentration) are strongly related to both the variables of food accumulation and pressure in child training toward compliance. For the 46 societies studied, both the food accumulation and socialization variables are related significantly to the other ecological and cultural variables, such as size of settlement and social stratification.

The correlation between food accumulation and socialization practices is positive for responsibility and obedience training and negative for achievement, self-reliance, and independence training. When the more global measure of socialization (i.e., pressure toward compliance versus assertion) is employed, these relationships still hold. Using this overall compliance-assertion score, Barry, Child, and Bacon (1959) found a correlation of .94 with degree of food accumulation; of the 23 societies above the median on the compliance-assertion rating, 20 are high food-accumulating, and of the 23 societies below the median, 19 are low food-accumulating. There is thus a strong similarity between socialization emphases and the broader ecological and cultural context.

So far in this chapter, we have explored the process of cultural transmission across cultures. We began by presenting a view of both culture and behavior as adaptations to the ecological contexts in which it developed and is currently displayed. By distinguishing among three forms of cultural transmission, we examined differential effects of context on the processes. Parents (engaged in vertical transmission) employ socialization (child-rearing) practices that appear to be adaptive to ecocultural setting. Other adult members of society (who provide the broader enculturation through oblique transmission) tend to place variable emphases on compliance and assertion, also depending on the ecocultural features of the society in which they operate. When the others are outsiders, they provide another form of oblique transmission in the form of acculturation influences on the developing individual. Finally, horizontal transmission from peers comes from within one's own cultural group; however, peers in multicultural settings (e.g., cities of immigration and international schools) increasingly serve to bring acculturative influences to bear. These latter influences are less well studied across cultures and require research (see Berry, Phinney, Sam, and Vedder [2006] for an example of a comparative study of youth acculturation; see Sam and Berry [2006] for an overview of the field of acculturation psychology).

6.0. A COMPARATIVE STUDY OF FAMILY

In this section, we present findings from a study based in part on the Ecocultural Framework (Georgas, Berry, van de Vijver, Kagitcibasi, & Poortinga, 2006). As such, it examines the relationships among ecocultural variables, social structural variables, family roles, and psychological variables. Figure 6.3 illustrates some of these variables, expanded from the Ecocultural Framework shown in Figure 6.1.

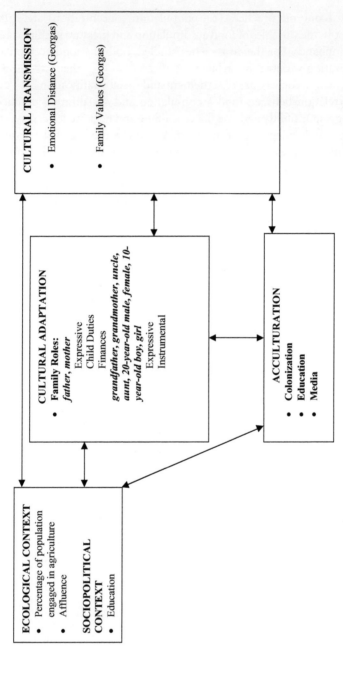

Figure 6.3. The Ecocultural Framework, cultural transmission, and family variables.

The study examined these relationships in 27 nations representing the geo-cultural zones of East Asia (South Korea, Japan, and Hong Kong); Oceania (Indonesia); South Asia (India); West Asia (Pakistan, Iran, Georgia, and Saudi Arabia); North Africa (Algeria); Central Africa (Nigeria and Ghana); North Europe (Britain, the Netherlands, Germany, and France); South Europe (Greece, Bulgaria, Turkey, Cyprus, and Spain); East Europe (Ukraine); North America (Canada and United States); Central America (Mexico); and South America (Chile and Brazil).

6.1. Method

6.1.1. *Sample*

An attempt was made to select countries so as to represent the major geographical and cultural regions of the world in order to maximize ecocultural variation in variables such as economic measures. The sample consisted of $N = 5,482$ university students from the 27 countries noted previously. The samples ranged from $N = 70$ in Ghana to $N = 450$ in Pakistan. A problem with such samples is that these students represent a specific age category of the population and are not necessarily representative of either their cohorts or other ages. In addition, they represent only the most educated sector of the population, which most likely will not continue the traditional forms of subsistence of their elders. However, there is good reason to use such a sample: University students often represent the age group and level of education that are at the cutting edge of cultural changes in terms of attitudes and values. Thus, the responses of university students should represent the leading edge of changes in a culture rather than the average level of responses that would be obtained using a representative sample of a culture.

6.1.2. *Variables*

The levels of analyses and the variables are as follows:

> The ecocultural variables are (1) the ecological variable: percentage of the pop-ulation engaged in agriculture; (2) the economic variable: affluence; and (3) the sociopolitical variable: education. In addition, we introduced (4) family variables: the family roles for nine family positions and the psychological variables; (5) emotional distance; and (6) family values.

The arrows in the Ecocultural Framework (see Figure 6.1) symbolize the potential relationships among the three levels. The ecocultural variables were analyzed only at the country level, whereas the other two levels were analyzed at both the country and the individual levels.

Culture. Culture was analyzed in terms of the Ecocultural Framework and based on the methodological approach described in Georgas and Berry (1995) and Georgas, van de Vijver, and Berry (2004). Ecocultural variables at the country level were collected from archival data from the World Development Report of the World Bank (2002a, 2002b).

Ecological variables were as follows: (1) agriculture, measured by percentage of the population engaged in agriculture; and (2) affluence, measured by the following economic variables: gross national product per capita in U.S. dollars, energy use per capita (in kilograms of oil equivalent), electricity consumption per capita in kilowatt hours, unemployment rate, percentage of the population employed in industry, percentage of the population employed in services, imports (in U.S. dollars), and exports (in U.S. dollars) (United Nations Statistics Division, 2002a, 2002b).

The sociopolitical variable was education, measured by the percentage of tertiary-education-level students enrolled in education, humanities, social sciences, natural sciences, and medicine; pupil–teacher ratio for pre-primary, primary, and secondary education; age of pre-primary, primary, and secondary enrollment; duration of each education level; and male and female tertiary-education enrollment percentages. These indices could be labeled "access to education"; that is, in countries with higher scores on education, more males and females enroll in tertiary education, fewer tertiary students specialize in a specific field, and countries with longer duration of pre-primary, primary, and secondary education have fewer numbers of pupils per teacher.

Family Roles. The family roles questionnaire was developed by Georgas and his colleagues on the basis of family literature and questionnaires from 30 countries. Based on pilot testing in Greece and discussions with colleagues in the project, 22 roles were selected. The roles are in the areas of psychological environment in the family, traditions, kinship relationships, hierarchical power, housework, school, play, behavior and support of children, finances, babysitting, and helping parents with economic activities. A 6-point scale was employed (from Almost Always to Never) to rate nine family positions: father, mother, grandfather, grandmother, uncle/aunt, 20-year-old male, 20-year-old female, 10-year-old boy, and 10-year-old girl. These family positions represent three generations and collateral relatives (i.e., aunts/uncles). Thus, the method was not based on the responses of members of each generation but rather on the students' perceptions of how each generation might respond to each family role.

The method for determining the factors of family roles across the 27 nations was as follows. The extraction method was Principle Component Analyses of the pooled data of the 22 family roles from all 27 nations for each of the nine family positions. A separate Principle Component Analysis of the data from each nation for each family position was then conducted. The next step was to compare the factor structure of each country for each family position with the factor structure of the pooled dataset, employing the Tucker phi criterion of at least 0.90 as a measure of the structural equivalence of the factors.

Three main roles were found for father and mother: *expressive* (e.g., providing emotional support to children, grandparents, and wife/husband; keeping the family united; keeping a pleasant environment); *financial* (e.g., contributing financially to the family, managing finances, giving pocket money to children, supporting career of children); and *childcare* (e.g., taking children to school, playing with children, helping children with homework).

Two main roles were found for the other seven family positions: *expressive* (e.g., providing emotional support, keeping the family united, conveying traditions) and *instrumental* (e.g., contributing financially, babysitting, helping parents with their work). Note that the financial and childcare roles of mother and father are instrumental roles. The analyses demonstrated a remarkable cross-cultural stability in the patterning of the 22 roles.

An unexpected finding was that the family roles resembled Parsons's (1943, 1949) expressive and instrumental roles and Durkheim's (1888, 1892) description of the last two stages of family change, in which the paternal family is reduced to the conjugal or nuclear family and in which the relationships between parents and children change from material or economic basis to "personal motives."

The psychological variables were as follows:

Emotional Bonds. The questionnaire of Georgas et al. (2001) employed scales based on concentric circles, derived from Bogardus's (1925) concepts of social distance and personal space. A 7-point scale was employed, from Very Far to Very Close. Two categories were employed in the analysis: bonds with members of the nuclear family (i.e., mother, father, brothers, and sisters), and bonds with members of the extended family (i.e., grandparents, uncles/aunts, and cousins).

Family Values. The family-values questionnaire was separated into two factors: (1) *hierarchical roles* of father and mother, and (2) *relationships within family and with kin.* These are traditional values related to extended family roles in agricultural societies, developed in Greece (Georgas, 1993, 1999). Deviations from these baseline measures of traditional family values would be a measure of changes from traditional values. A 7-point scale was employed, from Strongly Agree to Strongly Disagree.

6.1.3. *Hypotheses*

The hypotheses that guided the project were rooted in the Ecocultural Framework, as discussed in the first section of this chapter. As discussed previously, this framework has two fundamental exogenous variables: ecological and sociopolitical contexts. Ecological factors are important contributors to cultural and behavioral variation when people are living at the subsistence level because there are few alternatives to adapting directly to ecological press when there are no other resources available. Beyond this ecological press, when people are affected by external sociopolitical influences, they change socially and behaviorally (through the process of acculturation) in various ways. These ways are not always by assimilating these influences but also can be by integrating or combining external influences with one's traditional practices or by reaction and resistance to them.

However, the basic ecological factors and the cultural, social, and behavioral adaptations are considered to "set the stage" for this acculturative journey. Despite the nonrepresentative/university nature of samples, we expected to detect variations in social and behavioral characteristics that are due to differential ecological settings but are modified by the way in which they have undergone acculturation.

Our strategy is to analyze these social and behavioral variations, first as a function of ecological factors, then as a function of acculturative factors, and finally as a function of the interaction of the two sets of factors.

The ecocultural perspective proposes that the ways in which a society engages its natural habitat will encourage certain forms of social organization and individual development within these social institutions. This general perspective leads to a number of specific hypotheses that can be evaluated with findings obtained in this study. In more detail, we expect that the percentage of the population engaged in agriculture will lead to hierarchical forms of social organization (including the family), to tighter ways of socializing children, and to closer bonds among family members. Conversely, as societies change from agrarian toward industrial and postindustrial forms of economic activity, their affluence increases, leading to a set of opposite expectations. Additionally, as sociopolitical influences increase (especially by way of formal schooling), these opposite expectations are further promoted.

Specifically, we hypothesized that in societies high in agriculture, there will be tighter differentiation of the family roles across the three generations than in high-affluence societies; closer expressive and child-duty roles for the mother, grandmother, and 20-year-old females; higher financial and instrumental roles of the father, grandfather, and 20-year-old males; and higher family values placed on hierarchy and kin relationships as well as similarity in these family values across generations. Similarly, in high-agricultural societies, there should be closer emotional bonds with members of the nuclear family, particularly with kin, and similarity across the three generations.

In contrast, for high-affluent and high-education societies, there will be less close expressive roles and lower acceptance of family values of hierarchy and kin relationships. In addition, across all societies, the higher the expressive role, the closer should be the emotional bonds with the nuclear family and kin.

6.1.4. *Results and Discussion*

We expected that the hypotheses based on the Ecocultural Framework specifying the relationships articulated for percentage engaged in agriculture would also be found for affluence but in an inverse direction. Moreover, this ecological variable has links to sociopolitical variables because many of the changes in affluence and its current levels have resulted through contact with other cultures. Hence, we expected that the relationships between affluence and other variables in the study would be similar to those for education. This does not invalidate the independent theoretical background of each ecological and sociopolitical variable but rather attests to the strong interrelationships between these ecological and sociopolitical variables at the country level. Thus, this section describes the simple correlations among agriculture, affluence, and education and the family and psychological variables.

The predictions involved the association of the ecological, family-role, and psychological variables. It was expected that the percentage of the population in agriculture would be positively correlated with high expressive and instrumental roles, close emotional bonds with the nuclear and extended family members, and high hierarchy and kin family values; an opposite pattern was expected for affluence and education.

Table 6.1 presents the country-level correlations of percentage engaged in agriculture, affluence level, and education with the previous variables. The presentation of the correlations deals more with effect sizes than with significance of correlations. For our current sample sizes ($N = 27$), correlations are significant at the 5% level if their absolute values are larger than .38 and at the 1% level if their values are larger than .48.

The correlations (i.e., absolute values) of percentage engaged in agriculture with expressive roles of father and mother were very high ($r = .71$) and declined across the family positions of grandfather, grandmother, aunt, uncle, and 20-year-old males and females. That is, the correlations of expressive roles with percentage engaged in agriculture were positive and very high across all family positions except for 10-year-old children. The patterns of correlations between affluence and education with expressive roles are negative; that is, they are mirror images of the correlations with agriculture. In addition, the correlations of level of affluence with expressive roles were slightly lower than those of agriculture and those of education were slightly lower than affluence.

The pattern of correlations with instrumental roles was slightly more complex. Fathers from agricultural countries were highly correlated with the financial role, but no correlations were significant with child care (which appears to be universal across countries), while there were also no correlations between the financial role or the childcare role of mothers and agriculture (nor level of affluence or education). This also suggests that these roles are universal across ecological and sociopolitical contexts. As discussed previously, the financial and childcare roles of mother and father are essentially the instrumental role, so that the financial and childcare roles are not exactly comparable to the other family positions. The highest correlations between agriculture and instrumental roles were those of the 20-year-old males ($r = .82$) and the 20-year-old females ($r = .73$). Even the 10-year-olds' instrumental roles were highly correlated with

Table 6.1. *Country-level (N = 27) correlations of agriculture, affluence, and education with family roles of nine family positions*

	Father			Mother			Grandfather		Grandmother		Aunt/Uncle		Male 20 Years Old		Female 20 Years Old		Male 10 Years Old		Female 10 Years Old	
	Exp.	Fin.	Care	Exp.	Fin.	Care	Exp.	Instr.	Exp.	Instr.	Exp.	Instr.	Exp.	Instr.	Exp.	Instr.	Exp.	Instr.	Exp.	Instr.
Percentage Working in Agriculture	.71	.67	.14	.71	.03	.01	.64	.42	.55	.19	.39	.66	.46	.82	.44	.73	.05	.59	.59	
Affluence	−.65	−.58	.11	−.61	.11	.16	−.61	−.19	−.48	.05	−.37	−.28	−.55	−.66	−.51	−.69	−.33	−.38	−.29	−.41
Education	−.55	−.45	.03	−.54	.15	.22	−.52	−.04	−.44	.21	−.43	−.29	−.52	−.56	−.50	−.49	−.39	−.44	−.37	−.46
Emotional Nuclear	.35	.51	.26	.47	.07	.29	.48	.27	.53	.29	.40	.26	.47	.52	.45	.58	.40	.11	.37	.14
Bonds Extended	.15	.43	.34	.31	.17	.54	.27	.28	.23	.36	.25	.33	.28	.30	.24	.48	.20	−.12	.16	−.09
Family Hierarchy	.79	.49	−.17	.60	−.27	−.38	.70	.33	.58	−.04	.44	.37	.65	.62	.62	.47	.34	.51	.31	.50
Values Kin	.80	.65	.22	.79	−.16	−.05	.78	.28	.72	.01	.63	.43	.85	.69	.84	.62	.44	.21	.43	.23

Notes: Correlations are significant at the 5% level if their absolute value is at least .38 and at the 1% level if their absolute value is at least .49 (N = 27).
Exp. = Expressive Role; Fin. = Financial Role; Care = Childcare Role; Instr. = Instrumental Role

Table 6.2. *Country-level (N = 27) correlations of agriculture, affluence, and education with emotional distance and family values*

| | Emotional Bonds (Georgas et al., 2006) | | Family Values (Georgas et al., 2006) | |
	Nuclear	Extended	Hierarchy	Kin
Percentage Working in Agriculture	.33	.26	.69	.64
Affluence	−.39	−.29	−.68	−.64
Education	−.29	−.05	−.59	−.60

the agriculture variable. These are essentially roles such as helping with housework, helping parents, and helping with the care of younger children – that is, older and younger children in agricultural societies do many more of these family tasks than in affluent societies.

Percentage engaged in agriculture (see Table 6.2) was marginally related ($r = .33$) to emotional bonds with members of the nuclear family but, surprisingly, not with members of the extended family ($r = .26$). The correlations of affluence were slightly higher, respectively, and those of education lower. On the other hand, agriculture was highly correlated with hierarchical family ($r = .69$) and relationships with family and kin values ($r = .64$), and the pattern of relationships with affluence and education were similar.

Finally, the pattern of the intercorrelations among the family roles for each position, the emotional bonds, and the family values are of considerable interest, as shown in Table 6.3. Fairly high correlations were found between emotional bonds with members of the nuclear family and expressive roles in all the family positions. However, relatively low correlations were found among emotional bonds with members of the extended family and expressive roles. This finding was counterintuitive and not expected.

These analyses described the correlations between the ecological and sociopolitical variables and the family at the country level. The means for each country of the family roles for each family position at the individual level are presented for the expressive and instrumental roles (Figures 6.3 and 6.4). The countries are separated into three country zones, based on the cluster analysis of the affluence level of each country, listed in order of declining index of affluence: (1) high-level affluence: United States, Canada, Germany, Japan, France, the Netherlands, United Kingdom, Hong Kong, South Korea, and Spain; (2) middle-level affluence: Greece, Saudi Arabia, Ukraine, Mexico, Bulgaria, Chile, Cyprus, Brazil, Turkey, Iran, and Georgia; and (3) low-level affluence: Indonesia, Pakistan, India, Algeria, Ghana, and Nigeria.

Table 6.3. *Correlations of the family roles for each family position with emotional bonds and family values*

		Father			Mother			Grandfather		Grandmother		Aunt/Uncle		Male 20 Years		Female 20 Years		Male 10 Years		Female 10 Years	
		Exp.	Fin.	Care	Exp.	Fin.	Care	Exp.	Instr.	Exp.	Instr.	Exp.	Instr.	Exp.	Instr.	Exp.	Instr.	Exp.	Instr.	Exp.	Instr.
Emotional	Nuclear	.35	.51	.26	.47	.07	.29	.48	.27	.53	.29	.40	.26	.47	.52	.45	.58	.40	.11	.37	.14
Bonds	Extended	.15	.43	.34	.31	.17	.54	.27	.28	.23	.36	.25	.33	.28	.30	.24	.48	.20	−.12	.16	−.09
Family	Hierarchy	.79	.49	−.17	.60	−.27	−.38	.70	.33	.58	−.04	.44	.37	.65	.62	.62	.47	.34	.51	.31	.50
Values	Kin	.80	.65	.22	.79	−.16	−.05	.78	.28	.72	.01	.63	.43	.85	.69	.84	.62	.44	.21	.43	.23

Notes: Correlations are significant at the 5% level if their absolute value is at least .38 and at the 1% level if their absolute value is at least .49 ($N = 27$).
Exp. = Expressive Role; Fin. = Financial Role; Care = Childcare Role; Instr. = Instrumental Role

116

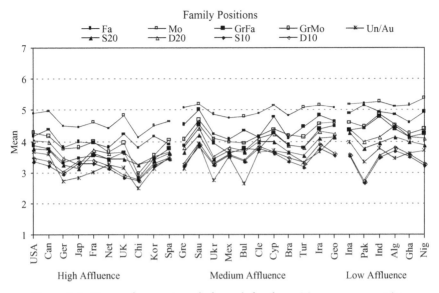

Figure 6.4. Means of expressive role for each family position across countries.

Means of the family roles for each family position, separated into high, medium, and low affluence levels, are shown in Figures 6.4 and 6.5. Consistently higher scores were reported for female positions; for instance, the mean of the mother across the three family roles (i.e., expressive role, finances, and childcare) was $M = 4.62$, whereas this mean for the father was $M = 4.12$. Similarly, the

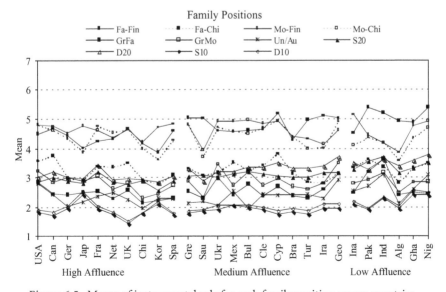

Figure 6.5. Means of instrumental role for each family position across countries.

mean score was $M = 3.50$ for the grandmother and $M = 3.25$ for the grandfather, $M = 3.58$ for the 20-year-old daughter and $M = 3.40$ for the 20-year-old son, and $M = 2.72$ for the 10-year-old daughter and $M = 2.64$ for the 10-year-old son. The importance of the various family positions for the family roles showed an interesting pattern. As expected, parents showed the highest scores ($M = 4.37$), indicating that they play the most central role in vital family functions, both expressive and instrumental. They are followed by the 20-year-old children ($M = 3.49$), who are followed by the grandparents ($M = 3.37$). Uncles and aunts showed a mean of 2.89, while the lowest scores were obtained for 10-year-old children ($M = 2.68$). Finally, means of expressive roles were larger than means of instrumental roles, with the exception of the financial role of the father, which was globally the most important role of the father.

The Regression Analyses. As discussed previously, the ecological variables of percentage engaged in agriculture and affluence and the sociopolitical variable of education were highly intercorrelated. A factor analysis of the economic indicator affluence, the education indicator, and the percentage of the population working in agriculture constituted a strong factor that explained 82.3% of the variance. We combined these three measures into one variable, called the *socioeconomic index.*

Regression analyses were carried out with the socioeconomic index for the expressive roles of all positions. The expressive roles of the father and the mother were both negatively associated with the socioeconomic index (median $\beta = -.52$ and $\beta -.53$, respectively); coefficients of all tests were significant. The expressive roles of both grandparents were also negatively related to the socioeconomic index (median $\beta = -.53$ for the grandfather and $\beta = -.43$ for the grandmother). However, no significant relationships were found for uncles and aunts. The expressive role of the 20-year-old sons and daughters were negatively related to the socioeconomic index (median $\beta = -.61$) but lower for the 10-year-old children (median $\beta = -.41$).

The instrumental role of the parents, split between finances and childcare, yielded squared multiple correlations that were lower than found in the analyses of the expressive role. Apart from this agreement, the findings were quite different for both parents. The financial role of the father diminished with the level of the socioeconomic index (median $\beta = -.47$; all four coefficients were significant, $p < .05$), but this was not the case for the mother (median $\beta = -.05$; the coefficient was not significant in any analysis). The childcare role of the father was unrelated to any country characteristic. As with the simple correlations, the socioeconomic index was unrelated to the childcare role; we found no evidence for the view that with increased socioeconomic level of countries (i.e., a higher score on the socioeconomic index), the father assumes a more active role in childcare.

A final observation concerns the comparison of the size of the squared multiple correlations for both parents. The median value of the father was .31, whereas the median value of the mother was .19. This finding suggests that the roles of the father are more affected by changes in the socioeconomic index than are the roles of the mother; however, it should be realized that this interpretation is tentative (for the current limited sample size, tests of differences in dependent multiple correlations require much larger differences in observed values to be significant).

Further evidence for this interpretation was found in the analysis of the grandparents. Higher values were found for the grandfather than for the grandmother. The absence of any influence of the socioeconomic index on the instrumental role, found for the parents, was replicated for the grandparents. It can be concluded that the expressive role of both grandparents becomes less salient with increases in the socioeconomic index, in particular for the grandfather, and that cross-cultural differences in their instrumental role may be affected by country characteristics other than studied here.

The socioeconomic index invariably yielded negative regression coefficients, which were significant for the instrumental role (median $\beta = -.47$). The final analyses involved the children. The socioeconomic index had a negative sign in all 32 analyses (4 children $\times$ 2 roles $\times$ 4 religions). Finally, the values of the squared multiple correlations were higher for the instrumental role than for the expressive role (with median values of .10 and .40, respectively). This is a reversal of the pattern found for all adult roles.

Close inspection of the country means of the roles per position (see Figure 6.3) makes clear that across positions, means of expressive roles tended to differ across countries in the same way, which suggests the existence of positive correlations across the positions. If the expressive roles of the nine positions are considered as items of a scale, an internal consistency of *Alpha* = .96 is found. Similarly, if the instrumental roles are taken to constitute a single scale, an internal consistency of *Alpha* = .83 is found. Both values point to consistent country differences in both roles. Furthermore, the expressive role revealed slightly larger squared multiple correlations than the instrumental role.

As hypothesized, these relationships suggest that engaging one's ecosystem through the practice of agriculture sets the stage for close family ties, in particular for the role of the mother in showing emotional and psychological support to family and kin and maintaining those ties. Conversely, with increased affluence, which is usually the result of a move away from agriculture toward industrial economic activity, these family relations become diminished. This reduction is further promoted in societies with advanced educational systems at all levels.

This pattern of relationships is explained by the interrelations among the three predictor variables noted herein. These intercorrelations were untangled in the multiple-regression analyses.

Note also the nonsignificant correlations between the mother's childcare duties and financial roles and the ecological and sociopolitical variables. This suggests that these roles are universally not related to either the affluence level, educational level, or agricultural level of these societies. Mothers appear to perform these roles to the same degree in all societies.

Again, only country-level affluence was found to be related to emotional distance – that is, negatively correlated with members of the nuclear family. It is surprising and contrary to family-studies predictions that affluence was not found to be correlated with emotional bonds with members of the extended family (i.e., grandmother, grandfather, aunt/uncle). It would appear that young people from agricultural societies have somewhat closer emotional ties with members of the nuclear family but, paradoxically, about the same level of emotional ties with kin as in more affluent Western countries. What is the explanation? One possible explanation is that maintaining close contacts and communication with members of the extended family – grandparents and fathers-in-law, aunts and uncles, collateral kin on both sides – is necessary to maintain equilibrium among these kin groups in agricultural societies. Much of it is ritualized in various family celebrations (e.g., weddings, baptisms, and funerals), which is necessary when extended families are involved in family corporate economic activities. Thus, there appears to be emotional closeness and interaction, but one must always be careful not to "rock the boat" by openly showing favoritism toward certain aunts or uncles lest it results in resentment or even open conflicts among different kin. Although some family studies have indicated that the relationships among kin in countries with functionally extended-family systems are close, harmonious, and happy, below the surface there are often resentments and jealousies among family members. There are a number of possible explanations for this phenomenon: for example, because of perceived economic favoritism of the grandparents to certain sons and daughters, because one member of the family has been successful, or because the brother (who may be the economic patriarch of the family) is perceived as showing favoritism to a sister. Thus, showing emotional favoritism openly in the extended family can be dangerous. One learns that one should try to treat all members of the extended family equally to avoid conflicts with kin.

The three ecological and sociopolitical variables were highly correlated and showed similar patterns with the family values: hierarchical values of the father and mother, and relationships within the family and kin. Hierarchical values of the father and mother were negatively correlated with affluence, negatively correlated with education, and positively correlated with percentage of the population engaged in agriculture. Relationships within the family showed the same pattern: negatively correlated with affluence and education and positively correlated with percentage of the population engaged in agriculture. This finding is consistent with the type of ecologically adapted pattern of socialization found in agricultural societies (Barry et al., 1959) in which children are trained for "responsibility" and "obedience." It is also consistent with evidence that highly differentiated social stratification is found in extended families in agricultural societies as compared with less stratification in nuclear families in nonagrarian societies (Nimkoff & Middleton, 1960). These hierarchical roles of the father and mother developed in agricultural societies, which value the father as the patriarch of the family, who has the power and makes the important decisions, whereas the mother's role is to obey the father and raise the children.

Affluence appears to be the primary statistical predictor, explaining most of the variance. That is, while agriculture and education are correlated with family roles, hierarchical, and family and kin variables, they are themselves dependent on the economic level of a society. Emotional bonds with the nuclear and extended family members are much less tied to the economic level of the societies. That is, societies acculturate, not only individuals. Societies adapt to economic, educational, media, and other cultural changes in the world. Some have adapted very successfully economically (e.g., South Korea and Taiwan), whereas others have not and consequently remain primarily agricultural societies. Economic development of a society results in many institutional changes. One of the most important is economic investment in the educational system, including better schools, facilities, more teachers, and so on. However, economic development also means a decrease in the percentage of the population engaged in agriculture, primarily subsistence agriculture, and a concomitant increase in other economic activities, such as industry, tourism, and services.

Thus, the level of affluence of a society appears to be the main predictor of many of the family and psychological variables. This finding is consistent with those reported by Georgas, van de Vijver, & Berry (2004). In that study, affluence was systematically related to a number of values as well as to personal well-being; religion was also related to those same variables but to a lesser extent. Together, those studies and the present study highlight the fundamental role of the affluence of a society in the patterning of social and psychological characteristics of the population. Because affluence is a complex variable, combining ecological (e.g., agriculture) and sociopolitical (e.g., education) factors, we consider these consistent findings as support for the ecocultural approach that has guided this project.

7.0. CONCLUSIONS

The ecocultural approach allows for the identification of background factors that may influence the social and cultural (including family) characteristics of a society and the development of individual behaviors that are adaptive to both the ecosystem and the cultural system. In this study of the similarities and differences in family and behavior, the ecocultural approach has been a valuable guide to understanding the relationships among the many variables of interest. The family has been placed center stage in these arrangements, being both adaptive to context and serving as the basis for individual development. This central role of family as the core agent of cultural transmission was illustrated by the pattern of correlations among background variables (e.g., the percentage of the population engaging in agriculture, affluence, and education), structural and functional features of family life (e.g., roles, bonds, and networks), and family values.

There have been numerous advantages to using the ecocultural approach in this study. First, it assisted in the identification of societies that provide sufficient ecological and cultural variation to examine similarities and differences in family arrangements. Second, it suggested which features of society and family are likely to be adaptive to these contexts and which should be included in the research. Third, it guided the decision regarding which personal outcomes should be examined in the survey of individuals sampled. Overall, the ecocultural approach has served as a theory-based way to structure relationships among a complex set of variables when attempting to understand linkages between cultural and family contexts and variations in cultural transmission and individual behaviors.

REFERENCES

Arnett, J. (1995). Broad and narrow socialization: The family in the context of cultural theory. *Journal of Marriage and the Family, 57*, 617–628.

Barry, H., Child, I., & Bacon, M. (1959). Relations of child training to subsistence economy. *American Anthropologist, 61*, 51–63.

Bennett, J. (1976). *The ecological transition.* London: Pergamon.

Berry, J. W. (1966). Temne and Eskimo perceptual skills. *International Journal of Psychology, 1*, 207–229.

Berry, J. W. (1967). Independence and conformity in subsistence-level societies. *Journal of Personality and Social Psychology, 7*, 415–418.

Berry, J. W. (1976). *Human ecology and cognitive style: Comparative studies in cultural and psychological adaptation.* Oxford, UK: Sage/Halsted.

Berry, J. W. (1979). A cultural ecology of social behaviour. In L. Berkowitz (Ed.), *Advances in experimental social psychology*, Vol. 12 (pp. 177–206). New York: Academic Press.

Berry, J. W. (1985). Cultural psychology and ethnic psychology. In I. Reyes, I. R. Lagunes, & Y. H. Poortinga (Eds.), *From a different perspective* (pp. 3–15). Lisse, the Netherlands: Swets & Zeitlinger.

Berry, J. W. (1994a). Ecology of individualism and collectivism. In U. Kim, H. C. Triandis, C. Kagitcibasi, S-C. Choi, & G. Yoon (Eds.), *Individualism and collectivism* (pp. 77–84). London: Sage Publications.

Berry, J. W. (1994b). An ecological approach to cultural and ethnic psychology. In E. J. Trickett, R. J. Watts, & Birman, D. (Eds.), *Human diversity* (pp. 115–141). San Francisco: Jossey-Bass.

Berry, J. W. (2001). Contextual studies of cognitive adaptation. In J. Collis & S. Messick. (Eds.), *Intelligence and personality* (pp. 319–334). Mahwah, NJ: Lawrence Erlbaum Associates.

Berry, J. W. (2003). Conceptual approaches to acculturation. In K. Chun, P. Balls-Organista, & G. Marin (Eds.), *Acculturation* (pp. 17–37). Washington, DC: American Psychological Association Press.

Berry, J. W. (2007). Acculturation. In J. E. Grusec & P. D. Hastings (Eds.), *Handbook of socialization: Theory and research* (pp. 533–558) (2nd ed.). New York: Guilford Press.

Berry, J. W., & Cavalli-Sforza, L. L. (1986). *Cultural and genetic influences on Inuit art.* Report to Social Sciences and Humanities Research Council of Canada, Ottawa.

Berry, J. W., Dasen, P. R., & Witkin, H. A. (1983). Developmental theories in cross-cultural perspective. In L. Alder (Ed.), *Cross-cultural research at issue* (pp. 13–21). New York: Academic Press.

Berry, J. W., Phinney, J. S., Sam, D. L., & Vedder, P. (2006). *Immigrant youth in cultural transition.* Mahwah, NJ: Lawrence Erlbaum Associates.

Berry, J. W., Poortinga. Y. H., Pandey, J., Dasen, P. R., Saraswathi, T. S., et al. (1997). *Handbook of cross-cultural psychology,* 3 volumes. Boston: Allyn & Bacon.

Berry, J. W., Poortinga, Y. H., & Segall, M. H. (2002). *Cross-cultural psychology: Research and applications* (2nd ed.). New York: Cambridge University Press.

Berry, J. W., & Sam, D. L. (1997). Acculturation and adaptation. In J. W. Berry, M. H. Segall, & C. Kagitcibasi (Eds.), *Handbook of cross-cultural psychology, Vol. 3, Social behavior and applications* (pp. 291–326). Boston: Allyn & Bacon.

Berry, J. W., van de Koppel, J. M. H., Sénéchal, C., Annis, R. C., Bahuchet, S., et al. (1986). *On the edge of the forest: Cultural adaptation and cognitive development in Central Africa.* Lisse, the Netherlands: Swets & Zeitlinger.

Bogardus, E. S. (1925). Measuring social distance. *Journal of Applied Sociology, 9,* 299–308.

Bond, R., & Smith, P. (1996). Culture and conformity: A meta-analysis. *Psychological Bulletin, 119,* 111–137.

Boyd, R., & Richerson, P. (1985). Why is culture adaptive? *Quarterly Review of Biology, 58,* 209–214.

Camillieri, C., & Malewska-Peyre, H. (1997). Socialization and identity strategies. In J. W. Berry, P. Dasen, & T. S. Saraswathi (Eds.), *Handbook of cross-cultural psychology, Vol. 2. Basic processes and human development* (pp. 41–68). Boston: Allyn & Bacon.

Cavalli-Sforza, L. L., & Feldman, M. W. (1981). *Cultural transmission and evolution: A quantitative approach.* Princeton, NJ: Princeton University Press.

Chun, K., Balls-Organista, P., & Marin, G. (2003). *Acculturation: Advances in theory, measurement and applied research.* Washington, DC: APA Books.

Dasen, P. R. (1975). Concrete operational development in three cultures. *Journal of Cross-Cultural Psychology, 6,* 156–172.

Durkheim, E. (1888). Introduction à la sociologie de la famille. *Annales de la Faculté des Lettres de Bordeaux, whole no. 10.*

Durkheim, E. (1892). La famille conjugale. *Revue Philosophique de la France et de l'Étranger, 90,* 1–14.

Feldman, M. W. (1975). The history of the relationship between environment and culture in ethnological thought. *Journal of the History of the Behavioural Sciences, 110,* 67–81.

Forde, D. (1934). *Habitat, economy and society.* New York: Dutton.

Georgas, J. (1988). An ecological and social cross-cultural model: The case of Greece. In J. W. Berry, S. H. Irvine, & E. B. Hunt (Eds.), *Indigenous cognition: Functioning in cultural context* (pp. 105–123). Dordrecht, the Netherlands: Martinus Nijhoff.

Georgas, J. (1993). Ecological-social model of Greek psychology. In U. Kim & J. W. Berry (Eds.), *Indigenous psychologies* (pp. 56–78). Newbury Park, CA: Sage Publications.

Georgas, J. (1999). Family as a context variable in cross-cultural psychology. In J. Adamopoulos & Y. Kashima (Eds.), *Social psychology and cultural context* (pp. 163–175). Beverly Hills, CA: Sage Publications.

Georgas, J., & Berry, J. W. (1995). An ecocultural taxonomy for cross-cultural psychology. *Cross-Cultural Research, 29,* 121–157.

Georgas, J., Berry, J. W., van de Vijver, F. J. R., Kagitcibasi, C., & Poortinga, Y. H. (Eds.) (2006). *Families across cultures: A 30-nation psychological study.* Cambridge: Cambridge University Press.

Georgas, J., Mylonas, K., Bafiti, T., Christakopoulou, S., Poortinga, Y. H., Kagitçibasi, Ç., et al. (2001). Functional relationships in the nuclear and extended family: A 16-culture study. *International Journal of Psychology, 36,* 289–300.

Georgas, J., van de Vijver, F. J. R., & Berry, J. W. (2004). The ecocultural framework, ecosocial indicators and psychological variables in cross-cultural research. *Journal of Cross-Cultural Psychology, 35,* 74–96.

Herskovits, M. J. (1949). *Man and his works: The science of cultural anthropology.* New York: Knopf.

Huntington, E. (1945). *Mainsprings of civilization.* New York: Wiley.

Kroeber, A. (1939). *Cultural and natural areas of native North America.* Berkeley: University of California Press.

Malinowski, B. (2001). *Scientific theory of culture and other essays. Selected works,* Vol. 9. London: Routledge.

Mishra, R. C., Dasen, P. R., & Niraula, S. (2003). Ecology, language, and performance on spatial cognitive tasks. *International Journal of Psychology, 38*(6), 366–383.

Mishra, R. C., Sinha, D., & Berry, J. W. (1996). *Ecology, acculturation and psychological adaptation: A study of Advasi in Bihar.* Delhi: Sage Publications.

Murdock, G. P. (1969). Correlations of exploitive patterns. In D. Damas (Ed.), *Ecological essays.* National Museum of Canada Bulletin No. 230, Anthropological Series No. 86.

Nimkoff, M. F., & Middleton, R. (1960). Types of family and types of economy. *American Journal of Sociology, 66,* 215–225.

Nsamenang, B. (1992). *Human development in cultural context.* Newbury Park, CA: Sage Publications.

Parsons, T. (1943). The kinship system of the contemporary United States. *American Anthropologist, 45,* 22–38.

Parsons, T. (1949). The social structure of the family. In R. N. Anshen (Ed.), *The family: Its functions and destiny.* New York: Harper.

Pelto, P. (1968). The difference between "tight" and "loose" societies. *Transaction, April,* 37–40.

Sam, D. L., & Berry, J. W. (Eds.) (2006). *Cambridge handbook of acculturation psychology.* Cambridge: Cambridge University Press.

Tomasello, M., Krüger, A., & Ratner, H. (1993). Culture learning. *Behavioural and Brain Sciences, 16,* 495–552.

Tylor, E. B. (1871). *Primitive culture.* London: Murray.

United Nations Statistics Division (2002a). *Demographic, social & housing statistics.* Retrieved September 2002 from http://unstats.un.org/unsd.

United Nations Statistics Division (2002b). *Energy statistics.* Retrieved September 2002 from http://unstats.un.org/unsd.

Werner, C. M., Brown, B. B., & Altman, I. (1997). Environmental psychology. In J. W. Berry, M. H. Segall, & C. Kagitcibasi (Eds.), *Handbook of cross-cultural psychology, Vol. 3: Social behavior and applications* (pp. 255–290). Boston: Allyn & Bacon.

Witkin, H., & Berry, J. W. (1975). Psychological differentiation in cross-cultural perspective. *Journal of Cross-Cultural Psychology, 6,* 4–87.

World Development Report of the World Bank (2002a). *Data & statistics.* Retrieved September 2002 from http://www.worldbank.com/data/countrydata.

World Development Report of the World Bank (2002b). *Data & statistics.* Retrieved September 2002 from http://www.worldbank.com/data/countrydata.

7

Intergenerational Relations and Cultural Transmission

GISELA TROMMSDORFF

INTRODUCTION

Continuity and change of cultures over generations are affected by cultural transmission. The intergenerational transmission of culture refers to the way values, knowledge, and practices that are prevalent in one generation are transferred to the next generation. Cultural transmission, thus, is seen as a process by which the reproduction of culture occurs in each successive generation (Corsaro, 1997). However, the persistent reproduction of culture is only one aspect of (absolute) cultural transmission; another aspect is selective transmission. Transmission can be more or less intended and planned; it can also be a direct or indirect consequence of certain activities and events. Furthermore, the direction of transmission and its process can vary. Cavalli-Sforza and Feldman (1981) originally drew a distinction between horizontal (i.e., within one generation) and oblique (i.e., between generations) transmission; in other studies, horizontal transmission includes both (Hewlett & Cavalli-Sforza, 1986). In line with research on socialization, more recent studies differentiate between three types of transmission: vertical transmission between parents and their offspring, oblique transmission functioning through socialization institutions and other agents (e.g., parents' peers), and horizontal transmission among peers (Berry, Poortinga, Segall, & Dasen, 2002).

Intergenerational transmission has been seen as based on the relationship between different cohorts who share the same historical and socialization background but who are not biologically related (cf. Mannheim, 1929/1964).

The study on "Value of Children and Intergenerational Relations in Six Cultures" is supported by grants from the Deutsche Forschungsgemeinschaft (DFG) (Tr 169/ 4–1, 2, 3) (Principal investigators: Gisela Trommsdorff, University of Konstanz, and Bernhard Nauck, Technical University of Chemnitz). Beate Schwarz, Isabelle Albert, and Boris Mayer, University of Konstanz, are collaborating in this project. I am grateful to Holly Bunje who gave valuable suggestions to improve the English language.

The focus of psychologists is on individuals who belong to the same family interacting with each other in the process of intergenerational transmission. This perspective refers to the transfer of values and resources between different biologically related generations within a family (usually parents and their offspring but also grandparents and their grandchildren).

Although the direction of transmission is usually assumed to take place from the older to the younger generation, recent studies on parent–child relationships have identified bidirectional and indirect effects. This view gains special importance in the study of intergenerational cultural transmission and the respective intergenerational relations from a life-span perspective in the cultural context (Trommsdorff, 2006). Accordingly, intergenerational cultural transmission cannot be confined to unidirectional and static analyses. To predict the process, the direction, and the outcome of the cultural transmission for biologically related generations (i.e., belonging to the same family with partially shared genetic and environmental conditions), a comprehensive theoretical framework is needed.

Here, we start from an ecocultural model of intergenerational relations as the basis for cultural transmission. It is assumed that the process, direction, and outcomes of cultural transmission are affected by the *persons* (*agents*) who are involved in the transmission process, their respective *relationships*, the *issues* (*contents*) that are transmitted, and the *cultural context* in which transmission takes place. The effect of these variables on the cultural transmission may be direct or indirect. The outcomes of transmission can be described by continuity and selectivity in the transmission of culture.

The *persons* (i.e., parents and their children) involved in the transmission process influence the process and the outcome of the transmission on the basis of their preferences, beliefs, and competencies, including their cultural knowledge. Here, the socialization experience of these persons, their social status, and their developmental age are all relevant. The developmental status of the persons affects their intention and means of transmitting cultural values. Their acceptance of these values may change over time, such as when grown-up children become parents and thus influence the transmission of values.

The *relationship* of the persons involved in the transmission process influences its process and outcome, including continuity and selectivity. Therefore, the parent–child relationship is seen as the basic *transmission belt* (Schönpflug, 2007). This relationship can be based on emotional closeness or normative obligation, on harmony or conflict, on a hierarchical or vertical structure, on a long or short history of shared experiences, and on interdependence or independence (cf. Trommsdorff, 2006). A person-oriented approach is thus related to the *relationship* approach, taking into account the various qualities of relationships in the process of cultural transmission.

Also, cultural transmission is assumed to depend on the *contents* of transmission and their respective importance for the individual person and for the culture, which can be related to more or less deep-rooted, important, widely shared, consistent, and well-integrated traditional values, cultural knowledge, and practices.

Furthermore, cultural transmission takes place in the wider *context*. The influence of these factors (i.e., persons, relationships, and contents) may differ depending on the conditions in the proximate or distant context. The contextual factors (e.g., heterogeneous or homogeneous, changing or stable societies) presumably affect the cultural beliefs and competence of the persons involved in the transmission process, their culture-specific relationship, and the cultural meaning of the topics to be transmitted. Multiple agents of transmission and their respective relationships can stabilize or undermine the vertical transmission of culture from one generation to the next, thus affecting cultural continuity. The oblique transmission may or may not coincide with the vertical transmission, and the horizontal transmission through peers may support or undermine the intergenerational transmission (Trommsdorff, 2006). Also, the wider *socioeconomic and cultural context*, including socioeconomic and cultural change (and crises) or continuity, may foster or constrain the intergenerational transmission and affect the impact of the previously mentioned moderating and mediating factors.

A theoretical framework of cultural transmission has to consider the relative and interactive effects of the persons involved in the transmission, their interpersonal relationships, the topics (i.e., contents) to be transmitted, and the contextual factors. For respective empirical studies, a complex design including at least three biologically related generations from different cultural contexts is necessary (Trommsdorff, 2001a, 2001b, 2006; also see Section 4.0 in this chapter). To study the dynamic aspects of cultural transmission, taking into account individual development, changing relationships, and changing environments, a longitudinal study should complement this design. In this way, conditions and outcomes of cultural transmission, its selectivity, and its contribution to cultural continuity or change could be specified. The obviously related methodological difficulties may indicate why very few empirical data to test such a model are available at present. Accordingly, this chapter can deal with only selected aspects of the complex issue of cultural transmission, focusing on intergenerational relations in the life span in different cultural contexts.

The first part of this chapter discusses cultural transmission and socialization; the second part discusses intergenerational relations in the life span as a basis for the transmission of culture; the third part deals with transmission in cultural contexts; and the fourth part presents an empirical approach to the study of intergenerational relationships and cultural transmission in different cultures. Finally, these discussions are summarized with a focus on social change and cultural continuity.

1.0. INTERGENERATIONAL CULTURAL TRANSMISSION AND SOCIALIZATION

1.1. Intergenerational Transmission as a Socialization Process

Research on intergenerational transmission is often confined to dealing with processes and effects of socialization that do not go beyond traditional socialization theories. Sometimes intergenerational transmission and socialization are even used as interchangeable concepts. Our position is that socialization and transmission are not the same. Socialization is only a part of intergenerational cultural transmission insofar as it is part of the transmission belts and usually aims at ensuring a certain outcome.

Previous socialization research encountered several shortcomings that could be avoided by future research on intergenerational cultural transmission (for a summary, see Trommsdorff, 2006). One of the shortcomings was the one-sided approach to the *nature–nurture controversy*, ignoring the interactive effects of genetic dispositions and environmental factors (e.g., Plomin, 2000). In much socialization research, the biological basis of socialization, learning, and development has been ignored. At the same time, only very selective aspects of the environment have been considered – mainly, the proximate environment focusing on parents.

Another shortcoming of previous socialization research was the assumption of *unidirectionality* of parenting, emphasizing parental behavior (i.e., discipline) as influencing the development of the children. The traditional view of the child as a passive recipient of parental influences ignored *interactions* between parent and child in the process of development. Research has suggested a *bidirectional approach* to socialization and development (Kuczynski, 2003) and has also dealt with the intentional elements in socialization. The explanation of the effects of parenting (Baumrind, 1991) has made it necessary to also account for intentional processes focusing on parental goals and expectations as part of parental theories (Goodnow & Collins, 1990). The perspective of the active role of the child (Bell, 1979; Maccoby & Martin, 1983) assumes the child's intentional processes of learning and imitation (Bandura, 1977, 1986; Grusec & Goodnow, 1994).

Another problem in traditional socialization research is the static view, focusing on the socialization of children and adolescents while ignoring further processes in adulthood from a *life-span perspective*.

A further shortcoming of socialization research was the neglect of the *context* in which development takes place. Only selected aspects of the proximate environment, usually the parents, were considered whereas the effects from the more *distant environment* were ignored. The neglect of contextual factors is a reason for another problem of previous socialization research: its *ethnocentric bias*. Most socialization theories have been empirically tested only in Western cultures, ignoring possible effects of the cultural context on socialization. This is surprising because early anthropological studies pointed out different social-ization practices and processes in other cultures (Benedict, 1934; Mead, 1935). Also, Bronfenbrenner (1979) strongly suggested studying individual develop-ment from an ecotheoretical perspective, taking into account the interactive effects of the micro-, meso, macro-, and chrono-systems. However, only recently have interactive effects among the family and the other socializing agents (e.g., peers or school and other institutions) been studied as part of a complex system of socialization (cf. Bugental & Goodnow, 2000; Collins, Maccoby, Steinberg, Hetherington, & Bornstein, 2000; Maccoby, 2000).

Although socialization research cannot provide a sufficient basis for a the-ory on cultural and intergenerational transmission, research on intergenera-tional cultural transmission may profit from past shortcomings in socialization research.

1.2. Intergenerational Transmission beyond Socialization Processes

In this section, we suggest a theoretical framework for the intergenerational transmission of culture by studying processes and outcomes of transmission as based on intergenerational relations over the life span in cultural contexts. In this framework, the bidirectionality in the parent–child relationship is assumed to function as a transmission belt during the life span and within a wider cultural context.

1.2.1. *Biological Basis of Intergenerational Transmission*
The biological conditions of intergenerational transmission can be observed in early infant development. One biological basis of transmission was elaborated by attachment theorists (Ainsworth, Blehar, Waters, & Wall, 1978; Bowlby, 1969), who asserted that a universal need for security and attachment in infants is related to the responsiveness of primary caretakers. When the caretakers provide the basis for secure attachment, the child can fulfill the need for curiosity and competence by exploration of the environment. This, in turn, fosters further social, emotional, and cognitive development over the life span (Thompson, 1999). Thus, attachment can be seen as a precondition for cultural learning and intergenerational cultural transmission including the partial transmission of attachment quality and possibly other aspects of intergenerational relations from one generation to the next (Trommsdorff, 2001a, 2002, 2006).

Social learning starts in early life through the biologically based ability for empathy (Gallese, 2003), shared attention, intentionality, understanding intentions of others (including theory of mind), and imitation (Meltzoff & Moore, 1998). The biologically based precursors of cultural transmission can be observed in infants' ability to engage in and readiness for selective imitation. Tomasello, Kruger, and Ratner (1993) suggested three consecutive ontogenetic learning models for cultural learning: imitative learning (starting at 9 months), instructed learning (starting at about 4 years), and collaborative learning (starting at about 6 or 7 years). Keller (2002) adds another component, which is assumed to be prevalent during the first two and a half to three months of life: "structured learning," which is based on social interactions and directed by emotions. This results in approach or avoidance tendencies as a biological basis of cultural learning.

Furthermore, other studies have shown that the interplay between the endocrine architecture of one's life history and psychological outcomes during one's life course affect parental competence and child growth (Worthman, 1999).

1.2.2. *Interpersonal Basis of Cultural Transmission*

Transmission: Outcome or Process. One goal of research in cultural transmission has been to explain the continuity of cultural values transmitted from parents to their children. Intergenerational transmission, therefore, can be regarded as the children's acquisition and acceptance of values. Consequently, research on intergenerational transmission has usually focused on the "outcome" of transmission and the question as to whether the transmission was "successful." First, it is problematic to measure the outcome of transmission by simply focusing on similarities of single values between parents and their children without investigating whether transmitters are motivated to create similarity by their transmission efforts, as discussed in Sections 4.0 and 5.0. Second, the focus on outcomes only catches one aspect of transmission and ignores the processes and direction of transmission, which may provide a more interesting approach in understanding the functionality and meaning of the "outcomes."

Transmission Processes: Unidirectionality in Intergenerational Transmission. The process of transmission has been explained in two ways: by assuming a unidirectional process of parents influencing their children and by assuming bidirectional processes including interactions between children and parents.

The first approach usually assumes that the outcome is intended by the parents while ignoring the children's intentions. This approach regards *parenting as the main transmission belt*. The focus of these studies is on the parents' behavior and their (direct) effects on the child's "internalization" of parental values.

Beyond Unidirectionality in Intergenerational Transmission. The second approach regards both *parents and children as the transmission belt*, assuming that transmission takes place on the basis of the activity of both the parents and the child. The model of *internalization* by Grusec and Goodnow (1994) is very fruitful for a theory on transmission belts; they assert that the child actively participates in the socialization process by interpreting, evaluating, either accepting or rejecting the parents' message, and, finally, possibly conforming and internalizing the message, thus matching their own intentions with those of their parents.

Furthermore, the child's behavior influences the way the parents interact with the child. This assumption of *bidirectionality* became the focus of socialization and internalization theories (Grusec & Kuczynski, 1997; Kuczynski, 2003). It allows for more refined predictions of transmission processes and can be seen as part of the model of internalization. It offers a fruitful approach to the explanation of intergenerational transmission as based on bidirectional intentionality.

Beyond Bidirectionality and Interactions in Intergenerational Transmission. The acknowledgment of the *child's intentionality and activity* in the process of development is seen here as a promising but not sufficient component for a theory on cultural transmission. A further precondition for successful transmission beyond the bidirectionality between child and parent is the *quality of the parent–child relationship.*

Successful internalization is predicted when the child feels accepted, when he or she regards the parents as adequate models, and when the parents communicate the message clearly. These are relevant aspects of the parent–child relationship that traditional socialization research has ignored. Thus, the study of intergenerational and cultural transmission has to go beyond the bidirectional perspective and consider intergenerational relations over the life span and in the cultural context. These are the topics of the next section.

2.0. INTERGENERATIONAL RELATIONS OVER THE LIFE SPAN

2.1. Theoretical Approach to Intergenerational Relationships

Why are intergenerational relations considered important for cultural transmission? It is assumed here that relationships between parents and their children can explain the direction, the process, and the outcome of intergenerational cultural transmission. Here, we conceptualize parent–child relationships as lifelong, biologically constituted personal relationships; they are based on interconnected experiences in the past and the expectation of interconnected experiences in the future. Parent–child relationships constitute the most extended relationships on the dimension of time, and their quality may change over the life course. They are only partially voluntary and start from an asymmetric distribution of resources. This view on parent–child relationships as a transmission belt implies that cultural transmission can affect both parents and their children.

Parent–child relationships differ from other relationships. They are not the same as intimate and close voluntary personal relationships. For decades, exchange theoretical approaches were used to explain close relationships (Homans, 1961; Kelley, 1983; Kelley & Thibaut, 1978; Thibaut & Kelley, 1959). Biological and evolutionary approaches (e.g., attachment theory; see Ainsworth et al., 1978; Bowlby, 1969) stimulated criticism to the traditional exchange theoretical approach; for example, the interdependence theory on close relationships (Rusbult & Van Lange, 2003) regards "relationship-specific motives" such as trust and commitment as influencing prosocial orientations and the persistence of the relationship. Beyond this approach, the importance of culture for the explanation of close relationships was suggested by Rothbaum, Pott, Azuma, Miyake, and Weisz (2000) and Trommsdorff (1995b, 2001a). We assume here that shared beliefs and goals related to the cultural context are a basic component of close relationships (Trommsdorff, 1991, 2001a). Those cultural beliefs, in turn, affect the process and the outcome of transmission.

2.2. Life-Span Approach to Parent–Child Relationships

From a life-span perspective, the question of how changes in intergenerational relations influence cultural transmission gains new meaning. Life-span approaches deal with changing developmental tasks and normative life events (Havighurst, 1972); life stages, transitions, and crises (Erikson, 1959); continuity and change of biological, cognitive, emotional, motivational, and social domains of the person; and selective optimization in multidimensional development (Baltes & Baltes, 1990). These approaches are usually applied to individual development but can also be related to changes and stability of parent–child relations during the life span and effects on cultural transmission.

First, we discuss this topic from the point of view of Western developmental theories. In Section 3.0, we focus on the limitations of this approach by considering the cultural context.

From *early childhood to adolescence*, asymmetry in parent–child relationships is assumed to become increasingly transformed into symmetric partnerships. This implies conflicting interests and negotiations between parents and children in the pursuit of individuality and individual needs fulfillment. From the Western perspective, parents are viewed as pursuing the goal of establishing their children's independence while simultaneously striving for continuity of values by having their children adopt their values. These seem to be inherently contradictory goals. The transmission of values in a context in which independence is highly valued does not necessarily imply conformity to parental values. Accordingly, the developmental task of *adolescents* has often been seen as establishing a unique identity distinct from that of their parents and of achieving autonomy. Emotional, attitudinal, conflictual, and functional independence are seen as the core elements in the process of separation–individuation (Hoffman, 1984).

How can these processes foster cultural transmission from parents to children? It seems quite plausible that cultural transmission only occurs selectively under this condition. Recent studies that have criticized the separation–individuation assumption and its individualistic bias argue that both autonomy from and relatedness to the parents is a more appropriate description for parent–child relationships in this developmental period. Because the connection to the parents is seen as a relevant precondition for the individuation process (Cooper, Grotevant, & Condon, 1983), the rebalancing of individuality and connectedness permits the achievement of individuated relationships. At the same time, the parents themselves undergo certain developmental changes, from their role as caretakers to the role as facilitators of their child's development (Cooney, 1997).

During further development, oblique and horizontal cultural transmission occurs and may moderate the vertical transmission process, which is increasingly characterized by bidirectional intentional influences and negotiation. *Young adulthood* has often been described by processes of negotiation between parents and offspring in order to ensure the independence of the children and reduce conflicts in parent–child relationships.

Parent–child relationships in *middle adulthood* are usually characterized by the adult offspring having their own children (i.e., the "sandwich generation"). Neugarten (1968) conceived of mid-life development as growing responsibility in the now more extended family. Related changes in the quality of the parent–child relationship gain importance as a result of a third separation–individuation process, when the adult parents grow older, retire from work, take on the role of grandparents, or experience psychological and cognitive dependency. These changes in later adulthood and old age again affect the relationships among the aging parents, their adult children, and their grandchildren.

The changing quality of the parent–child relationship in mid-life was conceptualized by Blenkner (1965) as the development of "filial maturity." In this period, the relationship between adult children and their parents is less influenced by the social norm of parental roles and more by the perceived personal needs of the aging parents.

Filial autonomy, the degree of reciprocity between the parent and the adult child, and the overall interdependence of the family members can be assumed to affect processes of cultural transmission over the life course.

2.3. Parent–Child Relationships over the Life Span and Cultural Transmission in a Changing Context

A serious shortcoming of research on parent–child relationships is the neglect of contextual factors. Parent–child relationships develop within a wider family system and are affected by the wider socioeconomic and cultural context. They take place in *changing contexts*, which imply changing developmental tasks over the life course (e.g., Crocket & Silbereisen, 2000; Elder, 1974, 1998; Trommsdorff, 2000, 2001a, 2001b, 2003). These studies provide insight about risk and buffering factors for development of family members interacting in a context of linked lives, which again are affected by the wider socioeconomic and cultural contexts. The changing structure of intergenerational relationships (e.g., parent–child, grandparent–grandchild) can still be seen as a transmission belt allowing for the continuation of family members' interconnected "linked lives" over the life course (e.g., Elder, 1998).

The question now arises about the effects of the changing environment on intergenerational cultural transmission. This question is especially relevant in times of dramatic socioeconomic and demographic changes such as increasing longevity and a related gender gap in life expectancy, decreasing fertility and increasing postponement of first-child birth, decreasing family stability, and increasing diversity of family structure (e.g., due to divorce, single-parent families, second or third marriage, changing gender roles) (cf. Bengtson, 2001; Trommsdorff & Nauck, 2005; Zarit & Eggebeen, 2002). Due to the worldwide increase in longevity, parents and children will share on average almost five decades as adults.

The impact of social and economic changes on intergenerational relations, including those between grandparents and grandchildren, can include changes in vertical or horizontal economic transfers and investments (Kohli & Szydlik, 2000), changes in the relationship quality (including emotional closeness, solidarity between the generations, patterns of intergenerational exchanges and support, family eldercare), and changes in the continuity or discontinuity of intergenerational relations over time, as well as similarities and differences between the generations with respect to values (e.g., Bengtson & Robertson, 1985; Cooney, 1997; King & Elder, 1997; Trommsdorff, 2006; Zarit & Eggebeen, 2002).

Rapidly changing cultural contexts can even induce a reversal in the direction of cultural transmission. Adolescents' adoption of changing cultural values can initiate a change in the direction of transmission, thereby effecting changes in the values, beliefs, and behavior of their parents. These value changes may enter into the intergenerational transmission of values to the youngest generation – the grandchildren. Results from our studies actually point to more similarities among grandparents and adolescent grandchildren than among grandparents and their adult children (Trommsdorff, Mayer, & Albert, 2004). Thus, intergenerational relationships can be seen as a source of change in the process of cultural transmission (Kuczynski & Navara, 2006; Valsiner, 1988). This view again takes seriously the active role of the child in the process of transmission and internalization (on the basis of bidirectionality), the function of intergenerational relationships in the life span and in the process of changing contexts, and the heterogeneity and dynamic nature of cultures and societies.

3.0. CULTURAL CONTEXT AND THE INTERGENERATIONAL TRANSMISSION OF CULTURE

The transmission of values (via socialization, internalization, or the like) and intergenerational relationships are embedded in a wider socioeconomic and *cultural context*. The transmission belts are affected by cultural values while also affecting the transmission of such values. A deficit in previous research on transmission has been the neglect of the wider social and cultural context in which it takes place. This is surprising because more than 80 years ago, early anthropological studies (e.g., by Ruth Benedict, Margaret Mead, Beatrice B. Whiting, and John W. M. Whiting) noted that different socialization practices and parent–child relationships, which are related to different child outcomes, can be observed in non-Western cultures. Only more recently has the question been posed whether transmission theories empirically tested in the Western world can be generalized to other cultural contexts (Bugental & Goodnow, 2000; Rothbaum & Trommsdorff, 2007; Rothbaum, Weisz, Pott, Miyake, & Morelli, 2000; Trommsdorff & Kornadt, 2003). Studies on acculturation also provide insight about the impact of contextual factors in the process of cultural transmission (see Knafo & Schwartz, chapter 11, and Schönpflug, chapter 2, this volume). A culture-informed approach to intergenerational transmission considers the culture-specific aspects of socialization, internalization, and intergenerational relationships. First, a general theoretical approach to culture and development is suggested. Second, culture-informed studies on parenting and parent–child relationships as a part of cultural transmission are discussed.

3.1. Culture and Individual Development

The transmission of culture is a traditional topic in cultural anthropology. For example, LeVine (1973) states:

> The transmission of culture from generation to generation is, in Mead's (1935) view, a process of communication in which many aspects of the growing individual's cultural environment relay ... messages reflecting the dominant configurations of his culture. ... They enter into communication with him by making certain (culturally approved) reactions to his cries, his performance of bodily functions, his attempts to move and grasp; much of this communication is nonverbal and implicit. It lays a basis for the later transmission of the same underlying messages in a thousand other ways, some of them explicit, as the child increasingly participates in the various aspects of adult culture. Child rearing is fundamental in the acquisition of cultural character, but it is only the first of many formative experiences, each reinforcing the other in communicating cultural configurations to the individual (p. 54).

In contrast to most theories of socialization that are confined to Western cultures, the question of the transmission of culture is related to the general question of how individual psychological processes are related to culture (Bruner, 1996). Some authors assume a unidirectional influence of culture on the mind. The traditional model of the *tabula rasa* fits with this notion. At the other extreme, culture and mind are seen as being interdependent and interconnected (Cole, 1996).

From the first perspective, the person is more or less the recipient of cultural influences. Empirical research on transmission of culture follows this approach and starts from a quasi-experimental design, comparing different cultures and related forms of transmission with respect to their effects on the person. This approach attempts to generalize empirical findings on causal relations across cultures and is typical of cross-cultural research and its nomothetical methodological basis. From the second perspective, the person actively constructs culture while also being affected by culture.

These perspectives have long been viewed as mutually contradictory. In the same line of reasoning, the assumptions of a "psychic unity of mankind" and "cultural relativism" contradict each other. However, for a culture-informed study of cultural differences and similarities, it is essential to consider culture-specificities in methods, data analyses, and interpretation of the data, thus combining an "etic" and an "emic" perspective (for an overview, see Trommsdorff & Friedlmeier, 2004; Trommsdorff & Mayer, 2005). The study of the transmission of culture could be seen as constructively connecting the "emic" and "etic" approaches, focusing on the individual person and intergenerational relations in cultural transmission. Accordingly, questions on the universality of (selective) cultural transmission can only be answered when taking into account the cultural context.

How to describe cultures? The study of the transmission of culture must deal with the difficult concept of culture. In anthropological research, more than 100 definitions of culture have been suggested (Kroeber & Kluckhohn, 1952). Benedict (1934) introduced the notion of "cultural pattern," whereas others preferred the notion of cultural models (D'Andrade & Strauss, 1992; Holland & Quinn, 1987; Shore, 1996), cultural templates (or schemata) (Geertz, 1973), or cultural practices (Shore, 1996). Cultural transmission thus includes the transmission of such cultural practices and knowledge. This process may follow more or less strict rules and thus preserve continuity or induce change.

From a psychological point of view, a definition of culture seems futile unless the psychological aspects of culture relative to the individual person are specified in terms of functional relationships (Trommsdorff & Friedlmeier, 2004). According to Geertz (1973), culture is a semiotic system (of meanings) and functions as an external control system for human behavior; it is seen as a selective factor in the evolutionary process and not as the final product. A psychological approach conceives of the function of culture as a factor in the process of socio-cultural change and individual development. Depending on the cultural context, the transmission of culture can be more or less constrained and thus ensure, respectively, continuity or change. Accordingly, cultural transmission is studied herein with respect to the transmission of cultural models and knowledge in the process of individual development and intergenerational relationships in context.

What are the contents of cultural transmission? A psychologically relevant definition of culture cannot avoid the question of the relationship between culture and mind (Bruner, 1996). Shore (1996) attempted to study culture and mind by relating " ... *both* 'external' institutions (culture-in-the world) *and* 'internal' mental representations (culture-in-the-mind)" (p. 5), conceptualizing culture *in* mind. According to Shore (1996), instituted models (i.e., institutionalized, objectified, and publicly available shared arrangements or empirically observable social institutions) are part of the external social world. They can organize the development of mental models in the newly socialized persons and can become (more or less) conventional mental models. However, these mental representations are not simply a copy of the cultural model, they are rather underlying complex processes of "meaning construction"; they are products of intentional behavior (p. 51).

The relationship between both the institutionalized and the mental models is complex. When cultural models are transformed into individual mental models, they undergo significant transformations. Accordingly, Shore (1996) poses three questions: (1) How are public forms of knowledge or culturally mediated mental models transformed into personal mental models?; (2) How do cultural practices connect models in the world to those in the mind?; and (3) What happens to those mental models during the transformation process? Because dominant cultural models can be challenged by alternative (counter) models, a further question concerning the selective transmission comes up: Why and how is *which* cultural model transformed into a personal model?

3.2. Cultural Transmission Belts

The underlying psychological question relevant to this chapter is how the transmission of culture functions. Culture provides various transmission belts (Schönpflug, 2001) or modes of acquiring the cultural "model" or scripts. In a more general sense, transmission takes place on the basis of shared cultural beliefs. In his famous *Völkerpsychologie,* Wundt (1900–1920) described how cultural beliefs are connected to certain symbols and rituals. For example, people who have the same totem belong to one family or to one tribe; they share the same cultural beliefs and practices and are involved in the transmission of those beliefs to the next generation.

Transmission of culture has been conceptualized as the repetition of the same idea in various contexts (i.e., "thematicity") (Quinn & Holland, 1987). This repetition may consist of practicing a certain behavior that is part of the family tradition, such as the lifelong practice of an art or artist production (e.g., Noh play in Japanese families). Repetition of cultural practices is part of the apprenticeship model (Rogoff, 2003). Another approach to explaining transmission of culture in other contexts was described by Vygotsky (1962) and Greenfield (2000) as "guided participation" of children in the world of adults. This is mostly the case in traditional cultures in which transmission belts are based on model learning and imitation of behavior rather than following abstract principles.

In this chapter, the focus is on cultural transmission based on biological intergenerational relationships. Traditionally, transmission of heritage, material, and cultural knowledge takes place in the family. Cultural transmission through biological and family relationships can be explained through the cultural and, hence, psychological meaning (e.g., the value of the family, children, and parent–child relationships). For example, in some cultures, biological relationships are less important for the transmission of cultural practices in cases where no male child is born. The adoption of a child (usually male) can become the basis for establishing an in-group family-like relationship; this compensates for the lack of biological continuation of the family, ascribing the role of a successor to the adopted child. Thus, the active construction of transmission (beyond the biologically based parent–child relationship) is part of the respective cultural belief system.

Accordingly, transmission has been viewed as being affected through "ethnopsychology" (Shore, 1996). This is in line with Bruner's (1996) view on the interrelation between culture and mind: " ... How a people believe the mind works will ... have a profound effect on how in fact it is *compelled* to work if anybody is to get on in a culture" (p. xvii). Here, it is assumed that the subjective beliefs of socialization agents (e.g., parents and teachers) as part of the cultural meaning system will affect the next generation's beliefs, "meaning making," and behavior, thus constituting "reality" (Bruner, 1996).

Universally, people develop theories to help them understand and respond to the world around them. These naïve theories usually reflect the shared beliefs of people who live in a given culture or environment. Such naïve ethnotheories are central to thinking and behavior and include cultural contents transmitted from one generation to the next. This assumption underlies the theoretical approach of Super and Harkness (1999; Harkness & Super, 2002), who describe the function of the developmental niche as a part of culturally based transmission. This assumption also underlies our own research on subjective theories and parental beliefs in the cultural context (Trommsdorff & Friedlmeier, 2004) and further cross-cultural studies on the intergenerational transmission of values (Albert, 2007; Trommsdorff, 2001a, 2002, 2007; Trommsdorff, Mayer, & Albert, 2004) (see Section 4.0).

Considering the culture-specific meaning system, the problem of *universality* or *culture-specificity* in transmission must be addressed. According to Berry (1967) and Cole and Scribner (1974), even basic processes of perception are "modeled" by a specific cultural context (e.g., different optical illusions of people raised in carpentered environments – straight lines, regular angles – versus "natural environments" – without artificial lines and no experience of two-dimensional perception). Shore (1996) suggested that these "cultural models" (D'Andrade & Strauss, 1992; Holland & Quinn, 1987) can be thought of as "cultural affordances" (p. 6) equivalent to physical affordances in the natural environment.

The debate about the universality or relativity of psychological processes is shortsighted when it focuses only on fully determined, universally shared processes or only on the variability and the seemingly arbitrary nature of cultural practices (Shweder, 1991). Shore (1996) suggested a third alternative, namely that "cultural phenomena are better characterized as conventional arrangements that may or may not be arbitrary" (p. 37). Accordingly, cultural practices are conceived of herein as human creations that are constrained and that vary within these constraints.

3.3. Cultural Pathways for Intergenerational Relationships and Cultural Transmission

Therefore, we suggest an integrated ecocultural and developmental approach to study parent–child relationships as part of cultural pathways (Trommsdorff, 2006, 2007). The respective cultural contexts are regarded as providing both certain constraints and opportunities for the development of parent–child relationships: (1) the ecocultural approach differentiates among several levels of the macro-, meso-, and micro-system (Bronfenbrenner, 1979); (2) the value approach differentiates between cultural values (e.g., independence and interdependence) (Kagitcibasi, 1996; Triandis, 1995); and (3) the model of the developmental niche describes proximate developmental factors such as parental ethnotheories and practices (Harkness & Super, 2002; Super & Harkness, 1999). These approaches can be integrated in a cultural model on developmental paths focusing on autonomy and relatedness in close parent–child relationships (Rothbaum, Pott et al., 2000; Rothbaum & Trommsdorff, 2007; Trommsdorff, 2006, 2007).

Independence and Interdependence as Basic Values. The relationship between culture and parent–child in the process of cultural transmission can be seen on various levels: Cultural values can influence and regulate parent–child relationships over the life span, and parent–child relationships can influence the development and change of value orientation in the child and in the parents. They can thereby affect the transmission of values to the next generation, which in turn affects the cultural value system. Thus, cultural values can be seen not only as input and output variables but also as a moderator affecting the quality of the parent–child relationship and the transmission. Accordingly, cultural values can be studied on various levels: At one level, the cultural values are represented in cultural meaning systems, rituals, and artifacts; at another level, the individual value orientations are represented by individual belief systems, goals, intentions, and individual behavior. Thus, the focus of research can be either on the macro-, micro-, or group level or on the level of the individual person (Bronfenbrenner, 1979; Matsumoto, 1999; Triandis, 1995).

Cultures and individual members of a culture can differ with respect to their values in regard to the self and the role of the person relative to the family and society. In certain cultures, the person tends to experience himself or her-self as rather separate from others; in other cultures, the person experiences himself or herself as interconnected, especially with members of the family and the in-group. These different qualities were conceptualized as *independence* and *interdependence* (Markus & Kitayama, 1991, 1994). In some cultures, a clear preference for independence and autonomy is highly valued, whereas in other cultures, interdependence and relatedness are preferred. This distinction of culture-specific value orientations has proven useful for the explanation of cultural differences in self-development, in the development of emotions and cognitions, in the development of interpersonal interactions and relations (Fiske, Kitayama, Markus, & Nisbett, 1998; Greenfield, Keller, Fuligni, & Maynard, 2003; Rothbaum, Pott, et al., 2000; Rothbaum, Weisz, et al., 2000; Trommsdorff & Dasen, 2001; Trommsdorff & Rothbaum, 2008), and in family systems (Kagit-cibasi, 1996). The culture-specific values of independence and interdependence affect the meaning of aspects of parent–child relationships such as relatedness, control, and autonomy.

Parent–child relationships can vary along *assurance* versus *trust* (Rothbaum, Pott, et al., 2000; Yamagishi, Cook, & Watabe, 1998). Some cultures are based on the need for assurance, which is related to close kin networks and an incentive structure for members of the in-group; this builds a sense of obligation, uncon-ditional loyalty, and filial piety. In contrast, other cultures are based on the need for security, which is related to changing in-groups and weak group ties, while there is hope for commitment (in the absence of assurance). Here, contracts or intimacy serve as the basis for close relationships. These very different qualities underlie the two types of relationships, characterized by *different meanings* and *dynamics of relatedness* (Rothbaum & Trommsdorff, 2007).

3.4. Cultural and Developmental Paths of Intergenerational Relationships over the Life Span

3.4.1. *The Cultural Meaning of Parent–Child Relationships and Parenting*
A culture-informed theory on parent–child relationships and cultural transmis-sion has to consider the culture-specific meanings of the respective behavioral indicators. This was the starting point for the culture-informed theoretical mod-ification of attachment theory by Rothbaum, Weisz, et al. (2000). The authors question the universality of the assumed concepts that underlie attachment the-ory and their culture-insensitive operationalization (e.g., caretakers' sensitivity) but do not question the universality of attachment theory.

Cross-cultural studies show that bidirectionality in parent–child relation-ships can have different meanings in different cultures (Trommsdorff & Kornadt, 2003). The Western view is usually confined to interpersonal nego-tiations between parents and children on the basis of relatively independent positions. However, in many East Asian cultures, parents' and children's roles are embedded in a hierarchical structure; the level and function of these roles pre-scribe certain behavior (Chao & Tseng, 2002; Trommsdorff & Kornadt, 2003). This behavior is embedded in a stable relationship of mutual obligation and based on emotional interdependence, as indicated by the concepts of filial piety and reciprocity (e.g., Kim, Kim, & Hurh, 1991; Schwarz, Trommsdorff, Kim, & Park, 2006; Wang & Hsueh, 2000).

Also, cross-cultural studies show that the "same" parenting may have differ-ent meanings in different cultures, and different parenting may have the same meaning in different cultures (Kornadt & Trommsdorff, 1984; Trommsdorff & Kornadt, 2003). For example, harsh punishment of children is seen as harm-ful for child development in Western cultures whereas it is positively valued in traditional Chinese families (Stevenson, Chen, & Lee, 1992; Stevenson & Zusho, 2002). In several East Asian (Japan) and Southeast Asian (Indonesian) cultures, as compared to Western (German) cultures, adolescents report more parental control and, at the same time, less conflict and more harmony in the parent–child relationship (Trommsdorff, 1995a).

These differences do not speak to cultural meaning unless the function of this parental behavior is studied. Cross-cultural studies show that the same parental behavior and goals may have different functions in different cultural con-texts, thus underlining the culture-specificities of parent–child relationships (for Asians, see the overview by Chao & Tseng, 2002). Our own studies on adolescents from different cultures showed that Japanese as compared to German youths felt rejected by their parents when experiencing low parental control (Trommsdorff, 1985). Similar results of Koreans living in North America compared to Koreans living in the Republic of Korea were reported by Rohner and Pettengill (1985). Results on negative effects of parental control on children and adolescents cannot be generalized across cultures but rather must be interpreted in an integrative, culture-informed theoretical framework on parent–child relationships.

From a culture-informed point of view, the basic cultural difference in parent–child relationships depends on whether observed behavior patterns are intended to establish and stabilize *interdependent* relationships based on cooperation and harmony or whether they are intended to develop *independent* relationships including conflicts and negotiations of power (Rothbaum, Pott, et al., 2000). These intentions are based on relevant experience in the past and they shape expectations for the future. A typical example would be an interaction sequence between a mother and a child in the case of conflicting goals (resulting in "misconduct" of the child) in a Japanese and a German dyad. This interaction sequence usually ends with the Japanese mother giving in whereas a conflict prevails in the German dyad (Trommsdorff & Kornadt, 2003). In Japan, the value of interdependence and maintaining harmonious relationships prevails, whereas in Germany, the value of independence dominates. The culture-specific parental intentions are part of the individual value system, constituting both the transmission belt and the (intended) outcome of the transmission process.

3.4.2. *Culture-Specific Developmental Paths in Parent–Child Relationships*
Starting from cultural differences in parent–child relationships, Rothbaum, Pott, et al. (2000) suggested a culture-specific model of development in Japan and in the United States representing a social-oriented and an individualist culture. The authors describe very different patterns of parent–child relationships based on needs for separation or closeness, for independence or interdependence, and for autonomy or relatedness. Consequently, either self-oriented or other-oriented goals characterize the cultural differences in those relationships. The authors are less interested in describing differences in the importance and strength than in differences in the *meaning and dynamics* of close relationships. The authors view the biological predispositions for relatedness as "passing through cultural lenses" during development (p. 1123). These cultural lenses are based on cultural values that emphasize interdependence and accommodation or independence and individuation. They affect the development of close relationships. Accordingly, the authors identify two prototypes: the *symbiotic harmony* and the *generative tension* (p. 1123). The cultural value of symbiotic harmony is based on the desire to maintain interdependence by fulfilling one's duties, by compliance with parents' wishes, and by meeting social expectations. For example, parent–child relationships in Japan are based on interdependence and characterized by harmony, cooperation, mutual obligations, and the need to reciprocate (Trommsdorff, 2006; Trommsdorff & Kornadt, 2003).

In contrast, the prototype of generative tension (which can be observed in the mother–child relationship in the United States) is based on the desire to establish and maintain independence and fulfillment of individual goals. Here, parent–child relationships are based on partnership, acceptance of conflicts, and negotiations of individual interests. The different pathways of intergenerational relationships affect cultural transmission in line with the respective culture-specific value orientations and cultural model.

3.4.3. *Lifelong Intergenerational Transmission in Cultural Context*
It is assumed here that the respective cultural models affect individual development and the transmission of values (Chao & Tseng, 2002; Rothbaum, Weisz, et al., 2000; Stevenson & Zusho, 2002; Trommsdorff & Kornadt, 2003). As an example of parent–child relationships in childhood, in the Western context, mothers tend to have their children focus on objects, whereas East Asian mothers prefer close body contact, including co-sleeping; they have their children focus on the relationship, based on empathy, mutual acceptance, relatedness, and assurance. Japanese mothers believe that conformity to social rules cannot be enforced on their children; instead, the children have to mature and believe in those rules and comply with them voluntarily (Lebra, 1994). Here, cultural transmission is based on interdependent parent–child relationships.

Transmission between parents and their adolescent and adult children continues throughout the life span. In East Asian cultures, social obligations toward the family and filial piety usually characterize the parent–child relationship over the life span. Asian adolescents and adult children are aware of their parents' sacrifice – especially their mother's. The obligation to reciprocate is based on emotional interdependence and underlies the adult children's motivation to care for adult parents. As part of the Confucian values of seniority and filial piety, the aged parents traditionally receive respect as the "honorable elders" (Palmore & Maeda, 1985; Wang & Hsueh, 2000). Furthermore, the shared belief in ancestors and the continuity of the family are part of cultural transmission and continuity in most Asian cultures (Trommsdorff, 2006; in press).

To summarize, cultural transmission occurs during the life span and in cultural context; it is affected by the changing developmental tasks in the parent–child relationship. The process, direction, and outcome of cultural transmission differ depending on the cultural context and the cultural model of independence or interdependence that organizes parent–child relationships over the life span. The study of intergenerational cultural transmission, focusing on the parent–child relationships from a life-span perspective, allows us to address questions of the quality of the parent–child relationship (e.g., with respect to interdependence or independence) and how it affects processes, direction, and outcomes of cultural transmission.

4.0. EMPIRICAL INVESTIGATION OF INTERGENERATIONAL CULTURAL TRANSMISSION

4.1. Research Questions and Methods

In this section, a currently ongoing cross-cultural study on intergenerational cultural transmission over the life span is briefly summarized. The goals and theoretical assumptions, methods, and selected empirical findings are presented.

Goals and Theoretical Framework of the Study. The general idea underlying this project is the theoretical model on intergenerational cultural transmission (i.e., value of children [VOC] and intergenerational relations). The present study attempts to test the theoretical model on the cultural and socioeconomic conditions of cultural transmission, taking into account past and present socialization of parents and children from three biologically related generations, their value orientations, and their relationship quality (Trommsdorff, 2001a, 2001b, 2003) (Figure 7.1).

The present study analyzes the different qualitative aspects of parent–child relationships and their function as mediating factors between the culture-specific value orientations (e.g., independence/interdependence, individualism/collectivism, VOC) and the individual investment (e.g., support) in the older or younger generation.

This study starts from an integrated approach (cf. Trommsdorff, 2006, 2007), taking into account ecological and socioeconomic factors, individual value orientations, and the developmental niche as part of the developmental

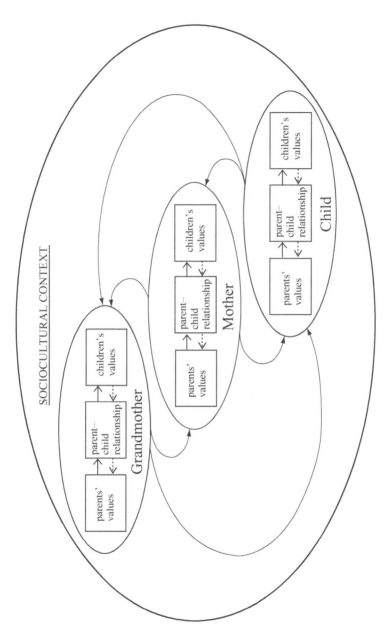

Figure 7.1. Parent–child relationships as transmission belt.

pathway. Beyond the biological connectedness, the shared cultural values concerning childhood, parenthood, and old age are assumed to influence the relationships between parents and their children over the life span and over the generations. The predominant cultural values (e.g., independence or interdependence) affect the pathways for the development of parent–child relationships and the related processes of the cultural transmission.

It is assumed that the parent–child relationship serves as the basis for further interactions, which in turn affect the further development and contribute to the transmission of cultural value orientations and relationship patterns. Furthermore, it is expected that the wider ecological and macro-structure provide both constraints and opportunities for these processes of intergenerational cultural transmission (cf. Nauck, 2001, 2005; Trommsdorff, 2001a, 2001b, 2003, 2006, 2007; Trommsdorff & Nauck, 2005, 2006).

Thus, the major goal of this project is to study universal and culture-specific relationships among context, value orientations, the quality of parent–child relationships (including the support given and received by parents and children), and their impact on intergenerational (i.e., selective, reciprocal, or unidirectional) transmission over the life course.

Methods. The present study on intergenerational cultural transmission follows a specific design that includes cross-sectional data on three biologically related generations (i.e., grandmothers, mothers, and adolescents) and a control group of young mothers with preschool children and different cultural contexts that represent different value orientations and family systems (i.e., Germany, France, Israel, Palestine, Czech Republic, Turkey, Republic of Korea, People's Republic of China, Indonesia, India, and South Africa). Subgroups in several of these countries (e.g., urban and rural samples) account for intracultural differences. The sample currently consists of more than 10,000 persons.

Procedure. All interviews were undertaken on a face-to-face basis by trained interviewers in each country. The instruments used are questionnaires based on pretests in those countries; they include some established and some newly developed scales to measure the following:

- the quality of the parent–child relationship (e.g., bidirectionality, emotional or instrumental relationship quality)
- value orientations (e.g., independence and interdependence, VOC, value of the family)
- transmission processes (e.g., parenting style)
- transmission outcomes (e.g., similarities, function of transmission for development)
- direction of transmission (e.g., from parents to children, from children to parents) (For a more detailed description, see Schwarz, Chakkarath, Trommsdorff, Schwenk, & Nauck, 2001; Trommsdorff, 2001a, 2001b, 2002; Trommsdorff & Nauck, 2005, 2006.)

First, empirical analyses from this project focused on bidirectional and multi-directional flows of transmission in the cultural context. For persons involved in the transmission process, we focused on grandmothers and mothers, mothers and adolescents, grandmothers, mothers, and adolescents.

4.2. Preliminary Results on Intergenerational Transmission of Values

Outcome of Intergenerational Transmission. Similarity of values has often been regarded as indicating the intended "successful" transmission of values from parents to their children due to successful parenting and a positive parent–child relationship (Grusec & Goodnow, 1994). Cultural values, socioeconomic changes, and developmental tasks may affect the parent–child relationship and moderate the transmission of values between the generations.

In accordance with the model of culture-specific developmental paths (Rothbaum, Pott, et al., 2000), it may be assumed that in countries where values of interdependence are high, similarities in value orientations among the older and younger generations will be stronger than in individualistic societies. Also, fewer similarities among generations and more intragenerational differences (i.e., inconsistencies) are expected in those countries where values of independence are more relevant (and/or where a transition to modernity is taking place). In the latter case, the older generation presumably prefers "modern" values of independence and individualism less than the younger generation, who may prefer both traditional and modern values. Thus, a general preference for individualistic values (and/or a sociocultural change toward modernity) as compared to a general preference for group-oriented (i.e., collectivistic) values on the aggregate level should be related to higher selectivity in the transmission of values, more intergenerational differences, and more intragenerational inconsistencies in value orientations.

(a) In one study, we tested intergenerational differences and similarities with respect to parental goals and values, thus focusing on the parents' intentions for child outcomes. Developmental timetables (i.e., the preferred age levels for the children showing a certain behavioral competence) were used because they indicate cultural values and knowledge about the "ideal" and preferred time of development. We compared mothers and their biological mothers (i.e., grandmothers) with respect to their preferred developmental timetables in German, Korean, and Indonesian samples (i.e., the pilot study) (Schwarz, Trommsdorff, Kim, & Park, 2006). Whereas differences between the Korean and German mothers and grandmothers occurred, the Indonesian dyads showed no differences. These results demonstrate that disagreements between grandmothers and mothers are less pronounced in a traditional-interdependent culture. In line with this reasoning, we compared developmental goals of German mothers and grandmothers. Here, differences between the two generations occurred in the expected direction: Developmental goals of obedience were more preferred and goals of independence were less preferred by grandmothers as compared to mothers (Trommsdorff et al., 2004).

(b) However, because the testing of mean differences in value orientations does not give insight into the meaning of the specific values that are "success-fully" transmitted, it is preferable to compare *value structures* (e.g., by latent class analysis) as a more valid approach to indicate whether and in which way generations differ. This analysis was carried out for a sample of two generations from a country undergoing significant socioeconomic and cultural change: the Czech Republic. Here, grandmothers belonged to a group with high values on all VOC dimensions whereas none of their adult daughters (i.e., mothers of ado-lescent children) belonged to this group; the adult daughters were represented in a group in which only the emotional VOC was high (Mayer & Trommsdorff, 2003). However, it must be analyzed in further studies whether those differences indicate effects of value changes or of individual development.

Processes of Intergenerational Transmission. As suggested in our model of intergenerational relations over the life span, the relationship quality between mothers and adolescents should influence the extent of transmission. According to the two-step model (i.e., the accurate perception of a value and its accep-tance) by Grusec and Goodnow (1994), it was assumed that intimacy in the relationship and perceived acceptance enhances communication between ado-lescents and their mothers, thereby increasing the accurate perception and the acceptance of maternal values. In contrast, conflicts between adolescents and their mothers increase the communication about values (cf. Knafo & Schwartz, 2003) but at the same time reduce the accuracy of perception and the acceptance of them.

Cross-cultural studies are needed to study the processes of transmission. This is one goal of our project, "Value of Children and Intergenerational Relations." In a recent study, we investigated how several general and domain-specific value orientations (e.g., individualism/collectivism, family values, and interdepen-dence) are transmitted from one generation to the next (Albert, 2007; Albert & Trommsdorff, 2003; Albert, Trommsdorff, & Sabatier, 2005). First, we tested the effects of the parent–child relationship as part of the transmission process for the German and French sample of mothers, grandmothers, and their ado-lescent children within the framework of the VOC study (Albert, 2007; Albert & Trommsdorff, 2003). The extent of transmission of values (i.e., general and domain-specific values such as individualism/collectivism, family, and interde-pendence) and the influence of the parent–child and grandparent–grandchild relationship quality on the extent of transmission of values were tested (i.e., regression analyses). The results showed that all four value orientations of the adolescents were predicted by the value orientations of the mothers. The pre-diction of individualism, however, was relatively weak in Germany, indicating a rather selective transmission of values. At the same time, mean values of mothers and adolescents on all scales differed in both countries; this indicates a relative as opposed to an absolute transmission. Apart from this, in Germany, intimacy and perceived admiration by parents turned out to be successful transmission belts for values of collectivism and the value of the family but not for individualism and interdependence, thus suggesting the need to refine the model by Grusec and Goodnow (1994) with respect to the contents and meaning of the values. Conflict had no moderating effect on value transmission. In France, any of these aspects of the relationship quality had an effect on transmission. Furthermore, all aspects of the relationship quality had direct effects on the value orientations of the adolescents in both countries. Results on the transmission between grandmothers and their adolescent grandchildren showed an unexpected moderating effect of intimacy on collectivism: The less intimacy was reported, the stronger was the transmission of collectivism in France. Here, a particular function of intergenerational relationships in nonadjacent dyads becomes obvious. Grandmother–grandchild relationships are more hierarchically organized than parent–child relationships, thus affecting the role of intimacy for value transmission. As expected, perceived admiration enhanced the transmission of interdependence from grandmothers to grandchildren, especially in France. These results support the notion that the relationship quality has an important impact on the process of transmission affecting the development of value orientations of adolescents. Furthermore, the results indicate that intergenerational cultural transmission must be studied with respect to the cultural meaning of the values in question and the culture-specific aspects of relationship quality.

In line with the model by Grusec and Goodnow (1994), we also assumed that parenting plays an important role in value transmission (Albert, 2007; Albert, Trommsdorff, & Sabatier, 2005). To clarify possible culture-specificities in the process of transmission, we tested the role of parenting as a mediator of transmission. The sample consisted of 510 German and French mother–adolescent dyads. The results showed intergenerational transmission of all values in both cultural samples; furthermore, cultural differences in parenting occurred, and parenting had culture-specific effects on the transmission of different values. In Germany, collectivism was transmitted via maternal acceptance and control, and interdependence was transmitted via maternal acceptance. In France, family values were transmitted via maternal control. Thus, culture-specificities in parenting and intergenerational relationships must be considered when explaining processes of transmission.

Furthermore, we studied the role of the cultural context for the transmission of values comparing intergenerational transmission of general and domain-specific values in Germany and Indonesia, two contexts that differ with respect to the developmental path of independence and interdependence (Albert, Trommsdorff, & Wisnubrata, 2006). Whereas the transmission of individualism was stronger in Indonesian families, the transmission of family values was stronger in German families. Apparently, values that are not shared by the society are rather transmitted within the family, whereas widely shared values are transmitted by various socialization agents, thereby reducing the impact of families on value transmission.

Beyond the transmission of values, more empirical evidence is needed on the process of transmission of other orientations. For example, attachment – an important personality and relationship variable – has often been assumed to be transmitted from parents to children. However, only scarce empirical evidence is available as far as the processes in the transmission of attachment are concerned. Therefore, as part of the "Value of Children and Intergenerational Relations" study, we compared German and Indian adolescents' and their mothers' attachment and analyzed how far maternal parenting mediates the relationship between mothers' and their adolescent children's attachment (Albert, Trommsdorff, & Mishra, 2007). The sample consisted of 300 Indian and 310 German mother–adolescent dyads. One major result was that Indian mothers reported using more control than German mothers. Furthermore, control and acceptance as parenting styles were more balanced in the Indian sample as compared to the German sample. In both cultures, attachment of mothers clearly predicted the attachment of adolescent children. However, the relationship between maternal and adolescent attachment was not mediated by parenting. The results are in line with the assumption that cultural pathways of development affect the meaning of parenting and of attachment. However, the specific mediators for the transmission of attachment in the respective cultures still must be clarified. Further studies are needed to identify the influential processes in the transmission of values and other general orientations and to study the moderating effects of culture on those processes.

4.3. Implications for the Study of Intergenerational Cultural Transmission

The studies on intergenerational cultural transmission have demonstrated that it is necessary to interpret the "outcomes" of transmission in a theoretical culture-informed framework and not only focus on single indicators of values and simple comparisons of means between different generations, as in many past studies on transmission. Intergenerational similarities in values measured at a single time-point do not necessarily indicate "successful" cultural transmission, and "unsuccessful" transmission is not necessarily indicated by intergenerational value discrepancies, as can be seen when including intentions of the transmitter and, furthermore, when considering the function of the transmitted orientations in the respective (possibly changing) context. However, other researchers have not made this distinction. Kohn and Schooler (1983) studied value similarities among generations (cohorts) with respect to political orientations, religious beliefs, and lifestyles. They argued that for Western countries, the transmission of values from one generation to the next is very modest and that internalization of values can only seldom be empirically documented. This skeptical summary of intergenerational transmission of values is not confirmed by psychological analyses on intergenerational cultural transmission. The results from our studies show that the implicit assumption that similarity of parents' and children's values indicates "successful" transmission can be wrong due to the more complex problem of *selective transmission* of values. Comparisons of mean values indicating the degree of "absolute" transmission have to be differentiated from correlations of values between parents and children that indicate "relative" transmission of values (Vermulst, De Brock, & Van Zutphen, 1991).

From a developmental perspective, intergenerational differences in values can be related to different stages in the individual life cycle and to a different historical impact on socialization. Similarities in values of parents and their children can therefore change in size and pattern during socialization and over the life span, and they can vary in different social groups and according to the respective contents (i.e., subjective meaning) of the values. Therefore, little can be said about "successful" transmission as long as it is unclear what the function of certain values is (e.g., with respect to the person's development). Certain value discrepancies between parents and children may occur for a certain period (especially during adolescence and emerging adulthood). The consequence may be more clarity and stability in the resulting later value orientations. Intrapersonal changes of and inconsistencies in values are a normal aspect of development, and discrepancies between values of parents and their children may be due to developmental dynamics, not indicating failure of cultural transmission but rather a certain developmental stage in the internalization of values and in the "successful" cultural transmission. Thus, transmission must be studied from a long-term perspective.

Furthermore, the contents of the values as part of the value system of the family must be considered (Trommsdorff et al., 2004). In a culture where individualistic values prevail, more contradictions, ambiguity, and negotiation of value priorities occur. In this context, different conditions for the transmission of values prevail as compared to traditional cultures, which are characterized by a more homogeneous value system.

To summarize, similarities or differences of single values between parents and their offspring do not tell us much about "successful" transmission. Also, a static perspective assuming direct transmission of values from parents to children and regarding value similarity as an indicator of successful transmission cannot account for the dynamic process of cultural transmission in the cultural context. The pattern and meaning of the values, their behavioral relevance, the quality of the intergenerational relations, and the function of these relationships in the process of transmission in the respective cultural context all have to be assessed in research on intergenerational cultural transmission.

5.0. OUTLOOK: INTERGENERATIONAL CULTURAL TRANSMISSION AND SOCIOCULTURAL CHANGE

Intergenerational cultural transmission has been studied in this chapter by considering the quality of the parent–child relationship over the life span in different cultural contexts. It has been shown that intergenerational transmission can change over the life span and depends on the development of parent–child relationships; the impact of culture on the transmission of culture through intergenerational relations cannot be ignored.

The transmission of culture may be seen as deriving from the child's internalization of values. However, this does not necessarily imply the child's conformity to parental values. Certain values can be enacted differently and may change their meaning during individual development and social change. Intergenerational transmission of culture can change the relationships between values and behavior and can induce innovations. This assumption takes into account both the active role of the child in the process of transmission and internalization and the heterogeneity of cultures and societies.

Further studies on intergenerational cultural transmission, therefore, should address the questions of how far continuity and stability of culture can be predicted from transmission processes and how far intergenerational relationships and cultural transmission can be seen as a source for innovation and change (Kuczynski & Navara, 2006; Valsiner, 1988). Therefore, the function of intergenerational relationships for cultural transmission, including selective continuity or drastic change, needs further investigation.

The child's and the parents' activity in the transmission process is influenced by the parent–child relationship and the cultural values. Specific values (e.g., independence) may have different cultural and/or subjective meanings according to the cultural context in which the value is prevalent and the actor's personality (e.g., development, intention, and worldview). A certain behavior may seem to indicate a specific value although it is meant to express a quite different value. Invalid measurement occurs when the cultural and the subjective meaning of the specific observed behavior is not considered. Human behavior may be based on different, even conflicting, motives. For example, compliance may have different meanings: suppressed resistance or fully endorsed internalized acceptance of values. Internalization of certain values can thus give rise to very different forms of behavior. The kind and degree of internalization is more adequately assessed by considering the subjective meaning of only those manifest behaviors that are strongly related to the self-concept. Therefore, the question is raised as to how far deviance from or acceptance of certain cultural values is a part of one's self-construal.

Under certain circumstances – and depending on the cultural context, the developmental age, and the situation – deviance is well accepted and seen as an indicator of successful transmission of values from parents to children. In several cultures (e.g., Japan and China), children are not expected to comply with cultural values and norms in early childhood. Children's noncompliance is regarded as a cultural value of childhood that enhances later successful transmission of values. The modern Japanese Kabuki player is an example of simultaneously cultural compliance and deviance. He should fully comply with traditional cultural norms while on stage; off stage, however, he may engage in "Western"-style modern behavior, thus serving as a model for the continuation and also discontinuation of certain traditional values. Therefore, more has to be known about relationships between the transmission of traditional culture and innovation.

The processes of cultural transmission in times of drastic socioeconomic and cultural change also need to be investigated. Our own studies have shown that ongoing demographic change induces changes in intergenerational relationships and changes in the VOC (from economic to emotional values) (Makoshi & Trommsdorff, 2002; Nauck, 2000; Trommsdorff & Nauck, 2006; Trommsdorff, Zengh, & Tardif, 2002).

Furthermore, the role of the transmission of culture for an individual's development should be clarified. A further task for future research is to study the gene-environment relationships in the process of transmission and its culture-specific functions.

REFERENCES

Ainsworth, M. D., Blehar, M. C., Waters, E., & Wall, S. (1978). *Patterns of attachment: A psychological study of the strange situation.* Hillsdale, NJ: Erlbaum.

Albert, I. (2007). *Intergenerationale Transmission von Werten in Deutschland und Frankreich.* Lengerich, Germany: Pabst Science.

Albert, I., & Trommsdorff, G. (2003, August). *Intergenerational transmission of family values.* Poster presented at the XIth European Conference on Developmental Psychology in Milan, Italy.

Albert, I., Trommsdorff, G., & Mishra, R. (2007). Parenting and adolescent attachment in India and Germany. In G. Zheng, K. Leung, & J. G. Adair (Eds.), *Perspectives and progress in contemporary cross-cultural psychology. Selected papers from the Seventeenth International Congress of the International Association for Cross-Cultural Psychology* (pp. 97–108). Beijing, China: China Light Industry Press.

Albert, I., Trommsdorff, G., & Sabatier, C. (2005, July). *Parenting and intergenerational transmission of values in Germany and France.* Paper presented at the 7th European Regional Congress of the International Association for Cross-Cultural Psychology, San Sebastian, Spain.

Albert, I., Trommsdorff, G., & Wisnubrata, L. (2006, July). Intergenerational transmission of values in different cultural contexts: A study in Germany and Indonesia. Paper presented at the 18th International Congress of the IACCP, Spetses, Greece.

Baltes, P. B., & Baltes, M. M. (1990). Psychological perspectives on successful aging: The model of selective optimization with compensation. In P. B. Baltes & M. M. Baltes (Eds.), *Successful aging: Perspectives from the behavioral sciences* (pp. 1–34). Cambridge, UK: Cambridge University Press.

Bandura, A. (1977). *Social learning theory.* Englewood Cliffs, NJ: Prentice Hall.

Bandura, A. (1986). *Social foundations of thought and action: A social cognitive theory.* Upper Saddle River, NJ: Prentice-Hall.

Baumrind, D. (1991). Effective parenting during the early adolescent transition. In P. A. Cowan & E. M. Hetherington (Eds.), *Family transitions: Advances in family research series* (pp. 111–163). Hillsdale, NJ: Erlbaum.

Bell, R. Q. (1979). Parent, child, and reciprocal influences. *American Psychologist, 34*, 821–826.

Benedict, R. (1934). *Patterns of culture.* Boston: Houghton Mifflin.

Bengtson, V. L. (2001). Beyond the nuclear family: The increasing importance of multi-generational bonds. *Journal of Marriage & Family, 63*, 1–16.

Bengtson, V. L., & Robertson, J. F. (Eds.). (1985). *Grandparenthood.* Beverly Hills, CA: Sage Publications.

Berry, J. W. (1967). Independence and conformity in subsistence-level societies. *Journal of Personality & Social Psychology, 7*, 415–418.

Berry, J. W., Poortinga, Y. H., Segall, M. H., & Dasen, P. R. (2002). *Cross-cultural psychology: Research and applications* (Vol. 2). New York: Cambridge University Press.

Blenkner, M. (1965). Social work and family relationships in later life with some thoughts on filial maturity. In E. Shanas & G. F. Streib (Eds.), *Social structure and the family: Generational relations* (pp. 46–59). Englewood Cliffs, NJ: Prentice-Hall.

Bowlby, J. (1969). *Attachment and loss: Vol. 1, Attachment.* New York: Basic Books.

Bronfenbrenner, U. (1979). *The ecology of human development: Experiments by nature and design.* Cambridge, MA: Harvard University Press.

Bruner, J. S. (1996). *The culture of education.* Cambridge, MA: Harvard University Press.

Bugental, D. B., & Goodnow, J. J. (2000). Socialization processes. In W. Damon & N. Eisenberg (Eds.), *Handbook of child psychology: Vol. 3, Social, emotional, and personality development* (5th ed., pp. 389–463). New York: John Wiley & Sons.

Cavalli-Sforza, L. L., & Feldman, M. W. (1981). *Cultural transmission and evolution: A quantitative approach.* Princeton, NJ: Princeton University Press.

Chao, R., & Tseng, V. (2002). Parenting of Asians. In M. H. Bornstein (Ed.), *Handbook of parenting: Vol. 4, Social conditions and applied parenting* (2nd ed., pp. 59–93). Mahwah, NJ: Erlbaum.

Cole, M. (1996). *Cultural psychology: A once and future discipline.* Cambridge, MA: Harvard University Press.

Cole, M., & Scribner, S. (1974). *Culture & thought: A psychological introduction.* New York: Wiley.

Collins, W. A., Maccoby, E. E., Steinberg, L., Hetherington, E. M., & Bornstein, M. H. (2000). Contemporary research on parenting: The case for nature and nurture. *American Psychologist, 55*, 218–232.

Cooney, T. M. (1997). Parent–child relations across adulthood. In S. Duck (Ed.), *Handbook of personal relationships* (2nd ed., pp. 451–468). Chichester, UK: Wiley.

Cooper, C. R., Grotevant, H. D., & Condon, S. M. (1983). Individuality and connectedness in the family as a context for adolescent identity formation and role-taking skill. *New Directions for Child Development, 22*, 43–59.

Corsaro, W. A. (1997). *The sociology of childhood.* Thousand Oaks, CA: Pine Forge Press.

Crocket, L. J., & Silbereisen, R. K. (Eds.). (2000). *Negotiating adolescence in times of social change.* Cambridge, UK: Cambridge University Press.

D'Andrade, R. G., & Strauss, C. (Eds.). (1992). *Human motives and cultural models.* New York: Cambridge University Press.

Elder, G. H., Jr. (1974). *The children of the Great Depression: Social change and life experience*. Chicago: University of Chicago Press.

Elder, G. H., Jr. (1998). The life course as developmental theory. *Child Development, 69,* 1–12.

Erikson, E. H. (1959). *Identity and the life cycle*. New York: International University Press.

Fiske, A. P., Kitayama, S., Markus, H. R., & Nisbett, R. E. (1998). The cultural matrix of social psychology. In D. T. Gilbert, S. T. Fiske, & G. Lindzey (Eds.), *The handbook of social psychology* (4th ed., Vol. 2, pp. 915–981). Boston: McGraw-Hill.

Gallese, V. (2003). The roots of empathy: The shared manifold hypothesis and the neural basis of intersubjectivity. *Psychopathology, 36,* 171–180.

Geertz, C. (1973). *The interpretation of cultures: Selected essays*. New York: Basic Books.

Goodnow, J. J., & Collins, W. A. (Eds.). (1990). *Development according to parents: The nature, sources, and consequences of parents' ideas*. Hillsdale, NJ: Erlbaum.

Greenfield, P. M. (2000). Three approaches to the psychology of culture: Where do they come from? Where can they go? *Asian Journal of Social Psychology, 3,* 223–240.

Greenfield, P. M., Keller, H., Fuligni, A. J., & Maynard, A. (2003). Cultural pathways through universal development. *Annual Review of Psychology, 54,* 461–490.

Grusec, J. E., & Goodnow, J. J. (1994). Impact of parental discipline methods on the child's internalization of values: A reconceptualization of current points of view. *Developmental Psychology, 30,* 4–19.

Grusec, J. E., & Kuczynski, L. (Eds.). (1997). *Parenting and the internalization of values: A handbook of contemporary theory*. New York: Wiley.

Harkness, S., & Super, C. M. (2002). Culture and parenting. In M. H. Bornstein (Ed.), *Handbook of parenting: Vol. 2, Biology and ecology of parenting* (2nd ed., pp. 253–280). Mahwah, NJ: Erlbaum.

Havighurst, R. J. (1972). *Developmental tasks and education*. New York: MacKay.

Hewlett, B. S., & Cavalli-Sforza, L. L. (1986). Cultural transmission among Aka pygmies. *American Anthropology, 88,* 922–934.

Hoffman, J. A. (1984). Psychological separation of late adolescents from their parents. *Journal of Counselling Psychology, 31,* 170–178.

Holland, D., & Quinn, N. (Eds.). (1987). *Cultural models in language and thought*. New York: Cambridge University Press.

Homans, G. C. (1961). *Social behavior*. New York: Harcourt, Brace & World.

Kagitcibasi, C. (1996). *Family and human development across cultures: A view from the other side*. Mahwah, NJ: Erlbaum.

Keller, H. (2002). Development as the interface between biology and culture: A conceptualization of early ontogenetic experiences. In H. Keller, Y. H. Poortinga, & A. Schölmerich (Eds.), *Between culture and biology: Perspectives on ontogenetic development* (pp. 215–240). New York: Cambridge University Press.

Kelley, H. H. (1983). *Close relationships*. New York: Freeman.

Kelley, H. H., & Thibaut, J. W. (1978). *Interpersonal relations: A theory of interdependence*. New York: Wiley.

Kim, K. C., Kim, S., & Hurh, W. M. (1991). Filial piety and intergenerational relationship in Korean immigrant families. *International Journal of Aging and Human Development, 33,* 233–245.

King, V., & Elder, G. H., Jr. (1997). The legacy of grandparenting: Childhood experiences with grandparents and current involvement with grandchildren. *Journal of Marriage & Family, 59,* 848–859.

Knafo, A., & Schwartz, S. H. (2003). Parenting and adolescents' accuracy in perceiving parental values. *Child Development, 74,* 595–611.

Kohli, M., & Szydlik, M. (Eds.). (2000). *Lebenslauf, Alter, Generation: Band 3. Generationen in Familie und Gesellschaft* [Life-course, age, generation: Vol. 3. Generation in family and society]. Opladen, Germany: Leske + Budrich.

Kohn, M. L., & Schooler, C. (1983). *Work and personality: An inquiry into the impact of social stratification.* Norwood, NJ: Ablex Publishing Corporation.

Kornadt, H.-J., & Trommsdorff, G. (1984). Erziehungsziele im Kulturvergleich [Child-rearing goals in cross-cultural comparison]. In G. Trommsdorff (Ed.), *Jahrbuch für Empirische Erziehungswissenschaft 1984: Erziehungsziele* (pp. 191–212). Düsseldorf, Germany: Schwann.

Kroeber, A. L., & Kluckhohn, C. (1952). Culture: A critical review of concepts and definitions. *Papers. Peabody Museum of Archaeology & Ethnology, Harvard University, 47*(1).

Kuczynski, L. (2003). Beyond bidirectionality: Bilateral conceptual frameworks for understanding dynamics in parent–child relations. In L. Kuczynski (Ed.), *Handbook of dynamics in parent–child relations* (pp. 1–24). Thousand Oaks, CA: Sage Publications.

Kuczynski, L., & Navara, G. (2006). Sources of innovation and change in internalization and socialization. In M. Killen & J. Smetana (Eds.), *Handbook of moral development* (pp. 299–327). Mahwah, NJ: Erlbaum.

Lebra, T. S. (1994). Mother and child in Japanese socialization: A Japan–U.S. comparison. In P. M. Greenfield & R. R. Cocking (Eds.), *Cross-cultural roots of minority child development* (pp. 259–274). Hillsdale, NJ: Erlbaum.

LeVine, R. A. (1973). *Culture, behavior, and personality.* Chicago: Aldine.

Maccoby, E. E. (2000). Parenting and its effects on children: On reading and misreading behavior genetics. *Annual Review of Psychology, 51,* 1–27.

Maccoby, E. E., & Martin, J. A. (1983). Socialisation in the context of the family: Parent–child interaction. In P. H. Mussen & E. M. Hetherington (Eds.), *Handbook of child psychology: Vol. 4, Socialization, personality and social development* (pp. 1–101). New York: Wiley.

Makoshi, N., & Trommsdorff, G. (2002). Value of children and mother–child relationships in Japan: Comparisons with Germany. In U. Teichler & G. Trommsdorff (Eds.), *Challenges of the 21st century in Japan and Germany* (pp. 109–124). Lengerich, Germany: Pabst Science.

Mannheim, K. (1929/1964). *Das Problem der Generationen* [The problem of the generations]. Köln, Germany: Westdeutscher Verlag.

Markus, H. R., & Kitayama, S. (1991). Culture and the self: Implications for cognition, emotion, and motivation. *Psychological Review, 98,* 224–253.

Markus, H. R., & Kitayama, S. (1994). A collective fear of the collective: Implications for selves and theories of selves. *Personality and Social Psychology Bulletin, 20,* 568–579.

Matsumoto, D. (1999). Culture and self: An empirical assessment of Markus and Kitayama's theory of independent and interdependent self-construal. *Asian Journal of Social Psychology, 2,* 289–310.

Mayer, B., & Trommsdorff, G. (2003, September). *Kindbezogene Wertstrukturen bei tschechischen Müttern und Großmüttern [Child-related value structures of Czech mothers and grandmothers]*. Poster presented at the 16th Meeting of the Section of Developmental Psychology of the German Psychological Association, Mainz, Germany.

Mead, M. (1935). *Sex and temperament in three primitive societies*. New York: William Morrow.

Meltzoff, A. N., & Moore, M. K. (1998). Infant intersubjectivity: Broadening the dialogue to include imitation, identity and intention. In S. Braten (Ed.), *Intersubjective communication and emotion in early ontogeny* (pp. 47–88). Cambridge, MA: Cambridge University Press.

Nauck, B. (2000). Social capital and intergenerational transmission of cultural capital within a regional context. In J. Bynner & R. K. Silbereisen (Eds.), *Adversity and challenge in life in the new Germany and in England* (pp. 212–238). Houndmills, UK: Macmillan.

Nauck, B. (2001). Der Wert von Kindern für ihre Eltern: "Value of children" als spezielle Handlungstheorie des generativen Verhaltens und von Generationenbeziehungen im interkulturellen Vergleich [The value of children for their parents: A special action theory of fertility behavior and intergenerational relationships in cross-cultural comparison]. *Kölner Zeitschrift für Soziologie und Sozialpsychologie, 53*, 407–435.

Nauck, B. (2005). Changing value of children: An action theory of fertility behavior and intergenerational relationships in cross-cultural comparison. In W. Friedlmeier, P. Chakkarath, & B. Schwarz (Eds.), *Culture and human development: The importance of cross-cultural research in the social sciences* (pp. 183–202). Hove, UK: Psychology Press.

Neugarten, B. L. (1968). *Middle age and aging: A reader in social psychology*. Chicago: University of Chicago Press.

Palmore, E. B., & Maeda, D. (1985). *The honorable elders revisited (Otoshiyori saikô)*. Durham, NC: Duke University Press.

Plomin, R. (2000). Behavioural genetics in the 21st century. *International Journal of Behavioral Development, 24*, 30–34.

Quinn, N., & Holland, D. (1987). Culture and cognition. In D. Holland & N. Quinn (Eds.), *Cultural models in language and thought* (pp. 1–40). New York: Cambridge University Press.

Rogoff, B. (2003). *The cultural nature of human development*. Oxford, UK: Oxford University Press.

Rohner, R. P., & Pettengill, S. M. (1985). Perceived parental acceptance–rejection and parental control among Korean adolescents. *Child Development, 56*, 524–528.

Rothbaum, F., Pott, M., Azuma, H., Miyake, K., & Weisz, J. (2000). The development of close relationships in Japan and the United States: Paths of symbiotic harmony and generative tension. *Child Development, 71*, 1121–1142.

Rothbaum, F., & Trommsdorff, G. (2007). Cultural perspectives on relationships and autonomy-control. In J. E. Grusec & P. Hastings (Eds.), *Handbook of socialization* (pp. 461–489). New York: The Guilford Press.

Rothbaum, F., Weisz, J., Pott, M., Miyake, K., & Morelli, G. (2000). Attachment and culture: Security in the United States and Japan. *American Psychologist, 55*, 1093–1104.

Rusbult, C. E., & Van Lange, P. A. M. (2003). Interdependence, interaction and relationships. *Annual Review of Psychology, 54*, 351–375.

Schönpflug, U. (2001). Intergenerational transmission of values: The role of transmission belts. *Journal of Cross-Cultural Psychology, 32*(2), 174–185.

Schwarz, B., Chakkarath, P., Trommsdorff, G., Schwenk, O., & Nauck, B. (2001). *Report on selected instruments of the value of children main study.* Unpublished manuscript, University of Konstanz, Konstanz, Germany.

Schwarz, B., Trommsdorff, G., Kim, U., & Park, Y.-S. (2006). Intergenerational support: Psychological and cultural analyses of Korean and German women. *Current Sociology, 54*(2), 315–340.

Shore, B. (1996). *Culture in mind: Cognition, culture, and the problem of meaning.* New York: Oxford University Press.

Shweder, R. A. (1991). *Thinking through cultures: Expeditions in cultural psychology.* Cambridge, MA: Harvard University Press.

Stevenson, H. W., Chen, C., & Lee, S. (1992). Chinese families. In J. L. Roopnarine & D. B. Carter (Eds.), *Parent–child socialization in diverse cultures* (pp. 17–33). Norwood, NJ: Ablex Publishing Corporation.

Stevenson, H. W., & Zusho, A. (2002). Adolescence in China and Japan: Adapting to a changing environment. In B. B. Brown, R. W. Larson, & T. S. Saraswathi (Eds.), *The world's youth: Adolescence in eight regions of the globe* (pp. 141–170). Cambridge, UK: Cambridge University Press.

Super, C. M., & Harkness, S. (1999). The environment as culture in developmental research. In S. L. Friedman & T. D. Wachs (Eds.), *Measuring environment across the life span: Emerging methods and concepts* (pp. 279–323). Washington, DC: American Psychological Association.

Thibaut, J. W., & Kelley, H. H. (1959). *The social psychology of groups.* New York: John Wiley and Sons.

Thompson, R. A. (1999). Early attachment and later development. In J. Cassidy & P. R. Shaver (Eds.), *Handbook of attachment: Theory, research, and clinical applications* (pp. 265–286). New York: The Guilford Press.

Tomasello, M., Kruger, A. C., & Ratner, H. H. (1993). Cultural learning. *Behavioral and Brain Sciences, 16,* 495–552.

Triandis, H. C. (1995). *Individualism & collectivism.* Boulder, CO: Westview Press.

Trommsdorff, G. (1985). Some comparative aspects of socialization in Japan and Germany. In I. Reyes Lagunes & Y. H. Poortinga (Eds.), *From a different perspective: Studies of behavior across cultures* (pp. 231–240). Amsterdam: Swets & Zeitlinger.

Trommsdorff, G. (1991). Sympathie und Partnerwahl: Enge Beziehungen aus interkultureller Sicht [Sympathy and partner selection: Close relationships from a cross-cultural perspective]. In M. Amelang, H.-J. Ahrens, & H. W. Bierhoff (Eds.), *Partnerwahl und Partnerschaft: Formen und Grundlagen partnerschaftlicher Beziehungen* (pp. 185–219). Göttingen, Germany: Hogrefe.

Trommsdorff, G. (1995a). Parent–adolescent relations in changing societies: A cross-cultural study. In P. Noack, M. Hofer, & J. Youniss (Eds.), *Psychological responses to social change: Human development in changing environments* (pp. 189–218). Berlin, Germany: De Gruyter.

Trommsdorff, G. (1995b). Person-context relations as developmental conditions for empathy and prosocial action: A cross-cultural analysis. In T. A. Kindermann & J. Valsiner (Eds.), *Development of person-context relations* (pp. 113–146). Hillsdale, NJ: Erlbaum.

Trommsdorff, G. (2000). Subjective experience of social change in individual development. In J. Bynner & R. K. Silbereisen (Eds.), *Adversity and challenge in life in the new Germany and in England* (pp. 87–122). Basingstoke, UK: Macmillan Press.

Trommsdorff, G. (2001a). Eltern-Kind-Beziehungen im interkulturellen Vergleich [Parent-child relations in cross-cultural comparison]. In S. Walper & R. Pekrun (Eds.), *Familie und Entwicklung: Perspektiven der Familienpsychologie* (pp. 36–62). Göttingen, Germany: Hogrefe.

Trommsdorff, G. (2001b). *Value of children and intergenerational relations: A cross-cultural psychological study.* Retrieved May 21, 2008, from http://www.uni-konstanz.de/FuF/SozWiss/fg-psy/ag-entw/.

Trommsdorff, G. (2002). An eco-cultural and interpersonal relations approach to development over the life span. In W. J. Lonner, D. L. Dinnel, S. A. Hayes, & D. N. Sattler (Eds.), *Online Readings in Psychology and Culture* (Unit 12, Chapter 1) (http://www.wwu.edu/~culture), Center for Cross-Cultural Research, Western Washington University, Bellingham, WA.

Trommsdorff, G. (2003). Parent–child relations in the life span: A cross-cultural perspective. In Korean Association of Child Studies (Ed.), *Parental beliefs, parenting, and child development from developmental perspectives* (pp. 9–66). Seoul, Republic of Korea: Korean Association of Child Studies.

Trommsdorff, G. (2006). Parent–child relations over the life span. A cross-cultural perspective. In K. H. Rubin & O. B. Chung (Eds.), *Parenting beliefs, behaviors, and parent–child relations. A cross-cultural perspective* (pp. 143–183). New York: Psychology Press.

Trommsdorff, G. (2007). Entwicklung im kulturellen Kontext [Development in cultural context]. In G. Trommsdorff & H.-J. Kornadt (Eds.), *Enzyklopädie der Psychologie: Themenbereich C Theorie und Forschung, Serie VII Kulturvergleichende Psychologie. Band 2: Erleben und Handeln im kulturellen Kontext* (pp. 435–519). Göttingen, Germany: Hogrefe.

Trommsdorff, G. (in press). Socialization of self-regulation for achievement in cultural context: A developmental-psychological perspective on the Asian miracle. In U. Kim & Y.-S. Park (Eds.), *Asia's educational miracle: Psychological, social, and cultural perspectives.* New York: Springer Press.

Trommsdorff, G., & Dasen, P. R. (2001). Cross-cultural study of education. In N. J. Smelser & P. B. Baltes (Eds.), *International encyclopedia of the social and behavioral sciences* (pp. 3003–3007). Oxford, UK: Elsevier.

Trommsdorff, G., & Friedlmeier, W. (2004). Zum Verhältnis zwischen Kultur und Individuum aus der Perspektive der kulturvergleichenden Psychologie [The relation between culture and the individual in cross-cultural perspective]. In A. Assmann, U. Gaier, & G. Trommsdorff (Eds.), *Positionen der Kulturanthropologie* (pp. 358–386). Frankfurt am Main, Germany: Suhrkamp.

Trommsdorff, G., & Kornadt, H.-J. (2003). Parent–child relations in cross-cultural perspective. In L. Kuczynski (Ed.), *Handbook of dynamics in parent–child relations* (pp. 271–306). London: Sage Publications.

Trommsdorff, G., & Mayer, B. (2005). Kulturvergleichende Ansätze [Cross-cultural approaches]. In H. Weber & T. Rammsayer (Eds.), *Handbuch der Persönlichkeitspsychologie und Differentiellen Psychologie. Handbuch der Psychologie* [Handbook of Personality Psychology and Psychology of Individual Differences, Handbook of Psychology] (pp. 220–228). Göttingen, Germany: Hogrefe.

Trommsdorff, G., Mayer, B., & Albert, I. (2004). Dimensions of culture in intra-cultural comparisons: Individualism/collectivism and family-related values in three generations. In H. Vinken, J. Soeters, & P. Ester (Eds.), *Comparing cultures: Dimensions of culture in a comparative perspective* (pp. 157–184). Leiden, the Netherlands: Brill Academic Publishers.

Trommsdorff, G., & Nauck, B. (Eds.). (2005). *The value of children in cross-cultural perspective: Case studies from eight societies.* Lengerich, Germany: Pabst Science.

Trommsdorff, G., & Nauck, B. (2006). Demographic changes and parent–child relationships. *Parenting: Science and Practice, 6*(4), 343–360.

Trommsdorff, G., & Rothbaum, F. (2008). Development of emotion regulation in cultural context. In S. Ismer, S. Jung, S. Kronast, C. v. Scheve, & M. Vandekerckhove (Eds.), *Regulating emotions: Social necessity and biological inheritance* (pp. 85–120). London/New York: Blackwell.

Trommsdorff, G., Zheng, G., & Tardif, T. (2002). Value of children and intergenerational relations in cultural context. In P. Boski, F. J. R. van de Vijver, & A. M. Chodynicka (Eds.), *New directions in cross-cultural psychology. Selected papers from the 15th International Conference of the International Association for Cross-Cultural Psychology* (pp. 581–601). Warszawa, Poland: Polish Psychological Association.

Valsiner, J. (1988). Epilogue: Ontogeny of co-construction of culture within socially organized environmental settings. In J. Valsiner (Ed.), *Social co-construction and environmental guidance in development* (pp. 283–297). Westport, CT: Ablex Publishing.

Vermulst, A. A., De Brock, A. J. L. L., & Van Zutphen, R. A. H. (1991). Transmission of parenting across generations. In P. K. Smith (Ed.), *The psychology of grandparenthood* (pp. 100–122). London: Routledge.

Vygotsky, L. S. (1962). *Thought and language* (E. Hanfmann & G. Vakar, Trans.). Cambridge, MA: The MIT Press.

Wang, Q., & Hsueh, Y. (2000). Parent–child interdependence in Chinese families: Change and continuity. In C. Violato, E. Oddone-Paolucci, & M. Genuis (Eds.), *The changing family and child development* (pp. 60–69). Aldershot, UK: Ashgate.

Worthman, C. M. (1999). Epidemiology of human development. In C. Panter-Brick & C. M. Worthman (Eds.), *Hormones, health, and behavior: A socio-ecological and life span perspective* (pp. 47–104). New York: Cambridge University Press.

Wundt, W. (1900–1920). *Völkerpsychologie: Eine Untersuchung der Entwicklungsgesetze von Sprache, Mythus und Sitte* [Völkerpsychologie: An analysis on the developmental laws of language, myths, and customs] (10 Vols.). Leipzig, Germany: Engelmann & Kröner.

Yamagishi, T., Cook, K. S., & Watabe, M. (1998). Uncertainty, trust, and commitment formation in the United States and Japan. *American Journal of Sociology, 104,* 165–194.

Zarit, S. H., & Eggebeen, D. J. (2002). Parent–child relationships in adulthood and later years. In M. H. Bornstein (Ed.), *Handbook of parenting: Vol. 5, Practical issues in parenting* (2nd ed., pp. 135–161). Mahwah, NJ: Erlbaum.

8

Intergenerational Transmission, Social Capital, and Interethnic Contact in Immigrant Families

BERNHARD NAUCK

INTRODUCTION

The extent of intergenerational transmission is seen in the context of migrant families as a major mechanism by which the adolescents' intraethnic and interethnic social contacts are shaped and their social identification is structured. To integrate these family-related aspects of the social incorporation of immigrants, classical theoretical models of assimilation processes have to be extended and modified. The following empirical analyses examine the role of intergenerational transmission in the social incorporation of second-generation adolescents. As a starting point for an adequate modeling of intergenerational transmission processes, a classical action-theoretical model by Esser (1980) was chosen. This theoretical model includes both contextual and individual mechanisms that affect the assimilation process: Opportunity structures, action barriers, and action alternatives are related to the perceptions, cognitions, and evaluations of the individual actor in a simple two-level (i.e., context and individual) process model of cognitive, structural, social, and identificational assimilation. According to this model, personal preconditions of the assimilation process are partly "imported" motivational and cognitive attributes that are confronted with the opportunities provided by the respective context in the receiving society and that "match" a specific social and structural placement as the starting point of an assimilation career. Discrimination is seen in this theoretical model as a major source of action barriers that thus restricts the action alternatives for social integration of minority members. The assimilation process itself is divided into subsequent stages of *cognitive assimilation* (i.e., acquisition of knowledge about the receiving society and its institutional structure, acquisition of language skills as the strategic means to gain access to this knowledge); *structural assimilation*

The data collection for the empirical analysis was funded by the *German Research Council*; the *Federal Ministry of Germany for Family, Elderly, Women and Youth*; and the *Volkswagen Foundation*. Parts of this chapter were published as "Intercultural Contact and Intergenerational Transmission in Immigrant Families" in the *Journal of Cross-Cultural Psychology, 32*, 2001, 175–189.

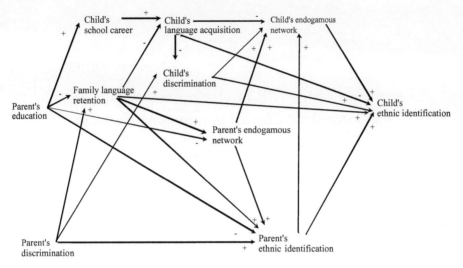

Figure 8.1. Intergenerational transmission in the acculturation process of second-generation migrants.

(i.e., social participation, placement in the occupational structure); *social assimilation* (i.e., informal social contact to members of the receiving society); and, if the precondition of personal integration of the various roles in the receiving society is met, *identification assimilation* (i.e., predominant identification with the receiving society) (Nauck, 1988). This model has its specific merits in that sequences of incorporation of immigrants and interethnic relations are investigated. However, the model also has its limitations because it is not explicit regarding the contextual and the actor's level and because it is strongly related to the individual situation of the first-generation migrants. The assimilation process of subsequent generations – in this case, of second-generation adolescents – can only be specified by replacing the "contextual" starting conditions (i.e., society of origin) with the family-of-origin situation of the adolescents (Nauck, 2001, p. 176). The family of origin is included as an intermediate contextual level, which transmits not only personal preferences and belief systems but also serves as an important locus of social control. It also functions as the major mechanism of initial structural and social placement in the receiving society. To test the theoretical assumptions, the model must be related to empirical constructs. The assumptions about the direction in the relationships between the respective constructs in Figure 8.1 strictly follow assimilation theory.

1. As is usual in survey analysis, no direct measures of the opportunity structure of the receiving society are available; therefore, "feelings of discrimination" by the parents is introduced as the exogenous, contextual variable. It is assumed that feelings of discrimination are strongly

intergenerationally related and transmitted and that discrimination itself decreases social assimilation.

2. The cultural capital of the parents is the other exogenous, individual variable and is measured by the parents' educational level, which is assumed to have a negative effect on the retention of the language spoken in the society of origin in the migrant family and on the endogamy of its social networks (and, thus, a positive effect on social assimilation) and a positive effect on the school career of the child (the child's cultural capital) and the child's cognitive assimilation.

3. The retention of the language of origin in the migrant family is a strong means by which to decrease the opportunities and necessities for the language acquisition of family members, as well as to shape their network structure, and thus it is a strong requisite for the retention of an ethnic identification.

4. Intergenerational transmission results in a strong relationship between the social assimilation of the parents and that of the child (i.e., their exogamous social network composition) and a strong influence of the parents' identificational assimilation on both the child's social assimilation and ethnic identification.

The empirical analysis is based on a dataset from a $5 \times 2 \times 2$ design of parent–child dyads of migrant families; that is, for five different groups of migrant families, generation dyads of the same gender (i.e., mothers and daughters, fathers and sons) were surveyed:

1. The study comprises five different groups of migrant families – namely, Greek, Italian, and Turkish labor migrant families in Germany; German repatriates from Russia in Germany; and Jewish immigrants from Russia in Israel. Each migrant group has its own characteristics that must be considered in the analysis. The groups indicate not only different nationalities and cultures of origin but also different institutional regulations with regard to residence permits, membership of different migration cohorts and waves, and different distributions of sociodemographic characteristics, as follows.

Italians are the migrant nationality in Germany with the smallest cultural distance (Steinbach, 2004), and they are also the oldest migrant cohort. One consequence of Italy being a member of the European Union is that among Italians, there are numerous migrants with long periods of residence as well as those who shift frequently between their society of origin and Germany.

Greeks have the second smallest cultural distance and are the second oldest migrant cohort. However, only since the end of the 1980s has Greece had the same membership status in the European Union as Italy. Limitations in residential status made shifting between Greece and Germany impossible for a long time, resulting in comparatively long residential periods in Germany. Recently, a larger proportion of Greek migrant workers adopted the Italian commuting pattern.

Turks are regularly looked on as the migrant-worker nationality with the greatest cultural distance from Germans, and they constitute the last signifi-cant wave of migrant workers in Germany. They are, by far, the largest migrant minority group in Germany; because of their number, in many urban areas they meet the structural preconditions for ethnic segregation and for the institu-tional completion of a minority subculture. At the same time, Turks differ from Italians and Greeks with respect to their residential status. Limitations in resi-dential status prevent commuting between the society of origin and Germany but do provide (together with the gap between the two societies' welfare situa-tion) ongoing incentives for chain-migration marriage and family reunification. The ongoing incorporation of earlier migrated families is thus masked by the coinciding influx of new waves of migrants.

German repatriates from Russia are the newest group of immigrants in Germany, with a first significant wave in the 1980s and an enormous increase after the breakup of the Soviet Union. They immediately receive German citi-zenship; take part in special, extensive integration programs; and fully benefit from the German social welfare system. Their legal status is based on the con-cept of having German ancestry and maintaining German cultural heritage. This produces a consensual fiction of "no cultural distance." In any case, the migration to Germany is usually a final one because remigration is typically not considered a realistic option. Administrative regulations have produced high residential segregation of German repatriates, at least at the beginning of their stay in Germany. Currently, the repatriates seem to show a tendency toward social closure and "ethnic" segregation (Steinbach, 2001).

The situation of *Russian immigrants in Israel* is comparable to that of the German repatriates. Having already received a first, significant wave of Russian Jews in the early 1970s, Israel faced an increase of about 10% of its population due to the enormous immigration after the breakup of the Soviet Union. They are full citizens of the Israeli state from the very beginning, take part in even more extensive "absorption" programs, and fully benefit from the comparatively extensive welfare system. Their legal status is based not on the *jus sanguinis*, as in the German repatriate case, but rather on their believing in the Jewish religion, which also establishes a consensual fiction of no cultural distance to other members of the Israeli state. The administrative regulations in Israel assume the absorption of these immigrants into the receiving society as soon as possible. The sheer number of the newest immigrant wave, together with predominant "push" factors of migration motivation, may have created the preconditions for a group consciousness of being different and, as in the German repatriate case, for "ethnic" segregation (Steinbach & Nauck, 2000).

The study design, therefore, contrasts two significantly different groups of immigrant families: the classic migrant-worker nationalities with the German repatriates and the Jewish emigrants to Israel, both stemming from Russia. The variations between the migrant groups in terms of human capital and acculturation strategies allow the testing of assumptions about the level and direction of change in ethnic identification and how it is transmitted intergenerationally.

2. The parent–child dyads in each migrant family consist of mother–daughter or father–son pairs (from different families). In contrast to the conventional cohort analyses of migration research, in which aggregate findings of separate immigrant generations are compared, this analysis is explicitly based on transmission processes within parent–child dyads of migrant families. The child generation includes children attending grades 7 through 9 of different school tracks; they are thus at the stage of preparing for the transition to the labor force or to college. The parents in these families are almost exclusively migrants of the first generation, whereas some of the groups of juveniles represent the second generation. Among the parents, 92.6% of the Greeks, 95.6% of the Italians, 96.7% of the German repatriates, and 100% of the Turks and the Russian Israelis were born in the society of origin; among the youths, 70.9% of the Italians, 71.5% of the Greeks, and 79.8% of the Turks were born in Germany, but only 1.1% of the German repatriates and none of the Russian Israelis were born in the receiving society.

3. The opportunity structure varies twofold in this design. With regard to the immigrant families from Russia, it varies according to the institutional structure of the receiving societies of Israel and Germany. On a second level, it varies according to the socioecological context within the respective society. Approximately half of the respondents live in highly urbanized contexts with a comparatively high population density with the same national origin and a correspondingly high opportunity for the institutional completion of an ethnic colony. The other half consists of respondents from a small-town context, which generally implies a higher standard of living among immigrant families, a lower density of migrant population, and thus little opportunity for the establishment of ethnic colonies.

Every cell of this design contains approximately 100 persons; specifically, the study consists of 397 interviews with Greek parent–child dyads, 406 Italian and 405 Turkish immigrants, 427 German repatriates, and 448 Russian Israelis ($N = 2,083$). The data collection took place between 1990 and 1992 for the Turkish families, between 1996 and 1997 for the Greeks and Italians, and between 1998 and 1999 for the German repatriates and Russian Israelis. The oral interviews were conducted by means of standardized questionnaires, which were available in the language of the society of origin (i.e., Greek, Italian, Turkish, and Russian) and in German or Hebrew, respectively, according to the language preference of the respondent. Parents and children were interviewed separately. The following variables were used in the empirical analysis.

Parents' education is based on statements about levels of schooling of the parents in the country of origin. Following the approach of Blossfeld and Jaenichen (1992), education is operationalized as a ratio-scaled variable according to the necessary years of schooling for the corresponding degree in the respective country; the values for the years of schooling of both parents are summed.

Family-language retention is based on a score of parents' and children's answers about whether the language of origin is the main communication language between parents and children and between brothers and sisters.

The *child's school career* is operationalized as the completion of stages in the school track system, including attendance of a kindergarten in the receiving society, attendance of special preparatory classes for foreign pupils, and secondary school tracks. The higher the score, the more complete the school career of the corresponding child in the highest school track of the receiving society.

The *child's language acquisition* is based on the subjective, ordinal-scaled statements of the child about his or her ability to understand, speak, read, and write the language of the receiving society.

The *parents' feelings of being discriminated against (parents' discrimination)* and the corresponding *child's discrimination* are based on four indicators for the parents (feeling *not at all* to *very strongly* discriminated against at work, in the neighborhood, when shopping, and by authorities) and three corresponding indicators for the children (at school, in the neighborhood, and when shopping).

The *parents' ethnic identification* and the *child's ethnic identification* are variables based on two ordinal-scaled indicators each, concerning the choice of daughters/sons-in-law (parents') or choice of a spouse (child's), and concerning the choice of first names for their grandchildren or children. Ethnic identification is thus measured as a preference for a son/daughter-in-law or a spouse from one's own national/migrant group and as a preference for first names related to the culture of origin.

Additionally, the empirical analysis is based on data about ego-centered social networks. These data are drawn from a network generator for both generations of migrants. This generator allows the respondent to list 20 names of persons with whom he or she has daily relationships (i.e., has a close personal relationship with, discusses important personal problems with, spends his or her spare time with, to whom he or she gives help, and from whom he or she receives help). Altogether, 26,017 network members are listed (12,704 by parents and 13,313 by their children).

The *network size* indicates the number of persons named by the respective respondent concerning the areas of activity within the network generator. The *spatial availability* indicates the proportion of network members within walking distance to the respondent. The contact frequency indicates the proportion of network members with at least weekly contact.

The *multiplexity* of the network is measured "close to theory" according to the basic assumptions of Coleman (1988, 1990) about social capital, according to which social capital is highest in those relationships, that are characterized by the highest possible spatial *availability*, by the highest frequency of *social contacts*, by the variety of *activities* (doing different things with the same person), and by the network *density* (network members not only interact with the respondent but maintain dense relationships among themselves). According to this approach, social capital consists of a product – the multiplication of the discussed dimensions of network properties. The dimensions are assessed in the following way: A named person is classified as being available if he or she is living in the immediate neighborhood; frequent contact is given, if there exists at least a weekly interaction; complex activities are taken as given, if with this person at least one expressive activity (e.g., a close personal bond, sharing meals, spending spare time together) and at least one instrumental activity (e.g., discussing personal things, giving or receiving help) are exercised; and density is given, if the network member is a member of the family or kin. Accordingly, network multiplexity consists of the sum of the product of "availability," "contacts," "activities," and "kinship membership" across all named network members.

The *kinship-centeredness* is measured by the proportion of persons belonging to the kinship of the respondent, including his or her family.

The *ethnic homogamy* of the network structure, on which the analysis focuses, is measured by the proportion of persons belonging to the same nationality (in the case of Greeks, Italians, and Turks) or by having the same origin (in the case of the German repatriates and the Russian Israelis).

The multivariate empirical models are specified as structural equation models with latent variables; the estimates are based on the criteria of maximum likelihood. The Goodness-of-Fit Index (GFI), the Adjusted Goodness-of-Fit Index (AGFI), and the Root Mean Square Residual (RMR) are reported for each empirical model. To achieve maximum comparability, the empirical models for all groups have the same structure.

1.0. EMPIRICAL RESULTS

1.1. Intergenerational Transmission of Cultural Capital and Ethnic Identification

In the first step, level differences among immigrant nationalities, generations, and gender are investigated, together with bivariate measures for intergenerational transmission. The percentages in the results of Table 8.1 are reduced to one significant category; the correlations, however, are based on the full range of the variables – in the case of language acquisition and retention and in the case of discrimination, additive indices of several single indicators are used.

The *educational level* (and thus the cultural capital that may be invested in the migration process) varies considerably between the included immigrant groups. Whereas almost all of the Jewish immigrants from Russia in Israel and approximately half of the German repatriate parents have at least a high school degree, this is the case for less than a quarter of the migrant-worker parents, with the highest schooling for the Turkish fathers and the lowest for the Greek

Table 8.1. *Transmission of cultural capital and ethnic identification in Italian (I), Greek (G), and Turkish (T) migrant families in Germany; German repatriate families (R); and Jewish repatriates from Russia in Israel (J)*

| | | Percentage | | | | Correlations | |
		Father	Mother	Son	Daughter	Father–Son	Mother–Daughter
Educational degree	I	20.4	23.4	21.4	17.0	.35	.32
(parents: secondary-school	G	20.5	15.7	20.5	13.7	.40	.07
degree or more; children:	T	33.2	20.0	20.3	18.0	.05	.28
in the highest school track)	R	44.2	52.4	14.0	17.5	.16	.30
	J	99.6	98.1	21.9	33.8	.03	.08
Family-language retention in	I	50.0	59.0	26.7	28.0	.56	.50
the communication between	G	56.5	56.9	34.0	27.9	.58	.55
parents and children (parents'	T	48.8	51.5	9.3	9.0	.22	.35
columns) and between	R	40.5	37.7	37.7	28.8	.76	.69
brothers and sisters	J	91.6	90.3	73.2	64.7	.40	.28
(children's columns)							
Language acquisition	I	19.9	19.5	76.2	81.0	.24	.15
(percentage speaking the	G	25.0	16.2	75.0	74.6	.38	.35
language of the receiving	T	4.4	2.0	53.7	60.0	.12	.28
society "very well")	R	19.1	17.5	50.2	53.3	.59	.49
	J	2.1	8.2	42.7	56.0	.36	.43
Children's language retention	I			33.5	33.9		
(percentage speaking the	G			38.0	41.6		
language of the society of	T			48.8	28.5		
origin "very well")	R			44.2	52.4		
	J			44.4	44.7		
Feelings of discrimination	I	10.7	11.0	.5	2.0	.53	.55
(percentage feeling "strongly"	G	10.5	11.7	1.5	1.5	.58	.57
discriminated in two or more	T	15.1	5.5	4.9	5.5	.19	.11
areas)	R	6.0	5.2	3.7	4.2	.63	.54
	J	4.2	4.3	2.9	2.4	.16	.21
Marriage endogamy	I	2.4	5.5	4.4	3.5	.34	.48
(percentage "never" accepting	G	4.0	9.1	9.0	6.1	.40	.46
a native-born son/daughter-in-	T	25.4	46.5	30.7	46.0	.30	.28
law or a native-born spouse,	R	4.2	3.3	5.6	6.2	.37	.29
respectively)	J	27.4	18.3	20.3	16.7	.26	.16
Return plans	I	13.1	12.5	6.3	8.0	.20	.17
(percentage planning to	G	22.0	27.9	13.0	10.2	.41	.28
return)	T	31.2	28.0	16.1	22.5	.16	.28
	R	10.8	11.0	.9	.0	*	*
	J	13.0	11.9	.4	.5	*	*

mothers among them; there is no difference in the level of education between the first and second generations of the Italian, Greek, and Turkish migrant families. The newly arrived repatriates in Germany and Israel show a significant gap in educational level. The young repatriates have an educational level at least as low as that of the classical migrant worker in Germany. In Israel, only about 22% of the migrant boys and 34% of the migrant girls are in the highest school track as compared to nearly 100% of their parents having graduated from high school. Accordingly, the intergenerational transmission is lowest in the most recently arrived Israeli group and highest in the first arrived Italian group.

A major mechanism for *ethnic-language retention* is related to whether this language is used in the family of origin for communication between parents and children and among siblings. Table 8.1 shows the percentages of families in which both parents and children consistently report that the language of the society of origin is used. Slightly more than half of the immigrant parents in Germany use solely the Italian, Greek, Turkish, or Russian language when speaking with their children, whereas more than 90% of the Russian immigrants in Israel use their ethnic language. Language retention is slightly higher in the mother–daughter dyads in the Italian, Greek, and Turkish families, and slightly higher in the father–son dyads in the repatriate families in both Germany and Israel. In all immigrant groups, language retention is lower in the communication between brothers and sisters as compared to the communication between parents and children. The contrast is highest in Turkish migrant families and lowest in German repatriate families. Accordingly, the intergenerational transmission of the family-language retention is quite high in the German repatriate families (and in Italian and Greek immigrant families) and low in the Turkish families (and in the Russian Jewish families). The level of family-language retention is not directly related to the level of the children's *mastery of the language of the society of origin* (i.e., of their parents); although three quarters of the Russian Jewish youngsters report using Russian for communication with their brothers and sisters, less than 50% report speaking this language "very well." The highest language losses are reported by the Turkish girls: less than one third claim to speak Turkish "very well" (but about 50% of the Turkish boys state that they do!). Both the intergenerational differences in the family-language retention and the children's mastery of the language of their parents show the difficulty of sustaining the culture of origin in the majority of immigrant families. Accordingly, neither "segregation" nor "integration" seems to be the major pathway of acculturation but rather "assimilation" and – perhaps – "marginalization." Which one of these two is the most probable depends on the acquisition of the language of the receiving society. It is not surprising that in all immigrant groups, the children's generation masters the language much better than their parents. However, both groups of parents – the Turkish parents in Germany and the Russian Jews in Israel – show relatively low levels of language acquisition. Both groups may be probable candidates for ethnic segregation but, due to the differences in the educational level, perhaps for different reasons. However, in the next generation, these differences have nearly disappeared and the rank order of the host-language mastery of the second generation merely mirrors the historical immigrant waves, with the Italians ranking first, the Greeks second, the Turks third, and the repatriates in both countries last, but with the most visible intergenerational transmission effect.

Strong intergenerational differences in the *feelings of discrimination* are reported: First-generation immigrant parents report discrimination to a significantly higher degree than their children. The most discrimination felt was reported by Turkish fathers (i.e., 15% report feeling "strongly" discriminated against in at least two of the areas of work, housing, shops, and authorities); the lowest discrimination was reported by Russian Jews in Israel. The immigrant groups differ considerably according to the intergenerational transmission of feelings of being discriminated against: The transmission effect is consistently high for both genders in the Italian, Greek, and German repatriate families, and it is low in the Turkish and Russian Jewish families. This may indicate a sharper separation of the living spheres of the generations in these families.

More active indicators for segregation (or, more precisely, nonassimilation) are those referring to *marriage endogamy* and *plans to return*. Marriage endogamy may be related to the creation of a more or less stable minority subculture, whereas plans to return indicate at least a reason not to invest too much in a permanent stay in the receiving society. The tendency toward marriage endogamy is highest in the Turkish families, especially in the female dyad, and second highest in the Russian Jewish families in Israel; this tendency is quite low in the Italian and Greek families and there is no difference in the German repatriates. In all five migrant groups, the intergenerational transmission of attitudes toward marriage endogamy is relatively high in both gender dyads. Plans to return differ again according to the migrant generation, being considerably higher in the first generation as compared to the second but on different group-specific levels. In the repatriate families in Germany and Israel, plans to return are practically absent; in the second generation, they are literally zero. At approximately 13%, the percentages for the Italian parents are only slightly higher than for the German repatriate parents. Plans to return are more pronounced in the Greek first generation, especially in the Turkish families, in which approximately 30% of the parents and 20% of the children report plans to return.

In general, the results show a clear intergenerational trend toward more cultural contact and less segregation in second-generation immigrants. However, these level differences are linked, as shown by the comparatively high correlations between the attitudes and behavior of both generations in the family dyads (Nauck, 1997). This transmission effect is higher in migrant families as compared to nonmigrant families and indicates a highly synchronized intergenerational pattern of coping with the migrant situation. This effect seems to be unrelated to the cultural capital available in the family: The transmission of educational success is the lowest among all investigated indicators (Nauck, Diefenbach, & Petri, 1998). It remains an open empirical question whether the mechanisms of the acculturation process are the same in all immigrant groups. The analysis of the level differences already revealed two extreme groups: The Turkish immigrant families in Germany on the one hand and the Jewish Russian families in Israel on the other. Both groups show comparatively high segregation tendencies: Both groups of parents have relatively poor knowledge of the language of the respective receiving society and thus a high tendency to use the language of origin for communication in the family, and both groups show the highest tendency toward marriage endogamy. However, whereas this is related to feelings of discrimination and to decisive plans to return in the case of the Turkish families, it seems also to be related to extremely high levels of education, lowest feelings of discrimination, and absence of plans to return in the case of the Russian Jews. This leads to the next research question: whether the same segregation behavior may have totally different causes and consequences.

1.2. Transmission of Network Structures in Migrant Families

Intergenerational transmission of the social relations of migrant family members can be analyzed with the help of similarity measures regarding the network characteristics of the parent and child generation. Table 8.2 shows the empirical findings for the gender-specific parent–child dyads in the five migrant groups regarding level differences in the network characteristics between generations (i.e., means) and the intergenerational similarities (i.e., correlations).

Comparing the two generations regarding the number of network members (i.e., *network size*), intergenerational transmission processes are quite strong: The more extended the network of the parents, the more extended it is for the child's generation. The network size in the male dyad is larger than in the female dyad in the Italian, Greek, and Turkish families, whereas the opposite is the case in the repatriate families from Russia, in both Germany and Israel. This result may be related to the patrilineal versus matrilineal organization of the families in the respective cultures, giving those family members more (extrafamilial) relationships on whose gender the lineage is centered.

In general, the *spatial availability* of and the *contact frequency* with network members is quite high. This is not specific to immigrant families but rather a general characteristic of relationships recalled in a network generator: Approximately 90% of the network members in all groups, in both generations and genders, are those with whom contacts are maintained at least on a weekly basis. This ceiling effect makes it almost impossible to calculate intergenerational transmission effects. Even the spatial availability is relatively high, although it is lower than in nonmigrant families (Nauck & Kohlmann, 1999). However, the percentage of network members who do not live in the neighborhood is consistently lower in Turkish migrant families than in all other groups. This may

Table 8.2. *Transmission of network characteristics in Italian (I), Greek (G), and Turkish (T) migrant families in Germany; German repatriate families (R); and Jewish repatriates from Russia in Israel (J)*

			Means			Correlations	
						Father–	Mother–
		Father	Mother	Son	Daughter	Son	Daughter
Network Size	I	5.73	5.52	5.63	5.60	.70	.64
	G	6.39	5.69	6.18	5.83	.61	.65
	T	7.48	6.46	7.86	6.58	.39	.41
	R	6.13	6.28	5.99	6.13	.73	.76
	J	3.72	3.69	4.15	4.22	.49	.15
Spatial Availability	I	.87	.87	.92	.91	.50	.45
(proportion of network	G	.84	.88	.88	.92	.51	.40
members within walking	T	.69	.78	.83	.84	.49	.34
distance)	R	.85	.83	.89	.87	.47	.68
	J	.80	.72	.86	.77	.32	.31
Contact Frequency	I	.92	.91	.96	.96	.38	.36
(proportion of network	G	.91	.92	.96	.97	.38	.19
members with at least	T	.88	.86	.99	.94	(−.04)	.17
weekly contact)	R	.96	.94	.99	.97	(.12)	.41
	J	.91	.89	.93	.86	.16	.23
Kinship-Centeredness	I	.85	.86	.69	.71	.34	.47
(proportion of kinship	G	.82	.86	.66	.67	.45	.51
within the network)	T	.87	.95	.67	.76	.20	.25
	R	.88	.87	.71	.70	.37	.57
	J	.81	.78	.61	.53	.68	.46
Social Capital	I	21.7	24.4	24.5	23.8	.52	.46
(sum-score of multiplex	G	23.0	25.7	25.6	24.9	.55	.48
network relationships)	T	30.6	28.8	33.4	23.0	.60	.41
	R	25.0	29.7	25.8	24.8	.54	.60
	J	18.0	17.7	16.3	15.9	.36	.37
Intraethnic Network	I	.88	.90	.75	.78	.58	.45
(proportion of network	G	.88	.91	.75	.77	.60	.59
members belonging to	T	.98	.97	.90	.91	.26	.11
their own ethnic/migrant	R	.94	.93	.83	.82	.33	.48
group)	J	.93	.90	.91	.84	.04	.25

indicate that they maintain relationships much more intensively with network members still living in the society of origin or in other places in a migrant situation. This finding thus supports the comparatively strong ethnic identification of Turkish migrant families, which makes them more likely to maintain "costly" relationships over long distances.

The high *proportion of kinship members* in the network of migrant families is both an effect of chain-migration, through which within a short period extended kinship relationships are reconstituted in the immigrant context, and of maintaining relationships within the society of origin, mainly within the kinship context. More than approximately 80% of the networks of parents in all immigrant groups consists of relatives. This proportion drops consistently to approximately two thirds for the child generation, but it is not clear whether this is an effect of assimilation or of the specific life stage (i.e., whether this effect will be stable over the life course or whether there will be a re-increase of the proportion of kinship members in later life stages [after marriage]). The kinship-centeredness of the social network is highest in German repatriate families and especially in Turkish migrant families, and it is extreme in the female dyad within this group: 95% of the network of Turkish mothers is relatives (and 76% of the network of Turkish immigrant girls). This clearly indicates that the action space of most of the Turkish females in the immigration context is closely related to the availability of an extended kinship system, especially with regard to social relationships with the opposite sex (Nauck & Kohlmann, 1999).

In general, the proportion of network members who belong to the same ethnic or migrant group (*intraethnic network*) is extremely high: More than 90% of the networks of immigrant parents and more than 75% of the networks of immigrant youth are intraethnic. However, this result should not be overestimated because its significance is only revealed in relation to proportion of kinship members. In general, the proportion of intraethnic networks being not kinship relationships is relatively small, especially in the parents' generation: Only about 5% of the intraethnic network of Italian, Greek, and German repatriate parents and only about 10% of their children's intraethnic networks are not relatives. Therefore, generally speaking, the social relationships of immigrants are shaped not along ethnic but rather along kinship lines. However, there are variations: 11% of the network members of Turkish fathers in Germany (but only 2% of Turkish mothers) and 12% of those of Russian Jewish parents in Israel are from the same group of origin but are not kinship members. Consistently, the proportion of nonkin among the intraethnic network increases for their children: 23% of the network of Turkish boys (but only 15% of Turkish girls) and approximately 30% of second-generation Russian Jews in Israel maintain nonkin-based intraethnic relationships. Clearly, the exception of the Turkish female dyad can be explained by ceiling effects and not by fundamental differences. Therefore, the general conclusion is that these two groups, which have already shown a high segregation tendency with respect to language use and ethnic identification, also show a much higher tendency toward a nonkinship-based intraethnic network and have the lowest proportion of members of the receiving society within their network. The highest proportion of interethnic network membership is found in Italian and Greek families, being already significantly higher in the first generation but with a further increase to approximately 25% in second-generation youth. German repatriates, on the other hand, have a network structure that is nearly as strictly ethnically closed as that of the Russian Jews or the Turkish migrants.

Results concerning the differences in the *social capital* are based on the assumption that social capital is created in multiplex, interrelated, frequent, close relationships. Thus, level differences in social capital of the family members in the five migrant groups ultimately answer the question of the fundamental differences between the most segregated groups of Turkish immigrants in Germany and of Russian Jews in Israel, being related to feelings of discrimination and decisive plans to return in the case of the Turkish families, and to extremely high levels of education, lowest feelings of discrimination, and absence of plans to return in the case of the Russian Jews. Whereas Turkish family members in Germany consistently have the highest social capital, Russian Jews in Israel consistently have the lowest, with both groups being significantly different from the "average" of the remaining Italians, Greeks, and German repatriates. These differences in social capital thus seem to be related to fundamentally different strategies of acculturation: Whereas the Turkish families in Germany employ a more collectivistic strategy mainly making use of the available social capital, the Russian Jewish families rely on a more individualistic strategy mainly making use of the available high cultural capital and having the smallest network size of all groups. Accordingly, intergenerational transmission is comparatively high in the "collectivistic" case of Turkish migrant families and relatively low in the "individualistic" case of Russian Jews.

But why do both strategies result in high segregation tendencies? A necessary precondition is, of course, the sheer number of the minority members that has to be met and which makes segregation much easier for Russian Jews and Turks as compared to Italians, Greeks, and German repatriates. It is hypothesized that a second precondition is the respective relationship with the majority and the resulting opportunity structure: Segregation tendencies increase with the relative closure of the receiving society toward the immigrant population. This is clearly the case, to a certain extent, for the Turkish population in Germany: They are most likely to show feelings of discrimination – and their defensive tendency (supported by evolutionarily successful "collectivistic" cultural patterns from the society of origin) to rely more on social than cultural capital may even enforce the social closure between the majority and minority. The situation for Russian Jews in Israel is quite different: Their cultural capital is equivalent or superior to the receiving society and – as the lack of feelings of discrimination indicates – a social closure might be absent. However, gains from the investment of the highly available cultural capital into assimilation may not be as salient as, for example, it is in the case for the Italians, Greeks, and German repatriates. Rather, investment in "weak ties" within one's own group of origin with equally highly specialized skills and abilities may be as profitable and, indeed, not entail any further need for assimilative efforts. Segregation increases if the opportunity structure of the receiving society either *does not* or *cannot* offer something to immigrants.

1.3. A Multivariate Empirical Test of the Theoretical Model

It is assumed that variations in the extent of intergenerational transmission of network characteristics will lead to different outcomes in the acculturation of the second generation. According to Coleman's thesis (1988), direct effects of social control proceed from overlapping close multiplex networks in both generations. Accordingly, it should be concluded that the transmission of segregation tendencies is higher in families with high social capital and low in families with low social capital (and high cultural capital instead). In the following discussion, an empirical test of these assumptions is conducted in two steps. First, results are provided for the entire sample (i.e., including Italians, Greeks, Turks, German repatriates, and Russian Israelis) (Table 8.3). Second, the specified micro model of intergenerational transmission is compared for the respective immigrant groups, thereby varying the macro differences of group-related differences in cultural and social capital and the opportunity structures of the receiving context.

Results from the structural equation model of the total population of migrant families already have important implications for the theoretical discussion. First, the results confirm many of the basic assumptions of assimilation theory as formulated in the basic model. Discrimination has a weak yet positive effect on language retention in migrant families, which, in turn, significantly decreases the child's acquisition of the language of the receiving society; the child's school career has the expected positive effect on language learning. The higher the educational level of the parents, the lower is the proportion of intraethnic members in their network; family-language retention instead increases the proportion of intraethnic network members. The results clearly show the "strategic" effect of family-language retention on the acculturation process because it is strongly related to the parents' ethnic identification ($b = .41$). The acquisition of the language of the receiving society increases and perceived discrimination decreases the proportion of interethnic members in the network of migrant youth. The proportion of intraethnic network members has the expected positive effect on ethnic identification, both for parents and their adolescent children.

Second, intergenerational transmission has a strong effect on the acculturation process in migrant families. The more parents feel discriminated against in the receiving society, the more their children of the same gender do ($b = .54$); the higher the proportion of intraethnic members in the networks of the parents, the higher it is in the networks of their children ($b = .31$). Especially strong is the transmission of ethnic identification between parents and children of the same gender ($b = .74$).

Third, two findings do not support the basic assumptions. (1) There is no direct transmission of cultural capital between generations. This result replicates previous findings from other datasets on immigrants in Germany (Nauck,

Table 8.3. *Results of structural equation modeling of intergenerational transmission in the acculturation process of second-generation migrants*

	Total Sample	Migrant Groups				
		Italians in Germany	Greeks in Germany	Turks in Germany	German Repatriates	Russian Israelis
RMR	.057	.067	.064	.054	.052	.058
GFI	.92	.89	.87	.93	.88	.92
AGFI	.89	.84	.82	.90	.83	.89
Paths						
Child's school career → Child's host-language acquisition	.20[a]	.33	.17	.26	.11	.04
Parents' education → Child's school career	.01	.26	.10	.29	.37	.13
Parents' education → Family-language retention	.38	−.21	−.04	−.29	.21	.22
Parents' education → Parents' endogamous network	−.14	−.19	−.22	−.05	−.15	−.06
Parents' education → Parents' ethnic identification	.03	−.13	−.14	−.51	.02	−.26
Parents' discrimination → Family-language retention	.06	.10	.00	.05	.20	−.01
Parents' discrimination → Child's discrimination	.54	.66	.67	.25	.73	.30
Parents' discrimination → Parents' ethnic identification	.04	.19	.17	.06	.23	.09
Family-language retention → Child's host-language acquisition	−.24	−.06	−.08	−.35	−.32	−.27

Family-language retention → Child's ethnic identification	−.05	.23	−.05	.04	.18	.21
Family-language retention → Parents' endogamous network	.11	.24	.19	.05	.11	.07
Family-language retention → Parents' ethnic identification	.41	.52	.39	.32	.26	.20
Child's host-language acquisition → Child's endogamous network	−.11	−.07	−.11	−.12	−.30	.00
Child's host-language acquisition → Child's discrimination	−.20	−.14	−.16	−.25	−.24	−.07
Child's host-language acquisition → Child's ethnic identification	−.24	−.21	−.30	−.25	−.16	−.25
Child's discrimination → Child's endogamous network	.05	.08	.07	.14	−.05	.13
Child's discrimination → Child's ethnic identification	.02	.05	−.14	.01	−.22	.20
Child's endogamous network → Child's ethnic identification	.13	.17	.18	.25	.13	.10
Parents' endogamous network → Parents' ethnic identification	.21	.23	.33	.06	.00	.13
Parents' endogamous network → Child's endogamous network	.31	.42	.47	.10	.38	.16
Parents' ethnic identification → Child's endogamous network	.31	.29	.26	.50	.09	.05
Parents' ethnic identification → Child's ethnic identification	.74	.89	.61	.49	.72	.24

RMR, root mean square residual; GFI, Goodness-of-Fit Index; AGFI, Adjusted Goodness-of-Fit Index.

Diefenbach, & Petri, 1998), in which no correlations were found between the educational level of the parents and the school success of their children in migrant families, whereas the effect is quite strong in the native German reference population. (2) There is a weak but positive relationship between the level of education and the parents' ethnic identification and a quite strong positive effect of the parents' educational level on family-language retention ($b = .38$). This latter finding clearly contradicts classical assimilation theory, according to which those immigrants with the highest individual opportunities should assimilate fastest.

Results for the subsample of Italian migrant families in Germany fit the general assumption of assimilation theory much better than results for the total sample. There is a positive effect of transmission of cultural capital between parents and children ($b = .26$); for example, for the "oldest" immigrant group, the social placement of the children is already related to the educational level of the parents. The level of education is negatively related to the ethnic identification of the parents ($b = -.13$). Family-language retention is highest in those families with low cultural resources ($b = -.21$), as assimilation theory would predict. In addition, the results show that compared with the total sample, the institutional effect of schooling on the children's language acquisition is much higher ($b = .33$) than the effect of the family's language retention ($b = -.06$), but language retention increases its direct effect on the child's ethnic identification ($b = .23$). Finally, the effect of the parents' feelings of discrimination on their ethnic identification is increased ($b = .19$). However, important for the evaluation of the general model is that the mechanisms of intergenerational transmission are strong in the acculturation of the second generation in this relatively well-established migrant group.

Results for the subsample of Greek migrant families in Germany basically go in the same direction as those for the Italians. The results, again, support assimilation theory, but the empirical relationships among the variables are already significantly weaker. One finding that does not confirm assimilation theory is that the child's ethnic identification is decreased by discrimination ($b = -.14$). As for the Italian families, the effects of intergenerational transmission within the model remain very strong, thus confirming the theoretical model in this regard.

Because practically all Turkish families in Germany (especially the parents' generation) have entirely intraethnic social networks (Nauck, Kohlmann, & Diefenbach, 1997), the estimates related to these two variables drop drastically, which leads to a total underestimation of close networks (and intergenerational transmission related to it) for this migrant group. Nevertheless, the remaining empirical results support assimilation theory at least as strongly as the results for the Italian subsample. Finally, the indirect effect of the parents' cultural resources on the children's language acquisition is strengthened in both directions via schooling success and family-language retention. Compared to Italian and Greek migrant families, the extent of intergenerational transmission in Turkish migrant families is obviously decreased yet still strong. This difference is caused by higher intergenerational differences in the level of assimilation in Turkish migrant families in Germany than those in Italian or Greek families (Nauck, 1997).

Results for the German repatriate families differ from those of the migrant families in some respects. Most important, there is a significant positive relationship between the parents' education and retention of the Russian language in the family ($b = .21$), which, in turn, decreases the child's language acquisition quite strongly ($b = -.32$). On the other hand, the educational level has only an indirect effect on the parents' ethnic identification via family-language retention ($b = .26$); it is also influenced by the parents' feelings of discrimination ($b = .23$) but not by the ethnic composition of the parents' network. The second significant deviance from the assimilation model is the relationship between the child's feelings of being discriminated against and his or her ethnic identification. As with the Greek families, ethnic identification of the children decreases when they feel they are discriminated against. In general, German repatriate families are no exception from the general result that intergenerational transmission is the most important effect in the acculturation process: The more the parents feel discriminated against, the more their children do ($b = .73$); the higher the parents' ethnic identification, the higher their children's ($b = .72$). The weaker relationship between their ethnic network structure ($b = .38$) again may be due to a lack of variance because of the high proportion of intraethnic network members, especially in the parents' generation.

Another quite different picture is provided by results for the Russian Jewish immigrant families in Israel. As with the German repatriate families, the parents' education positively influences the retention of the Russian language ($b = .22$), which itself significantly decreases the child's host-language acquisition ($b = -.27$), whereas the institutional effect of schooling (and the parents' transmission of cultural capital via school success) is rather small. Low levels of discrimination, small network sizes, and generally high proportions of network members who are immigrants from Russia also lead to the effect that neither discrimination nor network structure has the same strong effects on the acculturation process. Intergenerational transmission processes are also less strong in this empirical model (i.e., .30 for discrimination, .16 for network composition, and .24 for ethnic identification), albeit still significant.

2.0. DISCUSSION

The empirical results of this comparative study on the acculturation process in immigrant families of different origin and in different immigrant contexts have revealed some important insights.

There are systematic variations between the respective immigrant groups and generations with regard to the antecedent conditions – namely, the available cultural capital to be invested in the acculturation process (economic capital is of no importance for these groups because they normally enter the immigrant context without any economic capital) and the respective opportunity structure of the receiving society.

There are systematic variations between members of the parents' and children's generation, but the two are linked together through intergenerational transmission processes to a varying degree according to family cultures and acculturation strategies. These level differences lead to different outcomes with regard to social assimilation – namely, the ethnic composition of the individual networks in the two generations – and to identificational assimilation.

The empirical results have also revealed that there are systematic variations in the direction and intensity of the relationships among the variables in the empirical models. The first category of results can easily be explained by assimilation theory with varying group levels of resources and opportunity structures in different historical or geographic contexts; the second category can be explained if basic assumptions about cultural differences among the respective immigrant groups are added. The latter class of results, on the other hand, is quite difficult to explain and raises serious questions challenging assimilation theory in general. Why do some immigrant groups undergo cultural retention even though discrimination is clearly lacking and the immigrants have all the cultural means to assimilate, as it is the case for the German repatriates and the Russian Israelis? Why does high cultural capital lead predominantly to fast assimilation with regard to language acquisition in some cases (e.g., in Turkish and Italian families in Germany) but to a high family-language retention in others (e.g., in German repatriate and Russian Israeli families)? Why do feelings of being discriminated against lead to a decrease of ethnic identification in some groups like Turkish parents and Greek and German repatriate youths but to an increase in other groups or generations?

A possible solution may be to look for systematic variations in the available social capital of migrant families, which is comparatively high in both generations of Turkish migrant families and comparatively low in Russian Israeli families. This seems to suggest that those immigrant families with low cultural capital and low opportunities offered by the receiving society try to compensate for them with the nurtured social capital. They rely on the offers from close, multiplex relationships and, consequently, end up in a comparatively segregated, return-oriented milieu. This is the case for those Turkish families that do not follow the assimilation or integration track like other Turkish families with higher cultural capital, which invest it either solely in the receiving society or – in the rare case of extremely high resources – in both the receiving and the return context. On the other hand, Russian Israeli families (and Greek families in Germany) seem to have great difficulty in transferring their (high) cultural capital to their offspring; that is, assimilation and investment in relationships with the receiving society do not pay off for them and remain low. This is all the more true when the families' cultural capital is higher. Accordingly, language retention is highest in those Russian Israeli families with the highest cultural capital.

The empirical analysis has shown clearly the strong extent to which processes of intergenerational social placement and acculturation processes are knitted together and the strong importance that (generalized) cultural capital has on the process: The educational level of the parents has a strong, far-reaching influence on the acculturation process of their children. It has a direct influence on language retention in the family (although varying in its direction in the respective migrant group) and on the course of the children's school career and their language acquisition, and it impacts indirectly the social and identificational assimilation (i.e., intraethnic network composition and ethnic identification). The cultural capital that families are able to invest in intergenerational transmission processes after an international move seems to be of strategic importance for the course and speed of the acculturation processes in both generations. The impact of the contextual opportunity structures remains relatively small in this empirical analysis. This is partly the effect of indirect measurement via perceived discrimination and additional assumptions about macro effects of migration waves and the institutional structure of the respective immigration context. Moreover, the level of perceived discrimination is rather low in all investigated groups. Therefore, the results may be due to the specific constellation, and they might be understood as an investigation into the variations of culture contact, when major barriers and discrimination in the receiving context are missing. At least in the case of the Turkish migrants in Germany, the German repatriates, and the Russian Israelis, a comparatively stable, conflict-free, and at the same time socially segregated coexistence of minority and majority seems to exist. Comparative studies should show whether this would be similar for migrant minorities with intensive discrimination experiences. The examples of the Italian and Greek families in Germany show that intensified social contacts with members of the receiving society are not necessarily related to assimilation in the sense of a replacement of the culture of origin by the culture of the receiving society. Family-language retention prevails and offers the double option of the integration mode of acculturation, at least to the second generation. The examples of the repatriates in Germany and the Russian Israelis show that variations in ethnic identity may be studied not only as a consequence of culture contact, which is normally done in migration research, but also as an antecedent condition: At least parts of these two groups migrate because of their initially high ethnic identification with the receiving society. Accordingly, culture contact may decrease identification, especially if discrimination is perceived.

Further theoretical thoughts regarding the incorporation process of migrants into the receiving society should concentrate on the transmission of cultural and social capital in migrant families and their strategies of intergenerational social mobility within the system of social inequality in both societies.

Although intergenerational status transmission is a phenomenon often described in mobility research, such transmission processes are seldom considered in migration research and acculturation models. This extended perspective relates migration systematically to the predominantly dramatic changes in the resource and opportunity constellations that confront parents in their investment strategies for their offspring. Intergenerational relationships, as the strongest of all relationships, become even more important in the migration process for plausible reasons: Weak ties may be nonexistent in the migrant situation or involve intensive costs and less gain. Migration, as a long-term, costly family enterprise, may only be justified as an investment for and in the offspring.

A full theoretical understanding of this high-cost situation would then imply the modeling of the relationship of the varying economic, social, and cultural intergenerational transfers relative to the probability of expected outcomes in the receiving society alone (as in the case of German repatriates), in the receiving society and the society of origin (as in the case of Italian, Greek, and Turkish migrant families in Germany), and perhaps in other receiving contexts (as it may be the case for some Russian Israelis). Such a model must consider that children may be different intermediate goods in the respective social context. They may serve as a means for economic security when providing additional family income or providing transfer payments of material help in later life stages. They may also serve as a means for social recognition, based on the self-created close, individual relationship when providing emotional support and understanding, or as a positional good that provides status among others. Children may lose their specific quality as intermediate goods in the receiving context and may regain it in the case of return. Which kind of intermediate goods children are for their parents in the respective context, therefore, has far-reaching implications for the intensity, extent, and duration of parental investment and for the shape of intergenerational transmission (Nauck, 2005).

Results for the Turkish families clearly show, for example, that children are, to a great extent, intermediate goods for achieving economic security (Kagitcibasi, 1982). Accordingly, high parental investments in the cultural capital of their children would pay off only in a highly functionally differentiated society and are thus related to the receiving society alone. If a durable residence status in a welfare society does not seem to be secured or is not intended, priority has to be given to the accumulation of transferable economic capital and to the maintenance of strong, interrelated, and thus reliable social relationships. Those relationships may be achieved best within the kinship system because this social capital will be least devaluated during (further) regional mobility, and they will best serve purposes of maintaining the stability of the intergenerational relationships on which the parents will have to rely. Alternative options such as investing in "weak" ties in the receiving society may appear comparatively insecure and unreliable because the native-born majority has all of the advantages. This may render it plausible that even after many years of stay in Germany, investments in interethnic networks remain quite low and why investments in social capital are concentrated fully on intergenerational coorientation.

The method suggested herein of relating the different results of cultural contact during the migration process systematically to the constellation of cultural and social capital allows the dissolution of the one-dimensionality of the conceptualization of acculturation: Cultural knowledge related to the society of origin and to the host society, social contacts with members of the majority and minority population, and probably also loyalties toward and identification with both population groups can, on principle, vary independently from each other and assume any measure. However, double options and bicultural orientations are easy to achieve in typical low-cost situations, such as choices in eating habits, musical taste, and mass media communication consumption (and perhaps ethnic identification), on which most migration studies focus. Choices are more difficult to make if they imply long-term investments, like the acquisition or the retention of a second or third language and professional skills (as part of the cultural capital) or like the creation and maintenance of lasting, reliable, and rewarding social relationships, marital choices, and reproductive behavior (as part of the social capital), which both need long-lasting, intensive investments until they pay off and are thus much more self-binding. Therefore, in high-cost situations, when resources of time, money, and energy become scarce, double options become more improbable and the question of whether to assimilate or to segregate (or return, respectively) becomes salient again. It is for this reason that the most self-binding social relationships – namely, intergenerational relationships – are so crucial for the long-term outcomes of migration-caused culture contact and must be considered intensively in migration research.

REFERENCES

Blossfeld, H. P., & Jaenichen, U. (1992). Educational expansion and changes in women's entry into marriage and motherhood in the Federal Republic of Germany. *Journal of Marriage and the Family, 54*, 302–315.

Coleman, J. S. (1988). Social capital in the creation of human capital. *American Journal of Sociology, 94*, Supplement, S95–S120.

Coleman, J. S. (1990). *Foundations of social theory.* Cambridge: Harvard University Press.

Esser, H. (1980). *Aspekte der Wanderungssoziologie* (Aspects of a Sociology of Immigration). Darmstadt/Neuwied: Luchterhand.

Kagitcibasi, C. (1982). *The changing value of children in Turkey.* Honolulu, HI: East-West Center.

Nauck, B. (1988). Sozialstrukturelle und individualistische Migrationstheorien: Elemente eines Theorienvergleichs (Sociostructural and individualistic theories of migration: Elements of a comparison of theories). *Kölner Zeitschrift für Soziologie und Sozialpsychologie, 40*, 15–39.

Nauck, B. (1997). Migration and intergenerational relations: Turkish families at home and abroad. In W. W. Isajiw (Ed.), *Multiculturalism in North America and Europe:*

Comparative perspectives on interethnic relations and social incorporation (pp. 435–465). Toronto: Canadian Scholar's Press.

Nauck, B. (2001). Intercultural contact and intergenerational transmission in immigrant families. *Journal of Cross-Cultural Psychology, 32,* 175–189.

Nauck, B. (2005). The changing value of children: A special action theory of fertility behavior and intergenerational relationships in cross-cultural comparison. In W. Friedlmeier, P. Chakkarath, & B. Schwarz (Eds.), *Culture and human development: The importance of cross-cultural research in the social sciences* (pp. 183–202). Hove: Psychology Press.

Nauck, B., Diefenbach, H., & Petri, K. (1998). Intergenerationale Transmission von kulturellem Kapital unter Migrationsbedingungen: Zum Bildungserfolg von Kindern und Jugendlichen aus Migrantenfamilien in Deutschland (Intergenerational transmission of cultural capital under conditions of migration: The level of education of youth from migrant families). *Zeitschrift für Pädagogik, 44,* 701–722.

Nauck, B., & Kohlmann, A. (1999). Kinship as social capital: Network relationships in Turkish migrant families. In R. Richter & S. Supper (Eds.), *New qualities in the lifecourse: Intercultural aspects* (pp. 199–218). Würzburg: Ergon.

Nauck, B., Kohlmann, A., & Diefenbach, H. (1997). Familiäre Netzwerke, intergenerative Transmission und Assimilationsprozesse bei türkischen Migrantenfamilien (Family networks, intergenerational transmission and processes of assimilation in Turkish migrant families). *Kölner Zeitschrift für Soziologie und Sozialpsychologie, 49,* 477–499.

Steinbach, A. (2001). Intergenerational transmission and integration of repatriate families from the former Soviet Union in Germany. *Journal of Comparative Family Studies, 32,* 466–488.

Steinbach, A. (2004). *Soziale Distanz: Ethnische Grenzziehung und die Eingliederung von Zuwanderern in Deutschland* (Social distance: Ethnic borders and the integration of immigrants in Germany). Wiesbaden: Westdeutscher Verlag.

Steinbach, A., & Nauck, B. (2000). Die Wirkung institutioneller Rahmenbedingungen für das individuelle Eingliederungsverhalten von russischen Immigranten in Deutschland und Israel (The impact of institutional contexts for the integration of Russian immigrants in Germany and Israel). In R. Metze, K. Mühler, & K. D. Opp (Eds.), *Normen und Institutionen: Entstehung und Wirkungen. Theoretische Analysen und empirische Befunde (Norms and institutions: Emergence and influences. Theoretical analyses and empirical findings)* (pp. 299–320). Leipzig: Leipziger Universitätsverlag.

9

Developmental Processes Related to Intergenerational Transmission of Culture: Growing Up with Two Cultures

AMADO M. PADILLA

INTRODUCTION

This chapter examines the theoretical construct of biculturalism from a socialization perspective and focuses on children and adolescents who come from environments that foster dual-culture socialization. Before we can thoroughly discuss the issues in bicultural development, it is important to address a few general issues about socialization. Over the years, there have been numerous, excellent state-of-the-art summaries of the relevant research literature on socialization (Maccoby, 2000; Maccoby & Martin, 1983). In this research, we see the importance given to the role of parents and other family members in the socialization of children to the values, beliefs, and acceptable standards of behavior of a society. This is followed by an examination of the role played by peers and institutions, such as the school in shaping the social character of the individual (Minuchin & Shapiro, 1983). This literature informs us about the ways in which adults and their institutions transmit culture to children with the expressed purpose of incorporating children into membership in society. Although the aim of culture transmission generally is its continuity, there may also be transmission that results in cultural change (e.g., if the values of creativity and individuality are transmitted to the same or the next generations).

A gap in the literature on socialization is at the heart of this chapter. The implicit assumption in socialization research is that children are enculturated into a single culture; therefore, culture is not salient in understanding socialization processes because if everyone has nearly the same experience, then differences that occur between children and socializing agents are not due to culture per se. When culture has taken on relevance in socialization research, it has been in the form of cross-cultural research that aims to compare the socialization practices of two or more distinct cultural groups to determine how differences in child-rearing affect some aspect of a child's behavior (Chao, 1996).

The traditional view of socialization (Maccoby & Martin, 1983) does not take into account the fact that many individuals are members of two cultural groups and that their socialization may involve intergenerational transmission to two cultural orientations (Haritatos & Benet-Martinez, 2002). Bicultural socialization may occur simultaneously, as in the case of a child who is socialized to one culture by one parent and to another culture by the other parent, or by one cultural perspective from parents and another from grandparents and other family members (Silverstein & Chen, 1999). Another way that dual socialization occurs early in a child's life is when parents adhere to the lifestyle of one culture at home and teachers practice another culture at school. This "growing up" in two cultures and bicultural transmission is the theme of this chapter.

I first discuss why growing up in two cultures and becoming bicultural is a timely and necessary topic for discussion in understanding developmental processes in cultural transmission. To understand this point, it is necessary to present information on the changing demographic profile of the United States. The intent is to show how immigration is recasting the "face" of America and to suggest that there are sizeable numbers of immigrants and their children who wish to hold onto their heritage culture. From this flows the second major topic, which addresses the conditions that favor heritage cultural socialization that result in bicultural development. Third, I discuss the theoretical issues that relate to ethnic socialization that are critical to bicultural development. Finally, a review of the empirical literature is presented that enables a better understanding of the variations in the transmission of culture across generations.

1.0. CONTEXTS FOR DEVELOPMENT

1.1. A Demographic Profile of the United States

Demographers have shown that the influx of immigrants, especially from Latin America and Asia between 1965 and the present, constitutes the largest movement of people to this country since the period between 1880 and 1900 (Portes & Rumbaut, 2001). These newer immigrants also have a higher fertility ratio than is found among the American population, which is also contributing significantly to the changing demography of the United States (Portes & Rumbaut, 1990).

The U.S. Bureau of the Census reports that the Hispanic population grew 58% to 35.3 million people in the decade between 1990 and 2000, which makes Hispanics more numerous than the 34.6 million African Americans who, until this latest census, had been the largest minority group in the United States. In addition, the 2000 census showed that there were 10.2 million individuals who self-identified as Asian origin, 2.5 million American Indian or Alaska Native, and 0.4 million Native Hawaiians or other Pacific Islanders (U.S. Census Bureau, March 2001).

The demographic shifts taking place are dramatic because they include the addition of new immigrants who have not been in the mix before. For instance, the Afro-Caribbean population from such countries as Jamaica, Haiti, and Guyana, as well as Africans from Nigeria and Ghana, is growing rapidly (from 4.0% in 1990 to 6.2% in 2000). More precisely, the Afro-Caribbean population grew by more than 580,000 (more than 60%) and the African population grew by more than 300,000 (more than 130%) in a 10-year period. These two groups combined, despite being much smaller than the native African American population, contributed approximately 25% to the 3.7-million increase in the non-Hispanic Black population during the 1990s. Although they are not an often-recognized part of the American ethnic mosaic, both of these groups are emerging as large and fast-growing populations (Rong & Brown, 2001). For instance, Afro-Caribbeans now outnumber and are growing faster than such well-established ethnic minorities as Cubans and Koreans.

A similar diversity spread has been happening among Latinos in recent years. Although the Mexican-origin population is by far the largest group with approximately 21 million, followed by 3.41 million Puerto Ricans and 1.24 Cuban Americans, there have been sizable increases of Hispanic immigrants from Central and South America. In proportion to their number, it is the new Latinos for whom the figures are most changed. These new Hispanics increased in number by 2.4 million between 1990 and 2000. Conservatively, 335,000 additional Dominicans and Salvadorans have settled in the United States between 1990 and 2000, bringing the total to 1.42 million. Add to this another 91,000 Columbians who have entered after 1990 and this group's population is approximately 471,000. Other large groups include approximately 372,000 Guatemalans and 218,000 Hondurans who call the United States home. Three other groups are quickly approaching the three quarters of a million mark: Ecuadorians, Peruvians, and Hondurans. These groups all share a common language but are distinct in history and cultural forms that have evolved differently because of their geography, political and social institutions, respective immigration histories, and relationship with their European and indigenous roots.

In the decade between 1990 and 2000, the total Asian population increased from 7.2 million to 12.3 million, which represents a 69% growth rate of this population in a 10-year period. The Asian share of the total population rose from 2.9% to 4.4%, still much smaller than the country's African American or Latino groups but a much more considerable presence today than in the past and very prominent in some states and major cities.

The Chinese remain the largest single national-origin group, currently about 2.7 million and nearly a quarter of the Asian total. They are followed by 2.4 million Filipinos. Asian Indians are the fastest growing group: fifth largest in 1990 but now third, more than doubling in a decade, and reaching 1.9 million in 2000.

Three other groups have more than a million residents, and each represents about a tenth of Asians. Of these, the Japanese have the longest history in the country, but their growth from 847,562 in 1990 to 1.15 million in 2000 was modest in comparison to other groups. The other two Asian subgroups are Koreans, up by 54% from 798,849 in 1990 to 1.23 million in 2000, and Vietnamese, who doubled from 614,547 in 1990 to 1.22 million in 2000.

The impact that the growth of these new populations is having on regional economies and politics is also important to understand. For instance, in Florida, Hispanics now outnumber Blacks, and in California, the most populous state, they outnumber Blacks and comprise a third of the state's total population. Another way to gauge the transformation is by the sheer magnitude of immigration to this country. Whether measured in terms of size, composition, and geographic concentration, the numbers are impressive. The 2000 census reported a foreign-born population of more than 30 million people. Combining immigrants and the roughly 28 million U.S.-born children of immigrants, a fifth of the total national population is of recent foreign origin. Also relevant is the fact that the overwhelming majority of immigrants since 1960 are non-European. Of the post-1960 immigrants, slightly more than half (52%) have come from Latin America and the Caribbean, with Mexico alone accounting for 28% of the total. Another 29% have come from Asia and the Middle East. An added statistic is that Filipinos, Chinese, and Indochinese alone account for 15% of the immigrant pool.

For the first time ever, the 2000 census also gave Americans the option of identifying themselves as belonging to more than one race. Nearly 7 million people, or 2.4% of the nation, described themselves as multiracial. The option of identifying with more than one race was especially popular in regions where people of different races have long intermarried, such as Alaska and Hawaii, and in states like California, Texas, Florida, and New York, which have grown rapidly in their ethnic and racial mix. Today, 5% of all U.S. marriages involve couples of different racial backgrounds.

Within racial and ethnic groups, mixed-marriage rates vary widely. Hispanics and Asians, the nation's fastest-growing minority groups, marry partners of different races at about three times the rate of Whites. Asian women and Black men are more than twice as likely as Asian men and Black women to marry outside their groups. Whereas only 3.1% of Whites were involved in an interracial marriage in 2000, 16.3% of Asians and 16.3% of Hispanics were married to someone of a different race. The rates were highest for Asian women (21.4% versus 10.6% for Asian men) and Hispanic women (17.2% versus 15.1% for Hispanic men).

At the same time, the non-Hispanic White population is a shrinking share of the country, dropping to 69% in 2000 from 76% in 1990. Non-Hispanic Whites are now a minority in California and will soon be in Texas. In addition, there are other population shifts taking place. For instance, many non-Hispanic Whites are moving to what demographers call the New Sun Belt – states such as Georgia, North Carolina, and South Carolina – where new waves of immigrants from Asia and Latin America are also settling.

1.2. The Emergence of Minority-Majority Populations

Social theorists are pointing to emerging "minority-majority" populations in large immigrant states such as California. Because the newcomers are a youthful population, schools are the most dramatically impacted social institution affected by the population shift and the new minority-majority (EdSource, 2007). Furthermore, there is concern that the newcomers are not being absorbed into mainstream society as rapidly as immigrants in earlier times. This has generated considerable debate on reasons why these newcomers are not assimilating. One side of the debate has centered on the issue of "absorption" into mainstream culture and has presented data to show that absorption of immigrants has never been easy and that recent immigrant groups are becoming "Americanized" at approximately the same rate as earlier immigrants. Others acknowledge the slow absorption of recent immigrants into mainstream society and explain the slow assimilation through an analysis of social barriers and racism that prevent more rapid absorption (Segal, 2002; Suarez-Orozco & Suarez-Orozco, 2001). Still others argue that some immigrant groups, especially Mexicans, do not want to assimilate (Buchanan, 2002; Hanson, 2003).

In many respects, the intergenerational transmission of ethnic-heritage cultures is due then to important macro-level changes that have transpired in America during the last 4 decades. It is interesting how these macro-level changes that have altered the socialization practices of an increasing diverse population have gone unnoticed in mainstream psychology but not among ethnic psychologists. Today, the topics of ethnic socialization, ethnic identification, and biculturalism have taken on increased importance in ethnic psychology (Bernal, Trimble, Burlew, & Leong, 2003; Chun, Balls Organista, & Marin, 2002; Hall & Okazaki, 2002). However, an examination of the basic textbooks in psychology does not reflect the growing literature on biculturalism. In fact, little attention is still given to culturally diverse children and adolescents in developmental psychology (Padilla & Lindholm, 1992). In the following sections, ethnic socialization and the macro- and micro-social conditions that lead to child-rearing practices that result in socialization to two cultures are discussed. Also of importance are questions related to the ramifications of bicultural social transmission from the perspectives of the individual and society.

1.3. Bicultural Socialization and Biculturalism: Asset or Liability?

The behaviors ascribed to an individual who is bicultural were first noted in the sociological literature under the heading of dual-culture personality. This literature addressed the question of whether dual-cultural socialization is positive or negative for the individual involved (Park, 1928; Stonequist, 1937). Stonequist (1937, p. 2) focused greater attention on the negative consequences of dual-cultural socialization and argued that

> The individual who through migration, education, marriage, or some other influence leaves one social group or culture without making a satisfactory adjustment to another finds himself on the margin of each but a member of neither. He is a "marginal" man.

Stonequist and Park argued that making a satisfactory adjustment to a new culture was fraught with danger. According to the Park–Stonequist model, the marginal person feels isolated and closed off from members of either the culture of origin or the culture of the host group – or worse, isolated from both. Furthermore, according to this view, the person suffers from self-hatred, low self-esteem, and feelings of inferiority. The marginal person is marked by negativity and character traits that predispose the individual to serious mental health problems. It is important that Stonequist gave little attention to how an individual could make a satisfactory adjustment to two social groups.

The marginal-person model advanced by Park and Stonequist was the generally accepted view for nearly half a century. Despite repeated criticism about the lack of scientific evidence for marginality and the vagueness of the concept (Green, 1947; Mann, 1973), the ideas emanating from the concept of marginality are still present in current models of acculturation (Berry, 2003). However, in their critique of the construct of marginality and whether the construct has scientific validity, Del Pilar and Udasco (2004, p. 11) conclude that

> Being caught between cultures frequently does result in difficulties and adjustment problems. The marginality investigators failed to note that these difficulties and adjustment problems can take as many negative forms as are discussed in the voluminous diagnostic manual of psychiatric problems or as many positive forms as are reflected in the biographies of successful immigrants.... one concept cannot hope to cover all these variables.

In contrast to marginality, *biculturalism* began to emerge in the 1980s as a term to reference individuals who manage two cultures successfully. LaFromboise, Coleman, and Gerton (1993) defined a *bicultural person* as an individual who, by virtue of the socialization he or she received from their primary caretakers, is competent in two cultures. According to this view, it is possible to be a member of two cultures without being in serious psychological conflict about either. It is important that in this bicultural perspective, the person does not favor one culture over the other, the dual transmission of cultural information from parents and other caretakers is quite deliberate, and both cultures are received positively.

This new view of dual-culture transmission has enriched our thinking about socialization processes and how individuals participate to varying degrees as members of two cultural groups. Research in this area is exemplified in the work of numerous investigators (Bernal, Knight, Garza, Ocampa, & Cota, 1990; Hurtado & Gurin, 1987; Phinney & Chavira, 1995; Phinney, Ong, & Madden, 2000; Quintana, Castaneda-English, & Ybarra, 1999; Umana-Taylor & Fine, 2004). These researchers examined topics germane to ethnic socialization, ethnic identification, and biculturalism. For the "biculturalists," we see a more positive image of the bicultural person. The bicultural person is well adjusted and open to others and is a cultural broker between peoples of different backgrounds. The completely bicultural person is an individual who possesses two social identities congruent with the norms of each culture. The person is equally at ease with members of either culture and can easily switch from one cultural orientation to the other and do so often with native (or near native) like facility. Furthermore, this comfort with two cultures extends to interactions with individuals from cultures other than those in which the bicultural person has competence. This social flexibility is viewed by biculturalists as an advantage and as one of the reasons for bicultural exposure (LaFromboise et al., 1993). When behavioral conflicts do occur among people with bicultural backgrounds, as they inevitably must, psychotherapists call for interventions that strive to reaffirm the dual-cultural background of their clients (Szapocznik, Santisteban, Kurtines, Perez-Vidal, & Hervis, 1984), which is a far cry from saying that someone is "irreparably" damaged.

In summary, the theory of the dual-culture personality and marginality was not buttressed by empirical evidence (Mann, 1973). Today, empirical research on biculturalism is commonplace in the psychological literature. The missing element in much of this discussion, however, is why and how people become bicultural. Before we can focus on answers to those questions, we must first put in perspective the topic of identity development and the more specific examination of ethnic-identity formation.

1.4. Ethnic-Identity Development

Adolescents, irrespective of their cultural orientation, must deal with issues in the development of their personal identity (Erikson, 1968). For example, adolescents of Mexican origin are often asked by peers whether they identify as Mexican, Mexican American, American, Chicano, Latino, or Hispanic. There are important historical and political reasons for each of these ethnic labels that refer to individuals of Mexican heritage regardless of whether they are immigrants or later-generation American citizens. Each label packs important information about the cultural, social, and political stance of the parents and community in the larger context of immigration history and assimilation into American society. The multiple labels and their associated meanings are often confusing. Identity development creates serious concerns for ethnic adolescents, who often want to construct their own identities free of the ethnic and racial biases imposed on them by their grandparents, parents, teachers, peers, and other authority figures.

Erikson (1968) described the essence of identity and the crisis of identity formation during adolescence as the search by adolescents to define themselves in ways that are free of the family influence and in line with peers and non-related adult role models. For adolescents from a bicultural family, the search for an identity free from their immediate family (i.e., grandparents and parents) creates challenges not experienced by unicultural adolescents. For example, Mexican-immigrant parents often place their children in conflict when they demand that they maintain a "Mexican" identity although the young person may never have lived in Mexico. At school, the same young person is told that he or she lives in America and should think of himself or herself first and foremost as "American." However, whenever the young person is asked to complete an official school form, he or she generally must choose an identity among the following: non-Hispanic White, Mexican, Mexican American, Hispanic, Other. Often, adolescents question the relevance of those ethnic-related questions on the grounds that they make assumptions about their identity that are not accurate. For example, if the person was born in the United States, why is the question relevant? In the same way, if the young persons are American citizens, why are they being asked to identify with racialized categories that they may not identify with because they see their world in a much more complicated way than merely a collection of racial and ethnic categories (Olsen, 1997)? The confusion described by Erikson (1968) becomes salient for many adolescents who devise other ways to answer the "Who am I?" question: "I am me," "I am a human being," or, as one adolescent said, "I am who I am. That's it."

1.5. Cultural Transmission: Two Cultures, Not One

Four major conditions have the potential for creating a situation of bicultural social transmission. In discussing each condition, it is important to keep in mind whether the transmission of two cultural orientations experienced by a young person is carried out by the primary agents of socialization (i.e., parents and grandparents) or by secondary agents (i.e., teachers, peers, and other role models). It is important because these socializing agents may emphasize different aspects of culture during the transmission process. The important point is that cultural transmission is more complex for many persons who come from an immigrant-heritage background. Most contemporary models of parenting and socialization are applicable only to children growing up in unicultural contexts (Maccoby, 2000). However, as the demographic data show, this is not the situation in which many children live today.

2.0. IMMIGRANT CHILDREN AND ADOLESCENTS

Children and adolescents who immigrate to a new country must of necessity acquire the customs and behaviors of their adopted country. Depending on their age at the time of immigration, the young immigrants have already been socialized to the culture of their parents and, as a consequence, may experience considerable difficulty in adapting to their new surroundings because of the demand to learn the language and cultural practices of their hosts. In a study of university students, Mena, Padilla, and Maldonado (1987) found that immigrants who arrived before age 12 reported fewer acculturative stressors than students who immigrated after age 12. The ease with which young immigrants are able to adjust to a new culture depends on the type of support and assistance they receive from their primary caretakers while they make the transition to the new culture, as well as the peer and institutional supports in place to assist the youthful newcomers.

The school and peers are the main sources of cultural transmission of the new culture for immigrant children and adolescents, whereas the immigrant parents continue to maintain the cultural practices of their home country. Today, we commonly find schools that have adopted programs such as newcomer centers, English-as-a-Second Language (ESL) classes in the content areas (e.g., sheltered American History), bilingual education programs, and heritage-language classes (e.g., Korean for native speakers). The general intent of these programs is to transition immigrant students to an all-English curriculum as rapidly as possible while offering a supportive environment for their language and culture. The overall objective of these efforts is "Americanization," or assimilation to American culture while still valuing the cultural diversity of students. Often, American peers assist by providing English-language input and modeling youth-culture orientation. Slowly but surely, immigrants acquire enough of the language and culture of the host group to participate in the new culture. In the process, many youth also retain – to varying degrees – competence in their home culture, depending on their age at immigration.

In communities populated by immigrant groups, it is not uncommon to see children serving as translators and cultural brokers for their parents and other adult family members. Frequently, young bilingual children serve as translators between their parents and teachers, apartment managers, physicians, shopkeepers, and so on. For the young person, this is a situation of mandatory biculturalism because of the need to acquire competencies in the host culture in order to assist parents. This is an interesting twist on the way in which cultural transmission is commonly viewed. In this case, the immigrant children or adolescents are bringing the new culture that they are learning from teachers and peers to their parents. When this happens, they are the transmitters of the new culture and they are bringing the new culture to their parents rather than vice versa.

Although this situation may be beneficial for the parents, it can place a heavy burden on the child who serves as a cultural and linguistic broker while still in the process of learning the culture of the parents as well as that of the host group. For the parents, there is also the potential danger of surrendering too much power to their children because of their reliance on them as cultural brokers (Buriel, Perez, De Ment, Chavez, & Moran, 1998; Weisskirch & Alatorre Alva, 2002).

An equally difficult situation for immigrant parents and children entails the conflicts in values and modes of behavior that are presented to them because of the two cultures. For example, Sung (1985) described the bicultural conflicts experienced by Chinese immigrant children. Some of the conflicts identified by Sung involved the difference in independence training seen in American parenting but not in traditional Chinese parenting, where interdependence on the family is the acceptable mode of behavior. Sung also noted differences in respect for authority, especially toward teachers: Whereas Chinese teachers command great respect, American teachers are not held in the same high esteem by American students. In a series of studies, Chao (1994, 1996, 2000) showed how immigrant-Chinese parenting styles are different from American parenting styles based on the typology of authoritative, authoritarian, and permissive. A Chinese parent employs a type of "training" model that has elements of both authoritarianism and permissiveness, coupled with a high degree of emphasis on filial piety and parental warmth. Although Chao (2000) studied Chinese parents, she contends that the patterns of parenting are shared with other Asian groups, notably Japanese and Koreans. This parenting style contrasts with American parenting styles, which emphasizes joint decision making and mutual respect between parents and adolescents. It is interesting that Asian American adolescents become attuned to this difference in parenting styles between their immigrant parents and their American peers. On occasion, this results in serious intergenerational conflict between Asian parents and their children, who are less willing to "toe the line" when it comes to filial piety.

In a longitudinal study involving East Asian (i.e., Chinese, Japanese, Korean, and Vietnamese), Filipino, and Latino (i.e., Mexican, Salvadoran, and Nicaraguan) students, Tseng and Fuligni (2000) reported that when immigrant parents and their children both communicated in the home language, there was more cohesion and less conflict between the two generations. Adolescents from those homes reported that they were more emotionally connected with their parents. However, when the parents communicated in the home language and their children spoke English, all ethnic groups reported that they felt less connected with their parents and that there was less cohesion in the home. It is surprising that in those cases in which adolescents reported that they and their parents mutually communicated in English, they also reported more conflict with their father regarding daily household issues. Although the findings from this study are correlational, they suggest that cultural transmission in immigrant households flows more smoothly when parents are able to establish a pattern of interpersonal communication based on the home language of the parents. Tseng and Fuligni (2000) maintain that their findings suggest that in situations in which there is tension between the adolescent and the parent, the more acculturated adolescents use English as a means to distance themselves from their parents. Thus, the adolescents – by virtue of their proficiency in English and refusal to speak the home language – effectively curtail their parents' efforts at cultural transmission.

In a study of first-, second-, and third-generation Mexican-heritage students and their parents, Buriel and Cardoza (1993) found that first-generation students exhibit more cultural continuities between themselves and their parents because both were born in Mexico and spoke Spanish as their primary language. Cultural continuity was further augmented when members of both parent and student generations shared a common educational experience in Mexico. According to Buriel and Cardoza (1993), although the students were proficient in English (the survey was conducted in English) and despite the students' exposure to a Euro-American cultural milieu, they still had more in common with their parents, thereby facilitating cultural transmission, than was the case with their second-generation Mexican American counterparts.

In summary, the cultural differences in parenting practices identified by Sung (1985) and Chao (2000) with Asian immigrant youth are generalized across many different immigrant groups (Tseng and Fuligni, 2000). Furthermore, although it is possible to readily identify the cultural conflicts, still little is known about the dynamics of cultural transmission in the immigrant generation to inform parents about ways to minimize intergenerational conflict due to the effects of acculturation from secondary sources, such as school and peers. The transition to the new culture may be difficult for immigrants of all ages but for different reasons. Immigrant parents are often involved in their own acculturation and rely on their more rapidly acculturating children to assist them in their interactions with the host culture. Similarly, immigrant children often are left to their own devices to make decisions about how much of their home culture they wish to retain and/or practice.

3.0. SECOND-GENERATION INDIVIDUALS

In this section, the status of two distinct groups of children who are typically classified as second generation is addressed: (1) children born in the United States of parents who themselves are immigrants, and (2) children born in another country who immigrate before the age of 5. These two groups of children are indistinguishable when viewed behaviorally on such measures as proficiency in English, school achievement, and cultural assimilation (Portes & Rumbaut, 2001). Because the parents of second-generation children are immigrants who generally adhere to the traditional practices, values, and language(s) of their own upbringing, they often expect the same adherence to the home culture from their second-generation children. Children and adolescents in this situation usually have demarcated boundaries in the sources of culture transmission and in how they respond to these bifurcated cultural demands. The second-generation individuals, like their first-generation counterparts, frequently serve as the primary cultural and linguistic bridge between their parents and the host society. The major difference is that unlike the first generation, these youth frequently learn about the parents' culture in a social vacuum with little environmental support. In other words, the parents transmit their culture to their children while in the host culture. Thus, the home becomes the cultural focal point for most transmissions that involve the culture of the parents. This is all the more difficult when there is not an ethnic community that can continuously reinforce what the parents are doing in the home.

Thus, second-generation youth often learn the parents' culture in isolation and American culture at school, from peers, and through mass media. It is not surprising that second-generation youth often find themselves between "a rock and a hard place": They are expected to maintain the culture of the parents while they are also given mixed messages about how Americanized they should become. It is not uncommon to hear, "You're in America now and you must be an American," while also being told, "Don't forget who you are and where you come from" (Padilla, 2003). Pressure to conform to the home culture of the parents is often more challenging for immigrant and second-generation females than for males. This is even more difficult for female adolescents who come from traditional cultures, such as Muslims and Hindus, who adhere to much stricter gender roles than other immigrant groups, such as those from Asia or Latin America (Olsen, 1997; Sarroub, 2001).

For some ethnic females, when the two cultures clash – as they often do around issues of gender roles and dating (American culture) – girls are often caught in a double bind and forced to conform, with the possible consequence that they may feel a certain degree of resentment toward their parents who immigrated to the United States. These adolescents often complain that their parents want them to be "frozen in time" and in a culture that they know only from their parents. As native-born Americans, they are exposed to many of the social forces that ensure their enculturation as Americans. However, many are pulled back toward the culture of their parents and grandparents, who expect them to be loyal to their cultural roots. How parents, grandparents, and other extended family members socialize children in bicultural contexts will determine the child's eventual level of biculturalism (Silverstein & Chen, 1999).

In a study of the role of grandparents in the socialization of Mexican American children, Schmidt and Padilla (1983) found that both grandmothers and grandfathers were involved in the socialization of grandchildren. However, there was an important gender difference in how such socialization occurred. Grandmothers were more involved with granddaughters, especially when they were the offspring of their own daughters. Similarly, grandfathers were more involved in the socialization of male children of their own daughters (see also Euler, Hoier, & Rohde, Chapter 5, this volume). Grandparents reported that their interactions with grandchildren included the transmission of such cultural information as learning to cook ethnic dishes, talking about Mexico and its heroes, teaching Mexican songs and dances, and talking to grandchildren in Spanish. It is interesting that children of daughters spoke more Spanish to their grandparents than did children of sons of grandparents.

From the perspective of the grandparents, proficiency in Spanish appeared important in maintaining their culture. This finding was later confirmed in a 10-year longitudinal study of 353 grandparent–adult grandchild dyads (Silverstein & Chen, 1999). In that study, measures of acculturation that included Spanish proficiency were taken of grandparents of whom 41% were born in Mexico and of grandchildren of whom only 2% were born outside the United States. Findings revealed that more acculturated grandchildren reported less frequent interactions with grandparents. Furthermore, the Spanish-speaking ability of the grandchildren predicted greater social interaction and feelings of familism and closeness across generations. There was also a gender difference with granddaughters reporting more fluency in Spanish and more frequent interactions with grandparents. More acculturated grandchildren reported weaker affection for their grandparents than less acculturated grandchildren. Accordingly, acculturation differences as marked predominantly by Spanish-language proficiency across the generational span of grandparent–grandchild serve to disrupt the transmission of cultural information across generations. Apparently, in the absence of a Spanish-language bridge between the grandparent–grandchild dyads, there was a marked decline of interaction of any type between the generations. The weakened bonds of familism and affection among the acculturated grandchildren also heightened the difference in cultural orientations between the generations.

In two related studies conducted with Southeast Asians, it was found that differences in language acculturation across generations in the same family result in tension and conflict between the young and old (Detzner, 1996; Weinstein-Shr & Henkin, 1991). The apparent social distance and diminished cultural transmission across generations that is created by language acculturation call for more research because it addresses the matter of whether bilingual proficiency is a prerequisite of biculturalism. For many immigrant parents, bilingualism is essential; otherwise, how can their children communicate with them or understand the culture? Other parents are less insistent on bilingualism and do not see it as essential in the transmission of culture to their children. It is likely that immigrant parents and grandparents with more human capital (e.g., more education and higher income levels) are more likely to be bilingual themselves and capable of cultural transmission in either language depending on the circumstances, whereas parents with less human capital are restrained in linguistic flexibility and limit their communication about culture to the mother tongue.

We know that a shift from a non-English home language to English occurs generally within one generation (e.g., Lopez, 1982; Veltman, 1981). If we adhere strongly to a model that assumes that home language is critical to bicultural competence, how is it possible to still talk about biculturalism with second-generation youth if they possess little proficiency in the language of their elders? If immigrant parents do not insist on home-language proficiency, then in what aspect of their culture are they interested in transmitting to their children and how is this accomplished? The question of cross-generational cultural transmission is important and is in need of considerably more research among immigrant populations (see Nauck, Chapter 8, this volume).

In a longitudinal study, Portes and Rumbaut (2001) collected data from more than 5,000 adolescents and parents who had immigrated to the United States from 77 different countries. The second generation was defined as U.S.-born children of foreign parents or foreign-born children who were brought to the United States before adolescence. One significant finding was that there were benefits of selective acculturation – which as used by Portes and Rumbaut (2001, p. 274) is similar to how the term *biculturalism* is used in this chapter:

> Children who learn the language and culture of their new country without losing those of the old have a much better understanding of their place in the world. They need not clash with their parents as often or feel embarrassed by them because they are able to bridge the gap across generations and value their elders' traditions and goals. Selective acculturation forges an intergenerational alliance for successful adaptation that is absent among youths who have severed bonds with their past in the pursuit of acceptance by their native peers.

In summary, the second generation is positioned between the culture of the parents and American culture. By definition, many are enculturated in the parental culture, but how extensively depends entirely on the parents, the extended family, and the ethnic community that may or may not exist for them. Similarly, the second generation is exposed to American culture; how they embrace it depends on the hold that the parent's culture places on them and the extent of contact with members of the majority group. More longitudinal studies are needed similar to Portes and Rumbaut (2001) that examine the role that parents, grandparents, teachers, peers, and coworkers play in the adaptation of the second generation.

4.0. THIRD- AND LATER-GENERATION ETHNIC INDIVIDUALS

In this section, attention is given to third- and later-generation individuals who, like their parents, were born in the United States. Biculturalism is practiced by parents, grandparents, community leaders, and role models, who serve as the major conduits for cultural transmission to the third generation, but the process is not smooth and there is little longitudinal research to rely on in a review such as this. Today, there is no shortage of bicultural communities everywhere in the United States; for example, they can be found in the Chinatowns, Little Saigons, Little Italys, Latino barrios, Greek neighborhoods, Koreatowns, and Muslim American communities in all metropolitan centers. These ethnic communities offer supportive services to immigrants while also providing heritage-culture support through language schools for children, community centers for families, and places of worship – all of which serve to keep later-generation people connected to their heritage culture. For example, an examination of Mexican Americans in the Southwest offers an excellent case study of an ethnic group that is constantly being infused by newcomers from Mexico while also having developed a specific culture of their own because of their long-standing residence within the borders of the United States (Tatum, 2001). Many of these native-born Americans of Mexican heritage continue to steadfastly identify with a form of Mexican culture and maintain many of the values, beliefs, and customs of Mexico. It is important that many of these later-generation ethnic people are more loyal to their ethnic heritage than they are knowledgeable of its culture (e.g., history, art, and literature) and the Spanish language (Keefe & Padilla, 1987).

Because of their commitment to their ethnic heritage, later-generation Mexican American parents and grandparents may practice dual-culture socialization with their children. For reasons that differ across ethnic groups, the bicultural-oriented later-generation individuals maintain their biculturalism by choice and often view it as a benefit rather than a liability. For these individuals, acceptance of their membership in an ethnic community does not imply that they are "disloyal" Americans. Unfortunately, with the growing ethnic diversity in the United States, some social theorists have difficulty grasping the idea that multiculturalism does not imply disloyalty to America, nor does it pose dire consequences for the unity of the country (e.g., Schlesinger, 1991).

Involvement in ethnic-community activities by no means implies a rejection of American culture because prior research has shown that ethnic involvement and national identity are not strongly correlated. This is consistent with Der-Karabetian's (1980) finding among Armenian Americans and Zak's (1973) finding with Jewish Americans, and it supports the bicultural hypothesis of acculturation. Thus, participation in ethnic-community affairs is associated with a stronger sense of bicultural ethnic belonging. Exposure to the dominant majority culture with eventual assimilation into it does not need to result in the rejection of one's ethnic and cultural heritage.

In their acculturation model, Padilla (1980) and Keefe and Padilla (1987) distinguished between *cultural awareness* (CA) and *ethnic loyalty* (EL). CA is the cognitive dimension that specifies the knowledge that individuals possess of their culture (i.e., knowledge includes proficiency in Spanish and English; knowledge of the history, art, and music of both Mexico and the United States; and knowledge of current events that shape culture). EL, on the other hand, is the behavioral component of the model and it assesses a person's preference regarding language, cultural forms of leisure activities, and ethnic friendships. The rationale is that the affect that a person expresses toward a social group will also dictate the preferences that he or she holds toward activities and members of the group.

In using this distinction, Keefe and Padilla (1987) found that cultural awareness decreased markedly between the first and fourth generations. With the loss of specific cultural knowledge, including a language shift to English, parents and grandparents have little heritage culture to transmit to their children and grandchildren. Thus, later-generation respondents compensated by transmitting more messages about ethnic identification and loyalty and fewer messages about actual cultural content. Montgomery (1992) replicated this finding with a college-student population of Mexican American respondents in South Texas.

A major question of theoretical significance is why EL persists across generations in the face of decreasing or near total absence of cultural knowledge. To better understand this, Keefe and Padilla (1987) examined the factors that contributed to EL. The most salient factor was *perceived discrimination*. The higher their respondents scored on a measure of perceived discrimination, the higher the respondents scored on EL. Furthermore, regardless of how seemingly bicultural and/or Americanized respondents were, they were still relatively insulated within their ethnic group. For example, few had intimate friends outside their ethnic group and most had only limited social contacts with non–Mexican Americans. This was true even though the more acculturated or bicultural an informant was, the more likely he or she was to have coworkers from other ethnic groups. So, although acculturation may serve an adaptive function, it does not at the same time ensure that the ethnic person will be incorporated into a broader social network of nonethnic persons. A possible explanation for this comes from research on skin color.

Research on the impact of skin color on the life chances of Latinos indicates that even after controlling for background variables such as parents' education, age, and language ability, having a darker skin and a more Indian-looking phenotype has a negative effect on the educational and economic attainment of Latinos (Arce, Murguia, & Frisbie, 1987; Gómez, 2000; Vasquez, Garcia-Vasquez, Bauman, & Sierra, 1997). These research findings support the contention made by Portes and Rumbaut (2001) that newcomers pay a penalty for being immigrants or later-generation ethnic individuals who differ in phenotype from the host society, and even a greater penalty for being darker and more Indian-looking (or Asian or African) in phenotype. The cost is both psychological and economic – psychological in the sense of the discomfort of being stigmatized as different and economic because the greater the stigma, the lower the human capital that the person is able to acquire that then translates to social mobility in the American context of structural assimilation.

Building on the relevance of discrimination and stigma, Phinney and Chavira (1995) reported that Mexican American, African American, and Japanese American parents stated that they felt compelled to instill pride in their heritage while also having conversations with their children about discrimination that they might confront in the future. In another study of 45 dyads of Mexican American, English-speaking mothers and their 6- to 10-year-old children, the mothers reported that they discussed with their children issues of discrimination and prejudice (Knight, Bernal, Cota, Garza, & Ocampo, 1993). However, the way in which parents communicated information about discrimination was not straightforward but rather was connected to several variables associated with the mothers' cultural and familial circumstances. Specifically, the mothers who were more comfortable with their Mexican cultural background and less comfortable with the majority culture, and whose husbands' family had resided in the United States for fewer generations, were more likely to instill Mexican culture in their young children while also transmitting more messages about ethnic pride and discrimination. As for the children in these dyads, Knight et al. (1993) found that children whose mothers were comfortable with their Mexican background used more ethnic labels to describe themselves and, importantly, knew more about their culture; reported engaging in ethnic behaviors; and were more likely to prefer ethnic foods, friends, and social activities. In a study of older children (i.e., 7- to 13-year-olds), Quintana and Vera (1999) found that the older children had developed a more sophisticated understanding of the ethnic prejudice they faced. This, in turn, was associated with higher levels of ethnic knowledge and ethnic identification on the part of the older children. Parental ethnic socialization was not predictive of understanding prejudice in this study, but it did relate significantly to ethnic knowledge. Thus, the developmental process suggested is that children learn about their cultural heritage from their parents and, as they advance cognitively, they are increasingly able to understand the meaning of prejudice and how their ethnic group is targeted for discrimination. The result of this process is that the young person emerges with a sense of ethnic identity that is sharpened by a continuous flow of ethnic-related socializing experiences with parents, family members, and peers. Studies with older informants are needed to assess how ethnic knowledge, understanding of the dynamics of prejudice, and evolution of ethnic identity proceeds through adolescence and young adulthood.

Thus, for many second- and later-generation individuals, biculturalism is an adaptive strategy for coping with discriminatory practices. It is a more adaptable strategy than alienation from the society to which one belongs as a birthright but where discrimination may occur because of skin color and phenotype. In the literature, there is recognition of cultural transmission that incorporates more than just knowledge of culture from one generation to the next but that also prepares children for prejudice and discrimination. This corresponds to the rather extensive literature on racial socialization with African Americans but which is still lacking in the literature of other stigmatized groups (e.g., Hispanics and Asian Americans). In a study that examined the role of ethnic and social perspective-taking abilities and parental ethnic socialization, Quintana, Castaneda-English, and Ybarra (1999) found that parental ethnic socialization was positively correlated with ethnic-identity achievement among a population of mostly third- and later-generation Mexican American adolescents. However, the ability to take a different perspective was linked developmentally to cognitive processes, not to ethnic socialization. Quintana et al. (1999) speculated that higher levels of ethnic perspective-taking reflect cognitive processes and that these are related to self-protective properties found among stigmatized groups. Specifically, adolescents with a high level of ethnic perspective-taking understand that negative feedback about their ethnicity or ethnic group is likely due to ethnic prejudice, not to some internal characteristic or behavior. How an adolescent's higher cognitive processing and not ethnic socialization comes to offer this self-protective function is not well understood and requires more research.

We turn now to the final category that has the potential for dual-culture socialization: mixed-ethnic and/or racial-heritage children. In the case of mixed-heritage children, cultural transmission is no less complex; however, there are different dynamics because in the situations discussed so far, ethnic and cultural knowledge was communicated by parents who shared the same cultural knowledge. Here, the situation is different because the two parents represent different ethnic, racial, or cultural traditions and each contributes to the transmission of knowledge according to his or her own distinct background.

5.0. MIXED-ETHNIC AND/OR RACIAL-HERITAGE CHILDREN

Intermarriage has been touted as the desirable endpoint of a race-free society. Children of intermarried couples often acknowledge and embrace the cultural and racial identity of both their parents. Today, it is commonplace to find individuals of mixed-heritage backgrounds acknowledging their biculturalism and biracial origins (Obama, 1995).

The literature on mixed-ethnic/racial-heritage children has exploded in recent years (Coronado, Guevarra, Moniz, & Szanto, 2003; Nash, 1999; Root, 1996, 2001; Winters & DuBose, 2003). This literature shows that children of interracial (e.g., African American and White) marriages have received greater attention than have children of interethnic (e.g., Hispanic and non-Hispanic White) marriages (Rosenblatt, Karis, & Powell, 1995). However, offspring of interethnic marriages must also cope with complex problems because parents may differ not only in race but also in culture and language and often religious preference as well.

Murguia (1982) suggested that intermarriage encourages a movement away from a definite ethnic identity. He speculated that children of intermarriages are subject to more cultural diversity and, if not properly handled, may have difficulty in identifying with the lower-status ethnic group; however, not all research supports this position. For instance, in a study of 63 adolescents of marriages involving a Mexican-origin and a non-Hispanic parent, positive outcomes were found on measures of Mexican ethnic identity (Salgado de Snyder, Lopez, & Padilla, 1982). In that study, adolescents between the ages of 12 and 18 were interviewed to ascertain their ethnic identification and knowledge of their Mexican culture. Most of the adolescents (70%) identified as Mexican heritage and nearly all (89%) reported being proud of their Mexican heritage. In addition, 40% spoke some Spanish and most were familiar with Mexican cultural events. In these mixed marriages, when the mother was Mexican, the children were more likely to receive cultural transmissions regarding Spanish-language instruction, as well as lessons on history, traditions, holidays, and traditional foods. Salgado de Snyder et al. asked their informants about the advantages and disadvantages of their mixed-ethnic heritage; 56% of the respondents expressed advantages in having mixed parentage. Among the most frequently mentioned advantages were being able to learn about two different cultures, speaking two languages, and growing up without prejudices. Some respondents did report disadvantages, such as conflicting child-rearing styles between their parents based on their respective culture.

Biracial and multiracial children and families often face unique challenges. Identity development for biracial children is most strongly shaped by their respective parents' racial socialization and by the acceptance they receive from others during sensitive stages of development (Hughes & Johnson, 2001). Through their cultural transmissions, parents can prepare children for what society has to offer; however, it is not always easy to do so. According to Reddy (1994), uniracial parents in interracial relationships have a difficult time preparing their biracial children for what they will experience in society. With experiences unique to their particular ethnic group, it is difficult to fully understand the biracial experience. Often, biracial children have completely different phenotypes and societal experiences than either of their parents and thus have experiences that neither parent could fully appreciate, understand, or teach. Racial ambiguity and dual identity often create a number of difficult experiences, such as rejection, racism, isolation, and identity confusion. In some instances, uniracial parents are unable or unwilling to communicate these difficulties to their children.

Reddy (1994) outlined three main assumptions that parents and families of biracial children often forget. (1) Parents may not be aware in their child-rearing that their biracial children do not always identify with how they look. Parents assume that biracial children identify with the race that they phenotypically resemble. Although teachers, peers, and strangers may automatically categorize them in one racial group, the biracial person may not identify with that group. The process of shaping one's identity based on societal perceptions is known as the "looking-glass self" (Padilla & Perez, 2003). Various family and social experiences cause biracial children to accept or reject the looking-glass identity. Additionally, some parents encourage their children to embrace both cultural identities and avoid "choosing sides." (2) It is not unusual for a biracial individual to be excluded from a racial or ethnic group. Biracial adolescents report feeling isolated if they have few biracial peers. A biracial adolescent who looks ethnic but "acts White," for example, may be rejected by one group because of how he or she looks and by another because of how he or she acts. This is perhaps one reason why many parents choose to raise their children to identify with the group that they phenotypically resemble. (3) There is usually more than one possible positive racial-identity resolution, but finding these alternative solutions may be difficult. People can identify with how they look, identify with both cultures, identify with a single culture, identify as biracial, or create their own racial identity. How the young person identifies is largely influenced by parental/familial modes of cultural and racial transmission. Community diversity, presence or absence of significant family members, cultural and language practices, and socialization preferences largely shape the identity formation of biracial children.

Root (1996) cautioned parents about cultural-transmission practices that have the potential for creating a "fragmented identity" (i.e., identity conflict and confusion) in their children. Identity fragmentation can be minimized through open, supportive communication between parents and children. In a guide for parents with biracial children, Jackson Nakazawa (2004) states that teaching biracial children about all of their cultures and letting them know that it is okay (and wonderful) to be who they are and to look the way they do are very important first steps. The unconditional support of a loving family that offers a safe haven from racial categorization can be comforting and relieving from society's constant need to categorize, define, and treat accordingly. It is also important that parents consider and discuss the difficulties of prejudice and discrimination that their children might face.

Another strong social influence of identification is the peer group. As children develop, peers become an important referent group. The racial composition of peer groups can have a particularly strong impact on the way that biracial children choose to identify. Because peers increasingly become the social referent group as children get older and become young adults, opinions, beliefs, and other social cues can sway identification toward the larger cultural identification of the peer group and also influence the intergenerational transmissions that occur around themes of race, culture, and identity. Biracial children with weak parental involvement in their cultural development tend to be more susceptible to the social influences of their peers. Thus, peers can be a strong positive or negative determinant of racial identity for biracial children.

In addition to the familial- and peer-socializing influences, the community and its cultural messages can influence identity development. Community settings that are largely representative of a single culture and race can differentially impact the life of a biracial young person seeking to identify racially. Interracial families living in high ethnically dense communities – for example, Latino, Asian, and Black neighborhoods – are more likely to be exposed to Black, Latino, and Asian culture, thus influencing the socialization of biracial children.

Patterns of cultural transmission in childhood can facilitate or interfere with how biracial children experience in-group and out-group racism. It is not too uncommon to hear that a biethnic person is perceived as not dark enough or not culturally competent in the ethnic language or culture (Streeter, 1996). Some mixed-race individuals face ridicule based on their phenotypes while ironically also being pressured to identify with their phenotypic ethnic and/or racial community. The challenges that biracial students encounter from other ethnic students are made more difficult if they believe that they have to defend their parents.

In a study conducted in Hawaii and New Mexico on mixed-ethnic heritage individuals, Stephan and Stephan (1989, 1991) reported on positive features of mixed-ethnic parentage. In this research, they assessed the psychological functioning of mixed-heritage individuals to test whether they conformed to the negative characteristics predicted by the "marginalists" or whether respondents manifested positive features assumed by the "biculturalists." In Hawaii, the subjects were college students of Caucasian and Asian American heritage plus a group of mixed Caucasian Asian–heritage students. In New Mexico, the single-heritage respondents were non-Hispanic Whites and Hispanics and the mixed-heritage subjects were mixed non-Hispanic White and Hispanic students. The results showed that on measures of "Attitudes toward Caucasians (C) and Asian-Americans/Hispanics (A-A/H)," "Contact with Cs and A-A/Hs," and "Enjoyment of C culture and A-A/H culture," the mixed-heritage individuals fell midway between the single-heritage comparison groups whether in Hawaii or New Mexico. Furthermore, the mixed-heritage individuals projected an image of the perfect cultural bridge between the ethnic and mainstream groups. The only significant differences were on intergroup anxiety and self-esteem, with the Hawaiian Asian group expressing greater intergroup anxiety and lower self-esteem than either the Caucasians or the mixed-heritage groups. It is interesting that in Hawaii the mixed-heritage respondents were more likely to identify as Japanese than were the respondents in New Mexico, who showed more resistance to identify as Mexican-origin. This may be due to the higher social status of Japanese in Hawaii and the much lower social status of Mexicans in a border region like New Mexico. More research is necessary to examine the role of social status in the dual-cultural identity of mixed-heritage individuals.

Although there is still much to learn about mixed-ethnic/racial-heritage marriages and cultural-transmission practices within such households, the findings indicate that biracial individuals are well adjusted and socially competent in their two cultures. If there are problems that biracial individuals experience, they are due to in-group and out-group racism that affects majority and minority groups alike more than to any failings in the biracial individuals themselves. Biracial and bicultural individuals who are integrated into their dual-cultural heritage and who are open and positive about their background have life experiences that are rich and full. More developmental-oriented studies are needed that focus on how parents socialize children to be responsive to their dual-cultural and racial/ethnic heritage, as well as in how to manage discrimination directed toward them because of their biracial heritage. Finally, the crossing of color and cultural boundaries is no longer perceived with the same negative lens of earlier times. Mixed-race couples and their children are adding a new vitality to America (Obama, 1995).

CONCLUSION

Demographic shifts in the United States in the past 30 years have altered how we should think about socialization practices and the transmission of culture across successive generations. The traditional melting-pot view of America may never have been a reality for all immigrants, and today this is even more apparent with large numbers of immigrants coming from Latin America and Asian countries. These newer immigrants are literally changing the face of America, from white to various shades of brown. Furthermore, immigrant parents are more inclined now than at other times to pass their traditional culture to their children and grandchildren. This does not imply that the cultural linkages that bind us together as Americans are endangered; rather, biculturalism is seen as the wave of the future and an asset to be embraced.

Individuals who are socialized into the traditions and practices of two cultures are far more numerous than what is reflected in the professional literature. Furthermore, because of significant immigration – especially from Latin America and Asia – coupled with significant increases in exogamy (i.e., intermarriage) during the last 30 years, there is more reason for developmental psychologists to include bicultural transmission in their study of child and adolescent development.

Although the focus in this chapter has been on bicultural intergenerational transmission in Hispanics and Asian American families, it is important to acknowledge that the same processes that operate in cultural transmission in these two groups are to be found in many other immigrant groups, second- and later-generation ethnic Americans, and mixed-heritage individuals of many different backgrounds. More research is needed to fully comprehend dual-culture socialization processes and outcomes for children and adolescents. Recognition of bicultural socialization is an important area of study and, until such studies are undertaken, we will have an incomplete understanding of how many children balance the traditional cultural practices of the home and the larger American culture in which they live.

Today's psychological models used in the study of cultural transmission and biculturalism must examine new possibilities in the evaluation of lifestyles across generations, syntheses of cultures, and psychological adaptation. It is important to understand how stigmatization and negative stereotypes based on skin color and phenotype operate to motivate individuals to adopt bicultural strategies to cope with racism. In other words, stigma and perceived discrimination have effects that are different from what we might have anticipated. Immigrants and ethnic people are not shedding their culture to become American; instead, discrimination appears to motivate ethnic-group members to transmit their heritage knowledge from one generation to the next while also adopting the behavioral competencies necessary to become functioning members of an American culture to which they also belong.

The effort to understand complex and sensitive issues involving ethnic families and children may seem burdensome. However, the payoff is worth the effort if we are able to better understand the meaning of cultural transmission in families and societal contexts that are guided daily by more than a single culture. This approach also acknowledges that biculturalism creates new ways of envisioning developmental processes.

REFERENCES

Arce, C. H., Murguia, E., & Frisbie, W. P. (1987). Phenotype and life chances among Chicanos. *Hispanic Journal of Behavioral Sciences, 9,* 19–23.

Bernal, M. E., Knight, G. P., Garza, C. A., Ocampo, K. A., & Cota, M. K. (1990). The development of ethnic identity in Mexican American children. *Hispanic Journal of Behavioral Sciences, 12,* 3–24.

Bernal, G., Trimble, J., Burlew, A. K., & Leong, F. T. (Eds.) (2003). *Handbook of Racial and Ethnic Minority Psychology.* Thousand Oaks, CA: Sage Publications.

Berry, J. W. (2003). Conceptual approaches to acculturation. In K. M. Chun, P. Balls Organista, & G. Marin (Eds.), *Acculturation: Advances in theory, measurement, and applied research* (pp. 17–37). Washington, DC: American Psychological Association.

Buchanan, P. J. (2002). *The death of the West: How dying populations and immigrant invasions imperil our country and civilization.* New York: St. Martin's Press.

Buriel, R., & Cardoza, D. (1993). Mexican American ethnic labeling: An intrafamilial and intergenerational analysis. In M. E. Bernal & G. P. Knight (Eds.), *Ethnic identity: Formation and transmission among Hispanics and other minorities* (pp. 197–210). Albany, NY: State University of New York.

Buriel, R., Perez, W., De Ment, T. L., Chavez, D. V., & Moran, V. R. (1998). The relationship of language brokering to academic performance, biculturalism, and self-efficacy among Latino adolescents. *Hispanic Journal of Behavioral Sciences, 20,* 283–297.

Chao, R. K. (1994). Beyond parental control and authoritarian parenting style: Understanding Chinese parenting through the cultural notion of training. *Child Development, 65,* 1111–1120.

Chao, R. K. (1996). Chinese and European-American mothers' beliefs about the role of parenting in children's school success. *Journal of Cross-Cultural Psychology, 27,* 403–423.

Chao, R. K. (2000). Cultural explanations for the role of parenting in the school success of Asian American children. In R. D. Taylor & M. C. Wang (Eds.), *Resilience across contexts: Family, work, culture, and community* (pp. 333–363). Mahwah, NJ: Lawrence Erlbaum Associates.

Chun, K. M., Balls Organista, P., & Marin, G. (2002). *Acculturation: Advances in theory, measurement, and applied research.* Washington, DC: American Psychological Association.

Coronado, M., Guevarra, R. P., Moniz, J., & Szanto, L. F. (Eds.). (2003). *Crossing lines: Race and mixed race across the geohistorical divide.* Santa Barbara, CA: Multiethnic Student Outreach, University of California.

Del Pilar, J. A., & Udasco, J. O. (2004). Marginality theory: The lack of construct validity. *Hispanic Journal of Behavioral Sciences, 26*(1), 3–15.

Der-Karabetian, A. (1980). Two cultural identities of Armenian Americans. *Psychological Reports, 47,* 123–128.

Detzner, D. F. (1996). No place without a home: Southeast Asian grandparents in refugee families. *Generations, 20,* 45–48.

EdSource (2007). *Resource cards on California schools.* Mountain View, CA: EdSource.

Erikson, H. E. (1968). *Identity: Youth and crisis.* New York: W. W. Norton & Co.

Gómez, C. (2000). The continual significance of skin color: An exploratory study of Latinos in the Northeast. *Hispanic Journal of Behavioral Sciences, 22*(1), 94–103.

Green, A. W. (1947). A re-examination of the marginal man concept. *Social Forces, 26,* 167–171.

Hall, C. N., & Okazaki, S. (Eds.). (2002). *Asian American psychology.* Washington, DC: American Psychological Association.

Hanson, V. D. (2003). *Mexifornia: A state of becoming.* San Francisco, CA: Encounter Books.

Haritatos, J., & Benet-Martinez, V. (2002). Bicultural identities: The interface of cultural, personality, and sociocognitive processes. *Journal of Research in Personality, 6,* 598–606.

Hughes, D., & Johnson, D. (2001). Correlates in children's experiences of parents' racial socialization behaviors. *Journal of Marriage and Family, 63,* 981–995.

Hurtado, A., & Gurin, P. (1987). Ethnic identity and bilingualism attitudes. *Hispanic Journal of Behavioral Sciences, 9,* 1–18.

Jackson Nakazawa, D. (2004). *Does anybody else look like me? A parent's guide to raising multiracial children.* New York: Da Capo Press.

Keefe, S. E., & Padilla, A. M. (1987). *Chicano ethnicity.* Albuquerque, NM: University of New Mexico Press.

Knight, G. P., Bernal, M. E., Cota, M. K., Garza, C. A., & Ocampo, K. A. (1993). Family socialization and Mexican American identity and behavior. In M. E. Bernal & G. P. Knight (Eds.), *Ethnic identity: Formation and transmission among Hispanics and other minorities* (pp. 105–129). Albany, NY: State University of New York Press.

LaFromboise, T., Coleman, H. L., & Gerton, J. (1993). Psychological impact of biculturalism: Evidence and theory. *Psychological Bulletin, 114*(3), 395–412.

Lopez, D. E. (1982). *Language maintenance and shift in the United States today: The basic patterns and their social implications. Volume III: Hispanics and Portuguese* (p. 135). Los Alamitos, CA: National Center for Bilingual Research.

Maccoby, E. E. (2000). Parenting and its effect on children: On reading and misreading behavior genetics. *Annual Review of Psychology, 51*, 1–27.

Maccoby, E. E., & Martin, J. A. (1983). Socialization in the context of the family: Parent–child interaction. In P. H. Mussen (Ed.), *Handbook of child psychology. Vol. IV: Socialization, personality, and social development* (pp. 1–101). New York: John Wiley & Sons.

Mann, J. W. (1973). Status: The marginal reaction: Mixed-bloods and Jews. In P. Watson. (Ed.), *Psychology and race* (pp. 213–223). Upper Saddle River, NJ: Penguin Education.

Mena, F. J., Padilla, A. M., & Maldonado, M. (1987). Acculturative stress and specific coping strategies among immigrant and later-generation college students. *Hispanic Journal of Behavioral Sciences, 9*, 207–225.

Minuchin, P. P., & Shapiro, E. K. (1983). The school as a context for social development. In P. H. Mussen (Ed.), *Handbook for child psychology. Vol. IV: Socialization, personality, and social development* (pp. 197–274). New York: John Wiley & Sons.

Montgomery, G. T. (1992). Comfort with acculturation status among students from South Texas. *Hispanic Journal of Behavioral Sciences, 14*, 201–223.

Mura, D. (1991). *Turning Japanese: Memoirs of a Sensei*. New York: Anchor Books.

Murguia, E. (1982). *Chicano intermarriage: A theoretical and empirical study*. San Antonio, TX: Trinity University Press.

Nash, G. B. (1999). *Forbidden love: The secret history of mixed-race America*. New York: Henry Holt and Co.

Obama, B. (1995). *Dreams from my father: A story of race and inheritance*. New York: Times Books.

Olsen, L. (1997). *Made in America: Immigrant students in our public schools*. New York: The New Press.

Padilla, A. M. (1980). The role of cultural awareness and ethnic loyalty in acculturation. In A. M. Padilla (Ed.), *Acculturation: Theory, models, and some new findings* (pp. 47–84). Boulder, CO: Westview Press.

Padilla, A. M. (2003). *Becoming American: Acculturation, assimilation, and banishment*. Invited presentation to the Developmental Psychology Colloquium, University of California, Santa Cruz, November 17.

Padilla, A. M., & Lindholm, K. J. (1992). *What do we know about culturally diverse children?* Paper presented at the Annual Meeting of the American Psychological Association, Washington, DC, August 14.

Padilla, A. M., & Perez, W. (2003). Acculturation, social identify, and social cognition: A new perspective. *Hispanic Journal of Behavioral Sciences, 25*, 35–55.

Park, R. E. (1928). Migration and the marginal man. *American Journal of Sociology, 5*, 881–893.

Phinney, J. S., & Chavira, V. (1995). Parental ethnic socialization and adolescent coping with problems related to ethnicity. *Journal of Research on Adolescence, 5*, 31–53.

Phinney, J. S., Ong, A., & Madden, T. (2000). Cultural values and intergenerational value discrepancies in immigrant and non-immigrant families. *Child Development, 71*, 528–539.

Portes, A., & Rumbaut, R. G. (1990). *Immigrant America: A portrait*. Berkeley, CA: The University of California Press.

Portes, A., & Rumbaut, R. G. (2001). *Legacies: The story of the immigrant second generation*. Berkeley, CA: University of California Press.

Quintana, S. M., Castaneda-English, P., & Ybarra, V. C. (1999). Role of perspective-taking abilities and ethnic socialization in development of adolescent ethnic identity. *Journal of Research on Adolescence, 9,* 161–184.

Quintana, S. M., & Vera, E. M. (1999). Mexican American children's ethnic identity, understanding of ethnic prejudice, and parental ethnic socialization. *Hispanic Journal of Behavioral Sciences, 21,* 387–404.

Reddy, M. (1994). *Crossing the color line: Race, parenting, and culture.* New Brunswick, NJ: Rutgers University Press.

Rong, X. L., & Brown, F. (2001). The effects of immigrant generation and ethnicity on educational attainment among young African and Caribbean Blacks in the United States. *Harvard Educational Review, 71,* 536–565.

Root, M. P. (Ed.). (1992). *Racially mixed people in America.* Newbury Park, CA: Sage Publications.

Root, M. P. (Ed.). (1996). *The multiracial experience: Racial borders as the New Frontier.* Thousand Oaks, CA: Sage Publications.

Root, M. P. (2001). *Love's revolution: Interracial marriages.* Philadelphia: Temple University Press.

Rosenblatt, P. C., Karis, T. A., & Powell, R. D. (1995). *Multiracial couples: Black & White voices.* Thousand Oaks, CA: Sage Publications.

Salgado de Snyder, N., Lopez, C. M., & Padilla, A. M. (1982). Ethnic identity and cultural awareness among the offspring of Mexican interethnic marriages. *Journal of Early Adolescence, 2,* 277–282.

Sarroub, L. K. (2001). The sojourner experience of Yemeni American high school students: An ethnographic portrait. *Harvard Educational Review, 71,* 390–415.

Schlesinger, A. M., Jr. (1991). *The disuniting of America: Reflections on a multicultural society.* New York: W. W. Norton.

Schmidt, A., & Padilla, A. M. (1983). Grandparent–grandchild interaction in a Mexican American group. *Hispanic Journal of Behavioral Sciences, 5,* 181–198.

Segal, U. A. (2002). *A framework for immigration: Asians in the United States.* New York: Columbia University Press.

Silverstein, M., & Chen, X. (1999). The impact of acculturation in Mexican American families on the quality of adult grandchild–grandparent relationships. *Journal of Marriage and the Family, 61,* 188–198.

Stephan, C. W., & Stephan, W. G. (1989). After intermarriage: Ethnic identity among mixed Japanese American and Hispanics. *Journal of Marriage and the Family, 51,* 507–519.

Stephan, W. G., & Stephan, C. W. (1991). Intermarriage: Effects on personality, adjustment, and intergroup relations in two samples of students. *Journal of Marriage and the Family, 53,* 241–250.

Stonequist, E. V. (1937). *The marginal man: A study in personality and culture conflict.* New York: Russell & Russell, Inc.

Streeter, C. A. (1996). Ambiguous bodies: Locating Black/White women in cultural representations. In M. P. Root (Ed.), *The multicultural experience: Racial borders as the New Frontier* (pp. 305–320). Thousand Oaks, CA: Sage Publications.

Suarez-Orozco, C., & Suarez-Orozco, M. M. (2001). *Children of immigration.* Cambridge, MA: Harvard University Press.

Sung, B. L. (1985). Bicultural conflicts in Chinese immigrant children. *Journal of Comparative Family Studies, 16*, 255–269.

Szapocznik, J., Santisteban, D., Kurtines, W., Perez-Vidal, A., & Hervis, O. (1984). Bicultural effectiveness training: A treatment intervention for enhancing intercultural adjustment in Cuban American families. *Hispanic Journal of Behavioral Sciences, 6*, 317–344.

Tatum, C. M. (2001). *Chicano popular culture: Que hable el pueblo.* Tucson, AZ: The University of Arizona Press.

Tseng, V., & Fuligni, A. J. (2000). Parent–adolescent language use and relationships among immigrant families with East Asian, Filipino, and Latin American backgrounds. *Journal of Marriage and the Family, 62*, 465–476.

Umana-Taylor, A. J., & Fine, M. A. (2004). Examining ethnic identity among Mexican-origin adolescents living in the United States. *Hispanic Journal of Behavioral Sciences, 26*, 36–59.

U.S. Census Bureau (March 2001). Overview of race and Hispanic origin. Accessed July 15, 2004, at www.census.gov/population/www/socdemo/race.html.

Vasquez, L. A., Garcia-Vazquez, E., Bauman, S. A., & Sierra, A. S. (1997). Skin color, acculturation, and community interest among Mexican American students: A research note. *Hispanic Journal of Behavioral Sciences, 19*(3), 377–387.

Veltman, C. (1981). Anglicization in the United States: The importance of parental nativity and language characteristics. *International Journal of the Sociology of Language, 32*, 65–84.

Weinstein-Shr, G., & Henkin, N. (1991). Continuity and change: Intergenerational relations in Southeast Asian refugee families. *Marriage and Family Review, 16*, 351–367.

Weisskirch, R. S., & Alatorre Alva, S. (2002). Language brokering and the acculturation of Latino Children. *Hispanic Journal of Behavioral Sciences, 24*(3), 369–378.

Winters, L. I., & De Bose, H. L. (Eds.). (2003). *New faces in a changing America: Multiracial identity in the 21st century.* Thousand Oaks, CA: Sage Publications.

Zack, N. (1993). *Race and mixed race.* Philadelphia: Temple University Press.

Zak, I. (1973). Dimensions of Jewish-American identity. *Psychological Reports, 33*, 891–900.

10

The Transmission Process: Mechanisms and Contexts

UTE SCHÖNPFLUG AND LUDWIG BILZ

INTRODUCTION

Cultural transmission – as opposed to genetic transmission – requires some form of social learning. Thus, no one would claim cultural transmission if all members of a population learned a particular behavior only because they had all been exposed to the same set of contingencies from the physical environment. In this case, there is no cultural transmission because there is no social learning. Intergenerational cultural transmission is clearly the appropriate concept, on the other hand, when adults intentionally teach the younger generation or when the younger generation imitates adults. Such clear forms of transmission may not always be involved in the intergenerational transfer of information, however. The term *cultural* in cultural transmission indicates the transmission of cultural elements that are widely distributed, such as social orientations, knowledge, skills, and behaviors (e.g., rituals).

Cultural persistence is essentially a question of social transmission (Cavalli-Sforza & Feldman, 1981). Vertical social transmission from the parent generation to the offspring generation may prepare the ground for continuity in culture. It is less responsive to environmental variability (Laland, 1993). However, the process of cultural transmission does not lead to a constant replication of culture in successive generations; rather, it falls somewhere between an exact transmission (with hardly any difference between parents and offspring) and a complete failure of transmission (with hardly any similarity between the generations). Functionally, either extreme would be problematic for a society: Exact transmission would not allow for novelty and change and, hence, the ability to respond to new situations, whereas failure of transmission would not permit coordinated action between generations (Boyd & Richerson, 1985). In addition, Boyd and Richerson noted that vertical parent–offspring transmission is unbiased; *unbiased* refers to the relatively weak responsivity to environmental influences and to such collective transmission mechanisms as prestige or conformity transmission, which is *biased* (see also Schönpflug, Chapter 1, this volume).

If new members of a culture enter and leave a social system slowly, the mechanisms of transmission can be slow and diffuse. In this case, vertical transmission is the predominant path. If new members join and exit rapidly, or in large numbers relative to those who stay, then culture must be transmitted quickly and intensively if it is to be maintained. In this case, the horizontal transmission network functions most efficiently.

Our research focuses on vertical transmission from parents to offspring. We were interested in the selectivity of transmission contents, in the impact of cross-cultural and intracultural social contexts, and in various transmission mechanisms or *transmission belts*. We discuss some noteworthy findings that may help to provide some insight to the process of transmission and to the results of that process. Our research explores the transmission of values but other content areas were also included, such as the belief in a just world (Schönpflug & Bilz, 2004), xenophobia (Six, Geppert, & Schönpflug, Chapter 16, this volume), and social identity (Geppert, 2002).

The transmission of value orientations may be seen as a core issue of culture maintenance and culture change. Values provide standards for actions and thus regulate day-to-day behavior as well as important and critical life decisions (e.g., Gärling, 1999). Some global processes involved in the transmission of values are assumed to be (1) *socialization*, and (2) *enculturation*. Socialization involves the deliberate shaping of individuals to become adapted to the social environment. The common means of transmission by socialization are concrete child-rearing or child-training practices by parents and other educators or mentors. They may be more or less explicit teaching strategies or implicit mechanisms, such as observational learning. Socializers aim at educating the offspring generation to become functioning and adaptive members of the social community. Enculturation aims at developing persons into competent members of a culture including identity, language, rituals, and values (see also Berry & Georgas, Chapter 6, this volume). It may also take the form of either explicit, deliberate learning or implicit, unintentional learning.

The transmission process involves a selection of transmitted contents. Campbell (1975) argued that the fact that most moral beliefs are altruistic suggests that they have been shaped by group selection, through mentor, peer, and parent–offspring transmission. A transfer of this finding to the realm of values leads to the hypothesis that collectivistic values are more readily transmitted than individualistic values, as the former are of the type that are shaped by group selection while the latter are not. Collectivistic values may be functional to group maintenance and lead to the evolution of cooperation among groups of unrelated individuals.

This chapter introduces three lines of research followed up during recent years. The first line involves the selectivity of contents in the parent–offspring transmission process, the second line tries to clarify the impact of varying contexts on transmission, and the third line attempts to identify various mechanisms or transmission belts that enhance or prevent transmission. The criterion for transmission throughout our research is the similarity between transmitter and transmittee or adopter with regard to a given transmission content.

1.0. STUDY 1: INTERGENERATIONAL TRANSMISSION OF VALUES

Although intergenerational transmission is not asymmetrical – being oriented only from the older to the younger generation – our research focuses on the direction from parent to offspring. Kohn (1983; Kohn, Slomczynski, & Schoenbach, 1986) discovered that a parent's experiences of work, especially self-direction at work, have a positive influence on a child's personality. They also found retroactive transmission of children to parents but only in their American sample and not in their Polish sample. The strength of transmission in both directions seemed to be dependent on context. In Poland, mothers appeared to have a stronger influence on their children than fathers, and children seemed to have less influence on their parents. Kohn (1983) summarized his transmission research by stating that the similarity between adults and their children is only moderate and limited to certain domains: political and religious beliefs and lifestyle, value orientations, and general points of view concerning social reality.

Schönpflug and Silbereisen (1992) initiated a longitudinal study following the ideas of Kohn, Slomczynski, and Schoenbach (1986). They conceptualized transmission as taking place through communication in which social orientations and norms are transported. The communication variables considered were those relevant for estimating the degree of transmission, such as intensity and initiation of discussions on certain contents. Again, bidirectional transmission was only observed in German and not in Polish families. In German families, the mother had more influence on her child's beliefs about *societal keynote issues* (Bengtson & Troll, 1978) when the child was in early and middle adolescence; thereafter, in later adolescence, the father seemed to be more influential. In Polish families, both parents had an equal influence on their children when they were 14 years old, but 1 year later, mothers influenced their children more than fathers.

In another study from our initial research, two further aspects of transmission became important: the variation of *contents of transmission* – in this study, various values – and *transmission belts* or transmission-enhancing conditions. One kind of transmission belt investigated was relational: parenting styles and marital quality of the parents. The other kinds of transmission belt involved sociodevelopmental variables: father's education, phase in adolescent development (i.e., early, middle, and late adolescence), and sibling position.

The interdisciplinary longitudinal study included Turkish adolescents and their parents living as immigrant workers in Germany as well as Turkish adolescents and their families in Istanbul. The transmission of value orientations according to Schwartz (1992, 1994) was investigated (Schönpflug, 2001). The main issues of this study were the questions of whether some value orientations are more readily transmitted than others, whether we can identify the impact of various transmission belts, and whether varying context of the same cultural group makes a difference for both aspects.

1.1. Cultural Contexts and Transmission Belts

Parent–offspring transmission does not corroborate the adaptation to variable environments. In the case of family migration, the effectiveness of transmission from parents to children should be lower because the transmission of the culture of origin may be dysfunctional in the host country. Not only will the offspring generation be reluctant to accept transmission, but parents may also be reluctant to transmit their own orientations, which – in a new environment – to a certain extent constitute standards for nonadaptive behavior patterns. In addition, the acculturation of the children of migrants is usually faster than that of the parents (Schönpflug, 2007) and, hence, value discrepancy between the parent and the child generations increases with length of stay in the migration context (Phinney, Ong, & Madden, 2000).

In Schwartz's (1992) international study on value dimensions, Turkey turned out to be one of the collectivistic cultures, whereas Germany was recognized as being an individualistic society. Turkish migrants to Germany make a transition from a collectivistic to an individualistic social environment. Thus, effective transmission between generations in migrated groups necessarily leads to segregation from the majority culture in the host country when host culture and culture of origin of a migrated group differ. Migrant parents oriented toward maintenance of the culture of origin in the host country emphasize the transmission of culture of origin, whereas parents oriented toward adaptation in the host society withhold cultural transmission in order to let their children adapt functional behavior patterns from other sources of transmission. Therefore, parents living in the context of their culture of origin should transmit their value orientation more intensively than parents living in a migration context. In contrast to this line of thinking is Boyd and Richerson's (1985) insight stating that continuous cultures have slow and diffuse transmissions, whereas rapidly changing cultures should reveal rapid and – probably – more intense transmission. Their hypothesis might also hold for the migration situation, given that migrant parents want to constrain their children's acculturation.

1.2. Relational Transmission Belts

Some parenting styles are effective transmission belts, whereas others prevent transmission (van Ijzendoorn, 1992). Parenting styles that create a positive emotional interaction between parent and child most likely promote the transmission of values. One parenting style in question is empathetic parenting. The rigid-authoritarian parenting style may distance parent and child, thus diminishing chances for transmission.

A positive marital relationship implies estimating a mutually positive emotional quality and homogeneity of attitudes and orientations between conjugal partners. As early as 1981, Cavalli-Sforza and Feldman found that homogeneity in parental attitudes leads to more intense transmission of that attitude in the intergenerational context.

1.3. Developmental Perspective

The result of the transfer of social orientations (e.g., attitudes and values) and of skills and knowledge in the transmission process is similarity between the persons involved. In line with Cavalli-Sforza, Feldman, Chen, and Dornbusch and colleagues (1982), we assume that the similarity observed between parents and offspring may be considered as valid evidence of intergenerational transmission. From a developmental point of view, this process goes through various stages during a lifetime. Younger children are subject to intense transmission efforts by their socializers. With growing autonomy, the child adopts what the transmitter offers more and more selectively. By the time the child goes through adolescence, differential transmission results may be observed: Adolescents may revolt against parental transmission that they had previously adopted and may later on accept it again. Transmission is probably most effective at particular stages of development. According to more recent ideas put forward by Grolnick, Deci, and Ryan (1997), the growing autonomy of a child prevents the effective transmission of values in the family. As autonomy increases with age, the negative influences of a child's age on the effectiveness of transmission processes should be observed.

Education is a personal resource of a transmitter with positive effects on transmission. With increasing levels of education, fathers might find greater acceptability as models for their children. Greater acceptability as a model leads to more intense transmission (Bandura, 1986; Grusec, 1997); in addition, educated fathers might have greater skills for transmission.

Another developmental issue is the question of the influence of sibling position of the child under study. Harris (1998) argued that later-born children are more susceptible to peer or sibling influence than firstborn children and, hence, show less impact of parental transmission attempts. This effect may be independent of the age of the adolescent child. One observation that seems to be noteworthy is that the youngest siblings seem to be more similar to their parents than the older ones (Cavalli-Sforza et al., 1982). At the same time, they might be equally influenced by their older siblings. The parents' influence is then mediated through the older siblings, as Chen, Cavalli-Sforza, and Feldman (1982) found in a study about transmission in Taiwan.

In accordance with the various aspects reported from the literature, the following hypotheses were tested in our initial research:

1. The generation gap indicated by the parent–child difference in mean ratings of importance of values is larger for parent–child dyads with the experience of discontinuous cultural contexts (e.g., the experience of migration) than for parent–child dyads experiencing continuity in their sociocultural contexts because they stayed in their home country.
2. Collectivistic values are subject to vertical parent–offspring transmission between generations in the family, whereas individualistic values tend not to be transmitted in this way.
3. Irrespective of social context, the intensity of transmission is moderated by parenting styles based on commitment and closeness between the parent and the child generations (e.g., empathetic parenting) but is not enhanced by a rigid-authoritarian parenting style. In addition, the parents' positive quality of marital relationship enhances transmission between generations because it provides homogeneity of parental orientations.
4. The higher the parents' personal resources, the more probable the effective transmission of their values because they have greater acceptability as models and greater transmission skills.
5. The older and more autonomous the adolescents become, the less receptive to transmission they will be.
6. The higher the sibling position of the child, the less parent-to-child transmission is observed, as they tend to be more susceptible to sibling influence. However, if older siblings' transmission attempts are in line with those of their parents, the younger siblings will be more similar to their parents.

1.4. Methodological Approach and Results

Methodological Approach. The hypotheses were tested in a longitudinal study including 100 Turkish male adolescents and their parents living in Berlin and 100 Turkish male dyads living in Istanbul. Further details about the sample are described in Schönpflug (2001).

The contents of transmission were nine value categories published by Schwartz (1992), belonging to two major value dimensions: (1) *collectivistic values*: humanism, universalism, traditionalism, security, and conformism; and (2) *individualistic values*: power, self-direction, stimulating life, and hedonism. Sons' *perception of fathers' parenting styles* was partly conceptualized according to Baumrind (1991). For the study, only two parenting styles were defined: rigid-authoritarian and empathetic, resulting from a factor analysis including all

26 items from the children's questionnaire (Cronbach's alphas were .75 and .76, respectively). In addition, *marital harmony* was measured by a scale assessing attitude toward marriage: It consisted of five items from the fathers' questionnaire. Internal consistency for the five items was high (Cronbach's alpha = .87). *Level of father's education* and *sibling position of child* as indicated by the parent were introduced as further factors influencing the transmission result. All measurements were checked for response biases. The ratings differentiated well within and across the scales.

Generation Gap in Mean Importance of Values. To test hypothesis 1, group comparisons of means of values were made. There were significant father–son differences in value orientation. In the migration groups, collectivistic values seemed to be more important to fathers than to their sons, but not in the father–son dyads living in Turkey. Here, the sons rated all collectivistic value categories except traditionalism as being more important than their fathers did. All mean differences for collectivistic values between fathers and their sons in Berlin were significant. The Turkish father–son dyads in Turkey revealed significant father–son mean value differences in three collectivistic value categories (i.e., universalism, traditionalism, and conformism), but two were in the opposite direction: Sons rated humanism and universalism higher than fathers did. The generation-gap analysis between fathers and sons in the three samples revealed significant differences for three of the four individualistic value categories: universalism, power, and self-direction. For power, the fathers' mean value was higher than that of the sons', whereas for the other categories, the reverse was true. In the Southern German subsample, only stimulation and hedonism revealed a significant generation gap, with the sons' means being higher than the fathers'. In the Istanbul subsample, once again, stimulation, hedonism, and self-direction had significantly higher mean values in sons than in fathers.

To summarize, the generation gap is greatest in the Berlin sample, followed by the Istanbul sample, and is lowest in the Southern German sample; hypothesis 1 was therefore not consistently confirmed.

Transmission of Values. Hypothesis 2 predicts that there is more transmission of collectivistic than individualistic values within generational dyads. To test this hypothesis, nine stepwise multiple-regression analyses were performed, one for each value category. They included the sons' importance of a particular value category as a dependent variable and their fathers' importance of the same value category as a predictor in the first step. According to Larson and Almeida (1999), a significant β value may be interpreted as indicating the impact of the fathers' value system on their sons' value system. Region, age, and level of parental education were partialled out in the analysis. The children's school track was not controlled for because at the age level of the participants, the school system in Turkey does not differentiate between school levels. Table 10.1 indicates results of the multiple regressions: It reveals that transmission was observed in the case of collectivistic value categories but was not indicated by significant β values in

Table 10.1. *Transmission of values in Turkish father–son dyads (Study 1)* *(transmission-coefficients β from multiple-regression analyses)*

| | Criteria: Value Son | | | | | | | | |
| | Collectivistic Values | | | | | Individualistic Values | | | |
	Humanism	Universal-ism	Security	Tradi-tionalism	Conform-ism	Stimu-lation	Hedo-nism	Power	Self-Direction
Predictor									
Value Father	.24**	.21**	.28***	.21**	.20**				.18**
Controlled for									
Age					−.12*				
Region[1]			.18**				−.15*	.15*	
Parental Education									.12*
Sibling Position									

$* = p < .05; ** = p < .01; *** = p < .001.$
[1] Coded 1 = Berlin, 2 = Southern Germany, 3 = Istanbul.

the case of individualistic value categories. The only exception to this general result was the value category of self-direction. The variables that were controlled for rarely had a significant effect on the sons' importance ratings in each of the nine value groups. Region had a significant impact for the value categories of security, hedonism, and power, and parental education had a significant effect on the value category termed *self-direction*. The results may be understood as a confirmation of hypothesis 2.

Moderators of Transmission. The following six moderators of the transmission process were examined: empathetic and rigid-authoritarian parenting styles, marital relationship of parents, father's education, child's age, and sibling position. The two parenting styles and marital-relationship scale scores were dichotomized by median split and the multiple-regression analyses described previously were repeated separately for high and low levels of moderators. The empathetic and rigid-authoritarian styles yielded most transmissions when high and low levels were given, respectively. The transmission coefficients in Table 10.2 are controlled for age, parental education, and region.

Collectivistic values were generally transmitted when empathetic parenting was high. Security was an exception, showing no transmission under the two levels of this moderator. However, a stimulating life – an individualistic value – was also transmitted when empathetic parenting was high.

Collectivistic values were predominantly transmitted when rigid-authoritarian parenting was low. Again, one individualistic value group – namely, self-direction – was transmitted well under this level of the second moderator. Thus, transmission occurred in the absence of rigid-authoritarian

Table 10.2. *Transmission coefficients (β) of the two value dimensions of collectivism and individualism conditional on various moderators in Turkish father–son dyads (Study 1)*

		Father–Son Values	
Moderator	Level	Collectivism	Individualism (Self-Direction)
Empathetic	Low		
Parenting	High	.21**	
Rigid-Authoritarian	Low	.27***	(.20)**
Parenting	High		
Positive			
Marital	Low	.23**	
Attitude	High	.28**	(.29)**
Father's	Low		
Educational	Medium	.18*	
Level	High	.27**	
Age	12–14	.25*	(.24)**
in	15–16	.22*	
Years	17–19		
	First	.20*	
Sibling Position	Second	.26**	
	Third–Seventh	.27**	(.24)**

* = $p < .5$; ** = $p < .01$; *** = $p < .001$.

parenting. Security, by contrast, was transmitted under both levels of rigid-authoritarian parenting.

The third moderator included was the fathers' positive attitude toward being married. As predicted, the highly positive group of fathers transmitted more values to their sons than those fathers who evaluated their marriage less positively. Again, however, all five collectivistic value categories were transmitted, whereas only two of the individualistic value categories were transmitted: hedonism and self-direction; hypothesis 3 was thus partially corroborated.

Three further variables were introduced as moderators: educational level of the father, age of child, and sibling position (see Table 10.2). The educational level of the father was trichotomized into low, medium, and high levels. As the transmission coefficients show, most transmission took place at the medium and high levels of the fathers' education; hypothesis 4 was thus confirmed. The selection of values is the same as in the other analyses, as collectivistic value orientation was predominantly observed. When the age of the child was trichotomized into three age groups and introduced as a moderator variable, the transmission coefficients were significant for the two younger age groups but not for the oldest group in late adolescence. A sensitive period for transmission is apparently at a younger, less autonomous stage of development in early to middle adolescence. One exception is the value category of *stimulating life*. In the oldest group, this was the only transmitted value domain. In the younger age groups, the canonical collectivistic values were transmitted. These results support hypothesis 5.

The last moderator was sibling position of the child (see Table 10.2). The sibling position of the child was also trichotomized (i.e., first, second/third, and higher position) and used as a moderator. Contrary to expectations, transmission tended to be more prevalent among the later-born children as compared to first- and second-born children. Contrary to hypothesis 6 but in accordance with Cavalli-Sforza et al. (1982), the later-born children tended to reveal more transmission effects than the first- and second-born children. The first- and second-born children showed transmission effects only for humanism, security, and traditionalism, whereas later-born children showed transmission effects for these three values as well as universalism, conformism, and self-direction. Sibling position is not confounded with age of children ($r = .01$).

The moderators thus confirmed the general results of the global transmission analyses: Moderators corroborate the transmission of predominantly collectivistic values.

1.5. Discussion

This initial study aimed at clarifying two aspects of the process of intergenerational transmission: the selectivity of the transmission process with respect to the contents of transmission and the functioning of *transmission belts*. The transmitted contents investigated were collectivistic values and individualistic value categories. The transmission belts were interactional variables: (1) *relational*: empathetic and rigid-authoritarian parenting styles and marital harmony; and (2) *given resources of transmitters and adopters*: fathers' educational level, stage of adolescent development or age, and sibling position. Furthermore, (3) the *continuity of the cultural context in which the intergenerational transmission process was situated* was also understood as a transmission belt. The results found for transmission of values between Turkish fathers and sons living in Turkey and Germany corroborated most of our hypotheses.

The results reveal that the transmission of values between fathers and sons seemed to be restricted to the collectivistic value categories of humanism, universalism, security, traditionalism, and conformism. This general finding had only one exception: The value category of self-direction was also transmitted. Being collectivistic may well be compatible with being self-directed, whereas the high evaluation of power may not be compatible and, therefore, is not transmitted. Under conditions of special transmission belts, such as high empathetic parenting and high positive evaluation of marital status, the importance of a stimulating life, and hedonism were also transmitted; also, these two value categories seem to be compatible with the transmission of collectivism. Hence, transmission should not be understood as exclusively serving group maintenance: Fathers transmit and sons accept two self-enhancing values – namely, self-direction and stimulating life. Individuals do not tend to exclusively meet the needs of the group, even when socialized and enculturated in a generally collectivistic culture like the Turkish culture (Schwartz, 1992). We have to interpret these results in light of the dyad studied: fathers and sons. The gender-specificity of the results was explored in further research (see the following discussion).

A continuous cultural context does not lead to intensified transmission. Turkish father–son dyads living in Turkey did not show more transmission than Turkish father–son dyads living in a big city or in a provincial environment after work migration to Germany. Thus, continuous contexts lead rather to slow and diffuse transmission, as several authors had foreseen (Cavalli-Sforza et al., 1982; Boyd & Richerson, 1985). However, the analyses including fathers' educational level as a moderator revealed that collectivistic values are transmitted in families with medium and high educational levels but not in low-education families. We may conclude that the transmission of values requires (1) competence on the part of the fathers to use transmission strategies (e.g., empathetic parenting style) to convince their offspring to internalize certain values; and (2) highly evaluated qualities of the transmitter that render him an attractive model.

One developmental issue implied in this study is the test of the parental influence against possible sibling influence. A direct measure of peer impact of values was not included; however, with children's increasing sibling position, more sibling influence and less parental impact in values were expected. The results did not confirm this expectation: The later-born sons revealed a broader parental impact in values than the earlier-born sons. Later-born children seem to be more susceptible to internalizing group-oriented collectivistic values than first- and second-born children. In line with Cavalli-Sforza et al. (1982), we believe that the older children corroborate the parents' transmission attempts by transmitting the same message for whatever reason. More research is needed to further explore this issue.

A critical developmental issue in transmission research is the optimal time span in adolescence for the transmission of values. The results with age group as a moderator suggest that most similarity between fathers and sons is observable in early and middle adolescence. Thus, collectivistic value orientation seemed to be conveyed in the formative years of the first half of adolescence, but the perceived importance of a stimulating life – a compatible individualistic value category – was transmitted late in adolescence. Cultural continuity via effective transmission in the value domain is better ensured when the transmission of values starts early. As adolescents approach adulthood, collective values may no longer be willingly accepted. This conclusion might hold, however, only for adolescents growing up in an individualistic context.

2.0. STUDY 2: GOALS AS MEDIATORS OF TRANSMISSION
AND GENDER DIFFERENCES

Migrant groups should follow the principle forwarded by Cavalli-Sforza and Feldman (1981) that rapidly changing societies with members frequently coming and leaving should reveal intensive transmission attempts in order to maintain their culture by passing it on to the next generation. Yet, parental beliefs and values may have lost some or much of their adaptive value as the new generation grows up in a sociocultural context that differs from the context in which their parents were socialized and enculturated. Also, in this situation, parental models are challenged by competing role models, which are often more attractive or prestigious within the dominant culture of the host society. On the other hand, in the absence of convergent vertical, horizontal, and oblique cultural transmission in the host society, one may expect that intrafamilial cultural transmission is more intensely motivated and more intentionally directed and sustained by the parents. In addition, family solidarity may increase when families face discrimination from the majority society and a sense of being underprivileged. Nauck's (1997) findings documented gender and educational differences in intergenerational relations between Turkish parents and children. Therefore, we are confronted with two possible outcomes: reduced transmission under migration as opposed to under slowly changing continuous cultural context.

2.1. Transmission: A Goal-Mediated Process

Research by Phalet and Schönpflug (2001a, 2001b) looked at the mediating role of socialization goals as effective means of transmission. Parental goals for their child are found to direct and sustain goal-directed socialization practices. They influence the development of the child by encouraging goal-congruent behaviors (Goodnow, 1988). Parents in collectivistic cultures such as the Turkish culture stress conformity goals more (e.g., obedience and respect for parents) as opposed to parents in individualistic cultures; the latter predominantly stress autonomy goals, as is the case in the German culture. The socialization of the children toward achievement – but not necessarily individual autonomy – becomes more important with socioeconomic modernization in collectivistic societies.

Phalet and Schönpflug (2001b) explored the transmission-enhancing role of the socialization goals of conformity, autonomy, and achievement in the intergenerational transmission process of collectivistic and individualistic values and academic aspirations. Three further specifications of the hypotheses stated previously guided the development of a hypothetical model of conditional and mediated value transmission in Turkish immigrant families. (1) The contents and means of transmission differ between male and female dyads.

Specifically, fathers and sons are more collectivistic and stress conformity goals more than mothers and daughters. (2) Educational opportunities also influence the contents and means of transmission. Regardless of the gender of child and parent, academic aspirations and achievement goals of the parent become more important with better educational opportunities for the child. (3) Overall intensity of value transmission is expected to differ across the gender of parent and child, such that more transmission takes place in father–son dyads than in mother–daughter dyads.

The hypotheses were tested in the same longitudinal study as described previously but included Turkish adolescents and their parents in Germany and Turkish and Moroccan adolescents and their parents in the Netherlands. A total of 404 Turkish parent–child dyads in Germany were compared with 190 Turkish and Moroccan parent–child dyads in the Netherlands.

Parental and child collectivism was measured in terms of family relatedness versus separateness or distance from the family (Hui, 1988). Individualism was measured by items indicating independence of family influence in financial and educational issues. Achievement value was measured by the child's academic level of aspiration and the educational level aspired to by the parents for their children by naming as options the academic qualification levels possible in various hierarchically organized school tracks. Parental socialization goals were assessed on the basis of their rank order in an extensive list of socialization goals. Conformity, autonomy, and achievement goals were measured by one-item measures (Figure 10.1).

2.2. Analyses and Results

Structural equation models (i.e., LISREL) were used to test the hypothetical transmission model (Bollen, 1989). In line with the first hypothesis on selective transmission, significant transmission coefficients were found for collectivism ($\beta = .37$) but also for aspirations ($\beta = .35$). These direct effects indicate that the transmission process is at least in part independent of parental socialization goals. The findings confirm, however, the expected impact of parental values on their socialization goals (first hypothesis): Parental collectivism is associated with conformity goals but is negatively related to autonomy and achievement goals. Parental individualism had no direct impact on socialization goals.

As predicted by the second hypothesis, the direct transmission of collectivism was strengthened by an indirect transmission path leading through parental conformity goals to collectivism values in the children ($\beta = .40$). However, the model does not confirm the hypothesized mediating role of autonomy or achievement goals in the intergenerational transmission of aspirations.

The expected gender difference in collectivism was not found, although both mothers ($\gamma = .23$) and daughters ($\gamma = .18$) showed somewhat higher levels of

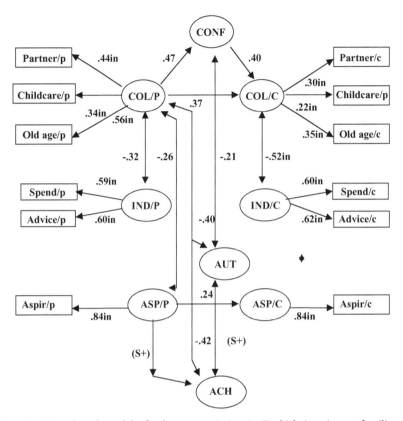

Figure 10.1. Cultural model of value transmission in Turkish immigrant families as mediated by socialization goals (conditional on gender and educational status) (Study 2). *Note:* COL/p/c (collectivism of parent or child): Partner/p/c "Parents should not interfere with their children's choice of a partner" (reversed); Childcare/p/c "It is better for the development of small children if they stay with their mothers"; Old age/p/c "When parents get old, it is better for them to go to an old people's home than to burden their children" (reversed). IND/p/c (individualism of parent or child): Spend/p/c "It should not concern my family whether I spend or save the money I have earned" and Advice/p/c "In educational matters it is best not to follow the advice of one's own family." Response format: 4 "fully agree" to 1 "fully disagree." ASP/p/c (aspiration of parent or child): Aspir/p/c (aspired level of graduation) 1 = don't care about finishing school; 2 = obligatory high school; 3 = middle school; 4 = senior high school including qualification for university entry; 5 = university final examination. (a) CONF (conformity goal of parent): "being an obedient daughter/son"; (b) AUT (autonomy goal of parent): "independent thinking and being autonomous"; (c) ACH (achievement goal of parent): "being successful in school."

individualism – in the narrow sense of distance from the family in financial and educational matters – than fathers and sons. Finally, gender differences in parental socialization goals not only showed (as expected) less conformity pressure on daughters ($\gamma = -.18$) but also much less autonomy

($\gamma = -.41$) and achievement pressure ($\gamma = -.47$) on daughters than on sons.

On the whole, the transmission of values from Turkish fathers to sons seems much closer to a goal-directed process than the transmission of values from mothers and daughters. Similar modeling of the gender-specific transmission process revealed that fathers seem to have an inhibitory effect of paternal individualism on filial collectivism through less strong conformity goals. Apparently, more individualistic fathers exert less conformity pressure on their sons and thereby weaken their commitment to collectivistic family values. Neither of the inhibitory transmission paths was significant in mother–daughter relationships. Apart from these gender-specific effects, the transmission of collectivism and academic aspirations was fully replicated in male and female comparison groups. It follows that the third hypothesis, which predicts more intense value transmission in father–son relations, is not supported.

In a final step, a cross-national comparison of Dutch and German acculturation contexts was conducted. To this end, the Dutch transmission model, which was mostly (although not fully) equivalent for Turkish and Moroccan ethnic groups, was compared to the German transmission model. Most of the associations and effects were invariant across national contexts in the selected multisample transmission model for parent–child dyads in Germany and in the Netherlands ($\chi^2(187,594) = 249.24$; $p = .0016$; *GFI* $= .90$; *CFI* $= .93$; *rmsea* $= .031$ without correlated errors). The tests of invariance across national contexts sustain partially equivalent transmission contents and paths in Germany and in the Netherlands (compared to the baseline model: $\chi^2(11) = 15.25$; $p > .10$). First, full factorial invariance is rejected ($\chi^2(2) = 15.94$; $p < .001$) due to different meanings of collectivism values in the two countries. Although parental and filial attitudes toward the choice of a partner are the single most reliable indicators of family relatedness in the Netherlands, attitudes toward childcare and old-age security are better indicators of relatedness in Germany. These differences in meaning should be remembered when comparing the transmission of collectivism values across national contexts. Second, full structural invariance is also rejected, but partial structural invariance is obtained for parental and filial values.

Third, full functional invariance of endogenous causal effects β is rejected ($\chi^2(10) = 109.74$; $p < .001$). Partial functional invariance reveals cross-national commonalities as well as national differences in transmission paths. Thus, the direct and indirect transmission of collectivism holds across national contexts, but the effect of parental collectivism on conformity goals is stronger in the German context than in the Dutch context. Moreover, the transmission of parental aspirations, and their effect on autonomy goals for the children, is specific to the German context. All negative or inhibitory transmission paths are also context-specific, except for a cross-national negative effect of parental individualism on conformity goals.

2.3. Discussion

One of the aims of our research on transmission was to analyze the process of value transmission from one generation to the next under conditions of rapid and deep cultural change of two contexts in the migration situation. The main research questions were concerned with selective transmission of contents, the effective means, and the differential contents and intensity of value transmission as a function of gender and educational status of Turkish-immigrant parent–child dyads.

Again, this second study also revealed the selective transmission of content: Collectivistic rather than individualistic values are transmitted, although different measurements were used. In addition, academic aspirations are transmitted. Collectivistic values are transmitted directly *and* via parental conformity goals for their children. Clearly, parental conformity goals function as effective means for the transmission of collectivism values from Turkish parents to children. The evidence with regard to parental achievement goals, however, is less clear. The transmission of academic aspiration continues to be direct in the presence of autonomy and achievement goals. Apparently, the *socialization for achievement* of Turkish children in Germany is less of a goal-directed parental endeavor than the socialization of family values. In summary, parental socialization goals function at least partly as mediators of intergenerational value transmission. The overall intensity of value transmission is very moderate, however. Many competing influences seem to prevent cultural replication from one generation to the next.

In comparing the transmission process across cultures, the impact of intracultural variation in gender and educational status on value transmission was also considered. Despite notable ethnic and national differences in the meaning of collectivism values, in the mediating role of conformity and achievement goals, the combined cross-ethnic and cross-national comparisons yield convergent results, which sustain the intergenerational transmission of core collectivism values across acculturation contexts.

Finally, the positive transmission paths are complemented by mostly culture-specific negative or inhibitory transmission paths. Thus, parental autonomy goals in the Netherlands and academic aspirations in Germany were found to interfere with the effective transmission of collectivism values. In all, the inhibitory transmission paths point to the divisive impact of intergenerational value conflicts in acculturating families, opposing normative solidarity to individual autonomy (in the Dutch context), or academic success (in the German context) for the children.

In the final analysis, the comparison of value transmission across acculturation contexts supports the cross-cultural generalizability of a selective and mediator model of value transmission. At the same time, the cross-ethnic and cross-national transmission models reveal interesting ethnic and national differences in the contents, the mediation, and the intensity of value transmission. In line with the fourth hypothesis regarding ethnic differences in acculturation patterns, the transmission of collectivism is more intense in Turkish parent–child dyads as compared to Moroccan dyads, due to a closer link between parental collectivism and heightened conformity pressure. The greater goal-directed effort of Turkish parents to transmit collectivistic values of relatedness between generations fits into the expected pattern of lagged or selective acculturation in tightly knit Turkish immigrant families and communities. Not only ethnic cultures but also national contexts of acculturation exercise their influence on the transmission process. In Germany, collectivistic values, along with achievement values, are more intensely transmitted between generations than in the Netherlands. It is interesting that ethnic cultures and national contexts do not affect the direct transmission path. Rather, cross-cultural variation in the intensity of transmission is located in the indirect transmission path, which is typically mediated by parental conformity goals.

3.0. STUDY 3: TRANSMISSION MECHANISMS AND FILTER

Although there is some agreement that transmission often takes place, little is known about the mechanisms and processes behind intergenerational similarities and relationships (Rosich & Meck, 1987). The course of the transmission process depends first of all on the three main components inherent in the transfer: the transmitter, the transmission content, and the adopter.

A basic question that has not been addressed as yet is whether all parents transmit. Most researchers would say *yes* without hesitation: The parent initiates the transmission process automatically, unless some contextual or pathological disruption of the parent–offspring relationship or the personality of the transmitter or adopter has occurred (Tomasello, Krüger, & Ratner, 1993). Given that all human parents potentially transmit, do parents differ in their motivation to transmit? In conditions of abrupt social change, such as the fall of a political regime, parents might refrain from transmitting certain transmission contents because they foresee that their own social orientations, skills, and knowledge will not be functional in the future life of their offspring. A similar case in question is changing the context during migration. Our new research approach addresses this question of motivation to explore the role of the strength of motivation to transmit certain content for the resulting parent–offspring similarity. The intensity of the parental transmission motivation is included in this study of the transmission of values within the family. Furthermore, the contents of transmission might be an appealing content that the adopter is eager to take over and/or the content is frequent or normative (i.e., a modal trait more or less transmitted by all socializers). Our final analyses also include estimates of the transmitter and the adopter of the distribution of the transmitted contents (i.e., the values) in their social environment.

The adopter – in this research, the children – are more or less receptive to the transmission efforts of their parents. During the rebellious autonomy- and identity-seeking adolescence, we found fewer transmission results in the form of similarity between parent and offspring as compared to younger and older children.

3.1. Social Transmission: An Analogy to Genetic Transmission?

As may be learned from the short history of transmission research (Schönpflug, Chapter 2, this volume), Cavalli-Sforza and Feldman (1981) presented evidence that the cultural transmission of social attitudes is analogous to the regularities of Mendelian dominant-recessive genetic transmission. The same question guided one part of our research. We looked at the transmission of the belief in a just world (Schönpflug & Bilz, 2004) from parent to child under the condition of a discontinuously changed context (i.e., the opening of the wall between East and West Germany). The results of Schönpflug and Bilz fully confirm the findings reported by Cavalli-Sforza and Feldman: If father and mother both hold a highly intensive just-world belief, the probability that their child will also hold a strong belief in a just world is very high. If only one parent holds a strong belief and the other a weak belief, then the child will hold either a strong or a weak belief in a just world. If both parents hold weak beliefs, the child will also share their weak beliefs. The claim of a parallel process of social and genetic transmission was thus demonstrated with different transmission contents and by different researchers.

3.2. The Filter Model

The basic conceptualization of the transmission process postulates that a direct transmission of values and other social orientations from father and/or mother to child exists. However, a number of variables may influence the intensity of the transmission process. We assume that various filters exist that regulate the transfer between the generations: Most important for the intensity of transmission appears to be the parents' motivation to transmit particular values or social orientations. The higher the motivation to transmit, the more probable a successful transfer of values is assumed to be from parent to offspring. A second important variable constituting the filter is the child's acceptance of the parental influence. The intensity of the functioning of both types of filter component is assumed to be differentiated between families with regard to their transmission rates. Families with high parental motivation to transmit particular values and a child that highly accepts the parental impact with regard to the given values

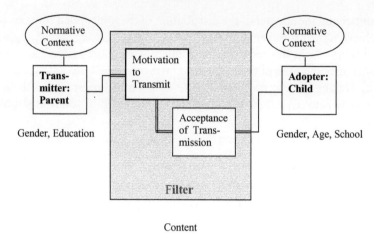

Content

Figure 10.2. The revised transmission model (Study 3).

should have the highest transmission rate. Do parents differ in transmission motivation and – if they do – which of the parents holds the highest motivation to transmit? Furthermore, if parental motivation to transmit and children's acceptance of parental influence are discrepant, then we assume that the motivation to transmit is the dominant mediator for transmission. Under conditions of high motivation to transmit and low acceptance of parental influence by the child, we expect a higher transmission rate than when the opposite conditions hold.

Furthermore, the model implies that the extent to which either parent or child perceives that their respective social contexts support the given value transmitted should influence the transmission rate as well but indirectly by impacting the motivation or the readiness to accept. The social context, with its normative value climate, should enhance transmission of values for normatively oriented persons and under conditions of weak motivation to transmit and/or low acceptance.

It is plausible to expect that parental transmission motivation decreases with the children's age. Once the children have become young adults, their parents reduce their transmission efforts. Intuitively plausible is also a curvilinear relationship between parental motivation to transmit and children's age. Until the end of puberty, parents might strive for impact on their children and then, with the onset of young adulthood, they reduce their efforts, also considering the fact that their children have reached a state of relative autonomy and independence. Autonomous and independent children tend not to accept parental influence as readily as younger children, and parents probably hold back their transmission attempts when children claim independence. Hence, the transmission result is expected to be age-dependent.

The basic model (see Figure 10.2) defines transmission as the process resulting in similarity between parental and child value or social orientation. In the model, an indirect path from the transmitter's own values via parental perception of value climate in their social context to the child's value is conceived. The readiness to accept parental influence and the child's perception of the value distribution in the surrounding social climate ultimately influences the child's own value orientation. The model predicts that the specified relationships will covary with age, gender, and school track of the child. The theoretical model is tested by searching for distinct constellations of the two variables: motivation (separate for mother and father) and acceptance of the child. The transmission rates of the distinct constellations within the family are analyzed. It should be remembered that the model is developed for specific contents of transmission – namely, values or other social orientations for which it makes sense to include the representation of the specific contents in the normative social contexts of the transmitters and the transmittees. The definition of cultural transmission implies that its content has to be distributed within a given cultural realm (Tomasello, Krüger, & Ratner, 1993) and the most frequent social orientation (i.e., skill, knowledge) has the greatest probability of being successfully transmitted (Henrich & Boyd, 1998).

3.3. Analyses and Results

Sample. The filter model was tested in a sample of 203 complete families with adolescent children (ages 15 and 16 years) from all school types from East Germany. A sample of 65 students from Martin Luther University in Halle (Saale, Saxony-Anhalt) studying various disciplines was added to explore age trends in transmission (see also Six, Geppert, & Schönpflug, Chapter 16, this volume).

Measures. The measures of the Schwartz, Lehman, and Roccas (1999) values questionnaire were used to obtain a variety of value categories. The value inventory measures 10 values with a 40-item scale. When applying a multidimensional scaling procedure, the Smallest Space Analysis, the 10 values may be grouped into 4 value categories: (1) *self-enhancement,* including hedonism, power, and achievement; (2) *self-transcendence,* including benevolence and universalism; (3) *conservation,* including conformity, security, and traditionalism; and (4) *openness* to change, including stimulation and self-determination.

In addition to each single value rating, a total of 40 value items, both parents rated independently their *motivation to transmit* the given value and the children rated how much they felt influenced by their parents in that same given value. Each parent's separate self-rated motivation to transmit for each given value was summarized over a defined category of values belonging to one of four value categories (Schwartz, Lehman, & Roccas, 1999). The child's self-rated *acceptance of parental influence* with regard to a given value category was treated in the same way.

One way to test the crucial variables of the basic model requires establishing distinct constellations of the father's and the mother's motivation to transmit

Table 10.3. *Results of the cluster analysis: Means of cluster variables and description of clusters including significance of mean differences (Study 3)*

Variables	Cluster			Significant Differences
	1 (LT)	2 (IT)	3 (HT)	
Father's Transmission Motivation	3.58	3.83	4.28	
Mother's Transmission Motivation	3.67	3.84	4.25	
Child's Perceived Parental Transmission Impact	2.81	4.12	3.44	
Size of Cluster (N = 203)	n = 58	n = 76	n = 69	
Child's Perception of Value in Social Context	3.97	4.16	4.04	1 < 2*
Father's Perception of Value in Social Context	3.88	3.89	4.11	1 < 3*
Mother's Perception of Value in Social Context	3.88	3.92	4.17	1 < 3*
Age of Child (Years)	15.78	17.07	17.23	all
Getting Along with Parents (1 = worse, 2 = equal to, 3 = better than peers)	2.07	2.45	2.22	1 < 2*
Father Employed (0 = no; 1 = yes)	.83	.92	.96	1 < 3*
Father's Educational Level (1 = basic to 5 = university)	4.00	4.75	4.23	1 < 2*
Child's School Track (1 = lower/middle track, 2 = high level track, 3 = college)	1.99	2.24	2.19	n.s.
Transmission Coefficients (β)[1]				
Self-Transcendence Father				
Mother		.43***		
Conservation Father			33**	
Mother				
Self-Enhancement Father			.56***	
Mother		.23*		
Openness to Change Father			.41***	
Mother				

[1] Controlled for father's, mother's, and child's general perception of context over all four value categories, child's age, gender, and school track.

* = $p < .05$; ** = $p < .01$; *** = $p < .001$.

and the child's acceptance of parental influence with regard to a given value category. The three variables were submitted to a centroid cluster analysis. The analysis was constrained to three clusters. A total of four such cluster analyses was performed, one for each value category. The resulting clusters were very similar, such that we felt justified in presenting one cluster analysis performed with all four value categories combined. The results are presented in Table 10.3.

The centroids of the cluster centroids characterize specific *family types*: Cluster 1 characterizes a family type with intermediate motivation to transmit from the father's and the mother's side and low perceived parental influence by the child. According to our theoretical approach, this cluster may be labeled Low Transmission (LT) Family Type because both filter variables are represented relatively weakly. Cluster 2 shows high parental motivation to transmit for the mother and the father alike but only intermediate acceptance of parental transmission by the child; this cluster may be termed High Transmission (HT) Family Type because, according to our thinking, the parental motivation influences transmission rate more than the child's acceptance. Cluster 3 shows intermediate transmission motivation by both the father and the mother yet high perceived parental impact by the child. This cluster may be labeled Intermediate Transmission (IT) Family Type. It is noteworthy that the individual levels of transmission motivation of either parent were never at the theoretical minimum of 1.00 but rather had an empirical minimum of 2.00 and a maximum of 5.50, whereas the child's acceptance variable had an empirical minimum of 1.00 and the same maximum of 5.50 as the parental variables. We may thus conclude that parents may have low motivation to transmit but the level does not seem to approach a theoretical minimum, whereas children may not admit to parental influence at all.

Table 10.3 also provides an overview of variables describing the family types. The children's estimation of the value in their social context is relatively weaker in LT, intermediate in HT, and strongest in IT families, in which the child admits the strongest parental influence. The two parents' estimates of values in the social context differ somewhat across family types. It is highest in HT families and similarly lower in both LT and IT families. The child's perception of the normativity of values in the social context is higher than that of the parents in the IT and the LT family, whereas in the HT family, the means are reversed: Parental estimates are higher than the child's. In the LT family, the child tends to still be in middle adolescence, whereas IT and HT families tend to have a child in late adolescence. Parents in LT families are somewhat younger than in IT and LT family types. Fathers in LT families seem to have a somewhat lower educational level and are relatively more unemployed than fathers in the other two family types. The mother variables did not differ between clusters. Gender of the child was also evenly distributed over the three family types. In addition, the child's self-rating of *getting along with parents* follows in terms of its size of the cluster variable of the child's admittance of parental impact on his or her own values; the ratings increase continuously from cluster 1 to cluster 3. The child's school track also increases parallel to the educational level of the father from cluster 1 to cluster 3, both being highest in the IT family type.

3.4. Differential Transmission in the Three Family Types

The empirical definition of the three family-type clusters allows the central theoretical assumptions to be tested that parents' motivation to transmit enhances their transmission rate and that children's higher admittance of parental impact is also associated with a higher transmission rate. The family types LT, IT, and HT should, therefore, show low, intermediate, and high transmission rates, respectively.

Transmission rates are estimated by β-values of the regression of the child's value preference on the parents' value preference obtained in a stepwise multiple regression including father's value; mother's value; and the father's, mother's, and child's estimates of normativity of value in context controlled for age, gender, and school track of the child. Four such stepwise multiple regressions were performed, one for each value dimension. The transmission coefficients are listed in Table 10.3. HT takes place in families in which the father and the mother have a relatively high motivation to transmit and the child's acceptance of parental impact is intermediate in three value dimensions (i.e., conservation, self-enhancement, and openness to change) and in the IT family type in which parental motivation is intermediate but the child's acceptance is relatively high (i.e., self-transcendence and openness to change). When all three variables are either intermediate or low, none of the transmission coefficients reached significance. We may conclude from these results that parental motivation and the child's acceptance of the parents were both important transmission filters. Parental motivation seems to dominate the child's acceptance in influencing the extent to which values are transmitted.

The influence of the normative role of the context of each family role included in this study seems to be of minor importance in families with above-average child acceptance of parental impact. The βs of the context variables generally do not reach statistical significance. However, when the child's acceptance is either low or intermediate with regard to parental influence, the child's estimation of the normativity of the context is a significant predictor of the child's values: for self-transcendence, $\beta = .26$, $p < .05$, and for conservation, $\beta = .40$, $p < .01$ in LT families. The father's and the mother's perception of values in their social context has no significant effect on the child's value. Thus, the context is a factor of influence on the child's values when parental motivation and child's acceptance of parental impact is relatively low, respectively. The context seemed to be irrelevant for children's values when children are oriented toward their parents, as in the IT family type.

The differential transmission coefficients for the mother and the father reveal that the mother or the father functions as transmitter, depending on the family type. The father's transmission domains are conservation in the HT and openness to change in the IT family, whereas the mother's transmission domains are self-transcendence in the IT family and self-enhancement and openness to change in the HT family.

3.5. Discussion

According to the basic model of transmission, motivation to transmit by the parents and readiness for acceptance by the child serve as filters in the transmission process. The definition of three family types with these two variables, separated for the father's and the mother's motivation to transmit, resulted in a family type with high parental motivation to transmit and relatively low readiness to accept parental influences with regard to value transmission by the child. Another family type had relatively high acceptance of parents from the child but relatively low parental motivation to transmit, and a third family type had balanced acceptance and motivation. Whereas a low level of readiness to accept influences was observed on the part of the child, parental transmission motivation was always at an intermediate level or higher and never below the average scores. The transmission rates corroborate the influence of parental motivation to transmit as a filter condition, but acceptance of parental influence by the child was also a filter condition. Both enhance transmission rates, with parental motivation being the more efficient factor for value transmission. We may thus conclude that interactive contributions from both the transmitter and the adopter regulate the transmission process.

In HT families, three of the four value categories were transmitted, the exception being self-transcendence. In IT families, only two value categories were transmitted: The father and the mother transmit openness to change and self-transcendence differentially. No value category was transmitted in LT families. Thus, our basic model was supported by the results of Study III.

Further characteristics of parents in LT, IT, and HT families revealed that younger parents transmit less; they are predominant in LT families. Boys and girls are equally distributed over the third HT family type. As was already known from Study I, in HT families, a high level of parental education prevails and children attend higher school tracks. Children reporting above-average acceptance of parental influence regarding value orientation in the IT families also state that they get along with their parents better than average. This supports the interpretation of the IT family type as one in which children appear to have reason to accept their parents as models. In IT families, the explicitly stated motivation of the parents to transmit is reduced as compared to the HT parents, probably because the readiness of the child to accept transmission is high.

CONCLUSIONS

The three theoretical and empirical approaches to the investigation of transmission in our research show a sequence of research proceedings from sociodemographic process variables such as the family role of the transmitter, the gender of transmitter and adopter to psychological process variables (e.g., selectivity of contents of transmission), and parental motivation to transmit, as well as the child's acceptance of the transmission influences. In addition, our research explored moderators and mediators of transmission, which we refer to as transmission belts and filters, respectively. We found that personal resources such as parental level of education, as well as interactive variables such as marital harmony, were efficient transmission belts. However, the sibling position of the child also was influential, with the youngest child being the most similar to parents. This special finding, as well as marital harmony, coincides well with the reports and interpretations of Cavalli-Sforza et al. (1982). When older siblings teach younger ones the same information as the parents do, or when a harmoniously agreeing couple exerts influence in the same direction on the child, we have in both cases an accumulation of transmitting efforts that lead to greater influence and similarity between parent and child.

Educational goals of parents mediate the transmission of specific values. Thus, the educational goal of conformity mediates the transmission of collectivistic values. These mediators are culture-specific and context-resistant at the same time. In Turkish and Moroccan migrants, collectivistic values are transmitted, whereas individualistic values are not. However, Turkish migrants in the Netherlands and Germany show other mediating processes for transmission. For Turks in Germany, the transmission of collectivistic values is compatible with achievement values, whereas for Turks in the Netherlands it is not. Hence, we may not expect a straightforward list of factors, mediators, and moderators that influence the transmission process at a universal or even at a culture-specific level. The cross-cultural comparisons are only in their infancy and require further research. Only after we have collected data in more cultural contexts will we be able to recognize more regularity in the transmission process.

The motivation to transmit has a somewhat stronger influence on the transmission result as compared to the child's acceptance of parental influence. Further explorations with other kinds of transmission contents are needed to indicate whether this conclusion is generally warranted.

We did not find low motivation to transmit with any of the contents studied: values, xenophobia (see Six, Geppert, & Schönpflug, Chapter 16, this volume), or belief in a just world (Schönpflug & Bilz, 2004). However, we cannot yet be certain that we will not find it with other types of contents. In such a case, we must look for still other sources of influence, such as the influence of the social environment (i.e., conformity transmission) (Henrich & Boyd, 1998), forerunners (Bengtson & Troll, 1978), or peers (ter Bogt et al., Chapter 18, this volume). The stronger influence of the child's estimation of the distribution of a given value in the social context in the LT family type indicates that in cases of low acceptance and low/intermediate motivation, the social environment may become influential as a *conformity transmitter*. Parents who do not want the social environment to gain a dominant influence on their child's social orientations, skills, knowledge, and behaviors may develop high motivation to transmit and create a readiness in the child to accept their transmission.

Parallel analyses to those reported performed for each value category with one-parent (i.e., the mother) families need to be conducted to add to our present knowledge. The role of the single mother as a transmitter might be strengthened in the absence of the father; it is also plausible to expect a weak impact, as the influences of both the father and the mother will not be accumulated. These specific analyses would reveal strengths and weaknesses of single-parent families. This is all the more relevant considering that the frequency of this family type is increasing.

The transmission process was expected to be domain-specific; therefore, the central issue of the transmission process was the extent to which parental transmission motivation depended on the content of the transmission. In addition, the question had to be asked about the extent to which the child's acceptance depends on the transmission content. Results obtained so far demonstrated that the transmission rate depended on the content of transmission, but we have not yet included any results concerning the dependence of the motivation and acceptance on content domain. This issue remains open for further analyses.

Furthermore, some paths of the basic model have not yet been analyzed – namely, the parents' estimation of the distribution of the values in the social context on their motivation to transmit and, similarly, the children's context estimation on their acceptance level. Further analyses will reveal more structural information of the variables in the model.

The research program outlined in this chapter is only just beginning to construct a solid basis of results that will allow the prediction of transmission under various constraints. Findings in line with those of other authors and our speculations reassure us that the measures introduced into the study are valid. Starting from this firm ground, further explorations of new shores should be promising.

REFERENCES

Bandura, A. (1986). *Social foundations of thought and action: A social cognitive theory.* Englewood Cliffs, NJ: Prentice Hall.

Baumrind, D. (1991). Effective parenting during the early adolescent transition. In P. A. Cowan & E. M. Hetherington (Eds.), *Family transitions* (pp. 111–163). Hillsdale, NJ: Erlbaum.

Bengtson, V. L., & Troll, L. (1978). Youth and their parents: Feedback and intergenerational influence in socialization. In: M. R. Lerner & G. B. Spanier (Eds.), *Child influences on marital and family interaction: A life span development* (pp. 215–240). New York: Academic Press.

Bollen, K. A. (1989). *Structural equations with latent variables.* New York: Wiley.

Boyd, R., & Richerson, P. J. (1985). *Culture and the evolutionary process.* Chicago: University of Chicago Press.

Campbell, D. T. (1975). On the conflicts between biological and social evolution and between psychology and moral tradition. *American Psychologist, 30*, 1103–1126.

Cavalli-Sforza, L. L., & Feldman, M. W. (1981). *Cultural transmission and evolution: A quantitative approach.* Princeton, NJ: Princeton University Press.

Cavalli-Sforza, L. L., Feldman, M. W., Chen, K. H., & Dornbusch, S. M. (1982). Theory and observation in cultural transmission. *Science, 218*, 19–27.

Chen, K.-H., Cavalli-Sforza, L. L., & Feldman, M. W. (1982). A study of cultural transmission in Taiwan. *Human Ecology, 10*, 365–381.

Gärling, T. (1999). Value priorities, social orientation and cooperation in social dilemmas. *British Journal of Social Psychology, 38*, 397–408.

Geppert, K. (2002). *Transmission von Fremdenfeindlichkeit und Werthaltungen in der Familie* [The transmission of xenophobia and values in the family]. Master's Thesis, Martin Luther University, Halle (Saale), Germany.

Goodnow, J. J. (1988). Parents' ideas, feelings, and actions: Models and methods from developmental and social psychology. *Child Development, 59*, 286–320.

Grolnick, W. S., Deci, E. L., & Ryan, R. M. (1997). Internalization within the family: The self-determination theory perspective. In J. E. Grusec & L. Kuczynski (Eds.), *Parenting and children's internalization of values: A handbook of contemporary theory* (pp. 135–161). New York: Wiley.

Grusec, J. (1997). A history of research on parenting strategies. In J. E. Grusec & L. Kuczynski (Eds.), *Parenting and children's internalization of values* (pp. 3–22). New York: Wiley.

Harris, J. R. (1998). *The nurture assumption: Why children turn out the way they do.* New York: The Free Press.

Henrich, J., & Boyd, R. (1998). The evolution of conformist transmission and the emergence of between-group differences. *Evolution and Human Behavior, 19*, 215–241.

Hui, C. H. (1988). Measurement of individualism–collectivism. *Journal of Research in Personality, 22*, 17–36.

Kohn, M. (1983). On the transmission of values in the family: A preliminary formulation. In A. C. Kerckhoff (Ed.), *Research in sociology of education and socialization* (Vol. 4, pp. 3–12). Greenwich, CT: JAI Press.

Kohn, M., Slomczynski, L., & Schoenbach, C. (1986). Social stratification and the transmission of values in the family. *Sociological Forum, 1*, 73–102.

Laland, K. N. (1993). The mathematical modeling of human culture and its implications for psychology and the human sciences. *British Journal of Psychology, 84*, 145–169.

Larson, R. W., & Almeida, D. M. (1999). Emotional transmission in the daily lives of families: A new paradigm for studying family processes. *Journal of Marriage and the Family, 61*, 5–20.

Nauck, B. (1997). Intergenerative Konflikte und gesundheitliches Wohlbefinden in türkischen Familien: Ein interkultureller und interkontextueller Vergleich [Intergenerative conflicts and physical well-being in Turkish families: A comparison between cultures and contexts]. In B. Nauck & U. Schönpflug (Eds.), *Familien in verschiedenen Kulturen* [Families in different cultures] (pp. 324–354). Stuttgart: Ferdinand Enke.

Phalet, K., & Schönpflug, U. (2001a). Intergenerational transmission of collectivism and achievement values in two acculturation contexts: The case of Turkish families in Germany and Turkish and Moroccan families in the Netherlands. *Journal of Cross-Cultural Psychology, 32*, 186–201.

Phalet, K., & Schönpflug, U. (2001b). Intergenerational transmission in Turkish immigrant families: Parental collectivism, achievement values and gender differences. *Journal of Comparative Family Studies, 32*, 489–504.

Phinney, J. S., Ong, A., & Madden, T. (2000). Cultural values and intergenerational value discrepancies in immigrant and non-immigrant families. *Child Development, 71*, 528–539.

Rosich, R. M., & Meck, N. E. (1987). Intergenerational relations and life-span developmental psychology. *Human Development, 30*, 60–65.

Schönpflug, U. (2001). Intergenerational transmission of values: The role of transmission belts. *Journal of Cross-Cultural Psychology, 32*, 174–185.

Schönpflug, U. (2007). *Migration.* In G. Trommsdorff & J. Kornadt (Eds.), Enzyklopädie der Kulturvergleichenden Psychologie [Encyclopedia of Cross-Cultural Psychology] (Vol. 3, pp. 1–48). Göttingen, Germany: Hogrefe.

Schönpflug, U., & Bilz, L. (2004). The transmission of the just world belief. In S. Dalbert & H. Sallay (Eds.), *The justice motive in adolescence* (pp. 43–63). London: Routledge.

Schönpflug, U., & Silbereisen, R. K. (1992). Transmission of values between generations in the family regarding societal keynote issues: A cross-cultural longitudinal study on Polish and German families. In S. Iwawaki, Y. Kashima, & K. Leung (Eds.), *Innovations in cross-cultural psychology* (pp. 269–278). Lisse, the Netherlands: Swets & Zeitlinger.

Schwartz, S. H. (1992). Universals in the content and structure of values: Theoretical advances and empirical tests in 20 countries. In M. P. Zanna (Ed.), *Advances in experimental social psychology* (Vol. 25, pp. 1–65). New York: Academic Press.

Schwartz, S. H. (1994). Beyond individualism–collectivism: New dimensions of cultural values. In U. Kim, H. C. Triandis, C. Kagitcibasi, S.-C. Choi, & G. Yoon (Eds.), *Individualism and collectivism: Theory, methods and applications* (pp. 85–121). Newbury Park, CA: Sage Publications.

Schwartz, S. H., Lehmann, A., & Roccas, S. (1999). Multimethod probes of basic human values. In J. Adamopoulos & Y. Kashima (Eds.), *Social psychology and cultural context: Essays in honor of Harry C. Triandis* (pp. 107–287). Newbury Park, CA: Sage Publications.

Tomasello, M., Krüger, A. C., & Ratner, H. H. (1993). Cultural learning. *Behavioral and Brain Sciences, 16*, 495–552.

van Ijzendoorn, M. H. (1992). Intergenerational transmission of parenting: A review of studies on nonclinical populations. *Developmental Review, 12*, 76–99.

11

Accounting for Parent–Child Value Congruence:
Theoretical Considerations and Empirical Evidence

ARIEL KNAFO AND SHALOM H. SCHWARTZ

INTRODUCTION

Values are desirable abstract goals that apply across situations. Values serve as guiding principles in people's lives, as criteria to select and justify actions and to evaluate people and events (Rohan, 2000; Rokeach, 1973; Schwartz, 1992). Values relate meaningfully to numerous important behaviors such as alcohol consumption (Schwartz, Melech, Lehmann, Burgess, Harris, & Owens, 2001), risky sexual behavior (Goodwin, Realo, Kwiatkowska, Kozlova, Nguyen Luu, & Nizharadze, 2002), vocational behavior (Knafo & Sagiv, 2004; Sagiv & Schwartz, 2004), and pro- and antisocial behaviors (Bond & Chi, 1997; Knafo, 2003a). Parents invest heavily in trying to influence their children's values. Yet, their success is quite limited; the relationship between parental and child values is far from being congruent (Homer, 1993; Knafo & Schwartz, 2001; Troll & Bengtson, 1979).

This chapter addresses the processes that lead to parent–child value congruence. By *value congruence*, we mean that parents and their children attribute similar importance to a value. Levels of parent–child value congruence vary as a function of the substantive content of values. Congruence is usually high for religious values and lower for most other values that have been studied (Kalish & Johnson, 1972; Miller & Glass, 1989). It is therefore important to consider the content of values when studying value transmission. The crucial content aspect that distinguishes among values is the type of motivational goal that they express (Schwartz, 1992). Evidence from diverse cultural, linguistic, and religious groups

The research was supported by grants from the National Science Foundation (Israel Academy of Sciences) and from the NCJW Center for Development in Education, and was facilitated by the Leon and Clara Sznajderman Chair of Psychology. The work of the first author was supported by a Kreitman Foundation fellowship while at Ben Gurion University and by a fellowship from the Martin and Vivian Levin Center for the Normal and Pathological Development of the Child and Adolescent. We thank the families for their participation in the study. We would also like to thank Anat Bardi, Moshe Berger, Olga Mazo, Gila Melech, Yuval Piurko, Tammy Rubel, Lilach Sagiv, Naomi Struch, and Noga Sverdlik for their comments on drafts of the manuscript.

in 67 countries supports the claim that 10 values are relatively comprehensive and are reliably discriminated across samples (Schwartz, 1992, 1994, in press a). The four studies discussed herein focus on these 10 values. Short definitions of each value in terms of its central goal are as follows: (1) *power:* social status, dominance over people and resources; (2) *achievement:* personal success according to social standards; (3) *hedonism:* pleasure or sensuous gratification; (4) *stimulation:* excitement, challenge, and novelty; (5) *self-direction:* independence of thought and action; (6) *universalism:* understanding, tolerance, and concern for the welfare of *all* people and nature; (7) *benevolence:* preserving and enhancing the welfare of people to whom one is close; (8) *tradition:* respect and commitment to cultural or religious customs and ideas; (9) *conformity:* restraint of actions and impulses that may harm others or violate social expectations; and (10) *security:* safety and stability of society, relationships, and self.

The purpose of this chapter is to investigate a model that accounts for parent–child value congruence through children's accuracy of perception and acceptance of parental values (Grusec & Goodnow, 1994). Study 1 tests this model with data from 591 Israeli families. Study 2 asks whether children perceive some values more accurately or accept some values more than others. Study 3 examines explanations for the variation in accurate perception and acceptance of specific values. Study 4 identifies and tests explanations of some gender differences in value-transmission processes. The general discussion explores potential causes of value congruence beyond parental influence and proposes directions for future research.

1.0. STUDY 1: A TWO-STEP MODEL FOR PREDICTING PARENT–CHILD VALUE CONGRUENCE

1.1. Research Issues

Congruence between the values of parents and children can be attributed to various sources (Dalton, 1982; Harris, 1995; Keller, Bouchard, Arvey, Segal, & Dawis, 1992). Most prominent is socialization through which parents influence the values of their children (Grusec & Kuczynski, 1997). Although we consider several alternative processes in the discussion section, this chapter focuses on processes through which parents may affect their children's values. For this purpose, we adapt a model proposed by Grusec and Goodnow (1994), who developed this model to analyze internalization of parental values by young children in disciplinary situations. We extend it to the analysis of value congruence.

1.2. Accuracy of Perception and Acceptance

Grusec and Goodnow suggested a two-step process of internalization. First, children must perceive which values their parents want them to endorse. Second, children must accept those values as their own. Value transmission may succeed or fail at either or both steps in this process. In the first step (i.e., perception), children may perceive their parents' values accurately or may misperceive them; in the second step (i.e., acceptance), children may choose to accept the values they perceive, but they may also reject them. This analysis extends directly to value congruence. If children perceive their parents' values accurately and then accept rather than reject them, value congruence should be high. In this view, children are active partners in the determination of value congruence.

There is some evidence that accurate perception of parental values relates to the level of parent–child value congruence. The more accurate children and adolescents are in perceiving their parents' values, the more congruence between their values and their parents' values (Cashmore & Goodnow, 1985; Okagaki & Bevis, 1999; Smith, 1982; Westholm, 1999; Whitbeck & Gecas, 1988). There is also some evidence that perceived parental values serve as a mediating link between parents' and children's values (Kohn, Slomczynski, & Schoenbach, 1986; Okagaki & Bevis, 1999; Westholm, 1999).

Our application of the two-step model implies that accuracy of value perception and acceptance of perceived values are preconditions for parent–child value congruence. Indeed, we see these as sufficient although not always necessary conditions. We therefore hypothesize that parent–child congruence regarding a particular value is high when children accurately perceive their parents' priorities for that value and accept those priorities. We further hypothesize that parent–child congruence is moderate if either accuracy or acceptance is moderate and the other is moderate or high. Absent either accurate perception or acceptance, we expect the congruence level to be low.

To illustrate how the two steps contribute to congruence, consider a study of opinion congruence (Acock & Bengtson, 1980). In this study, children perceived their father's opinion of welfare recipients with some accuracy, but their own opinion differed from their father's. Accurate perception together with rejection of the perceived father's opinion yielded weak opinion congruence. In contrast, children accepted the opinion that they perceived their mother as endorsing regarding government's role in business, but they misperceived their mother's actual opinion. In both instances, opinion congruence was low but for different reasons. In the first instance, children rejected their parents' opinion; in the second, they misperceived their parents' opinion. Such processes are likely to apply to value congruence as well.

The two-step model can help to pinpoint why the degree of value congruence between parents and their children varies as a function of the type of value. For some values, both accuracy of perception and acceptance may often be high, leading to high congruence. For others, either accuracy or acceptance or both may be low, which would lead to low congruence.

The two-step model postulates two causal processes (Paths a and b in Figure 11.1). Parents' socialization values have a causal impact on perceived parental values to the extent that perception is accurate. Perceived parental values have

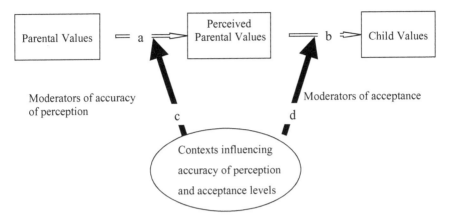

Figure 11.1. The two-step process of achieving value congruence.

a causal impact on children's own values to the extent that they are accepted. Conceptualizing value transmission in this way defines children's perception of parental values as a mediator between parents' and children's values. To the extent that perceived parental values do indeed serve as a mediator, controlling their effects on children's values should reduce the correlation between parents' values and their children's values (Baron & Kenny, 1986; Kohn, Slomczynski, & Schoenbach, 1986).

This may appear to be a "transmission" model in that it focuses on parents socializing children (Kuczynski, Marshall, & Schell, 1997). However, through their role as perceivers and acceptors of parental values, children have a major impact in this model. Characteristics of parents (e.g., Schönpflug, 2001), of children (Knafo & Schwartz, 2004a), and of the social context (Boehnke, 2001; Knafo, 2003b) may all affect parents' success in transmitting values because they may increase or decrease children's accuracy in perceiving their parents' values and their acceptance of the values they perceive (Paths *c* and *d* in Figure 11.1).

The following sections examine accuracy in perceiving parental values and acceptance of them as processes affecting value congruence, based mainly on data from 591 Israeli families. Earlier reports, based on this dataset, examined how parenting variables relate to adolescents' accuracy in perceiving parental values (Knafo & Schwartz, 2003) and to their acceptance of parental values (Knafo & Schwartz, 2005).

1.3. Method

1.3.1. *Procedure and Respondents*
The study population was families of Jewish high school students from state and state-religious schools in Israel of varied socioeconomic levels.[1] Families

---

[1] See Knafo and Schwartz (2003) for a detailed description of the sample and procedure.

of adolescents were recruited by telephone and were included if the adolescent and at least one parent agreed to participate (46%). Data were gathered in 603 families. We disqualified 12 families because of incomplete questionnaires, leaving a final sample of 591 families. Of the adolescents, 56% were female and 44% were male, with a mean age of 17.1 years ($SD = .7$). In 52% of the families, two parents participated; only one parent participated in the remaining families. There were 306 mother–daughter dyads, 224 mother–son dyads, 187 father–daughter dyads, and 175 father–son dyads.

1.3.2. *Instruments*

Values. We employed a modification of the Portrait Values Questionnaire (PVQ) (Schwartz, in press b; Schwartz, Lehmann, & Roccas, 1999; Schwartz et al., 2001). Multitrait–multimethod analyses indicate that the PVQ measures the same 10 values as the Schwartz Value Survey (SVS) (Schwartz, 1992). The PVQ presents respondents with a more concrete and less cognitively complex task than the SVS, making it suitable for parents with little or no formal schooling. The PVQ includes short verbal portraits of 40 people. Each portrait describes a person's goals, aspirations, or wishes that point implicitly to the importance of a single value. For example: "Thinking up new ideas and being creative is important to him. He likes to do things in his own original way" describes a person for whom self-direction values are important. "It is important to her to be rich. She wants to have a lot of money and expensive things" describes a person who cherishes power values. The verbal portraits present the person's values by describing each person in terms of what is important to him or her – the goals and wishes he or she pursues.

To measure *own* values, adolescents indicated "How much like you is this person?" for each portrait. They checked one of six boxes labeled as follows: *very much like me, like me, somewhat like me, a little like me, not like me,* and *not like me at all.* Thus, we inferred adolescents' own values from their self-reported similarity to people described in terms of particular values. Responses were converted to a 6-point numerical scale and each adolescent's responses were centered on his or her own mean.[2] To measure *perceived parental values,* adolescents were asked, "How would your father/mother want you to respond to each item?" To measure *socialization values,* parents indicated, "How would you want your son/daughter to respond to each item?"[3] About 20 minutes, during

---

[2] Centering was performed because parents and their own children share a general tendency to report values as more or less important (correlation between the mean rating of all 40 items by adolescents and parents: $r = .30$). Failure to control for this shared response tendency would inflate parent–child congruence correlations.

[3] Measuring the values that parents *want* their children to endorse rather than parents' *own* values has two significant implications. The measured value congruence between parents and children reflects the success of intended socialization. It shows the degree to which children have adopted the values that parents wish to transmit. However, this "value congruence" does

which adolescents answered other questions, intervened between reporting own values and perceived parental values.

Smallest Space Analyses (SSA) (Guttman, 1968) of the values of adolescents and their parents yielded structures similar to the prototypical, circular structure of values (Schwartz, 1992). Here, however, two subtypes of security values – individual and group – were distinct. To increase measurement reliability, we used structural equation modeling (i.e., AMOS [Arbuckle, 1997]) to construct latent variables for each type of value. The sets of single items intended to index the values served as the observed variables. For each value, we constructed three separate latent variables: children's own value, parents' value for their children, and parental value that children perceived. For the individual subtype of security values, it was not possible to construct latent variables with the same indicators for parents and children, which suggests nonequivalence in the meaning of individual security. Because nonequivalence precludes comparison, we excluded this value from further analyses.[4] For conceptual reasons and to make the models identifiable, we constrained the single-item indicators of a value to have the same loading on all three latent variables involving that value (Taris, Semin, & Bok, 1998).

1.4. Results

1.4.1. *Predicting Congruence Levels with Accuracy and Acceptance*

We assessed the relationships among the latent variables using structural equations. We performed all analyses on each of the 10 values, separately for each of the 4 dyadic combinations of mothers and fathers with sons and daughters. To improve model fit, we included correlated errors between items answered by the same source (i.e., parents or children), when appropriate. The goodness of fit of the theoretical models that included perceived parental values as the mediator between parents' socialization values and their children's own values tested the hypotheses. We performed separate multigroup analyses (Arbuckle, 1997) for fathers and mothers, with the models for sons and daughters estimated simultaneously. The comparative fit index (CFI) and root mean square error of approximation (RMSEA) for the father and the mother analyses for each value indicated the fit of the models to the data. CFIs of 0.9 or greater and RMSEAs of 0.05 or smaller generally indicate an adequate fit of model to data (Ullman,

---

not measure the correspondence between parents' and children's actual values. In some cases (e.g., migration), parents acknowledge the need to differentiate between the values they want for themselves and for their children (Kuczynski et al., 1997). Still, the values parents wish to transmit correlate highly with their own values (correlations of .60 to .80) (Knafo & Schwartz, 2001; Whitbeck & Gecas, 1988).

[4] We included only items that loaded significantly on their hypothesized factors in every 1 of the 12 cases (3 latent values [adolescents', parents', and perceived parents' values] × 4 subgroups [fathers, mothers, daughters, and sons]). This left a final count of 29 items.

Table 11.1. *Father's socialization values: Adolescents' accuracy of perception, acceptance, and value congruence*

Value	(1) Congruence Coefficients	(2) Accuracy Coefficients	(3) Acceptance Coefficients	(4) Congruence Path Coefficient after Mediation
SONS N = 175				
Tradition	.81**	.92**	.94**	.63*
Benevolence	.42**	.50**	.64**	.19
Universalism	.29**	.40**	.80**	−.01
Self-Direction	.06	.40**	−.10	.11
Stimulation	.24**	.38**	.30**	.08
Hedonism	.21*	.26*	.25*	.17
Achievement	.17*	.31**	.46**	.02
Power	.35**	.44**	.75**	.08
Security (Group)	.42**	.27	.38**	.28**
Conformity	.24*	.24	−.23	.39
DAUGHTERS N = 187				
Tradition	.87**	.82**	.99**	.25
Benevolence	.09	−.01	.52**	.24
Universalism	.20*	.53**	.35**	.08
Self-Direction	.58**	.68**	.58**	.42
Stimulation	.43**	.38**	.34**	.23*
Hedonism	.29**	.38**	.35**	.21*
Achievement	.44**	.51**	.54**	.32*
Power	.40**	.46**	.65**	.17
Security (Group)	.34**	.29*	.64**	.23*
Conformity	.34**	.47**	.34**	.24*

* $p < .05$ (1-tailed); ** $p < .01$ (1-tailed).

1996). All CFIs and all but three RMSEAs met these criteria. Power and group security in the mother analyses and tradition in the father analyses fell slightly short.

Table 11.1 presents the levels of parent–child value congruence, accuracy of perception, and acceptance of perceived parental values, across the 10 values, among sons and daughters, for fathers. Table 11.2 presents the findings for mothers. Column 1 in each table gives the measure of congruence – the standardized regression coefficient obtained by regressing children's values on the values their fathers (mothers) wanted them to endorse. Column 2 presents the measure of accuracy – the coefficient from regressing perceived parental values on parents' socialization values. Column 3 presents the measure of acceptance – the coefficient from regressing children's values on the parental values that they perceived.

Table 11.2. *Mother's socialization values: Adolescents' accuracy of perception, acceptance, and value congruence*

Value	(1) Congruence Coefficients	(2) Accuracy Coefficients	(3) Acceptance Coefficients	(4) Congruence Path Coefficient after Mediation
SONS N = 224				
Tradition	.76**	.93**	.72**	.54*
Benevolence	.24**	.28*	.64**	.09
Universalism	.40**	.41**	.65**	.20*
Self-Direction	.37**	.46*	.39*	.21
Stimulation	.37**	.14	.40	.24*
Hedonism	.29**	.19	.42**	.22*
Achievement	.06	.09	.43**	.04
Power	.44**	.31**	.79**	.17
Security (Group)	.56**	.42**	.90**	.20
Conformity	.38**	.04	.13	.33*
DAUGHTERS N = 306				
Tradition	.80**	.93**	.80**	.57*
Benevolence	.24**	.43**	.58**	−.01
Universalism	.11	.07	.71**	.10
Self-Direction	.36**	.78**	.63**	−.17
Stimulation	.28**	.37**	.22*	.22*
Hedonism	.10	.19*	.24*	.09
Achievement	.40**	.40**	.59**	.20*
Power	.54**	.46**	.72**	.16
Security (Group)	.25**	.12	.57**	.13*
Conformity	.35**	.54**	.40**	.25*

* $p < .05$ (1-tailed); ** $p < .01$ (1-tailed).

1.4.2. Mediation of Congruence by Perceived Parental Values

We next ask whether the mediation proposed by the two-step model accounts for the observed levels of parent–child value congruence. Operationally, we test whether introducing perceived parental values as a mediator between parents' and adolescents' values reduces the direct path between them. To illustrate these analyses, Figure 11.2 presents the path model for mothers' and daughters' power values. The congruence coefficient was 0.54; the standardized path coefficients were 0.46 for accuracy of perception and 0.72 for acceptance; and the direct path from parental to child power values, net of mediation, was 0.16. Thus, mediation through perceived parental values accounted for almost all of the congruence between the power values mothers wanted their daughters to endorse and the daughters' own power values.

Column 4 of Tables 11.1 and 11.2 presents path coefficients between parent and child values after introducing perceived parental values as a mediator. In

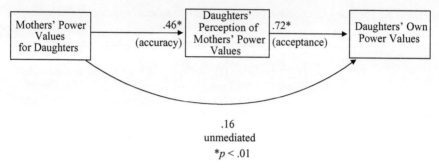

Figure 11.2. Predicting female adolescents' power values with the two-step process.

most cases, the mediation considerably reduced the association. Specifically, mediation reduced the variance accounted for by parental values by at least 40% in 32 of 40 cases (i.e., 10 values × 4 dyads). Of 35 cases in which parental values predicted children's values significantly (see column 1 in Tables 11.1 and 11.2), 18 paths were reduced to insignificance. Thus, the two steps of accuracy and acceptance substantially mediate the congruence between children's values and those of their parents, although not completely.

1.4.3. *Relationships of Congruence to Accuracy of Perception and Acceptance*

We hypothesized previously that accuracy of perception and acceptance both contribute to parent–child congruence. Thus, we would expect that the higher the acceptance and the more accurate the perception, the higher the congruence level. These hypotheses translate into an interaction prediction in addition to the two main effects. Parent–child congruence should correlate with the multiplicative product of the accuracy and acceptance coefficients.

As hypothesized, the congruence coefficients (column 1) correlated highly with the accuracy of perception coefficients (column 2) across the 10 values: father–son, 0.81; father–daughter, 0.84 (see Table 11.1); mother–son, 0.80; and mother–daughter, 0.81 (see Table 11.2) – all $p < .01$. The congruence coefficients also correlated substantially with the acceptance coefficients (column 3) across the 10 values: father–son, 0.68; father–daughter, 0.72; mother–son, 0.48; and mother–daughter, 0.55 – all $p < .05$. Moreover, congruence correlated even more strongly with the multiplicative interaction of accuracy and acceptance, as hypothesized: father–son, 0.89; father–daughter, 0.94; mother–son, 0.84; and mother–daughter, 0.88 – all $p < .01$.

To test the hypothesis formally, we treated the 40 coefficients as independent data points. We regressed congruence on accuracy and acceptance and then added the interaction term in a hierarchical regression. Because of the issue of multicollinearity, all variables were centered about their means (Baron & Kenny, 1986). Together, accuracy of perception ($\beta = 0.63$, $t = 6.01$, $p < .01$) and acceptance ($\beta = 0.31$, $t = 2.97$, $p < .01$) explained 68% of the variance in congruence. The interaction term alone predicted 77% of the variance in congruence. The interaction term added significantly ($\beta = 0.39$, $t = 4.27$, $p < .01$), with a total of 78% of the variance in congruence explained by accuracy, acceptance, and their interaction.

1.5. Discussion: Evidence for the Role of Accuracy of Perception and Acceptance

Several findings support the application of the Grusec and Goodnow (1994) model. As hypothesized, the two steps of accuracy and acceptance substantially mediated the congruence between adolescents' own values and their parents' socialization values for the 10 values, although the mediation was not complete. In addition, across values and dyadic gender-compositions, the combination of accuracy in perceiving parental values and acceptance of them strongly predicted parent–child value congruence.

Although the two-step model received much support, some anomalous findings point to the need to go beyond it to understand parent–child value congruence fully. In some cases, a substantial relationship between parents' and children's values remained even when perceived parental values were controlled statistically. This implies that variables not in the value-transmission model of Figure 11.1 influence parent–child value congruence.[5] In addition, not all differences in either accuracy of perception or acceptance led to differences in congruence. Consider conformity values: Daughters exhibited moderate accuracy and acceptance of both their parents' conformity values, whereas sons exhibited low accuracy and acceptance. Indeed, sons even rejected their father's conformity values (see the negative acceptance coefficient in Table 11.1). Nonetheless, sons, like daughters, showed moderate congruence with their parents for conformity values. Clearly, processes other than accuracy of perception and acceptance must account for father–son value congruence for conformity. We consider alternative sources of parent–child congruence in the general discussion.

2.0. STUDY 2: DIFFERENCES ACROSS VALUES IN ACCURACY, ACCEPTANCE, AND CONGRUENCE

2.1. Research Issues

Just as observers perceive some traits more accurately than others (Funder, 1995), so they may perceive some values more accurately than others. Just as adolescents ascribe more legitimacy to parental demands in some domains than

---

[5] For example, demographic similarity between parents and children can account for some of the similarity in values. We did not control for these effects because, indeed, parent–child influence may mediate in part the impact of the social context on children, and statistically controlling demographic similarity may eliminate actual socialization effects. In Study 3, we investigate in detail the role of demographic variables in predicting processes relevant to value influence in the family.

in others (Smetana, 1995), they may ascribe more legitimacy to some parental socialization values than to others and accept them more. That is, particular values may elicit consistently higher levels of accuracy and/or acceptance across individuals and other values may elicit consistently lower levels. Consequently, parent–child value congruence should also vary systematically across values.

We reason that the level of accuracy or acceptance of a particular value depends on the nature of its motivational content. In the following sections, we generate hypotheses that specify relationships of value content to levels of accuracy and acceptance. However, we must first establish whether the content of values does relate systematically to accuracy of perception, acceptance, and congruence. To answer this question requires comparing different groups. For this purpose, we use – in addition to the current sample – two smaller samples in which values were measured with a different instrument. Together, the three samples enable us to seek consistent variations – across age groups, gender compositions of dyads, and diverse methods – in accuracy, acceptance, and congruence of different values.

2.2. Method

Two groups participated: One group included 43 adolescents and their parents, the other group included 47 young adults and their parents, in Israel. The young adults responded as part of a course project. Each recruited one adolescent (not their own sibling). Both parents participated in most families (i.e., adolescents 95%, young adults 89%). The adolescent sample was 66% female, with a mean age of 16.5 years ($SD = 2.44$); the young adult sample was 75% female, with a mean age of 23.2 years ($SD = 1.77$). Samples did not differ in family income, parents' education, or religiosity.

We measured values with the Schwartz Value Survey (SVS) (Schwartz, 1992), which includes 57 value items, each briefly defined in parentheses (e.g., Social Order [stability of society]). Respondents rated the importance (or perceived importance) of each value on a 9-point scale. Detailed discussions of the theoretical grounding, validity, and reliability of this instrument appear in Schwartz (1992, 1994, 1996, in press a, b). Young adults and adolescents rated their own values as well as the values they perceive that their parents want them to endorse.[6] Parents responded to the survey once. They rated the importance they want their child to attribute to each value as a guiding principle in his or her life. Because maternal and paternal values correlated positively for all values ($r = 0.34$ to 0.83,

---

[6] Children had the opportunity to attribute different preferred values to their two parents, but they reported the same values for each in the majority of cases. We therefore averaged perceived father and mother values where they differed. Other studies show high correspondence between children's perceptions of the values of their two parents as well as actual value agreement between the father and the mother (Acock & Bengtson, 1980; Cashmore & Goodnow, 1985; Rohan & Zanna, 1996).

median $r = 0.60$), we averaged the values of mothers and fathers to obtain single indexes of parents' values.

The Smallest Space Analysis (SSA) (Guttman, 1968) of responses supported use of the standard sets of single value items to index 8 of the 10 values (Schwartz, 1992, 1994) in both samples. Two changes were necessary to make the values of parents and their children comparable: We distinguished two components of universalism values identified in earlier theory and research – nature (i.e., appreciating and protecting the natural environment) and social concern (i.e., understanding people who are different and treating them justly) (Sagiv, 1994). The SSAs also suggested that parents and children understood security values differently. Because nonequivalence of meaning precludes comparison, we excluded security values from further analyses. We averaged the items intended to measure each value to obtain importance scores for each of the 10 values, after centering each person's responses on his or her own mean.

2.3. Results

2.3.1. *Consistency across Age Groups*
Table 11.3 presents the standardized regression coefficients (correlations) in the sample of young adults (top panel) and of adolescents (bottom panel) for value congruence (column 1), accuracy of perception (column 2), and acceptance (column 3). The correlation of the coefficients for the 10 values in one sample with those in the other was $r = 0.35$ for congruence, $r = 0.58$ for accuracy, and $r = 0.48$ for acceptance. This indicates some consistency across the two life stages regarding the specific values that are perceived more or less accurately, accepted more or less, and on which parents and children are more or less congruent. However, consistency is far from perfect.

Age-group differences in accuracy of perception or in acceptance of specific values can account for many of the differences in the congruence of specific values. Consider the example of conformity values: They showed no congruence among adolescents ($r = 0.08$) but some among young adults ($r = 0.23$). The analyses point to acceptance as a source of this difference. Adolescents perceived their parents' conformity values quite accurately ($r = 0.56$) but did not accept them at all ($r = 0.08$). On the other hand, young adults exhibited moderate acceptance of perceived parental conformity values ($r = 0.27$) and at least weak accuracy of perception ($r = 0.21$).

The differences in accuracy and acceptance of parental conformity values among adolescents and young adults may reflect different objective conditions of contact with parents. Leaving home reduces the intensity of parent–child conflict and power struggles (Aquilino, 1997). The adolescents lived in their parents' homes and, therefore, were subject to ongoing, implicit or explicit conformity pressures. The young adults had all spent at least 2 to 3 years away from their parents' homes in the army, and most were now living independently.

Table 11.3. *Accuracy of perception, acceptance of parental values, and congruence of children's values with parents' socialization values*

Value	(1) Congruence Coefficients	(2) Accuracy Coefficients	(3) Acceptance Coefficients
YOUNG ADULTS N = 47			
Tradition	.59**	.73**	.63**
Benevolence	.12	.14	.25*
Social Concern (Universalism)	.54**	.50**	.41**
Nature (Universalism)	.44**	.57**	.53**
Self-Direction	.25*	.46**	.29*
Stimulation	.21	.37**	.49**
Hedonism	.38**	.59**	.53**
Achievement	.10	.37**	.26*
Power	.18	.57**	.30*
Conformity	.23	.21	.27*
ADOLESCENTS N = 43			
Tradition	.65**	.72**	.66**
Benevolence	.41**	.38**	.43**
Social Concern (Universalism)	.28*	.39**	.38**
Nature (Universalism)	.37**	.54**	.63**
Self-Direction	.33*	.43**	.25*
Stimulation	.18	.42**	.35*
Hedonism	.21	.47**	.34*
Achievement	.29*	.42**	.57**
Power	.45**	.65**	.41**
Conformity	.08	.56**	.08

* $p < .05$ (1-tailed); ** $p < .01$ (1-tailed).

Greater recent and current exposure to parental conformity pressures among adolescents may produce not only greater accuracy but also greater rebellion and lower acceptance of perceived parental conformity values. Hence, despite higher accuracy of perception in the adolescent sample, congruence was lower because of very low acceptance.[7]

2.3.2. Consistency across Different Value Instruments
Did the same values show high or low accuracy, acceptance, and congruence in the two studies that measured values among adolescents with the PVQ versus the SVS? Nine values were common to both studies (i.e., tradition, benevolence,

---

[7] The dependence of congruence for specific values on the combination of accuracy and acceptance is also supported in these samples. Across the 10 values, substantial correlations were found between congruence coefficients and the multiplicative accuracy × acceptance interaction term ($r = .85$ among adolescents and .83 among young adults; both $p < .01$).

universalism [social concern], self-direction, stimulation, hedonism, power, achievement, and conformity).[8] The correlation of accuracy coefficients in one study with those in the other, across the nine values, was 0.65. Correlations were 0.77 for acceptance and 0.73 for congruence (all $p < .01$). This indicates substantial consistency regarding the particular values perceived more or less accurately, accepted more or less, and showing high or low parent–child congruence. This consistency emerged despite using different value instruments and samples recruited in very different ways.

2.3.3. Consistency across Different Parent–Adolescent Gender Combinations
We next examined the extent to which the accuracy, acceptance, and congruence coefficients for each value were consistent across the four dyadic gender combinations in the PVQ sample (see Tables 11.1 and 11.2). We correlated the coefficients across the 10 values for each of the 6 possible pairings of the 4 dyads: father–son, father–daughter, mother–son, and mother–daughter. Correlations for accuracy ranged from $r = 0.43$ to 0.85 (median 0.54), for acceptance from $r = 0.50$ to 0.76 (median 0.59), and for congruence from $r = 0.41$ to 0.82 (median 0.60). These correlations reveal considerable consistency across dyads in the particular values that exhibit high or low accuracy, acceptance, or congruence.

Taken together, the results support the conclusion that particular values exhibit characteristically higher or lower levels of accuracy, acceptance, and congruence. Results for value congruence, aggregated across all the analyses, reveal that transmission of values from parents to children was most successful for tradition values followed by power values and least successful for hedonism values followed by benevolence values. Moreover, the level of accuracy of perception and of acceptance of particular values largely predicted the level of congruence for those values. Therefore, to understand which values show more or less parent–child value congruence, Study 3 investigates factors that may influence accuracy in perceiving particular values and acceptance of them.

3.0. STUDY 3: EXPLAINING VARIATION IN PERCEPTION AND ACCEPTANCE OF SPECIFIC VALUES

3.1. Hypotheses

Accuracy of Perception. The trait and attitude literatures identify two factors that affect accuracy of perception and also may be relevant to values. Observers perceive targets' self-reported traits more accurately if the traits are evaluatively

---

[8] To make the analyses comparable across the SVS and PVQ studies, we combined the scores for fathers and mothers in the larger sample that used the PVQ. We also weighted the male and female subsamples to match the gender composition of the SVS adolescent sample (66% female) because there were some gender effects among adolescents in levels of congruence, accuracy, and acceptance (see the following discussion).

neutral than if they are extremely socially desirable or undesirable (Funder, 1995; John & Robins, 1994). Presumably, this is due to self-enhancement bias in self-reports for desirable traits and defensiveness bias in self-reports for undesirable traits. The value equivalent of social desirability is the importance attributed to particular values in the surrounding society. Parents' may bias reports of their socialization values upward for extremely important values in the society and downward for extremely unimportant values. We therefore hypothesize lower accuracy in adolescents' perception of the values that are extremely important or extremely unimportant in society as compared with values of moderate societal importance. The extremely important values in the population studied here were benevolence and security; the least important were power and stimulation (Knafo & Schwartz, 2004b).

For some social attitudes, transmission succeeds more when parents and children share the same social environment (Dalton, 1982). Parents' membership in groups (e.g., religious) or social categories (e.g., social class) conveys information about their attitudes and values to their children, especially if the group is known to endorse particular values (e.g., universalism values in an environmental group). Adolescents can then infer parental values from the values manifestly important to the group. Some values are linked to sociodemographic characteristics (e.g., tradition values to religion, conformity and self-direction values to social class) (Kohn & Schooler, 1983). Adolescents are likely to be exposed to their parents' friends who share the parents' characteristics and the values linked to them, which increases the salience of those values and makes it easier for adolescents to infer them accurately. We, therefore, hypothesize that accuracy of perception is higher for values that are predictable by the sociodemographic characteristics of parents.

Acceptance. The legitimacy that adolescents grant to parental authority in a value domain is likely to influence acceptance of parents' values. Smetana (1995, 2000) noted that adolescents consider their parents' authority more legitimate when they try to influence them with regard to moral, conventional, and prudential issues rather than personal issues. Relationships of specific values to those types of issues suggest hypotheses regarding the values likely to elicit more or less acceptance.

Moral issues refer to others' rights or welfare. Universalism, benevolence, and power values are most concerned with the welfare of others. The first two values call for promoting others' welfare, the latter justifies self-interest at the expense of others. *Conventional* issues are those governed by arbitrary social norms. Conformity values focus on upholding conventions. Tradition values concern both moral and conventional issues. *Prudential* issues pertain to safety and avoiding harm to the self. Security and – to a lesser degree – conformity values concern prudential issues. *Personal* issues are those whose consequences affect only the actor; adolescents tend to consider them legitimately outside their parents' regulation (Smetana, 2000). Hedonism, stimulation, self-direction, and achievement values concern primarily personal issues (Schwartz, 1992). Based on the lower legitimacy of parental authority in personal issues, we hypothesize the following: Adolescents' acceptance of perceived parental values is lower for hedonism, stimulation, self-direction, and achievement values than for other values.

Families tend to spend time with others with similar backgrounds, personal characteristics, and – to some extent – values. Exposure of adolescents to those others with whom their parents share values is likely to provide social support for those values. It may imbue them with greater authority and legitimacy. The values likely to receive such social reinforcement are those related to family demographic characteristics. Adolescents may be more accepting of those parental values that are typical of families with similar background characteristics. We therefore hypothesize that acceptance is higher for those values associated more strongly with family demographic characteristics.

3.2. Method

The data from Study 1 tested the hypotheses. To reduce the number of analyses, we combined sons and daughters. To estimate the extent to which perceived parental values reflect family demographic characteristics, we regressed the importance of each perceived value on four key demographic variables in a stepwise regression: (1) *family religiosity* from adolescents' response to the question: "How would you define your family, in terms of religiosity?" (3 = religious; 2 = traditional; 1 = nonreligious); (2) *parents' educational attainment* in years of schooling; (3) *parents' age*; and (4) *family ethnicity* (3 = both parents born in Muslim countries [Sephardic]; 1 = both parents born in Christian countries [Ashkenazi]; 2 = mixed or other origin). The proportion of variance in the importance of a perceived parental value accounted for by these demographic variables indicates the extent to which the value reflects family demographic characteristics.

Columns 1 and 2 of Table 11.4 present the coefficients of accuracy and acceptance for each value, separately for fathers (top panel) and mothers (bottom panel). Column 3 of Table 11.4 reports the proportion of variance explained by demographic characteristics for each value.

3.3. Results and Discussion

Accuracy. As hypothesized, accuracy of perception was higher for values that were predictable by parents' sociodemographic characteristics. The proportion of variance in perceived parental values accounted for by demographic variables correlated strongly with accuracy in perceiving values (fathers, $r = 0.63$, $p < .05$; mothers, $r = 0.81$, $p < .01$).

We tested the hypothesis that adolescents are less accurate in perceiving those values that are extremely important or unimportant in society than the values

Table 11.4. *Accuracy and acceptance of perceived fathers' and mothers' socialization values and variance accounted for by demographic characteristics*[9]

Value	(1) Accuracy Coefficients	(2) Acceptance Coefficients	(3) Variance Proportion Accounted for by Demographics
FATHERS N = 362			
Tradition	.85**	.90**	.25
Benevolence	.27**	.64**	.05
Universalism	.45**	.58**	.03
Self-Direction	.92**	.34**	.06
Stimulation	.37**	.31**	.04
Hedonism	.35**	.29**	.08
Achievement	.36**	.49**	.01
Power	.44**	.72**	.04
Security (Group)	.25**	.47**	.03
Conformity	.40**	.16**	.03
MOTHERS N = 540			
Tradition	.93**	.78**	.20
Benevolence	.34**	.72**	.09
Universalism	.24**	.65**	.05
Self-Direction	.68**	.59**	.07
Stimulation	.30**	.31**	.00
Hedonism	.18**	.30**	.01
Achievement	.29**	.55**	.06
Power	.37**	.72**	.02
Security (Group)	.23**	.65**	.00
Conformity	.45**	.35**	.02

* p < .05 (1-tailed); ** p < .01 (1-tailed).

of moderate societal importance with a planned comparison. We compared the 8 accuracy coefficients for the values of greatest societal importance (i.e., benevolence, security) and least societal importance (i.e., power and stimulation), for fathers and mothers, with the 12 accuracy coefficients for the remaining 6 moderately important values. As hypothesized, mean accuracy was lower for values of extremely high or low societal importance ($M = 0.32$) than for those of moderate importance ($M = 0.51$; $t(18df) = 1.92$; $p < .05$, 1-tailed).

These two sets of findings point to the importance of the social environment in adolescents' perception of their parents' values. Social characteristics that distinguish their own family and its social circle from others can help adolescents

---

[9] The proportions of variance in perceived parental values are based on stepwise regressions, with family religiosity, family ethnicity, parents' age, and parents' education as predictors. Details of the analyses are available from the authors.

infer more accurately which values are more or less important to their parents. The importance of those values is made more salient by exposure to the social circle. In contrast, it is difficult for adolescents to discern their own parents' priorities accurately for values that are viewed consensually in the surrounding society as highly desirable (important) or not (unimportant). This may be because parents bias their overt expression of these values toward societal norms.

Acceptance. As hypothesized, acceptance was higher for values that were predictable by parents' sociodemographic characteristics. The proportion of variance in perceived parental values accounted for by demographic variables correlated positively with acceptance of values (fathers 0.57, mothers 0.61; both $p < .05$, 1-tailed). This finding supports theorizing that exposure of adolescents to social environments that give greater legitimacy to their parents' socially linked value priorities increases acceptance of those values.

A planned comparison tested the hypothesis that acceptance levels are lower for values concerned with personal issues (i.e., self-direction, stimulation, hedonism, and achievement) than for values that concern moral, conventional, or prudential issues. We compared the 8 acceptance coefficients for values concerned with personal issues (4 values × 2 parents) with the 12 coefficients for values concerned with the other issues (6 values × 2 parents). As hypothesized, mean acceptance was lower for personal-issue values ($M = 0.40$) than for the other values ($M = 0.62$; $t(18df) = 2.68$; $p < .02$, 1-tailed). The idea that adolescents see parental influence as less legitimate in the personal domain (Smetana, 2000) can explain those results. Because adolescents feel that their parents' have less legitimacy in trying to impose values in the personal domain, they are more likely to ignore or reject what their parents want for them.

4.0. STUDY 4: EFFECTS OF THE GENDER COMPOSITION OF PARENT–CHILD DYADS ON VALUE TRANSMISSION

4.1. Research Issues

Early theories of identification and value internalization ascribed great importance to the gender composition of the parent–child dyad. Some theorists argued that intergenerational value transmission is primarily from parents to their same-sex rather than their opposite-sex children (Freud, 1927; Parsons, 1955). Indeed, when asked about their desire to be like their parents, adolescents usually reveal a same-sex preference (Hoffman, 1971; Knafo & Schwartz, 2005; Winch, 1962).

Troll and Bengtson (1979) noted three opposing theoretical assertions in the literature: (1) fathers influence child values more than mothers; (2) congruence is higher in same-sex than in opposite-sex dyads; and (3) daughters are more susceptible to parental influence than sons. They summarized many studies as follows: "We cannot conclude that gender effects are important in transmission. While some studies support the common assumption that fathers are more influential than mothers are, other studies do not. Sex of child does not appear to be a relevant variable in parent–child congruence" (Troll & Bengtson, 1979, p. 145). A German study exemplifies such inconsistency: Boehnke (2001) found strong same-sex effects only for power values and higher congruence for daughters mainly for tradition values.

We propose that the specific content of the different values may explain some of the inconsistency of gender effects. That is, the effect of the gender composition of the parent–child dyad depends on the particular value in question. As discussed previously, the patterns of accuracy and acceptance coefficients for the different values showed some consistency across genders; however, there still were gender differences (see Tables 11.1 and 11.2). We therefore generate and test hypotheses regarding how the gender composition of dyads, together with the particular content of a value, may jointly influence levels of accuracy and acceptance and thereby influence value congruence.

4.2. Interparental Agreement, Accuracy, and Acceptance

Accuracy in perceiving parental values is greater when there is value agreement between the father and the mother in the family (Knafo & Schwartz, 2003). Parental agreement may provide more consistent and less confusing value messages that are easier to perceive accurately. Because adolescents tend to look to their same-sex parent as a model, they may attend more to this parent's value messages and perceive them fairly accurately even in the presence of parental disagreement. Parental disagreement may interfere more with the children's accurate perception of the values of opposite-sex parents because they attend to them less. We therefore hypothesize that in opposite-sex parent–child dyads, perception of parental values is more accurate the greater the value agreement between parents. In same-sex parent–child dyads, accuracy of perception may relate to parental value agreement but less strongly.

In a similar vein, we expect parental value agreement to promote the acceptance of perceived parental values mainly for the opposite-sex parent. If adolescents look up to their same-sex parent more, their acceptance of the values of the opposite-sex parent may largely depend on the latter's agreement with the same-sex parent. We therefore hypothesize that in opposite-sex parent–child dyads, acceptance of perceived parental values is greater when there is more value agreement between parents; we do not expect this relationship in same-sex dyads.

We computed interparent agreement scores for each value by correlating the importance ratings of that value by the two parents, across the set of families. Separate interparent agreement scores were computed for the parents of sons and of daughters. We then tested the hypotheses by correlating the accuracy of perception scores and the acceptance scores (see columns 2 and 3 of Tables 11.1 and 11.2) with those agreement scores, across the 10 values. As hypothesized for the opposite-sex dyads, parental agreement correlated positively with accuracy of perception of parental values (father–daughter, $r = 0.69$; mother–son, $r = 0.78$; both $p < .05$, 1-tailed); for same-sex dyads, correlations were positive but not significant (father–son, $r = 0.34$; mother–daughter, $r = 0.14$; both n.s.). Also as hypothesized, parental agreement correlated positively with acceptance in opposite-sex dyads (father–daughter, $r = 0.52$, $p < .06$, 1-tailed; mother–son, $r = 0.60$, $p < .05$, 1-tailed) but not in same-sex dyads (father–son, $r = -0.06$; mother–daughter, $r = 0.43$, both n.s.).

4.3. Gender-Typing of Values and Acceptance

Troll and Bengtson (1979, p. 145) averred that "The more sex roles are expected to be differentiated, the more one would expect sex linkage in personality transmission." This implies that same-sex preference should be stronger for values that are relevant to gender roles. The idea that children learn gender-typed behavior by attending to the behavior of relevant same-sex models suggests the same conclusion (Bussey & Bandura, 1999).

Which values are gender-neutral and which are more gender-typed? Theories of gender differences propose that women are more communal (i.e., caring, nurturant) and person-oriented, whereas men are more agentic (i.e., instrumental, assertive) and task-oriented (Bakan, 1966; Parsons, 1955). Research reveals that on average, the sexes do differ along this dimension (Eagly & Wood, 1991; Golombok & Rust, 1993; Knafo, Iervolino, & Plomin, 2005). The values that most clearly express the agentic versus communal distinction are self-enhancement (particularly power) and self-transcendence (particularly benevolence), respectively. Fathers and sons in the families studied herein attributed more importance to self-enhancement values (i.e., power and achievement) than mothers and daughters; the reverse was true for self-transcendence values (i.e., benevolence and universalism) (Knafo & Sagiv, 2004; Knafo & Schwartz, 2004b). Hence, we infer that self-enhancement and self-transcendence values are gender-typed in the current population.

The gender-typing of those values has implications for the acceptance of parental values. We expect sons to take their father as the model for these values and daughters to take their mother as their model. On the other hand, we expect no same-sex preference for the modeling of gender-neutral values. We, therefore, hypothesize that acceptance of self-enhancement and self-transcendence values is greater than acceptance of gender-neutral values in same-sex parent–child dyads. We expect no difference in acceptance of gender-typed versus gender-neutral values in opposite-sex dyads.

The acceptance coefficients in column 3 of Tables 11.1 and 11.2 support the hypothesis. In same-sex dyads, the mean acceptance coefficient for the four gender-typed values was significantly higher than the mean coefficient for the six gender-neutral values ($M = 0.66$ versus $M = 0.37$, $t(18$ df$) = 2.32$, $p < .05$).

In opposite-sex dyads, the mean acceptance coefficients for gender-typed versus gender-neutral values did not differ ($M = 0.57$ versus $M = 0.52$, t (18df) $= 0.55$, n.s.).

Troll and Bengtson (1979) concluded that the gender composition of the parent–child dyad is not relevant to value transmission. Our examination of specific values revealed a more complex picture. Gender composition does matter for some values. Parental agreement on the importance of a particular value affects both accuracy in perceiving and acceptance of that value – but only in opposite-sex parent–child dyads. Gender-typing of values affects acceptance but only in same-sex dyads.

We explained both findings as reflecting the importance of the same-sex parent as a model for values. However, the effects of modeling may also depend on the specific content of the value in question. A striking finding for father–son dyads illustrates this phenomenon. There were only two negative acceptance coefficients in the study: one for conformity values and one for self-direction values. Both appeared in these dyads, indicating that sons rejected both their father's conformity and self-direction values. These values concern issues of obedience versus autonomy. Adolescent sons may reject their father's values because conflict over obedience and autonomy may be especially intense in these dyads as opposed to other parent–child dyads. This provocative finding warrants further research.

5.0. GENERAL DISCUSSION

The Two-Step Model. This research supports the extension of the Grusec and Goodnow (1994) two-step model to value acquisition. Accuracy in perceiving parental socialization values and acceptance of those values account for most of the variance in parent–child value congruence. We have demonstrated that accuracy, acceptance, and – as a consequence – congruence vary systematically by value content and parent–child dyadic gender composition.

Of course, in the absence of a longitudinal design, we can only infer support for one or another causal process that may contribute to value congruence from correlations. Most of the findings were compatible with a causal process of value transmission from parents to children via the parental values that children perceive. The role of parenting in determining accuracy, acceptance, and congruence attests to the causal impact of parents' values on their children's values (Furstenberg, 1971; Knafo & Schwartz, 2001, 2003; Okagaki & Bevis, 1999; Rohan & Zanna, 1996). However, alternative causal explanations for observed parent–child congruence cannot be ruled out.

This research was conducted in a single society with a particular sequence of life-stage roles (i.e., high school student, soldier, and college student) and particular values salient in public discourse (i.e., tradition and security); hence, some findings may be culture-dependent. However, the basic two-step process of value transmission is probably quite culture-general; studies in Australia, Poland, Sweden, and the United States yielded results congruent with it (Cashmore & Goodnow, 1985; Kohn et al., 1986; Westholm, 1999). Of course, the relative importance of the two steps may be culture-dependent. For example, perception of the parents' values may contribute less to achieving parent–child value congruence in cultures in which the range of acceptable values is limited – so-called narrow-socialization cultures (Arnett, 1995). There, children may attain accuracy by inferring what their own parents' values must be from other sources. Research on parent–child value congruence across cultures will be enlightening.

Beyond Accuracy of Perception and Acceptance. Although the processes in the two-step model received much support in this research, some anomalous findings point to the need to go beyond it to fully understand parent–child value congruence. In some cases, a substantial correlation between parents' and children's values remained even when perceived parental values were controlled statistically. This implies that variables not in the value-transmission model of Figure 11.1 influence parent–child value congruence. In addition, not all differences in either accuracy of perception or acceptance led to differences in congruence. Consider conformity values: Daughters exhibited moderate accuracy and acceptance of both their parents' conformity values, whereas sons exhibited low accuracy and acceptance. Indeed, sons even rejected their father's conformity values. Nonetheless, sons – like daughters – showed moderate congruence with their parents for conformity values. Clearly, processes other than accuracy of perception and acceptance must account for father–son value congruence for conformity.

We briefly comment on three other processes that may produce parent–child value congruence: (1) children's influence on their parents' values; (2) shared, genetically based temperaments; and (3) environmental influences that reinforce or contradict parental values.

Children's Influence on Parents. Longitudinal studies indicate that parents influence their children more strongly than children influence parents (Kohn et al., 1986; Taris, 2000). However, children do influence their parents in the course of living together (Ambert, 1992; Kuczynski et al., 1997). For example, adolescents may draw their parents' attention to the nonconventional behavior of the teen peer group and thereby influence their parents to emphasize conformity values less and stimulation values more. Children may also indirectly influence their parents' values by exposing them to social environments that emphasize values consistent with the children's values. For example, children may initiate joint activities between their own family and the families of their peers. This exposes parents to other parents who may mutually influence one another's values (Ambert, 1992).

If children help to shape their parents' values, they should be able to perceive these parental values more accurately. Moreover, children should more readily accept values that they themselves have a hand in shaping. Thus, value congruence traceable to children's influence on their parents would also be reflected in accuracy and acceptance. Another way to focus on the children's role in the process is by asking which children characteristics enhance their accuracy of perception or acceptance of parental values. For example, adolescents who explore various options when forming their identity perceive their parents' values more accurately than low-exploration adolescents (Knafo & Schwartz, 2004a).

Kuczynski et al. (1997) reversed the common focus of research and examined the influence of children on their parents. They argued that parents transform and interpret the messages they receive from their children. Thus, the two-step process may also apply to children's influence on parents' values. A study by Hastings and Grusec (1997) supported this idea for accuracy. They found that the more accurately that parents perceived adolescents' thoughts and feelings during disagreements, the fewer the conflicts and the more satisfactory their resolution. One way that accurate perception may reduce conflict is by increasing the parents' understanding of the adolescents' standpoints and changing the parents' own views as a result. Future research might systematically examine the application of the two-step process of accuracy and acceptance to children's influence on parents.

Genetic Influences. Parents and their children may attribute similar levels of importance to specific values because of shared genetic preferences (e.g., for high arousal). Of course, DNA codes for proteins, not for value priorities, but one may speculate that individual genetic differences may ultimately cause differences in complex traits, such as altruism (Bachner-Melman et al., in press), which may serve as motivational anchors for values. Thus, genetic similarity between parents and children is a potential source of parent–child value congruence. Although the evidence is still scarce, it suggests that genetic effects on values may be important. For example, a study of twins reared together and apart concluded that about half the explained variance in religious values can be ascribed to genetics (Waller, Kojetin, Bouchard, Lykken, & Tellegen, 1990). Another study, with twins reared apart, reported heritability coefficients of 18% to 56% for six work values (Keller et al., 1992), and an adoption study found significant heritability for conservative attitudes (Abrahamson, Baker, & Caspi, 2003). Moreover, children's genetic propensities help to shape their own environment by evoking particular responses from parents and others (Scarr & McCartney, 1983). Such gene-environment correlations may enhance parent–child congruence.

The value whose importance is most likely to depend on temperament and genetics is stimulation (Schwartz, 1992, 1994). Contrary to the expectation based on simple genetic causality, however, congruence was only moderate for stimulation. Perhaps their different age-specific roles weaken the congruence between adolescents and their parents for stimulation values. The genetic influence may manifest itself more in later life stages (Eaves, Martin, Heath, Schieken, Meyer, et al., 1997). Gene-environment interactions may make genetic influences on values more complex (Plomin, DeFries, & Lohelin, 1977; Scarr & McCartney, 1983). Consider a child who inherits an extroverted temperament that inclines her to value stimulation. However, the child's genetic tendency to take risks elicits parental socialization that urges her to be more cautious and to value security. Such negative, evocative gene-environment correlations (Scarr & McCartney, 1983) may explain the low to moderate parent–child congruence in stimulation values.

Genetic tendencies may also influence children's susceptibility to parental influence (Belsky, 2000). For those genetically inclined to be susceptible, accuracy of perception and acceptance and the parenting variables that influence them may be more relevant to value congruence. Comparing parent–child value congruence in adopted and natural children may reveal genetic influences. Adopted children may be less attuned genetically to their parents' meanings and therefore perceive their parents' values less accurately. Moreover, if adopted children project their own values onto their adoptive parents, they may be less accurate to the extent that value priorities are genetically grounded. The role of genetics in determining congruence for different values merits investigation.

Environmental Influences. Shared environments may influence parents' and children's values in the same direction. For example, living in a dangerous environment could increase the importance of security values for both parents and their children. Moreover, parents' partial control over the value-forming environments to which their children are exposed (e.g., restricting television viewing, choosing a neighborhood to live in) may increase congruence. If these environments are compatible with parental values, they reinforce the values parents want for their children. The influence of the environment may also promote parent–child value congruence through social processes external to the family (Harris, 1995) – processes not dependent on accuracy and acceptance. Educational settings are especially relevant environments for acquiring values (Alwin, 1990; Kohn & Schooler, 1983). Exposure to particular educational settings and school peer groups may explain why significant unexplained variance remained in parent–child congruence regarding tradition values, even after controlling accuracy and acceptance.

A potentially fruitful path for future research on environmental influences is to examine the fit between the value environment that parents provide and the value environment of the school. Knafo (2003b) reported that accuracy of perception, acceptance, and congruence was all lower in families in which the fit between parental religiosity and school religiosity was poor. Similarly, Russian immigrant adolescents in Israel who attend a Russian-only school (presumably high parent–school fit) accepted their parents' values to a greater extent than adolescents in heterogeneous schools (Knafo, Assor, Schwartz, & David, Chapter 12, this volume).

6.0. CONCLUSION

This study demonstrated that the two-step model adapted from Grusec and Goodnow (1994) can account for much of the variance in parent–child value congruence: Congruence was high when accuracy of perception and acceptance were high and low when either or both of those processes were low. There were cases, however, that did not fit this pattern, which pointed to the need to go beyond the two-step model. We discussed three additional sources of value congruence: children's influence on their parents' values; shared, genetically based temperaments; and environmental influences that reinforce parental values – each deserves further research.

This is the first study to address the two-step model with a broad, relatively comprehensive set of values. In addition, it is the first to propose explanations for variation across specific values in accuracy and acceptance. We identified several factors that help explain why particular values may be perceived more or less accurately and accepted or rejected. We also identified a number of interactions between the gender composition of parent–adolescent dyads and value content in predicting accuracy and acceptance. Future research that attends to differences among specific values will doubtless identify additional factors and interactions that influence the processes of value acquisition and change.

REFERENCES

Abrahamson, A. C., Baker, L. A., & Caspi, A. (2003). Rebellious teens? Genetic and environmental influences on the social attitudes of adolescents. *Journal of Personality and Social Psychology, 83*, 1392–1408.

Acock, A. C., & Bengtson, V. L. (1980). Socialization and attribution processes: Actual versus perceived similarity among parents and youth. *Journal of Marriage and the Family, 40*, 501–515.

Alwin, D. F. (1990). Cohort replacement and changes in parental socialization values. *Journal of Marriage and the Family, 52*, 347–360.

Ambert, A. M. (1992). *The effect of children on parents.* New York: Haworth Press.

Aquilino, W. (1997). From adolescent to young adult: A prospective study of parent–child relations during the transition to adulthood. *Journal of Marriage and the Family, 59*, 670–686.

Arbuckle, J. L. (1997). *AMOS Users Guide: Version 3.6.* Chicago: Smallwaters Corp.

Arnett, J. J. (1995). Broad and narrow socialization: The family in the context of a cultural theory. *Journal of Marriage and the Family, 57*, 615–628.

Bachner-Melman, R., et al. (in press). Dopaminergic polymorphisms associated with self-report measures of human altruism: A fresh phenotype for the dopamine D4 receptor. *Molecular Psychiatry.*

Bakan, D. (1966). *The duality of human existence: Isolation and communion in Western man.* Boston: Beacon Press.

Baron, R. M., & Kenny, D. A. (1986). The moderator–mediator variable distinction in social psychological research: Conceptual, strategic, and statistical considerations. *Journal of Personality and Social Psychology, 51,* 1173–1182.

Belsky, J. (2000). Conditional and alternative reproductive strategies: Individual differences in susceptibility to rearing experience. In J. Rodgers, D. Rowe, and W. Miller (Eds.), *Genetic influences on human fertility and sexuality: Theoretical and empirical contributions from the biological and behavioral sciences* (pp. 127–146). Boston: Kluwer.

Boehnke, K. (2001). Parent–offspring value transmission in a societal context: Suggestions for a utopian research design with empirical underpinnings. *Journal of Cross-Cultural Psychology, 32,* 241–255.

Bond, M. H., & Chi, V. M. Y. (1997). Values and moral behavior in mainland China. *Psychologia: An International Journal of Psychology in the Orient, 40,* 251–264.

Bussey, K., & Bandura, A. (1999). Social cognitive theory of gender development and differentiation. *Psychological Review, 106,* 676–713.

Cashmore, J. A., & Goodnow, J. J. (1985). Agreement between generations: A two-process approach. *Child Development, 56,* 493–501.

Dalton, R. J. (1982). The pathways of parental socialization. *American Politics Quarterly, 10,* 139–157.

Eagly, A. H., & Wood, W. (1991). Explaining sex differences in social behavior: A meta-analytic perspective. *Personality and Social Psychology Bulletin, 17,* 306–315.

Eaves, L. J., Martin, N. G., Heath, A. C., Schieken, R. M., Meyer, J. M., Silberg, J. S., Neale, M. C., & Corey, L. A. (1997). Age changes in the causes of individual differences in conservatism. *Behavior Genetics, 27,* 121–124.

Freud, S. (1927). *The ego and the id.* London: Hogarth Press.

Funder, D. C. (1995). On the accuracy of personality judgment: A realistic approach. *Psychological Review, 102,* 652–670.

Furstenberg, F. F. (1971). The transmission of mobility orientation in the family. *Social Forces, 49,* 595–603.

Golombok, S., & Rust, J. (1993). The measurement of gender role behaviour in pre-school children: A research note. *Journal of Child Psychology & Psychiatry, 34,* 805–811.

Goodwin, R., Realo, A., Kwiatkowska, A., Kozlova, A., Nguyen Luu, L. A., & Nizharadze, G. (2002). Values and sexual behaviour in Central and Eastern Europe. *Journal of Health Psychology, 7,* 1–12.

Grusec, J. E., & Goodnow, J. J. (1994). Impact of parental discipline methods on the child's internalization of values: A reconceptualization of current points of view. *Developmental Psychology, 30,* 4–19.

Grusec, J. E., & Kuczynski, L. (Eds.). (1997). *Parenting and the internalization of values: A handbook of contemporary theory.* New York: Wiley.

Guttman, L. (1968). A general nonmetric technique for finding the smallest coordinate space for a configuration of points. *Psychometric, 33,* 469–506.

Harris, J. R. (1995). Where is the child's environment? A group socialization theory of development, *Psychological Review, 102,* 458–489.

Hastings, P., & Grusec, J. E. (1997). Conflict outcome as a function of parental accuracy in perceiving child cognitions and affect. *Social Development, 6,* 76–89.

Hoffman, M. L. (1971). Identification and conscience development. *Child Development,* *42,* 1071–1082.

Homer, P. M. (1993). Transmission of human values: A cross-cultural investigation of generational and reciprocal influence effects. *Genetic, Social, and General Psychology Monographs, 119,* 343–367.

John, O. P., & Robins, R. W. (1994). Accuracy and bias in self-perception: Individual differences in self-enhancement and the role of narcissism. *Journal of Personality and Social Psychology, 66,* 206–219.

Kalish, R. A., & Johnson, A. I. (1972). Value similarities and differences in three generations of women. *Journal of Marriage and the Family, 34,* 49–54.

Keller, L. M., Bouchard, T. J., Jr., Arvey, R. D., Segal, N. L., & Dawis, R. V. (1992). Work values: Genetic and environmental influences. *Journal of Applied Psychology, 77,* 79–88.

Knafo, A. (2003a). Authoritarians, the next generation: Values and bullying among adolescent children of authoritarian fathers. *Analyses of Social Issues and Public Policy, 3,* 199–204.

Knafo, A. (2003b). Contexts, relationship quality, and family value socialization: The case of parent–school ideological fit in Israel. *Personal Relationships, 10,* 373–390.

Knafo, A., Iervolino, A., & Plomin, R. (2005). Masculine girls and feminine boys: Genetic and environmental contributions to atypical gender development in early childhood. *Journal of Personality and Social Psychology, 88,* 400–412.

Knafo, A., & Sagiv, L. (2004). Values and work environment: Mapping 32 occupations. *European Journal of Psychology of Education, 19,* 255–273.

Knafo, A., & Schwartz, S. H. (2001). Value socialization in families of Israeli-born and Soviet-born adolescents in Israel. *Journal of Cross-Cultural Psychology, 32,* 213–228.

Knafo, A., & Schwartz, S. H. (2003). Parenting and accuracy of perception of parental values by adolescents. *Child Development, 73,* 595–611.

Knafo, A., & Schwartz, S. H. (2004a). Identity status and parent–child value congruence in adolescence. *British Journal of Developmental Psychology, 22,* 439–458.

Knafo, A., & Schwartz, S. H. (2004b). *Value transmission in the family: Effects of family background and implications for educational achievement.* Jerusalem: NCJW Research Institute for Innovation in Education (Hebrew).

Knafo, A., & Schwartz, S. H. (2005). *Identification with parents, parenting, and parent–child value similarity among adolescents.* Submitted manuscript, The Hebrew University.

Kohn, M. L., & Schooler, C. (1983). *Work and personality.* Norwood, NJ: Ablex.

Kohn, M. L., Slomczynski, K. M., & Schoenbach, C. (1986). Social stratification and the transmission of values in the family: A cross-national assessment. *Sociological Forum, 1,* 73–102.

Kuczynski, L., Marshall, S., & Schell, K. (1997). Value socialization in a bidirectional context. In J. E. Grusec & L. Kuczynski (Eds.), *Parenting and the internalization of values: A handbook of contemporary theory* (pp. 23–50). New York: Wiley.

Miller, R. B., & Glass, J. (1989). Parent–child similarity across the life course. *Journal of Marriage and the Family, 51,* 991–997.

Okagaki, L., & Bevis, C. (1999). Transmission of religious values: Relations between parents' and daughters' beliefs. *Journal of Genetic Psychology, 160,* 303–318.

Parsons, T. (1955). Family structure and the socialization of the child. In T. Parsons & R. F. Bales (Eds.), *Family, socialization, and interaction process.* Glencoe: The Free Press.

Plomin, R., DeFries, J. C., & Lohelin, J. C. (1977). Genotype-environment interaction and correlation in the analysis of human behavior. *Psychological Bulletin, 84,* 309–322.

Rohan, M. J. (2000). A rose by any name? The values construct. *Personality and Social Psychology Review, 4,* 255–277.

Rohan, M. J., & Zanna, M. P. (1996). Value transmission in families. In C. Seligman, J. M. Olson, & M. P. Zanna (Eds.), *The psychology of values: The Ontario symposium, Vol. 8* (pp. 253–276). Hillsdale, NJ: Erlbaum.

Rokeach, M. (1973). *The nature of human values.* New York: The Free Press.

Sagiv, L. (1994). *Cross-national variation in the components and meaning of universalism values.* Paper presented at the Twelfth International Conference of the International Association for Cross-Cultural Psychology, Pamplona, Spain.

Sagiv, L., & Schwartz, S. H. (2004). Values, intelligence, and client behavior in career counseling: A field study. *European Journal of Psychology of Education, 19,* 237–254.

Scarr, S., & McCartney, K. (1983). How people make their own environments: A theory of genotype-environment effects. *Child Development, 54,* 424–435.

Schönpflug, U. (2001). Intergenerational transmission of values: The role of transmission belts. *Journal of Cross-Cultural Psychology, 32,* 174–185.

Schwartz, S. H. (1992). Universals in the content and structure of values: Theoretical advances and empirical tests in 20 countries. In M. P. Zanna (Ed.), *Advances in experimental social psychology, Vol. 25* (pp. 1–65). New York: Academic Press.

Schwartz, S. H. (1994). Are there universal aspects in the content and structure of values? *Journal of Social Issues, 50,* 19–46.

Schwartz, S. H. (1996). Value priorities and behavior: Applying a theory of integrated value systems. In C. Seligman, J. M. Olson, & M. P. Zanna (Eds.), *The psychology of values: The Ontario symposium, Vol. 8* (pp. 1–24). Hillsdale, NJ: Erlbaum.

Schwartz, S. H. (in press a). Basic human values: Their content and structure across countries. In A. Tamayo & J. Porto (Eds.), *Valores e trabalho* [Values and work]. Brasilia: Editora Universidade de Brasilia.

Schwartz, S. H. (in press b). Robustness and fruitfulness of a theory of universals in individual human values. In A. Tamayo & J. Porto (Eds.), *Valores e trabalho* [Values and work]. Brasilia: Editora Universidade de Brasilia.

Schwartz, S. H., Lehmann, A., & Roccas, S. (1999). Multimethod probes of basic human values. In J. Adamopoulos & Y. Kashima (Eds.), *Social psychology and culture context: Essays in honor of Harry C. Triandis* (pp. 107–123). Newbury Park, CA: Sage Publications.

Schwartz, S. H., Melech, G., Lehmann, A., Burgess, S., Harris, M., & Owens, V. (2001). Extending the cross-cultural validity of the theory of basic human values with a different method of measurement. *Journal of Cross-Cultural Psychology, 32,* 519–542.

Smetana, J. G. (1995). Parenting styles and conceptions of parental authority during adolescence. *Child Development, 66,* 299–316.

Smetana, J. G. (2000). Middle-class African American adolescents' and parents' conceptions of parental authority and parenting practices: A longitudinal investigation. *Child Development, 71,* 1682–1686.

Smith, T. E. (1982). The case for parental transmission of educational goals: The importance of accurate offspring perceptions. *Journal of Marriage and the Family, 44*, 661–674.

Taris, T. W. (2000). Quality of mother–child interaction and the intergenerational transmission of sexual values: A panel study. *The Journal of Genetic Psychology, 161*, 169–181.

Taris, T. W., Semin, G. R., & Bok, I. A. (1998). The effect of quality of family interaction and intergenerational transmission of values on sexual permissiveness. *The Journal of Genetic Psychology, 159*, 225–237.

Troll, L., & Bengtson, V. (1979). Generations and the family. In W. R. Burr, R. Hill, F. I. Nye, & I. L. Reiss (Eds.), *Contemporary theories about the family, Vol. 1* (pp. 127–161). New York: The Free Press.

Ullman, J. B. (1996). Structural equation modeling. In B. G. Tabachnick & L. S. Fidell (Eds.), *Using multivariate statistics* (3rd ed.). New York: Harper Collins.

Waller, N. G., Kojetin, B. A., Bouchard, T. J., Lykken, D. T., & Tellegen, A. (1990). Genetic and environmental influences on religious interests, attitudes, and values: A study of twins reared apart and together. *Psychological Science, 1*, 138–142.

Westholm, A. (1999). The perceptual pathway: Tracing the mechanisms of political value transfer across generations. *Political Psychology, 20*, 525–551.

Whitbeck, L. B., & Gecas, V. (1988). Value attributions and value transmission between parents and children. *Journal of Marriage and the Family, 50*, 829–840.

Winch, R. (1962). *Identification and its familial determinants.* Indianapolis, IN: Bobbs-Merrill.

12

Culture, Migration, and Family-Value Socialization: A Theoretical Model and Empirical Investigation with Russian-Immigrant Youth in Israel

ARIEL KNAFO, AVI ASSOR, SHALOM H. SCHWARTZ,
AND LIMOR DAVID

INTRODUCTION

Values are a core component of culture (Hofstede, 1980; Schwartz, 1999). Early theorists described values as the cultural heritage, passed from one generation to the next, that allows individuals to function efficiently in their social environment and to preserve the structure of society (Mannheim, 1952; Mead, 1934). Cross-cultural studies of intergenerational value transmission are few in number, however. This chapter addresses some of the core issues relevant to the study of value transmission across cultures. We focus on the interplay of culture, migration, and parenting style as they relate to socialization processes.

We first propose two different processes through which parenting style and culture may affect value socialization. We then consider the role of parenting style in diverse cultures, focusing on Russian-immigrant and veteran-Israeli youth.[1] Then we examine acculturation attitudes and acculturation contexts as they relate to value socialization in immigrant families. Finally, we briefly discuss implications of the findings for cross-cultural studies of value socialization.

The family is an open system in which parents and children influence one another and in which input from the environment influences them both (O'Connor, Hetherington, & Clingempeel, 1997; Whitchurch & Constantine, 1993). Figure 12.1 presents five contexts that constitute this system: parental, child, parent–child dyadic, family, and ecological. Ecological refers to the wider

---

[1] *Russian immigrants* refers to Russian-speaking immigrants to Israel from all parts of the former Soviet Union.

Parts of the research were carried out while the first author was at Ben Gurion University and at the Social, Genetic, and Developmental Psychiatry Research Centre, Institute of Psychiatry, King's College London. Research reported in this chapter was supported in part by a grant from the Israel Science Foundation to the second author. The work of the first author was partly supported by a Kreitman Foundation Fellowship. Israel Science Foundation Grant No. 921/02 supported the work of the third author on this chapter. Correspondence should be addressed to Ariel Knafo, Department of Psychology, Faculty of Social Sciences, The Hebrew University of Jerusalem, Jerusalem 91905, Israel. E-mail address: msarielk@huji.ac.i

community and culture in which the family is embedded (Bronfenbrenner, 1986). For each context, Figure 12.1 specifies a nonexhaustive list of the aspects likely to affect parent–child value congruence.

Most studies of value transmission have focused on the effect of parenting practices on parent–child value congruence (Rohan & Zanna, 1996; Whitbeck & Gecas, 1988). We also examine the role of parenting style. Parenting style, however, is only one – albeit important – aspect of the context in which parent–child value congruence develops. Other aspects include, for example, parents' education, child's age and birth order, and gender composition of the parent–child dyad (Schönpflug, 2001). Taking a family-systems perspective, we focus on two intertwined aspects of the ecological context: culture and migration. We examine their role in socialization together with parenting style.

1.0. STUDY 1: PARENTING STYLE, CULTURE, AND CULTURE TRANSMISSION

1.1. Research Issues

Despite the interest in parenting styles and discipline techniques, little attention has been given to the possibility that particular parenting behaviors may have different impacts on the intergenerational transmission process in different cultures; Study 1 examines this possibility. We investigate how culture and parenting style jointly influence parent–child value congruence, closeness, and conflict. This chapter refers to children's *perceived* value congruence when children express for themselves the same values that they perceive their parents are holding. That is, children accept the values they attribute to their parents.[2]

Culture and parenting style function together to influence children and parent–child relationships in two major ways. First, parenting style may *mediate* the effects of culture. For example, a hierarchical culture may lead to more coercive or controlling parenting (Chirkov & Ryan, 2001). This culturally influenced parenting style, in turn, may affect children's subjective well-being or acceptance of parental values. The upper panel of Figure 2 represents this process of influence in which parenting style is a mediator (Baron & Kenny, 1986). Second, culture may *moderate* the effects of parenting style on children; the nature of those effects depends on the culture of the society. For example, Leung, Lau, and Lam (1998) found that authoritative parenting enhanced adolescents' academic achievement in the United States and Australia but autocratic parenting did not, whereas the opposite was true in Hong Kong. The lower panel of Figure 12.2 represents the process in which culture is a moderator.

[2] Knafo and Schwartz (chapter 11, this volume) provide a detailed analysis of the roles of accuracy in perceiving parents' values and acceptance of perceived parental values in the development of value congruence.

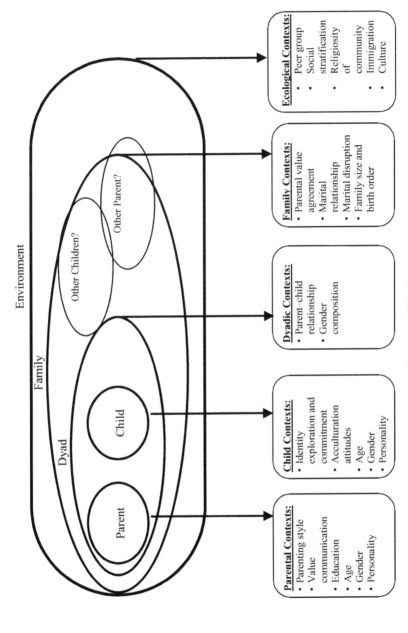

Figure 12.1. The family system and contexts of parent–child value congruence.

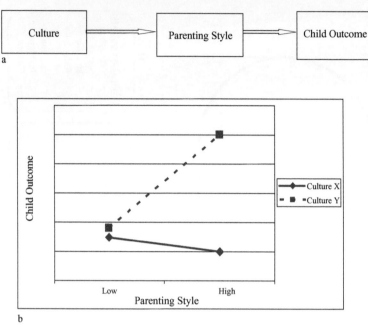

Figure 12.2. Potential effects of culture and parenting style on child outcomes. a. Cultural influence through parenting style. b. Culture-dependent parenting-style effects.

1.2. Parenting Style as a Mediator of Cultural Influence

This section considers two parenting techniques: *autonomy support* and *love withdrawal*. Autonomy-supportive parenting aims to enhance children's inclination to behave in ways they experience as authentic and self-determined. Autonomy support refers to such behaviors as taking the child's perspective; providing rationales for parental expectations; and considering the child's opinions, feelings, and abilities (Assor, Kaplan, & Roth, 2002; Grolnick & Ryan, 1989). Love withdrawal entails parents making their affection for their child conditional on the extent to which the child complies with their demands (Assor, Roth, & Deci, 2004; Coopersmith, 1967).

Autonomy Support. Compared to Western cultures, the cultures of the former Soviet Union valued conservatism and hierarchy more and devalued autonomy and egalitarianism (Schwartz & Bardi, 1997). The political and educational systems in the former Soviet Union revolved around cohesion and control (Klugman, 1986). Traditional Soviet pedagogy sought to foster obedience and group-mindedness (Bronfenbrenner, 1970). This same culture is likely to express itself in parenting behavior. Parents are likely to organize the family hierarchically, to restrict their children's actions, and to articulate expectations for compliance with their demands. Where such a culture prevails, parents are more likely to consider it legitimate to be demanding. In the absence of alternative parenting models, children also may accept demanding parenting as more legitimate. Moreover, they may experience any negative feelings that parental coercion evokes in them as less acceptable. Research on parenting style in the former Soviet Union supports those expectations. Soviet parents viewed children's submission as an ideal and they emphasized norms and rules rather than children's individuality (Mirsky & Prawer, 1992; Sen'ko, 1993). They granted children little right to participate in decision making.

Restricting children is also a common and accepted disciplinary method among Russian-immigrant parents in Israel (Shor, 1999). They are more demanding and monitor their children more closely than veteran-Israeli parents (Zaslavsky & Moore, 2003). On average, Russian-immigrant parents exhibit a more autocratic style of parenting; they express less warmth and demand more obedience than veteran-Israeli parents. Such autocratic parenting correlates negatively with parental responsiveness, a characteristic of autonomy-supportive parenting (Knafo & Schwartz, 2003a). Israeli culture emphasizes autonomy and egalitarianism more than former Soviet cultures (Schwartz, 1999). Parents of native Israeli youth may manifest this cultural difference by allowing their children more autonomy and considering them more as equals. In light of this analysis, we expect lower autonomy-supportive parenting among Russian-immigrant parents than among veteran-Israeli parents.

Love Withdrawal. The Soviet child-rearing literature recommended that parents respond to children's disobedience by temporarily withdrawing affection (Bronfenbrenner, 1970; Geiger, 1968). Russian parents in Russia and Israel reportedly employ love withdrawal (e.g., actively ignoring the child) frequently (Klugman, 1986; Shor, 1999). One study found no difference between veteran-Israeli and Russian-immigrant parents in the extent of love withdrawal (Knafo & Schwartz, 2003b). However, it did find evidence of greater legitimacy for this parenting practice among Russian immigrants. Based on past findings, we expect more love withdrawal among parents from the former Soviet Union than among veteran-Israeli parents.

Consequences of Different Parenting Techniques. Assuming that the expected cultural differences in parenting style exist, how do they affect value transmission? Past research revealed no difference in the extent to which adolescent children of native Israelis and of Russian immigrants accepted the values they perceived their parents to hold (Knafo & Schwartz, 2001). The type of parenting style may not affect the *extent* of acceptance of parental values; the *quality* of acceptance, however, may depend on how parents convey their values. *Quality of acceptance* refers to the way in which youth experience their acceptance of parents' values – the reasons they attribute to themselves for accepting these values. Do they experience accepting their parents' values more as an autonomous and self-determined act or more as the result of coercion?

Children of autonomy-supportive parents tend to identify with their parents and to accept their opinions because they view them as sensible and just (Peterson, Smirles, & Wentworth, 1997). Children of parents who do not support autonomy may also tend to agree with their parents. When they do, however, it is for "controlled" reasons such as obedience, desire to please parents, avoidance of parental punishment, or feelings of guilt (Assor, Roth, & Deci, 2004).

Knafo and Assor (2005) reported that autonomous acceptance of parental values relates to autonomy-supportive parenting. In contrast, we expect love withdrawal to induce the acceptance of parental values out of fear of punishment, feelings of guilt, or hope of external rewards because it threatens rather than supports the child. That is, we expect children subjected to love withdrawal or little autonomy-supportive parenting to accept perceived parental values for controlled reasons. Therefore, assuming that Russian-immigrant parents exhibit more love withdrawal or emphasize less autonomy in their parenting than veteran-Israeli parents, the quality of their children's acceptance of parental values should differ. We hypothesize that children of veteran-Israeli parents exhibit more autonomous acceptance of perceived parental values than children of Russian-immigrant parents; the reverse holds for controlled acceptance.

The causal process of value transmission underlying this hypothesis is one in which parenting style mediates the effects of culture on the quality of acceptance of parental values. Specifically, we postulate that differences in the levels of cultural hierarchy and autonomy to which Russian-immigrant and veteran-Israeli parents are exposed lead to differences in their use of love withdrawal and autonomy-supportive parenting practices. In turn, these differences in practices lead to differences in the nature of the children's acceptance of perceived parental values, to more controlled versus autonomous acceptance.

1.3. Culture as a Moderator of the Effects of Parenting Style

Research in Western societies shows that autonomy-supportive parenting enhances children's well-being and their relationships with parents, whereas controlling parenting has the opposite effects (Grolnick, Deci, & Ryan, 1997). Might the positive effects of autonomy support and negative effects of controlling be limited to Western cultures, as Iyengar and Lepper (1999) suggest? For example, Quoss and Zhao (1995) reported that autocratic parenting, characterized by low responsiveness, fostered negative attitudes toward parents in Western cultures but positive attitudes in Asian cultures. Grusec, Rudy, and Martini (1997) proposed that parents in non-Western cultures can behave in an autocratic fashion and still succeed in creating positive child-rearing conditions.

Other studies (mostly guided by self-determination theory) suggest that children in non-Western countries also strive for autonomy and react negatively to controlling parenting (Chirkov, Ryan, Kim, & Kaplan, 2003; Katz & Assor, 2003). For example, Chirkov and Ryan (2001) reported that perceived autonomy support related positively to academic motivation and well-being for both

Russian and U.S. students. Katz and Assor (2002) found that parental imposition of activities that were inconsistent with children's interests undermined intrinsic motivation in both Bedouin and Jewish Israeli children, using behavioral measures of motivation. However, when motivation was assessed via self-report, parental imposition undermined motivation only for the Jewish children.

Studies of parenting-style antecedents of parent–child value congruence are also largely from Western(ized) cultures. They found that autonomy-supportive parenting promotes an accurate perception of parental values by adolescents and that nonresponsive parenting (i.e., love withdrawal and autocratic parenting) hinders an accurate perception (Knafo & Schwartz, 2003a). These studies also reported that autonomy-supportive parenting enhances acceptance of parents' values by adolescents and nonresponsive parenting reduces acceptance (Knafo & Schwartz, 2003b; Peterson, Smirles, & Wentworth, 1997). There is little evidence, however, regarding parenting effects on the extent and quality of parent–child value agreement in non-Western cultures.

Knafo and Schwartz (2003b) reported different impacts of parenting style on adolescent attitudes toward parents and on acceptance of perceived parental values in veteran-Israeli and Russian-immigrant families. Autocratic parenting and love withdrawal related negatively to closeness to parents and to acceptance of their values in the Israeli-born group. In the Russian-immigrant group, love withdrawal had no negative effects. The authors suggested that controlling practices may affect well-being less negatively in Russian families because they see such practices as more legitimate. More generally, parenting styles may have more or less harmful effects in a society depending on the legitimacy granted to the styles in the respective culture.

In summary, there is controversy regarding how cross-culturally consistent the effects of particular parenting styles are on socialization and, more specifically, transmission outcomes. We address this issue by comparing the correlates of parental love withdrawal in two cultures, one that legitimizes this technique (i.e., Russian) and one that does not (i.e., native Israeli). Specifically, we study relationships of love withdrawal to children's subjective well-being, to their relationships with their parents, and to acceptance of perceived parental values. For Israeli-born youth, we expect negative associations of love withdrawal with these child-relationship outcomes. For Russian immigrants, we anticipate weaker negative effects of love withdrawal. The study also examines whether the socialization outcomes of parental autonomy support are equally positive in the two cultural groups.

1.4. Method

1.4.1. *Participants and Procedure*
Forty Russian-immigrant undergraduate students in Israel participated in a study of parenting style, motivation to agree with parental values, and subjective well-being (Knafo & Assor, 2005). To form a matched sample, for each immigrant

student we selected one veteran-Israeli student of the same sex and attending the same class in business administration, accounting, education, psychology, or economics. Participants completed questionnaires assessing autonomous and controlled motivations for accepting parents' values, perceived autonomy support by parents, agitation, guilt, and happiness (Knafo & Assor, 2005). We drew on the following additional variables: students' acceptance of parental values, perceived parental love withdrawal, and conflict with parents. Questionnaires were administered in a classroom setting and the students received course credit for their participation.

1.4.2. *Instruments*
Parenting Style. Five 4-point agree–disagree items measured *perceived autonomy-supportive parenting*. Three items came from a parental responsiveness measure (e.g., "When my parents make decisions, they try to consider what I want") (Knafo & Schwartz, 2003a) and two were added to capture value-related aspects of autonomy support (e.g., "My parents enable me to find my own personal way to express the principles they believe in"). A 5-item scale measured *perceived love withdrawal* (e.g., "My parents won't talk to me when I do something against their will"). Three items were taken from Knafo and Schwartz (2003a). The Cronbach alpha was $\alpha = .75$ for autonomy support and $\alpha = .85$ for love withdrawal.

Subjective Well-Being. Respondents indicated the extent to which they had experienced each of 10 feelings in the past few weeks on a 4-point scale. We assumed that feelings over several weeks reflected overall subjective well-being more accurately than feelings at one specific point in time. Agitation was indexed by four items (e.g., "nervous," $\alpha = .82$), guilt by three items (e.g., "guilty," $\alpha = .79$), and happiness by three items (e.g., "happy," $\alpha = .75$). A smallest-space analysis (Guttman, 1968) of the correlations among the items confirmed the discrimination into three distinct feelings.

Autonomous and Controlled Reasons for Acceptance. Knafo and Assor (2005) constructed a measure of perceived autonomous versus controlled reasons for accepting parents' values using the format of the Perceived Locus of Causality measure (Ryan & Connell, 1989). Respondents first read a simple definition of values (i.e., "Values are goals in life with which we decide what is good and what is not"). Then, to reduce responding based on perceptions of what is socially desirable, they were told that "people differ in the extent to which they agree with their parents' values." They then read the introductory phrase, "When you agree with your parents, it is because...," which was followed by a list of possible reasons for accepting parental values. Respondents rated each reason on a 7-point agree–disagree scale. Six items indexed autonomous motivation ($\alpha = .87$; e.g., "Because I understand the logic behind my parents' values") and six items indexed controlled motivation ($\alpha = .87$; e.g., "Because I don't want to disappoint my parents").

Perceived Conflict with Parents. Two 4-point agree–disagree items indexed conflict (α = .78; e.g., "Recently, there were occasions when I had a tough dispute or argument with my parents").

Acceptance of Perceived Parental Values. Respondents read short descriptions of each of the 10 Schwartz (1992) values and rated their importance to themselves and to their parents on a 4-point scale (i.e., 0 = not at all important; 3 = very important).[3] Acceptance was measured by correlating the respondents' own values with the values they perceived their parents as wanting them to endorse.

1.5. Results

1.5.1. *Parenting Style as a Mediator of Cultural Influence*
Average Between-Culture Differences. The upper panel of Table 12.1 presents the means and standard deviations for love withdrawal and autonomy-supportive parenting in the two cultural groups. As hypothesized, Russian-immigrant youth perceived their parents as higher in love withdrawal than veteran-Israeli youth ($t(78) = -3.59, p < .01$). Russian-immigrant youth also perceived their parents as lower in autonomy-supportive parenting; however, the difference was not significant, perhaps due to sample size ($t(78) = 1.47$, n.s.).

The second panel of Table 12.1 presents the data for the extent of and reasons for acceptance of perceived parental values. We expected no difference in the extent of acceptance and, indeed, found none ($t(78) = 0.32$, n.s.). As hypothesized, Russian-immigrant youth reported more controlled reasons for acceptance than veteran-Israeli youth ($t(78) = -2.55, p < .01$). Russian-immigrant youth also reported fewer autonomous reasons; however, this difference was not significant ($t(78) = 0.65$, n.s.).

Mediation of Cultural Influence Through Parenting Style. The two cultural groups differed in both the use of love withdrawal and the reasons for which children accepted their parents' values. We now ask: Did parental love withdrawal mediate the effects of culture on the reasons why children accept their parents' values? We assessed this with a series of regressions. Treating culture as a dummy variable (i.e., veteran Israelis = 0; Russian immigrants = 1), culture predicted controlled reasons for accepting parents' values ($\beta = -.28, t = -2.55, p < .01$). Culture also predicted perceptions that parents use love withdrawal ($\beta = .38, t = 3.59, p < .01$). Moreover, use of love withdrawal predicted controlled acceptance of parental values ($\beta = .57, t = 6.12, p < .01$). To assess mediation, we regressed controlled reasons for accepting parents' values on love withdrawal

---

[3] A subsample of 44 participants responded to the original Schwartz (1992) Value Survey 2 weeks later. Except for the benevolence and self-direction values, value scores assessed with the two methods correlated significantly ($r = .35$ to .78, median $r = .45$). Hence, these items measure reasonably well the broad range of values described by Schwartz (1992) and are suitable for the purpose of computing a congruence measure.

Table 12.1. *Means and standard deviations (in parentheses) of parenting style, acceptance of perceived parental values, and reasons for acceptance of perceived parental values (Study 1)*

	Russian-Immigrant Families	Veteran-Israeli Families
Perceived Parenting Style		
Love withdrawal*	1.16	0.68
	(0.59)	(0.60)
Autonomy-supportive parenting	2.15	2.30
	(0.44)	(0.46)
Value Agreement with Parents		
Acceptance of perceived parental values	0.54	0.51
	(0.38)	(0.42)
Controlled motivation for acceptance*	3.58	2.92
	(1.13)	(1.18)
Autonomous motivation for acceptance	4.99	5.13
	(0.83)	(1.19)

* Significant difference between the two cultural groups ($p < .01$).

and then added culture to the prediction equation. Using love withdrawal as a mediator reduced the effect of culture on controlled acceptance to insignificance (i.e., β dropped from $-.28$ to $-.07$ [$t = -.73$, n.s.]).

These results point to a mediation process of the type shown in the upper panel of Figure 12.2. Russian-immigrant parents exhibit greater love withdrawal than veteran-Israeli parents. As a result, although both groups accept their parents' values to the same degree, Russian-immigrant youth do so more because of controlled reasons than veteran-Israeli youth.[4]

1.5.2. *Culture as a Moderator of the Effects of Parenting Style*
The upper panel of Table 12.2 presents the correlations of love withdrawal and autonomy-supportive parenting with three affective aspects of subjective well-being (i.e., guilt, agitation, and happiness), conflict with parents, and acceptance of perceived parental values for Russian immigrants. The lower panel presents the same data for Israeli-born youth.

Love withdrawal correlated positively and autonomy-supportive parenting negatively with guilt, agitation, and conflict in both cultural groups. The differences between the correlations for the two parenting styles were significant in each case. As expected, love withdrawal had weaker negative effects in the

---

[4] That being said, it should be noted that youths perceive their parents as using autonomy support more than love withdrawal in *both* cultures. Moreover, youths experience their agreement with parents as more autonomous than controlled in both cultural groups (see Table 12.1). Reported differences are between cultures and not within cultures.

Table 12.2. *Correlations of parenting styles with youths' subjective well-being,
parent–child conflict, and acceptance of perceived parental values (Study 1)*

	Love Withdrawal	Autonomy-Supportive Parenting
Russian-Immigrant Families		
Guilt[a]	.32*	−.23
Happiness	.24	−.12
Agitation[a]	.33*	−.18
Perceived conflict with parents[a]	.48**	−.39**
Acceptance of perceived parental values	−.10	−.06
Veteran-Israeli Families		
Guilt[a]	.37**	−.20
Happiness	−.12	.00
Agitation[a]	.55**	−.52**
Perceived conflict with parents[a]	.80**	−.36*
Acceptance of perceived parental values[a]	−.28*	.36*

* $p < .05$, 1-tailed; ** $p < .01$, 1-tailed.
[a] Correlation difference between love-withdrawal and autonomy-supportive parenting is significant at $p < .05$ (1-tailed).

Russian-immigrant group, although only the effect on conflict with parents differed significantly between groups ($r = .48$ versus $r = .80$, $z = 2.48$, $p < .01$). The correlations of parenting style with happiness were not significant. It is interesting, however, that the weak correlation of happiness with love withdrawal was positive in the Russian-immigrant group ($r = .24$) and negative in the veteran-Israeli group ($r = −.12$), and the correlation difference was marginally significant ($z = 1.57$, $p < .06$). Finally, replicating Knafo and Schwartz (2003b), for Israeli-born youth, autonomy support related positively to acceptance of perceived parental values ($r = .36$, $p < .05$), whereas love withdrawal related negatively to acceptance ($r = −.28$, $p < .05$). For Russian-immigrant youth, these parenting techniques had no effect on acceptance. In summary, the effects of parenting style on children and on parent–child relationships differed in the two cultural groups.

1.6. Discussion

The findings provide support for both processes through which culture and parenting style intertwine to influence children and parent–child relationships. Evidence for parenting style as a mediator of cultural effects comes from the finding that perceived parental love withdrawal mediated the impact of cultural group (Russian immigrant versus veteran Israeli) on controlled agreement with parental values. Evidence for culture as a moderator of parenting-style effects comes from the numerous differences between the cultural groups in the effects of love withdrawal and autonomy support on youths' feelings, conflict with parents, and acceptance of perceived parental values. There was a consistent pattern of stronger negative effects for love withdrawal and positive effects for autonomy support among Israeli-born than among Russian-born youth. Not all differences were significant, of course, perhaps reflecting the relatively small sample sizes (i.e., 40 in each group). Moreover, autonomy support had positive effects and love withdrawal had negative effects in both groups. Thus, culture affected the size rather than the direction of some of the outcomes of parenting style.

The contexts in which parents and children are embedded also merit investigation. Russian immigrants to Israel are not only Russian, they are also immigrants. The immigration experience may affect cultural transmission processes as well. For example, immigrant parents' values tend to change more slowly than the values of their children (Feather, 1975; Knafo & Schwartz, 2001). Although most parents may find it difficult or even objectionable to change, the extent to which their children want to adopt the values of the majority culture may show significant variance. We therefore expect to find associations between adolescents' acculturation attitudes and the processes of cultural transmission. Study 2 addresses this topic.

Another aspect of the transmission context is the extent to which immigrants live within their own in-group culture or are exposed to other cultures. The proportion of immigrants in a region can reflect this (Phinney, Ong, & Madden, 2000). Knafo and Schwartz (2003b) compared Russian-immigrant families living in regions where they constituted a small (6%) and a substantial (24%) minority. Love withdrawal correlated positively with accepting perceived parental values in the context with many immigrant families. Where the proportion of immigrant families was low, love withdrawal correlated negatively with acceptance, as it did in veteran-Israeli families. The authors interpreted this context effect as due to the influence of exposure to the majority culture versus one's in-group culture on views regarding the legitimacy of love-withdrawal parenting. Study 2 uses a different operationalization for exposure to the majority or in-group culture to reassess this contextual effect. It compares immigrant adolescents attending a Russian school with those in a majority-dominated school.[5]

2.0. STUDY 2: IMMIGRATION AND CULTURAL TRANSMISSION

2.1. Research Issues

The study of cultural transmission is perhaps most interesting but also more complex in the case of immigrant youth. In monocultural studies, in addition to

---

[5] Both Knafo and Schwartz (2003b) and Study 2 in this chapter examine the extent of accepting parental values, not the quality of acceptance. Even if love withdrawal leads to high acceptance, this acceptance may be mostly for controlled reasons. Further research should address the nature of acceptance.

parental values to guide their value choices, children are exposed to one broad culture that they partly share with their parents. Immigrant youth face a more complex task. In addition to their parents' value-modeling, they are exposed to two distinct and sometimes contradictory value environments. It is not surprising that adapting to these value environments challenges young immigrants and may influence their well-being (Berry & Sam, 1997; LaFromboise, Coleman, & Gerton, 1993).

Most immigrants adapt their own values to be closer to the values that prevail in the new environment. Children tend to adopt those values more than their parents (Feather, 1975; Georgas, Berry, Shaw, Christakopoulou, & Milonas, 1996). Immigrant adolescents perceive their parents' value messages as less consistent than nonimmigrant adolescents. Confusion about parents' values may partly account for somewhat lower parent–adolescent value congruence in immigrant families (Knafo & Schwartz, 2001).

Many factors affect the extent to which immigrant youth adopt the values of their parents or the host society. As with all youth, the factors in Figure 12.1 are important (e.g., the personality of parents and of children and the characteristics of the parent–child dyad and the family). Specific to the immigration context are the acculturation attitudes of immigrant youth – that is, their attitudes toward the preferred ways of dealing with their culture of origin and the host culture. Study 2 also considers a context variable: the proportion of immigrants in the immediate environment. In addition, it explores interrelationships and interactions among those variables. For example, does the contextual variable of proportion of other immigrants in the environment moderate impacts of parenting style on child outcomes?

2.1.1. *Acculturation Attitudes*

Berry and Sam (1997) distinguished four acculturation strategies based on polar attitudes toward the culture of origin and the new culture. *Assimilation* refers to accepting the culture of the host society and rejecting one's culture of origin. *Integration* refers to positive attitudes toward both cultures, and it is often considered the most adaptive strategy. *Separation* refers to maintaining one's culture of origin while rejecting the culture of the host society. *Marginalization* refers to rejection of both cultures.

The culture of origin for Russian-immigrant adolescents in this study is represented by the perceived values of their parents. Separation and integration attitudes entail accepting their culture of origin and, hence, their parents' values. In contrast, assimilation and marginalization attitudes entail rejecting the culture of origin and, hence, their parents' values. Those who accept their culture of origin are more likely to identify with their parents and accept them as carriers of this culture. We hypothesize that adolescents who endorse high levels of separation and integration attitudes accept their perceived parents' values and identify more with their parents than adolescents who endorse assimilation or marginalization attitudes.

Feelings of closeness to parents do not necessarily involve seeing parents as role models. We therefore offer no hypothesis for the relationship of acculturation attitudes to closeness. We do, however, explore the relationship of acculturation attitudes to closeness and to parenting style.

2.1.2. *Acculturation Context*

As discussed previously, the relative proportions of immigrants and host-society members to whom immigrant youth are exposed may affect their acceptance of perceived parental values. If they frequently encounter value messages opposed to those they receive at home, immigrant youth may question the validity of parental values. The values of peers or teachers may be especially challenging (Goodnow, 1997). Knafo (2003), for example, found that acceptance of parents' values was lower among youth who attended schools whose religious orientation differed from that of their own parents. Immigrant youth in Israel may attend ethnically homogeneous schools with other immigrant youth. Alternatively, they may attend ethnically heterogeneous schools with students from the host society and other immigrant groups. The challenge of exposure to values different from those of their parents is, of course, greater in the heterogeneous schools. We, therefore, hypothesize that Russian-immigrant youth who study in ethnically homogeneous (i.e., Russian) schools accept their parents' values more than those who study in ethnically heterogeneous schools.

The competing value messages that immigrant youth receive at home and from the host society may increase value conflict between parents and children (Pettys & Balgopal, 1998). Immigrant adolescents may embrace new ideas and values encountered at school (Rosenthal, Ranieri, & Klimidis, 1996). If parents object to their changed values, the emotional distance between parents and children may increase (Holmbeck, 1996). We therefore hypothesize that Russian immigrant youth feel closer to their parents if they study in ethnically homogeneous schools than if they study in ethnically heterogeneous schools.

As discussed previously, immigrant parents exhibit greater value inconsistency. This may lead their children to view them as less fair or as hypocritical. Immigrant youth who are exposed to alternative value models may therefore choose models other than their parents with which to identify. We therefore hypothesize that Russian immigrant youth identify more with their parents if they study in ethnically homogeneous schools than if they study in ethnically heterogeneous schools.

Consider next how the level of exposure to the host society and to the culture of origin may affect acculturation attitudes. Adolescents are likely to prefer the dominant culture to which they are exposed because dominance implies greater legitimacy and provides greater familiarity. They may adopt this culture and reject the alternative culture – be it the culture of origin or of the host society. Hence, we hypothesize that separation attitudes are stronger among immigrant youth in ethnically homogeneous than in ethnically heterogeneous schools.

We further hypothesize that assimilation attitudes are stronger among immigrant youth in ethnically heterogeneous than in ethnically homogeneous schools.

2.1.3. *Interaction of Acculturation Context with Parenting Style*

The current study directly tests the proposal that culturally appropriate parenting behaviors are more legitimate and beneficial in acculturation contexts in which the immigrant culture is prevalent (Knafo & Schwartz, 2003b). In Study 1, love withdrawal had more negative effects on acceptance of perceived parental values, youths' subjective well-being, and parent–child relationships among Israeli-born than among Russian-immigrant youth. Immigrant adolescents in heterogeneous schools may see love withdrawal as less legitimate than their counterparts in homogeneous schools because the former are exposed more to the dominant culture. We therefore hypothesize that love withdrawal will be manifest in more negative effects on acceptance of perceived parental values and on parent–child relationships among immigrant adolescents in heterogeneous than in homogeneous schools.

Assuming that adolescents attending ethnically heterogeneous as opposed to homogeneous schools view love withdrawal as less legitimate, then the more love withdrawal their parents use, the less likely the adolescents are to accept their parents' Russian culture. High use of love withdrawal may also signify that immigrant parents have not adapted to the surrounding cultural environment as much as their adolescent children have, which may increase the emotional distance between them. These processes are likely to produce rejection of parents as models and, hence, a greater preference for assimilating into the surrounding society. Among immigrant adolescents who attend homogeneous, all-Russian schools, high use of love withdrawal by parents is less likely to be viewed as illegitimate and, therefore, should have little impact on acculturation attitudes. We therefore hypothesize that parents' love withdrawal correlates more positively with assimilation attitudes among immigrant youth in heterogeneous schools than in homogeneous Russian schools.

2.2. Method

2.2.1. *Participants and Procedure*

Respondents were 54 Russian-immigrant adolescents in central Israel, consisting of 21 males and 33 females with a mean age of 14.2 years ($SD = .5$). They had migrated to Israel from the former Soviet Union 3 to 14 years prior to data collection in 2003 ($M = 9.7$; $SD = 2.6$). Most (78%) lived with both of their parents, 17% with their mother only, and 6% with their father only.

Of the total, 30 adolescents studied in an ethnically homogeneous Russian school and 24 in heterogeneous schools. In the latter schools, classes had two to six Russian immigrant students, and the majority of students (86% on average) were veteran Israelis. The groups did not differ in terms of mean age, time since immigration, sex distribution, or marital status of parents. Adolescents volunteered to complete questionnaires during after-school activities.

2.2.2. Instruments

Parenting Style. The same items as in Study 1 were used to measure perceived autonomy-supportive parenting and perceived love withdrawal.

Acculturation Attitudes. We assessed the four acculturation attitudes with 19 items adapted from Ben-Shalom and Horenczyk (2003). For each attitude, one item referred to each of five domains: friends, holidays, culture in general, future marriage partners, and language (there was no marginalization item for language). Responses were on a 5-point agree–disagree scale. Cronbach's alpha was $\alpha = .72$ for separation, $\alpha = .76$ for assimilation, $\alpha = .71$ for integration, and $\alpha = .56$ for marginalization.

Identification with Parents. Three items from Knafo and Schwartz (2004) measured identification on a 4-point agree–disagree scale (e.g., "I would like to be like my parents": $\alpha = .66$).

Closeness to Parents. Two items measured closeness on a 4-point agree–disagree scale (e.g., "I love meeting, talking, and spending time with my parents": $\alpha = .77$).

Acceptance of Perceived Parental Values. The same items were used as in Study 1.

2.3. Results

2.3.1. Acculturation Attitudes

The majority of adolescents (83%) scored highest on integration of all the acculturation attitudes. Although interesting in its own right, the limited variance of the integration attitude precluded the use of individual differences on integration to examine effects of acculturation attitudes on parent–child value congruence. We therefore assigned participants to groups according to the other attitude that most characterized them. This yielded three groups: separation ($N = 22$), assimilation ($N = 18$), and marginalization ($N = 14$).

Table 12.3 presents the means and standard deviations for accepting perceived parental values, identification with parents, closeness to parents, and parenting style in the three groups. A planned comparison, using the error term from a one-way ANOVA, contrasted adolescents characterized by separation attitudes with adolescents characterized by assimilation and marginalization. As we hypothesized previously, the separation-attitude group accepted their parents' perceived values more than adolescents in the assimilation or marginalization groups ($t(51) = 1.90$, $p < .05$, 1-tailed). Also as hypothesized, the separation group identified more with their parents than other adolescents ($t(51) = 2.80$, $p < .01$). Acculturation-attitude groups did not differ in terms of closeness to parents, autonomy-supportive parenting, or love withdrawal.

Table 12.3. *Means and standard deviations (in parentheses) of accepting perceived parental values, parent–child relationship quality, and parenting style perceived by adolescents for groups discriminated by acculturation attitude (Study 2)*

	Dominant Acculturation Attitude		
	Separation	Assimilation	Marginalization
Parent–Child Relationship			
Acceptance of perceived parental values*	0.46	0.29	0.20
	(0.42)	(0.33)	(0.49)
Closeness to parents	2.19	1.92	2.04
	(0.70)	(0.69)	(0.72)
Identification with parents**	1.92	1.20	1.57
	(0.62)	(0.78)	(0.67)
Parenting Style			
Love withdrawal	1.25	1.48	1.29
	(0.43)	(0.67)	(0.70)
Autonomy-supportive parenting	2.03	2.13	2.24
	(0.58)	(0.69)	(0.50)

* $p < .05$, 1-tailed; ** $p < .01$, 1-tailed, for contrast between separation group and other groups.

2.3.2. Acculturation Context

Table 12.4 compares Russian-immigrant adolescents who study in ethnically homogeneous versus heterogeneous schools. The upper panel of Table 12.4 presents the means and standard deviations for accepting perceived parental values, closeness, and identification. Adolescents studying in homogeneous schools accepted their parents' values more ($t(52) = 3.12$, $p < .01$), felt closer to them ($t(52) = 1.95$, $p < .05$, 1-tailed), and identified more with them ($t(52) = 3.62$, $p < .01$) than adolescents in heterogeneous schools, all as hypothesized previously.

The second panel of Table 12.4 presents the acculturation attitudes of adolescents in homogeneous versus heterogeneous schools. As hypothesized previously, those in homogeneous schools had stronger separation attitudes ($t(52) = 1.70$, $p < .05$, 1-tailed), whereas those in homogeneous schools had stronger assimilation attitudes ($t(52) = 4.23$, $p < .01$). The bottom panel of Table 12.4 indicates that the levels of their parents' love withdrawal and autonomy-supportive parenting reported by students in the two schools did not differ.

2.3.3. Interaction of Acculturation Context with Parenting Style

We hypothesized that love withdrawal would affect acceptance of perceived parental values and parent–child relationships more negatively and assimilation attitudes more positively among immigrant adolescents in heterogeneous than in homogeneous schools. The upper panel of Table 12.5 presents the correlations of love withdrawal with acceptance of perceived parental values, closeness, and identification in the two types of schools. Love withdrawal related positively to

Table 12.4. *Means and standard deviations (in parentheses) of acceptance of perceived parental values, parent–child relationship quality, acculturation attitudes, and parenting style (Study 2)*

	Ethnically Homogeneous Russian Schools	Ethnically Heterogeneous Schools
Parent–Child Relationship		
Acceptance of perceived parental values**	0.48	0.15
	(0.40)	(0.38)
Closeness to parents*	2.22	1.85
	(0.68)	(0.68)
Identification with parents**	1.89	1.22
	(0.56)	(0.79)
Acculturation Attitudes		
Separation*	2.23	1.82
	(1.00)	(0.70)
Assimilation**	1.60	2.44
	(0.78)	(0.66)
Integration	3.97	4.06
	(0.73)	(0.78)
Marginalization*	1.67	2.13
	(0.76)	(0.87)
Perceived Parenting Style		
Love withdrawal	2.12	2.11
	(0.56)	(0.64)
Autonomy-supportive parenting	1.28	1.40
	(0.54)	(0.65)

* $p < .05$, 1-tailed; ** $p < .01$, 1-tailed, for difference between two groups.

closeness to parents among adolescents in homogeneous schools but *negatively* to closeness to parents among adolescents in heterogeneous schools ($r = .17$ versus $r = -.48$; $z = 2.40$ for correlation difference). A similar but weaker effect was found for identification. Love withdrawal correlated negatively but weakly with accepting perceived parental values in the heterogeneous schools and not at all in the homogeneous schools. Together, these results partially support our hypothesis.

The lower panel of Table 12.5 presents the correlations of love withdrawal with acculturation attitudes. There was a positive correlation of love withdrawal with assimilation attitudes among adolescents in ethnically heterogeneous schools, as expected; however, this correlation was not significantly greater than in the homogeneous schools. Hence, support for the hypothesis that love withdrawal increases assimilation attitudes more among immigrant adolescents in heterogeneous than in homogeneous schools was weak.

Table 12.5. *Correlations of perceived parental love withdrawal with acceptance of perceived parental values, parent–child relationship quality, and acculturation attitudes (Study 2)*

	Total	Ethnically Homogeneous Russian Schools	Ethnically Heterogeneous Schools
Acceptance of perceived parental values	−.13	−.03	−.17
Closeness to parents	−.17	.17	−.48**
Identification with parents	−.05	.20	−.15
Acculturation Attitudes			
Separation	−.12	−.11	−.09
Assimilation	.27*	.17	.36*
Integration	.11	.01	.20
Marginalization	.07	.10	−.01

* $p < .05$, 1-tailed; ** $p < .01$, 1-tailed.

3.0. GENERAL DISCUSSION

This chapter addressed issues in cultural transmission while taking into account culture and migration. The first study focused on two ways in which culture enters into transmission. We proposed that culture affects preferred parenting styles, which, in turn, affect transmission. Exemplifying this process, Russian-immigrant parents were perceived as using more love withdrawal, which, in turn, led to more controlled acceptance of perceived parental values by Russian-immigrant adolescents. We also proposed that the cultural context influences the effectiveness of parenting practices. To exemplify this process, we examined outcomes of the use of love withdrawal in Israeli-born versus Russian-immigrant families. As in past studies (Knafo & Schwartz, 2003b), love withdrawal had more negative effects in the Israeli-born group than in the Russian-immigrant group. It related to increased conflict with parents and to lower subjective well-being in adolescents.

The second study examined effects of migration as a context for acceptance of parents' values and parent–child relationships. We compared immigrant adolescents who attended ethnically homogeneous (i.e., all-Russian) schools with those who attended heterogeneous schools with large majorities of students from the host society. Transmission was probably more successful in families whose children attended the homogeneous schools. The immigrant adolescent children accepted their Russian parents' values more, had better relationships with their parents, and had acculturation attitudes that were more favorable to their culture of origin and less favorable to the host culture. The school context moderated the degree to which parental use of love withdrawal was effective. For adolescents who experienced more exposure to the majority Israeli culture because they attended heterogeneous schools, love withdrawal related somewhat more negatively to closeness to parents and somewhat more positively to assimilation as an acculturation strategy.

Adolescents' Role in Cultural Transmission. This chapter examined effects of parenting variables on cultural transmission. However, the studies also provided unique evidence that adolescents also influence transmission processes. The findings that adolescents' characteristics influence acceptance of parents' values support a bilateral view of value acquisition in the family (Kuczynski, Marshall, & Schell, 1997). Parents may transmit values but adolescents may adopt or reject them.

Only a few studies have included psychological characteristics of the child in their accounts of cultural transmission (Furstenberg, 1971; Knafo & Schwartz, 2004; ter Bogt, Meeus, Raaijmakers, & Vollebergh, 2001). The findings regarding the correlates of different acculturation attitudes in Study 2 highlight the role of adolescents in the development of parent–child value congruence. Adolescent immigrants with separation attitudes accepted the perceived values of their parents the most; they may identify less with Israeli culture and more with their parents' values, which represent Russian culture for them.

Even if adolescents accept their parents' values, it is important to distinguish the nature or quality of the acceptance. To what extent do adolescents experience themselves as making an autonomous choice or as being controlled by externally imposed forces? As Knafo and Assor (2005) have shown, the degree of perceived autonomy has implications for youths' subjective well-being. Autonomous agreement was found to be related to well-being and controlled agreement to agitation and guilt. We found that the effects of love-withdrawal parenting depended on the cultural context and that the quality of adolescents' acceptance related to love withdrawal. Thus, both parents and adolescents contribute to the quality of adolescents' acceptance of parental values, and the cultural context moderates those contributions. Such complex interactions merit further study.

Love Withdrawal in Cultural Context. Study 1, like past research (Knafo & Schwartz, 2003b; Zaslavsky & Moore, 2003), suggests that culturally appropriate parenting behavior is more effective. The legitimacy attributed to particular parenting practices signifies their appropriateness. Study 2 specified a contextual variable that influences legitimacy in the migration context: the extent of exposure to the dominant, majority culture. Immigrants may maintain relatively separate institutions that minimize exposure (e.g., homogeneous Russian schools) or they may experience substantial exposure to the host culture (e.g., heterogeneous schools). For adolescents in Study 2, love withdrawal was more detrimental to relationships with their parents when exposure to the host culture was substantial rather than minimal.

Although love withdrawal had fewer negative effects on socialization processes among Russian immigrants than among veteran Israelis, its consequences were also negative in the Russian-immigrant group. Thus, love withdrawal was related to feelings of guilt and agitation and to conflict with parents in both groups. Moreover, even immigrant adolescents experienced their acceptance of parental values as more externally controlled to the extent that their parents used love withdrawal. Thus, although love withdrawal may be less detrimental to Russian-born versus Israeli-born youth, it is at least somewhat problematic in both groups.

The current studies assessed the consequences of love withdrawal via self-reports. The finding that love withdrawal was less problematic among Russian-born youth, particularly in all-Russian contexts, might reflect the way in which consequences were measured. Future research should assess consequences of love withdrawal with indicators other than self-reports. Perhaps youths in highly controlling, hierarchical cultures and families are reluctant to voice criticism or to express negative feelings toward parents in self-reports; their resentment might emerge if other measures are employed. A study of Bedouin children in Israel supports this view (Katz & Assor, 2002, 2003). Children in this hierarchical culture did not express their resentment verbally in response to parental coercion. However, they showed opposition to imposed parental expectations in their behavior. Thus, the legitimacy of publicly expressing negative feelings toward parents, such as the legitimacy of love withdrawal, may depend on culture.

Moderation of Parenting Style Effects by Cultural Context. The current research reinforces the argument that findings about parenting style cannot automatically be generalized across cultures (Grusec et al., 1997; Knafo & Schwartz, 2003b). Equally important, this research demonstrates the fact that varying cultural contexts *within* societies may moderate the consequences of parenting practices. We found that migration and homogeneity or heterogeneity in the school or residential region exhibited moderating effects.

Our studies focused on love withdrawal, a type of parenting of special relevance in Russian culture. Future research should examine other parenting practices – the consequences of which may be sensitive to different cultural contexts. Are there parenting practices that have near-universal effects on parent–child relationships, on child outcomes such as subjective well-being, and on cultural transmission? Self-determination theory argues that autonomy-supportive parenting should have positive effects regardless of culture (Chirkov & Ryan, 2001; Grolnick et al., 1997). Here, too, such a parenting style had positive correlates in the Russian-born and the Israeli-born groups. However, many parenting variables may have culture-specific effects. Research should seek to identify parenting practices that are especially beneficial or detrimental, legitimate or illegitimate, in particular cultures but not in others.

Choice of School for Children. Parents whose values differ from those of the surrounding society may choose special schools that convey values similar to their own. This shelters their children from exposure to the majority values. It may make parents' values clearer to adolescents, increase the perceived truth-value of these values, and thereby enhance parent–child value congruence (Knafo, 2003). The effect of choosing all-immigrant schools in the current study illustrated this process: Immigrant adolescents in those schools accepted their parents' perceived values more, had acculturation attitudes that were more compatible with preserving their parents' culture, and enjoyed better relationships with their parents. It is possible that those children were highly in accord with their parents' values before they agreed to be sent to ethnically homogeneous schools. It is impossible to address this possibility without a longitudinal design; however, even in that case, ethnically homogeneous schools are likely to perpetuate the values that children were exposed to at home, a process that is likely to retain (or further increase) a high level of acceptance of parental values.

Nonetheless, many parents send their children to heterogeneous schools that expose them to the values of the surrounding society. Parents may do this because there is no choice, but some may do so because they believe it will help their children to adapt to society (Kuczynski et al., 1997) or because the school has a better academic standard. The risk, of course, is that the children will acquire values to which their parents object. Minority parents may combat this risk by efforts to strengthen their children's ethnic identity (Thornton, Chatters, Taylor, & Allen, 1990); however, the environment often overrides parents' efforts (Garbarino, Kostelny, & Berry, 1997). A particular disadvantage of immigrant parents is that their children tend to perceive them as less consistent than other parents in their value messages (Knafo & Schwartz, 2001). This may weaken the parents' ability to socialize their children in the competition with peers, teachers, and other sources of influence. Perceived parental inconsistency and value competition with the encompassing environment may also contribute to the poorer quality of parent–child relationships that we observed among immigrant adolescents in ethnically heterogeneous schools.

Strengths and Limitations of the Current Studies. An important strength of the current studies is the examination of cultural-transmission processes within a context that included numerous parent and child variables. In addition to studying parenting style and the success of parental-value transmission, we explored adolescents' reasons for accepting perceived parents' values; their closeness to, identification with, and conflict with parents; and their subjective well-being. This broad perspective also permitted investigation of some of the interactions among influences on cultural transmission.

The small number of participants in both studies limited our ability to detect moderate or weak group differences with confidence. Replication with larger samples is needed. Study 1 reduced random error by closely matching the Russian-immigrant and veteran-Israeli groups on relevant background variables. Most results were compatible with related findings from past research, which suggests that replications might confirm these current findings.

A second limitation concerns the fact that we assessed parenting style using adolescents' reports of how their parents behaved rather than by observation or reports by the parents themselves. It was reasonable to use adolescents' self-reports to assess variables that are, by definition, phenomenological constructs (e.g., subjective well-being, acculturation attitudes, values and reasons for holding them). As for parenting style, future studies might benefit from obtaining parent reports or third-party observations. Of course, the impact of parenting style is often mediated by how it is perceived by youths (Neiderhiser, Pike, Hetherington, & Reiss, 1998). Moreover, the hypothesized associations of parenting style with objective variables (e.g., cultural group) in the current study support the validity of adolescents' reports of parenting style.

We assessed acceptance of perceived parental values rather than actual parent–child value congruence. As we discuss elsewhere (Knafo & Schwartz, Chapter 11, this volume), acceptance is just one step through which actual parent–child value congruence is achieved. The other important step is accuracy of perception of parental values (Grusec & Goodnow, 1994; Knafo & Schwartz, 2003a). Implications of immigration attitudes and context, parenting style, and culture on accuracy of perception should also be studied.

The relative lack of findings for our parenting measures among the Russian immigrants may be interpreted as attesting to the irrelevance of the concept of love withdrawal or of our measure to this ethnic group. The relevance of love withdrawal to the Russian context has been documented elsewhere (Bronfenbrenner, 1970; Klugman, 1986). The measure used in this study did yield meaningful results with Russian-immigrant families (e.g., see Tables 12.2 and 12.5); however, as we predicted, it tended to relate less strongly to immigrants' well-being than was the case with veteran-Israeli youth. Future studies on this ethnic group should explore parenting dimensions that relate *more strongly* to the adaptation of Russian-immigrant youth than to Israeli-born youth.

The small sample sizes precluded the study of possible differences between fathers and mothers in parent–child value congruence, parenting style, or other variables. Nor was it possible to analyze separately the data for sons and daughters. Analyses of same- and different-sex parent–child dyads should be undertaken with larger samples.

4.0. CONCLUSIONS

This chapter asked how culture and migration affect cultural transmission. Two studies investigated this question, using Russian immigrants in Israel as an exemplary cultural group. This is one of the first attempts to study value transmission with a focus on cross-cultural issues. The data on love withdrawal and its relationship with controlled versus autonomous acceptance of perceived parental values supported the view that culture – through its expression in such cultural practices as parenting styles – affects the transmission process. The studies also demonstrated the role of adolescents' acculturation attitudes and of the acculturation context provided by the school in cultural transmission. Both studies further illustrated the importance of the appropriateness of parenting practices to particular cultures and contexts as an influence on cultural transmission.

Cross-cultural studies provide a unique opportunity to study cultural transmission from a comparative perspective. We previously discussed some of the complexities and possible directions; other variables with which culture may interact in determining the transmission process also warrant investigation. The gender of the child or parent, for example, may have different implications for transmission in different cultures. The design of our study precluded the examination of gender interactions with culture, but they are probably common. For instance, Kohn, Slomczynski, and Schoenbach (1986) reported that mothers in Poland and the United States had different effects in the transmission process.

Cultural variation in the nature of identity formation is also relevant to the transmission process (Knafo & Schwartz, 2004). Cultures differ in their tolerance for identity exploration (Erikson, 1994; Waterman, 1999). Do adolescents adopt their own parents' values less in cultures that allow or encourage them to explore their identities? Does greater exploration increase the experience of autonomy versus external control among those who accept their parents' values?

Cultures also differ in the degree to which they constrain members to hold a narrow set of taken-for-granted values. Homogeneous cultures are especially likely to promote a specific, narrow set of values (Arnett, 1995; Welch, 1984). Cultural practices and daily routines may communicate values in a way that makes them appear so "natural" that they require no explanation or justification (Goodnow, 1997). The absence of competing value messages in a society is likely to increase the extent of parental influence in cultural transmission. For example, among African Pygmies, where there were no schools and only a few age peers, parental influence was the major process of cultural transmission (Cavalli-Sforza, 1993).

Cultures may also differ in the legitimacy they attribute to the relative influence of younger and older generations on one another. Cultures that emphasize the cultural dimensions of hierarchy and embeddedness (Schwartz, 1999) or power-distance (Hofstede, 1980) are more likely to constrain youth to accept the values of the older generation. Cultures that emphasize autonomy, egalitarianism, and individualism are more likely to grant legitimacy to influence from the younger to the older generation. Future research can test these hypotheses.

The findings of these studies present a complex picture in which the influence of parents on their children depends on parents' own characteristics, on the characteristics of the children, and on cultural and situational factors. We have also identified additional sources of complexity that make the cross-cultural study of cultural transmission especially challenging. There is much yet to do to unravel the influences of parental values, parenting behavior, family relationships, and cultural context in the process of cultural transmission.

REFERENCES

Arnett, J. J. (1995). Broad and narrow socialization: The family in the context of a cultural theory. *Journal of Marriage and the Family, 57*, 615–628.

Assor, A., Kaplan, H., & Roth, G. (2002). Choice is good, but relevance is excellent: Autonomy-enhancing and suppressing teacher behaviors predicting students' engagement in schoolwork. *British Journal of Educational Psychology, 72*, 261–278.

Assor, A., Roth, G., & Deci, E. L. (2004). The emotional costs of perceived parents' conditional regard: A self-determination theory analysis. *Journal of Personality, 72*, 47–89.

Baron, R. M., & Kenny, D. A. (1986). The moderator–mediator variable distinction in social psychological research: Conceptual, strategic, and statistical considerations. *Journal of Personality and Social Psychology, 51*, 1173–1182.

Ben-Shalom, U., & Horenczyk, G. (2003). Acculturation orientations: A facet theory perspective on the bidimensional model. *Journal of Cross-Cultural Psychology, 34*, 176–188.

Berry, J., & Sam, D. (1997). Acculturation and adaptation. In J. Berry, M. Segall, & C. Kagitcibasi (Eds.), *Handbook of cross-cultural psychology: Vol. 3, Social behavior and applications* (2nd ed.). Boston: Allyn & Bacon.

Bronfenbrenner, U. (1970). *Two worlds of childhood: U.S. and U.S.S.R.* New York: Russell Sage.

Bronfenbrenner, U. (1986). Ecology of the family as a context for human development: Research perspectives. *Developmental Psychology, 22*, 723–742.

Cavalli-Sforza, L. L. (1993). How are values transmitted? In M. Hechter, L. Nadel, & R. E. Michod (Eds.), *The origin of values* (pp. 305–317). New York: Aldine de Gruyter.

Chirkov, V., & Ryan, R. M. (2001). Parent and teacher autonomy support in Russian and U.S. adolescents. *Journal of Cross-Cultural Psychology, 32*, 618–635.

Chirkov, V., Ryan, R. M., Kim, Y., & Kaplan, U. (2003). Differentiating autonomy from individualism and independence: A self-determination theory perspective on internalization of cultural orientations and well-being. *Journal of Personality and Social Psychology, 84*, 97–110.

Coopersmith, S. (1967). *The antecedents of self-esteem.* San Francisco: Freeman & Co.

Erikson, E. H. (1994). *Identity: Youth and crisis.* New York: Norton.

Feather, N. T. (1975). *Values in education and society.* New York: The Free Press.

Furstenberg, F. F. (1971). The transmission of mobility orientation in the family. *Social Forces, 49*, 595–603.

Garbarino, J., Kostelny, K., & Berry, F. (1997). Value transmission in an ecological context: The high-risk neighborhood. In J. Grusec & L. Kuczynski (Eds.), *Handbook of parenting and the transmission of values* (pp. 307–332). New York: Wiley.

Geiger, H. K. (1968). *The family in Soviet Russia.* Cambridge, MA: Harvard University.

Georgas, J., Berry, J., Shaw, A., Christakopoulou, S., & Milonas, K. (1996). Acculturation of Greek family values. *Journal of Cross-Cultural Psychology, 27*, 329–338.

Goodnow, J. J. (1997). Parenting and the "transmission" and "internalization" of values: From social-cultural perspectives to within-family analyses. In J. E. Grusec & L. Kuczynski (Eds.), *Handbook of parenting and the transmission of values* (pp. 333–361). New York: Wiley.

Grolnick, W. S., Deci, E. L., & Ryan, R. M. (1997). Internalization within the family: The self-determination theory perspective. In J. E. Grusec & L. Kuczynski (Eds.), *Parenting and children's internalization of values: A handbook of contemporary theory* (pp. 135–161). New York: Wiley.

Grolnick, W. S., & Ryan, R. M. (1989). Parent styles associated with children's self-regulation and competence in school. *Journal of Educational Psychology, 81,* 143–154.

Grusec, J. E., & Goodnow, J. J. (1994). Impact of parental discipline methods on the child's internalization of values: A reconceptualization of current points of view. *Developmental Psychology, 30,* 4–19.

Grusec, J. E., Rudy, D., & Martini, T. (1997). Parenting cognitions and child outcomes: An overview and implications for children's internalization of values. In J. E. Grusec & L. Kuczynski (Eds.), *Parenting and the internalization of values: A handbook of contemporary theory* (pp. 259–282). New York: Wiley.

Guttman, L. (1968). A general nonmetric technique for finding the smallest coordinate space for a configuration of points. *Psychometrica, 33,* 469–506.

Hofstede, G. (1980). *Culture's consequences: International differences in work-related values.* Beverly Hills, CA: Sage Publications.

Holmbeck, G. N. (1996). A model of family relational transformations during the transition to adolescence: Parent–adolescent conflict and adaptation. In J. A. Graber, J. Brooks-Gunn, & A. C. Petersen (Eds.), *Transitions through adolescence: Interpersonal domains and context* (pp. 167–199). Mahwah, NJ: Erlbaum.

Iyengar, S. S., & Lepper, M. R. (1999). Rethinking the value of choice: A cultural perspective on intrinsic motivation. *Journal of Personality and Social Psychology, 76,* 349–366.

Katz, I., & Assor, A. (2002). *The effect of autonomy support on intrinsic motivation in Jewish and Bedouin children: The meaning of autonomy in different cultures.* Paper presented at the American Educational Research Association (AERA) conference, New Orleans, LA, United States.

Katz, I., & Assor, A. (2003). *"Even if he asks her, she shouldn't tell": Bedouin children react to stories on autonomy support and suppression.* Paper presented at the Society for Research in Child Development (SRCD) conference, Tampa, FL, United States.

Klugman, J. (1986). The psychology of Soviet corruption, indiscipline, and resistance to reform. *Political Psychology, 7,* 67–82.

Knafo, A. (2003). Contexts, relationship quality, and family value socialization: The case of parent–school ideological fit in Israel. *Personal Relationships, 10,* 373–390.

Knafo, A., & Assor, A. (2005). *Adherence to parental values: Desirable when autonomous, problematic when controlled.* Unpublished manuscript. Jerusalem, Israel: The Hebrew University.

Knafo, A., & Schwartz, S. H. (2001). Value socialization in families of Israeli-born and Soviet-born adolescents in Israel. *Journal of Cross-Cultural Psychology, 32,* 213–228.

Knafo, A., & Schwartz, S. H. (2003a). Parenting and accuracy of perception of parental values by adolescents. *Child Development, 73,* 595–611.

Knafo, A., & Schwartz, S. H. (2003b). Culture-appropriate parenting and value transmission in families of Israeli-born and Soviet-born adolescents in Israel. In T. Horowitz, S. Hoffman, & B. Kotik-Friedgut (Eds.), *From pacesetters to dropouts: Post-Soviet youth in comparative perspective* (pp. 69–87). New York: Rowan and Littlefield.

Knafo, A., & Schwartz, S. H. (2004). Identity status and parent–child value congruence in adolescence. *British Journal of Developmental Psychology, 22,* 439–458.

Kohn, M. L., Slomczynski, K. M., & Schoenbach, C. (1986). Social stratification and the transmission of values in the family: A cross-national assessment. *Sociological Forum, 1,* 73–102.

Kuczynski, L., Marshall, S., & Schell, K. (1997). Value socialization in a bidirectional context. In J. E. Grusec & L. Kuczynski (Eds.), *Parenting and the internalization of values: A handbook of contemporary theory* (pp. 23–50). New York: Wiley.

LaFromboise, T., Coleman, H. I. K., & Gerton, J. (1993). Psychological impact of biculturalism: Evidence and theory. *Psychological Bulletin, 114,* 395–412.

Leung, K., Lau, S., & Lam, W. L. (1998). Parenting styles and academic achievement: A cross-cultural study. *Merrill-Palmer Quarterly, 44,* 157–172.

Mannheim, K. (1952). *Essays on sociology and social psychology* (P. Kecskemeti, Ed.). London: Routledge & Kegan Paul.

Mead, G. H. (1934). *Mind, self and society.* Chicago: University of Chicago Press.

Mirsky, J., & Prawer, L. (1992). *To immigrate as an adolescent: Immigrant youth from the former Soviet Union in Israel.* Jerusalem: Van Leer Institute and The Association for the Development and Advancement of Manpower in Social Services in Israel.

Neiderhiser, J. M., Pike, A., Hetherington, E. M., & Reiss, D. (1998). Adolescent perceptions as mediators of parenting: Genetic and environmental contributions. *Developmental Psychology, 34,* 1459–1469.

O'Connor, T. G., Hetherington, E. M., & Clingempeel, W. G. (1997). Systems and bidirectional influences in families. *Journal of Social and Personal Relationships, 14,* 491–504.

Peterson, B. E., Smirles, K. A., & Wentworth, P. A. (1997). Generativity and authoritarianism: Implications for personality, political involvement, and parenting. *Journal of Personality and Social Psychology, 72,* 1202–1216.

Pettys, G. L., & Balgopal, P. R. (1998). Multigenerational conflicts and new immigrants: An Indo-American experience. *Families in Society, 79,* 410–422.

Phinney, J. S., Ong, A., & Madden, T. (2000). Cultural values and intergenerational value discrepancies in immigrant and non-immigrant families. *Child Development, 71,* 528–539.

Quoss, B., & Zhao, W. (1995). Parenting styles and children's satisfaction with parenting in China and the United States. *Journal of Comparative Family Studies, 26,* 265–280.

Rohan, M. J., & Zanna, M. P. (1996). Value transmission in families. In C. Seligman, J. M. Olson, & M. P. Zanna (Eds.), *The psychology of values: The Ontario symposium,* Vol. 8 (pp. 253–276). Hillsdale, NJ: Erlbaum.

Rosenthal, D., Ranieri, N., & Klimidis, S. (1996). Vietnamese adolescents in Australia: Relationships between perceptions of self and parental values, intergenerational conflict, and gender dissatisfaction. *International Journal of Psychology, 31,* 81–91.

Ryan, R. M., & Connell, J. P. (1989). Perceived locus of causality and internalization: Examining reasons for acting in two domains. *Journal of Personality and Social Psychology, 57,* 749–761.

Schönpflug, U. (2001). Intergenerational transmission of values: The role of transmission belts. *Journal of Cross-Cultural Psychology, 32,* 174–185.

Schwartz, S. H. (1992). Universals in the content and structure of values: Theoretical advances and empirical tests in 20 countries. In M. P. Zanna (Ed.), *Advances in experimental social psychology, Vol. 25* (pp. 1–65). New York: Academic Press.

Schwartz, S. H. (1999). A theory of cultural values and some implications for work. *Applied Psychology: An International Review, 48,* 23–47.

Schwartz, S. H., & Bardi, A. (1997). Influences of adaptation to communist rule on value priorities in Eastern Europe. *Political Psychology, 18,* 385–410.

Sen'ko, T. V. (1993). Parents' ideas about ideal children. *Russian Education and Society, 35,* 19–27.

Shor, R. (1999). Inappropriate child-rearing practices as perceived by Jewish immigrant parents from the former Soviet Union. *Child Abuse and Neglect, 23,* 487–499.

ter Bogt, T. F. M., Meeus, W. H. J., Raaijmakers, Q. A. W., & Vollebergh, W. A. M. (2001). Youth centrism and the formation of political orientations in adolescence and young adulthood. *Journal of Cross-Cultural Psychology, 32,* 229–240.

Thornton, M. C., Chatters, L. M., Taylor, R. J., & Allen, W. R. (1990). Sociodemographic and environmental correlates of racial socialization by Black parents. *Child Development, 61,* 401–409.

Waterman, A. S. (1999). Identity, the identity statuses, and identity status development: A contemporary statement. *Developmental Review, 19,* 591–621.

Welch, M. R. (1984). Social structural expansion, economic diversification, and concentration of emphases in childhood socialization. *Ethos, 12,* 363–382.

Whitbeck, L. B., & Gecas, V. (1988). Value attributions and value transmission between parents and children. *Journal of Marriage and the Family, 50,* 829–840.

Whitchurch, G. G., & Constantine, L. I. (1993). System theory. In P. Boss (Ed.), *Sourcebook of family theory and methods* (pp. 325–353). New York: Plenum.

Zaslavsky, T., & Moore, M. (2003). The influence of immigration to Israel on the parental behavior of immigrants from the former Soviet Union. In T. Horowitz, S. Hoffman, & B. Kotik-Friedgut (Eds.), *From pacesetters to dropouts: Post-Soviet youth in comparative perspective* (pp. 88–102). New York: Rowan and Littlefield.

13

Immigrant Parents' Age Expectations for the Development of Their Adolescent Offspring: Transmission Effects and Changes after Immigration

EVA SCHMITT-RODERMUND AND RAINER K. SILBEREISEN

INTRODUCTION

Immigration often takes place from traditional developing countries into modern industrialized cultures and is related to a whole range of changes in the living conditions of an individual. The confrontation with an unfamiliar value system is one of the most important challenges in the life of an immigrant (Schmitt-Rodermund & Silbereisen, 2008). Whereas adolescents tend to adjust relatively quickly to such a situation – in part because of their higher competence in language acquisition – their parents sometimes have more trouble developing new perspectives and acquiring new skills (Feldman, Mont-Reynaud, & Rosenthal, 1992; Süss, 1995). Unemployment of the breadwinner may add to a situation of shifted roles within the family in favor of the adolescents (Hehl & Ponge, 1997). The goal of this chapter is to shed light on the process of adaptation for parents of immigrant adolescents. The target group of the study consists of ethnic Germans who arrive in what they deem their country of origin from states that were formerly known as the Eastern Bloc. However, their ancestors have lived in Russia, Poland, or Romania for many generations and, therefore, they can be considered true immigrants (Silbereisen & Schmitt-Rodermund, 2000). They have kept their in-group language of German and customs (e.g., the celebration of Christmas). This group is being studied to clarify issues related to value orientations, especially age expectations or timetables for adolescent developmental transitions to behavioral autonomy. Do parents adhere to their traditional perspectives, or do some of them change their expectations about the autonomy development of their children toward earlier ages during the time they stay in the new country? To what extent does the new social context contribute to the parents' possible change of expectations, and to what extent are parental expectations influenced by their children's expectations and vice versa? Before presenting expectations about possible changes and their sources, some work on value orientations held by immigrants is discussed.

1.0. VALUE ORIENTATIONS, DEVELOPMENTAL TIMETABLES, AND IMMIGRATION

Value orientations that endorse the connectedness to others, solidarity, integration with other people, and control of one's emotions are called *collectivistic*. The interests of the group – be it the family or the community – come first. Values that focus on the emotional, social, and economic independence from others are called *individualistic*. They stress the importance of individual autonomy and may be characterized by the assumption that individuals know best what is good for themselves (Kim, Triandis, Kagitcibasi, Choi, & Yoon, 1994). Although there has been extended discussion on whether the two orientations are orthogonal or actually represent the two ends of a continuum, most researchers agree that modern, industrialized cultures may be described as less collectivistic and more individualistic, whereas traditional cultures are more collectivistic than individualistic (Hofstede, 2001). When individuals migrate from a collectivistic country to an industrialized country, they usually face a change to an individualistic mainstream culture. This difference between their own views and those held by the host culture in the new country may be susceptible to at least some change and adaptation in orientations and attitudes.

Value orientations are known to direct parents' expectations for the developmental timetables of their children and the younger generation's ideas about what to achieve during the life course. Cultural groups with a collectivistic background stress the importance of early timing in areas that serve the group (e.g., preparing meals for younger siblings or showing obedience to others), whereas groups with a more individualistic background favor early transitions to individual autonomy (e.g., independence in expressing needs). Compared to mothers from the United States, Japanese mothers expected their children to show self-control and emotional security earlier. American mothers expected verbal and social abilities to appear earlier in life (Hess, Kashiwagi, Azuma, Price, & Dickson, 1980). These findings were mirrored by studies comparing individualistic and collectivistic groups from other cultural backgrounds (Goodnow, Cashmore, Cotton, & Knight, 1984; Roer-Stier & Rivlis, 1998; Rosenthal & Gold, 1989; Trommsdorff, 1989). Similar differences were apparent when adolescents of the respective cultures were compared in their age expectations about their own development. Youths from collectivistic backgrounds expected transitions to autonomy at a later point in time compared to agemates from individualistic backgrounds. Adolescents from individualistic backgrounds reported earlier ages for their first romantic relationship, whereas those from collectivistic contexts placed this transition as late as young adulthood (Feldman & Quatman, 1988; Feldman & Rosenthal, 1990, 1991; Rosenthal & Bornholt, 1988; Schmitt-Rodermund & Silbereisen, 1999; Stewart, Bond, Deeds, & Chung, 1999).

Consequently, adult immigrants of collectivistic backgrounds experience quite a contrast not only between their own value orientations and those of the individualistic host culture in general but also concerning their own "adolescent timetables" and the respective expectations of mainstream-culture youths and their parents. Through media use but also via direct contact of immigrants with members of the host culture, adolescents and parents realize indirectly in which ways they differ from beliefs held by members of the majority group, and these differences may instigate a gradual change over time. Usually, the rank order of parents' and adolescents' age expectations is very similar. Although the particular ages may vary, parents with late timetables tend to have children who hold late expectations about their own development as well (Juang, Lerner, McKinney, & von Eye, 1999; Stewart et al., 1999). In immigrant groups, however, the similarity between parents and adolescents seems to decrease during the time spent in the host country. Cross-sectional research comparing groups of adolescent immigrants of collectivist backgrounds found the timetables of second-generation adolescent immigrants to be more similar to those of local youths than to the developmental expectations of the first generation (Feldman & Rosenthal, 1990, 1991). However, for parents, no such differences in age expectations were found as a function of the time spent in the host country (Goodnow et al., 1984). This finding may not be surprising given that group comparisons among adult immigrants of differential length of residence also did not reveal any differences in value orientations. Among adult immigrants, length of residence has no effect on adaptation of values toward attitudes usually held by people whose heritage culture roots in the host country (Rosenthal, Bell, Demetriou, & Efklides, 1989). To our knowledge, there have been no longitudinal studies conducted that confirm the absence of any adaptation in values and related constructs for adults. Studies of adolescents revealed that they, indeed, adapt their developmental timetables in parallel to the duration of their stay in the host country and probably to the range of experiences in the new cultural context (Schmitt-Rodermund, 1997; Schmitt-Rodermund & Roebers, 1999; Schmitt-Rodermund & Silbereisen, 1999).

2.0. THE CASE OF ETHNIC GERMAN IMMIGRANTS

This chapter explores whether or not there are adaptive changes in ethnic German immigrant parents' expectations for the development of their offspring that relate to their length of residence in Germany. Those immigrants have moved from a collectivistic context to a country that can be considered highly individualistic (Alsaker & Flammer, 1999; Hofstede, 2001; Krebs & Schnell, 1987; Lantermann & Hänze, 1995). The value orientations of ethnic German immigrants are clearly oriented toward the needs of the group rather than the individual (Schmidt & Dannhauer, 1989; Süss, 1995). Previous studies on developmental timetables of immigrant parents compared groups with differing lengths of residence cross-sectionally. For the current study, a longitudinal dataset with four measurement points is used: 0, 6, 12, and 18 months after the initial interview with immigrant families from Poland, Romania, and the former Soviet Union. In accordance with results of the studies conducted by Goodnow, Feldman, Rosenthal, and others (Deeds, Stewart, Bond, & Westrick, 1998; Feldman & Rosenthal, 1990, 1991; Goodnow et al., 1984; Rosenthal et al., 1989; Stewart et al., 1999), we assumed that adults, on average, showed no trend in their autonomy expectations toward earlier transitions over time.

Irrespective of the fact that parents, on average, can be assumed to maintain their expectations concerning their offspring's developmental timetables, moderating factors may be at work that are responsible for changes in the developmental timetables in subgroups of the parents. We already know from previous work that adolescents change their timetables toward the earlier expectations of local youths to different degrees. Some hardly changed at all or even reported later ages for youthful transitions over time, whereas others reported considerably earlier ages for the transitions to autonomy every 6 months. The degree to which adolescents adapted their age expectations for autonomy to the views held by their local agemates related to the quality of their family relationships. Those who experienced a high frequency of dispute and a low level of parent–child exchange held earlier timetables with length of residence (Schmitt-Rodermund & Silbereisen, 1999).

Typically, parents' behavior, through their parenting practices, is deemed the regulator for adolescents' behavior. For example, adolescent delinquency is usually seen as a product of low parental monitoring (Wiesner & Silbereisen, 2003); however, it is not only the parents who take action and influence their children by their parenting behaviors. Kerr and Stattin (2003) point out that parental behavior to some extent is reactive rather that proactive in that parents change their practices toward less control on the whereabouts of their offspring and decrease support in reaction to their children's delinquency. The same may be true with respect to value orientations. Negotiations with parents are part of normative development to adulthood and help to transform the parent-dominated childhood relationship into a more egalitarian and independent relationship. As a product of this process, parents increasingly compromise with their adolescents (Smetana, Daddis, & Chuang, 2003). In terms of developmental timetables, it is feasible to assume that parents change their expectations toward earlier ages as a direct consequence of their children's attempts to renegotiate the degrees of freedom in choosing their own action priorities. However, if adolescents show little activity in this regard, parents are likely to keep their late expectations for adolescent autonomy.

Consequently, the level of agreement observed between parents and children could be due to one of two processes; the first is that parents influence their children's orientations. According to Schönpflug (2001) and many others, parents are indeed influential regarding value orientations or other important issues in the lives of adolescents (e.g., career decision making) in both immigrant and nonimmigrant families (Collins, 1990; Kohn, Slomczynski, & Schoenbach, 1986;

Nauck, 1997; Phalet & Schönpflug, 2001; Steinberg, 1990; Steinberg & Silverberg, 1986; Taris, 2000; Vollebergh, 2001). Thus, immigrant parents endorsing late adolescent timetables can be expected to have children who change less during immigration toward the earlier expectations of their local peers and vice versa. Less change on the part of the adolescents implies more similarity to the persistent parental orientations. The second source for parent–child similarity may be the parents' changes due to their children's negotiations. Adolescents who express an earlier developmental timetable may have parents who, over time, come to share the views of their offspring.

3.0. PARENT–ADOLESCENT SIMILARITY IN TIMETABLES

Accordingly, Schönpflug (2001) found that immigrant sons with positive parenting experiences held value orientations similar to those of their father, whereas sons who considered the parenting style of their parents as strict and unpleasant did not share their father's views to the same extent. Schönpflug (2001) concluded that the transmission of values from parents to children works well only in the presence of transmission belts – in this case, a good quality relationship between fathers and sons. Rosenthal, Ranieri, and Klimidis (1996) found a similar association indicating that girls who perceived higher value discrepancies with their parents also reported more conflict within the family. Their interpretation focuses on a girl's difficulties in dealing with two cultures and, other than Schönpflug or ourselves, assumes the value discrepancy as antecedent to a more precarious parent–daughter relationship. Despite these interpretational differences, both lines of research support a strong association between the social-emotional climate in a family and the similarity of values and age expectations, respectively, between parents and children.

Schönpflug (2001) further proposed that the quality of the family relationship may moderate the influence that parents have on their children's values. Shared variance in parents' and children's beliefs or values is usually interpreted as a result of the influence of the parental generation on the children, and Schönpflug states no exceptions. In agreement, Kohn (1983) showed that the transmission from parents to children occurs in both individualistic and collectivist families. For more individualistic societies such as the United States, however, transmission of values from children to parents was also found (Kohn, 1983).

For a collectivistic group such as ethnic German immigrants in Germany, it may be argued that transmission of values and opinions from adolescents to parents is not likely. On the other hand, immigrant adolescents are influenced by their local, more individualistic agemates. As a consequence, they may start arguing with their parents about the accepted timing of their transitions. Attempts by adolescent children to convince their parents to grant them more freedom are often initiated with a heightened level of conflict and disagreement,

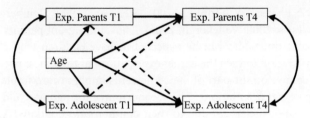

Figure 13.1. Model for the analysis of parental influence on the changes in adolescents' timetables and vice versa. *Note:* The dotted lines represent the two paths for which differential effects in the two groups (lower and higher levels of conflict) were expected. All effects were controlled for the age of the adolescent.

followed by a gradual adaptation on the part of the parents (Smetana et al., 2003).

In summary, we assume the following:

1. On average, with length of residence, immigrant parents do not adapt their expectations for their children's autonomy to earlier ages as their children do. However, the degree of conflict is likely to be a moderating factor. In families with low levels of conflict, parents are likely to adhere to the late age expectations for their children's autonomy, or they may even hold increasingly later timetables the longer they live in Germany. Parents in families with higher levels of conflict can be expected to change their expectations toward earlier ages, thereby following the adaptations of their children.

2. Over time, parents influence their children, especially if there are low levels of conflict in the family. In this case, we expect adolescents of parents who share late developmental timetables for autonomy to change less toward the earlier timetables of local peers and vice versa. In families with high levels of conflict, the influence from parents to adolescents is expected to be less strong. Moreover, in those families, adolescents are likely to influence their parents. Youths with early timetables are expected to be successful in changing their parents' views to earlier ages over time. Figure 13.1 depicts the model that integrates these assumptions. In addition, it specifies further relationships – namely, the adolescents' age influences both parental and adolescent expectations both concurrently and later.

4.0. DESIGN OF THE STUDY

The sample used for these analyses included 220 ethnic German immigrant families from countries of the former Soviet Union, Poland, and Romania. Data were collected from target children aged between 10 and 16 years at the first wave of measurement, and from their parents, who were interviewed separately.

Table 13.1. *Demographic characteristics of the sample (N = 220)*

	M	SD	Min	Max
Years of residence at T1	1.47	0.79	0.11	3.60
Years of residence at T4	3.28	0.81	1.70	5.63
Age adolescent T1	13.25	1.77	9.56	16.63
Age mother T1	38.54	6.04	28.61	66.75
Age father T1	40.86	6.80	30.21	74.59
Collectivist value orientation parents T1	4.01	1.33	0	6
Collectivist value orientation parents T4*	4.87	1.34	0	6
Years of education mother	9.64	2.00	5	19
Years of education father	9.29	2.14	1	19

	N	%		
Country of origin				
Poland	49	22.3		
Romania	55	28.6		
Former Soviet Union	87	48.1		
Girls	110	50.0		
Owned a home in country of origin	99	45.6		
Lived in provisional accommodation at T1	116	54.0		
Owned a home at T4	12	5.5		
White-collar job in country of origin: father	50	22.7		
White-collar job in country of origin: mother	106	48.2		
Father unemployed at T1	102	46.4		
Father unemployed at T4	38	17.3		

Note: For years of residence, parentheses indicate the range. Otherwise, parentheses show *N* of cases.
* The difference between T1 and T4 collectivism is not significant.

Originally, 242 families had participated in the study; 22 families missed one or more measurement points and were excluded from the analyses. All remaining 220 families had taken part in each of the four interviews, separated by a 6-month period. Table 13.1 shows relevant characteristics of the sample.

As shown in Table 13.1, families faced some difficult living conditions, at least at T1. Most of them managed better over time, but there were some unemployed fathers left at T4. According to official statistics, the percentage of unemployment of fathers at T4 in this sample matches that of the population of ethnic German immigrants in general and is almost twice as high as among native Germans (Schmitt-Rodermund, in press).

Four interviews were conducted at 6-month intervals. For approximately 3 hours, families were interviewed in person by trained interviewers. The families were recruited through advertisements in local newspapers and by utilizing various institutional and personal contacts of the members of the six participating research sites. The families were paid the equivalent of $80 (USD) per interview. Because many of the families still lived in provisional homes, often sharing a single room, some of the adolescents' data was assessed by written questionnaire. In this way, we achieved independence of parents' and adolescents' reports. Because of problems with the German language, some adolescents were interviewed using a Polish or Russian version of the questionnaire. Two different issues were measured: (1) developmental timetables by parents and adolescents, and (2) the level of conflict at T3.

Developmental Timetables. Parents were asked to report at what age (in full years) they would expect their offspring to have accomplished seven topics of behavioral autonomy: (1) not required to tell parents where they are going, (2) come home at night as late as they want, (3) spend money (wages or allowances) however they want, (4) go out dancing in discotheques, (5) drink alcohol other than in the company of parents, (6) fall in love, and (7) have a steady boyfriend or girlfriend. Adolescents were asked the same questions in a questionnaire that they filled privately while their parents were interviewed (Feldman & Quatman, 1988; Rosenthal & Bornholt, 1988). Following the coding system used by Feldman and colleagues, the responses were recoded using a scale ranging from 1 (earlier than or equal to age 10.5), 2 (from age 10.51 to 12.5), 5 (from age 16.51 to 18.5), to 6 (equal to or later than age 18.51). The response "never" was indicated by a score of 7. Originally, we had distinguished two different types of autonomy – namely, autonomy from parental supervision and autonomy in social relationships (Schmitt-Rodermund & Silbereisen, 1999). Because the two areas of autonomy were highly correlated (i.e., the two scores were correlated at about $r = .50$ for all waves and parents and children, respectively), we decided to take the average of the two scores as a single measure for the expected timing of behavioral autonomy for parents and adolescents. Of the seven items, the internal consistencies (alpha) ranged from .67 to .77. The average alpha of parents and children and the four waves was .73.

Conflict. At T3, parents indicated the levels of dispute in their families using five age-typical conflict themes drawn from Spiel (1992). They were asked to rate the intensity of recent arguments (e.g., concerning their children's company during leisure, their homework for school) on a 6-point scale with 0 indicating no conflict at all and 5 representing the highest intensity. The internal consistency (alpha) was .71. The average across the five items was used in a median-split procedure to compute a dichotomous variable that indicated whether a family was in dispute over a series of topics. The group with higher levels of conflict (47.3%) had values of 1.81 and higher.

5.0. RESULTS

5.1. Parental Change of Developmental Timetables over Length of Residence

To test the first hypothesis, an ANOVA was conducted for the parental expectations for autonomy. The wave of measurement (1–4) was the within-group

Expected Ages for Transitions to Autonomy

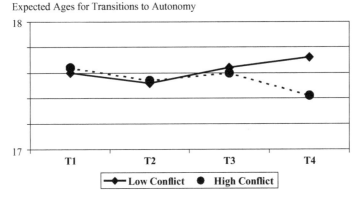

Figure 13.2. Parental timetables categorized by level of conflict.

factor and the level of conflict was the between-group factor. Age of the children served as a control variable. As expected, there was no main effect of the within-group factor, but an interaction effect with level of conflict ($F(3,213) = 3.050$, $p = .03$) was found. Parents who had reported that they experienced higher levels of conflict with their children changed their age expectations for their development toward autonomy to earlier timetables, whereas parents from families with low conflict levels changed toward somewhat later ages over time. Figure 13.2 shows the respective means for the four waves.

5.2. The Direction of the Influence

The second hypothesis was tested by estimating a cross-lagged model using structural equation modeling with AMOS (Arbuckle & Wothke, 1999). For this purpose, data from the first and the fourth measurement points were used. As a first step, covariances and zero-order correlations were computed for families with both high (above the diagonal) and low (below the diagonal) levels of conflict. Table 13.2 shows the coefficients of the respective variables; the similarity between parents and children is relatively high in both of the two waves (T1 and T4) and in families with high and low conflict. In all cases, the correlation coefficients are around t-40, with the exception of T1 (low levels of conflict). Taken together, the coefficients do not indicate a higher similarity between parents' and adolescents' views under conditions of a harmonious family life.

A saturated model was computed separately for the groups with lower and higher levels of conflict. The adolescent's age was included as a control variable. Figure 13.3 shows separate results for the groups with higher and lower levels of conflict. Significant paths ($p < .05$) are indicated by arrows in bold print. The R^2 is given in the upper-right corner of the outcome variables. Paths that were included in the models but proved to be insignificant are shown as thin dotted lines without a coefficient indicated.

Table 13.2. *Intercorrelations and covariances of the variables included in the cross-lagged models (high levels of conflict: above the diagonal; low levels of conflict: below the diagonal; top row, correlations; bottom row, covariances)*

	Exp Par T1	Exp Ad T1	Exp Par T4	Exp Ad T4	Age Ad T1
Exp Par T1	– –	.44 ***	.59 ***	.42 ***	.22 *
		.23	.22	.20	.24
Exp Ad T1	.23 *	– –	.36 ***	.48 ***	−.07 n.s.
	.14		.16	.27	−.09
Exp Par T4	.61 ***	.17 n.s.	– –	.43 ***	.30 **
	.22	.07		.18	.28
Exp Ad T4	.36 ***	.46 ***	.42 ***	– –	−.02 n.s.
	.19	.29	.16		−.03
Age Ad T1	.42 ***	−.02 n.s.	.36 ***	.16 n.s.	– –
	.54	−.03	.34	.21	

At first, the results appear to be similar for the two groups. In both groups, both high or no or low levels of conflict, parents seemed to adjust their expectations about their adolescent children's development according to the children's ages (the effect of age on parents' T4 expectation in the group with low conflict just missed significance). The older the adolescents, the later were the timetables

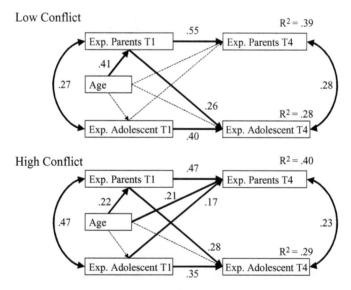

Figure 13.3. Results of cross-lagged models for families with low and high levels of conflict. *Note:* Significant effects are indicated by a bold line and the coefficient is given. Nonsignificant paths are shown as dotted lines with no coefficient.

of the parents at T1, and there were fewer changes toward earlier timetables seen at T4.[1] However, the age expectations of the adolescents – both the entrance level and the degree of change over time – were not affected at all by their age. Thus, whereas parents seem to draw on their offspring's chronological age when forming expectations about the ages of transitions to autonomy, adolescents do not seem to adjust their expectations as a function of age.[2]

Parents and children revealed high levels of stability in their expectations for autonomy – parents even more so than adolescents. This was basically true for both conflict groups, although the group with higher levels of conflict showed somewhat less stability in both parents and children, thereby indicating room for change over time.

Finally, in both groups, parents seem to exert an influence on their children. Parents who expected later ages for the transitions to autonomy in their children at T1 had offspring who changed less toward earlier timetables at T4. (When the T1 entrance level is statistically controlled, as in this case, the remaining variance is due exclusively to changes between T1 and T4.) It is interesting that this effect showed up in much the same way for both groups – those with lower and higher levels of conflict – and the coefficients are virtually identical. According to Schönpflug (2001), we expected that the influence from parents to children would be stronger in families with good relationships between parents and adolescents. Thus, the hypothesis that parents would be less influential in groups with higher levels of conflict must be rejected. But, it is important to remember that the general level of conflict is relatively low. With a maximum of 5, a median of 1.8 shows that parents and adolescents do not often discuss contrary opinions. However, the result is the same even when a group of the top 25% conflictual families is tested against the other 75%.

A closer look at the results reveals a clear difference between the two groups. As expected, adolescents from families with higher levels of conflict seemed to succeed in influencing their parents' age expectations over time. Adolescents who held earlier expectations at T1 let their parents change their timetables toward earlier ages at T4 only in families with high levels of conflict ($\beta = .17$, $p = .05$). In families with low levels, adolescents had no such influence on their parents' expectations for autonomy ($\beta = .05$, $p = $ n.s.). Thus, the expectation that adolescents would influence their parents under the condition of higher levels of family dispute could be confirmed. Unfortunately, the difference was not large enough to result in a significant effect when the two models (i.e., low and high conflict) were tested against each other ($\chi^2 = 1.474$, $df = 1$, $p = $ n.s.).

---

[1] In additional analyses, parents' age, socioeconomic status, and parental value orientations were statistically controlled. The results stayed exactly the same, which is why only the age of the adolescent was included as a control variable.

[2] See Schmitt-Rodermund and Silbereisen (1999) and Schmitt-Rodermund (1997) for details on the relationship of adolescents' age and their developmental timetables.

However, such tests on differences in path weights are known to be conservative and therefore tend to underestimate possible differences.

6.0. DISCUSSION

The aims of this chapter were twofold. First, we wanted to confirm that immigrant parents' age expectations for the pace of their children's development, on average, do not change over time of residence in the new country. Group comparisons had revealed that value orientations were likely to stay the same after immigration; however, to our knowledge there were no longitudinal data available that supported this view, either for values or for other related constructs such as age expectations for behavioral autonomy. Utilizing the current, prospective study, we did not find any change of parental timetables over time, at least not as an overall effect. No matter how long the respective family had lived in Germany, the ethnic German parents deemed the achievement of behavioral autonomy relatively late during the transition to adulthood. We hypothesized that this would hold true for one group in particular: those who live in harmony with their children. For families with higher levels of conflict, we predicted that the parents would gradually adapt their timetables toward earlier ages, based on their adolescents' heightened attempts to renegotiate constraints on their freedom. These expectations also were confirmed. We found an interaction between the length of residence and the style of family communication. In families with conflictual relationships, parents changed their developmental timetables across time toward earlier ages, whereas in families with low levels of conflict, the timetables were stable or even shifted toward later ages – probably as a reaction to their children's behavior.

Second, we were interested in examining the direction and relative strength of the statistical effects. Do the data fit a model, according to which immigrant parents influence the pace of their children's adaptation toward the earlier developmental timetables of local youths? Or is it feasible to assume that adolescents also influence parents in their adaptation over time? Could it be that the adolescents' efforts to renegotiate autonomy-related issues contribute to the parents' earlier timetables over time in the group with higher levels of conflict? Following Schönpflug's (2001) notion of transmission belts, we hypothesized that in families with low levels of conflict, parents would influence their children but not vice versa. In families with high levels of conflict, however, we assumed that parents' influence on the children would be reduced and, furthermore, that the adolescents would influence the degree of their parents' adaptation to earlier views. Most of these expectations were confirmed.

Indeed, there was a strong effect of the parents' timetables on the adolescents' shift toward earlier age expectations for autonomy among local youths. Parents who held late expectations for the ages of their offspring's development toward autonomy had children who adapted less toward earlier timetables. Contrary to our expectation, this was not only true in families with low levels of conflict but also in those with a less peaceful family life. Concerning the effect of adolescents' own age expectations, however, we found that they indeed pushed the expectations of their parents toward earlier ages under conditions of conflictual family relationships but not in those families with low levels of conflict.

Taken together, the observed similarity between parents and their adolescent offspring may not only be the result of a strong influence of the parents on the children. However, this direction of influence accounts for the degree of change in the adolescents' timetables after immigration, following Schönpflug's (2001) assumptions. Yet, there are other families in which children push their parents to adopt different timetables over time by means of conflict and renegotiation. In those families, similarity between parents and children is lower, which may contribute to different opinions. Different opinions in youth-related topics, in turn, are likely to increase adaptation on the part of the parents. The granting of more autonomy may bring about relief from ongoing conflict and, thus, feelings of stress for parents. Moreover, adolescents who ask for an increase in the degrees of freedom may also have more social competence and higher self-esteem, factors that convince parents to reward the more adult-like behavior of their offspring with autonomy. Earlier research on individuation among adolescents of differential pubertal timing showed that early developers not only ask for more freedom in decision making but also receive more freedom and are treated on equal terms by their mother. Same-aged late developers, on the other hand, not only behave more "child-like" but also receive no additional degrees of freedom in decision making, even if they complain and negotiate with their mother (Weichold, Silbereisen, Schmitt-Rodermund, Vorwerk, & Miltner, in press). Future research must ask how much pubertal timing plays a role in the synchronization of parental and adolescent age expectations in an immigration context and whether conflict may be a mediator rather than a moderator in that process.

According to results of the current study, the views on adult immigrants probably need to be adapted. Although many parents are likely to adhere to their original views and orientations, some do change as a result of specific experiences in the new country. However, we need a better understanding of why these adults change their views. Is our assumption true that the children are responsible for this by constant begging and fighting, or is there a third factor that accounts for both the higher levels of conflict and the changes in the parents' views, such as a more liberal approach toward life in general and parenting in particular? So far, however, we do not have any indication of that direction. The results hold, even when we statistically control for differences in parental value orientations, parental age, and the socioeconomic status of the family.

Nevertheless, we need more research that taps more directly into what causes parents to develop doubts about adequacy of their developmental timetables that they hold for their adolescents. Is it that they simply know more about their children through more communication that comes with conflict and become convinced that their son or daughter will have their first romantic relationship sooner than they first assumed? Or do they learn about local adolescents through their children's reports or other sources and, consequently, adapt toward these standards despite their disapproval? The first suggestion would build on a reactive strategy on the part of the parents: Adolescents act differently in the flow of their first romantic relationship, and parents are compelled to correct their views about the timetables of their son or daughter. Mothers and fathers observe the behavior of local youths and, in all likelihood, see that even when earlier in many autonomy-related aspects, they do not necessarily have more problem behavior. The parents may realize that keeping their offspring away from early autonomy could alienate them from their local peers. However, this explanation does not fully explain the effects because all immigrant parents have access to the same observations but do not all reach the same conclusions.

The second variant would be a proactive approach, in which parents grant more freedom before their offspring ask for it in conflictual negotiations, just because they know about the needs of their sons and daughters through mutual exchange. To find out whether it has the same effect as conflicts and to explain such a hypothesis, we need to explore the role of nonconflictual communication (e.g., How much information about their lives do adolescents share with their parents? How much time do parents and adolescents spend together in mutual exchange and joint activities?).

Although the current study realized a prospective-longitudinal design, our conclusions concerning the effects and influence of parents and children cannot be considered confirmation of a causal relationship. After all, we only demonstrated the nature of the covariation among the variables with a conceptual model; the scope and breadth of the variables assessed leave room for improvement. Nevertheless, the study is an important step in better understanding the effects of parent–child communication as a medium for transmitting changes in values and attitudes.

REFERENCES

Alsaker, F. D., & Flammer, A. (1999). *The adolescent experience: European and American adolescents in the 1990s.* Mahwah, NJ: Erlbaum.

Arbuckle, J. L., & Wothke, W. (1999). *AMOS 4.0 user's guide.* Chicago, IL: Small Waters Corporation.

Collins, W. A. (1990). Parent–child relationships in the transition to adolescence: Continuity and change in interaction, affect, and cognition. In R. Montemayor, G. R. Adams, & T. G. Gullota (Eds.), *From childhood to adolescence: A transitional period?* (pp. 85–106). Newbury Park, CA: Sage Publications.

Deeds, O., Stewart, S. M., Bond, M. H., & Westrick, J. (1998). Adolescents between cultures: Values and autonomy expectations in an international school setting. *School Psychology International, 19,* 61–77.

Feldman, S. S., Mont-Reynaud, R., & Rosenthal, D. A. (1992). When East moves West: The acculturation of values of Chinese adolescents in the U.S. and Australia. *Journal of Research on Adolescence, 2,* 147–174.

Feldman, S. S., & Quatman, T. (1988). Factors influencing age expectations for adolescent autonomy: A study of early adolescents and parents. *Journal of Early Adolescence, 8,* 325–343.

Feldman, S. S., & Rosenthal, D. A. (1990). The acculturation of autonomy expectations in Chinese high-schoolers residing in two Western nations. *International Journal of Psychology, 25,* 259–281.

Feldman, S. S., & Rosenthal, D. A. (1991). Age expectations of behavioral autonomy in Hong Kong, Australian and American youth: The influence of family variables and adolescents' values. *International Journal of Psychology, 26,* 1–23.

Goodnow, J. J., Cashmore, J., Cotton, S., & Knight, R. (1984). Mother's developmental timetables in two cultural groups. *International Journal of Psychology, 19,* 193–205.

Hehl, F. J., & Ponge, I. (1997). Der Prozess der Aussiedlung: Veränderung von familiären Strukturen [The process of emigration: Changes in familial structures]. *System Familie, 10,* 10–20.

Hess, R. D., Kashiwagi, K., Azuma, H., Price, G. G., & Dickson, P. (1980). Maternal expectations for mastery of developmental tasks in Japan and the United States. *International Journal of Psychology, 15,* 259–271.

Hofstede, G. (2001). *Culture's Consequences: Comparing Values, Behaviors, Institutions, and Organizations Across Nations* (2nd ed.). Beverly Hills, CA: Sage Publications.

Juang, L. P., Lerner, J. V., McKinney, J. P., & von Eye, A. (1999). The goodness of fit in autonomy timetable expectations between Asian-American late adolescents and their parents. *International Journal of Behavioral Development, 23,* 1023–1048.

Kerr, M., & Stattin, H. (2000). What parents know, how they know it, and several forms of adolescent adjustment: Further support for a reinterpretation of monitoring. *Developmental Psychology, 36,* 366–380.

Kerr, M., & Stattin, H. (2003). Parenting of adolescents: Action or reaction? In A. C. Crouter & A. Booth (Eds.), *Children's influence of family dynamics: The neglected side of family relationships* (pp. 121–151). Mahwah, NJ: Lawrence Erlbaum.

Kim, U., Triandis, H. C., Kagitcibasi, C., Choi, S. C., & Yoon, G. (Eds.) (1994). *Individualism and collectivism: Theory, method, and applications.* Thousand Oaks, CA: Sage Publications.

Kohn, M. L. (1983). On the transmission of values in the family: A preliminary formulation. In A. C. Kerckhoff. (Ed.), *Research in sociology of education and socialization* (Vol. 4, pp. 3–12). Greenwich, CT: JAI.

Kohn, M. L., Slomczynski, K. M., & Schoenbach, C. (1986). Social stratification and the transmission of values in the family: A cross-national assessment. *Sociological Forum, 1,* 73–102.

Krebs, U., & Schnell, B. (1987). Alltägliche Bezugssysteme als Maß der Integration deutscher Spätaussiedler aus Rumänien [Measures of integration of ethnic German immigrants from Romania]. *Psychologische Beiträge, 29,* 676–689.

Lantermann, E. D., & Hänze, M. (1995). Werthaltungen und materieller Erfolg bei Aussiedlern [Values and economic success among ethnic German immigrants]. *Zeitschrift für Sozialpsychologie, 26,* 15–23.

Nauck, B. (1997). Intergenerative Konflikte und gesundheitliches Wohlbefinden in türkischen Familien: Ein interkultureller und interkontextueller Vergleich [Intergenerational conflicts and health-related well-being among Turkish families: An intercultural and intercontextual comparison]. In B. Nauck & U. Schönpflug (Eds.), *Familien in verschiedenen Kulturen* (pp. 324–354). Stuttgart, Germany: Enke.

Phalet, K., & Schönpflug, U. (2001). Intergenerational transmission of collectivism and achievement values in two acculturation contexts: The case of Turkish families in Germany and Turkish and Moroccan families in the Netherlands. *Journal of Cross-Cultural Psychology, 32*, 186–201.

Roer-Strier, D., & Rivlis, M. (1998). Timetable of psychological and behavioral autonomy expectations among parents from Israel and the former Soviet Union. *International Journal of Psychology, 33*, 123–135.

Rosenthal, D. A., Bell, R., Demetriou, A., & Efklides, A. (1989). From collectivism to individualism? The acculturation of Greek immigrants in Australia. *International Journal of Psychology, 24*, 57–71.

Rosenthal, D. A., & Bornholt, L. (1988). Expectations about development in Greek- and Anglo-Australian families. *Journal of Cross-Cultural Psychology, 19*, 19–34.

Rosenthal, D. A., & Gold, R. (1989). A comparison of Vietnamese-Australian and Anglo-Australian mothers' beliefs about intellectual development. *International Journal of Psychology, 24*, 179–193.

Rosenthal, D., Ranieri, N., & Klimidis, S. (1996) Vietnamese adolescents in Australia: Relationships between perceptions of self and parental values, intergenerational conflict, and gender dissatisfaction. *International Journal of Psychology, 31*, 81–91.

Schmidt, N., & Dannhauer, H. (1989). Die erziehungspsychologische Problematik der Kinder von Spätaussiedlern aus osteuropäischen Ländern [The problems of parenting and education in children of ethnic German immigrants]. *Unsere Jugend, 41*, 12–20.

Schmitt-Rodermund, E. (1997). *Akkulturation und Entwicklung: Eine Studie unter jungen Aussiedlern.* [Acculturation and development]. Weinheim: Beltz-Psychologie Verlags Union.

Schmitt-Rodermund, E. (in press). Immigration. In R. M. Silbereisen & M. Hasselhorn (Eds.), *Enzyklopädie der Psychologie*, Serie V (Entwicklung), Vol. 5: *Psychologie des Jugendalters* [Encyclopedia of psychology, Series V, Vol. 5: Psychology of adolescence]. Göttingen: Hogrefe.

Schmitt-Rodermund, E., & Roebers, C. M. (1999). Akkulturation oder Entwicklung? Veränderungen von Autonomieerwartungen bei Einheimischen und Kindern aus Aussiedlerfamilien [Acculturation or development? Changes in autonomy expectations among local and ethnic German immigrant adolescents]. *Psychologie in Erziehung und Unterricht, 46*, 161–176.

Schmitt-Rodermund, E., & Silbereisen, R. K. (1999). Determinants of differential acculturation of developmental timetables among adolescent immigrants to Germany. *International Journal of Psychology, 34*, 219–233.

Schmitt-Rodermund, E., & Silbereisen, R. K. (2008). Akkulturation und Entwicklung: Jugendliche Immigranten [Acculturation and development – adolescent immigrants]. In R. Oerter & L. Montada (Eds.) *Entwicklungspsychologie* (6th Edition) (pp. 859–873). Weinheim: Psychologie Verlags Union.

Schönpflug, U. (2001). Intergenerational transmission of values: The role of transmission belts. *Journal of Cross-Cultural Psychology, 32,* 174–185.

Silbereisen, R. K., & Schmitt-Rodermund, E. (2000). Adolescent immigrants' well-being: The case of ethnic German immigrants in Germany. *International Journal of Group Tensions, 29,* 79–100.

Smetana, J. G., Daddis, C., & Chuang, S. S. (2003). "Clean your room!": A longitudinal investigation of adolescent–parent conflict and conflict resolution in middle-class African American families. *Journal of Adolescent Research, 18,* 631–650.

Spiel, C. (1992). *Adolescents and parents perceive each other: Do match and mismatch indicate the quality of relationships?* Paper presented at the V. European Conference on Developmental Psychology, Seville, Spain, 6–9 September.

Steinberg, L. (1990). Autonomy, conflict, and harmony in the family relationship. In S. S. Feldman & G. R. Elliott (Eds.), *At the threshold: The developing adolescent* (pp. 255–276). Cambridge, MA: Harvard University Press.

Steinberg, L., & Silverberg, S. (1986). The vicissitudes of autonomy in early adolescence. *Child Development, 57,* 841–851.

Stewart, S. M., Bond, M. H., Deeds, O., & Chung, S. F. (1999). Intergenerational patterns of values and autonomy expectations in cultures of relatedness and separatedness. *Journal of Cross-Cultural Psychology, 30,* 575–593.

Süss, W. (1995). Zur psychosozialen Situation der Aussiedlerkinder und – jugendlichen (The psychosocial situation of repatriate children and adolescents). *Sozialwissenschaften und Berufspraxis, 18,* 131–146.

Taris, T. W. (2000). Quality of mother–child interaction and the intergenerational transmission of sexual values: A panel study. *Journal of Genetic Psychology, 161,* 169–181.

Trommsdorff, G. (1989). Sozialisation und Werthaltungen im Kulturvergleich. In G. Trommsdorff (Ed.). *Sozialisation im Kulturvergleich* (pp. 97–121). Stuttgart: Enke.

Vollebergh, W. A. M. (2001). Intergenerational transmission and the formation of cultural orientations in adolescence and young adulthood. *Journal of Marriage and the Family, 63,* 1185–1198.

Weichold, K., Silbereisen, R. K., Schmitt-Rodermund, E., Vorwerk, L., & Miltner, W. H. R. (in press). Links between timing of puberty and behavioral indicators of individuation. *Journal of Youth and Adolescence.*

Wiesner, M., & Silbereisen, R. K. (2003). Trajectories to delinquent behaviour in adolescence and their covariates: Relations with initial and time-averaged factors. *Journal of Adolescence, 26,* 753–771.

PART THREE

INTRACULTURAL VARIATIONS

14

Intergenerational Transmission of Moral Capital across the Family Life Course

MERRIL SILVERSTEIN AND STEPHEN J. CONROY

INTRODUCTION

The prescription to honor one's mother and father – the fifth commandment[1] in the Old Testament – is a moral imperative found in almost all cultures of the world. However, this adage far from guarantees that children will actually feel responsible for supporting their aging parents and leaves open the question of how such obligations come into being. This can be especially problematic in developed societies where bureaucratic mechanisms may supplant kinship groups to serve basic needs of the elderly and where social change in families – such as divorce, step-parenting, and geographic separation – has produced uncertainty about the willingness and ability of adult children to fulfill their filial duties. In this chapter, we examine the intergenerational transmission of moral capital from older to younger generations as a mechanism by which responsibility to the elderly is reinforced through families. We define *moral capital* in terms of the internalized social norms that obligate children to care for and support their older parents, a concept at the intersection of self-interest (for parents) and altruism (for children) as viewed through the prism of sociological and economic theories of exchange.

How are we to understand the extraordinary efforts made by adult children to serve the needs of their older parents? In the absence of a strong bioevolutionary explanation for why children support their parents (as there would be in the case of parents supporting their children), one is drawn to a social explanation such as reciprocity or normative structures. How do parents ensure that their children will provide for them in their old age? From where does filial duty to

---

[1] Religious traditions actually vary somewhat in their numbering and division of the Ten Commandments. Following St. Augustine, Roman Catholics and Lutherans (among other Christian traditions) consider this to be the fourth Commandment (McKenzie, 1965).

We would like to acknowledge Daphna Gans for her contribution to this program of research, and Linda Hall for her assistance in the preparation of this manuscript.

older parents derive? Are familistic values a form of moral capital that parents invest in their children for social insurance in old age?

In this chapter, we review theoretical and empirical literature from several disciplines that reflect on strategies used by parents to optimize the chances that they will receive support from their children in old age. As we discuss herein, the social and behavioral sciences have emphasized mechanisms of reciprocity and power in coming to grips with why adult children support their older parents. Missing from this literature is the notion that the transmission of filial values from one generation to another inculcates in children a responsibility to respond to the needs of aging parents. We consider the socialization of children to familistic values to be an investment in their moral capital, much like the investment in a child's education represents an investment in the child's human capital. In our discussion, we treat moral capital as a blend of social and cultural capital – concepts with deep roots in sociology and economics, as well as political science.

We begin this chapter by discussing the concept of moral capital in families as it fits within the sociological and economic literature on family transfers, and then we present an empirical illustration testing the correspondence between the values of parents and children measured over 3 decades.

1.0. MORAL CAPITAL: A WORKING DEFINITION

In exploring the issue of moral capital, we address questions about the family that touch on its importance as one of the most fundamental social organizations in society. In small-group applications, the concept of the moral economy can be traced to the work of Mauss (1923/1967), who stressed moral obligations over pecuniary motives for the exchange of resources in tribal societies. The simple act of providing a gift to another triggers the obligation to reciprocate as part of an integrative dynamic that reinforces cohesion of the kinship group and ensures its survival as a distinct social and cultural entity. Giving to others and building an obligation for later repayment is considered the social glue out of which emerges small-group stability – including family solidarity (Homans, 1950). Mutual dependence builds cohesion in relationships with high levels of primacy and to which there are few alternatives, such as those that tend to be found in families (Emerson, 1981).

In carving out intellectual space for the concept of moral capital, it is useful to distinguish moral capital from two other forms of capital that have a basis in families – namely, social and cultural capital. Social capital has a long and varied history in the social sciences but can be roughly defined as the benefits that accrue from the initiation and maintenance of social relationships and social networks as well as the solidarity, trust, and reciprocity that arises from them (Coleman, 1988; Putnam, 1995, 1996). Whereas definitions of social capital vary in terms of their locus (e.g., individuals, relationships, networks, and communities), a notion common to many definitions is that social capital is built through the investment of social, emotional, or material resources that build in others the obligation to reciprocate.

The sociological approach to intergenerational transfers as an exchange process is rooted in the precept that reciprocity is enforced by normative principles that obligate the repayment of an incurred social debt. Social-exchange theorists have argued that the norm of reciprocity is a principle of obligation to repay – in some fashion – the receipt of valued assets, services, or sentiments (Emerson, 1981; Gouldner, 1960; Molm & Cook, 1995). This insight gained new power through the concept of social capital as the product of social exchange, a resource built up through social interaction and the provision of favors to others (Coleman, 1988). Furstenberg and Kaplan (2004), writing specifically about social capital in families, provide a strictly normative basis for social capital, describing it as the "stock of social goodwill created through shared norms and sense of common membership" (p. 221). Putting the "exchange" and "normative" approaches together provides the leverage for better understanding how social capital is accumulated and then redeemed in family contexts. In other words, what compels individuals in whom social capital is invested to fulfill their duty toward the original investors is a normative form of social regulation specific to the type of relationship and social institution in question. Thus, filial obligations and moral sentiments that define *for a given relationship and social context* the appropriate duty of one family member toward another move us closer toward the idea of moral capital as both a valued good and a form of social solidarity in kinship groups.

The field of economics also lacks a consensus definition of *social capital* (Durlauf, 2002) and even maintains sharp criticism of the term itself (Arrow, 2000; Solow, 2000). Glaeser, Laibson, and Sacerdote (2002) define *social capital* at the individual level as "a person's social characteristics – including social skills, charisma, and the size of his Rolodex – which enables him to reap market and non-market returns from interactions from others" (p. F438), thus placing it in a similar neoclassical economic framework as physical and human capital. Sison (2003) claims, however, that social capital is morally agnostic: One could have high amounts of social capital – for example, willing business accomplices – and be morally bankrupt. Organized crime families, for example, instill in their members the need to respect and obey elders and demand conformity to an internal code of conduct that may lead to criminal acts. That "social capital could equally serve the purposes of a mafia clan as those of a philanthropic NGO" (Sison, 2003, p. viii) precipitates the need for further distinction between social and moral capital.

Cultural capital provides another vantage point from which to view the moral elements of social behavior in families. Bourdieu (1986) defines *cultural capital* as a set of symbolic resources that provide individuals the cultural intelligence to negotiate the social world in ways that best serve their interests.

Furthermore, cultural capital, as a form of learned cultural knowledge, is explicitly or implicitly transmitted from parent to child such that the advantages it engenders are reproduced across generations. If social capital represents the reserve of goodwill that resides in others, cultural capital can be said to represent the knowledge to behave toward others in expected and socially acceptable ways – essentially, the rules of social engagement for particular relationships. For example, friendships – because they are voluntary and more fragile than family relationships – are guided by a norm of short-term reciprocity and strive for balance in exchanges between the partners – or face the risk of dissolution. On the other hand, parent–child relationships – because they are long-term, permanent relationships – are able to tolerate long and multiple periods of imbalanced exchanges without much risk, especially if period-specific imbalances are expected to even out over the life course. Knowing these relationship "rules" is a necessary condition to building stable social relationships of the type that builds social capital.

We suggest that, in families, moral capital be viewed as forming at the intersection of social and cultural capital. When applied to intergenerational families in later life, moral capital resides in adult children as an obligation to provide assistance for their older parents. Being a "good" (i.e., attentive, responsible) parent early on builds a reserve of goodwill in children, but gratitude may not be enough to guarantee that support from one's adult children will be forthcoming; it may also take a moral commitment on the part of children to fulfill their end of the bargain. Alternatively, a "bad" parent who has little social capital invested in offspring may rely solely on his or her ability to socialize children to values of filial duty in order to ensure intergenerational support.

Following Bourdieu's (1986) contention that all forms of capital can be converted into one another, moral capital can be converted into social capital if parents know that they can count on their children to follow the cultural scripts of their role position. Similarly, moral capital may be transformed into human capital to the extent that the effort of transmitting values and norms to children yields a higher return to parents than would otherwise have been generated in the economy (Frank, 1988). The notion that treating others morally achieves positive economic outcomes for the firm (Fukuyama, 1995) is no less true for the family.

Moral Capital in Families. We use the term *moral capital* to refer to the normative precepts that are inculcated in children by parents, other family members, teachers, community institutions, and media to abide by cultural guidelines and act in ways that serve the greater good. Whereas *human capital* describes the value of individuals in the labor market, usually associated with investments in education and job training, and *social capital* refers to the value of interpersonal social investments for achieving desired ends, *moral capital* embodies the value of *values* – the certainty with which one can anticipate from others a set of behaviors consistent with the values and duties associated with their role position in a social organization. Notwithstanding the notion that moral capital is "what makes a person good as a human being" (Sison, 2003, p. 31) and not necessarily profitable or financially successful, there are important financial and social implications of it, especially in families over time.

In the social organization of the family, the transmission of familistic norms from parents to children increases the probability that in the future, parents will be able to count on their children for needed support. The generalized expectation that children are obligated to support their aging parents in times of need (Cicirelli, 1988, 1990) is essentially an insurance function of children but one that is to some degree structured by their moral training. However, most discussions of the interpersonal dynamics involved in the investment and redemption of social capital treat the moral underpinnings of the transaction as a constant. That is, investments in social relationships are assumed to provide fairly certain payoffs in the future. In informal "economies" such as the family, intergenerational transfers of labor, time, money, and emotion build a form of social equity that may be drawn against in the future. However, because there are few formal sanctions imposed on children who renege on the informal contract with parents, families face a classic intergenerational "commitment problem" (Frank, 1988). Enforcement must rely on the internalization of norms for what constitutes appropriate behavior in the parent–child relationship.

The risk of moral hazard – that is, of having noncompliant children – is greater in developed nations where filial-duty laws requiring children to support aging parents have been abandoned or are no longer enforced (Blair, 1996–1997). At the same time, the failure of children to behave in traditionally appropriate ways with respect to their older parents is less consequential in the developed world, where private markets (e.g., pensions and long-term disability insurance) and public provisions (e.g., Social Security and Medicare) serve as alternatives to family support for elders. Whether one views this apparent change as a reasonable response to altered institutional conditions (because parental needs are met in other ways) or as a moral failing characteristic of an increasingly individuated society, the intrafamilial source of this arguably waning filial imperative is something about which we know fairly little. However, even in modern societies such as the United States, adult children are assigned the duty (based on systems of civil, cultural, or religious beliefs) to support older parents in need, casting doubt on the conclusion that the contract between generations is truly abrogated (Blieszner & Mancini, 1987; Burr & Mutchler, 1999; Cicirelli, 1993; Rossi & Rossi, 1990; Seelbach, 1977, 1978; Stein, Wemmerus, Ward, Gaines, Freeberg, & Jewell, 1998). The obligation to provide care for older family members is an enduring moral precept of most social groupings, even if it is not always fulfilled in practice. (Japan is a good example of the still strong moral commitment but weakening filial practice of children; see Ogawa & Retherford, 1993.) Thus, the basis for intergenerational solidarity – intimacy, contact, exchange of services, and feelings of filial obligation – is maintained despite the expanded role of the welfare state (Daatland & Herlofson, 2003; Litwak & Kulis, 1987; Silverstein & Litwak, 1993; Warnes, 1994).

2.0. INTERGENERATIONAL TRANSMISSION IN THE FAMILY AS PROCESS

The process by which values are transmitted across generations is not a static phenomenon but rather one that unfolds over the family life course. When studying the transmission of values toward old-age support, there is an implied latency period in which the initial socialization of children by parents may not come to be fulfilled until decades later. A useful model for understanding how social capital is produced and consumed over time in families is the *support bank* (Antonucci, 1990). A support bank is a latent reserve of social capital that parents build early in the family life cycle by investing time, labor, and money in their children. This social capital is later drawn on in the form of social support from children when the parents develop age-associated dependencies. Whereas at any one point in time, the balance of the exchange between parents and children may be unequal, the balance sheet over the entire span of the relationship may look more equal. Thus, partners in the intergenerational relationship variously play the role of provider and of receiver, depending on the type and timing of their developmental needs (Hollstein & Bria, 1998).

Research suggests that earlier parental investments in their dependent children may later be reciprocated with instrumental forms of assistance from them as adults, suggesting a quid pro quo in observed transfers over time (Henretta, Hill, Li, Soldo, & Wolf, 1997; Silverstein, Conroy, Wang, Giarrusso, & Bengtson, 2002; Whitbeck, Simons, & Conger, 1991). However, research by Hofferth, Boisjoly, and Duncan (1999) showed no correspondence between retrospectively assessed transfers of money and time to kin and the perception that others will be available to provide assistance in case of need. Research by Silverstein et al. (2002) additionally demonstrated that children provide support to their parents even in the absence of early investments. Both sets of results suggest two alternatives: that transfers are driven purely by altruism or by normative prescriptions.

Exchange dynamics in families follow a different temporal pattern than that found in market and other nonkin relationships. Particularly, with regard to parent–child relationships, there can be a long time lag between a child's receipt of resources from parents and his or her provision of support to parents when they experience old-age dependencies. There may be a considerable period of latency in the relationship until a crisis emerges that calls on children to respond. Long gaps of time between transfers may depreciate the value of the parents' original investment, and less frequent social interaction brought on by normal "empty-nesting" in late adolescence and early adulthood may threaten confidence in the social capital of children. As a result, parents may come to count more on the internalized values of children than on gratitude for contributions by parents going back to childhood. That even parents with minimal investments can expect some support from their children (Silverstein, et al., 2002) further highlights the importance of norms under conditions when the reciprocity principle does not hold or weakens over long periods.

Social norms enforce and reinforce acts of reciprocity and serve as the implicit reason why preferences for repayment exist at all. It is through norms of familism that the intergenerational contract of reciprocity compels adult children to repay long-term social debts to their parents. Thus, any immediate "leverage" wielded by parents to control the actions of children (as is suggested in the case of bequests) gives way to obligations based on a "fairness" norm – the internalized notion that past debts should be repaid. These normative mechanisms are key guides to understanding when and how much support is expected from others. Such norms are products of a collective belief system but are manifest at the individual level in terms of the felt obligation to provide and the expectation to receive support in a particular relationship under particular circumstances. However, little research has focused on the extent to which support provided by adult children to their aged parents is motivated by altruism, self-interest, or normatively prescribed obligations (for an exception, see Caputo, 2002).

Given that social and human capital in families may lay dormant for many decades, it is possible that the value of this "investment" will depreciate over time due to memory lapses or be remembered differently by parent and child, raising the possibility that the child as an adult may renege on the implicit contract to reciprocate. The potential for uncertainty in what is essentially a contractually unregulated transaction demands that motivation be enforced by internalized commitments or a sense of duty on the part of the adult child (Litwak, 1985).

Developmental psychologists and family sociologists have shown the importance of parental influences on their children's values, ideologies, and identities (Bengtson, Biblarz, & Roberts, 2002; Glass, Bengtson, & Dunham, 1986; Taris & Semin, 1997). Recent challenges to this view notwithstanding (Harris, 1998), it seems clear that long-term longitudinal data across generations are needed to examine the degree of parental influence on the attitudes, values, personality, and behaviors of children over the life course. What may appear to be a departure from parental attitudes and values in adolescence may transform into conformity later in life, particularly when children negotiate the transitions of middle age (Putney & Bengtson, 2002).

3.0. INTERGENERATIONAL TRANSFERS AND THE ROLE OF MORAL CAPITAL IN ECONOMICS

Much has been written in economics about intergenerational transfers of assets and human capital. Becker's seminal work in the area (Becker, 1975, 1991; Becker & Tomes, 1976) addresses transfers primarily from the perspective of parent-to-child flows, with parents choosing to invest in the human capital (e.g., knowledge and skills) of their children to increase the children's human capital and, hence, their earnings potential. Still, the majority of research in this area has focused on the transfer of assets from parents to children (in developed nations) or children to parents (in less developed nations; see Lillard & Willis, 1997). In other words, there is an implicit assumption that the intergenerational transfers of interest occur in a unidirectional rather than bidirectional manner. Based on recent research (Silverstein et al., 2002; Sloan, Zhang, & Wang, 2002), we feel this oversight is unwarranted.

Some economists have considered investments in children as an alternative to private markets to reduce the risk of having unmet health, material, and economic needs in later life (Pauly, 1990). To his credit, Becker (1991, p. 255) noted that the classic way that economists have addressed intergenerational transfers (i.e., downstream) may be an oversimplification of reality and that parents invest in their children based on the anticipated returns and the alternatives available:

> In many societies, poorer and middle-income parents are supported during old age by children instead of by the sale of gold, jewelry, rugs, land, houses, or other assets that could be accumulated by parents at younger ages. Our analysis suggests that these parents choose to rely on children instead of on assets, because rates of return on investments in children are higher than they are on other assets.

Furthermore, Becker (1991, p. 255) suggests a mechanism (i.e., "social sanction") whereby children may be forced to uphold their end of an implicit intergenerational contract:

> In effect, poorer and middle-level parents and children often have an implicit contract, enforced imperfectly by social sanctions, that parents invest in children in return for support during old age. Both parents and children would be made better off by such contracts if investments in children were to yield a high return, where included in the yield would be any insurance provided by children against an unusually long old age.

Becker formalized this discussion further in his Nobel lecture (1992, p. 50) and suggested that parents may attempt to instill "guilt, obligation, duty, and filial love that indirectly, but still very effectively, can 'commit' children to helping them out (in old age)."

Thus, when classic assumptions of altruism (Bernheim & Stark, 1988; Stark, 1989) and unidirectionality of transfers are relaxed, modeling intergenerational transfers becomes more complex – in essence, it becomes a classic moral-hazard problem of the type that parents may be uncertain about their anticipated return to their investments in children. That is, even if parents and children signed formal contracts in which parents agreed to invest in their children's human capital early on and, in return, children agreed to support their parents in old age, adult children would have an incentive (based purely on self-interest) to behave opportunistically and renege on their contract.

Indeed, the problem of moral hazard looms large in the neoclassical economics literature that is rooted in theories of rational self-interest. As we have discussed, Becker (1991) maintained that parents will opt out of investing in the human capital of children if alternative market investments provide a greater return. However, parents may take "irrational" risks with their children for several possible reasons. For example, social expectations to be a "good parent" may cause a parent to invest in a child with poor or uncertain prospects. Additionally, parents face an uncertain future with their children and must entertain the possibility that returns from children may go unrealized. Parents may reduce this uncertainty by socializing their children to adopt norms of filial responsibility.

Although not specifically addressing the bidirectional transfers issue, work by Bernheim and Stark (1988) suggested that assuming at least some selfish behavior on the part of individuals may provide a more reasonable model of human behavior. Extending previous work, Stark (1989) argued that perfect altruism may not necessarily optimize the well-being of all parties. In fact, perfectly altruistic individuals may become more "exploitable," as when children fail to make an effort in the presence of an altruistic parent who freely provides resources to them – a phenomenon known as *shirking*. In the presence of shirking behavior, parents may restrict the flow of resources to the noncompliant child (Gatti, 1999). However, if parents acknowledge shirking behavior as a *possible* outcome in their children, the early training of children to values of filial responsibility may circumvent it.

Furthermore, there are serious empirical questions about whether perfect altruism exists in these intergenerational relationships. For example, Altonji, Hayashi, and Kotlikoff (1992, 1997) found consistent evidence against the altruism motivation for *inter vivos* transfers from parents to adult children. Similarly, research has demonstrated evidence for exchange (Cox, 1987), reciprocity (Sussman, Cates, & Smith, 1970), and "strategic bequest" motivations (Bernheim, Shleifer, & Summers, 1985) for intergenerational transfers. Nevertheless, some researchers have found evidence for altruism, at least under certain conditions (Dunn & Phillips, 1997; Logan & Spitze, 1995; McGarry, 1999; McGarry & Schoeni, 1995). In the few studies that have investigated upstream intergenerational transfers, evidence for motivations has been mixed (Lillard & Willis, 1997; Silverstein et al., 2002; Sloan, Zhang, & Wang, 2002). In summary, while assumptions of perfect altruism may provide convenient modeling advantages, the empirical findings – at a minimum – cast doubt on the overall robustness of this assumption. Thus, the need to address the potential moral-hazard problem remains.

We posit here that one way of reducing the moral-hazard problem is by early investments in children's moral capital. In the economics literature, the concept of moral capital (Ratnapala, 2003, p. 216) has been defined as the stock of morals (including virtues and observance of rules forbidding certain types of action) that promotes or is promoted by production of goods and services (Rosenberg, 1990). In the case of intergenerational exchange, we use the term to imply a stock of *values* that incorporate a code of conduct that promotes the transfer of time, affection, and assets from one generation to the next. If children are imbued with a sense of reciprocity, altruism, obligation to care for those in need, and so forth, then they may be more likely to support parents who are in need of assistance. In other words, parents would be naïve to merely invest in the human capital of their children without a similar or proportional investment in their moral capital.

Moral capital transferred to children could be viewed in the wider context of the multigenerational family in which the expression of filial responsibility for older parents serves as a model for the next generation (Cox & Stark, 1992). Thus, moral capital that resides in adult children provides an opportunity for self-gain by demonstrating this asset to younger generations. However, adult children still have an incentive to renege in the final period. Furthermore, a "social sanctions" enforcement mechanism would have little effect on adult children who were amoral (for a societal sanction) or unattached emotionally to their parents (for a parental sanction). We remain open to other possible motivations for transfers across generations, whose roots may lie in the multitude of generations that humans spent as hunter-gatherers without formal institutions to provide care and assistance to elders (Cosmides & Tooby, 1992).

Our thesis does not exclude other ways of reducing the risk from moral hazard. For example, parents may create an emotional bond with their children by showing them love, kindness, consideration, and care when they are young. When children reach adulthood, this emotional bonding makes them feel empathetic for their parents and, hence, increases the likelihood that they will support them. Previous research by the authors (Silverstein et al., 2002) suggests that "affective solidarity" is an important contributor to old-age support. Still, concerns discussed previously about the possible depreciation over time of emotional investments underline the need for investments in moral capital as a hedge against opportunism.

In any case, as noted in Barro (1974) and elsewhere, the motivation of intergenerational transfers (in particular, whether individuals are altruistically or normatively motivated) has important policy implications. Specifically, public programs (e.g., pay-as-you-go Social Security) that force the transfer of assets from younger to older generations partially neutralize the impact of altruistic children who adjust (i.e., reduce) their private transfer to accommodate the public one. This principle can also be seen in how families respond when public programs are cut. For instance, recent evidence from Sweden suggests an increase in the proportion of elders served by families over the same historical period that public policies restricted eligibility for in-home services (Sundstrom, Johansson, & Hassing, 2002). Many Asian nations that have few public provisions for their older population mandate that adult children provide eldercare as both a duty and a legal requirement. In these contexts, sociocultural values and the needs of the state are in alignment, with the burden put squarely on families in order to conserve government resources – what Cherlin (2005) calls the "public functions" of the family. Viewed in this light, moral capital serves both a family and a public function in the sense that informal caregiving to older adults allows the state to forgo public provisions of care.

4.0. AN EMPIRICAL EXAMPLE OF MORAL TRANSMISSION IN AGING FAMILIES

We present here a test of our moral capital transmission hypothesis in a longitudinal sample of parents and their children during 3 decades, in what we label a *generational-sequential design*. A key advantage of this design is that the transmission of values and norms across generations is assessed for parents and children when they are approximately the same age, thereby controlling for age effects.

In our conceptualization of the transmission process, we propose that parental values are inculcated in their children and then become internalized as normative beliefs concerning appropriate behavior at the relevant time. *Values* are defined as generalized principles that guide preferences for desired outcomes (e.g., belief in the centrality of family life). *Norms* are defined as the guiding rules for specific behaviors that conform to values in specific social contexts (e.g., responsibility for elderly parents). Finally, *normatively appropriate behavior* is the realization of norms in action toward the valued object (e.g., social support to older parents). The analysis we describe examines how value orientations toward family life as expressed by parents in 1971 are related to the endorsement of filial responsibility as expressed by their children in 1997/2000. In our empirical test, we do not directly address the issue of whether filial responsibility is manifest in support, leaving that to future work. However, we note that strong effects have typically been observed between expressions of filial obligation and supportive behavior of adult children (Bromley & Blieszner, 1997; Parrott & Bengtson, 1999; Rossi & Rossi, 1990; Silverstein & Litwak, 1993; Silverstein, Parrott, & Bengtson, 1995; Stein et al., 1998; Silverstein, Conroy, & Gans, 2008).

4.1. Sample

We addressed our research questions using data from the University of Southern California Longitudinal Study of Generations, a study of 2,044 individuals, ages 16 to 91, from 328 three-generation families. Eligible sample members were generated from the families of grandparents randomly selected in 1971 from the membership of a large (i.e., 840,000-member) prepaid health maintenance organization in the Los Angeles area. The sample pool was generally representative of White, economically stable, middle- and working-class families. Self-administered questionnaires were mailed to the grandparents and their spouses (G1), their adult children (G2), and their adolescent grandchildren (G3). Surviving respondents were surveyed again in 1985, 1988, 1991, 1994, 1997, and 2000. The unique longitudinal and intergenerational design of this survey provided an opportunity to prospectively examine the long-term basis of intergenerational transmission.

We analyzed data within 474 nuclear families. Represented in these families are 379 (G2) mothers and 322 (G2) fathers responding to the 1971 survey, and 291 (G3) daughters and 194 (G3) sons responding to either the 2000 or 1997 survey. Because preference was given to the 2000 responses if both years were available, reports by 58 children were taken from the 1997 survey. When there were more than two sons or two daughters from which to choose, the oldest and youngest were selected. On average, fathers were 45.6 years old and mothers were 42.4 years old in 1971, and daughters and sons were slightly older when assessed in 1997/2000, averaging 47.9 and 47.8 years old, respectively.

4.2. Measures

Generalized values toward the salience of family life are measured for parents with the following five considerations adapted from Heller's (1976) familism scale: (1) as many activities as possible should be shared by married children and their parents; (2) if a person finds that the lifestyle he or she has chosen runs so against his or her family's values that conflict develops, he or she should change; (3) marriage should be regarded as extending established families, not just creating new ones; (4) a person should talk over important life decisions with family members before taking actions; and (5) family members should give more weight to each others' opinion than to the opinions of outsiders. Responses were coded from 1 = "strongly disagree" to 4 = "strongly agree." Reliability alpha of the items was .60. A scale ranging from 5 to 20 was constructed to indicate the value of familism as expressed by parents.

Normative beliefs about the responsibility of adult children toward aging parents was measured using a 6-item scale that asks, "Regardless of the sacrifices involved, how much responsibility should adult children with families of their own have to (1) provide companionship or spend time with elderly parents who are in need; (2) help with household chores and repairs and/or provide transportation for elderly parents who are in need; (3) listen to the problems and concerns of elderly parents and provide advice and guidance; (4) provide for personal and health care needs of the elderly parent (e.g., bathing, grooming, and medications); (5) provide financial support and/or assist in financial and legal affairs of elderly parents who are in need; and (6) provide housing for the elderly parents who are in need." Each item was rated on a 5-point scale ranging from "none" to "total." The responses for six items were summed to come up with a "total degree of filial responsibility." The index score ranged from 6 to 30. The reliability coefficient alpha was .89.

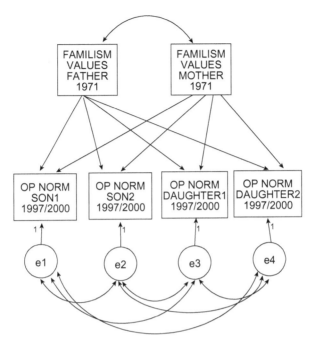

Figure 14.1. Intergenerational transmission of family norms: 1971–2000.

4.3. The Transmission Model

Our transmission model, shown in Figure 14.1, estimates the effect of familism values expressed by mothers and fathers in 1971 on norms toward support for older parents ("OP Norm") as expressed by two daughters and two sons in 2000. In the model, we estimate two types of effects: (1) direct transmission from parents to offspring (equality constraints imposed on effects for offspring of the same gender); and (2) associations between (a) offspring error terms (to account for common sibling environments independent of parents and equality constraints imposed on same-sex and cross-sex associations), and (b) mothers and fathers (to account for assortative mating).

Because only some families have complete data for all four members (due to variations in family size, gender configuration, and participation rates), we use pattern-mixture modeling to analyze these unbalanced pedigrees (McArdle & Hamagami, 1992). In pattern-mixture modeling, families are essentially organized into groups based on their pattern of complete and incomplete data. In families with incomplete configurations, parameter estimates that cannot be estimated directly are "borrowed" from families within which the relevant gender-specific relationships are intact. This approach provides unbiased estimates of parameters for the population providing that the usual assumptions of maximum likelihood estimation (MLE) are met, together with the assumption

Table 14.1. *Standardized parameter estimates for intergenerational transmission model*

Model Parameters	Standardized Estimates	t-Value
Direct Effects		
Father-to-son1	−.027	−.304[a]
Father-to-son2	−.024	
Father-to-daughter1	.148	2.067*[a]
Father-to-daughter2	.138	
Mother-to-son1	.048	.592*[a]
Mother-to-son2	.043	
Mother-to-daughter1	.086	1.283[a]
Mother-to-daughter2	.080	
Correlations		
Same-sex sibling error terms	.249 (S)	2.558*[a]
	.253 (D)	
Cross-sex sibling error terms	−.074 to −.062	−.672[a]
	(range)	
Father-mother	.162	2.654**
Goodness of Fit	**Fit Statistic**	**p-Value**
Chi-square/df	9.86/8	.275
NFI	.998	–
RMSEA	.022	–

* $p < .05$; ** $p < .01$.
[a] Denotes that unstandardized estimates for gender-specific relationships were constrained to be equal, resulting in one statistical test for each type of intergenerational pairing. Note that standardized estimates may vary when unstandardized estimates are constrained to be equal.

that data are missing completely at random or random conditional on observed variables (Little & Rubin, 1987). Under these assumptions, the MLE approach offers a practical way to use full information and account for all pedigree configurations in order to minimize attrition biases.

The results shown in Table 14.1 reveal that the model fits well and that there are significant spousal and same-sex sibling correlations. However, the translation of general parental attitudes into specific norms endorsed by offspring holds only for father–daughter dyads. There are reasons to expect that this effect, in particular, would be strong. If Becker (1991) was correct in stating that parents *strategically* invest in their children's human capital, then in the case of moral capital, the greatest advantage would be to transmit familism to those offspring who are potentially more receptive to the message. Because daughters are more willing than sons to be caregivers in American families (Aronson, 1992), parents would anticipate that their daughters more readily absorb values of familism and systematically direct parental investments of moral capital toward them.

A possible alternative explanation is that women are more capable of moral reasoning and either acquire or maintain their stock of moral capital more efficiently than men. In reviewing research that employed the Defining Issues Test – a widely used test of moral reasoning about social dilemmas based on Kohlberg's (1981) theory of moral development – Rest (1986) concluded that across a variety of studies, females consistently scored higher than males. Gilligan (1982) theorized that women and men approach moral issues from different perspectives, with women approaching from a "care" and men from a "justice" orientation. As such, girls may be more receptive to moral issues than boys. Family-care work, which includes eldercare responsibilities, is known to be a more important part of the female-role repertoire, at least in the cultural context of the United States.

But why are fathers more likely than mothers to share these values with their daughters? Again, drawing on the notion of strategic advantage, it would seem likely that fathers may be more likely than mothers to gain influence over their children by instilling moral precepts rather than by bonding emotionally (at least in this pre–baby-boom cohort of parents in which the gendered division of labor was more clear than it is today). Alternatively, perhaps it is the fathers – known to have weaker social-support networks in older age – who have the most to gain by investing in their own children. Admittedly, these ex post facto interpretations are speculative but consistent with other findings from these data showing that affection with children is more consequential for support received by mothers than by fathers (Silverstein, Parrott, & Bengtson, 1995). Elaborating on the model to include emotional integration and time spent with children (which may be a strategy used more by mothers), as well as intergenerational financial transfers, will allow a formal test of the various ways that the long reach of parents extends into the middle age of their children. Similar endeavors to analyze differences between all-male and mixed-gender families would be fruitful.

5.0. CONCLUSION

Our review of the literature on moral capital transmission between generations in families has cut across several disciplines and, in doing so, has suggested an integrative paradigm for better understanding social processes in the family. Capitalizing on theories from sociology, social psychology, demography, and economics helps to better understand how adult children come to develop a sense of duty to their older parents. We conceptualize filial commitment as a form of moral capital that parents invest in their children with the expectation that it will take root and flower into a commitment to eldercare responsibilities later in their life. The production of familistic norms in children is beneficial to families and society, but it should not be confused with simple altruism. However, because the self-interest of parents is served when children are successfully socialized to norms that reinforce family responsibility, normative beliefs may also be viewed as a set of transmittable values that attract reciprocation in the form of old-age support.

We note with interest that the founding father of the "classical school" of free-market economics, Adam Smith (1779), recognized the limits of rational self-interest for explaining the motivations behind interpersonal transactions in families. In his book, *The Theory of Moral Sentiments*, Smith wrote: "How selfish soever man may be supposed, there are evidently some principles in his nature which interest him in the fortune of others and render their happiness necessary to him though he derives nothing from it except the pleasure of seeing it." Smith seems to suggest that market and affective relationships operate in different spheres and are guided by different principles. Yet, this may be an oversimplification, in that morality and self-interest coincide in the same relationships, in the same spheres. In the business world, this approach blends utilitarian and moral values as a formula for success. Famed billionaire investor, Warren Buffett, is quoted as saying (Pandya, 1999), "You need integrity, intelligence and energy to succeed. Integrity is totally a matter of choice – and it's habit-forming." We have suggested in this chapter that moral sentiments and rational self-interest are not mutually exclusive in families as well, and that moral capital exists in the space between selfishness and selflessness, between strategic investment and simple altruism.

Our analysis supporting transmission between fathers and daughters should not distract future work from examining all types of gender pairings. Considering a larger set of investment currencies (i.e., emotion, time, and money) and using more reliable measures of exogenous values may portray a more complex picture of the transmission of eldercare norms than was possible in the current research. Furthermore, the motivation to actually provide care to older parents may vary by a child's gender, such that a unit-increase in norms may produce a stronger behavioral response in daughters than in sons. We also note that focusing on values that to some degree are reflexive (i.e., apply to the relationship between the sender and the receiver) may produce different transmission patterns than those found by other analyses in this volume that examine transmissible content that is more dispositional than interpersonal in nature.

Whereas the intergenerational transmission of moral capital is an intrafamilial process, its implications for the wider society are substantial. There is an interaction between this and external processes of exchange. For example, in the absence of formal markets and/or governmental transfer programs (e.g., Social Security and Medicare), we would expect the returns to investments in moral capital to be higher – because the *consequences* of opportunistic behavior of adult children are higher (i.e., poverty, isolation, and even death). In effect, these families are playing without a safety net. Similarly, private markets and government programs that reduce the risk of nonrepayment in old age may reduce the returns to investments in moral capital and weaken the incentives to transmit familistic values to new generations. Given the inverse relationship between returns to moral capital investment and access to public-transfer programs, it is not surprising that developing nations with the weakest public support for the elderly have the strongest cultural traditions of family care for them. These strong filial traditions can be seen as a public good that saves government from making public expenditures, providing a rationale for restricting public programs in support of the elderly. However, this argument as a justification to restrict government programs may reinforce the exploitation of well-intentioned but self-sacrificing family members, especially daughters and daughters-in-law who bear most of the burden of filial-care duties. Ultimately, these decisions rest on societal and family values that legitimate the proper balance of care between society and families for supporting older citizens and the ways by which the stock of moral capital is built and expended.

REFERENCES

Altonji, J., Hayashi, F., & Kotlikoff, L. (1992). Is the extended family altruistically linked? Direct tests using micro data. *American Economic Review, 82*, 1177–1198.

Altonji, J., Hayashi, F., & Kotlikoff, L. (1997). Parental altruism and inter vivos transfers: Theory and evidence. *Journal of Political Economy, 105*, 1121–1166.

Antonucci, T. (1990). Social supports and social relationships. In R. H. Binstock & L. K. George (Eds.), *Handbook of aging and the social sciences* (3rd ed., pp. 205–226). New York: Academic Press.

Aronson, J. (1992). Women's sense of responsibility for the care of old people: "But who else is going to do it?" *Gender & Society, 6*, 8–29.

Arrow, K. (2000). Observations on social capital. In P. Dasgupta & I. Serageldin (Eds.), *Social capital: A multifaceted perspective* (pp. 3–5). Washington, DC: The International Bank for Reconstruction and Development.

Barro, R. (1974). Are government bonds net wealth? *Journal of Political Economy, 82*, 1095–1117.

Becker, G. S. (1975). *Human capital.* New York: Columbia University Press.

Becker, G. S. (1991). *A treatise on the family* (enlarged edition). Cambridge, MA: Harvard University Press.

Becker, G. S. (1992). *The economic way of looking at life.* Nobel Lecture, December 9.

Becker, G. S., & Tomes, N. (1976). Child endowments and the quantity and quality of children. *Journal of Political Economy, 84*, S143–S162.

Bengtson, V. L., Biblarz, T. J., & Roberts, R. E. L. (2002). *How families still matter: A longitudinal study of youth in two generations.* New York: Cambridge University Press.

Bernheim, D., Shleifer, A., & Summers, L. (1985). The strategic bequest motive. *Journal of Political Economy, 33*, 1045–1076.

Bernheim, D., & Stark, O. (1988). Altruism within the family reconsidered: Do nice guys finish last? *American Economic Review, 78*, 1034–1045.

Blair, J. (1996–1997). "Honor thy father and thy mother" – but for how long?: Adult children's duty to care for and protect elderly parents. *Journal of Family Law, 35*, 765–782.

Blieszner, R., & Mancini, J. A. (1987). Enduring ties: Older adults' parental role and responsibilities. *Family Relations, 36*, 176–180.

Bourdieu, P. (1986). The forms of capital. In Richardson, J. G. (Ed.), *Handbook of theory and research for the sociology of education* (pp. 241–258). New York: Greenwood Press.

Bromley, M. C., & Blieszner, R. (1997). Planning for long-term care: Filial behavior and relationship quality of adult children with independent parents. *Family Relations, 46,* 155–162.

Burr, J. A., & Mutchler, J. E. (1999). Race and ethnic variation in norms of filial responsibility among older persons. *Journal of Marriage and the Family, 61,* 674–687.

Caputo, R. K. (2002). Rational actors versus rational agents. *Journal of Family and Economic Issues, 23,* 27–50.

Cherlin, A. J. (2005). *Public and private families.* Boston: McGraw Hill.

Cicirelli, V. G. (1988). A measure of filial anxiety regarding anticipated care of elderly parents. *The Gerontologist, 23,* 478–482.

Cicirelli, V. G. (1990). Relationship of personal social variables to belief in paternalism in parent caregiving situations. *Psychology and Aging, 5,* 458–466.

Cicirelli, V. G. (1993). Attachment and obligation as daughters' motives for caregiving behavior and subsequent effect on subjective burden. *Psychology and Aging, 8,* 144–155.

Coleman, J. S. (1988). Social capital in the creation of human capital. *American Journal of Sociology, 94,* Supplement, S95–S120.

Cosmides, L., & Tooby, J. (1992). Cognitive adaptations for social exchange. In J. H. Barkow, L. Cosmides, & J. Tooby (Eds.), *The adapted mind: Evolutionary psychology and the generation of culture* (pp. 163–228). New York: Oxford University Press.

Cox, D. (1987). Motives for private income transfers. *Journal of Political Economy, 95,* 508–546.

Cox, D., & Stark, O. (1992). *Intergenerational transfers and the demonstration effect* (working paper). Cambridge, MA: Harvard University Press.

Daatland, O. D., & Herlofson, K. (2003). "Lost solidarity" or "changed solidarity": A comparative European view of normative family solidarity. *Ageing & Society, 23,* 537–560.

Dunn, T., & Phillips, J. (1997). *Do parents divide resources equally among children? Evidence from the AHEAD survey.* Syracuse, NY: Center for Policy Research, Maxwell School of Citizenship and Public Affairs.

Durlauf, S. N. (2002). Symposium on social capital: Introduction. *The Economic Journal, 112,* F417–F418.

Emerson, R. M. (1981). Social exchange theory. In M. Rosenberg & R. H. Turner (Eds.), *Social psychology: Sociological perspectives* (pp. 30–65). New York: Basic Books.

Frank, R. H. (1988). *Passions within reason: The strategic role of the emotions.* New York: W. W. Norton & Company.

Fukuyama, F. (1995) *Trust: The social virtues and the creation of prosperity.* New York: The Free Press.

Furstenberg, F. F., & Kaplan, S. B. (2004). Social capital and the family. In J. Scott, J. Treas, & M. Richards (Eds.), *The Blackwell companion to the sociology of families* (pp. 218–232). Oxford: Blackwell Publishing Ltd.

Gatti, R. (1999). Family altruism and incentives. *Policy Research Working Paper, Series 2505.* The World Bank.

Gilligan, C. (1982). *In a different voice: Psychological theory and women's development.* Cambridge, MA: Harvard University Press.

Glaeser, E. L., Laibson, D., & Sacerdote, B. (2002). An economic approach to social capital. *The Economic Journal, 112* (November), F437–F458.

Glass, J., Bengtson, V. L., & Dunham, C. (1986). Attitude similarity in three-generation families: Socialization, status inheritance, or reciprocal influence? *American Sociological Review, 51*, 685–698.

Gouldner, A. W. (1960). The norm of reciprocity: A preliminary statement. *American Sociological Review, 25*, 161–178.

Harris, J. R. (1998). *The nurture assumption.* New York: The Free Press.

Heller, P. L. (1976). Familism scale: Revalidation and revision. *Journal of Marriage and the Family, 38*, 423–429.

Henretta, J. C., Hill, M. S., Li, W., Soldo, B. J., & Wolf, D. A. (1997). Selection of children to provide care: The effect of earlier parental transfers. *Journals of Gerontology, Series B: Psychological and Social Sciences, 52B*, 110–119.

Hofferth, S. L., Boisjoly, J., & Duncan, G. J. (1999). The development of social capital. *Rationality and Society, 11*, 79–110.

Hollstein, B., & Bria, G. (1998). Reciprocity in parent–child relationships? Theoretical considerations and empirical evidence. *Berliner Journal für Soziologie, 8*, 7–22.

Homans, G. C. (1950). *The human group.* New York: Harcourt, Brace and World.

Kohlberg, L. (1981). *The philosophy of moral development.* New York: Harper & Row Publishers.

Lillard, L. A., & Willis, R. J. (1997). Motives for intergenerational transfers: Evidence from Malaysia. *Demography, 34*, 115–134.

Little, R. J. A., & Rubin, D. B. (1987). *Statistical analysis with missing data.* New York: Wiley.

Litwak, E. (1985). *Helping the elderly: The complementary roles of informal networks and formal systems.* New York: Guilford Press.

Litwak, E., & Kulis, S. (1987). Technology, proximity, and measures of kin support. *Journal of Marriage and the Family, 49*, 649–661.

Logan, J., & Spitze, G. (1995). Self-interest and altruism in intergenerational relations. *Demography, 32* (August), 353–364.

Mauss, M. (1923/1967). *The gift: Forms and functions of exchange in archaic societies.* Translated by Ian Cunnison. New York: Norton (original work published in 1923).

McArdle, J. J., & Hamagami, E. (1992). Modeling incomplete longitudinal and cross-sectional data using latent growth structural models. *Experimental Aging Research, 18*, 145–166.

McGarry, K. (1999). Inter vivos transfers and intended bequests. *Journal of Public Economics, 73*, 321–351.

McGarry, K., & Schoeni, R. (1995). Transfer behavior in the health and retirement study: Measurement and the redistribution of resources within the family. *Journal of Human Resources, 30*, S184–S226.

McKenzie, J. L. (1965). *Dictionary of the Bible.* New York: MacMillian Publishing Co., Inc.

Molm, L. D., & Cook, K. S. (1995). Social exchange and exchange networks. In K. S. Cook, G. A. Fine, & J. S. House (Eds.), *Sociological perspectives on social psychology* (pp. 209–235). Boston, MA: Allyn and Bacon.

Ogawa, N., & Retherford, R. D. (1993). Care of the elderly in Japan: Changing norms and expectations. *Journal of Marriage and the Family, 55*, 585–597.

Pandya, M. (1999). Portrait of Warren Buffet, chairman of Berkshire Hathaway, Inc. (April 21), from a presentation at a Wharton executive series. Accessed on September 24, 2004, at http://leadership.wharton.upenn.edu/l_change/Interviews/Interview%20with%20Warren%20Buffett.doc.

Parrott, T. M., & Bengtson, V. L. (1999). The effects of earlier intergenerational affection, normative expectations, and family conflict on contemporary exchanges of help and support. *Research on Aging, 21*, 73–105.

Pauly, M. V. (1990). The rational nonpurchase of long-term-care insurance. *Journal of Political Economy, 98*, 153–168.

Putnam, R. D. (1995). Bowling alone: America's declining social capital. *Journal of Democracy, 6*, 65–71.

Putnam, R. D. (1996). The strange disappearance of civic America. *The American Prospect, 24*, 34–38.

Putney, N., & Bengtson, V. L. (2002). Socialization and the family: A broader perspective. In R. A. Settersten, Jr., & T. J. Owens (Eds.), *Advances in life-course research: New frontiers in socialization* (pp. 165–194). London: Elsevier.

Ratnapala, S. (2003). Moral capital and commercial society. *The Independent Review, 8*, 213–233.

Rest, J. R. (1986). *Moral development: Advances in research and theory.* New York: Praeger Publishers.

Rosenberg, N. (1990). Adam Smith and the stock of moral capital. *History of Political Economy, 22*, 1–18.

Rossi, A. S., & Rossi, P. H. (1990). *Of human bonding: Parent–children relationship across the life course.* New York: Aldine de Gruyter.

Seelbach, W. C. (1977). Gender differences in expectations for filial responsibility. *The Gerontologist, 17*, 421–425.

Seelbach, W. C. (1978). Correlates of aged parents filial responsibility expectations and realizations. *Family Coordinator, 27*, 341–350.

Silverstein, M., Conroy, S. J., & Gans, D. (2008). Commitment to Caring: Filial Responsibility and the Allocation of Support by Adult Children to Older Mothers. In Szinovacz, M. E., & Davey, A. (Eds.), *Caregiving contexts: Cultural, familial and societal implications* (pp. 71–92). New York: Springer Publishing Company, LLC.

Silverstein, M., Conroy, S. J., Wang, H., Giarrusso, R., & Bengtson, V. L. (2002). Reciprocity in parent–child relations over the adult life course. *Journal of Gerontology: Social Sciences, 57*, S3–S13.

Silverstein, M., & Litwak, E. (1993). A task-specific typology of intergenerational family structure in later life. *The Gerontologist, 33*, 258–264.

Silverstein, M., Parrott, T. M., & Bengtson, V. L. (1995). Factors that predispose middle-aged sons and daughters to provide social support to older parents. *Journal of Marriage and the Family, 57*, 465–475.

Sison, A. J. G. (2003). *The moral capital of leaders: Why virtue matters.* Northampton, MA: Edward Elgar.

Sloan, F., Zhang, H., & Wang, J. (2002). Upstream intergenerational transfers. *Southern Economic Journal, 69*, 363–380.

Smith, A. (1779). *The theory of moral sentiments.* Library of Economics and Liberty. Retrieved January 17, 2004, from http://www.econlib.org/library/Smith/smMS1.html.

Solow, R. (2000). Notes on social capital and economic performance, in P. Dasgupta & I. Serageldin (Eds.), *Social capital: A multifaceted perspective* (pp. 6–10). Washington, DC: The International Bank for Reconstruction and Development.

Stark, O. (1989). Altruism and the quality of life. *American Economic Review, 79,* 86–90.

Stein, C. H., Wemmerus, V. A., Ward, M., Gaines, M. E., Freeberg, A. L., & Jewell, T. (1998). "Because they're my parents": An intergenerational study of felt obligation and parental caregiving. *Journal of Marriage and the Family, 60,* 611–622.

Sundstrom, G., Johansson, L., & Hassing, L. B. (2002). The shifting balance of long-term care in Sweden. *The Gerontologist, 42,* 350–355.

Sussman, M., Cates, J., & Smith, D. (1970). *The family and inheritance.* New York: Russell Sage Foundation.

Taris, T. W., & Semin, G. R. (1997). Passing on the faith: How mother–child communication influences transmission of moral values. *Journal of Moral Education, 26,* 211–221.

Warnes, A. M. (1994). Cities and elderly people: Recent population and distributional trends. *Urban Studies, 31,* 4–5.

Whitbeck, L. B., Simons, R. L., & Conger, R. D. (1991). The effects of early family relationships on contemporary relationships and assistance patterns between adult children and their parents. *Journal of Gerontology: Social Sciences, 46,* S301–S337.

15

Similarity of Life Goals in the Family:
A Three-Generation Study

ALEXANDER GROB, WIBKE WEISHEIT, AND VERONICA GOMEZ

INTRODUCTION

Assumptions about family resemblances are widely held among people all over the world. Old sayings like "it's in the blood," "an apple doesn't fall far from the tree," and "like father, like son" reflect people's beliefs in this regard. Psychologists from various backgrounds such as family psychology, behavior genetics, and attachment theory have proposed mechanisms explaining why characteristics such as life goals might run in the family. Yet, convincing arguments suggest that there are few overlaps in terms of life goals: Family members share different parts of their biographies with each other, belong to different societal cohorts, and have been socialized in different historical contexts.

Little attention has been given to life goals from this similarity perspective. This lack of interest is surprising because shared goals are one feature of defining family (Schneewind, 1999). According to this definition, a family's community feeling is characterized by shared goals, shared experiences of positive and negative emotionality, knowledge, and values. Although some research focused on the relationship between parenting and children's goals (Kasser, Ryan, Zax, & Sameroff, 1995), little is known about the resemblance in goals of two or even three family generations. Three-generation family studies in general are quite rare, representing a sharp contrast to the increasing mutual lifetime of family generations. This increase has led to a growing importance of multigenerational families (Bengtson, 2001), providing many opportunities to be in contact and share ideas.

This study extends previous research on family resemblance by focusing on life goals and including three generations. Within families as well as at the cohort level, we examined the life goals of grandparents, parents, and adolescent and

We thank Stefanie Johl, Katrin Kuerschner, Anette Lemmler-Lauerbach, Simone Morschel, Maria Steinhauer, and Sabine Wenke-Wippermann for their assistance with data collection and data entry at the University of Bonn, Germany. The data were analyzed when the first and the senior author had appointments at the University of Bern, Switzerland.

young-adult children. We suggest that although many differences in life goals exist between the generations, the assumption of intrafamilial resemblance is tenable.

1.0. GOALS AND VALUE CONCEPTS IN PERSONALITY PSYCHOLOGY

Life goals are conceptualized as internal representations of desired states in terms of outcomes, events, and processes and as the personally meaningful objectives people pursue in their daily lives (Austin & Vancouver, 1996). This conceptualization resembles the definition of values, and the distinction between values and goals is not always clearcut, especially in empirical analyses. Values include what people find desirable or undesirable, but values do not necessarily imply energy or action. A hierarchical structure of the motivational system that sets motives and values over goals has been proposed (Bandura, 1986; Carver & Scheier, 1990; Emmons, 1989; Nurmi, 1989; Pervin, 1983). Long-term, general values are the basis for middle- and short-term goals that in turn direct people's thoughts and behaviors. As such, values are trans-situational goals that serve as guiding principles (Schwartz, Sagiv, & Boehnke, 2000).

Various dimensions to describe goals have been suggested – for example, importance and commitment, probability of goal attainment, specificity-representation, temporal range, level of consciousness, and complexity (Austin & Vancouver, 1996). We concentrate on two dimensions: (1) the importance of a goal, and (2) the perceived personal control over the goal's attainment. As another dimension to describe goals, their content is used. Goals reflect the issues of self, power, achievement, interpersonal concerns, leisure, and health (Novacek & Lazarus, 1990; Nurmi, 1992; Wickert, Lambert, Richardson, & Kahler, 1984). The assumption of basic psychological needs was the basis for the categorization of intrinsic and extrinsic goals (Deci & Ryan, 1985; Kasser & Ryan, 1993). Whereas intrinsic goals serve to fulfill the assumed innate needs for relatedness, autonomy, and competence, extrinsic goals include material success, status, and approval. With regard to perceived control, the number of people involved in the control behavior was proposed as a structuring factor in goals, resulting in the assumption of domain-specific control that varies among the personal, the interpersonal, and the societal domains (Grob, Flammer, & Wearing, 1995). Although goal importance and perceived control represent two separate dimensions in goals, they are interrelated (Grob, Little, Wanner, Wearing, & Euronet, 1996): People strive for control over goals in domains they find important.

To summarize, goals that people pursue in their life are assumed to be located on a middle level of the motivational system, varying along many dimensions. Because individuals in a family create "co-biographies" (Hagestad, 1986, p. 687) – a system of interacting lives – the anticipated future parts of their biographies might be related to one another as well. Therefore, the question arises of whether and why similarities in the goal domain exist among family members.

2.0. LIFE GOALS AND THE FAMILY

2.1. Mechanisms Contributing to Similarities among Family Members

Many theories address mechanisms that might contribute to similarities in the family. Behavior genetics explain similarities by common genes and shared environmental conditions and dissimilarities by the nonshared environment unique to every individual within the family (Plomin & Daniels, 1987; Rowe, 1997; Turkheimer & Waldron, 2000). Evolutionary psychology stresses the adaptivity of value transmission: Transmitted values make adaptive behavior possible under variable environmental conditions without the need to specify this behavior for every situation (Cavalli-Sforza, 1993; Michod, 1993).

Family resemblance can also be explained by the interaction among family generations that affects how children encounter the world: either by the process of parenting (Bowlby, 1969; Bretherton, 1985) and filiating (Valsiner, Branco, & Dantas, 1997), by messages passed on in terms of family myths (Martin & Olson, 1996; Samuel & Thompson, 1990), or by transgenerational mandates (Stierlin, 1994; Whitaker & Keith, 1981). There is evidence that internal working models of self and parent are the "vehicles whereby conventional, moral and ethical rules are initially transmitted" (Bretherton, Golby, & Cho, 1997, p. 129), enhancing the children's willingness to accept parental values and behaviors (Grusec & Goodnow, 1994). Parents who support autonomy, give structure through clear and explainable rules, and show involvement in their children's lives provide conditions for the satisfaction of children's basic needs in interaction with the environment. They have children who act in an intrinsically motivated manner (Grolnick, Deci, & Ryan, 1997; Kasser et al., 1995; Kasser, Koestner, & Lekes, 2002) and who perceive personal control (Schneewind, 1989). Moreover, family-interaction processes occur across three generations. Some grandparents define themselves as the ones who dispense family wisdom and who live on in their grandchildren (Kivnick, 1985; Neugarten & Weinstein, 1964), and some grandchildren see their grandparents as confidants or mentors who provide inspiration and encouragement (Franks, Hughes, Phelps, & Williams, 1993).

Only recently has the literature dealt with the fact that children influence their parents as well (Grusec, Rudy, & Martini, 1997; Lerner, 1993; Valsiner et al., 1997). Consequently, the processes across two as well as three generations are bidirectional. These latter approaches stress the crucial role of family-interaction variables in generating working models with various implications for how individuals behave and how they plan their life. However, the assumed process may also make family members different to one another. Hence, the possibility exists that parents serve as *anti-models*; that is, they might constitute precisely what children do *not* want to be or do. In this case, parents still provide a frame of reference – represented in a mental model – to set oneself off against. The developmental implications of possible conflicts resulting from this process need not be negative (Goodnow, 1994); on the contrary, experimentation with aspects of a model person can be interpreted as an essential "mechanism by which individual uniqueness is constructed under the flow of social suggestions" (Valsiner, 1994, p. 258). This kind of transgenerational process might lead to fewer similarities between family members; however, are these assumptions of similarity-fostering mechanisms reflected in empirical evidence in the domain of life goals?

2.1.1. *Family Similarities in Life Goals and Values*

Research on transgenerational similarities in goals has mainly focused on educational aspirations, therefore representing a specific and concrete aspect of goal-setting in life (Kandel & Lesser, 1969; Kerckhoff & Huff, 1974; Smith, 1991; Trusty & Pirtle, 1998; Wilson & Wilson, 1992). Regarding a wider range of goals covering various life domains, there is a remarkable lack of research: Research on family similarities in life goals across generations does not exist, even across two generations.

However, results from research on values might be transferred to this field of interest, drawing on the idea that values as well as goals are part of a hierarchical motivational system. Concerning value similarities in the family, some knowledge is available. One study included family members of three generations (Bengtson, 1975) and revealed that values from the dimension of collectivism versus individualism were equally affected by family and generation influences in the grandparent–parent pairs. In the parent–child pairs, however, there was only a strong family effect, whereas in the grandparent–child pairs, there was only a strong generation effect for those values. Values from the dimension of humanism versus materialism were not related between generations. Two-generation family studies confirm this finding of selective processes depending on the content: Family effects were found for collectivistic but not for individualistic values (Schönpflug, 2001); for tradition, hedonism, and stimulation values (Boehnke, 2001); and for hedonism and esteem values but not for social values (Homer, 1993). Across different values, parent–child correlations varied heavily from strong negative to strong positive coefficients (Rohan & Zanna, 1996). Instead of asking for their own values for their own life, another line of research relates children's values to what parents want their children to hold dear. Using this approach, a family effect was found for conformity values (Kohn, Slomczynski, & Schoenbach, 1986) and for goals in the domains of self-acceptance, affiliation, and financial success but not for community-feeling goals (Kasser et al., 1995), suggesting content-specific differences. Perceived control over the attainment of different life goals has also not been analyzed through the transgenerational lens. General control expectancies, however, were found to covary between parents and children (Hoffman & Levy-Shiff, 1994; Miller & Rose, 1982; Schneewind, 1989, 1995). In summary, one may suspect that the frequency of transgenerational similarities varies according to the domain under study.

2.1.2. Gender Influences on Family Resemblance

In view of these transgenerational dynamics, gender might influence family similarities in life goals. First, same-gender pairs might resemble each other more than opposite-gender pairs because identification or imitation is made easier, as suggested by psychoanalytic and social-learning theory. Second, mothers are still the primary caretakers in most families, hold the main responsibility in parenting, and are seen as the most important person in the first part of an individual's life span. Finally, research on relationship quality shows that the overall trend in terms of closeness in the parent–adult-child dyad is mother–daughter, mother–son, father–daughter, father–son (Bengtson, 1996; Rossi & Rossi, 1990). Across three generations, grandmothers were found to be closer to their grandchildren than grandfathers, and maternal grandparents were found to be closer than paternal grandparents (Eisenberg, 1988; Smith, 1995; Troll, 1996). Therefore, women in families are described as "kin-keepers" who monitor support activities, arrange meetings of the members, and spread the family news (Troll, 1996). To conclude, same-gender pairs might resemble each other more than opposite-gender pairs, and women in families might resemble each other more than men.

Because research on family similarities in terms of self-reported goals is lacking, so too is empirical evidence about the possible influences of gender. Research on values shows inconsistent results. The correspondence of adolescents' goals with what their mothers wanted them to value was equal for girls and boys (Kasser et al., 1995). Some studies indicate that parent–child similarity exists only between mothers and their children (Rodriguez, Ramirez, & Korman, 1999) or that patterns are different between mothers and fathers for a broad range of values (Boehnke, 2001), whereas others found no gender differences concerning the similarity (Kohn et al., 1986; Okagaki & Bevis, 1999; Rohan & Zanna, 1996). For perceived personal control, the results are also inconsistent (Hoffman & Levy-Shiff, 1994; Miller & Rose, 1982; Schneewind, 1989, 1995).

In summary, several theoretical considerations suggest that grandparents, parents, and grandchildren resemble each other in their life goals. Although there is little research on this resemblance, studies on values indicate that similarities might exist, at least to some degree. Nevertheless, the processes contributing to similarity addressed previously show a great variation between families. Interaction variables such as (grand)parenting, relationship quality, and family climate – as well as the conditions under which those processes occur, such as family structure, socioeconomic status, or culture – strongly differ between families (Amato & Keith, 1991a, 1991b; Constantine, 1993; Eisenberg, 1988; Elder, Robertson, & Conger, 1993; Kopera-Frye & Wiscott, 2000; Larson, Benson, Wilson, & Medora, 1998; Smith, 1995), which might affect the incidence of resemblance found. Families create their own set of meanings and their own construction of reality (Hagestad, 1986) that can be more or less in accord with what we find when averaging across families. Therefore, as a function of these variables, resemblance found in the literature might be very high in one type of family and very low in another. In the research presented here, these variables are not addressed further; nevertheless, they should be considered as possible moderators.

2.2. Mechanisms Contributing to Dissimilarities among Family Members

2.2.1. *Developmental Factors in the Process of Creating Dissimilarities*

The family provides the environment and the guidelines for individual development across the life span. In addition, society and culture affect development, supplying the wider context in which family members as individuals and the family system as a whole are embedded and with which they interact (Hagestad, 1986; Lerner & Kauffman, 1985). Because family members of three generations are confronted with the same conditions at different time points and with different conditions at the same point in their life course, developmental and societal factors are intertwined. Thus, the dynamics of individual development in the societal context might contribute to dissimilarities between family generations. This aspect is elaborated on with respect to life goals in the following discussion.

Developmental factors refer to individuals' biological, psychological, and social needs and the tasks they want to accomplish in different periods of their life (Erikson, 1959; Havighurst, 1948). Seen from a cross-sectional perspective, grandparents, parents, and children in one family are occupied with different themes and projects. *Societal factors* reveal their influence on individual development in terms of a normative reference system that includes societal standards for behavior in different life stages (Erikson, 1959; Havighurst, 1948; Kohli, 1985). In trying to meet these age-graded societal expectations, family members of different ages organize their behavior and plan their near future in different ways. Furthermore, those belonging to the same age group within a society are exposed to the same sociohistorical forces at the same point in life. Members of one generation select the same knowledge from their experience of those forces, providing them with a generational identity that is different from other generations' identities (Mannheim, 1928/1929). This generational identity is thought to manifest itself in particular shared attitudes, plans, and goals; hence, family members of various ages might differ in their goals because they have different generational identities. Findings on developmental and societal factors in goals are addressed in the next section.

2.2.2. *Goals across the Life Span*

The development of goals across the life span has begun to attract researchers' attention only since the 1990s. Studies have demonstrated that for participants from adolescence to old age, the importance of their goals reflects the developmental tasks of the corresponding age period. Individualistic values and life goals (i.e., an exciting life, personal freedom, a sense of accomplishment, physical appearance, education, and work) follow a linear age trend, becoming less important (Bengtson, 1975; Cross & Markus, 1991; Grob, Little, & Wanner, 1999; Nurmi, Pulliainen, & Salmela-Aro, 1992; Strough, Berg, & Sansone, 1996). Materialistic values such as financial comfort and possessions are valued most in middle adulthood, whereas public and health concerns are most important for older people (Bengtson, 1975; Grob et al., 1999; Heckhausen, 1997; Nurmi et al., 1992). Interpersonal life goals are consistently valued as important by members of all age groups (Grob et al., 1999). The summarized research is all cross-sectional, however, and represents momentary descriptions. Age differences, in fact, may represent a cohort effect, reflecting the individualism trend in Western societies (Bangerter, Grob, & Krings, 2001). Longitudinal studies are needed to examine the dynamics of goals across the life span, changing during major life transitions (Salmela-Aro, Nurmi, Saisto, & Halmesmäki, 2000).

2.2.3. *Perceived Control*

Perceived control over goal attainment shows a different development. As they get older, people perceive less and less control over their goals (Cross & Markus, 1991; Heckhausen, 1997; Nurmi et al., 1992), but the trajectories seem to be domain-specific. In one study, perceived control over personal and interpersonal life goals was high, increasing until age 30, decreasing until age 60, and then remaining stable. Perceived control over societal life goals, in contrast, was low and decreased farther across the life span (Grob et al., 1999).

Societal factors, in terms of normative reference systems, affect individual development, but these systems are not fixed for good. Furthermore, not all members of a society subscribe to the same norms to an equal extent. The agreement on the "right" time in the life cycle to address certain tasks varies across cohorts and across life domains. In a three-generation family study (Roscoe & Peterson, 1989), young women, their mothers, and their grandmothers showed the highest agreement on age norms concerning the family, less agreement on norms concerning occupation, and least agreement on norms concerning leisure. This transgenerational agreement further varies as a function of the age for which the norms are postulated. People born between the World Wars (1920–1925), those belonging to the early baby-boomer generation (born 1945–1950), and those belonging to generation X (born 1970–1975) reported on their goals for different points in the life course (Bangerter et al., 2001). Whereas the cohorts agreed on the most important goals for age 75 (health), only the two younger cohorts rated the same goals as most important for age 50 (family and work), and only the two older cohorts rated the same goals as most important for age 25 (family, occupation). Perceiving control similarly is subject to changes over time. In a study on general control expectancies, middle-aged women and men and older women in 1971 perceived less personal control than people of the same respective age and gender in 1991, whereas young adults scored equally at the two assessment waves (Gatz & Karel, 1993). Older and young adults perceived less personal control than middle-aged adults in 1971, and older adults perceived less control than middle-aged or young adults in 1985 and 1991. This shows that young adults gained control over time, as compared to the other two groups. In summary, cohort effects were found with regard to goal importance and perceived control over life goals.

2.2.4. *Gender Effects in Dissimilarities*

In the context of developmental and societal influences, different role expectations with which women and men are confronted might lead to gender effects in goals. Many differences between women's and men's goals have been reported. Women's goals in the domain of interpersonal relationships evolved around mutual, shared participation and other people, whereas men's goals were more often self-focused (Strough et al., 1996). In the transition to parenthood, women mentioned more goals concerning parenthood, the child's health, and the child's birth than men, who mentioned more achievement- and property-related goals (Salmela-Aro et al., 2000). In another study, women emphasized goals from the domains of education, self, traveling, and health, and men were more concerned with leisure and more global goals (Nurmi, 1992). Among adolescents, girls focused more on family-related goals (Greene & Wheatley, 1992); education-related goals (Nurmi, 1989); self-related goals (Grob & Flammer, 1999); self-acceptance, community feeling, and affiliation (Kasser et al., 1995); or valued all goals higher than boys (Grob et al., 1995). Boys valued financial success more than girls (Cross & Markus, 1991; Kasser et al., 1995). Concerning *perceived control* over goals, adolescent girls experienced more control in the societal domain than boys (Grob et al., 1995). In one study, women perceived less personal control in general (Gatz & Karel, 1993), whereas no gender differences were reported in another study (Lang & Heckhausen, 2001). The inconsistencies in the empirical evidence on gender differences in the domain of life goals might be due to varying samples (e.g., age span, cohorts included, and educational background) and measurement (e.g., dimensions and domains of goals).

In summary, goals that individuals hold dear are affected by the interaction of developmental factors, societal expectations, and historical time. This interaction may result in dissimilarities among members of different family generations.

3.0. RESEARCH QUESTIONS

3.1. Hypotheses

Various processes are supposed to influence family resemblance. In conclusion, two perspectives are to be considered when dealing with the question of transgenerational processes: (1) the development from one family generation to the next, and (2) the development of the individual across the life span – both embedded in historical and societal context. In the research presented here, both perspectives are integrated in a study on members of three biologically related family generations. Basic features of this study are addressed in the following discussion.

We were interested in self-reports because research on intergenerational relationship quality reveals some inconsistencies between the different viewpoints of family members. In general, these findings indicate that older family members tend to report more positive perceptions of a relationship than younger family members (Bengtson, 1996; Fingerman, 1995; Levitt, Guacci, & Weber, 1992; Winkeler, Filipp, & Boll, 2000). Furthermore, the perception of another person's life goals may be subject to many biases (Homer, 1993; Rohan & Zanna, 1996; Westholm, 1999). Nevertheless, in some studies on values and goals, one family member answered for the others (Iversen & Farber, 1996; Page & Washington, 1997; Smith, 1991; Trusty & Pirtle, 1998), thereby distorting information about similarities. To discover what people find important in their life and how much control they perceive, they had to be asked themselves.

Relationships among family members' values have been reported in some studies (Bengtson, 1975; Kasser et al., 1995; Rohan & Zanna, 1996; Schönpflug, 2001), suggesting that parents who put more emphasis on a goal than other parents have children who value this goal more strongly than other children.[1] Thus, it is assumed that the relative position of family members as compared to their age group might be related across generations (i.e., within-family covariation). First, we expected the goal importance of family members in the parent–child dyad to be related. Most of the grandchildren in our study still lived in their parents' house or had moved out only recently, whereas middle-aged parents and grandparents, in general, have lower intensity and frequency of contact. Second, we therefore expected to find more covariation in the younger (i.e., parent–adolescent-child) than in the older-parent–child (i.e., grandparent–parent) dyad. Third, referring to research on values, we assumed no relationships in terms of the importance of life goals between grandparents and grandchildren. In addition, family similarities might vary as a function of gender. Finally, we expected mothers and children to be more similar than fathers and children and parents and daughters to be more similar than parents and sons. We expected to find these gender differences in both the younger- and the older-parent–child dyads. With regard to grandparents and grandchildren, we expected to find more similarities among women than among men.

Furthermore, family similarities in perceived control over goals were investigated. We expected family correlations in terms of generally perceived control

---

[1] Throughout the text, we use the terms *old*, *middle-aged*, and *young adults* when referring to the age cohort. When focusing on the generational position within the family, we use the term *grandparents* or *generation 1 (g1)* for the oldest family generation, *middle-aged parents* or *generation 2 (g2)* for the middle family generation, and *grandchildren* or *generation 3 (g3)* for the youngest family generation. Because both the g1–g2 dyad and the g2–g3 dyad include parent–child relationships, we specify the cases in which age matters: g1–g2 dyads are addressed as older-parent–child dyads, and g2–g3 dyads are addressed as younger-parent–child dyads.

over different goals. Domain-specificity of perceived control over goals was reported (Grob et al., 1995), but there are no studies on domain-specificity in terms of family resemblance in perceived control. Therefore, we explored whether family similarities in perceived control differ between the goals.

Turning to differences between people, research on goals indicates that goal importance and perceived control are a function of age (Cross & Markus, 1991; Grob et al., 1999; Heckhausen, 1997; Nurmi et al., 1992) and historical time (Bangerter et al., 2001; Gatz & Karel, 1993). The goals of older grandparents, middle-aged parents, and young-adult children should reflect the developmental tasks of the corresponding age group. More specifically, we expected to find self-focused goals to be more important for young adults than for the two older-age cohorts and societal goals to be more important for older adults than for the two younger cohorts. Furthermore, we expected perceived control over self-focused, interpersonal, and societal goals to be highest in the youngest cohort and to decrease in the middle and oldest cohorts.

Assuming that goals reflect gender-role expectations, we expected gender differences in importance. Goals relating to the traditional female role, like being a good parent, should be more important for women than for men. Goals relating to the traditional male role (e.g., being successful at work) or goals from the domain of power should be more important for men than for women. Because people may imagine fewer obstacles in goal attainment when following the traditional path, we expected gender differences in perceived control over goals as well.

The most prominent problem of previous research on transgenerational similarities in goals is that it is lacking. Referring to this gap 25 years ago, Kohn stated that "the object of research on the transmission of values in the family has generally been not to *demonstrate* a similarity in parents' and children's values, but to *explain* a similarity that was assumed to exist" (Kohn, 1983, p. 1; italics added). For both the concept of values and for life goals, this statement still accounts for the research situation today. The current study aims to change this situation by addressing the question of how similar family members of three generations are in terms of their life goals. The resemblance among the generations was examined in different ways.

First, we looked at how family members' self-reported goals are associated across generations. We assumed to find some within-family covariation for goal importance and perceived control over goals, expecting stronger family similarities among women than among men.

Second, we analyzed the mean-level similarity in self-reported goals between the cohorts. We expected self-focused goals to be most important for young adults, whereas societal goals to be most important for old adults as compared to the other cohorts, respectively. We assumed that goals relating to the traditional female-gender role would be more important for women than for men, whereas goals relating to the traditional male-gender role would be more important for men.

Third, regarding perceived control over goals, we expected a linear-age trend in both goal-specific and overall perceived control, with young adults perceiving more control over their goals than middle-aged adults, who in turn should perceive more control than old adults. Furthermore, we expected women to perceive more control over traditional female-role–related goals and men to perceive more control over traditional male-role–related goals.

3.2. Method

3.2.1. *Sample*

Target participants were members of families with three generations and the youngest generation aged 16 to 25 years. We concentrated on four gender combinations, with grandchild and grandparent being of the same gender. An additional criterion for participation was that family members were biologically related.[2] In the case of divorced or separated parents, the parent with whom the child had lived was asked to participate. Parents-in-law were not included.

The sample consisted of 926 participants: 320 grandchildren aged 16 to 25 ($M = 18.8$, $SD = 2.58$), 318 parents aged 35 to 64 ($M = 47.0$, $SD = 5.01$), and 288 grandparents aged 54 to 95 ($M = 74.9$, $SD = 6.72$). Of the sample, 72% were female (i.e., 73% of the grandchildren, 68% of the parents, and 75% of the grandparents). As a result of historical location and sampling procedure, the educational level varied strongly among the generations: 42% had a university degree (i.e., 69% of the grandchildren, 42% of the parents, and 13% of the grandparents). Of the sample, 43% were married (i.e., 1% of the grandchildren, 78% of the parents, and 52% of the grandparents), and 14% were widowed (i.e., none of the children, 3% of the parents, and 43% of the grandparents). Grandmothers were more likely than all of the other groups to be widowed.

Complete data were collected from 261 family triads. From 149 families, 3 biologically related women participated; from 34 families, 3 men participated; and from 78 families, persons of different genders participated (i.e., grandmother, father, and granddaughter from 50 families; grandfather, mother, and grandson from 28 families). Within-family analyses were conducted with this subsample of complete families, whereas cohort and gender analyses were conducted with the whole sample.

3.2.2. *Procedure*

Data assessment took place in the summer of 2000 and spring of 2001 in Germany. The two subsamples are reported together because target participants and procedures were the same. Families participating in this study were

---

[2] Step-parents were included when they had entered the family before the child was 11 years old. This was the case in 2 of 262 families, in which the step-parent of one member of the parent generation participated.

contacted via members of the youngest generation in presentations of the research project in school classes and announcements on bulletin boards. Some families responded to a newspaper article about the research project or were recruited in old people's homes. People interested in participating were given questionnaires for themselves and the respective members of the other family generations to fill in at home. Alternatively, participants could leave the addresses of the other family members who were then mailed questionnaires. Each member of the family mailed the questionnaires back separately; 35% of the distributed questionnaires were returned.

3.2.3. *Measures*

The life-goals questionnaire was constructed for the study with 18 goals included in the 2000 version and half of those in the 2001 version. Each goal was presented on a separate page, together with the questions concerning the goal. For both the goal's importance ("How important is this goal to you?") and for the perceived control over attainment of the goal ("To what extent do you have personal control in reaching this goal?"), participants gave a rating on a 5-point scale, ranging from "not at all" (1) to "very important" (5) and from "no control at all" (1) to "complete control" (5), respectively. Participants were asked to refer responses to their current life. To assess overall control expectancy, the perceived control ratings were averaged across all goals. Reliabilities for this scale ("overall perceived control") were satisfactory in the whole sample ($\alpha = .80$) and in the gender and cohort subsamples ($\alpha = .71$ to $\alpha = .80$).

Complete goal-item formulations are reported in the appendix at the end of this chapter. They were chosen to represent self-focused goals (i.e., time for oneself, challenging experiences, self-acceptance, fun, health, and financial success), interpersonal goals (i.e., friendships, intimate relationship, satisfactory work life, being a good parent, admiration from others, and job security), and societal goals (working for the environment and for justice, contributing to the common good, political engagement, prestige, power) (Grob et al., 1995), and to reflect intrinsic and extrinsic motivations (Kasser & Ryan, 1993). However, the assumed structure for goal importance and for perceived control over goals was not found in all subsamples.[3] As a consequence, data were analyzed at the item level, accepting lower reliabilities and considering that items may have evoked different interpretations in subgroups. For didactic reasons, however, we maintained the previously mentioned categorization of self-focused, interpersonal, and societal goals that reflects the different contents.

---

[3] To aggregate goal ratings and then compare groups at the scale level, it must be ensured that goals mean the same for all groups. An approach to similarity in meanings is to analyze the interrelationships between goals in different age groups (Bengtson, 1975; Homer, 1993). Confirmatory factor analyses failed to detect the assumed structure or any other structure that was consistent across the total sample, as well as the gender and cohort subsamples.

4.0. RESULTS

Results of the family analyses are reported first, followed by results of the cohort analyses. In each section, results concerning gender are addressed.

4.1. Family Effects

We assumed that family members resemble each other in terms of what they find important in their life and how much control they perceive over the attainment of those goals. To examine this resemblance, correlations were computed for each of the three dyads (i.e., grandchildren–parents, parents–grandparents, grandchildren–grandparents) for both goal importance and perceived control over goals. Only significant results are reported ($p < .05$).

4.1.1. *Goal Importance*
In the total sample, significant positive correlations were observed for the importance of eight goals in the younger-parent–child dyad and six goals in the older-parent–child dyad. These observed correlations were distributed differently in the younger- and the older-parent–child dyads. The importance of time for oneself ($r = .15$), self-acceptance ($r = .19$), fun ($r = .16$), admiration ($r = .26$), and job security ($r = .29$) covaried exclusively between middle-aged parents and grandchildren. The importance of working for a clean environment ($r = .18$), working for justice ($r = .21$), and engaging in politics ($r = .17$) covaried exclusively between grandparents and parents. Only the importance of health ($r = .26$ in the younger-parent–child dyad and $r = .16$ in the older-parent–child dyad), friendships ($r = .21$ and $r = .18$, respectively), and prestige ($r = .15$ and $r = .21$, respectively) covaried in both groups, suggesting a continuous transmission effect across three generations. Goals of grandparents and grandchildren were not related at all.

To compare the strength of the correlations between the different generation combinations, contrasts between correlation coefficients were tested for significance ($p < .05$). For all goals, parent–child correlations in the younger and in the older dyads were tested against each other and against grandparent–grandchild correlations, if at least one of the compared correlations was marginally significant ($p < .10$; 34 contrasts altogether). Eight of the contrasts reached significance. For job security, stronger correlations were found for the younger-parent–child dyad than for the older-parent–child dyad. Compared to the grandparent–grandchild dyad, correlations in the younger-parent–child dyad were stronger for the importance of self-acceptance, financial success, friendships, admiration, and job security; correlations in the older-parent–child dyad were stronger for the importance of justice and prestige.

Regarding family members' gender, correlations in terms of goal importance between mothers and children were expected to be stronger than correlations between fathers and children, and correlations between parents and same-gender children were expected to be stronger than correlations between parents and opposite-gender children. Analyses indicated significant positive correlations in terms of goal importance mainly in the mother–child dyad, especially in the younger-mother–child dyad and with daughters. Between both grandmothers and mothers and mothers and young-adult daughters, the importance of challenging experiences ($r = .18$ and $r = .28$ in the younger- and older-mother–child dyads, respectively), health ($r = .30$ and $r = .20$, respectively), and friendships ($r = .24$ and $r = .26$, respectively) covaried, suggesting a continuous transmission effect. Only between middle-aged mothers and their daughters did the importance of fun ($r = .22$), admiration ($r = .25$), and job security ($r = .32$) covary significantly, and only between grandmothers and mothers was the importance of working for justice ($r = .18$) and prestige ($r = .34$) related. Grandmothers and granddaughters resembled each other in terms of the importance of finding time for oneself ($r = .19$). Family correlations in terms of goal importance among men were related to work and societal life, but no significant correlation occurred in either the younger- or the older-father–son dyad. Significant positive correlations existed between middle-aged fathers and their sons for the importance of job security ($r = .52$) and admiration ($r = .48$) and between grandfathers and fathers for the importance of a satisfactory work life ($r = .39$) and working for justice ($r = .57$). It was also in the male dyads in which a striking negative correlation was found – namely, for the importance of political engagement between middle-aged fathers and sons ($r = -.40$). Cross-gender family correlations were observed between mothers and sons for the importance of self-acceptance ($r = .50$), fun ($r = .40$), engagement in politics ($r = .53$, younger dyad), and health ($r = .34$, older dyad) and between fathers and adolescent daughters for the importance of health ($r = .45$) and admiration ($r = .47$).

To compare the strength of the relationships between the different gender combinations, contrasts between correlation coefficients were tested for significance ($p < .05$). Mother–child correlations were compared to father–child correlations, mother–daughter correlations were compared to mother–son correlations, and father–daughter correlations were compared to father–son correlations. Comparisons were made in both the younger- and the older-parent–child dyads. Again, comparisons were made only in cases in which at least one of the compared correlations was marginally significant ($p < .10$). Altogether, 56 contrasts resulted; 10 were significant, but only 6 of the significant contrasts were in the expected direction, with higher coefficients in same-gender pairs, in female pairs, and between mothers and children than between fathers and children.

Also, we assumed that grandparent–grandchild similarities would be more likely in females than in males. One significant positive correlation between grandmothers and granddaughters occurred for the importance of time for oneself ($r = .19$), and one significant negative correlation between grandfathers and grandsons occurred for the importance of admiration ($r = -.33$). None of the other correlations reached significance, and none of the contrasts between the correlations was significant.

In summary, we found correlations in terms of goal importance between family members but only for some goals and mainly in dyads with females. In most of the goals, however, the *strength* of the relationships did not differ in the assumed direction as a function of gender.

4.1.2. *Perceived Control over Goal Attainment*

In the total sample, overall perceived control was related in younger-parent–child dyads ($r = .18$) and older-parent–child dyads ($r = .14$) but not in the grandparent–grandchild dyad. Regarding goal-specific perceived control, significant positive correlations were found for four goals in the younger-parent–child dyads and for five goals in the older-parent–child dyads. Perceived control over a satisfactory work life was the only one that covaried both between grandparents and parents ($r = .18$) and between parents and children ($r = .15$), suggesting a continuous transmission across three generations. In addition, between middle-aged parents and their young-adult children, perceived control over health ($r = .18$), an intimate relationship ($r = .13$), a satisfactory work life ($r = .15$), and political engagement ($r = .20$) covaried. Between grandparents and parents, significant correlations were found for perceived control over financial success ($r = .16$), friendships ($r = .17$), a satisfactory work life ($r = .13$), and prestige ($r = .17$). Again, no correlations occurred between grandparents and grandchildren.

Contrasts between correlation coefficients indicated few significant differences between younger- and older-parent–child dyads and grandparent–grandchild dyads (5 of 29 contrasts were significant). Correlations in perceived control over power were stronger in older-parent–child dyads than in younger-parent–child dyads. Also, correlations in perceived control over a satisfactory work life and politics were stronger in parent–child dyads than in grandparent–grandchild dyads, whereas the reverse was the case for perceived control over contributing to the common good. It is noteworthy that no significant differences were found between family correlations in overall perceived control.

Considering gender, the most correlations were observed in mothers and daughters, especially in the older dyad. Mothers' and daughters' perceived control over an intimate relationship and a satisfactory work life were consistently positively related across generations ($r = .27$ and $r = .19$ in the older- and the younger-parent–child dyads, respectively). Only between middle-aged mothers and their daughters was perceived control over political engagement positively related ($r = .35$), and only between grandmothers and mothers did perceived control over time for oneself ($r = .21$), challenging experiences ($r = .22$), close friendships ($r = .28$), and contributing to the common good ($r = .21$) covary. A negative correlation was found between middle-aged mothers and their daughters with respect to perceived control over power ($r = -.21$). The only significant correlation between men occurred for perceived control over health ($r = .52$, father–young-adult son). Cross-gender correlations were found only between grandfathers and mothers for perceived control over a satisfactory work life ($r = .51$) and fun ($r = .39$) but not between mothers and sons and not in the younger-parent–child dyad. The strength of the correlations in perceived control did not differ by gender (11 of 44 contrasts reached significance) in either grandparent–grandchild or parent–child dyads.

Summarizing results of the within-family analyses we observed that, in general, similarities in goal importance and perceived control over goals existed across only two generations and only for some goals. The picture becomes more complex when considering gender. For both goal dimensions, the most significant relationships occurred between females, but the strength of the relationships did not differ by gender.

4.2. Cohort Differences

4.2.1. *Goal Importance*

To examine whether members of different cohorts and genders differ in their goals, mean-level comparisons among the children, parent, and grandparent groups were computed for the 18 goals. We looked first at the strictest test in multivariate analyses of variance across all goals with the cohort and gender factors. Then, we computed univariate analyses of variance for each goal. Those effects that were not significant at the multivariate level were not interpreted at the univariate level. All mean-level analyses and post hoc tests were computed at the 1% level of significance. In addition, we controlled for educational background.

The mean goal importance by cohort is illustrated in Figure 15.1. Goals are listed according to their mean importance in the total sample. Being a good parent was rated as most important in the total sample, followed by a satisfactory work life and self-acceptance. Close friendships, job security, and an intimate relationship also ranked highly. With the exception of self-acceptance, these goals evolved around the themes of close interpersonal relationships and work life. Self-focused goals such as health, fun, time for oneself, and challenging experiences were located in the middle of the hierarchy of importance, whereas societal and more extrinsic goals such as prestige, power, admiration, and political engagement ranked lowest. The pattern was different in the three cohorts. Young adults rated a satisfactory work life highest, followed by close friendships and being a good parent. Fun, self-acceptance, and an intimate relationship ranked next, whereas societal goals were among those with the lowest importance. Middle-aged adults emphasized the goals of being a good parent, a satisfactory work life, and an intimate relationship the highest. Self-acceptance, job security, and health were also of higher importance. Extrinsic goals like

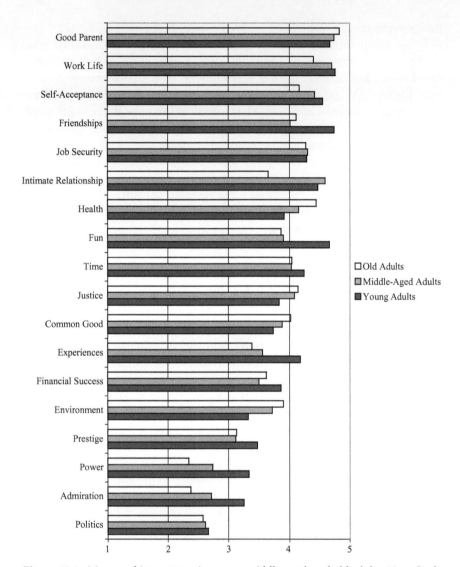

Figure 15.1. Mean goal importance in young, middle-aged, and old adults. *Note:* Goals are listed according to importance in the total sample. Goal-item formulations are abbreviated (see Appendix). 1 = not at all important; 2 = not very important; 3 = somewhat important; 4 = important; 5 = very important.

admiration by others and goals from the societal domain were less important in this group. Older adults attributed most importance to being a good parent, health, and a satisfactory work life; job security, self-acceptance, and working for justice were also important to them. Again, admiration by others and societal goals were among the least valued goals. Rank-order correlations between the goal hierarchies of the groups were $r = .87$ ($p < .001$) for older and middle-aged adults, $r = .80$ ($p < .01$) for middle-aged and young adults, and $r = .67$ ($p < .01$) for older and young adults. To conclude, the goal hierarchies of the three cohorts in our study were quite similar to one another. Relationships with other people and goals from the domain of work were most important in our participants' life.

In absolute terms, young-adult children were expected to rate self-focused goals as more important than middle-aged parents and old grandparents, and grandparents were expected to find societal goals more important than the other two groups. Gender differences were also expected. We found significant main effects for cohort ($F(2, 673) = 15.38$, $p < .001$), gender ($F(1, 673) = 7.54$, $p < .001$), and significant Cohort X Gender interaction ($F(2, 673) = 2.57$, $p < .001$) in the multivariate analysis. At the univariate level, the interaction effect was significant for the importance of time for oneself, self-acceptance, close friendships, an intimate relationship, and working for justice, accounting for a maximum of 3% of the variance. Post hoc analyses revealed that time for oneself was more important for middle-aged women than middle-aged men, whereas in the youngest and oldest cohorts, no gender differences occurred. This goal was more important for young than for old women, whereas among men, cohort differences were not observed. Self-acceptance was more important for women than for men in the two younger cohorts; however, again in the oldest cohort, gender differences did not occur. Among women, it was more important for the young and middle-aged than for the old, and again no cohort differences occurred among men. Middle-aged women valued close friendships more than middle-aged men, whereas no gender differences were observed in the youngest and in the oldest cohorts. Among both women and men, this goal was more important for the youngest cohort than for the middle and old cohorts, with a higher mean difference for men. Concerning the importance of an intimate relationship, all subsamples scored higher than the group of grandmothers. Young and middle-aged women valued this goal higher than old women, whereas no cohort differences occurred among men. Working for justice was valued higher by old men than by young men, whereas no cohort differences were observed among women. In those cases in which the interaction effect was significant, we did not interpret significant main effects of cohort and gender. Simple main effects are addressed in the next section.

Gender effects (without an interaction Cohort X Gender) were observed in 5 of the 18 goals. Health and being a good parent were more important for women than for men, whereas financial success, political engagement, and power were more important for men than for women. Each gender effect accounted for a maximum of 3% of the variance.

Cohort differences occurred in 10 of the 18 goals. A linear cohort effect was found for the importance of admiration and power, which were valued most by the young, less by the middle-aged, and least by the old adults. A linear-age effect also occurred for the importance of health, which was valued most by the old, less by the middle-aged, and least by the young adults. Young adults valued challenging experiences, fun, and prestige more than middle-aged and old adults and financial success more than middle-aged adults. Thus, four of the five extrinsic goals were valued more by young adults than by middle-aged and old adults. Young adults rated working for a clean environment as less important than middle-aged and old adults and contributing to the common good less than old adults. Old adults rated a satisfactory work life lower than middle-aged and young adults.[4]

In summary, the results show that the goals people find important in their life reflect the developmental tasks of the corresponding age and gender group. Goals from the traditional female-gender-role domain were more important for women, whereas goals from the traditional male-gender-role domain were more important for men. Young adults valued self-focused goals and extrinsic goals more than middle-aged and old adults. An exception to this pattern was health, which was valued most by old adults. In addition, old adults valued societal goals more than middle-aged and young adults.

4.2.2. *Perceived Control over Goal Attainment*

Cohort means of perceived control over goals are illustrated in Figure 15.2, in which goals are listed according to perceived control in the total sample. Participants perceived most control over being a good parent, followed by good physical health and self-acceptance. Friendships, an intimate relationship, and fun also ranked highly in perceived control, whereas societal goals ranked lowest. This hierarchy of perceived control over goals differed between the cohorts.

Young adults perceived most control over being a good parent, health, and fun, and least control over working for justice, admiration by others, job security, and working for a clean environment. Among middle-aged adults, being a good parent, an intimate relationship, and self-acceptance ranked highest in perceived control, whereas being an important member of society, admiration by others, and working for justice ranked lowest. Among old adults, perceived control was lower in general. Older adults perceived most control over being a good parent, health, and time for oneself and least control over power, political engagement, and admiration by others. Rank-order correlations between the perceived control hierarchies of the groups were $r = .83$ for old and middle-aged adults, $r = .85$ for middle-aged and young adults, and $r = .81$ for old and young adults (all $p < .001$). Thus, how much control people perceive over certain goals relative to other goals was similar across cohorts: Participants perceived more

---

[4] Because the age range of the middle-aged parent and the old grandparent group overlapped to some extent (29 parents and 20 grandparents are within the age range of 54 to 64), we conducted similar analyses by age instead of family generation membership. The sample was divided into seven age groups. These results pointed in the same direction as the cohort analyses. Controlling for education did not affect any of the results.

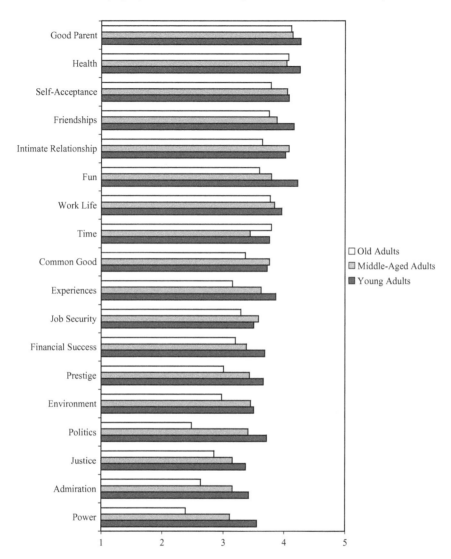

Figure 15.2. Mean perceived control about goals in young, middle-aged, and old adults. *Note:* Goals are listed according to perceived control in the total sample. Goal-item formulations are abbreviated (see Appendix). 1 = no control at all; 2 = a little control; 3 = some control; 4 = a lot of control; 5 = complete control.

control over personal and interpersonal goals than over societal goals or goals from the work domain.

Turning to the absolute level of perceived control over goal attainment, we expected young-adult children to perceive more control in general and more goal-specific control than middle-aged parents, who in turn were expected to perceive more control than old grandparents. Furthermore, we assumed that women would perceive more control over specific goals relating to the female-gender role than men, whereas the reverse would be the case for goals relating to the male-gender role. Regarding gender, we expected no differences in overall perceived control over goals. Interaction effects of Cohort X Gender occurred neither in the multivariate nor in the univariate analyses. At the multivariate level, the gender effect ($F(1, 673) = 4.73$, $p < .001$) and the cohort effect ($F(2, 673) = 8.65$, $p < .001$) were significant. At the univariate level, gender effects were found in goal-specific perceived control with respect to 4 of the 18 single goals but not in overall perceived control. Men perceived more control than women over financial success, job security, and prestige, whereas women perceived more control over health. Gender effects accounted for a maximum of 4% of the variance. Cohort effects occurred in overall perceived control, explaining 12% of the variance ($F(2, 926) = 62.90$; $\eta^2 = .12$). Overall perceived control was higher among young than among middle-aged adults, who in turn perceived more overall control over goals than old adults. Cohort effects were also found in goal-specific perceived control over 15 of the 18 single goals, accounting for up to 13% of the variance. Perceived control over challenging experiences, fun, health, admiration by others, working for justice and a clean environment, prestige, and power followed a linear age trend. Young adults perceived more control than middle-aged adults over all these goals, with the latter perceiving more control than old adults. Perceived control over the goals of time for oneself, financial success, and friendships was higher in young adults than in middle-aged and old adults. Finally, young and middle-aged adults perceived more control than old adults over self-acceptance, an intimate relationship, contributing to the common good, and political engagement. These results were confirmed in analyses by age and controlling for educational background. To summarize, the results show that perceived control over goals declined with age, irrespective of goal content. Also, men perceived more control than women over traditional male domains like work and power, whereas women perceived more control over health.

Judging from these analyses, members of three family generations differ in the importance of different life goals and the control they perceive over the attainment of those goals. The goals rated as important by young-adult children, middle-aged parents, and old grandparents reflected the developmental tasks of the corresponding age and gender group. Perceived control over goals declined across cohorts.

5.0. DISCUSSION

This study aimed at examining how similar family members of three generations are with respect to the importance attributed to life goals and the perceived control over those goals. In examining this question, we took two perspectives: First, we focused on how these two goal dimensions were related across generations; and second, we compared the two goal dimensions by generational status.

The results indicate intergenerational family similarity in importance and perceived control only for some life goals, only in the parent–child dyad, and mainly in dyads with females. The more parents rated health, friendship, and prestige as important to their life, the more their children valued those goals as important as well. Parents perceiving control over goals in general had children who also perceived control. At the level of different life domains, perceived control over a satisfactory work life was related between parents and children. Those relationships were found between both middle-aged parents and their young-adult children and between grandparents and middle-aged parents, pointing to a continuous transmission effect across generations. Also, patterns of similarity in the parent–child dyad were different according to gender, with more similarity among women and negative correlations only among men.

The findings on family resemblance in life goals are new in the literature. Previous research on values in the family has shown that similarities in what family members find important in their life differ remarkably according to the domain under study (Bengtson, 1975; Boehnke, 2001; Homer, 1993; Rohan & Zanna, 1996; Schönpflug, 2001). In one study on life goals in the family, mothers' goals for their children were related to children's own goals (Kasser et al., 1995). However, resemblance in family members' self-reported goal importance has not been examined to date. Although family effects in terms of general control expectancies were reported (Hoffmann & Levi-Shiff, 1994; Miller & Rose, 1982; Schneewind, 1989, 1995), the current research is the first to address perceived control over goals in the family, suggesting that family resemblance in perceived control varies between domains.

Furthermore, this is the first study to examine the resemblance of three family generations with regard to goals. Grandparents' and grandchildren's goal importance and perceived control over goals were unrelated in our study, supporting Bengtson's (1975) finding concerning values. Separating our sample by gender, we found one exception: The importance of time for oneself positively covaried between grandmothers and granddaughters, whereas no relationships occurred for perceived control. Overall perceived control over goals and perceived control over self-acceptance were related between grandmothers and granddaughters. Also, age of parents and children made a difference with respect to the patterns of similarity. Only in the younger-parent–child dyad were family similarities observed for the importance of time for oneself, self-acceptance, fun, admiration by others, and job security; only in the older-parent–child dyad were family similarities found for the importance of political engagement and working for a clean environment and for justice. Thus, among older participants, we found primarily the importance of societal life goals to be associated between family generations, whereas relationships among younger participants evolve around more self-focused topics. From a developmental perspective, one may view these findings as a function of age and various transitions that influence goal-setting. However, neither age of parent–child dyad nor gender moderated remarkably the strength of the correlations, which was contrary to our expectations. We cannot decide from our data whether this result emerged due to societal changes or, in the case of gender effects, due to unbalanced sample sizes.

When comparing the groups of grandparents, parents, and children at the mean level, we detected that the goals of our participants reflected the developmental tasks of the corresponding age groups. Goals from the self-focused domain were more important for the youngest cohort, and societal goals were more important for the oldest cohort than for the other two cohorts. Extrinsic goals like financial success, admiration, and prestige were perceived as being under greater personal control among members of the youngest cohort, adding to previous results on age differences (Cross & Markus, 1991; Grob et al., 1999; Heckhausen, 1997; Nurmi et al., 1992). In addition, societal gender-role expectations were reflected in goal importance and perceived control. Women scored higher than men in goals relating to traditional female topics such as health, understanding oneself, and parenthood. Men attributed more importance than women to domains that are still male-dominated such as work, power, and financial success. In addition to suggesting that people choose goals relating to developmental tasks, this may mean that goals change across the life span as a result of the degree to which their attainment leads to appreciation in society.

Salient themes of adolescents and young adults and their parents include creating a life of one's own in terms of lifestyle, relationships with peers, and financial independence, as well as in terms of issues relating to work and leisure time. At this point of the family life cycle, these preoccupations manifest themselves in everyday life patterns and in parent–child interactions. Because young adults and their parents often continue living together or stay in close contact, the everyday tangibility of self-focused goals might explain the domain-specific relationships found. In contrast, discourse between middle-aged parents and their old-aged parents may include different topics. Older people and middle-aged parents have settled and seek contact with one another more deliberately – at least in the case of our participants who were not in need of care. Their exchange may rather be about self-transcendent topics such as societal development so that reciprocal influences in goals are more likely to occur in this domain. However, this explanation draws heavily on the assumption that the more family members exchange, the more they resemble each other. In fact, the reverse may be the case.

Family resemblance in perceived control did not follow this pattern characterized by an emphasis on self-focused topics in the younger dyads and on societal topics in the older dyads. In addition, cohort analyses showed a strong linear age trend. Perceived control over goals declined from cohort to cohort, supporting a well-established finding in developmental psychology (Cross & Markus, 1991; Grob et al., 1999; Heckhausen, 1997; Nurmi et al., 1992), but goals did not follow this trend to the same degree. This means that whereas people maintain important strivings, they do not perceive control over their attainment. Implications of such dynamics for how people encounter the world and how happy they feel are well documented (Brunstein, 1993, 1999; Lang & Heckhausen, 2001).

Thus far, we have discussed our findings in the context of developmental psychology; an alternative interpretation is that they reflect societal changes. Historical processes, especially those experienced before age 25, are thought to leave their mark on how people plan their future (Mannheim, 1928/1929). The middle- and old-aged participants in our study spent their youth in times of radical societal changes, marked by clear political opponents and national alliances. At the level of the individual, the life course was also quite clear because the order and the time points of future transitions were relatively fixed. Therefore, societal topics attracted more attention because of their fundamentality, whereas personal life decisions were given less space. Adolescents and young adults in Western society today, in contrast, grew up in quiet times and experienced freedom in nearly all aspects of life. They saw the opening of former Eastern Bloc countries. Society has provided fewer guidelines for the personal aspects of life, whether occupational choices or leisure activities, referred to as the "destandardization" of the life cycle (Kohli, 1985, p. 22). Bengtson's (1975) finding of stronger family effects in the younger-parent–child dyad than in the older-parent–child dyad for individualistic values (i.e., exciting life, personal freedom, true friendship, and achievement) in the 1970s may suggest that societal changes toward individualization were already present at that time. Because freedom of choice may be experienced as a lack of orientation and as an excessive demand, children might orient toward their parents, who have already found their position in society. In the reverse direction, societal pressures of being up-to-date and rapid changes in technology and the leisure market provide an argument for parents to search for guidelines in their children, who are best informed about recent lifestyle trends. It is a matter for future research to examine which role developmental and societal factors play in family resemblance in terms of goals.

In this study, family similarities were observed only for some goals, and the amount of shared variance in life goals among members of different family generations was small. These findings might be interpreted as evidence that, in general, parents' goals have only few implications for children's goals and vice versa. Alternatively, they might mean that children deliberately decide to strive for different goals than their family members – in order to master the process of individuation by emulating parents in some domains of life while doing differently in others. Finally, several factors might moderate family resemblance in goals. Family effects might be quite strong in some families and very weak in others. We subscribe to this latter interpretation in proposing that the picture is more sophisticated: Theories on transgenerational processes suggest transmission belts such as parenting, relationship quality, homogeneity in significant others' values, as well as socioeconomic conditions, family structure, education, and working conditions (Schönpflug, 2001). These variables vary among families (Amato & Keith, 1991a, 1991b; Elder et al., 1993; Larson et al., 1998; Smith, 1995), explaining the low transmission effects in our study. Hence, the question arises of whether there are families in which (grand)parents represent ideal models to be emulated by younger family generations and what the characteristics of those model parents are. We claimed that model people might also be people to set oneself off against, providing a frame of reference for one's own life without emulating them. In addition, relationship quality might moderate family resemblance. One hypothesis is that people who describe their relationship as closer are more similar to each other in terms of what they value. However, the reverse hypothesis also seems tenable: Perhaps a close relationship allows for the tolerance of family differences (Goodnow, 1994). Which of these factors specifically play a role in transgenerational (dis)similarities is open to future research.

Among the strengths of the study was the family design. Information about families varies according to the source of information for the domain under study (Clarke, Preston, Raksin, & Bengtson, 1999; Landry & Martin, 1988; Levitt et al., 1992). Nevertheless, some studies include members of one family generation as informants who answer for the others. In our study, participants from three family generations self-reported their life goals, giving us confidence that we assessed what persons subjectively hold dear in their life.

Despite these strengths, the study is limited by the skewed sample composition in favor of the women. With current life expectancy, children will grow up with grandparents but lose their grandfathers when they are in adolescence and lose their grandmothers when they are young adults (Rossi & Rossi, 1990). This lineage pattern manifests itself in the composition of three-generational samples. The small sample sizes in families with men may provide an explanation for the few family relationships we found in dyads with men. Note that some correlations in those families were quite strong but did not reach significance due to sample size. Following today's adolescents and their parents into the future when they have children and grandchildren appears to be a promising avenue. This will allow us to delve further into transgenerational processes not only in women, like in many three-generational studies in psychology (Levitt et al., 1992; Roscoe & Peterson, 1989), but also in men. Another caveat is the question of whether members of different cohorts attribute the same meaning to the goal formulations. Our data did not fit to structural invariance across the different subsamples such that we deemed analysis on the item level to be more appropriate. However, given the fact that single items are less reliable than disattenuated-scale information, the consistent intrafamilial and across-age findings are impressive. This argumentation has a phenomenological correspondence in the long-term trajectories of life goals, which are dynamic aspects of personality that change with transitions in the life course (Salmela-Aro et al., 2000) and are subject to historical and societal forces (Bangerter et al., 2001). The correlational character of the study obstructs the disentangling of aging-related effects from effects relating to cohort phenomena as well as causal interpretations. Hopefully, future research will address these issues by using longitudinal designs.

In dealing with transgenerational resemblance, the first step is to identify psychological domains in which family similarities and differences are assumed and to describe them carefully. As a next step, the question then arises of which factors pull the outcomes of transgenerational processes in a specific direction and with which consequences. Using an innovative design, this study was a first attempt to chart the relationship between life goals of members of three family generations. Perhaps the most important lesson to be learned from this study is that we can detect similarities in terms of correlations in goals between middle-aged parents and their young-adult children as well as between old-aged parents and their middle-aged children. In accordance with previous research, life goals were age-related and could be portrayed across the life span. A historical perspective on life goals requires that we regard goal importance and perceived control over goals as well as family relationships in those dimensions in the light of societal changes, possibly contributing to fewer resemblance differences and fewer gender differences in resemblance but to more absolute cohort differences. Finally, in what respect the intrafamilial and intergenerational resemblance varies between and within nations and cultures represents the next challenging question.

REFERENCES

Amato, P. R., & Keith, B. (1991a). Parental divorce and the well-being of children: A meta-analysis. *Psychological Bulletin, 110,* 26–46.

Amato, P. R., & Keith, B. (1991b). Parental divorce and adult well-being: A meta-analysis. *Journal of Marriage and the Family, 53,* 43–58.

Austin, J. T., & Vancouver, J. B. (1996). Goal constructs in psychology: Structure, process, and content. *Psychological Bulletin, 120,* 338–375.

Bandura, A. (1986). *Social foundations of thought and action: A social cognitive theory.* Upper Saddle River, NJ: Prentice-Hall.

Bangerter, A., Grob, A., & Krings, F. (2001). Personal goals at age 25 in three generations of the twentieth century: Young adulthood in historical context. *Swiss Journal of Psychology, 60,* 59–64.

Bengtson, V. L. (1975). Generation and family effects in value socialization. *American Sociological Review, 40,* 358–371.

Bengtson, V. L. (1996). Continuities and discontinuities in intergenerational relationships over time. In V. L. Bengtson (Ed.), *Adulthood and aging: Research on continuities and discontinuities* (pp. 271–303). New York: Springer.

Bengtson, V. L. (2001). Beyond the nuclear family: The increasing importance of multi-generational bonds. *Journal of Marriage and the Family, 63,* 1–13.

Boehnke, K. (2001). Parent–offspring value transmission in a societal context. Suggestions for a Utopian research design – with empirical underpinnings. *Journal of Cross-Cultural Psychology, 32,* 241–255.

Bowlby, J. (1969). *Attachment and loss: Vol. 1, Attachment.* New York: Basic Books.

Bretherton, I. (1985). Attachment theory: Retrospect and prospect. *Monographs of the Society for Research in Child Development, 50*, 3–35.

Bretherton, I., Golby, B., & Cho, E. (1997). Attachment and the transmission of values. In J. E. Grusec & L. Kuczinsky (Eds.), *Parenting and children's internalization of values: A handbook of contemporary theory* (pp. 103–134). New York: Wiley.

Brunstein, J. (1993). Personal goals and subjective well-being: A longitudinal study. *Journal of Personality and Social Psychology, 65*, 1061–1070.

Brunstein, J. C. (1999). Persoenliche Ziele und subjektives Wohlbefinden bei aelteren Menschen [Personal goals and subjective well-being among older adults]. *Zeitschrift fuer Differentielle und Diagnostische Psychologie, 20*, 58–71.

Carver, C. S., & Scheier, M. F. (1990). Origins and functions of positive and negative affect: A control-process view. *Psychological Review, 97*, 19–35.

Cavalli-Sforza, L. L. (1993). How are values transmitted? In M. Hechter, L. Nadel, & R. E. Michod (Eds.), *The origin of values* (pp. 305–317). New York: de Gruyter.

Clarke, E. J., Preston, M., Raksin, J., & Bengtson, V. L. (1999). Types of conflicts and tensions between older parents and adult children. *The Gerontologist, 39*, 261–270.

Constantine, L. L. (1993). The structure of family paradigms: An analytical model of family variation. *Journal of Marital and Family Therapy, 19*, 39–70.

Cross, S., & Markus, H. (1991). Possible selves across the life span. *Human Development, 34*, 230–255.

Deci, E. L., & Ryan, R. M. (1985). *Intrinsic motivation and self-determination in human behavior*. New York: Plenum.

Eisenberg, A. R. (1988). Grandchildren's perspectives on relationships with grandparents: The influence of gender across generations. *Sex Roles, 19*, 205–217.

Elder, G. H., Jr., Robertson, E. B., & Conger, R. D. (1993). Tradierung einer Lebensweise: Vom Grossvater zum Vater und Sohn im laendlichen Amerika [Transmission of lifestyle: From grandfather to father and son in rural America]. In K. Lüscher & F. Schultheis (Eds.), *Generationenbeziehungen in "postmodernen" Gesellschaften [Intergenerational relationships in "postmodern" societies]* (pp. 125–142). Konstanz, Germany: Universitaetsverlag.

Emmons, R. A. (1989). The personal striving approach to personality. In L. A. Pervin (Ed.), *Goal concepts in personality and social psychology* (pp. 87–126). Hillsdale, NJ: Erlbaum.

Erikson, E. H. (1959). Identity and the life cycle. *Psychological Issues, 1*, 1–171.

Fingerman, K. L. (1995). Aging mothers' and their adult daughters' perceptions of conflict behaviors. *Psychology and Aging, 10*, 639–649.

Franks, L. J., Hughes, J. P., Phelps, L. H., & Williams, D. G. (1993). Intergenerational influences on Midwest college students by their grandparents and significant elders. *Educational Gerontology, 19*, 265–271.

Gatz, M., & Karel, M. J. (1993). Individual change in perceived control over 20 years. *International Journal of Behavioral Development, 16*, 305–322.

Goodnow, J. J. (1994). Acceptable disagreement across generations. In J. G. Smetana (Ed.), *Beliefs about parenting: Origins and developmental implications* (pp. 51–64). San Francisco: Jossey-Bass.

Greene, A. L., & Wheatley, S. M. (1992). "I've got a lot to do and I don't think I'll have the time": Gender differences in late adolescents' narratives of the future. *Journal of Youth and Adolescence, 21*, 667–686.

Grob, A., & Flammer, A. (1999). Macrosocial context and adolescents' perceived control. In F. D. Alsaker & A. Flammer (Eds.), *The adolescent experience: European and American adolescents in the 1990s. Research monographs in adolescence* (pp. 99–113). Mahwah, NJ: Erlbaum.

Grob, A., Flammer, A., & Wearing, A. J. (1995). Adolescents' perceived control: Domain specificity, expectancy, and appraisal. *Journal of Adolescence, 18*, 403–425.

Grob, A., Little, T. D., & Wanner, B. (1999). Control judgments across the life span. *International Journal of Behavioral Development, 23*, 833–854.

Grob, A., Little, T. D., Wanner, B., Wearing, A. J., & Euronet (1996). Adolescents' well-being and perceived control across fourteen sociocultural contexts. *Journal of Personality and Social Psychology, 71*, 785–795.

Grolnick, W. S., Deci, E. L., & Ryan, R. M. (1997). Internalization within the family: The self-determination theory perspective. In J. E. Grusec & L. Kuczinsky (Eds.), *Parenting and children's internalization of values: A handbook of contemporary theory* (pp. 135–161). New York: Wiley.

Grusec, J. E., & Goodnow, J. J. (1994). Impact of parental discipline methods on the child's internalization of values: A reconceptualization of current points of view. *Developmental Psychology, 30*, 4–19.

Grusec, J. E., Rudy, D., & Martini, T. (1997). Parenting cognitions and child outcomes: An overview and implications for children's internalization of values. In J. E. Grusec & L. Kuczinsky (Eds.), *Parenting and children's internalization of values: A handbook of contemporary theory* (pp. 259–282). New York: Wiley.

Hagestad, G. O. (1986). Dimensions of time and the family. *American Behavioral Scientist, 29*, 679–694.

Havighurst, R. J. (1948). *Developmental tasks and education.* New York: Longman.

Heckhausen, J. (1997). Developmental regulation across adulthood: Primary and secondary control of age-related challenges. *Developmental Psychology, 33*, 176–187.

Hoffman, M. A., & Levy-Shiff, R. (1994). Coping and locus of control: Cross-generational transmission between mothers and adolescents. *Journal of Early Adolescence, 14*, 391–405.

Homer, P. M. (1993). Transmission of human values: A cross-cultural investigation of generational and reciprocal influence effects. *Genetic, Social, and General Psychology Monographs, 119*, 345–367.

Iversen, R. R., & Farber, N. B. (1996). Transmission of family values, work, and welfare among poor urban Black women. *Work and Occupations, 23*, 437–460.

Kandel, D. B., & Lesser, G. S. (1969). Parental and peer influences on educational plans of adolescents. *American Sociological Review, 34*, 213–233.

Kasser, T., Koestner, R., & Lekes, N. (2002). Early family experiences and adult values: A 26-year, prospective longitudinal study. *Personality and Social Psychology Bulletin, 28*, 826–835.

Kasser, T., & Ryan, R. M. (1993). A dark side of the American dream: Correlates of financial success as a central life aspiration. *Journal of Personality and Social Psychology, 65*, 410–422.

Kasser, T., Ryan, R. M., Zax, M., & Sameroff, A. J. (1995). The relations of maternal and social environments to late adolescents' materialistic and prosocial values. *Developmental Psychology, 31*, 907–914.

Kerckhoff, A. C., & Huff, J. L. (1974). Parental influences on educational goals. *Sociometry, 37,* 307–327.

Kivnick, H. Q. (1985). Grandparenthood and mental health. Meaning, behavior, and satisfaction. In V. L. Bengtson & J. F. Robertson (Eds.), *Grandparenthood* (pp. 151–158). Thousand Oaks, CA: Sage Publications.

Kohli, M. (1985). Die Institutionalisierung des Lebenslaufs: Historische Befunde und theoretische Argumente [The institutionalization of life course: Historical findings and theoretical arguments]. *Koelner Zeitschrift fuer Soziologie und Sozialpsychologie, 37,* 1–29.

Kohn, M. L. (1983). On the transmission of values in the family: A preliminary formulation. *Research in the Sociology of Education and Socialization, 4,* 1–12.

Kohn, M. L., Slomczynski, K. M., & Schoenbach, C. (1986). Social stratification and the transmission of values in the family: A cross-national assessment. *Sociological Forum, 1,* 73–102.

Kopera-Frye, K., & Wiscott, R. (2000). Intergenerational continuity: Transmission of beliefs and culture. In B. J. Hayslip & R. Goldberg-Glen (Eds.), *Grandparents raising grandchildren: Theoretical, empirical, and clinical perspectives* (pp. 65–84). New York: Springer.

Landry, P. H. J., & Martin, M. E. (1988). Measuring intergenerational consensus. In D. J. Mangen & V. L. Bengtson (Eds.), *Measurement of intergenerational relations* (pp. 126–155). Thousand Oaks, CA: Sage Publications.

Lang, F. R., & Heckhausen, J. (2001). Perceived control over development and subjective well-being: Differential benefits across adulthood. *Journal of Personality and Social Psychology, 81,* 509–523.

Larson, J. H., Benson, M. J., Wilson, S. M., & Medora, N. (1998). Family of origin influences on marital attitudes and readiness for marriage in late adolescents. *Journal of Family Issues, 19,* 750–768.

Lerner, R. M. (1993). The influence of child temperamental characteristics on parent behaviors. In T. Luster & L. Okagaki (Eds.), *Parenting: An ecological perspective* (pp. 101–120). Hillsdale, NJ: Erlbaum.

Lerner, R. M., & Kauffman, M. B. (1985). The concept of development in contextualism. *Developmental Review, 5,* 309–333.

Levitt, M. J., Guacci, N., & Weber, R. A. (1992). Intergenerational support, relationship quality, and well-being. *Journal of Family Issues, 13,* 465–481.

Mannheim, K. (1928/1929). Das Problem der Generationen [The problem of generations]. *Koelner Vierteljahreshefte Soziologie, 7,* 157–330.

Martin, P., & Olson, S. (1996). Die Uebertragung von Interaktionsmustern zwischen Generationen [The transfer of interaction patterns between generations]. In W. Edelstein, K. Kreppner, & D. Sturzbecher (Eds.), *Familie und Kindheit im Wandel [Changes in family and childhood]* (pp. 287–295). Potsdam, Germany: Verlag fuer Berlin-Brandenburg.

Michod, R. E. (1993). Biology and the origin of values. In M. Hechter, L. Nadel, & R. E. Michod (Eds.), *The origin of values* (pp. 261–271). New York: de Gruyter.

Miller, J. Z., & Rose, R. J. (1982). Familial resemblance in locus of control: A twin-family study of the internal–external scale. *Journal of Personality and Social Psychology, 42,* 535–540.

Neugarten, B. L., & Weinstein, K. K. (1964). The changing American grandparent. *Journal of Marriage and the Family, 26,* 199–204.

Novacek, J., & Lazarus, R. S. (1990). The structure of personal commitments. *Journal of Personality, 58,* 693–715.

Nurmi, J.- E. (1989). Development of orientation to the future during early adolescence: A four-year longitudinal study and two cross-sectional comparisons. *International Journal of Psychology, 24,* 195–214.

Nurmi, J. E. (1992). Age differences in adult life goals, concerns, and their temporal extension: A life course approach to future-oriented motivation. *International Journal of Behavioral Development, 15,* 487–508.

Nurmi, J. E., Pulliainen, H., & Salmela-Aro, K. (1992). Age differences and adults' control beliefs related to life goals and concerns. *Psychology and Aging, 7,* 194–196.

Okagaki, L., & Bevis, C. (1999). Transmission of religious values: Relations between parents' and daughters' beliefs. *The Journal of Genetic Psychology, 160,* 303–318.

Page, M. H., & Washington, N. D. (1997). Family proverbs and value transmission in single Black mothers. *Journal of Social Psychology, 127,* 49–58.

Pervin, L. A. (1983). The stasis and flow of behavior: Toward a theory of goals. In M. M. Page (Ed.), *Nebraska symposium on motivation* (pp. 1–53). Lincoln, NE: University of Nebraska Press.

Plomin, R., & Daniels, D. (1987). Why are children in the same family so different from one another? *Behavioral and Brain Sciences, 10,* 1–16.

Rodriguez, N., Ramirez, III, M., & Korman, M. (1999). The transmission of family values across generations of Mexican, Mexican American, and Anglo American Families: Implications for mental health. In R. H. Sheets & E. R. Hollins (Eds.), *Racial and ethnic identity in school practices: Aspects of human development* (pp. 141–155). Mahwah, NJ: Erlbaum.

Rohan, M. J., & Zanna, M. P. (1996). Value transmission in families. In C. Seligman & J. M. Olson (Eds.), *The psychology of values: The Ontario symposium, Vol. 8. The Ontario symposium on personality and social psychology* (pp. 253–274). Mahwah, NJ: Erlbaum.

Roscoe, B., & Peterson, K. L. (1989). Age-appropriate behaviors: A comparison of three generations of females. *Adolescence, 24,* 167–178.

Rossi, A. S., & Rossi, P. H. (1990). *Of human bonding: Parent–child relations across the life course.* New York: de Gruyter.

Rowe, D. C. (1997). Genetics, temperament, and personality. In R. Hogan, J. Johnson, & S. Briggs (Eds.), *Handbook of personality psychology* (pp. 367–386). New York: Academic Press.

Salmela-Aro, K., Nurmi, J.-E., Saisto, T., & Halmesmäki, E. (2000). Women's and men's personal goals during the transition to parenthood. *Journal of Family Psychology, 14,* 171–186.

Samuel, R., & Thompson, P. (1990). *The myths we live by.* Florence: Taylor and Francis/Routledge.

Schneewind, K. A. (1999). *Familienpsychologie [Family psychology]* (Vol. 2., rev. ed.). Stuttgart: Kohlhammer.

Schneewind, K. A. (1989). Eindimensionale Erfassung von Kontrollueberzeugungen bei Erwachsenen und Kindern: LOC-E und LOC-K [Unidimensional scales for assessing generalized control beliefs in adults and children: LOC-E and LOC-K]. In

G. Krampen (Ed.), *Diagnostik von Attributionen und Kontrollüberzeugungen [Diagnostics of attributions and locus of control]* (pp. 80–92). Goettingen, Germany: Hogrefe.

Schneewind, K. (1995). Impact of family processes on control beliefs. In A. Bandura. (Ed.), *Self-efficacy in changing societies* (pp. 114–147). Cambridge: University Press.

Schneewind, K. A. (1999). *Familienpsychologie [Family psychology]* (Vol. 2, rev. ed.). Stuttgart, Germany: Kohlhammer.

Schönpflug, U. (2001). Intergenerational transmission of values. The role of transmission belts. *Journal of Cross-Cultural Psychology, 32*, 174–185.

Schwartz, S. H., Sagiv, L., & Boehnke, K. (2000). Worries and values. *Journal of Personality, 68*, 309–346.

Smith, P. K. (1995). Grandparenthood. In M. H. Bornstein (Ed.), *Handbook of parenting, Vol. 3: Status and social conditions* (pp. 89–112). Mahwah, NJ: Erlbaum.

Smith, T. E. (1991). Agreement of adolescent educational expectations with perceived maternal and paternal educational goals. *Youth and Society, 23*, 155–174.

Stierlin, H. (1994). *Individuation und Familie [Individuation and family]*. Frankfurt am Main, Germany: Suhrkamp.

Strough, J., Berg, C. A., & Sansone, C. (1996). Goals for solving everyday problems across the life span: Age and gender differences in the salience of interpersonal concerns. *Developmental Psychology, 32*, 1106–1115.

Troll, L. E. (1996). Modified-extended families over time: Discontinuity in parts, continuity in wholes. In V. L. Bengtson (Ed.), *Adulthood and aging: Research on continuities and discontinuities* (pp. 246–268). New York: Springer.

Trusty, J., & Pirtle, T. (1998). Parents' transmission of educational goals to their adolescent children. *Journal of Research and Development in Education, 32*, 53–65.

Turkheimer, E., & Waldron, M. (2000). Nonshared environment: A theoretical, methodological, and quantitative review. *Psychological Bulletin, 126*, 78–108.

Valsiner, J. (1994). Culture and human development: A co-constructionist perspective. *Annals of Theoretical Psychology, 10*, 247–298.

Valsiner, J., Branco, A. U., & Dantas, C. M. (1997). Co-construction of human development: Heterogeneity within parental belief orientations. In J. E. Grusec & L. Kuczynski. (Eds.), *Parenting and children's internalization of values: A handbook of contemporary theory* (pp. 283–304). New York: Wiley.

Westholm, A. (1999). The perceptual pathway: Tracing the mechanisms of political value transfer across generations. *Political Psychology, 20*, 525–551.

Whitaker, C. A., & Keith, D. V. (1981). Symbolic-experiential family therapy. In A. S. Gurman & D. P. Kniskern (Eds.), *Handbook of family therapy* (pp. 187–224). New York: Brunner/Mazel.

Wickert, F. W., Lambert, F. B., Richardson, F. C., & Kahler, J. (1984). Categorical goal hierarchies and classification of human motives. *Journal of Personality, 52*, 285–305.

Wilson, P. M., & Wilson, J. R. (1992). Environmental influences on adolescent educational aspirations. *Youth and Society, 24*, 52–70.

Winkeler, M., Filipp, S.-H., & Boll, T. (2000). Positivity in the aged's perceptions of intergenerational relationships: A "stake" or "leniency" effect? *International Journal of Behavioral Development, 24*, 173–182.

Appendix. *Life goal formulations presented in the questionnaire*

Goal Content	Item	Abbreviation
Self-Focused	To find time for yourself	Time
	To have challenging experiences	Experiences
	To understand and accept yourself	Self-acceptance
	To have fun	Fun
	To have good physical health	Health
	To attain financial success	Financial success
Interpersonal	To experience close friendships	Friendships
	To have a meaningful intimate relationship with someone	Intimate relationship
	To have a satisfactory work life	Work life
	To be a good mother or father	Good parent
	To be admired by others	Admiration
	To have job security	Job security
Societal	To work for a clean environment	Environment
	To contribute to the common good	Common good
	To engage in politics	Politics
	To work for justice in society	Justice
	To be famous	Prestige
	To be an important member of the community or society	Power

16

The Intergenerational Transmission of Xenophobia and Rightism in East Germany

BERND SIX, KRISTINA GEPPERT, AND UTE SCHÖNPFLUG

INTRODUCTION

The functional analysis of social processes reveals the importance of controlled transmission of the ideological patterns of a society. The stability of a society depends to a considerable extent on the structure of a social ideology (Six, 2002, p. 74), if ideology is understood as a system of social beliefs and orientations that exist as a frame of reference commonly accepted by a group or a society. Another premise is that an ideology includes patterns of interpretations for the explanation of social processes as well as a frame for evaluations that provides information regarding what is right or wrong, good or bad, but also provides rules that serve as standards for behavior in social contexts. Elements of such ideologies are values, norms, attitudes, prejudices, and stereotypes, which exist in numerous facets in various content areas. In his list of "isms," Saucier (2000) reports more than 500 different general value orientations – for example, authoritarianism, conservatism, Machiavellism, humanism, egalitarianism, ethnocentrism, racism, and liberalism. The concrete transformation of such general mental orientations into attitudes and prejudices results in a wide repertoire of social orientations that has to be controlled if the maintenance of a social system is to be guaranteed.

The intense interest in the maintenance of ruling social conditions may be illustrated by the strong reactions to threats to these conditions. The race riots in South Africa and the United States, the propagation of anti-authoritarian education, the change from materialistic to postmaterialistic value preferences, egalitarianism in gender relationships, or ecological protection programs have, in part, led to strong reactions from the leading elites. The processes of such conflict-ridden relationships between leading elites and minorities without privileges show that rarely may any party gain acceptance by the other. The result would be changes and shifts in the structure of such ideological systems. A similar mutual influence may be found in the established patterns of socialization in the family, school, and peer group, to name only the most important institutions for socializing the younger generation. In the introduction to his well-known hand-book of socialization, Goslin (1969, p. 5) pointed out that all persons involved in the socialization process are simultaneously "socializers" and "socializees." This bidirectional and reciprocal process guarantees the transmission of con-tents of socialization and is, at the same time, the basis of variations and changes resulting from this process of socialization. The primary socialization institu-tions tend to overrate their potential influence; this may be the reason why the socialization process has been conceived of as a learning process or, more specifically, a conditioned learning paradigm, in which given goals have to be achieved. Reciprocal or bidirectional models have not been easily accepted but seem to be a more adequate conceptualization than a unidirectional process.

1.0. XENOPHOBIA AND ITS TRANSMISSION

Explanations for the transmission of ethnocentrism, xenophobia, social prej-udices, and stereotypes do not usually go beyond a listing of socialization institutions (e.g., family, peer group, school, work, and media), the different disciplinary perspectives of sociocultural analyses (e.g., sociology, anthropol-ogy, and psychology), and the specification of established subdisciplines (e.g., microsociology, social psychology, and developmental psychology). If they then proceed to the slippery ground of providing explanations, the focus of investiga-tion is frequently on violent extreme rightist delinquents, neonationalistic youth groups, or racist delinquents. Their ideology is explained by their membership of violence-prone groups. At this time, young people have already acquired a relatively fixed pattern of discrimination against those who are not mem-bers of their in-group and who may therefore become potential targets of their violence-prone activities. To elaborate, in the following discussion we outline our reservations about the critical statement put forward by Willems (1992, p. 433), who concludes from the various explanatory approaches for violence motivated by xenophobia:

> Furthermore our explanations of violence and of the development of social move-ments are, on the one hand, too individualistic or macro sociological as far as they refer to features of individual actors or features of (social) movements; on the other hand, they are too macro-oriented, when they generally refer to conditions of soci-etal structure that may be the basis for victims of modernization and degradation and imply potentials for protest movements. Processes of interaction . . . and their conditions are frequently neglected, however.

We have to qualify our agreement with Willem because xenophobia develops at an earlier age than in adolescence, the time when it is usually measured. An adequate level of analysis might be achieved if interactional structures reflect-ing cognitive and emotional structural systems constitute the focus of research, not individual agents or global societal structures. One of the prototypical interaction systems is the family and another is the peer group. Hence, the inclusion of familial constellations protects our research from Willem's critique.

Kuczynski, Marshall, and Schell (1997) developed a bidirectional model of socialization, which has the advantage of including working models that correspond to the basic components of the socialization process. The working models constitute inherent dynamic components of the model: Parents as well as their children but also people or groups from the sociocultural context (e.g., siblings, peers, and media) process beliefs, values, attitudes, and motives in a specific way and develop specific working models that are responsible for the potential of dynamic changes in the socialization process. The internal processing of the contents of the working models is referred to as *internalization*, whereas the transformation of those contents into observable behaviors and social interactions is labeled *externalization*. The externalization processes of parents and children influence the parent–child interaction to equal extents, whereas the parent–child interaction itself impacts on the internalization of parents and children. Thus, the transmission of attitudes and values will be part of the interactions between parents and their children. Schönpflug (2001; Phalet & Schönpflug, 2001) specified this approach, indicating that cultural-context variables deserve more attention. The authors were also able to corroborate the relevance of their speculations in their research.

2.0. XENOPHOBIA AND VALUES: TWO CONCEPTS AND THEIR RELATIONSHIP

Providing a definition of the concept of *xenophobia* is difficult because it is frequently used in everyday language and, therefore, the meaning oscillates. Consequently, the meaning may overlap with the concept of "hostility towards foreigners," a concept that also has no strictly circumscribed meaning. Both concepts refer not to a general hostility toward strangers or foreigners but rather toward groups and individuals who are perceived as threatening. A person might have prejudices against Danes, Swedes, Englishmen, or Dutch people, but most likely there will be no general hostility toward persons or groups from those countries because they are not perceived as potentially threatening. The target groups of xenophobia differ not only in terms of the regional and national context but also in the international context. In Germany, xenophobia is directed toward foreigners from the states of the European Community, toward foreign workers, or employees from non–European Community countries, refugees, asylum seekers, and repatriates, who are German citizens by law but are looked at and evaluated as strangers. The categorization presented is usually not the one used by those who hold hostile attitudes toward strangers; instead, skin color, appearance, clothing, and language are frequently used for the identification of a person as a stranger.

In everyday language, speakers do not distinguish xenophobia as a social attitude or prejudice and discriminating behaviors. Xenophobia implies a spectrum encompassing the expression of negative opinions at one end, via rudeness, to aggressive behavior and massive violence at the other. The concept of xenophobia may be subsumed under one of the many variants of social prejudice, which also include the concept of stereotype. The diversity of subconcepts of social prejudice is not discussed here (see Zick, 1997); instead, *xenophobia* is defined as an ethnic prejudice and is thus related to racism, hostility toward foreigners, rightism, and nationalism. Xenophobia may be understood as the negative evaluation of people or groups from minorities, who are perceived as having their origin in other cultures and nations and whose presence threatens those persons or groups belonging to a majority. In this study, we focus on the concept of xenophobia because the concept of rightism differs slightly with regard to its central conceptual elements (i.e., xenophobia toward foreigners and nationalism). In addition, rightism also involves anti-Semitism (Frindte, Neumann, Hieber, Knote, & Müller, 2001) and the potential readiness for violence or actual violent behaviors associated with anti-Semitism. As Frindte et al. (2001) found in a study with 1,033 students from schools in Thuringia (East Germany), rightism consists of two factors: (1) features of rightist orientation, and (2) violence. The highest loading (.91) on the first factor resulted from the variable of xenophobia. It was not possible to include other facets of rightism and xenophobia (e.g., anti-Semitism or readiness for violence) in the study because school authorities refused to permit such an investigation.

The inclusion of values in the research of transmission of xenophobia and their function as a transmission belt or mechanism is based on two different trends in research on transmission, which reveal the significance of values for social attitudes. First, values – as the more general orientations – exert an influence on more specific beliefs and attitudes so that a multitude of attitudes exists and only a small number of value categories. However, single values may influence more than one attitude. These considerations are found in the writings of Rokeach (1973). In a more recent study (Haddock & Zanna, 2000), significant relationships between attitudes and values were reported. Homer and Kahle (1988) were able to successfully show that the impact of values on behavior is mediated by attitudes. The theoretically close connection between values and prejudices reveals itself in concepts of the so-called "new" or "modern" racism and its diverse variants such as symbolic racism (Sears & Henry, 2005), aversive racism (Dovidio & Gaertner, 2004), and ambivalent racism (Katz & Hass, 1988). It is not possible to consider all of these variants herein, but the common element to these concepts is some kind of dualism of values. It reveals itself in the acceptance and preference of values like egalitarianism, tolerance, and humanity on the one hand and – via relevant prejudices and discriminating behaviors – in the practice of opposite behaviors on the other hand.

3.0. AIM OF THE STUDY AND HYPOTHESES

Although only a small number of studies have considered the transmission of political attitudes (Cavalli-Sforza & Feldman, 1981), we hypothesize that xenophobia is vertically transmitted from parents to their adolescent children. This hypothesis is tested under different conditions. In particular, Boehnke's (2001) critique that studies on transmission frequently failed to analyze the parents and the children by gender guided our analyses.

It was explored whether the transmission of xenophobia proceeds in a similar manner to the transmission of values, whether the transmission is gender-specific and/or gender-bound, and which factors influence the transmission of xenophobia. In addition to the known factors of influence for the transmission process, such as the children's age, factors were introduced such as the socioeconomic situation of the parents and the extent to which the parents and children identify with the current political situation in East Germany after reunification.

A further research aim was to explore the role of values assessed according to the Schwartz value categories (Schwartz, Lehmann, & Roccas, 1999): Do they enhance the transmission of xenophobia – in other words, do they function as transmission belts? So far, some results are available that reveal transmission belts for the transmission of values. Rohan and Zanna (1996) investigated, for instance, the influence of authoritarian attitudes of parents on the similarity or dissimilarity among parents and their adult children. Schönpflug (2001) found differences in the intensity of value transmission when marital harmony, parenting style, father's education, or sibling position moderated transmission.

In our own research, parental values were considered transmission belts for the transmission of xenophobia. More specifically, it is tested whether, for example, strong traditionalistic parental attitudes exert more influence on the xenophobic attitudes of their children or whether a strong benevolence value held by parents' impacts children's level of xenophobia. In more detail, the following hypotheses were tested:

1. Xenophobia of students of a higher educational school track is lower than that of students of lower level school tracks.
2. Female students in higher level school tracks show less xenophobia than male students.
3. There are significant correlations between parents' and their children's intensity of xenophobia.
4. The economic situation of fathers influences the level of xenophobia of parents and their adolescent children.
5. The level of parents' xenophobia may predict the level of children's xenophobia; fathers' and mothers' levels of xenophobia have a differential impact on sons' and daughters' xenophobia.
6. Significant correlations are expected between value categories and xenophobia.

7. Male and female adolescents differ in their value preferences.
8. Values function as transmission belts for the intergenerational transmission of xenophobia.

4.0. METHOD

4.1. Sample

The participants were sampled in two steps. The first step started in June 2000 and ended in December of the same year. During that time, four lower level high schools ("Hauptschule" and "Mittelschule") and five higher level schools ("Gymnasium") with a total of $N = 376$ students in the federal state of Saxony-Anhalt in East Germany were included in the data collection. The target sample was planned to include 540 students on the basis of two classes (i.e., 9th and 10th grades) from each school (the number of students per class is typically 30). Thus, approximately 82% of the target student sample participated in the study. A total of 137 boys (36.5%) and 237 girls (62.9%)[1] participated; 147 were students of lower level high schools (39.2%) and 228 (60.8%) were students of the higher level school track. Both fathers and mothers of 145 families (38.7%) completed the questionnaire for parents, 61 mothers (16.3%) and 9 fathers (2.4%) answered alone, and the parents of 160 families (42.7%) did not return their questionnaires. On average, the students were 15.3 years old ($SD = 0.84$), the fathers were 42.8 years old ($SD = 6.5$), and the mothers were 40.5 years old ($SD = 4.7$).

During the second step, data were collected in a rural area in Saxony, East Germany. The target sample comprised a total of 306 students and their parents: The students attended three lower level high schools ('Mittelschule') from the age of 14 to 17 years in the 9th and 10th grades. Only 158 students (51.6%) between the ages of 14 and 17 years responded, consisting of 68 boys (43.0%) and 90 girls (57.0%). There were 44 mothers (27.8%) and 7 fathers (4.0%) who responded alone, whereas for 59 of the students (37.3%) both parents participated. The average age of the students was 15.3 years ($SD = 0.76$), the average age of the fathers was 42.3 years ($SD = 4.94$), and the average age of the mothers was 40.3 years ($SD = 4.7$).

Once the students and their parents had agreed to participate, the students were visited during school hours. After a short introduction, the students responded to the questionnaire in their classroom together with their classmates. The procedure took up to 50 minutes. The students received two questionnaires to take home to their parents with an instruction letter. Among other instructions, the parents were asked to respond independently. The students were also given two envelopes, one for each parent questionnaire, that carried a family

---

[1] If the given frequencies do not add up to the total number of students, the questionnaires had missing values for the information given.

code. After completion of the questionnaire, the parent was supposed to enclose the questionnaire in one of the two envelopes and seal it. The students brought the closed questionnaires back to school, where the researchers collected them.

4.2. Measures

Parallel measures were included in the questionnaire for the parents and for their adolescent children. The measures were as follows:

1. *Xenophobia.* Xenophobia was assessed by a rightism scale developed by Oesterreich (2001). The scale has 12 items that cover 6 topics: "identification with national greatness" (items 1 and 2), "hostility towards foreigners" (items 3 through 6), "undemocratic actions against representatives of the former GDR" (items 7 through 9), "law and order mentality" (item 10), and "playing down the crimes of the national-socialist regime in the thirties and early forties in Germany" (items 11 and 12). The response scale ranged from 1 ("not at all true") to 4 ("completely true"). A factor analysis based on all 12 items revealed a strong main component that explained 42.8% of the variance. The internal consistency of the scale indicated by Cronbach's alpha was 0.87. The same 12 items were not meaningful to the adolescents because they did not know enough about the national-socialist regime or the former GDR. Therefore, a shorter version of the first six items of the original scale was compiled, which measured well both the adolescents' and the parents' xenophobia and rightist attitudes.

   For the total sample ($N = 521$), a factor analysis of the six-item scale resulted in a one-dimensional solution, explaining 47% of the total variance. Cronbach's alpha was .77. This factor solution was found in both regional samples. For the parents, similar or better solutions were found in both regions: The one-dimensional solutions explained 46% and 57% of the total variance, and Cronbach's alphas were .84 and .81 for fathers and mothers, respectively.

2. *Value Orientations.* To assess the value preferences of students and their parents, the Portrait Questionnaire (PQ40) developed by Schwartz, Lehmann, & Roccas (1999) was employed. The PQ40 is based on Schwartz's studies (1992) and includes 10 value categories (i.e., self-determination, stimulating life, hedonism, achievement, power, security, conformity, tradition, benevolence, and universalism). Because the focus of our study is on the transmission of xenophobia, we did not expect all of the values to be able to assume the function of a transmission belt for its intergenerational transmission. According to results of research on prejudice, the values of achievement, power, security, conformity, traditionalism, benevolence, and universalism could be potentially relevant for the enhancement or reduction of prejudice.

3. *Regional Social Identity.* To clarify whether identification with being an East German and former citizen of the GDR is related to xenophobia, a regional identification scale was introduced into the questionnaire. In an attempt to answer the question of whether the level of xenophobia differs for people who reveal identification with East Germany (i.e., *assimilation*) as opposed to those who distance themselves from belonging to that region (i.e., *differentiation*), a social-identity scale was introduced (Schönpflug, 2000, 2005). The scale was an adaptation of the social-identity concept developed by Brewer (1991). Membership groups define the social identity of their members. Brewer assumes two central needs to relate to one's own social or ethnic group: the need to belong (i.e., assimilation) and the need to differentiate oneself from one's membership group. An optimal status of "distinctiveness" is achieved when a balanced state between the two needs has been reached, which is usually the case when a person is included in the group at an intermediate level. The scale was given to both parents and students. The scale for measuring differentiation from belonging to the regional group of East Germans included five items (e.g., for students: "I am embarrassed when in a [nonregional] peer group my East German origin becomes known"). The scale for assimilation had 9 items (e.g., for parents: "If possible, I prefer to live near my own [regional] countrymen"). Both scales had response formats from 1 ("not at all") to 4 ("completely true"). In addition, both adolescents and parents rated the extent to which they "feel" themselves to be "Europeans," "Germans," and "East Germans" on a similar 4-point response scale.

Furthermore, the students and their parents answered sociodemographic questions. The adolescents stated age, grade, and type of school, gender, and region of residence. The parents provided information about age, gender, family status, years of formal education, level of qualification achieved, profession, and employment status. The parents rated the evaluation of their current professional status as being worse than (1), equal to (2), or better than (3) their situation before the reunification of Germany.

5.0. RESULTS

5.1. Mean Differences in Xenophobia

The means and standard deviations for the levels of xenophobia of the subsamples are shown in Table 16.1. The mean level of xenophobia of all adolescents ($N = 521$) is $M = 2.20$ ($SD = 0.67$). The Saxony subsample revealed a lower level of xenophobia as compared to a subsample from the Saxony-Anhalt region, which was matched with regard to school track ($M = 2.21$, $SD = .64$, and $M = 2.40$, $SD = .75$, respectively). A t-test revealed a significant mean difference

Table 16.1. *Means (M) and standard deviations (SD) of xenophobia levels of the total sample and three subsamples, separated by gender*

			Region		
		Total	Saxony (Lower School Track)	Saxony-Anhalt (Lower School Track)	Saxony-Anhalt (Higher School Track)
Sample	M	2.20	2.21	2.40	2.06
	SD	.69	.64	.76	.65
Boys	M	2.37	3.32	2.42	2.38
	SD	.72	.62	.82	.69
Girls	M	2.09	2.12	2.40	1.90
	SD	.64	.60	.69	.56
Xenophobia	α	.77	.72	.80	.77
	N	521	154	141	226

($t(293) = 2.435$, $p < .05$) between the two regional lower school track subsamples. The students of the higher level school track had the lowest level of xenophobia ($M = 2.06$, $SD = .65$), which differed significantly from the means of the subsample of students of the lower school track in the same region ($t(364) = 4.63$, $p < .00$).

The means reflect the well-known finding of a negative relationship between educational level and xenophobia: The students of the higher school track revealed the lowest level of xenophobia. This general result is mainly due to the female students' differences in xenophobia. Female students had generally lower levels of xenophobia: $M = 2.39$, $SD = .75$ for male and $M = 2.08$, $SD = .65$ for female students, respectively ($t(519) = 4.22$, $p < .00$). However, the differences were not significant in all subsamples: A regional comparison between the two lower school tracks revealed that girls in the rural region of Saxony showed lower levels of xenophobia than the girls in the same school track in a bigger city in Saxony-Anhalt: A one-way analysis of variance including the three subsamples (i.e., lower level school track in Saxony, lower level and higher level in Saxony-Anhalt) as independent variable and female students' level of xenophobia as the dependent variable resulted in a significant mean difference between the subsamples ($F(2,316) = 18.18$, $p < .001$). Post hoc Scheffé tests showed significant differences between the xenophobia of girls in lower school tracks in the two regions ($M = 2.12$, $SD = .60$ for Saxony, and $M = 2.40$, $SD = .69$ for Saxony-Anhalt) but also between the mean xenophobia of girls in different school tracks in Saxony-Anhalt ($M = 2.40$, $SD = .69$ for lower level school tracks, and $M = 1.90$, $SD = .56$ for higher levels). There were no significant mean differences for boys among the three subsamples.

The association between parents' and their children's level of xenophobia can only be estimated separately for each parent because the response frequencies of the two parents differed considerably. The correlation between fathers and their child was $r = .31$; the correlation between mothers and their child was $r = .26$ (both significant at $p < .001$). Thus, further analyses based on correlations are possible. More specifically, only the correlation between boys and their fathers was significant ($r = .25$, $p < .001$), whereas the girls' xenophobia correlated at $r = .40$ with their father's prejudice. The correlation between mothers and daughters was $r = .36$ ($p < .001$). As expected, the correlation of xenophobia between mothers and fathers was relatively high ($r = .61$, $p < .001$), indicating homogeneity in attitudes between marital partners.

The correlations between the students' identification with being an East German (i.e., assimilation) and holding xenophobic attitudes was $r = .19$; for the parents, no significant correlations were observed. Distancing oneself from East German identity (i.e., differentiation) did not correlate with their level of xenophobia for either the children or the parents. One-item ratings of how much the children feel themselves to be Europeans, Germans, and East Germans correlated significantly with their xenophobia: $r = -.17$, $r = .29$, and $r = .16$, all $p < .00$, respectively. Moreover, significant correlations were observed for fathers between all three identification variables and the fathers' xenophobia: $r = -.25$, $r = .28$, and $r = .18$, all $p < .001$, respectively; the corresponding correlations for mothers were $r = -.05$, $p > .05$; $r = .25$, and $r = .20$, both $p < .00$.

The extent to which the family situation influences the level of xenophobia held by family members is depicted in Figure 16.1. The self-report of the fathers regarding how well positioned they feel after the reunification of Germany as compared to their professional situation before reunification showed clear effects on xenophobia: Fathers themselves, mothers, and their adolescent children showed the strongest xenophobic attitude when fathers reported being in a worse situation after than before reunification. Xenophobia ratings were reduced for all family members when fathers reported their situation after reunification as equal to how it was before. The xenophobia of fathers, mothers, and children was lowest when they felt better off. Self-reports of the professional situation of mothers did not result in any mean differences in xenophobia. A two-factor ANOVA was performed with the father's rating of his professional situation as the first between-group factor; the gender of the child as the second between-group factor; and the family role with the father's, mother's, and child's level of xenophobia as the within-subject factor. This resulted in a significant main effect of the father's professional situation: $F(2,197) = 7.19$, $p < .001$. The within-subject factor of family role was significant ($F(1,197) = 5.69$, $p < .02$, $M = 2.34$, $SD = .71$, $M = 2.07$, $SD = .71$, and $M = 1.87$, $SD = .68$ for father, mother, and child, respectively) and of the Family role x Gender interaction as well ($F(1,197) = 8.98$, $p < .003$). The corresponding xenophobia means for the male students were as follows: father's $M = 1.97$, $SD = .68$; mother's $M = 2.04$, $SD = .73$; and male child's $M = 2.45$, $SD = .75$. For the female students, the corresponding means and standard deviations were $M = 2.07$, $SD = .73$;

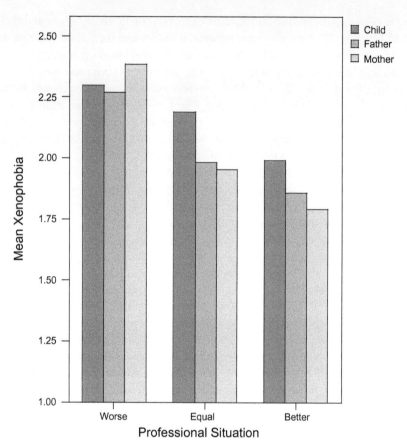

Figure 16.1. Level of xenophobia of all family members as dependent on the self-rated professional situation of the father after reunification of Germany as compared to before (interaction between father's professional situation and family role; see text).

$M = 2.04$, $SD = .66$; and $M = 1.99$, $SD = .65$ for the father, mother, and daughter, respectively. No other main effects or interactions were significant.

5.2. Intergenerational Transmission of Xenophobia

The extent to which the parents transmit xenophobia to their children was analyzed by means of multiple regressions. More specifically, the child's xenophobia was regressed on either the father's or the mother's level of xenophobia. The corresponding standardized regression coefficient β was interpreted as a transmission coefficient (Larson & Almeida, 1999). The effect of the father's and the mother's own level of xenophobia on the child's level was examined separately for fathers and mothers to avoid problems due to multicollinearity (i.e., the correlation between mother's and father's xenophobia was $r = .62$). The

Table 16.2. *Regression of adolescent children's xenophobia on their fathers'
and mothers' xenophobia*[1]

Predictor	B	SE B	β	$R^2_{Attenuated}$	N
Xenophobia Father	.250	.075	.259***	.15	147
Xenophobia Mother	.239	.068	.241**	.17	198

[1] Two separate analyses controlled for the children's gender, age, and school track.
*** Significant at $p < .001$; ** significant at $p < .01$; * significant at $p < .05$.

regression analyses were controlled for gender, age, and school track of the child.
For the total sample, the first multiple regression led to the results presented in
Table 16.2.

The transmission coefficients indicated a balanced transmission for fathers
and mothers (i.e., $β = .259$ for fathers and $β = .241$ for mothers). Apart from
the well-known gender effect, the other two control variables had no significant
effects on the child's xenophobia. Therefore, two separate multiple regressions
were performed, one for each gender. Control variables were the same as in the
previous analyses. The results are presented in Table 16.3; they show a distinct
predominant impact of both parents on daughters but not on sons. The control
variable of age had a significant effect only on sons' xenophobia when mothers'
xenophobia was the predictor in the analyses ($β = .285$, $p < .05$), indicating
that from mid to late adolescence, xenophobia increases for boys. School track
is important for the analyses – including mothers' and fathers' impact on their
daughters ($β = -.213$, $p < .01$) – revealing that in the higher level school track,
less xenophobia was observed.

Table 16.3. *Regressions of sons' and daughters' xenophobia on their fathers'
and mothers' xenophobia*[1]

Predictor	B	SE B	β	$R^2_{Attenuated}$	N
Criterion					
Son's Xenophobia					
Xenophobia Father	.213	.145	.201	.027	52
Xenophobia Mother	.257	.138	.249	.087	91
Criterion					
Daughter's Xenophobia					
Xenophobia Father	.259	.083	.308**	.153	63
Xenophobia Mother	.279	.074	.314***	.150	130

[1] Four separate regression analyses for each combination of gender of child and of parent,
controlled for age and school track of child.
*** Significant at $p < .001$; ** significant at $p < .01$; * significant at $p < .05$.

Table 16.4. *Correlations of xenophobia with value categories preferred by the same family role*

| | Xenophobia | | |
Value Category	Father $N = 145$	Mother $N = 198$	Child $N = 365$
Benevolence	−.10	−.01	−.16**
Universalism	−.10	−.05	−.34***
Traditionalism	.05	.28***	−.15*
Security	.33***	.40***	.23**
Conformity	.14	.26***	−.01
Self-Determination	.03	−.05	−.16**
Achievement	.21*	.25**	.14*
Power	.16	.11	.23**
Hedonism	.24**	.32***	−.03
Stimulating Life	.07	.17*	.08

*** Significant at $p < .001$; ** significant at $p < .01$; * significant at $p < .05$.

To examine the transmission effect under conditions of different levels of xenophobic attitude held by the adolescents, their xenophobia values were trichotomized separately for each gender group. The fathers' xenophobia had a significant effect on their children only when they held low levels of xenophobia ($\beta = .242$; $p < .05$), whereas the mothers transmitted to children with both low and high xenophobia ($\beta = .238$ and $\beta = .259$, both $p < .05$, respectively).

5.3. Transmission of Xenophobia Moderated by Value Preferences

Correlations of Xenophobia with Value Categories. To explore which value categories correlate with xenophobia, Pearson correlation coefficients were computed between each family member's xenophobia and their own value preferences (Table 16.4). Security and achievement seemed to be the value categories that correlated consistently and positively with xenophobia for all three family roles. Mothers' and fathers' hedonism correlated positively with their own xenophobia, and mothers' and children's traditionalism correlated with hedonism positively for mothers and negatively for children. Only for the children did power correlate significantly with xenophobia. For the mothers, the value of a stimulating life correlated significantly with xenophobia.

To examine the size of the transmission coefficients under conditions of low, medium, and high levels of a given value category, the categories were trichotomized, and parallel multiple regressions for low, medium, and high levels of a given value category were performed. If the transmission coefficient for xenophobia increased significantly with an increasing level of values, the value was considered a transmission belt. Other forms of analysis of the moderator

Table 16.5. *Transmission coefficients for xenophobia of fathers and mothers for three levels of the children's value categories of achievement, security, and traditionalism*

| | Adolescent Value Category | | | | | | | | |
| | Achievement | | | Security | | | Traditionalism | | |
Predictor	Low	Medium	High	Low	Medium	High	Low	Medium	High
Xenophobia									
Father[1]	.30*				.30*		.26*		
Mother	.23**	.41***				.41***		.39***	.33**
Control Variables									
Gender of Child									
Father	−.34*	−.31*	−.44**	−.36*	−.32*	−.45	−.45**	−.22	.03
Mother	−.28*	−.37**	−.39**	−.28**	−.38**	−.42**	−.42***	−.24*	−.02
$R^2_{Attenuated}$									
Father	.09	.16**	.37***	.09	.21*	.36***	.15*	.09*	.17
Mother	.08*	.22*	.33***	.08*	.23***	.34***	.15**	.23***	.14*

[1] Separate analyses for father and mother predictors to avoid multicollinearity.

*** Significant at $p < .001$; ** significant at $p < .01$; * significant at $p < .05$.

function of a value were rendered impossible by the high correlations of main terms with the corresponding interaction term.

The trichotomized values of achievement, security, and traditionalism as preferred by the child are shown in Table 16.5. All three value categories are transmission belts for the mother's and the father's transmission because they showed increasing levels of significant transmission coefficients. Low levels did not show any significant transmission coefficients. Further value categories resulted in similar transmission coefficients, with the exception of hedonism: Only when children held a low level of achievement did the father's and the mother's xenophobia have a significant impact on the child's xenophobia. The corresponding transmission coefficient for the mothers was $\beta = .23$, $p < .05$ and for the fathers was $\beta = .30$, $p < .05$. For mothers also a medium level of achievement value lead to the transmission of xenophobia ($\beta = .41$). Hence, it was possible to observe levels of values held by the child that enhance transmission coefficients such as achievement, security, traditionalism (as shown in Table 16.5) and conformity (for an analysis with the mother as predictors only), and self-determination that follow the same pattern. Other values such as stimulation, power, and conformity (for the fathers only) seemed to be efficient transmission belts only at low and high levels.

6.0. DISCUSSION

The issue of xenophobia in a globalizing world raises the fundamental question of whether xenophobia is adaptive or dysfunctional for the development of modern societies. The research presented in this chapter attempts to answer this question by looking at the intergenerational transmission of xenophobia in the family context. Cultural orientations are probably transmitted if they have an adaptive function. From a social-psychological point of view, this adaptive function might be found in an increase in in-group identification. Xenophobia has the effect of establishing social distance between the self or one's membership group and the stranger or foreigner. Transmitting xenophobia to the offspring implies the maintenance of social distance over generations of a society. In addition, despite the relevance of the familial intergenerational transmission of sociopolitical attitudes that can be observed as a basic pattern at a very young age (Aboud, 1988), it can be assumed that adolescents have "their own way of thinking" that is inspired by other sources of transmission, such as peers, other adults, media, or simply the *zeitgeist*.

On the basis of these considerations, the regional variation in the level of xenophobia observed in this study appears surprising. In two regions with the same past of the GDR communist regime, one rural and the other a larger city, xenophobia was lower in the rural region when lower level school tracks were compared. From a wider historical perspective, it may be speculated that the rural region included in the study was part of a trade network and the population, therefore, was used to being in contact with strangers in their everyday life and did not feel threatened. This tentative explanation is consistent with propositions made by Brown and Hewstone (2005) and Pettigrew and Tropp (2000), suggesting a negative association between extent of contact and level of xenophobia or ethnic prejudice.

Moreover, the educational difference between students of lower and higher level school tracks is consistent with the well-known finding that even in adolescence, higher levels of formal education are already associated with less xenophobia and less ethnic and social prejudice (Hopf, 1999; Wagner & Zick, 1995).

Furthermore, the consistently found evidence for lower levels of xenophobia and prejudices in girls and women is again documented in the research (Alba, Schmidt, & Wasmer, 2000; Hopf, Rieker, & Sanden-Marcus, 2002; Oesterreich, 2001; Schumann & Winkler, 1997). However, in our research, the gender and school-track effects interacted. The school-track effect in our study is mainly due to the differences in educational level of the female students. Although boys were generally higher in xenophobia than girls, they did not reveal significant school-type differences. The gender differences in xenophobia are maintained across the two regions. In the group of lower track high school students in the bigger-city area, boys and girls showed hardly any difference in xenophobia, whereas in the rural region, the typical dominance in xenophobia of boys compared to girls was found. The greatest gender difference occurred in the higher level school track: Boys held significantly stronger xenophobic attitudes compared to girls.

The general hypothesis that xenophobia is transmitted from parents to their children was corroborated by the correlation-based analyses presented in this chapter. The moderate sizes of the transmission coefficients may – in part – be due to the one-dimensional, six-item scale that was introduced in this research. Prejudices – including xenophobia – imply a system of beliefs, evaluations, and knowledge that encompasses a broad spectrum of content areas of differing significance and stability, as well as being influenced by different sources. These components were found to be hierarchically structured. A single one-dimensional scale touches on only a small fraction of this "universe of contents," its position remaining unknown. Thus, the transmission of xenophobia from parents to their children observed in the context of our research allows only a glimpse into the complex transmission process.

Another finding is also consistent with the interpretation of extreme rightism among the parent and youth generations in Germany: If people perceive their professional situation as bad – in this case, as worse than before the reunification – they tend to discriminate against foreigners. Our question of whether the fathers and the mothers perceive their current professional situation as worse than, equal to, or better than before reunification resulted in decreasing xenophobia values for all three family members. Thus, one source of rightism or xenophobia seems to be a perceived downgrading of one's own position. Whether we are dealing here with some form of scapegoating or a mechanism involving a channeling of negative emotions onto the target group of strangers or foreigners cannot be clarified by our results. The finding that social prejudice is related to an individual's economic situation has been reported by many American studies concerned with race riots in situations of economic recession (Jones, 1997; see also the critical discussion by Green, Glaser, & Rich, 1998).

Our data suggest that the fathers' and the mothers' xenophobic attitudes point in the same direction in the transmission process: Their aim is to transmit their own attitude to their adolescent offspring. However, when the gender of the child was considered, a differential impact of the two parents on sons and daughters was observed. Both parents transmitted less to sons than to daughters, and the mothers transmitted more efficiently to daughters than the fathers. Thus, we can tentatively conclude from our data that there is transmission of xenophobia predominantly along the gender lineage. The weaker parental influence on sons may have its origin in the greater emotional autonomy of male adolescents as compared to female adolescents. In addition, the boys may show greater peer-group orientation than the girls, which makes them susceptible to horizontal transmission.

The examination of the transmission effect under conditions of different levels of xenophobic attitude held by the adolescents revealed that the fathers' xenophobia had a significant effect on their children only when the children held low levels of xenophobia, whereas the mothers transmitted to children with low as well as high xenophobia. It can be speculated that adolescents perceive their parents' low or high level of xenophobia, compare it with their own level, and are more inclined to internalize their parents' views if their own are weak. In the case of increased susceptibility to the mother's influence when the adolescent holds a strong xenophobic attitude, it might be suspected that these adolescents are more emotionally dependent on their mother. At this stage, this research does not enable us to discern the possible sources of the differential transmission result.

The same interpretation may be given for the strong effect of parents, especially mothers on daughters, which was previously found in research by Nauck and Schönpflug (1997) and Phalet and Schönpflug (2001). The authors concluded that the relatively strong transmission effect of mothers on daughters might be due to the close emotional bond between mothers and daughters. At the same time, daughters might be less influenced by peer groups than sons.

The impact of the parents' social identity on the transmission of xenophobia was weaker than expected. Only the mother seemed to play a role in the transmission of xenophobia when it is made conditional on social identity. The reason for the relative irrelevance of regional identity might be based on the undifferentiating assessment of regional identity; however, it might also be traced back to a lack of mental representations of social identification of the type addressed.

This research corroborates the hypothesis that value orientations might moderate the transmission of xenophobia and, therefore, might function as transmission belts. Almost all values enhance the transmission of xenophobia in a significant way. However, some values enhanced transmission only when a given value category was moderately or strongly preferred by the child (e.g., achievement, security, traditionalism, self-determination, and having a stimulating life, as well as conformity; the latter two only for the mothers). Other values, by contrast, enhanced transmission only when a given category was weakly preferred (i.e., universalism for fathers and hedonism for both parents). For yet other values, this was the case only when the category was strongly preferred (e.g., stimulating life, conformity, and power for the fathers). A final pair of values – benevolence and self-determination – showed that the fathers can transmit xenophobia significantly only when their children hold intermediate levels of these two value categories.

From the correlations of adolescents' values with their xenophobic attitude, it may be concluded that universalistic, benevolent, self-determined, and traditionalistic adolescents showed lower xenophobia; security-, power-, and achievement-oriented adolescents expressed higher levels. Other values preferred by the child did not show any association with their level of xenophobia.

The case of achievement orientation and its moderating effect on the representation and transmission of xenophobia should be seen in light of the findings by Phalet and Schönpflug (2001) in migrant populations that migrants from collectivistic societies adopt achievement values from individualistic host societies relatively easily because increased achievement orientation increases the chances of survival in the host society. If achievement orientation also increases xenophobia for migrant populations, it is most likely directed toward the social majority of the host country and thus aids integration.

In a study such as this, the mechanisms of transmission of prejudices and values from parents to child and vice versa cannot be fully explored. In accordance with Stiksrud (1997), the type and intensity of transmission is concluded from the similarity between the parents and their children in the same family. It might be concluded that transmission is most intense and successful when parents and children are highly similar. However, without longitudinal data, we cannot be sure whether similarity is the origin or the result of intense transmission. The kind of reasoning that claims transmission to be the source of similarity, however, is supported by results from migration research. For instance, as Knafo and Schwartz (2001) showed for their migrant populations, the transmission of values was not complete over all 10 value categories or all levels of value preferences. They claimed that the new social context after migration led to an inconsistent externalization of the values on the part of the parents. The children clearly perceive these inconsistencies because they are more advanced in the acceptance of the values of the host society.

The parents in our sample were fully socialized in the GDR, and after the reunification of Germany, their context has also changed considerably. The parents still adhere to more collectivistic values, whereas their children have accepted more individualistic values. Given that the children tend to accept values that are similar to their own, the level of transmission between former GDR parents and their more assimilated children should be less intensive compared to other social contexts with more social continuity. More research using the same research instruments is needed to further clarify this issue. However, the moderation of the transmission of prejudices may be achieved not only by values but also by other moderators such as parenting style (Belsky, Jaffee, Sligo, & Silva, 2005; Schönpflug, 2001), attachment (Sabatier & Lannegrand-Willems, 2005), family climate (Taris, Semin, & Bok, 1998), and acceptance of parents (Schönpflug & Bilz, 2004).

In the same sample, Schönpflug and Bilz (2004) demonstrated in terms of belief in a just world that if parents hold equally strong attitudes to one another, they are more likely to have children with strong attitudes. In this study, the fathers' and the mothers' xenophobia correlated fairly highly, but the two parents were still found to transmit xenophobia differentially. We suggest that differential dependencies on values may be the source of this differential transmission rate of the mothers and the fathers. Values as moderators are differentially effective for the fathers, mothers, and children as participants of the transmission process of xenophobia. This indicates that growing up in the same social context alone does not guarantee value similarity in all subgroups and, therefore, equal effectiveness in xenophobia transmission. Taking this argument further, we may conclude that influences other than those that can be summarized as 'heritage of the GDR' must account for the levels of xenophobia found in our study. At least up to late adolescence, the influence of the individual parent initiates differences in the levels of the child's xenophobia and also – as was demonstrated by Schönpflug (2001) – of the child's values.

REFERENCES

Aboud, F. (1988). *Children and prejudice.* Oxford: Blackwell.

Alba, R., Schmidt, P., & Wasmer, M. (2000). *Deutsche und Ausländer: Freunde, Fremde oder Feinde: Empirische Befunde und Theoretische Erklärungen [Germans and foreigners: Friends, strangers or enemies: Empirical findings and theoretical explanations].* Wiesbaden: Westdeutscher Verlag.

Belsky, J., Jaffee, S., Sligo, J., & Silva, P. (2005). Intergenerational transmission of warm-sensitive-stimulating parenting: A prospective study of mothers and fathers of 3-year-olds. *Child Development, 76,* 384–396.

Boehnke, K. (2001). Parent–offspring value transmission in a societal context: Suggestions for a utopian research design – with empirical underpinnings. *Journal of Cross-Cultural Psychology, 32*(2), 241–255.

Brewer, M. B. (1991). On being the same and different at the same time. *Personality and Social Psychology Bulletin, 17,* 475–482.

Brown, R., & Hewstone, M. (2005). An integrative theory of intergroup contact. *Advances in Experimental Social Psychology, 37,* 255–343.

Cavalli-Sforza, L. L., & Feldman, M. W. (1981). *Cultural transmission and evolution: A quantitative approach.* Princeton, NJ: Princeton University Press.

Dovidio, J. F., & Gaertner, S. L. (2004). Aversive racism. *Advances in Experimental Social Psychology, 36,* 1–52.

Frindte, W., Neumann, J., Hieber, K., Knote, A., & Müller, C. (2001). Rechtsextremismus = 'Ideologie plus Gewalt' – Wie ideologisiert sind unsere Gewalttäter? [Rightism = 'ideology plus violence' – to what extent are our violent delinquents ideologized?] *Zeitschrift für Politische Psychologie, 9,* 81–98.

Goslin, D. A. (Ed.) (1969). *Handbook of socialization: Theory and research.* Chicago, IL: Rand McNally.

Green, D., Glaser, J., & Rich, A. (1998). From lynching to gay bashing: The elusive connection between economic conditions and hate crimes. *Journal of Personality and Social Psychology, 78,* 82–92.

Haddock, G., & Zanna, M. P. (2000). Cognition, affect, and the prediction of social attitudes. In W. Stroebe & M. Hewstone (Eds.). *European Review of Social Psychology, Vol. 10* (pp. 75–99). Chichester, UK: Wiley.

Homer, P. M., & Kahle, L. R. (1988). A structural equation test of the value-attitude-behavior hierarchy. *Journal of Personality and Social Psychology, 54,* 638–646.

Hopf, W. (1999). Ungleichheit der Bildung und Ethnozentrismus [Inequality of education and ethnocentrism]. *Zeitschrift für Pädagogik, 45*(6), 847–865.

Hopf, C., Rieker, P., & Sanden-Marcus, M. (2002). *Familie und Rechtsextremismus. Familiale Sozialisation und rechtsextreme Orientierungen junger Männer* [Family and rightism. Young men's familial socialization and extreme rightism]. Weinheim: Juventa.

Jones, J. M. (1997). *Prejudice and racism* (2nd. ed.). New York: McGraw-Hill.

Katz, I., & Hass, R. G. (1988). Racial ambivalence and American value conflict. Correlational and priming studies of dual cognitive structures. *Journal of Personality and Social Psychology, 55*, 893–905.

Knafo, A., & Schwartz, S. H. (2001). Value socialization in families of Israeli-born and Soviet-born adolescents in Israel. *Journal of Cross-Cultural Psychology, 32*, 213–228.

Kuczynski, L., Marshall, S., & Schell, K. (1997). Value socialization in a bidirectional context. In J. E. Grusec & L. Kuczynski (Eds.), *Parenting and children's internalization of values: A handbook of contemporary theory* (pp. 23–50). New York: John Wiley & Sons.

Larson, R. W., & Almeida, D. M. (1999). Emotional transmission in the daily lives of families: A new paradigm for studying family process. *Journal of Marriage and the Family, 61*, 5–20.

Nauck, B., & Schönpflug, U. (1997). *Familien in verschiedenen Kulturen* [Families in different cultures]. Stuttgart, Germany: Enke.

Oesterreich, D. (2001). *Autoritäre Persönlichkeit und Gesellschaftsordnung* [Authoritarian personality and social order]. Weinheim: Juventa.

Pettigrew, T. F., & Tropp, L. R. (2000). Does intergroup contact reduce prejudice? Recent meta-analysis findings. In S. Oskamp (Ed.), *Reducing prejudice and discrimination* (pp. 93–115). Mahwah, NJ: Erlbaum.

Phalet, K., & Schönpflug, U. (2001). Intergenerational transmission of collectivism and achievement values in two acculturation contexts: Turkish and Moroccan families in Germany and Turkish and Moroccan families in the Netherlands. *Journal of Cross-Cultural Psychology, 32*, 186–201.

Rohan, M. J., & Zanna, M. P. (1996). Value transmission in families. In C. Seligman, J. M. Olson, & M. P. Zanna (Eds.), *The psychology of values: The Ontario symposium, Vol. 8* (pp. 253–276). Hillsdale, NJ: Erlbaum.

Rokeach, M. (1973). *The nature of human values.* New York: The Free Press.

Sabatier, C., & Lannegrand-Willems, L. (2005). Transmission of family values and attachment: A French three-generation study. *Applied Psychology: An International Review, 54*, 378–395.

Saucier, G. (2000). "Isms" and the structure of social attitudes. *Journal of Personality and Social Psychology, 78*, 366–382.

Schönpflug, U. (2000). Akkulturation und Entwicklung [Acculturation and development]. In I. Gogolin (Ed.), *Migration, gesellschaftliche Differenzierung und Bildung* [Migration, societal differentiation, and education] (pp. 129–155). Opladen: Leske & Budrich.

Schönpflug, U. (2001). Intergenerational transmission of values: The role of transmission belts. *Journal of Cross-Cultural Psychology, 32*(2), 174–185.

Schönpflug, U. (2005). Ethnische Identität und Integration [Ethnic identity and integration]. In U. Fuhrer & H.-H. Uslucan (Eds.), *Familie, Akkulturation und Erziehung* [Family, acculturation, and education] (pp. 206–225). Stuttgart, Germany: Kohlhammer.

Schönpflug, U., & Bilz, L. (2004). Transmission of the belief in a just world in the family. In C. Dalbert & H. Sallay (Eds.), *The justice motive in adolescence and young adulthood* (pp. 43–63). London: Routledge.

Schumann, S., & Winkler, J. (Eds.) (1997). *Jugend, Politik und Rechtsextremismus in Rheinland-Pfalz* [Youth, politics, and rightism in Rheinland-Pfalz]. Frankfurt am Main, Germany: Lang.

Schwartz, S. H. (1992). Universals in the content and structure of values: Theoretical advances and empirical tests in 20 countries. *Advances in Experimental Social Psychology, 25,* 1–65.

Schwartz, S. H., Lehmann, A., & Roccas, S. (1999). Multimethod probes of basic human values. In J. Adamopoulus & Y. Kashima (Eds.), *Social psychology and culture context: Essays in honor of Harry C. Triandis* (pp. 107–278). Newbury Park, CA: Sage Publications.

Sears, D. O., & Henry, P. J. (2005). Over thirty years later: A contemporary look at symbolic racism. *Advances in Experimental Social Psychology, 37,* 95–150.

Six, B. (2002). Theorien ideologischer Systeme: Autoritarismus und Soziale Dominanz [Theories of ideological systems: Authoritarianism and social dominance]. In D. Frey & M. Irle (Eds.), *Theorien der Sozialpsychologie* (pp. 74–100). Bern, Switzerland: Huber.

Stiksrud, A. (1997). *Jugend im Generationen-Kontext* [Youth in the context of the generations]. Opladen: Westdeutscher Verlag.

Taris, T. W., Semin, G. R., & Bok, I. A. (1998). The effect of quality of family interaction and intergenerational transmission of values on sexual permissiveness. *The Journal of Genetic Psychology, 159,* 237–250.

Wagner, U., & Zick, A. (1995). The relation of formal education to ethnic prejudice: Its reliability, validity, and explanation. *European Journal of Social Psychology, 25,* 41–56.

Willems, H. (1992). Fremdenfeindliche Gewalt, Entwicklung, Strukturen, Eskalationsprozesse [Xenophobic violence, development, structures and processes of escalation]. *Gruppendynamik, 23,* 433–448.

Zick, A. (1997). *Vorurteile und Rassismus: Eine sozialpsychologische Analyse* [Prejudices and racism: A social psychological analysis]. Münster: Waxmann.

17

Intergenerational Transmission of Violence

HACI-HALIL USLUCAN AND URS FUHRER

INTRODUCTION

Both in clinical and in developmental psychology, there seems to be clear evidence that experiences of violence in childhood lead to a heightened risk of parents later using violence toward their own children. In general, beaten children are the beating parents of the next generation. Although this insight has not been confirmed as direct causal evidence, the postulated relationship is not really disputed. Straus (1980b) was able to prove this linear positive relationship between the frequency of experiences of violence and the probability of one's own use of violence: In his study, mothers who were victims of domestic violence as teenagers showed – with nearly 30% – the highest rate of active child maltreatment. Other empirical studies have also shown a link between an adult's acceptance of violence and his or her own early violence experience. Bower and Knutson (1996) questioned approximately 1,359 students and ascertained that the participants with experiences of violence in their childhood were inclined to play down the severity of the violence suffered.

Some of the results of research on intergenerational transmission of violence suffer from methodological difficulties because they are based only on clinical findings with a small sample size, which does not allow inferences to be made in favor of or against the general theoretical assumptions. One of the main weaknesses in clinical findings is that a control group is often lacking. These methodological problems have been avoided in some studies by including control groups and through prospective study designs with risk groups. Such studies were even able to differentiate between the childhood experiences of parents who beat their children and parents who do not use violence against their children (Herrenkohl, Herrenkohl, & Toedter, 1983; Straus, 1980a, 1980b). For example, Hunter and Kilström (1979) examined 282 risk mothers whose children were born prematurely or with disabilities. Of those mothers, 49 reported that they were maltreated or neglected by their parents in their childhood. In a second interview after 1 year, 10 mothers stated that they had used violence against their children; of those, 9 had experienced violence in their own childhood. One of the most important conclusions of these studies was the finding that despite being maltreated, some parents did not prefer violence as a parenting instrument. These "refusers" of violence had a positive relationship with at least one of their parents during their childhood and, furthermore, they actually had considerably higher social support (Wetzels, 1997). Moreover, the nonrepeaters had both healthier children and fewer ambivalent attitudes toward their child's birth than the repeaters. Parents who broke the cycle of violence were more overtly angry with respect to their earlier abuse and they were emotionally able to give detailed accounts of their own abusive experiences (Kaufman & Zigler, 1989). Lackey and Williams (1995) were able to demonstrate that despite a violent family history, strong social bonds for men have inhibitory effects on being violent against their family members.

In a study including a risk group, Egeland and Stroufe (1981a) showed in their 16-year longitudinal study that the rate of violence transmission by the group with their own violent experiences was considerably high: Of the 47 mothers who were maltreated as children, 44 maltreated or neglected their own children within a period of 2 years. Approximately 34% of those who were victims of violence in their childhood used violence toward their own children and physically punished them. The rate of violence in the group without violent experiences in their childhood, however, was only about 3%.

In reference to Wetzels' 1997 findings, Engfer (2000) reported that children who experience marital violence have an eight-times heightened risk of becoming a victim of violence and a three-times heightened risk of being victimized by sexual abuse compared to children who do not experience violence between their parents. Studies in the 1990s in Germany showed that 10% to 15% of all parents inflicted severe punishments on their children, and roughly 10% of all children in Germany had been victims of parental violence.

It seems to be undisputed that cultural context affects both parenting style (Darling & Steinberg, 1993) and the amount of violence in a society through the extent to which it tolerates violence as an appropriate method of conflict resolution, by teaching norms and values that support violent behavior – especially the norm of masculinity – or by rejecting any kind of aggressive interpersonal interaction. Thus, it is assumed that the impact and interpretation of violence is different in cultures in which violence is more common than in those that inhibit violence. Concerning domestic violence, there is a noticeable cultural variance: For instance, nearly 60% of Turkish juveniles have been exposed to paternal violence at least once in their life (Uslucan, 2003). Furthermore, studies conducted in the 1990s and between 2001 and 2003 showed that violence on an individual level as well as on a familial and community levels was – compared to Western European societies – more common and significantly higher in Turkish society (http://www.aile.gov.tr/Arastirma12.htm; http://www.aile.gov.tr/Arastirma18.htm; http://www.kriminoloji.com/siddet%

20cocuk.htm). Parents who use violence as an educational tool in a culture or a community that favors violence do not consider themselves "bad parents" if members of the community around them engage in the same parental violence. However, there are differences in the frequency of child maltreatment not only between cultures but also within a culture (e.g., ethnic or class differences) (Garbarino & Ebata, 1983).

Although some critics regard the intergenerational-transmission thesis as a myth (Gelles & Cornell, 1985), most of the research results indicate that many people who were victimized by violence in their family of origin have a higher risk of being subsequently susceptible to using violence in their own family. Egeland (1993), for example, gave a conservative transmission-rate estimate of 40%; Kaufman and Zigler (1993) reported a rate of 30%. They assumed that the best value for the true transmission rate is 30%, ± 5%. This means that nearly one third of all individuals who were physically abused, sexually abused, or neglected will treat their offspring with one of those forms of maltreatment; whereas two thirds, in defiance of their own treatment, will treat their children with normal and adequate care. With regard to Germany, Engfer (2000) reported a transmission rate of 14.3%, meaning that these parents were both victims of violence in their childhood and actually beat their own children. Methodologically, it is necessary to point out that variations in the estimation rates often depend on the time interval of the follow-up studies. For example, if parents were asked just 1 year after they were first questioned, the rates were lower than if they were asked many years later (Kaufman & Zigler, 1993).

Nevertheless, although it must be concluded that the impression of an inevitable cycle of violence is quite clear, it is necessary to keep in mind that most parents who experienced violence in their childhood do not use violence when they raise their own children. Also, in some studies in which parents abused their children, the majority were not abused in their own childhood (Widom, 1989). The same pattern was found among juvenile delinquents: The majority of abused juveniles did not become delinquent, and the majority of delinquents in most studies were not abused as children (Widom, 1989), a finding that was partially confirmed by our own investigation.

Being abused as a child may increase the risk of becoming an abusive parent, a delinquent, or an adult criminal. However, despite the fact that a history of abuse is one of the greatest risk factors in the etiology of child maltreatment, there is no straight pathway from early child abuse to later involvement in violence. For instance, early experiences of violence may sometimes lead not only to further aggressive behavior but also to depression and self-punishing behavior. In our terminology, *aggression* and *violence* are used synonymously, although they are constructs of different intellectual disciplines: The concept of aggression is more common in psychology, whereas violence is used more frequently in sociology. However, the focus should not be on the question of the existence of an intergenerational transmission but rather on the circumstances under which it occurs and on the variables that mediate this intergenerational cycle. It should also be emphasized that the greater the severity and frequency of the victimization, the greater the likelihood of severe and frequent violent acts outside the family.

For the theoretical explanation of the transmission process, it is necessary to identify ontogenetically acquired factors that predispose individuals to aggression or violence and also to look at their interaction with the actual fostering or inhibiting risk factors. It would then be possible to explain violent acts as a simultaneous accumulation of risks and lack of buffer factors. By explaining the causes of violence, we can address the issue in terms of probability. We can identify factors that increase or decrease the chances of violence, but we cannot say with any certainty that a given person with these characteristics will be violent.

Kaufman and Zigler (1989, p. 146) suggested that it is time to overcome the question, "Do abusive children become abusive parents?," and to ask instead, "Under what conditions is the transmission of abuse most likely to occur?" It seems evident that an accumulation of stressors and a lack of resources are the interacting conditions for the transmission of violence.

In many cases, the risk factors increase through positive feedback; in other words, if several risk factors can be identified, their effects increase, and it will be more difficult to break the cycle of violence (Ratzke & Cierpka, 2000). What seems to be of interest is the assessment of the risk of former violent experiences in terms of a later engagement in violence and the methods of intervention to break the cycle (Belsky, 1980, 1993; Kaufmann & Zigler, 1989; Wetzels, 1997). In Belsky's ecological model, the determinants of abuse and both compensatory and risk factors are included (Kaufman & Zigler, 1989, p. 139). Table 17.1 summarizes the determinants of abuse according to those authors.

There are several theoretical positions explaining the transmission of violence. In the following section, we focus on the learning theory, attachment theory, psychopathological approach, and sociological perspective.

1.0. THEORETICAL APPROACHES

1.1. Learning Theory

It is beyond doubt that great parts of our behavior are learned; this also applies for aggressive behavior, as the research on aggression in the last 30 years has demonstrated. But how is this behavior learned?

Learning takes place through different mechanisms, one of which consists of rewards and punishments. Behavior increases if it is followed by positive consequences and decreases if it is followed by negative consequences. If a child achieves his or her goal through an aggressive act, the child may learn that aggression is beneficial. Aggression may also be self-satisfying if it is accompanied by feelings of excitement – in this case, aggression has its own rewards. However,

Table 17.1. *Determinants of abuse: Compensatory and risk factors*

	Ontogenetic Level	Microsystem Level	Exosystem Level	Macrosystem Level
Compensatory Factors	History of positive relationship with one parent	Healthy children	Social support	Cultural promoting of a sense of shared responsibility for the community's children
	Awareness of past abuse	Supportive spouse	Few stressful events	Cultural opposition to violence
	High IQ; special talents Physical attractiveness	Economic security/savings	Strong religious affiliations Positive school experiences and peer relationships in childhood	Economic prosperity
	Good interpersonal skills		Therapeutic interventions	
Risk Factors	History of abuse	Marital discord	Unemployment	Cultural acceptance of corporal punishment
	Low self-esteem	Children with behavior problems; premature or unhealthy children	Isolation; poor social support	Cultural view of children as possessions
	Low IQ Poor interpersonal skills	Single parent Poverty	Poor peer relations as child	Economic depression

we should not need to experience rewards and punishments directly, as the social-learning theory has shown (Bandura, 1973; Bandura, Ross, & Ross, 1961). At times, it can be sufficient to watch the experiences of others, even those of people at a distance (e.g., on television). In this case, people are more likely to imitate behavior that earns other people rewards and avoid behavior that brings harm to others. By imitating another person's behavior, we want to develop their characteristics. This applies in particular to role models whom we may admire or idolize, such as parents or sporting figures. We believe that if we imitate them, then we can be like them. Family members, due to their availability and their nurturing and rewarding qualities, are the prime sources of imitation (Herzberger, 1996). A child may learn aggressive acts by watching the abusive behavior of parents and developing a set of rules that supports this behavior. Repeated exposure to aggression (e.g., in the mass media) may lead to the belief that violence is normative and an acceptable behavior. It desensitizes an individual to the consequences of aggression. It is said that aggressive parents provide their children with a script for the parental role, which they will later enact with their own children. However, Simons, Whitbeck, Conger, and Chyi-In (1991) found that there is no direct path from experienced to enacted violence. A child does not perfectly imitate the same specific aggressive behavior but rather adopts the *aggressive style* of interaction.

During their own childhood, on the one hand, children learn through love, tenderness, and affection. On the other hand, through physical punishment and neglect, children learn how parents regulate their emotions to control the child's behavior. In such contexts, children learn that physical punishment belongs to the "normal" repertoire of parental behavior and that it corrects supposedly undesirable development and undisciplined behavior. Children accept it as a suitable intervention. Furthermore, the observation of violent parents leads to imitation of behavioral aggression, to cognitive incorporation of violent acts, and to proviolent attitudes; the child adopts the parental beliefs that violence is an acceptable means of expressing anger and reacting to stress or a way in which to control others. In the same context, they fail to learn valuable skills (e.g., non-violent conflict resolution) because they have no appropriate parental models.

If children frequently witness violent behavior between their parents, they not only learn a pattern of conflict resolution – namely, that aggression is accepted in loving relationships within the family (Kalmus, 1984) – but they also establish a deep distrust in social relationships, insofar as they learn that loving people can also be cruel. This may sometimes lead to weaker self-esteem.

If parents have no professional training in child-rearing, they bring up their children in the same way as they were brought up themselves. Their own educational biography is the "cultural script" in the education of their own children. Along this line of reasoning, it is plausible to assume that to the extent that children learn aggressive strategies for solving problems, they lack learning models of beneficial problem-solving skills.

1.2. Attachment Theory

Attachment is to be understood as an enduring emotional bond, which is developed mainly during the first year of an infant's life, in which a child is completely dependent on his or her caretaker. This bond has an important function for a child: In establishing a secure attachment and a stable emotional relationship with his or her caretaker, a child develops a sense of trust and security. Disturbances in the development of a secure attachment may be related to an inability to develop close and fulfilling relationships in adulthood (Barnett, Miller-Perrin, & Perrin, 1997).

Attachment patterns – both secure and insecure (i.e., insecure-avoidant and disorganized attachment) – are activated in emotionally strained and critical situations. According to the work of Belsky (1993), children who suffer from violence may develop hostile personality characteristics, which lead them to use violence in their social environment. The lack of sensitive caretakers, maltreatment, and rejection by parents may lead to weak self-esteem and mistrust in interpersonal relationships. In a clinical study by Egeland and Stroufe (1981b), for example, the majority of abused or neglected children were anxiously attached. It is claimed that the earlier the maltreatment occurs, the greater the likelihood of an insecure attachment. According to attachment theory, the detrimental experiences are integrated into the internal working model of social relationships and the self so that they become especially effective in the process of intergenerational transmission of violence. The assumption is that maltreated parents develop a mental working model from their own childhood experiences, in which other people are internally unavailable, unreliable, and apt to reject others. From this perspective, they have a distorted perception of their own children and also regard their minor misconduct as a massive rejection of their own person. Herrenkohl et al. (1983), for example, suggested that the combination of emotional abuse and physical maltreatment is one important key to understanding the transmission process.

If a considerable part of mental energy is expended to regulate one's own relationships, which are experienced as fragile, only a limited amount of the parents' resources remain for the upbringing of their own children. Families with violence problems are generally multiproblem families; that is, there is not only violence but also other problematic conditions. Parents with insecure attachments are presumably less resistant to stress and show less responsivity to their children's needs. They produce a higher propensity toward anxiety due to their limited competencies in comforting their children, which in turn results in worse parental control. It is also well supported that people with rather insecure attachment experiences regard their environment as being more hostile and interpret unwanted childish behavior patterns as targeted at themselves.

However, an integration of troubled childhood experiences does not necessarily lead to a disorganized self or to violence. If people can succeed in gaining cognitive access to the triggers of their problematic emotional reactions, if they can reflect on their own behavior and relate it to their self, then they have the opportunity to change it. For instance, Main and Goldwyn (1984) showed that mothers who were confronted with violent and rejecting maternal behavior in their childhood rarely used violence if they were mentally confronted with their own feelings and experiences as rejected children.

In addition to these active cognitive adaptations, it seems that another factor plays an important role as a buffer regarding the transmission of violence: a person's current experience with his or her partner. A positive partnership is generally accompanied by a reduced risk of intergenerational transmission of violence, as the findings of Caliso and Milner (1992) revealed. Presumably, this positive experience of partnership can be seen as a reorganization of the internal working model. In contrast, it can be concluded that the highest risk for children to being exposed to the violence of their mother exists among those mothers who were not only victimized in their childhood but who also experienced revictimization by their partners in adulthood. These results reemphasize the importance of including the ecological context in the explanation of the intergenerational transmission of violence.

To simultaneously break the cycle of violence and reduce the intergenerational transmission, abused women need to learn about the emotional needs of their children. Egeland (1993), for example, was able to demonstrate that despite their risk status, only 3% of the mothers who were loved, nurtured, and emotionally supported as children were currently maltreating their children. Being raised in a warm and accepting environment seems to be a protective factor against maltreatment in the next generation. Egeland, Jacobvitz, and Stroufe (1988) pointed out that in comparison to the "continuity group," the group that broke the cycle had an emotionally supportive adult in childhood and had undergone extensive therapy in their lifetime.

1.3. Psychopathological Approach

The psychopathological approach is closely related to both psychoanalytic and attachment theory. It attributes the transmission of violence to problematic personality traits of the parents, which result from harsh punishment and rejections in their own childhood. These personality traits are activated when parents form a relationship with their own children. Research findings from the 1970s and 1980s identified a subgroup of severely disturbed individuals with psychiatric symptoms who abused children, but this group constituted less than 10% in the samples studied (Kempe & Helfer, 1972; Straus, 1980a). Wolfe (1985) reported that consensus exists among researchers that only 5% of abusing parents have extremely psychopathological symptoms. For Germany, research findings indicate that these relationships may be found for nearly 30% of abusive parents (Engfer, 2000). In addition to depression and other mental disorders and instabilities, the personality trait of heightened irritability seems to be crucial, which aggravates a patient interaction with a child. Although some studies claim that a successful educational career can be a protective factor that breaks the cycle of violence, in most cases, children who were beaten have developmental deficits in many school-relevant aspects, which hinder them in breaking the cycle.

One of the problematic points of the psychopathological approach is that the deficiencies of the parents can only be identified post hoc; that is, the fact that their own abuse history is reconstructed retrospectively. Further criticism is that this model follows a monocausal argumentation; not only the personality traits of parents but also those of other family members, of the peer group, and one's own affect the child's behavior. Children are the co-agents of both their own development and the parent–child relationship. Apart from this, some of the deficiencies of childhood (e.g., violence, neglect, and maltreatment) can be compensated through care families and in foster homes. A methodological problem of the psychopathological approach is that information regarding the parents' own maltreatment and abuse is gained in therapeutic contexts; in this respect, therefore, the sample size is small and the relationships identified cannot be generalized (Engfer, 1986).

1.4. The Sociological Perspective

The sociological perspective identifies the following factors for the transmission of violence: (1) a social acceptance of violence in the children's upbringing; (2) a stressful family situation through unemployment, poverty, or the like; and (3) a lack of social support in times of crisis. Typically, social-support systems are seen as stress-buffering and, therefore, as reducing violence. Social support can be differentiated in two aspects: emotional support and instrumental support. Emotional support is granted by social networks (i.e., sympathy from and acceptance by social contacts increase self-esteem and emotional well-being). In this context, the spouse has the greatest stress-buffering effect. Instrumental support is realized through information, advice, help, and economic and financial aids. Social-support systems also have a normative function: They set norms of behavior and they control the individual network member (Belsky & Vondra, 1989; Engfer, 1986).

However, the assumptions of the sociological approach are to be questioned if social factors on the macro level (e.g., norms of aggressive behavior or unemployment) intervene abruptly in the micro level of the individual, making it conceivable that social inequality and misery are not accompanied by subjective dissatisfaction or unhappiness. For example, the detrimental consequences of unemployment, such as strain and stress, may also be used by the parents in a constructive way because they have more time for their children. Frustrations do not result from the objective hardships but rather from the difference between subjective aspirations and externally caused objective deprivations. Some frustrations resulting from social hardships do not lead to aggression but rather more to resignation, disappointment, and psychosomatic diseases.

Beyond this, the sociological perspective cannot explain why violence is targeted only against a particular child or member of the family. It cannot be disputed that members of lower social classes have a higher risk of illness and lower resistance to stress and are more often confronted with daily hassles and critical life events. Nevertheless, the main question is how to interpret and cope with these problems. If they are interpreted as aversive and unmanageable, then – and only in those contexts – it is assumed that the risk of neglecting (rather than maltreating) the child will increase. It also appears to be the case that families in which maltreatment occurs have greater life burdens, such as unemployment, several children to be cared for, maternal and child illness, and marital conflicts. However, it is difficult to identify the exact relationship between a stressor (i.e., stressful life event) and violent acts. The sociological perspective in particular neglects the stressors that emerge from the child's own personality.

2.0. DETERMINANTS OF INTERGENERATIONAL TRANSMISSION OF VIOLENCE

2.1. Characteristics of Abusive Parents

Although no single profile of perpetrators exists, violence research does identify some attributes that lead to an elevated risk of physical child abuse in families. Compared to nonabusive parents, abusive parents have unrealistic expectations and negative perceptions regarding their children. These parents often think of their child as being bad, slow, and difficult to discipline, and they view the behavior of the child as opposed to themselves and as being intended to annoy them (Barnett et al., 1997). Abusive parents also show some deficits in child-management skills; in most cases, they have marital conflicts and experienced violence in their own childhood. Often, a correlation among poverty, social marginality, and violence can be identified. National surveys of family violence in the United States found a correlation between low socioeconomic status (SES) and violence: The largest proportion of abusive families was found in the low-SES group (Gil, 1973; Pelton, 1978). Additional relevant characteristics are as follows:

1. *Stability Versus Instability of Partnership.* For example, people with unstable and disharmonious marital relationships or single parentship, who are overstrained by the upbringing of their offspring, show higher rates of violence.
2. *Education and Social Stratum.* Members of the lower social classes are overrepresented in nearly all surveys regarding child abuse; in many

cases, their life conditions are marked by poverty, unemployment, and overcrowded living conditions. Unemployed parents, because they stay home for longer periods, are possibly frustrated about their life situation and are thus more easily irritated by their child's behavior.

3. *Family Size.* In families with several children, child abuse is overrepresented; having many children can lead to an overstraining of the parents. Family size can also be seen as an indicator of disorganized or less organized familial situations, such as not concerning oneself with pregnancy prevention or exploiting children in problematic marital relationships.

4. *Parents' Criminal Records*: Parents who abuse their children, in many cases, also have been charged with other offenses such as stealing, deception, and violence.

5. *Gender of Delinquent.* Reports indicate slightly higher rates of violence for females (53%) compared to males (47%). The primary cause of gender disparity may be the disproportionate level of child-rearing responsibilities. In two-parent families, the father is more often involved in child abuse, whereas in single-parent families, the mother is more likely to abuse her child. Alexander, Moore, and Alexander (1991) attested that there are different patterns of transmitting violence: In contrast to women, men seem to model violent behavior directly – namely, as a function of experiencing abuse by their own father.

6. *Age of the Parents*: Younger parents are more susceptible to committing child abuse. Anglo-American studies in particular indicate that in cases of severe infant abuse, the likelihood of abusiveness in young mothers is three times higher compared to the average age of the population. The mean age of perpetrators of physical child abuse is 32 years (Barnett et al., 1997). Other studies were able to show that abusive families are generally young families, many of whom were still in their teens when the first child was born.

7. *Social Isolation of the Family*: Abusive parents live in a more isolated manner than nonabusive parents. They lack important resources of social support, and the isolation leads to a lack of social control.

2.2. Characteristics of Victims of Physical Child Abuse

The research on violence has identified the following aspects with regard to child characteristics of abuse:

1. *Age of the Child.* Although child abuse occurs at every age level, it can be shown that there is an accumulation of violence in certain groups. Creighton (1984) estimates that nearly 50% of all abused children are older than 5 years and nearly 29% are older than 10 years. Other findings reveal that the risk of physical maltreatment declines with age. Prevalence

rates for the United States indicate that the majority of child victims fall between the ages of infants and 5 years (51%), followed by children between the ages of 6 and 11 years (26%), and then children between the ages of 12 and 17 years (23%) (Barnett et al., 1997). The peak period for abuse seems to be between the toddler and preschool ages (Egeland, 1993). This may give rise to one of the main problems in the estimation of the transmission rate, in that parents of children from infancy to the the age of 3 years are neglected in studies – as, for example, occurred in the nationally representative study by Straus (1980a), who interviewed 1,146 two-parent families with a child between the ages of 3 and 17 years.

2. *Gender.* Results concerning gender are not consistent. Some studies determined that boys are more often physically abused (National Family Violence Survey, Straus & Gelles, 1990), whereas in other studies, the frequency of abuse is relatively equal across gender. Results of the American Association for Protecting Children (AAPC) from 1988 demonstrate that for minor acts of physical violence, males and females are equally at risk; however, for major acts, boys are slightly more (54%) at risk than girls (46%) (Barnett et al., 1997). However, in most of the studies, the rate of abused boys is higher than that of girls; only during puberty do girls seem to be more frequent victims of parental violence than boys.

3. *Sibling Position of the Child.* In most cases, the firstborn child is more victimized than subsequent children. It may be assumed that this correlates with the young age of the mother, which is a risk factor for child abuse.

4. *Perinatal Charges.* The percentage of premature infants with a birth weight lower than 2,500 grams is two to three times higher among abused children. Birth weight can be seen as an indicator of a problematic pregnancy, lack of or inadequate medical care, and insufficient nourishment and childcare. In addition, it can be related to the young age of the mother.

5. *Conduct Problems of the Child as Causes of Violence.* Factors of parental violence toward younger children are enuresis and encopresis, disobedience, and defiance by the child. Older children, by contrast, encounter parental violence through lying, stealing, and school problems (Engfer, 1986).

6. *"Difficult Children."* A further risk group consists of "difficult" children, who are irritable and have trouble sleeping and eating, probably through their temperamental disposition. Compared to "easy" children, they are often victims of parental violence. This risk grows if the parents are also inexperienced in child-rearing and are overwhelmed with their parental tasks, as well as having a low tolerance for stress. In many cases, their impatience and perturbation increases with the child's restlessness and overactivity. The child's behavior might elicit violence in parents as the only alternative for managing the current situation. As a consequence, this kind of intervention by parents may lead to further behavioral problems

of the child, such as oppositional behavior, which might ultimately be responded to with further aggressive acts by the parents. Therefore, little by little, desensitization toward aggression as a means of behavior control emerges.

3.0. EFFECTS OF CHILD ABUSE

Child abuse causes harm not only during childhood; it also leads to a significant and far-reaching impact on the child's future competencies and behavior. In other words, abused children are more likely to show cognitive, behavioral, and socioemotional difficulties for the rest of their lifetime, discussed as follows.

1. Compared to nonabused children, abused children exhibit lower intellectual and cognitive functioning and have more learning disabilities. For example, they score lower on reading and mathematics tests and are more likely to repeat a grade in school (Barnett et al., 1997). Abused children show deficiencies in their cognitive and social development (Engfer, 1986).

2. Abused children show more aggressive and antisocial behavior (even after statistically controlling for other relevant factors such as poverty and family instability). They are often more violent toward their peers than children who do not suffer from victimization. Presumably, they expect rejection and hostility and perceive or interpret actions of others in social relationships as being hostile and provocative. In addition to the inadequate perception, they believe that they have to attack the other person in order to prevent being attacked. If they are successful in terms of self-assertion through violence, the readiness toward violence may be reinforced.

3. One of the deleterious consequences of violence in childhood may be the weakening of one's ability to develop strong social bonds; that is, victims have problems with both attaching to caregivers and regulating social interactions. They not only have insecure attachments (i.e., avoidance and resistance to parents) but also show lower qualities of social interaction with adults and peers. In addition, they have a higher incidence of emotional difficulties such as lower self-esteem and frequent feelings of hopelessness and depression (Barnett et al., 1997).

4.0. THE MAGDEBURG JUVENILE VIOLENCE STUDY (MJVS)

4.1. Research Issues

In our own empirical study, we attempted to retrospectively test the hypothesis of the intergenerational transmission of violence. We looked at the relationships between experiences of violence in childhood – namely, being victimized by parents, engagement in violent activities, and victimization in peer contexts. We assume that juveniles who were victimized as children or physically punished by their parents tend to interpret their social context as being more hostile and threatening and are more apt to react with violence.

To interpret the following results of the study, consider that although juvenile violence is increasing in several European countries, including Germany (Greve & Wetzels, 1999), Sweden (Sarnecki, 1991), and Norway (Estrada, 1999), the data primarily relate to violence of a less serious nature and do not include, for example, violence leading to the death of the victim, which is a relatively rare event. However, generally speaking, when comparing the Nordic countries, the level of criminal victimization is reported to be lower in Norway than, for example, in Sweden or Denmark. Otherwise, using the example of Turkey for purposes of contrast, it was shown that nearly 13% of juveniles from the ages of 13 to 18 have been involved in violent acts as offenders (Uslucan, 2003).

4.2. Method

We analyzed adolescents aged 12 to 17 in five neighborhoods of the city of Magdeburg, Germany. The adolescents answered questions about their family climate, parental risks, and experiences with domestic violence; their personal irritability; and their attitudes toward violence, as well as their involvement in violent acts. The aim of the study was to show the different effects of family disintegration on specific dimensions of violence, acceptance of violence, violent acts, and victimization. In this chapter, we report cross-sectional data from the first wave of the questionnaire study. In particular, we focus on the relationship among parenting context in the family, juvenile conduct problems, and delinquency.

The reliabilities of the measurement instruments were satisfactory (Table 17.2); most of the scales had reliabilities (i.e., Cronbach's alpha) above .75. Likert scales with a 5-point response format measured the acceptance of the presented item ranging from "do not accept" (=1) to "accept completely" (=5); scales measuring the frequency of the presented item ranged from "never" (=1) to "always" (=5). The statistical analyses were computed with the mean values.

We questioned 1,140 students from different schools in Magdeburg; participation was voluntary. The sample included 3 12-year-old students (0.3%), 159 13-year-olds (13.9%), 385 14-year-olds (33.7%), 375 15-year-olds (32.8%), 190 16-year-olds (16.6%), and 28 17-year-olds (2.4%). The average age was 14.6 years. Participants were nearly equally distributed in terms of gender: 561 (49.1%) were male and 564 (49.3%) were female; the rest did not indicate their gender.

Table 17.2. *Measures (scales)*

Author	Scale and Item Example	Reliability (Cronbach's Alpha)
Sturzbecher (1997)	Family Climate Example: I can rely on my family members. Number of items: 9	$\alpha = 0.82$
Sturzbecher (1997)	Irritability Example: I freak out very quickly. Number of items: 9	$\alpha = 0.86$
Straus (1990)	Conflict Tactics Scale (CTS) Example: My father/mother had beaten me before I was 12 years old. Number of items: 6	$\alpha = 0.85$ (f) $\alpha = 0.82$ (m)
Straus (1990)	Conflict Tactics Scale (CTS) Example: My father/mother had rejected me before I was 12 years old. Number of items: 6	$\alpha = 0.68$
Lösel & Bliesener (1994)	Parental risk factors Example: My parents drink too much alcohol. Number of items: 6	$\alpha = 0.63$
Sturzbecher (1997)	Acceptance of violence Example: To be respected, you have to use violence. Number of items: 5	$\alpha = 0.85$
Olweus (1993)	*Bully/Victim Questionnaire* Engagement in violent acts Example: How often have you beaten another person? Number of items: 5	$\alpha = 0.82$
Olweus (1993)	Victimization Example: How often have you been beaten by another person? Number of items: 5	$\alpha = 0.78$
Covariates	Age, gender, and social status of parents	

4.3. Results

In this section, we present descriptive results regarding violence experiences of juveniles in their familial context (as victims) and peer context (as victims and perpetrators).

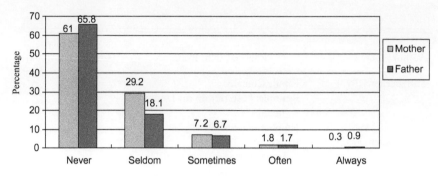

Figure 17.1. Frequency of domestic violence (Item Example: My mother/father beat me).

4.3.1. *Juvenile Violence in the Developmental Context*

Figure 17.1 shows that most of the adolescents reported having never or seldom been victims of domestic violence; more than 60% had never been beaten and between 18% and 29% were seldom victimized. However, nearly 9% were sometimes or often victims of paternal violence; the rate of maternal violence was also approximately 9%. Regarding the social status of the punishing parents, we were not able to identify a clear tendency in the group of mothers, but a tendency could be discerned among the fathers: Fathers who were househusbands showed the highest violence rates (16.7%), followed by jobless fathers (7.4%) and manual workers (4.1%). Whereas the gender differences concerning the victimization by parents are relatively small (i.e., 9.4% of males and 10.4% of females were beaten by their father; 8.3% of males and 9.8% of females were beaten by their mother), the variance among the age groups was more noteworthy, as shown in Table 17.3.

The data indicate that there was a peak of suffering domestic violence at the age of 16 years; this appeared to be valid for both maternal and paternal violence. We assume that at this age, autonomy and detachment attempts of juveniles lead to more conflicts with parents; parents who cannot cope with these changes in their adolescent children's life fall back on violence as an educational tool.

Table 17.3. *Domestic violence in different age groups (added scores of the categories "sometimes" to "always")*

Age (in years)	Maternal Violence (in %)	Paternal Violence (in %)
13 ($N = 157$)	9.6	6.7
14 ($N = 384$)	4.7	7.7
15 ($N = 374$)	11.3	11.3
16 ($N = 189$)	14.8	15.1
17 ($N = 28$)	10.7	12.5

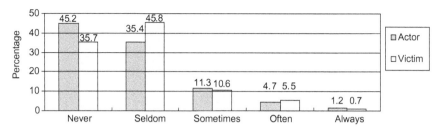

Figure 17.2. Frequency of engagement in violent activities (Item Example: Have you beaten another person/were you beaten by another person?).

Concerning one's own violent behavior (Figure 17.2), we observed that most of the students had never or rarely been engaged in violent activities and had seldom been victims of violence (nearly 80%); 17.2% reported being sometimes or more frequently engaged in violent activities; and nearly 6% reported that they were often or always engaged in violent activities. The scores for whether they had been victims of violence were similar: Approximately 16% had experienced violence from others, nearly 6% of them often or always.

Effect sizes of $d \leq 0.2$ describe small effects, $d \leq 0.5$ describe intermediate effects, and $d \geq 0.8$ describe strong effects (Bortz & Döring, 1995). The effect size d was computed as the mean difference between the groups with and without violent experiences (not the total sample) and then divided by the average standard deviation of both (i.e., violent versus nonviolent) groups. A group was categorized as having "experienced violence" if the mean value of domestic violence for separate paternal and maternal violence was $M \geq 2$; that is, if they had experienced violence more than once – from sometimes to always – from their parents.

As shown in Table 17.4, the family climate in the total sample was $M = 3.8$, which is above the theoretical scale mean of 3.0. In other words, in general, juveniles perceived the climate in their families as comfortable and satisfactory; however, this perception was clearly reduced in juveniles with experiences of domestic violence (i.e., $M = 3.22$ for paternal violence and $M = 3.19$ for maternal violence). The differences between the total sample and the "violence group" corresponded with large effect sizes (i.e., $d = 0.92$ for paternal violence, $d = 0.82$ for maternal violence). Furthermore, domestic violence and parental punishment were notably higher in the violence group than in the total sample; the violence group conceded more parental risks and regarded itself as more irritable. In particular, differences in the perception of the familial climate between the groups showed large effects, but effects were moderate concerning the attitudes toward violence and active violent behavior. The risk of victimization again showed large effect sizes between the groups (i.e., $d = 0.78$; $d = 1.0$).

As Table 17.5 reveals, most of the students were not exposed to violence from their parents; nearly 96% of the sample reported never or seldom experiencing

Table 17.4. Means, standard deviations, and effect sizes of familial and violence variables[1]

	Family Climate		Domestic Violence (m)		Domestic Violence (f)		Parental Punishment		Parental Risks		Irritability		Accept Violence		Violence Acts		Victimization	
N of total sample	1,101		1,115		1,053		1,033		1,036		1,075		1,102		1,095		1,104	
	M	SD	M	SD	M	SD	M	SD	M	SD	M	SD	M	SD	M	SD	M	SD
Total	3.8	0.65	1.19	0.34	1.18	0.4	1.88	0.58	1.5	0.44	2.76	0.82	2.11	0.94	1.54	0.59	1.75	0.6
Paternal Violence (PV) (N = 33)	3.22	0.69	1.7	0.79	2.93	0.8	2.64	0.8	2.06	0.94	3.19	0.88	2.35	1.04	1.84	0.68	2.26	0.79
Maternal Violence (MV) (N = 29)	3.19	0.86	2.79	0.58	1.83	1.01	2.66	0.7	2.29	1.03	3.35	0.88	2.63	0.88	1.71	0.6	2.46	0.9
Effect Size d — PV	0.92		1.0		3.62		1.3		0.86		0.53		0.26		0.51		0.78	
Effect Size d — MV	0.82		4.2		0.98		1.26		1.14		0.72		0.59		0.31		1.0	

[1] The effect size *d* represents the practical significance of the mean differences between the total sample and the sample with extreme domestic violence experiences (paternal and maternal).

408

Table 17.5. *Domestic violence and engagements in violence*

		Perpetrator		
		Yes	No	Total
Paternal Violence	Yes	11 (26.2%)	31 (73.8%)	42 (4.2% of total N)
	No	101 (10.5%)	863 (89.5%)	964 (95.8% of total N)
	Total	112 (11.1% of total N)	894 (88.9% of total N)	1,006 (100%)
Maternal Violence	Yes	5 (18%)	23 (82%)	28 (2.6% of total N)
	No	119 (11.4%)	922 (88.6%)	1,041 (97.4% of total N)
	Total	124 (11.6%)	945 (88.4%)	1,069 (100%)

violence from their father, whereas 42 subjects (4.2%) reported domestic violence (sometimes to always) by their father. The rate of maternal violence was lower: 97.4% never or seldom experienced violence from their mother, whereas 28 subjects reported having experienced violence from their mother sometimes or more often (2.6%). These findings are in line with national and international reports on domestic violence (Lösel & Bliesener, 2003; Wetzels, 1997). Regarding the transmission rate of violence in youth, it is clear that the rate of violent offenders with a history of abuse is less than that in the group without a history of abuse. In the group with paternal violence, 11 (26.2%) of the 42 juveniles who had experienced abuse were involved in further violence. This rate is notably lower in the group suffering from maternal violence: 5 (18%) of 28 juveniles with a history of abuse were involved in further violent acts. However, both rates were higher than the statistically expected rates: The expected rate of perpetrators for the group with paternal violence was 4.7% (the obtained value was 11%), whereas the expected rate for perpetrators with maternal violence was 3.2% (the obtained value was 5%). The mean values of perpetrators with a history of abuse in both cases (i.e., maternal and paternal violence) were higher than the group without a history of abuse (for paternal violence $M = 1.84$ versus $M = 1.52$; for maternal violence $M = 1.71$ versus $M = 1.53$), but the differences were only significant for paternal violence ($F(1,1004) = 9.07, p < .003$).

4.3.2. *Differential Impacts of Domestic Violence on Juvenile Violence*
As shown in Table 17.6, an interesting finding is that domestic violence in early childhood heightens the risk of being victimized. In our study, *victimization* is defined as suffering violence in the peer context. The rates for victimization for those with a history of abuse are notably higher than for perpetrators. Furthermore, it seems to make a difference whether domestic violence stems from the father or the mother. Whereas following a history of parental abuse, the rate of victimization seems, at 50%, to be nearly equal in the two categories (i.e., parental and maternal abuse), the risk of victimization after a history of maternal abuse is significantly higher (58.6%). The obtained rates in both cases

Table 17.6. *Domestic violence and victimization*

| | | Victimization | | |
		Yes	No	Total
Paternal Violence	Yes	21 (48.8%)	22 (51.2%)	43 (4.2% of total N)
	No	187 (19.2%)	787 (80.8%)	974 (95.8% of total N)
	Total	208 (20.5% of total N)	809 (79.5% of total N)	1,017 (100%)
Maternal Violence	Yes	17 (58.6%)	12 (41.4%)	29 (2.7% of total N)
	No	208 (19.8%)	841 (80.2%)	1,049 (97.3% of total N)
	Total	225 (20.9% of total N)	853 (79.1% of total N)	1,078 (100%)

are clearly higher than those that are statistically expected: The expected rate of victimization for the group with paternal violence is 8.8% and the obtained value is 21%; the expected rate for victimization with maternal violence is 6.1% and the obtained value is 17%. We can conclude that regarding victimization, the cycle of violence is far more apparent: Experiencing domestic violence in early childhood dramatically heightens the risk of being victimized in one's peer group.

Those juveniles who are victimized early in their childhood are – rather than becoming the later perpetrators – far more likely to become the later victims.

4.3.3. *Juvenile Violence and the Interplay of Personal and Familial Risks*
Concerning the acceptance of violence – as a cognitive prerequisite of active violence – the correlations with the indicated variables, as shown in Table 17.7, were all significant.

In addition to personal irritability, parental punishment and parental risk factors such as drug or alcohol abuse resulted in the highest correlation coefficients. As expected, family climate showed a negative correlation because it was measured as an index of positive interactions in the family. For the prediction of the acceptance of violence, personal irritability of the child was an important predictor; the second best predictor was family climate.

Regarding the active engagement in violence, the correlations were all highly significant ($p < .001$) with the indicator variables. In addition to a high irritability factor, both a negative family climate and parental punishments were the decisive factors for an active involvement in violence. For victimization, we were able to show (see Table 17.7) that, in particular, parental punishments during early childhood had the highest correlation, followed by personal irritability and maternal violence during childhood. Among those variables, all correlations were highly significant ($p < .001$) with the indicator variables. The best predictors

Table 17.7. *Correlations and standardized regression coefficients between violence and indicators of familial disintegration (N = 1,143)*

	Acceptance of Violence		Engagement in Violent Acts		Victimization	
	r	β	r	β	r	β
Family climate	−.17***	−.07*	−.23***	−.14***	−.14***	.02
Domestic violence – mother	.14***	.03	.17***	.04	.29***	.13***
Domestic violence – father	.11**	.00	.17***	.08*	.25***	.08*
Parental risk factors	.18***	.05	.20***	.04	.27***	.10**
Parental punishment	.20***	.04	.22***	.08*	.33***	.16***
Irritability	.38***	.34***	.32***	.25***	.30***	.20***
R^2 (explained variance)		.16		.15		.19

Notes:
r: Correlation coefficient (Pearson); controlled for age and gender.
β: Standardized regression coefficient.
*** $p < .001$; ** $p < .01$; * $p < .05$.

of victimization were irritability ($\beta = 0.20$; $p < .001$) and parental punishment ($\beta = 0.16$; $p < .001$).

The bivariate analyses illustrate that the acceptance of violence and active violent behavior was highly and positively correlated ($r = 0.53$; $p < .001$). Moreover, the relationship between acceptance and engagement in violent acts in a group was significant ($r = 0.57$; $p < .001$). These correlations were notably higher than those typically found between attitudes and behavior in psychology.

In accordance with other findings in the domain of the intergenerational transmission of violence, the results revealed significant relationships between domestic violence experienced in childhood and current involvement in violent behavior. Family climate, domestic violence, punishing parental styles, and personal irritability explained 16% of the variance of the acceptance of violence, 15% of the engagement in violent activities, and 19% of victimization (see Table 17.7).[2]

5.0. DISCUSSION

The detailed mechanisms of the intergenerational transmission of violence are far from well established. We discussed some of the prominent theories about

[2] This study was supported by the Kultusministerium des Landes Sachsen-Anhalt (FKZ: 2986A/0088R) with a grant to Urs Fuhrer and Karl-Peter Fritzsche.

why people are apt to act violently and attempted to identify risk factors on several ecological levels for the persistence of violence across generations. There is clear evidence that the transmission of cultural values and behavior patterns is mainly due to parenting. We were able to show in our empirical study that parenting styles characterized by positive emotional interaction between parent and child inhibits the transmission of violence (positive family climate), whereas parenting styles with violence as an educational means promotes the transmission of violence. In this regard, we demonstrate mechanisms that are contrary to those suggested by Schönpflug (2001) for the transmission of cultural values.

Results of our study confirm the hypothesis of the intergenerational transmission of violence. We were able to demonstrate that students who were punished physically by their parents were more likely to be involved in violent acts and in aggressive behavior toward others than students without experiences of violence in early childhood (see Table 17.4). The results for victimization were more clear: We were able to show that juveniles with a history of abuse (i.e., who were victimized by their parents) show a significantly higher risk for further victimization in their peer context. In addition, more precise analyses revealed that mainly maternal domestic violence entails a higher risk of victimization.

It can be assumed that juveniles who as children were frequently punished physically by their parents develop a weaker sense of personal worth, have low self-confidence (high experience of loss), and lack assertive strategies to manage conflicts. This may lead to further withdrawal and isolation in peer contexts, which disposes them to victimization (e.g., in school). They "learn" to accept violent behavior directed at them and – to a moderate extent – also learn to use violence as their own strategy for solving conflicts in everyday life. In terms of the assumptions of learning theory, they may be desensitized to the consequences of violence. Analogous to the concept of "learned helplessness" (Seligman, 1979), they develop learned "victim careers." Here, we can discern a kind of "negative" transmission insofar as it is not the active violent behavior patterns of parents that are transmitted but rather one's own passive suffering from early childhood to adolescence. According to this line of reasoning, we cannot confirm, for example, psychoanalytic assumptions that claim an "identification with the aggressor" (Freud, 1936) in order to explain the current violence of victims of early-childhood abuse. It seems that in accordance with Simons et al. (1991), it is not the direct path from experienced to enacted violence that will be transmitted but rather the aggressive style of interaction. In general, the assumptions of learning theory seem to be most suitable for interpreting our findings, although we were also able to confirm that the home-staying/joblessness of the father, in particular, led to a heightened risk of using violence toward his children. Thus, the sociological perspective also finds some support in our results.

Regarding active violence, our findings confirm the suggested 30%, ±5% (Kaufman & Zigler, 1993) rule of thumb for the estimation rate of violence transmission.

By differentiating the aspects of violence in "violence acceptance," "violent acts," and "victimization," and by regarding the effects of maternal and paternal violence separately, we were able to show different developmental effects of parental violence on juveniles: Intergenerational transmission of violence was more obvious for victimization and less so for violent acts. In summary, we were able to identify two main determinants of juvenile violence: the temperament (i.e., irritability) as a personal variable and the experienced domestic violence as a context variable. Therefore, prevention and intervention programs to reduce violence should focus primarily on techniques of anger regulation for children and parenting methods for adults as, for example, is the case in the well-established Triple P – Positive Parenting Program (Sanders, 1999).

The results of our study should be complemented by (1) a longitudinal analysis to explore the details of the transmission process, which we already completed with regard to victimization (Uslucan & Fuhrer, 2004); and (2) the analysis of parent–child dyads in a longitudinal and cross-cultural comparison, which we explored in the project "Violence in Families of Turkish Origin" (Fuhrer & Uslucan, 2002; Mayer, Fuhrer, & Uslucan, 2005). An analogous and more elaborated research design for the study of value transmission is discussed by Boehnke (2001) and Boehnke, Hadjar, and Baier (Chapter 19, this volume).

6.0. CONCLUSIONS AND METHODOLOGICAL REMARKS

First, it should be mentioned that violence is a continuous variable ranging from verbal abuse to varying degrees of physical abuse. For greater precision, it is necessary to use a specific concept of violence. Violence, and especially familial violence, is a social construction. It is conceivable that violence in other cultures may also be common but may not be recognized as a social problem. We refer to violence in a restrictive sense, according to which violence is intentional and related to physical harm.

The methodological problems of estimating the transmission rate are that (1) the sample size is often too small, (2) a control group often does not exist, (3) the data are often self-reports, and (4) they are retrospective data. When relying on case-study materials as primary data sources, they must be interpreted cautiously (Kaufman & Zigler, 1987); as retrospective data, they have even less validity. One further aspect that is responsible for the variance of the rate is the definitional criterion: The broader the definition of abuse, the greater the link between a history of abuse and current abuse. The nominal and operational definitions of violence are not even sufficiently resolved; there are no generally accepted formal definitions of "history of abuse" and "current abuse."

Nevertheless, we should keep in mind that child abuse is a low-base-rate phenomenon (Kaufman & Zigler, 1993). However, on the other hand, we should also be aware that children with a history of abuse are not only at risk of suffering excessive aggression and poor parenting but also of forming a number of other negative developmental traits such as depressive disorders (Kaufman, 1991) and other psychiatric problems.

Due to the high degree of sensitivity of the problem, it is difficult to collect data because of the legal consequences for the perpetrator and their stigmatization. Another basic problem concerns sample size – in particular, in terms of large representative samples such as the National Survey of Families and Households, the National Survey on Children, and the National Longitudinal Survey of Youth. In a large sample size, even very small effects can be statistically significant but cannot necessarily be interpreted as clinically significant (Deal & Anderson, 1995).

Further problems concern the sources of the data, as follows:

1. With self-reports by the perpetrator, there are the problems of memory lapses and decreased reliability of retrospective data. The perpetrators may lie, minimize, or overestimate the severity of violence or perceive their own violence as justified and thus not as reportable.
2. The recollections of victims may be influenced by the relationship between perpetrator and victim, perhaps resulting in lower report rates.
3. Informant reports (e.g., witnesses or observers of violence, teachers) or direct observations by scientists in laboratory situations (e.g., measurement of physiological responses during a quarrel) seem more reliable but lack ecological validity (Barnett et al., 1997).
4. To methodologically determine the different causal effects of violence transmission and to understand the mechanisms involved in breaking the cycle of violence, we require longitudinal studies with four different groups: (1) parents with a history of abuse who currently abuse their children, (2) parents with a history of abuse who do not abuse their children, (3) parents without a history of abuse who currently abuse their children, and (4) parents without a history of abuse who do not abuse their children.

Further research should try to solve these problems and thereby improve our understanding of the transmission of violence in families.

REFERENCES

Alexander, P. C., Moore, S., & Alexander, E. (1991). What is transmitted in the intergenerational transmission of violence? *Journal of Marriage and the Family, 53,* 657–668.
Bandura, A. (1973). *Aggression: A social learning analysis.* Englewood Cliffs, NJ: Prentice Hall.

Bandura, A., Ross, D., & Ross, S. A. (1961). Transmission of aggression through imitation of aggressive models. *Journal of Abnormal and Social Psychology, 67*, 575–582.

Barnett, O. W., Miller-Perrin, C. L., & Perrin, R. D. (1997). *Family violence across the lifespan*. Thousand Oaks–London–New Delhi: Sage Publications.

Belsky, J. (1980). Child maltreatment: An ecological integration. *American Psychologist, 35*, 320–335.

Belsky, J. (1993). Etiology of child maltreatment: A developmental-ecological analysis. *Psychological Bulletin, 114*, 413–433.

Belsky, J., & Vondra, J. (1989). Lessons from child abuse: The determinants of parenting. In D. Cichetti & V. Carlson (Eds.), *Child maltreatment: Theory and research on the causes and consequences of child abuse and neglect* (pp. 153–203). Cambridge: Cambridge University Press.

Boehnke, K. (2001). Parent–offspring value transmission in a societal context. *Journal of Cross-Cultural Psychology, 32*, 241–255.

Bortz, J., & Döring, N. (1995). *Forschungsmethoden und Evaluation* [Research methods and evaluation]. Berlin: Springer.

Bower, M. E., & Knutson, J. F. (1996). Attitudes toward physical discipline as a function of disciplinary history and self-labeling as physically abused. *Child Abuse & Neglect, 20*, 689–699.

Caliso, J., & Milner, J. (1992). Childhood history of abuse and child abuse screening. *Child Abuse & Neglect, 16*, 647–659.

Creighton, S. J. (1984). Trends in child abuse: 1977–1982. *The fourth report on the children placed on the NSPCC special units registers*. London: National Society for the Prevention of Cruelty to Children.

Darling, N., & Steinberg, L. (1993). Parenting style as context: An integrative model. *Psychological Bulletin, 113*, 487–496.

Deal, J. E., & Anderson, E. R. (1995). Reporting and interpreting results in family research. *Journal of Marriage and the Family, 57*, 1040–1048.

Egeland, B. (1993). A history of abuse is a major risk factor for abusing the next generation. In R. J. Gelles & D. R. Loseke (Eds.), *Current controversies on family violence* (pp. 197–208). Thousand Oaks–London–New Delhi: Sage Publications.

Egeland, B., Jacobvitz, D., & Stroufe, L. A. (1988). Breaking the cycle of abuse. *Child Development, 59*, 1080–1088.

Egeland, B., & Stroufe, L. A. (1981a). Developmental sequelae of maltreatment in infancy. In R. Rizley & D. Cicchetti (Eds.), *New directions for child development: Developmental perspectives in child maltreatment* (pp. 79–92). San Francisco: Jossey Bass.

Egeland, B., & Stroufe, L. A. (1981b). Attachment and early maltreatment. *Child Development, 52*, 44–52.

Engfer, A. (1986). *Kindesmißhandlung* [Child abuse]. Stuttgart, Germany: Enke.

Engfer, A. (2000). Gewalt gegen Kinder in der Familie [Violence against children in families]. In U. T. Egle, S. O. Hoffmann, & P. Joraschky (Hrsg.), *Sexueller Mißbrauch, Mißhandlung und Vernachlässigung* [Sexual abuse, violence and neglect] (pp. 23–40). Stuttgart, Germany: Schattauer.

Estrada, F. (1999). Juvenile crime trends in post-war Europe. *European Journal on Criminal Policy and Research, 7*, 23–42.

Freud, A. (1936). *The ego and the mechanisms of defense.* New York: International Universities Press.

Fuhrer, U., & Uslucan, H.-H. (2002). *Gewalt in Familien türkischer Herkunft* [Violence in Turkish families]. Unpublished proposal for a grant to the German State Department of the Family, Seniors, Women and Youth.

Garbarino, J., & Ebata, A. (1983). The significance of ethnic and cultural differences in child maltreatment. *Journal of Marriage and Family, 45,* 773–783.

Gelles, R. J., & Cornell, C. P. (1985). *Intimate violence in families.* Beverly Hills, CA: Sage Publications.

Gil, D. (1973). *Violence against children: Physical child abuse in the United States.* Cambridge, MA: Harvard University Press.

Greve, W., & Wetzels, P. (1999). Kriminalität und Gewalt in Deutschland: Lagebild und offene Fragen [Delinquency and violence in Germany: The situation and open questions]. *Zeitschrift für Sozialpsychologie, 30,* 95–110.

Herrenkohl, E. C., Herrenkohl, R. C., & Toedter, L. J. (1983). Perspectives on the intergenerational transmission of abuse. In D. Finkelhor, R. J. Gelles, G. T. Hotaling, & M. A. Straus (Eds.), *The dark side of families: Current family violence research* (pp. 305–316). Thousand Oaks–London–New Delhi: Sage Publications.

Herzberger, S. (1996). *Violence within the family: Social psychological perspectives.* Oxford: Westview Press.

Hunter, R. S., & Kilström, N. (1979). Breaking the cycle in abusive families. *American Journal of Psychiatry, 136,* 1320–1322.

Kalmus, D. (1984). The intergenerational transmission of marital aggression. *Journal of Marriage and the Family, 46,* 11–19.

Kaufman, J. (1991). Depressive disorders in maltreated children. *Journal of American Child and Adolescent Psychiatry, 30,* 257–265.

Kaufman, J., & Zigler, E. (1987). Do abused children become abusive parents? *American Journal of Orthopsychiatry, 57,* 186–192.

Kaufman, J., & Zigler, E. (1989). The intergenerational transmission of child abuse. In D. Cichetti & V. Carlson (Eds.), *Child maltreatment: Theory and research on the causes and consequences of child abuse and neglect* (pp. 129–150). Cambridge: Cambridge University Press.

Kaufman, J., & Zigler, E. (1993). The intergenerational transmission of abuse is overstated. In R. J. Gelles & D. R. Loseke (Eds.), *Current controversies on family violence* (pp. 209–221). Thousand Oaks–London–New Delhi: Sage Publications.

Kempe, C., & Helfer, R. (1972). *Helping the battered child and his family.* Philadelphia: J. B. Lippincott.

Lackey, C., & Williams, K. R. (1995). Social bonding and the cessation of partner violence across generations. *Journal of Marriage and the Family, 57,* 295–305.

Lösel, F., & Bliesener, T. (1994). Some high-risk adolescents do not develop conduct problems: A study of protective factors. *International Journal of Behavioral Development, 17,* 753–777.

Lösel, F., & Bliesener, T. (2003). *Aggression und Delinquenz unter Jugendlichen* [Aggression and delinquency among adolescents]. Neuwied, Germany: Luchterhand.

Main, M., & Goldwyn, R. (1984). Predicting rejection of her infant from mother's representation of her own experiences: A preliminary report. *International Journal of Child Abuse and Neglect, 8*, 203–207.

Mayer, S., Fuhrer, U., & Uslucan, H. (2005). Akkulturation und intergenerationale Transmission von Gewalt in Familien türkischer Herkunft. [Acculturation and intergenerational transmission of violence in familes of Turkish origin]. *Psychologie in Erziehung und Unterricht, 52*, 168–185.

Olweus, D. (1993). *Bullying at school: What we know and what we can do.* Oxford: Cambridge.

Pelton, L. H. (1978). Child abuse and neglect: The myth of classlessness. *American Journal of Orthopsychiatry, 48*, 608–617.

Ratzke, K., & Cierpka, M. (2000). Familien von Kindern mit aggressiven Verhaltensweisen [Families of children with aggressive behavior]. In U. T. Egle, S. O. Hoffmann, & P. Joraschky (Hrsg.), *Sexueller Mißbrauch, Mißhandlung und Vernachlässigung* [Sexual abuse, violence and neglect] (pp. 99–115). Stuttgart, Germany: Schattauer.

Sanders, M. R. (1999). The Triple P – Positive Parenting Program: Towards an empirically validated multi-level parenting and family support strategy for the prevention and treatment of child behavior and emotional problems. *Child and Family Psychology Review, 2*, 71–90.

Sarnecki, J. (1991). Juvenile delinquency in Sweden. In A. Snare (Ed.), *Youth, crime and justice: Scandinavian studies in criminology, Vol. 12* (pp. 11–25). Oslo: Norwegian University Press.

Schönpflug, U. (2001). Intergenerational transmission of values: The role of transmission belts. *Journal of Cross-Cultural Psychology, 32*, 174–185.

Seligman, M. E. P. (1979). *Erlernte Hilflosigkeit* [Learned helplessness]. Munich: Urban & Schwarzenberg.

Simons, R. L., Whitbeck, L. B., Conger, R. D., & Chyi-In, W. (1991). Intergenerational transmission of harsh parenting. *Developmental Psychology, 27*, 159–171.

Straus, M. A. (1980a). Societal stress and marital violence in a national sample of American families. In F. Wright, C. Bahn, & R. W. Rieber (Eds.), *Annals of the New York Academy of Sciences: Vol. 347, Forensic Psychology and Psychiatry* (pp. 229–250). New York: New York Academy of Sciences.

Straus, M. A. (1980b). Stress and physical child abuse. *Child Abuse and Neglect, 4*, 75–88.

Straus, M. A. (1990). Measuring intrafamily conflict and violence: The conflict tactics (CT) scales. In M.A. Straus & R. J. Gelles (Eds.), *Physical violence in American families: Risk factors and adaptations to violence in 8,145 families* (pp. 29–47): New Brunswick, NJ: Transaction.

Straus, M. A., & Gelles, R. J. (1990). *Physical violence in American families: Risk factors and adaptations to violence in 8,145 families*: New Brunswick, NJ: Transaction.

Sturzbecher, D. (1997). *Jugend und Gewalt in Ostdeutschland* [Youth and violence in East Germany]. Göttingen: Verlag für Angewandte Psychologie.

Uslucan, H.-H. (2003). Soziale Verunsicherung, Familienklima und Gewaltbelastung türkischer Jugendlicher. [Social insecurity, family climate and violence exposure of Turkish adolescents]. *Zeitschrift für Türkeistudien, 15*, 49–73.

Uslucan, H.-H., & Fuhrer, U. (2004). Viktimisierungen und Gewalthandlungen im Jugendalter. [Victimisation and juvenile violent acts]. *Psychologie in Erziehung und Unterricht, 51*, 178–188.

Wetzels, P. (1997). Gewalterfahrungen in der Kindheit [Experiences with violence in childhood]. Baden-Baden: Nomos.

Widom, C. S. (1989). Does violence beget violence? A critical reexamination of the literature. *Psychological Bulletin, 106*, 3–28.

Wolfe, D. A. (1985). Child-abusive parents: An empirical review and analysis. *Psychological Bulletin, 97*, 462–482.

http://www.aile.gov.tr/Arastirma12.htm

http://www.aile.gov.tr/Arastirma18.htm

http://www.kriminoloji.com/siddet%20cocuk.htm

18

"Don't Trust Anyone over 25": Youth Centrism, Intergenerational Transmission of Political Orientations, and Cultural Change

TOM F. M. TER BOGT, WIM M. J. MEEUS,
QUINTEN A. W. RAAIJMAKERS, FRITS VAN WEL, AND
WILMA A. M. VOLLEBERGH

INTRODUCTION

In his seminal work on generational identity and the intergenerational transmission of ideas, Mannheim (1928) already stated that under "normal" social conditions, the ideas of youth resemble those of adults. Only in times of intense social turmoil is it likely that young people start realizing that the conditions they have to face while growing up have changed drastically from those under which their parents grew up and that their worldview should change accordingly. The culturally most sensitive part of a cohort of young people might voice its opinions and create a consciousness that might become the trademark of a larger group of a youth generation, consciously setting itself apart from the habits and ideas of an older generation.

Mannheim (1928) wrote this part of his work in post–World War I Germany, where a demoralized young-adult generation, wary of war and nationalistic slogans, expressed intense dissent with the optimistic bourgeois outlook that had prevailed in the last decades of the 19th century and the first decades of the 20th. The war itself, the socialist revolution attempts of 1918–1919, and the highly unstable social and political climate in the Weimar Republic fostered a generational consciousness among a group of young adults who had left their youth in the trenches of the Great War. To those young men, the future looked bleak and all bourgeois claims of imminent progress and grand visions of Germany's geopolitical prominence, as espoused throughout the countries' educational system, seemed a fraud.

Although he was keen to note that most of the time, the young follow the old, Mannheim was among the first to address the role that adolescents and young adults, united as a generation with a distinct ideology, may have in changing the cultural climate of societies they grow up in (Abma, 1990). During the 20th century, young people were at the forefront of different social movements and, notably after World War II, instigated new ways of ideologically or affectively confronting the world. In this chapter, we empirically examine the special role young people with a strong orientation toward their peers and an equally strong aversion to the adult world may have in changing political orientations in a broad sense. Thus, one of the origins of cultural change is relocalized within the family, as an effect of the failure of parents to transmit their ideas to their young or, conversely, of the active resistance of children to the ideas of their parents.

1.0. YOUTH AND CULTURAL CHANGE

Mannheim (1928), in fact, was responding to a cultural shift with pre–World War I roots. Around the turn of the century, Germany saw the advent of what – for the first time – had to be called "youth culture" in a modern sense (Gillis, 1974). In 1897, Hermann Hoffman, a student living in Berlin, started hiking in the vicinity of the city with a group of grammar school students. In 1901, the movement of the Wandervogel was officially founded and, within a decade, branches of this loosely organized youth movement were established all over Germany. At first, this was a boys-only movement, but within a few years, girls were also allowed to become members. The Wandervogel crossed the country from the North Sea to the Alps. Through their clothes and image, this group of young people broke with the ideas and habits of the petit-bourgeois stratum from which they were recruited. The Wandervogel themselves were convinced that they could get along as men and women in a "pure" (i.e., nonsexualized) way, but they met with stiff resistance from adults, who thought that girls and boys wandering and camping out together with no adults around to curtail adolescent lust, was an insult to decency and they called for a ban of the movement (Becker, 1946/1960; Stachura, 1981).

In the criticism of a rapidly industrializing Germany, a number of elements kept recurring. The Wandervogel promoted a romantic vision of unspoiled country life; they thought that social interaction among people in the country was more authentic than among people in the city. They distrusted the pleasures of city life: entertainment and nightlife and the accompanying use of alcohol and cigarettes. Above all, the Wandervogel felt that youth had to set an example for the elderly. After all, had not the older generation just lost all credibility? The Wandervogel turned against their strict upbringing at home, the authoritarian climate in both school and church, and the pompous nationalism that permeated cultural and intellectual life. By returning to nature, beauty, and camaraderie and by declining materialism, authoritarianism, and narrow-mindedness, this generation held up a mirror to the face of the older generation and thereby claimed its role in history *as youth.* They were unified by the creed that young people were essential for the cultural development of the nation and that their vision was crucial for cultural revitalization (Becker, 1946/1960; Stachura, 1981; ter Bogt, 2000). In this sense, the Wandervogel were an example for all successive youth movements that tried to do the same.

In his book, *L'enfant et la Vie Familiale Sous l'Ancien Régime*, the French historian Philippe Ariès (1960) showed that for the development of an adolescent consciousness, the instigation of an educational system in all industrialized countries in the 18th and 19th centuries was of crucial importance. Instead of learning from parents and tutors (i.e., in continuous close contact with adults), young people were isolated from society and concentrated within special institutions – namely, schools. Especially in the last century, school age was systematically prolonged for almost every adolescent. It thus comes as no surprise that adolescents started to identify themselves as a separate group and that the higher educated – for example, the Wandervogel – would do so first (ter Bogt, 2000). As a reaction to the social categorization, a self-categorization was to follow. Ariès calls the definition of a population group between children and adults – adolescents and their experience of being young together – a historical construction. A strong orientation toward peers, later defined by social scientists as *youth centrism*, is a relatively new phenomenon that was inconceivable before the 20th century.

Throughout the 20th century, groups of young people maintained ideas and developed concepts that went against the grain of dominant culture (Elsler, 1971). Most of the attempts to formulate new cultural ideals and corresponding new ways of behaving met fierce resistance because adults were outraged by youth cultural displays of "bad" behavior and "immoral" attitudes (Cohen, 1972; Springhall, 1998). Historians have documented the role that young people played in major political and cultural shifts. Whereas their exact prominence as prime cultural movers may be disputed, even conservative observers have noted that although they may not have instigated cultural shifts, they were at least among the first to respond to changes at hand (Righart, 1995).

From the 1950s onward, in the historical and sociological literature, the role of adolescents has been described in the development of a more pleasure- and consumption-oriented society; the loosening of authoritarian attitudes and puritan sexual practices; greater equality of the sexes; acknowledgment of minority rights; attention to environmental values; and, in general, a permeation of postmaterialist values (Inglehart, 1977, 1997; Vollebergh, 1991). However, youth cultural movements do not systematically favor liberal, left-wing political, or cultural orientations. A substantial part of German youth fused the Nazi regime with youthful enthusiasm (Koch, 1975) and, in postwar Europe, young people have been avid supporters and propagators of right-wing extremist ideals (Wilkinson, 1981). Young people may passionately proliferate their ideals and self-confidently hold up against adult pressure, but the content of their idealism may differ radically. They have shown themselves able to promote both right- and left-wing ideologies or support ideas rooted in religious symbolic universes (ter Bogt, 2000).

In the social sciences, the special features of adolescence were recognized early. In 1905, Hall published his landmark study on a social category that had become more visible in the previous decades. In the next quarter of a century, his book, *Adolescence: Its Psychology and its Relations to Physiology, Anthropology, Sociology, Sex, Crime, Religion, and Education,* would become one of the most influential works for youth studies. As early as 1940, American sociologist Kingsley Davis published a work on what he called the parent–youth conflict. Whereas Mannheim saw generational conflicts as youthful expressions confined to times of profound social change, Davis was one of the first to consider a generation gap as a structural characteristic of modern society. In this type of society with – by definition – always rapidly changing social environments, children can no longer rely on the knowledge of their own parents. The fast obsolescence of the adult worldview in modern society makes for a social sphere in which young people can find relevant, up-to-date ideas on society and their future position in it. Parsons (1942) also sought the necessity and functionality of youth culture as a mediator between childhood and adult life in updating and preparing young people with the help of their peers for their role as grown-up citizens. He valued a certain tension between parents and their children and an orientation of young people toward their peers as a functional part of modern social life. Much later, in the 1970s and 1980s, British neo-Marxists criticized these functionalist thinkers for their lack of interest in class differences in the position and attitudes of youth; however, the sociologists from the Centre of Contemporary Cultural Studies in Birmingham posed the viewpoint that youth cultures and the worldview they help to shape are not only crucial for the ideas their members hold but also contribute to the public debate in their time (Abma, 1990). Members of the working-class youth culture may not use the traditional strategies of the labor movement, but with their dress codes, expression, and ideas, they pursue a "symbolic guerrilla" war (Hebdige, 1979) against bourgeois hegemony. Common to those functionalist and neo-Marxist views of the social position and role of youth cultures is that the cultural formations are responses to social changes and they themselves help to further change the world (ter Bogt & Meeus, 1994).

2.0. POLITICAL ORIENTATIONS

Adolescence is a critical period for the development of an identity and a world-view. Young people identify with their peers and take on a certain psychological distance from their parents. This does not imply a complete split between children and their parents; the older generation is highly effective in passing on its attitudes. Mannheim's (1928) ideas of the customary transmission of ideas from one generation to the next are corroborated by most empirical studies from the last decades. Although young people may have their own world with their peers, as functionalist and neo-Marxist sociologists pose, results of those studies reveal a striking resemblance between the opinions of parents and those of their children, and this similarity is not confined to the period in which children are young and living with their parents (Acock & Bengtson, 1980; Dalhouse & Frideres, 1996; Jennings & Niemi, 1981; Miller & Glass, 1989; Raaijmakers, 1993).

When trying to educate them, parents pass on their opinions directly to their children (Acock & Bengtson, 1980; Beck & Jennings, 1975; Moen, Erickson, & Dempster-McClain, 1997; Petit, Clawson, Dodge, & Bates, 1996; Vollebergh, Iedema, & Raaijmakers, 2001). However, in addition to direct parental transfer, at least two other processes are operative. Generally, both groups share the same environment and have the same social status. Sociocultural forces may propel both parents and their children in the same direction where the formation of attitudes is concerned (Glass, Bengtson, & Dunham, 1986; Vollebergh et al., 2001). Furthermore, transmission is not a one-way process. Especially during late adolescence and young adulthood, the relationship between parents and children tends to become more egalitarian. Children can hold their ground while discussing issues, and they start to influence the opinions of their parents. This too may result in more similarity of views (Cooney, 1997). Vollebergh et al. (2001) tried to model the different processes governing the formation of attitudes in the context of the family. They convincingly showed that all three processes – sociocultural inheritance, parental influence, and adolescent influence – were independently effective in the molding of opinions.

In this study, the focus is on two political orientations: *economic* and *cultural conservatism*. Middendorp (1978, 1991) followed Rokeach (1973) in dividing political attitudes into the domains of left/right and libertarian/conservative. We follow the conceptualization used by Felling, Peters, and Schreuder (1983) for the same dimensions: economic conservatism and cultural conservatism. Economic conservatives feel that existing economic conditions – that is, the liberal market economy – should not be changed. Differences in income, status, and wealth are justified and the labor movement, whether socialist parties or unions, should not become a dominant social force. Independently of these types of attitudes relating to economics and power, a second field of attitudes can be distinguished. Felling and his colleagues note, as Rokeach had previously, that lifestyle issues and moral judgments about the way people should lead their life form a different attitudinal field of political-cultural orientations. Cultural conservatism can be described as a traditionalistic outlook on life regarding social and familial roles of men and women, the status of "own" and "foreign" culture, and the rights of gays and other minority groups with nonmainstream lifestyles. In empirical research, it is operationalized as a combination of a nonegalitarian view of male–female relationships, suspicion toward immigrants and their culture, and an aversion to relationships and forms of cohabitation other than the civil marriage (Middendorp, 1978, 1991; Vollebergh, 1991; Vollebergh, Iedema, & Meeus, 1999).

In the Netherlands, the tendency during the period from 1970 to 1992 was a reinforcement of economic conservatism in combination with a decline of cultural conservatism. Cohort differences in changes regarding economic issues are weaker than those regarding cultural conservatism. Thus, like older people, new generations of adolescents have become more in favor of a market economy that sustains inequality in property and control, but they have been surpassing the older cohorts in wanting to fend off authorities probing into what they feel is their private life. It is important to mention that *within* cohorts, opinions were less prone to historical change, especially with regard to cultural conservatism. This suggests that opinions on cultural issues seem to be formed in a particular phase of life and that they remain fairly resistant to change afterwards. Economic conservatism is more of a general indicator of historical shifts in attitudes (Vollebergh et al., 1999). Differences in content and in susceptibility to historical contexts legitimize the separate analysis of cultural and economic conservatism. However, both the economic and cultural conservatism of youngsters are influenced by the environment in which they grow up. Parental income and level of education are – next to the adolescents' own level of education – strong predictors of those variables. The strength of the determinants does not change during adolescence. In developing their own views, adolescents cannot escape the confinements of their class and education. The environmental pressures appear to provide a relatively stable context for the internalization of political orientations. Past research has shown that sociocultural factors are strong predictors of adolescent orientations (Vollebergh et al., 2001).

As discussed previously, adolescents ground their conservatism, or lack of it, in the opinions that their parents hold, and they also transfer some of their attitudes to their parents. Across the two domains of economic and cultural conservatism, parental influence is – next to sociocultural inheritance – a strong determinant. Children influence their parents to a lesser degree than the reverse. Transfer of attitudes is a two-way process, although parents seem to be more effective in pushing through their views. Parents continue to be more influential than their children; however, in line with the growing independence of adolescents on their way to adulthood, their influence diminishes (ter Bogt & Meeus, 1994). Furthermore, older adolescents have stabilized their own views; they are more consistent in venting the internalized opinions (Vollebergh et al., 2001).

3.0. THE PSYCHOLOGY OF YOUTH CENTRISM

Adolescents distinguishing themselves as youth centrists exhibit a strong identification with peers and peer culture combined with distrust and loathing of the adult world and its institutions. Youth centrism, then, might act as a buffer against the parental transmission of opinions. This research issue is discussed in this chapter.

The concept of youth centrism originates from the concept of teenage ethnocentrism developed in British studies conducted in the 1960s by Schofield (1965). It can be defined in terms of the following: (1) rejection of parental influence and marked orientation toward peers; (2) criticism of adult institutions (e.g., family, school, state) and their representatives (e.g., parents, teachers, police, politicians); (3) strong belief in a generation gap; and (4) belief that young people can resist the "adult world."

Psychologically, youth centrism implies ingroup–outgroup differentiation (Rabbie & Horwitz, 1969); that is, young people constitute the valued ingroup, whereas adults form the outgroup. The other processes that Tajfel (1978) understood to be related to such a social categorization – the construction of social identity and social comparison – are also included in the concept of youth centrism. Young people who score highly on youth centrism compare themselves positively with adults; hence, their own group constitutes for them the basis for a positive identity.

The scale tapping youth centrism has been used in studies of parent–adolescent relationships, the definition of adolescence as a life phase, educational achievement, and occupational position. These studies show a remarkably consistent picture of youth centrists as opposed to their counterparts, the non–youth centrists. The relationship between youth centrists and their parents is less satisfactory than it is in the case of non–youth centrists. Youth centrists talk less with their parents and offer them fewer opportunities to recount their experiences (Zinnecker, 1982). A series of studies has shown that youth centrists receive less social support from their parents in comparison to non–youth centrists. This finding has been reported for social support in the domains of personal relationships, school, and leisure (Meeus, 1989; Meeus, Helsen, & Vollebergh, 1996; Meeus, Raaijmakers, & Vollebergh, 1992).

At relatively early ages, 15 to 17 years old, youth centrists claim certain adult privileges. They desire to apply their own norms in the areas of sex, timetables of going out and coming home, control of their money, and choice of living quarters (Zinnecker, 1982). However, this does not mean that youth centrists aspire to adult status in other domains; in fact, compared with non–youth centrists, they aspire to achieve complete adult status at a much later point in time than non–youth centrists.

These findings support the conclusion that youth centrists put greater stress on the importance of adolescence as an independent phase of life than non–youth centrists (Zinnecker, 1982). They are not trying to reach adulthood quickly; however, on the other hand, they wish to possess a number of adult privileges before they reach formal adult status. At school and at work, youth centrists experience greater difficulties than their counterparts. Their level of achievement is lower (Meeus et al., 1996), they repeat grades more often (Zinnecker, 1982), their educational level is lower (Maassen & Meeus, 1993; Vinken, 1997, 1999; Watts & Zinnecker, 1988), and they more frequently quit school without any qualifications (Zinnecker, 1982). They have more trouble acquiring an apprenticeship, and unemployment is more widespread among them (Vinken, 1997, 1999; Zinnecker, 1982). Youth centrists do not receive more social support from their peers compared with non–youth centrists (Meeus, 1989), nor do they have more social contacts or operate more in peer groups. They do, however, shape their contacts differently: They tend to consort with informal, spontaneously organized bands of friends, whereas non–youth centrists are more likely to meet their peers in established associations (e.g., they establish group contacts in their school or job) (Zinnecker, 1982).

Youth centrism is not an ideologically unified phenomenon. Meeus (1988) differentiated youth centrists into two subgroups. On the one hand, he recognizes youth centrists with a predominantly working-class background who are attracted to conservative sociocultural views; on the other hand, he sees young people with – for the most part – a higher level of education who tend to hold more liberal, left-wing opinions. Culturally, youth centrism is not a uniform phenomenon. Meeus's (1988) distinction recalls other class-based classifications of youth culture – for example, Willis's (1978) description of distinctions between working-class "bikers" and middle-class "bohemians," both cultural rebels but of different types. Although all youth centrists may be critical of the adult world, different types of youth centrists may disapprove of different aspects of what they conceive to be the values, ideas, and habits of adults. Vinken (1997, 1999) showed that youth centrists themselves may shift their opinions somewhat while growing up. Following a cohort of young people for 8 years – 1986 to 1994 – he concluded that "steady" youth centrists moved in the direction of less economic conservatism but their cultural conservatism remained a stable feature of their worldview.

In the 1980s and early 1990s, youth centrists, on the whole, favored cultural conservatism more often than their adult-centered peers. Regarding other political and cultural attitudes – economic conservatism, postmaterialism, and political interest – they hardly differed from non–youth centrists (Vinken, 1997, 1999). It may be concluded that during the last decade, youth centrists were the most avid supporters of neoconservative opinions in the cultural field and, as such, were among the first to break with a general tendency in the development of cultural attitudes in a liberal direction that has characterized the ideological climate in the Netherlands ever since the mid-1960s.

Although their sociocultural orientation may vary, these results suggest consistently that all youth centrists distance themselves from adults personally, socially, and culturally. Their resistance to adults in general and to the institutions of education and employment governed by rules seems to be an extension of the poor relationship with their parents. Because a poor parent–adolescent relationship is the core element, it is plausible that youth centrism is a moderator variable for the development of political orientations in adolescence.

4.0. YOUTH CENTRISM AS A MODERATOR OF THE TRANSMISSION OF ATTITUDES: A FAMILY APPROACH

Mannheim (1928) stated that a generation gap is characteristic only of a society in turmoil and, with it, youths alienated from basic social values. On the other hand, functionalist thinkers claim that parent–youth conflict is endemic in modern society and that a generation gap is functional for the adjustment of young people to changing social conditions, not a sign of social and cultural crisis. Neo-Marxists conceive of working-class youth cultural groups as groups subverting bourgeois values that rule the adult world. Empirical research from the last decades showed that, in general, young people's ideas resemble those of their parents. Based on results of those empirical studies, it is difficult to determine the accuracy of the ideas of Mannheim, the functionalists, and the neo-Marxists. That the views of adolescents strongly resemble those of their parents could be a sign that social changes in the past few years have not been radical enough to justify the existence of a specific generation (Mannheim, 1928) of a specific youth culture (Parsons, 1942). The fact that the views of adolescents resemble in many ways those of their parents could also corroborate the idea that transgenerationally stable, class-oriented subcultures exist (neo-Marxists) and that adolescents, just like their parents, do (or do not) rebel against the "bourgeois hegemony." Therefore, our study does not imply a verification of the theoretical ideas of Mannheim, the functionalists, or the neo-Marxists.

Both historians and sociologists have pointed out the importance of youth cultures with regard to social changes. In this study, we go one step farther back. We explore the role of youth centrism in conveying political orientations from one generation to another. When youth centrists do rebel against taking on their parents' ideas, it reveals a potentially important nexus in the formation of youth cultures. In their ideological rebellion against their parents – combined with a strong peer orientation – youth centrists could play an important role in processes of youth culture formation and as a result of social changes. Whereas sociologists and historians have always concentrated on the influence of social circumstances on the development of youth cultures, we trace the sociopsychological background of transgenerational transmission (sometimes successful and sometimes not) of ideas, and we relocalize the origins of cultural differentiation within the family.

The central questions in this study are: (1) Do the attitudes of young people holding a specific attitude – that is, youth centrism – resemble their parents' attitudes less than other non–youth centrist youngsters?; (2) Are youth centrists, during adolescence, less susceptible to the transfer of the political orientations of their parents?; and (3) Do they, in turn, influence their parents less than their non–youth centrist peers?

Youth centrism has been studied in a developmental context (Vinken, 1997). To this perspective, we add a multi-actor approach. We try to answer those questions in a longitudinal study addressing the transmission of political attitudes from parents to their children.

5.0. A MODEL OF THE DEVELOPMENT OF POLITICAL ORIENTATIONS

In Figures 18.1 and 18.2, the unbroken lines represent adaptations of a conceptual model of political socialization by Vollebergh et al. (2001). Social class

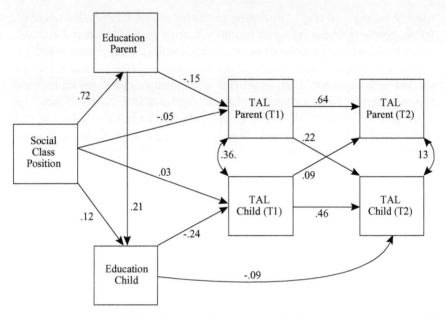

Figure 18.1. Basic model for Tolerance of Alternative Lifestyles (TAL). *Note:* Goodness of fit: $\chi^2(7) = 6.35$, $p = .500$. Broken lines indicate paths that were added to the conceptual model to reach satisfactory fit.

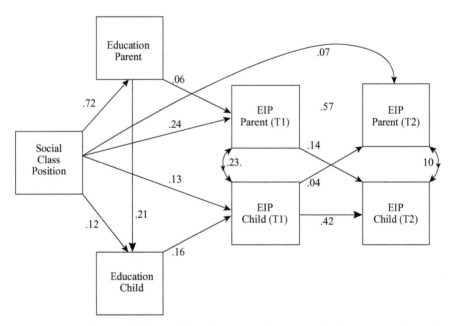

Figure 18.2. Basic model for Equality of Income and Property (EIP). *Note:* Goodness of fit: $\chi^2(7) = 10.85$, $p = .145$. Broken lines indicate paths that were added to the conceptual model to reach satisfactory fit.

determines the level of education of both parents and children to a certain extent, although the educational level of parents also influences that of their children (Bourdieu & Passeron, 1970; Hunstinx, 1998). Social class, as an indicator of social and cultural capital, also predicts the degree to which both parents and adolescents approve of economic and cultural conservatism. With these paths, factors defining social inheritance are covered. Furthermore, a correlation between attitudes of parents and those of their children is assumed to be present at Time 1 (T1) and Time 2 (T2). At T1 and T2, defining and directing paths in a causal chain is not legitimate because it is unclear which attitudes precede and potentially influence the other; therefore, potential mutual influence is represented through a correlation. The basic model specifies parents influencing their children between T1 and T2 and children influencing their parents during the same period. In this way, similarity and reciprocal influencing are conceptualized in this model. Finally, the stability of both parental and adolescent opinions is defined by the paths from their successive opinions at T1 to those at T2.

Past research has shown that it is reasonable to expect that social class is a strong determinant especially of economic conservatism (Knutsen, 1995). Cultural conservatism, on the other hand, is associated strongly with educational level. However, both education and social class form a stable background for the development of economic and cultural conservatism. Due to their age, parents have more stabilized opinions than their children, who are in the process of finding out what they want to hold as their own views (Vollebergh et al., 2001).

5.1. Method

5.1.1. Sample

Respondents were sampled from the Utrecht Study on Adolescent Development (USAD) 1991–1997, a longitudinal study of adolescents, young adults, and their parents (Meeus & 't Hart, 1993). The USAD study is based on a nationwide panel of about 9,000 households. Of these, all households were selected with adolescents and young adults between the ages of 12 and 24 years (3,926 households), which were initially contacted in 1991. Of these, a total of 2,471 (62.9%) households participated. This sample contained 3,394 adolescents and young adults (ages 12 to 24 years) who may be considered representative of the Dutch population of that age (Meeus & 't Hart, 1993). The sample was again contacted in 1994, resulting in a response of 1,871 (75.7%) households. In 1,115 (59.6%) of the 1,871 households, a parent and a child participated who had also been interviewed in 1991 ($N = 1,115$, N girls $= 601$ [53.9%], N boys $= 514$ [46.1%], minimum age of parent $= 29$ years, maximum age of parent $= 90$ years, mean age of parent $= 44.8$ years).

It was tested whether this sample of parent–child dyads significantly differed in any way from the original sample participating in the first measurement. We concluded that the selection was not systematically distorted, in terms of either background variables (i.e., age, educational level, gender, income) or measured attitudes.

5.1.2. *Measures*

All theoretical concepts were assessed by means of a written survey using Likert-type scales. Examples of the scales and the Cronbach's alpha are given herein. The correlations between scales and variables were used as input for a structural analysis model (i.e., AMOS) (Arbuckle, 1999).

Youth centrism was measured by an 11-item Dutch version of the original German scale (Zinnecker, 1982). As in earlier Dutch studies (Meeus, 1988; Meeus et al., 1996), the reliability of the scale proved to be satisfactory (Cronbach's alpha = .90). To analyze the possible moderating effects of youth centrism, the scores on this scale were categorized into quartiles.

Cultural conservatism was measured with the Tolerance of Alternative Lifestyles (TAL) scale (van der Avort, 1988), which measures the tolerance toward nontraditional forms of living together such as cohabitation with an unmarried partner, homosexual cohabitation, and so on. The scale consisted of six items. Internal reliability was adequate (i.e., Cronbach's alpha was greater than .80 for both children and parents for both measurements). This scale is both conceptually and empirically strongly related to core elements of cultural conservatism such as family traditionalism, enhancement of authoritarian parent–child relationships, and so on, and thus can be seen as a good indicator of nonconservative orientations toward cultural issues (Raaijmakers, 1993; van Dam, 1993).

Economic conservatism was measured using the Equality of Income and Possession (EIP) scale, borrowed for this purpose from Middendorp's study (1978) and adapted for the study of adolescents by Meeus (1986). The scale consists of three items that measure endorsement of efforts to reduce the socioeconomic differences in Dutch society (i.e., income, status, and occupation). Its internal reliability was adequate (Cronbach's alpha exceeded .80 for both children and parents at both times of measurement). This scale addresses one of the core issues in socioeconomic affairs – that is, reducing versus enhancing socioeconomic inequality – and is seen as a good indicator of nonconservative attitudes with reference to the socioeconomic domain (Middendorp, 1991; Raaijmakers, 1993).

Missing items on all of these scales were substituted by their relative mean (for a detailed discussion of this procedure, see Raaijmakers, 1999).

Social position of parents was assessed by asking parents about the highest level of education achieved by the main breadwinner of the family and their social class (five categories: 1 = blue collar/working class, 5 = upper class). In the analysis, the 1991 measurement was used. To assess the educational level of adolescents, four levels of educational attainment were classified on either the basis of the current level of education of young people still in school or by the highest level achieved by those no longer in the educational system. The level of educational attainment of adolescents was measured twice (in 1991 and again in 1994). Because the correlation between these two measurements was high, the analysis draws on the first measurement.

5.2. Preliminary Data Analyses

Using AMOS (version 4.0; Arbuckle, 1999) to arrive at fitting models, the conceptual models had to be adapted by adding one further path (indicated by broken lines in Figures 18.1 [TAL] and 18.2 [EIP]). Statistics reported at the bottom of Figures 18.1 and 18.2 indicate a satisfactory fit.

The basic models depicted in Figures 18.1 and 18.2 were reanalyzed in a multigroup analysis to explore the model fit for the four groups differing in youth centrism. Next, possible differences among the four groups were analyzed. It was examined whether subsequently freeing different paths of the basic model – thereby allowing different coefficient weights for the four groups differing in youth centrism – also resulted in significant improvements of the model-fit statistics. The order in which the model paths were allowed to vary between the groups was fixed. First, the path representing the similarity in political attitudes of parents and their children at T1 (Parent T1→Child T1) was set free. Second, the path representing the transmission of ideas from children to their parents (Child T1→Parent T2) was freed. Third, the path depicting the transmission in the opposite direction (Parent T1→Child T2) was freed. Next, the correlation in political attitudes of parents and their children at T2 (Parent T2→Child T2) was allowed to vary among the groups. Finally, all remaining paths were also set free, thereby allowing possible effects of the various social-background variables to be different for each of the four groups.

A model was considered to be an improvement of the basic model whenever its χ^2 value differed statistically significantly ($p < .05$) from the χ^2 value of the basic model. Next, further possible improvements by freeing subsequent paths were tested against this improved model, and so on.

5.3. Results

Results of the multigroup analysis on the effects of youth centrism on the parent–child relationships in cultural and economic attitudes are reported in Tables 18.1 and 18.2. In both cases, setting free one of the parent–child paths delivered a significant improvement of the basic model (see Table 18.1). However, as expected, setting free one or more of the paths – referring to possible differential effects of social-background variables – did not result in any further significant improvement of the model fit.

Table 18.1. *Parent–child paths for four groups differing in youth centrism: Multigroup analysis and model fit*[1]

	TAL	EIP
Basic Model: All paths fixed	$\chi^2(70) = 79.91$ $p = .20$	$\chi^2(70) = 95.97$ $p = .02$
Parent T1 ↔ Child T1 free	$\chi^2(67) = 65.96$ $p = .51$	
Child T1 → Parent T2 free	–	$\chi^2(64) = 82.63$ $p = .06$
Parent T1 → Child T2 free	–	–
Parent T2 ↔ Child T2 free	–	–
Basic Model: All paths free	–	–

Note: TAL = Tolerance of Alternative Lifestyles; EIP = Equality of Income and Property.
[1] Only statistically significant ($p < .05$) improvements of resulting χ^2 are reported.

With respect to the cultural domain (i.e., TAL), a clear difference between the groups was found in the correspondence of attitudes of the parents and their children at T1: With the decreasing degree of youth centrism, this correspondence increased, in which the high level of correspondence of the group with the lowest degree of youth centrism was most salient ($r = .49$) (see Table 18.2). Setting free the other parent–child paths did not result in any further significant improvement of the model fit, suggesting no moderating effects of youth

Table 18.2. *Multigroup analysis: Parent–child relationships in cultural and economic political attitudes*

Coefficients of groups differing in youth centrism[1]		TAL	EIP
Correlation Parent T1 ↔ Child T1			
Youth Centrism High	1	.27	
	2	.31	
	3	.33	
Low	4	.49	
Regression Weight (β) Child T1 → Parent T2			
Youth Centrism High	1		−.06
	2		.09
	3		.01
Low	4		.12

Note: TAL = Tolerance of Alternative Lifestyles; EIP = Equality of Income and Property.
[1] Only statistically significant ($p < .05$) differences between groups are reported.

centrism on the successive development of the TAL attitude of both parents and their children.

A somewhat different picture emerged from the analysis of the economic domain (i.e., EIP). Although no differences among the four groups in the initial correlation with parental attitudes could be observed, some differences appeared in the influence that each group exerted on the development of parental attitudes. For adolescents scoring low on youth centrism, this influence was moderately positive ($\beta = .12$) (see Table 18.2); adolescents with high scores in youth centrism, however, influenced their parents in the opposite direction ($\beta = -.06$). However, this moderating effect of youth centrism on the influence of adolescents on their parents was not accompanied by comparable effects on the influence the parents had on their children, nor could any significant difference be observed in the correspondence between the attitudes of parents and their children at the second time of measurement.

The dynamics of the development of economic and cultural conservatism differ, which legitimizes separate treatment of these variables in structural analyses. The results confirm conclusions from earlier research by Vollebergh et al. (2001) in which social-background variables were described as forming a stable background for the development of political attitudes. The four groups do not differ in the way in which class and parental and adolescent educational levels determine their views.

6.0. DISCUSSION

As expected, youth centrism seems to be an effective moderator of political orientations. The four groups react differently to parental efforts to socialize their children's attitudes. However, youth centrism does not affect cultural and economic attitudes in exactly the same way. Cultural conservatism is an attitude that has developed to a great extent when children reach middle adolescence. In this study, marked differences among the four different groups were already in place at T1. Indeed, young people high in youth centrism differ from their non–youth centrist peers with regard to parent–child similarity of views, as indicated by Parent T1→Child T1 correlations increasing from $r = .27$ for youth centrists to $r = .49$ for non–youth centrists (see Table 18.2). However, the results for cultural conservatism also point to the fact that the strong youth centrists do not stand apart from other youths; it is the group of strong non–youth centrists that differentiates itself from its peers. Youth centrists may have a rebellious self-image; however, a positive correlation (albeit a low one) between their cultural ideas and those of their parents indicates that they do not oppose their parents radically and, as such, they resemble peers with lower levels of youth centrism. It is interesting that the group of the adult–centrist youths sets itself apart, showing a far greater similarity of ideas with its parents than the rest of its peers.

During adolescence, no differences in the *process* of development of cultural conservatism were found among the four groups. This means that during this period, parents of youth centrists are no less effective in transferring their ideas and that youth centrists also are no less communicative. The ideological cleft between parents and their children remains as narrow (or wide) as it was, resulting in about the same amount of similarity (or difference) at T2. For this generation, adolescence is not a period in which young people drift farther away from the cultural attitudes of their parents – a fact also indicated by the nonmodeled zero-order correlations of parent–child attitudes of $r = .36$ and $r = .38$ at T1 and T2 for the whole group, respectively.

At T1, no significant changes exist among the four groups in the parent–child correspondence of economic attitudes. Also, in the transmission of parental economic conservatism during adolescence, no differences were found. Only when it comes to children influencing their parents during this stretch of time do strong youth centrists differentiate themselves from strong non–youth centrists. The first group effectively increases the dissimilarity between its economic views and those of its parents, whereas the second group works to increase similitude in those orientations. This process is indicated by the negative youth centrism child T1→Parent T2 path coefficient of $\beta = -.06$ and the positive non–youth centrism coefficient of $\beta = .12$ (see Table 18.2). For the whole group, parent–child economic conservatism correlations (zero-order) are $r = .28$ and $r = .25$ at T1 and T2, respectively. However, the similar magnitude of those correlations may mask an underlying process in which youth centrists distance themselves from their parents, whereas non–youth centrists do exactly the opposite – as indicated by the respective negative and positive values of the child–parent paths. Our first research question – Do they, in turn, influence their parents less than their non–youth centrist peers? – implies that the attitudes of youth centrists resemble their parents' attitudes less than is the case for non–youth centrist adolescents. For both cultural and economic attitudes, the conclusion can be drawn that youth centrists differentiate themselves from their parents but that the timing is different for the two attitudes. Whereas youth centrists were already breaking away from their parents' views at T1 in terms of cultural attitudes, they are in the process of doing so during adolescence when it comes to economic orientations. It may be concluded that youth centrism is an operative factor distinguishing certain groups of young people.

The answer to our second research question – Are youth centrists, during adolescence, less susceptible to the transmission of the political orientations of their parents? – must be answered negatively. Both for economic and cultural conservatism, youth centrists are influenced by their parents in the same way as the other groups. Here also, the self-image of youth centrists is misleading. Their critique of the adult world does not prevent them from being influenced by people who, at first sight, eminently represent that adult world: their parents. The question presents itself of how youth centrists perceive the parents. Adolescents may think their parents belong to the outgroup of "them," the world of despicable adults. In that case, youth centrists unwillingly and maybe unknowingly resemble "them." Or they may think parents belong to "us," only in a strange way being somewhat older, with youth centrists identifying no less positively with their parents than other adolescents.

The answer to our third research question – Do youth centrists influence their parents less than their non–youth centrist peers? – might be an indicator for the acceptance of the first interpretation (i.e., adolescents grudgingly taking on the views of their parents). It was expected that youth centrists transfer their ideas to a lesser degree, but the results show an even more dramatic process: Compared with their non–youth centrist peers, they seem to negatively influence their parents, at least where economic orientations are concerned. Youth-centrist adolescents actively alienate the older generation from their views, whereas adult centrists attract their parents to their opinions. This difference between groups confirms that youth centrism can dynamically moderate opinions during adolescence. Communication in families with youngsters high on youth centrism seems to be at least partly disturbed. Parents might get bored with the (economic) opinions of their offspring and turn away from them, even while they are successful in forcing their opinions on their children. Their children might perceive that their opinions do not count – further proof of not being taken seriously by grown-ups, even when the adults are their own parents.

In summary, youth centrism is an interesting moderator because youth centrists' political opinions resemble parental views less than those of (extreme) non–youth centrists. Furthermore, although youth centrists do not completely oppose the ideas of their parents, as indicated by low zero-order correlations between the views of parents and youth-centrist children, they alienate their parents from them during adolescence. On the other hand, their opposites – adult centrists – show a great deal of sensibility to their parents' attitudes and, in turn, effectively persuade their parents to close the gap between the ideas of the two generations.

Our results indicate that for adolescents, the socioeconomic background in which they grow up – class and education – is important for the ideas they develop. Within all social environments, the transfer of ideas from generation to generation is a smooth process for adult centrist youths. Because they constitute the majority of youth, a certain transgenerational constancy and ideological homogeneity is secured, at least when parents themselves are not too divided. On the other hand, our results also show that within the family environment, differences can occur between parents and children. Although the self-image of youth centrists as being diametrically opposed to their parents is negotiable, youth centrists do adopt relatively little of their parents' (non)cultural conservatism, and they alienate their parents actively regarding economic (non)conservatism. We attempted to trace the differences between old and young back to their family; a typical characteristic of some youths – their rebellion against the adult world – proves to be an active factor in the development of ideological disagreement between adolescents and their parents and, as a result, potentially between generations.

However, these results do not allow any conclusions to be drawn about the direction in which this disagreement is developing. Our model shows that youth centrists deviate from their parents' views irrespective of the type of opinions the older generation holds, which may also explain the fact that various types of youth centrists have been identified. Although all youth centrists have a tendency to oppose the adult world, the perception of what that adult world encompasses is probably different for every group discerned. Culturally conservative youth centrists may see adults and, thus, also their parents as the main cause of moral weakness in society, as well as decadence, lack of authority, and an intolerable erosion of the male and female roles. For culturally nonconservative youth centrists, the opposite applies; they will be more likely to accuse adults of rigidity, authoritarianism, and sexism, and they feel that they, as adolescents, can point out the right directions.

This implies two things for the role that adolescents and, more specifically, youth centrists may play in processes of social change. An older generation that is culturally and economically homogeneous creates the greatest chance of youth centrists turning en masse to the same oppositional position. Although youth centrists never comprise the majority of their cohort – as a group that conspicuously rebels against the adult world – they may have the critical mass to demand their role as prime critics of the existing situation of society and thus function as agents of social change. An older generation that is ideologically divided may splinter a potential youth-centrist–motivated rebellion; however, even under the latter condition, it is not unlikely that adolescents who bear a similar type of grudge against the adult world will seek each other's company and confirm each other's opinions. This implies that even when the older generation is characterized by ideological multiversity, tiny groups of youth centrists with the same type of opinions may initiate or support rebellious movements of any type.

Youth centrism in itself is not a sufficient condition for prominent adolescent criticism of the adult world transforming into a social movement; however, under a wide range of social conditions, it could contribute to rebellion. In retrospect, it is difficult to trace whether it was youth centrists who, in the 1950s, bore a warm heart toward rock and roll with its predilection for looser sexual relations and, more generally, a hedonist life attitude. Were the working-class youth centrists the first to undermine what they perceived as the old-fashioned work ethic and Victorian sexual morality of their parents? With hindsight, it is also difficult to determine whether the bohemians of the 1960s – who adhered to a hippy-like worldview, did "not trust anyone over 25," and were later called the first postmaterialists – could be found among middle-class youth centrists. It is also difficult to discern whether this applied to the students who, in 1968, throughout the Western world, saw the signs of an upcoming socialist revolution and enthusiastically contributed to that cause (ter Bogt, 2000). Future research into cultural change should include the youth-centrist factor to better understand the origins of cultural change.

Throughout the last century, historians and sociologists have pointed at the role youth movements may have had in processes of social change. In the 1980s, authors like Zinnecker and Meeus energetically addressed the youth-centrist paradigm and, as late as 1997, Vinken published a major study on the topic. However, in recent years, youth centrism has been an underdeveloped research area. We believe that it may take another generation of disenfranchised youth to again put adolescents and, in particular, youth centrists at the center of the historical stage. It may be the youth centrists themselves who prove that youth centrism deserves a place in theories that model social change.

REFERENCES

Abma, R. (1990). *Jeugd en tegencultuur: Een theoretische verkenning* [Youth and counterculture: A theoretical explanation]. Nijmegen, the Netherlands: SUN (doctoral dissertation, University of Nijmegen).

Acock, A. C., & Bengtson, V. L. (1980). Socialization and attribution: Actual versus perceived similarity among parents and youth. *Journal of Marriage and the Family, 42,* 501–515.

Arbuckle, J. L. (1999). *AMOS 4.01.* Chicago: SmallWaters Corp.

Ariès, P. (1960). *L'enfant et la vie familiale sous L'Ancien Régime* [Centuries of childhood]. Paris: Plon.

Beck, P. A., & Jennings, M. K. (1975). Parents as "middlepersons" in political socialization. *Journal of Politics, 37,* 83–107.

Becker, H. (1946/1960). *German youth: Bond or free?* London: Butler & Tanner.

Bourdieu, P., & Passeron, J.-C. (1970). *La reproduction: Eléments pour une théorie du système d'enseignement* [Reproduction: Elements of a theory on the system of social assignment]. Paris: Editions de Minuit.

Cohen, S. (1972). *Moral panics and folk devils.* London: MacGibbon & Kee.

Cooney, T. M. (1997). Parent–child relations across adulthood. In S. Duck (Ed.), *Handbook of personal relationships: Theory, research and interventions* (pp. 451–468). Chichester, UK: Wiley.

Dalhouse, A. C., & Frideres, J. S. (1996). Intergenerational congruency: The role of the family in political attitudes of youth. *Journal of Family Issues, 17,* 227–248.

Davis, K. (1940). The sociology of parent–youth conflict. *American Sociological Review, 5,* 523–535.

Elsler, A. (1971). *Bombs, beards and barricades: 150 years of youth in revolt.* New York: Stein & Day.

Felling, A., Peters, J., & Schreuder, O. (1983). *Burgerlijk en onburgerlijk Nederland* [Middle-class and non-middle-class attitudes in the Netherlands]. Deventer: Van Loghum Slaterus.

Gillis, J. R. (1974). *Youth and history: Tradition and change in European age relations, 1770–present.* New York: Academic Press.

Glass, J., Bengtson, V. L., & Dunham, C. C. (1986). Attitude similarity in three-generation families: Socialization, status inheritance or reciprocal influence? *American Sociological Review, 51*, 685–691.

Hall, G. S. (1905). *Adolescence: Its psychology and its relations to physiology, anthropology, sociology, sex, crime, religion, and education.* New York: Appleton.

Hebdige, D. (1979). *Subculture: The meaning of style.* London: Methuen.

Hunstinx, P. (1998). *Milieu, sekse, etniciteit en schoolloopbanen* [Social background, gender, ethnicity and school careers]. Unpublished doctoral dissertation, Utrecht University, the Netherlands.

Inglehart, R. (1977). *The silent revolution: Changing values and political styles among Western publics.* Princeton, NJ: Princeton University Press.

Inglehart, R. (1997). *Modernization and postmodernization: Cultural, economic, and political change in 43 societies.* Princeton, NJ: Princeton University Press.

Jennings, M. K., & Niemi, R. G. (1981). *Generations and politics: A panel study of young adults and their parents.* Princeton, NJ: Princeton University Press.

Knutsen, O. (1995). The impact of old politics and new politics value orientations on party choice: A comparative study. *Journal of Public Policy, 15*, 1–63.

Koch, H. W. (1975). *The Hitler youth: Origins and development 1922–1945.* London: MacDonald & Jane's.

Maassen, G., & Meeus, W. M. J. (1993). De verhouding tussen jongeren en volwassenen [The relationship between adults and adolescents]. In W. M. J. Meeus & H. 't Hart (Eds.), *Jongeren in Nederland* [Young people in the Netherlands]. Amersfoort, the Netherlands: Academische Uitgeverij.

Mannheim, K. (1928). Das Problem der Generationen [The problem of generations]. *Kölner Vierteljahreshefte für Soziologie, 7*, 157–185, 309–330.

Meeus, W. M. J. (1986). De twee gezichten van het jeugdig conservatisme [The two faces of conservatism in youth]. In M. Matthijssen, W. M. J. Meeus, & F. Van Wel (Eds.), *Beelden van Jeugd* [Images of youth] (pp. 109–128). Groningen, the Netherlands: Wolters Noordhof.

Meeus, W. M. J. (1988). Adolescent rebellion and politics. *Youth & Society, 19*, 426–434.

Meeus, W. M. J. (1989). Parental and peer support in adolescence. In K. Hurrelmann & U. Engel (Eds.), *The social world of adolescents* (pp. 167–185). New York: de Gruyter.

Meeus, W. M. J., Helsen, M., & Vollebergh, W. A. M. (1996). Parents and peers in adolescence: From conflict to connectedness. Four studies. In L. Verhofstadt-Denève, I. Kienhorst, & C. Braet (Eds.), *Conflict and development in adolescence* (pp. 103–116). Leiden, the Netherlands: DSWO-Press.

Meeus, W. M. J., Raaijmakers, Q., & Vollebergh, W. A. M. (1992). Political intolerance and youth centrism in adolescence: An overview of Dutch research and some recent longitudinal findings. In G. Breakwell (Ed.), *The social psychology of political and economic cognition* (pp. 97–120). London: Academic Press.

Meeus, W. M. J., & 't Hart, H. (1993). *Jongeren in Nederland* [Youth in the Netherlands]. Amersfoort, the Netherlands: Academische Uitgeverij Amersfoort.

Middendorp, C. P. (1978). *Progressiveness and conservatism: The fundamental dimensions of ideological controversy and their relationship to social class.* The Hague/Paris/New York: Mouton.

Middendorp, C. P. (1991). *Ideology in Dutch politics: The democratic system reconsidered 1970–1985.* Assen/Maastricht, the Netherlands: van Gorcum.

Miller, R. B., & Glass, J. (1989). Parent–child attitude similarity across the life course. *Journal of Marriage and the Family, 51,* 991–997.

Moen, P., Erickson, M. A., & Dempster-McClain, D. (1997). Their mother's daughters? The intergenerational transmission of gender attitudes in a world of changing roles. *Journal of Marriage and the Family, 59,* 281–293.

Parsons, T. (1942). Age and sex in the social structure of the United States. *American Sociological Review, 7,* 604–616.

Petit, G. S., Clawson, M. A., Dodge, K. A., & Bates, J. E. (1996). Stability and change in peer-rejected status: The role of child behavior, parenting and family ecology. *Merrill Palmer Quarterly, 42,* 267–294.

Raaijmakers, Q. A. W. (1993). Opvattingen over politiek en maatschappij [Beliefs on politics and society]. In W. M. J. Meeus & H. 't Hart (Eds.), *Jongeren in Nederland* [Youth in the Netherlands] (pp. 106–132). Amersfoort, the Netherlands: Academische Uitgeverij Amersfoort.

Raaijmakers, Q. A. W. (1999). Effectiveness of different missing data treatments in surveys with Likert-type data: Introducing the relative mean substitution approach. *Educational and Psychological Measurement, 59,* 725–748.

Rabbie, J. M., & Horwitz, M. (1969). The arousal of ingroup–outgroup bias by a chance win or loss. *Journal of Personality and Social Psychology, 69,* 223–228.

Righart, H. (1995). *De eindeloze jaren zestig: Geschiedenis van een generatieconflict* [The sixties: History of a generation conflict]. Amsterdam, the Netherlands: Arbeiderspers.

Rokeach, M. (1973). *The nature of human values.* New York: The Free Press.

Schofield, M. (1965). *The sexual behaviour of young people.* London: Longmans.

Springhall, J. (1998). *Youth culture and moral panics: Penny gaffs to gangsta rap 1830–1996.* London: Macmillan Press.

Stachura, P. D (1981). The German youth movement 1900–1945. London: Macmillan Press.

Tajfel, H. (1978). Social categorization, social identity and social comparison. In H. Tajfel (Ed.), *Differentiation between social groups* (pp. 61–76). London: Academic Press.

ter Bogt, T. F. M. (2000). De geschiedenis van jeugdcultuur en popmuziek [The history of youth culture and pop music]. In ter Bogt, T. F. M., and Hibbel, B. (Eds.), *Wilde jaren: Een eeuw jeugdcultuur* [Wild years: A century of youth culture] (pp. 11–168). Utrecht, the Netherlands: Lemma.

ter Bogt, T. F. M., & Meeus, W. M. J. (1994). Adolescentie: Historische achtergrond en theorievorming [Adolescence: Historical background and theory]. In W. M. J. Meeus (Ed.) *Adolescentie: Een psychosociale benadering* [Adolescence: A psychosocial approach] (pp. 10–55). Groningen, the Netherlands: Wolters-Noordhoff.

van Dam, B. (1993). *Een generatie met verschillende gezichten* [A generation with different faces]. Nijmegen, the Netherlands: ITS.

van der Avort, A. J. P. M. (1988). *Vrijzinnigheid in relaties, hedendaagse attitudes in de primaire levenssfeer* [Freedom in relations, recent attitudes on primary relationships]. Nijmegen, the Netherlands: ITS.

Vinken, H. (1997). *Political values and youth centrism.* Doctoral dissertation. The Netherlands: Tilburg University.

Vinken, H. (1999). Youth centrism and conservatism: The political value of resisting the adult world. *Zeitschrift für Soziologie der Erziehung und Sozialisation, 19*, 405–420.

Vollebergh, W. A. M. (1991). *The limits of tolerance.* Doctoral dissertation. The Netherlands: Utrecht University.

Vollebergh, W. A. M., Iedema, J., & Meeus, W. M. J. (1999). The emerging gender gap: Cultural and economic conservatism in the Netherlands 1970–1992. *Political Psychology, 20*, 291–327.

Vollebergh, W. A. M., Iedema, J., & Raaijmakers, Q. A. W. (2001). The formation of cultural orientations in adolescence: Status inheritance, intergenerational transmission and internalization of attitudes. *Journal of Marriage and the Family, 63*, 1185–1198.

Watts, M. W., & Zinnecker, J. (1988). Youth culture and politics among German youth: Effects of youth centrism. In J. Hazekamp, W. M. J. Meeus, & Y. te Poel (Eds.), *European contributions to youth research* (pp. 93–101). Amsterdam, the Netherlands: Free University Press.

Wilkinson, P. (1981). *The new fascists.* London: Grant McIntyre.

Willis, P. E. (1978). *Profane culture.* London: Routledge & Kegan Paul.

Zinnecker, J. (1982). Die Gesellschaft der Altersgleichen [The society of peers]. In A. Fischer (Hrsg.), *Jugend '81* [Youth '81] (pp. 422–673). Opladen: Leske+Budrich.

19

Value Transmission and *Zeitgeist* Revisited

KLAUS BOEHNKE, ANDREAS HADJAR, AND DIRK BAIER

INTRODUCTION: *ZEITGEIST* AND INTRAFAMILIAL TRANSMISSION PROCESSES

In a family, similarity between parent and offspring values can originate from three sources: (1) direct and mediated value-transmission effects of parents' values on the values of their children; (2) processes of adaptation of the parents to values and attitudes of their children; and (3) parents and children being affected similarly by the context within which they live (Boehnke, 2001; Knafo, 2003; Kohn, 1983; Urban & Singelmann, 1998). Intrafamilial processes of value transmission do not take place in an isolated family-only environment but rather in a specific societal context. All members of the family are in permanent contact with this context through peers, mass media, schooling, or work groups. As such, context effects can proceed from the educational system, the socioeconomic situation, or the societal value climate.

There are a growing number of studies dealing with context effects on intergenerational transmission. Urban and Singelmann (1998) define the context implicitly as the amount of variance of the child's values that is not explained by the father's and the mother's values. Other studies deal with context more explicitly. Knafo (2003) analyzes how parents' attitudes – in interplay with the school environment – influence children's values. His findings suggest that a stronger value transmission pertains in high-fit contexts – that is, when parents share the values of the children's school environment. Knafo explains this as follows: A high fit between the educational ideology of parents and the school environment leads to less value conflict within the family. Less conflict in the family is related to a better parent–child relationship, which in turn fosters successful value transmission.

This chapter relies on data originating from the study, "Dominance ideologies, gender roles and delinquency in the life of adolescents," which was financed by the Deutsche Forschungsgemeinschaft through a grant to the first author and to Hans Merkens, Free University of Berlin.

Kohn (1983; Kohn, Slomczynski, & Schoenbach, 1986) includes the broader societal context by integrating variables of the workplace. He shows that the influence of the mother and the father on the child's values depends not only on cultural context but also on social class, and he relates this finding to differential degrees of occupational or educational self-determination of the father and the mother. Hadjar and Baier (2003) report that the socioeconomic situation of the family has an impact on the gender-specificity of value-transmission processes: Whereas in lower class families, the father is the main agent of value transmission, in higher class families, both the mother and the father influence the values of their children to an equal degree. This difference is explained on the grounds of different parental styles: Lower class families tend to deploy more authoritarian parental behavior, which usually favors an unquestioned dominance of the father. In families with higher socioeconomic status, a more democratic parental style is usually favored, allowing for a less gendered value transmission.

Another explanation focuses on the active role children take in their own socialization: Different contexts may stand for different opportunity structures, which function as frames for the acceptance of certain values. For example, a higher class context is perceived as more successful by the children and, therefore, values cherished in that social-class context are more likely to be accepted by them (Baier & Hadjar, 2004) than values cherished by children growing up in a lower class.

Boehnke (2001, 2004) deals with *zeitgeist* as another context variable. He defines *zeitgeist* as the modal current value climate of a society. He was able to show that *zeitgeist* has an effect on the intergenerational transmission of values as they are defined and measured by Schwartz (1992). For values less endorsed in society, such as power and tradition values, he found considerably more parent–child similarity than for values endorsed by most members of society. Boehnke interpreted his findings as suggesting that families presumably have to communicate more about values atypical than typical for a given society. Through this more intense communication process, he assumed value transmission to be intensified and thus stronger for societally less endorsed values.

This chapter focuses once more on *zeitgeist*, "a value climate [. . .] that influences value priorities of both parents and offspring" (Boehnke, 2001, p. 244). *Zeitgeist* is a rather vaguely defined concept in contemporary social science (Zetterberg, 1992, 1997, 1998). In this study, *zeitgeist* is conceptualized as a dominant mainstream position taken by a majority of people of a given society toward a certain social value. Empirically, *zeitgeist* is the mean of preferences for a certain social value in a given society and therefore a constant, although people perceive and accept the *zeitgeist* to a different degree. There are at least two different ways to analyze *zeitgeist* influence. First, *zeitgeist* can be seen as a *disturbance term* that influences value transmission between parents and children. To measure the amount of variance in children's values that is explained by the particular value climate and to solve the question of whether there is an impact, *zeitgeist* is introduced as a control variable into the transmission model, as shown in Study I. Here, we merely assume a vague, general effect. Second, the value climate can be seen as an *explanatory variable*, in which the research question changes into how *zeitgeist* influences the process of value transmission or – more precisely – whether and how a specific family's relationship to the *zeitgeist* influences value transmission in that family. This problem can only be solved by models in which *zeitgeist* is a moderator variable that separates different groups (Study II). In this study, we postulate systematic effects of the *zeitgeist*.

A central problem of an operationalization and of data analysis is the nature of *zeitgeist* as being a constant at the time it is measured. In the two studies presented herein, we worked with two different options to transform *zeitgeist* into a variable measuring a particular family's relationship to it. One of the options is to create a random variable from the distribution of values in the sample. The other option is to create a variable that expresses the distance of a family from the *zeitgeist* conceptualized as the mean of all sampled families.

1.0. HIERARCHIC SELF-INTEREST: A CORE VALUE OF MODERN SOCIETIES

The substantive content of value transmission in both studies is Hierarchic Self-Interest (HSI), a value orientation at the core of industrialized societies. The theoretical background of this concept and then its measures are presented. We chose this value orientation for our analyses because HSI has been shown to be a powerful predictor of xenophobia, ethnocentrism, right-wing extremism, and related phenomena and is thus closely connected to an ever-recurring problem in German society (Küpper & Heitmeyer, 2004).

Theoretical Background. HSI is the individual expression of societal dominance ideologies (Hagan, Hefler, Claßen, Boehnke, & Merkens, 1998). Dominance ideologies contain the notion that success in all areas of life means to "perform better than others," to outperform rivals. These ideologies are found in the center of modern industrial societies that tend to be highly competitive and are strongly tied to the logic of free-market capitalism (Hadjar, 2004). Indications of the existence of such ideologies are found in classical and contemporary sociology. Smith (1776), Simmel (1978/1900), and Weber (1930) more or less agreed that capitalism and market economy are based on specific value systems of a rational lifestyle, de-emotionalization, competition, maximization of wealth, self-interest, and self-love. MacPherson (1962) called these mechanisms of capitalist societies "possessive individualism." In societies that are characterized by inequality, competition, and isolation, the individual's striving for wealth is also central to his or her social relationships: "market society is necessarily [...] a series of competitive and invasive relations" (MacPherson, 1962, p. 271).

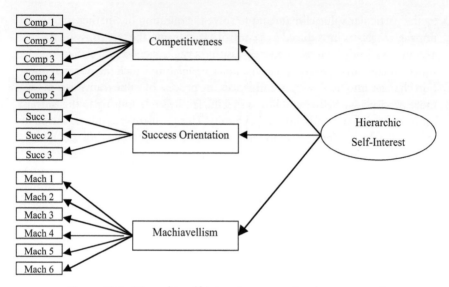

Figure 19.1. Hierarchic self-interest as a second-order construct.[a]
[a] See also Boehnke and Hadjar (2004).

On the individual or micro level, these dominance ideologies are measurable as the value syndrome HSI (Hadjar, 2004; Hagan et al., 1998). Classified in the sense of Schwartz's (1992) value theory, HSI encompasses power and achievement values and comes close to being a comprehensive measure of the self-enhancement dimension of Schwartz's value circumplex. Similar to the authoritarianism construct introduced by Adorno, Frenkel-Brunswik, Levinson, & Sanford (1950), the HSI syndrome is a second-order construct that encompasses several first-order factors (Boehnke & Hadjar, 2004). According to the nature of a syndrome, these factors may vary and additional factors may be integrated. For the following analyses, HSI includes three elements (Figure 19.1).

The factor of *competitiveness* refers to the desire to be better than others as asserted in Social Comparison Theory (Festinger, 1954). Festinger emphasized that individuals need to evaluate their abilities by social comparison with reference groups. An important aspect concerning the HSI construct is Festinger's assumption that people always try to gain better assessments while comparing. Here, the factor of hierarchy enters; this element of HSI is related to the hierarchical structure of society; perceived differences in success, status, and wealth; and positional competition (Hirsch, 1977).

Success orientation applies to the urge for rationality in working or learning processes and the impulse to produce material values. This dimension is derived from the materialism–postmaterialism concept of Inglehart (1977). Aspects of materialism – such as the urge for higher achievement and material wealth – are of special importance for the construct of HSI. HSI thereby also approximates what Inglehart more recently called *survival values* (Inglehart, 1997).

In sociology and political sciences, the term *Machiavellism* refers to a manner of governing the state that was explored by Machiavelli in the 15th and 16th centuries (Machiavelli, 1984/1532). Central to this concept is a ruling class characterized by hard labor, ambition, acumen, strong will, and self-confidence but that lacks altruism, morals, and wisdom. Christie and Geis (1970) derived a psychological concept from this macro-level description, making the features measurable on the individual level. Being Machiavellistic means asserting one's own goals against the interests of others at almost any cost.

Measures. The instruments to measure the three HSI factors are introduced only briefly. All items had to be rated by parents and offspring on a scale ranging from 1 (no agreement) to 5 (strong agreement). Competitiveness was measured by five items from a scale introduced by Jerusalem (1984). This scale has good psychometric properties, as indicated by an average Cronbach's α of .77 (five items). To operationalize success orientation, we used 3 items by Boehnke (1988), who developed a 12-item materialism–postmaterialism scale for adolescents. The part of the scale used herein contains only materialism items. This three-item scale has a high consistency (average Cronbach's $\alpha = .76/3$ items). For the Machiavellism dimension, six items were selected from a Machiavellism scale by Henning and Six (1977) and an item set devised for studies in East Germany by the Academy of Pedagogical Sciences of the German Democratic Republic (Akademie der pädagogischen Wissenschaften der DDR, 1989). This scale has a satisfactory internal consistency (average Cronbach's $\alpha = .71/6$ items).

An indication for the second-order structure of HSI can be derived from a confirmatory factor analysis with AMOS (Hadjar, 2004) or from analyses of the internal consistency of the second-order factor. Constructing a second-order scale from the three scale scores leads to a meta-scale with an average Cronbach's α of .68 (Table 19.1).

Two studies are presented that include the intrafamilial transmission of values for which the impact of the *zeitgeist* is controlled, as discussed in the next section.

2.0. VALUE TRANSMISSION STUDY I

Research Design. The basis for our analyses in both studies presented herein is the German panel dataset originating from the international project "Dominance Ideologies, Gender Roles, and Delinquency in the Life of Adolescents" conducted in Berlin and Toronto (Boehnke, Merkens, & Claßen, 1998). During a follow-up survey in 1999 (T1) and 2000 (T2), questionnaire data from 341 family quadruplets were collected. A quadruplet encompassed a school student (i.e., target child), one opposite-sex sibling, and both parents. The target children came from 68 Berlin schools (our sampling points) and were in the eighth and ninth grades during the first wave of data collection. Whereas at T1 the entire quadruplets were interviewed, at T2 only target children and their opposite-sex siblings were surveyed.

Table 19.1. *Instruments and consistency coefficients (Cronbach's α)*

Variable	Sample Item	$^{\alpha}$Father (Time 1)[a]	$^{\alpha}$Mother (Time 1)	$^{\alpha}$Son (Time 1)	$^{\alpha}$Daughter (Time 1)	$^{\alpha}$Son (Time 2)	$^{\alpha}$Daughter (Time 2)
Competitiveness (5 Items)	I'm only satisfied when my achievement is above average.	.78	.83	.72	.77	.75	.77
Success Orientation (3 Items)	The most important thing in life is achievement.	.77	.78	.74	.74	.77	.73
Machiavellism (6 Items)	It's not important how you win but that you win.	.77	.72	.73	.64	.72	.68
Hierarchic Self-Interest (3 Scale Scores)	(Second Order Construct)	.70	.66	.67	.66	.73	.68

[a] Parents were measured only once, whereas offspring were measured twice; see details in the text.

Sample. The sample of 341 family quadruplets can be described briefly as follows: At the first wave of data-gathering, the mean age of the adolescents was 14 years for both girls and boys. About one third of the families lived in the Eastern districts of Berlin and two thirds came from the Western part of the city, which fits with the actual distribution of East and West Berliners. The economic situation of the average family quadruplet in our sample was rather good. Only 17.5% of the families earned less than US$35,000 per year, 38.9% earned between US$35,000 and US$50,000, and 22.9% earned between US$50,000 and US$65,000. The family income of 20.7% of the sample was higher than US$65,000. For our sample of German family quadruplets, an above-average socioeconomic situation seems plausible insofar as the parents of adolescent children are older and therefore more integrated into their careers and the stratification system than parents of young children. We see our sample as representative of metropolitan "intact" families with at least two children living in the household.

Research Questions and Design. Similar to Boehnke, Ittel, and Baier (2002), this study undertook an analysis of the impact of the value climate at a given time (i.e., the *zeitgeist*) on intrafamilial value transmission. Therefore, *zeitgeist* was introduced as a control variable into the transmission models so that its effect could be separated from effects of value transmission.

To estimate the amount of variance in children's HSI (T2) determined by the *zeitgeist*, we followed the strategy proposed by Boehnke et al. (2002). A *zeitgeist* variable was constructed to transform the constant *zeitgeist* – that is, the mean for HSI in all of the 341 families – into a variable. First, the dataset consisting

Father HSI	Mother HSI	Son HSI	Daughter HSI (I)	Randomly Selected Father HSI	Randomly Selected Mother HSI	Randomly Selected Son HSI (I)	Randomly Selected Daughter HSI (I)	*Zeitgeist* HSI
...	...	...	...	...	...	...	...	...
3.19	3.13	3.67	3.29	...	...	...	...	...
2.07	2.28	4.11	1.60	...	...	...	...	...
3.09	2.91	2.71	2.50	...	...	...	...	...
2.03	2.58	3.34	2.76	...	...	...	...	...
2.67	2.84	3.72	2.59	2.03	2.91	4.11	3.29	3.09
...	...	...	...	...	...	...	...	...

Figure 19.2. Illustration of construction of the *zeitgeist* variable (segment of dataset).

of 341 cases (i.e., family quadruplets) was randomized, with family as the case. Second, for fathers, the score of the male parent-generation person preceding the target family "i" in the randomized dataset (i.e., the score of father "i-1") was added to family "i's" data as a variable. Third, for mothers, the score of the second previous female parent-generation person in the randomized dataset (i.e., the score of mother "i-2") was added to family "i's" data as a variable. Fourth, for sons, the score of the third previous male child-generation person in the randomized dataset (i.e., the score of son "i-3") was added to family "i's" data as a variable. Fifth, for daughters, the score of the fourth previous female child-generation person in the randomized dataset (i.e., the score of daughter "i-4") was added to family "i's" set as a variable. Sixth, the four pseudo-variables were averaged to become the variable *zeitgeist HSI* (Figure 19.2).

Through this strategy, *zeitgeist* was conceptualized as the value preference of the most generalized other – in the sense of Mead (1934) – to whom the subject of transmission has no direct relationship. Whereas significant others are neighbors, schoolmates, and peers (Knafo, 2003; Kohn, 1983), the generalized other stands for the entire society – here represented by the whole sample. The mean score of the *zeitgeist* HSI variable is 2.79, thus lying slightly below the theoretical scale mean of 3.0. *Zeitgeist* HSI was a variable that varied around the constant sample mean of the *zeitgeist* variable, thereby transforming the *zeitgeist* mean into a variable that could be integrated into multivariate analyses. As expected, correlations among the family members and their randomly selected counterparts, in general, did not deviate substantially from 0, but there were two significant correlations: a correlation of $r = -.16$ between fathers' HSI and

Table 19.2. *Correlations of HSI scores with* zeitgeist *HSI scores*

	Randomly Selected Father HSI	Randomly Selected Mother HSI	Randomly Selected Son HSI (Time 1)	Randomly Selected Daughter HSI (Time 1)	*Zeitgeist* HSI
Father HSI	−.06	–	–	–	−.16**
Mother HSI	–	−.04	–	–	−.08
Son HSI (Time 1)	–	–	.00	–	−.03
Daughter HSI (Time 1)	–	–	–	−.09*	.02

* $p < .10$; ** $p < .01$.

the *zeitgeist* HSI variable (i.e., mean of all randomly selected "family" members) and a marginally significant correlation between the daughter and her randomly selected counterpart.[1] Both correlations are negative (see Table 19.2). For the correlation between fathers' HSI and *zeitgeist* HSI, this means, for example, that the fathers' HSI tends to be lower when the generalized other has a high HSI. For daughters, it also means that they mark HSI lower when their generalized peers mark it higher, although the effect is not substantial.

Results. As the correlations in Table 19.3 show, there are significant value-transmission processes between fathers and mothers and their offspring. The father seems to be more important than the mother for the transmission of HSI. Whereas the father influences the sons' and the daughters' values at T2 to the same extent ($r_{father/son} = .31$, $r_{father/daughter} = .30$), there is less impact of the mother on her daughter ($r_{mother/son} = .26$, $r_{mother/daughter} = .19$). Stability coefficients (i.e., the correlations of offspring values across time) were quite high: For sons, they were $\beta = .66$; for daughters, they were $\beta = .60$. The father–mother value congruence was $r = .38$. This finding indicates that parental HSI orientations are not overly homogeneous. Value congruence between daughters and sons is lower still (T1: $r = .22$, T2: $r = .31$), but we find that value congruence of siblings increases over time. This increase is marginally significant ($p < .10$). Our findings concerning the genderedness of value transmission are not in line with common notions from psychology: We were unable to find a clear pattern that intergenerational value transmission is stronger within same-sex dyads, like Freud and Parsons suggested (Knafo, 2003). On the other hand, we found

[1] For two normally distributed variables, the average correlation of one variable with the same variable from all theoretically possible file neighbors would be 0. However, for skewed and hyper- or hypo-kurtotic distributions, this is not the case. Exactly this mathematical rule concurs with our understanding of "zeitgeist" as a societal value climate that temporarily produces a higher preference for certain values.

Table 19.3. *Intercorrelations among family members and HSI means and standard deviations*

	Father HSI	Mother HSI	Son HSI (Time 1)	Daughter HSI (Time 1)	Son HSI (Time 2)	Daughter HSI (Time 2)	Mean[a]	Standard Deviation
Father HSI	1						2.72	0.65
Mother HSI	.38**	1					2.59	0.63
Son HSI (Time 1)	.32**	.27**	1				3.07	0.63
Daughter HSI (Time 1)	.28**	.26**	.22**	1			2.80	0.60
Son HSI (Time 2)	.31**	.26**	.66**	.28**	1		3.04	0.67
Daughter HSI (Time 2)	.30**	.19**	.23**	.60**	.31**	1	2.75	0.59

** $p < .01$.
Generation main effect (Time 1 only): $F_{(1/336)} = 96.96 \ p < .01$.
Generation main effect (offspring Time 2): $F_{(1/336)} = 60.61 \ p < .01$.
Gender main effect (Time 1 only): $F_{(1/336)} = 49.12 \ p < .01$.
Gender main effect (offspring Time 2): $F_{(1/336)} = 57.03 \ p < .01$.
Gender main effect (offspring only, both times): $F_{(1/337)} = 61.12 \ p < .01$.
Generation X gender interaction (Time 1 only): $F_{(1/336)} = 5.61 \ p < .05$.
Generation X gender interaction (offspring Time 2): $F_{(1/336)} = 7.69 \ p < .01$.
Time main effect (offspring only): $F_{(1/337)} = 5.27 \ p < .05$.
Time X gender interaction (offspring only): $F_{(1/337)} = 0.27 \ p = .60$.

evidence – in line with Troll and Bengtson (1979) – that fathers influence child values more than mothers (see Table 19.3).

To assess the relative size of the impact of the *zeitgeist* (i.e., the current value climate in value-transmission processes), we calculated zero-order correlations and semipartial correlation coefficients (Table 19.4). We also included one more context variable: the socioeconomic status of the family as determined by the occupational prestige of either the mother or the father (whichever was higher). Occupational prestige was measured using the so-called magnitude prestige scale (Wegener, 1988) in which respondents merely indicate their occupation, which is then coded according to the rules published by Wegener. For example, a doctor receives a fairly high score of 186, whereas an unskilled worker receives a fairly low score of 20.

We partialled the parent–offspring correlation for the other parent-value score, for the sibling-value score, for the *zeitgeist*, and for the socioeconomic status. We then calculated proportions of explained variance in the children's value preference by entering mother value (Block 1), father value (Block 2), sibling value (Block 3), *zeitgeist* value (Block 4), and socioeconomic status (Block 5) into a regression analysis. Table 19.4 shows that the correlations between parent value preferences and offspring value preferences (T2) are reduced considerably when attenuating for other parent, sibling, *zeitgeist*, and socioeconomic status influence. Table 19.4 also shows that about 16% of the son's HSI and 12.5% of

Table 19.4. *Correlations of parental value preferences and offspring value preferences partialed for other influences (offspring values measured 1 year later)*

	Mother's HSI		Father's HSI		Percentage of Variation in Offspring Values Explained by					
	Zero-order corr.	Semi-partial corr.	Zero-order corr.	Semi-partial corr.	Total R^2_{adj}	Mother values	Father values	Sibling values	*Zeitgeist*	SES
Son's HSI (Time 2)	.26**	.15**	.31**	.26**	16.0	6.6[a] 26.1%	9.1 36.0%	7.7 30.4%	0.1 0.4%	1.8 7.1%
Daughter's HSI (Time 2)	.19**	.08	.30**	.27**	12.5	3.8 20.7%	8.1 44.0%	5.0 27.2%	0.2 1.1%	1.3 7.1%

** $p < .01$.

[a] The R^2s given for the different agents are R^2s acquired when entering that agent into the regression analysis first; this procedure was chosen to treat every agent fairly when comparing relative impact. It has the consequence that the individual R^2s do not add up to the total R^2.

the daughter's HSI are explained by the independent variables of the regression model. It can also be shown that the father is the most important agent of value transmission, followed by the siblings and the mother. In addition, the *zeitgeist* influence and the influence of a family's class background are rather low. This result is compatible with the findings of Boehnke et al. (2002), who found a substantial influence of the *zeitgeist* on the transmission only for xenophobic attitudes but not for HSI.

3.0. VALUE TRANSMISSION STUDY II

Research Questions and Design. Study I showed that there is a small but noticeable effect of the variable of *zeitgeist* on the transmission process, but it did not reveal any conditions that lead to the effect we detected. We now propose that there is not just a more or less diffuse effect but rather an effect that follows a certain pattern. Study II acknowledges explicitly that the current societal value climate – what we call the *zeitgeist* – is perceived and accepted by families in different ways. Following Grusec and Goodnow's (1994) and Knafo's (2003) concept of a two-step process of internalization and transferring this to *zeitgeist* internalization leads to the assumption that families have to perceive the *zeitgeist* accurately (Step 1: perception) and then have to choose whether to accept or reject the *zeitgeist* values (Step 2: reaction). Every family – in fact, every family member – behaves in a specific manner toward the *zeitgeist* and positions itself relative to it. Whereas Study I focused on the common *zeitgeist*, Study II concentrates on the idea that the specific distance between a family and the *zeitgeist* influences intrafamilial value-transmission processes. The main hypothesis of Study II is that value transmission in mainstream families differs from transmission processes in families that have value preferences distant from *zeitgeist* values. Value transmission and parent–child value congruence – so we assume – are significantly stronger in families distant from the *zeitgeist*. Mainstream families tend to communicate much less about values than families with a value orientation distant from the mainstream. Because the latter do not accept the *zeitgeist* as their own value position, those families have to reflect on their values substantially more than families whose values are in line with the *zeitgeist*. Non-*zeitgeist* families additionally tend to be more isolated, a situation that also leads to a stronger value transmission.

According to Goodnow (1997) and Knafo (2003), parents who are aware of their "otherness" regarding their value position are likely to put more effort into value transmission to prevent their children from internalizing opposing values of, for example, their school or peer environment. They "try either to shield their children from opposing values or to prearm them with counterarguments" (Knafo, 2003, p. 373). We hypothesize that all of these processes lead to a stronger cohesion and higher value congruence within a family.

To test our assumption, we constructed a variable that measures the distance of a family from the *zeitgeist*. First, we averaged the HSI scores of all four family members for Time 1 to obtain a family HSI. Looking at the sample as a whole, this variable is – of course – identical to the *zeitgeist* variable constructed for Study I: It has a mean of 2.79 and a standard deviation of .43. For Study II, however, we proceeded differently: We z-standardized the variable to obtain a variable ZHSI$_{Fam}$ with a mean of 0 and a standard deviation of 1. Finally, we dichotomized this variable by giving all families within the range from −1 to +1 a 0, and all other families – that is, those that are at a greater distance from the mean of 0, either to the negative or the positive side – a 1. In this way, we were able to measure a family's distance from the *zeitgeist*; 61.6% of the sample was classified as close to the *zeitgeist*, 38.4% as distant from the *zeitgeist*.[2]

Finally, to show that the quality of intrafamilial communication processes is different in families close to or distant from the *zeitgeist*, we used two indicators. The first is a scale introduced as a family coherence scale by Sagy and Antonovsky (1992), which can also be interpreted as a proximal measure for communication intensity (Communication Style I). We used four items of the scale in our study and posed them to all family members. Reliabilities for the four-item scale varied between Cronbach's $\alpha = .71$ and Cronbach's $\alpha = .74$ among the family members. A sample item read, "Life in our family is interesting." Items had to be answered on a scale ranging from 1 (low approval) to 7 (high approval). Second, we asked for an evaluation of decision processes in the family using three items from a scale developed by Kagitcibasi (1967; modified by Lederer, 1983) to measure a democratic parental style (Communication Style II). A sample item read, "When our family has to reach an important decision, the opinion of all family members including the children is taken into consideration." We see this as a proxy for intrafamilial communication intensity. This scale was only used among offspring. Consistencies of the three-item scale varied between Cronbach's $\alpha = .51$ and Cronbach's $\alpha = .55$. Here, items had to be answered on a scale ranging from 1 to 5.

Results. To test the assumption that value-transmission processes are stronger in families distant from the *zeitgeist*, we calculated across-time parent–offspring correlations separately for the two types of families (Table 19.5).

Table 19.5 clearly shows that it is families distant from the *zeitgeist* that have strong value-transmission processes, whereas in families close to the *zeitgeist*, transmission processes are rather weak.

---

[2] To avoid confounding the categorization of the families as close to or distant from the *zeitgeist*, and the across-time parent–offspring correlation (which is to a certain degree given when parent ratings are used both for the classification of the family and as part of the across-time correlations), one could carry out the classification of families on the basis of offspring T1 HSI ratings only. We have tested this and results are essentially the same.

Table 19.5. *Intrafamilial value transmission in relation to distance from* zeitgeist
(correlations)

	Close to *Zeitgeist*		Distant from *Zeitgeist*	
	Son's HSI (Time 2)	Daughter's HSI (Time 2)	Son's HSI (Time 2)	Daughter's HSI (Time 2)
Father HSI	.08	.15*	.52**	.43**
Mother HSI	−.05	.04	.58**	.39**

* $p < .05$; ** $p < .01$.

To validate our assumption that the reason for the linkage between *zeit-geist* distance and value transmission is the fact that in families distant from the *zeitgeist* communication processes are more intense, we tested whether the two family types differed on our two proximal measures of communication intensity. It should be kept in mind that our *zeitgeist* variable is neutral to the contents of value preferences. Families distant from the *zeitgeist* can be families in which the preference for HSI is substantially above *or* below the average of the sample.

Here also, the findings are clear (Table 19.6): Families close to the *zeit-geist* evaluate their family life – among other things – as less interesting than families distant from the *zeitgeist*. Children in the latter type of families also report inclusion in family decision processes more frequently than children in families close to the *zeitgeist*. The second measure of family communication style differentiates only with marginal statistical significance between the two distance-from-*zeitgeist* groups.

Table 19.6. *Family communication style as dependent on distance from* zeitgeist *(means and standard deviations)*

	Close to *Zeitgeist*	Distant from *Zeitgeist*	*t* Value
Intense Family Communication I	5.18 (0.62)	5.33 (0.62)	−2.15*
Intense Family Communication II	3.42 (0.56)	3.52 (0.58)	−1.69+

+ $p < .10$; * $p < .05$.

4.0. DISCUSSION AND CONCLUSIONS

Zeitgeist is a difficult sociological concept. Loosely formulated, one may see it as a concept somewhere between fashion and culture. Fashions[3] characterize short-term preferences for fairly concrete objects such as clothing, automobile designs, and media figures. *Culture*, a term we dare not attempt to define here, stands for something that has grown over decades, if not centuries or millennia, and encompasses an orientation more toward abstract than concrete phenomena. *Zeitgeist* is somehow in the middle of the two, probably closer to fashion in its contents than to culture. It is more abstract a concept than fashion because it does not usually pertain to concrete objects (e.g., color of clothes or design of neckties) but is something that changes fairly rapidly, possibly more frequently in recent decades than before.

This chapter is not the place to elaborate analytically on the distinction among fashion, *zeitgeist*, and culture. What is sought here is a way to include *zeitgeist* influences in one-shot or short-term panel studies of values and their intergenerational transmission. The current study took two approaches to include *zeitgeist* into its analyses. Study I conceptualized it as the value preferences of randomly selected others; Study II incorporated *zeitgeist* by positioning every family vis-à-vis the population mean, obviously estimated on the grounds of the sample mean. For both approaches, there would have been more appropriate strategies had data for them been available. For Study I, a less technical approach could have been taken had respondents been asked for an evaluation of average preferences of HSI in German society. In Study II, knowledge about mean HSI from an independent estimate of the population mean would have been more elegant, but both types of data were unavailable.

However, even in cases like the current study, in which no additional data are available, it is possible to show the influence of the *zeitgeist* on intrafamilial value-transmission processes. Evidence from this study can be summarized as in the following discussion.

Families with an atypical preference of hierarchic self-interest at Time 1 (i.e., families that show either a particularly high or a particularly low preference for the HSI value syndrome) emerge as achieving a stronger across-time parent–offspring transmission of value preferences. How can this finding be interpreted? Families with an atypical preference of HSI could either be highly entrepreneurial and competitive families that have no problems with elbowing their way through life, or they could be families that strongly reject a "capitalist," self-enhancement outlook on life. Both types of families, in a way, are outsiders in German society. To convey to their offspring that the particular family-specific

---

[3] We do not mean to speak of *haute couture* here (i.e., fashion in the sense of innovation) but rather of aesthetics trends of everyday life.

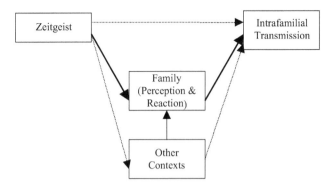

Figure 19.3. *Zeitgeist* and the intrafamilial value transmission process – a model.

value orientation is "good," parents from those families need more communication with their children than parents from mainstream families. Getting children to assimilate the cherished values of the family does not "come easy" (as can be assumed if cherished family values are in accordance with the societal mainstream), but transmission needs an investment, a more intense intrafamilial communication.

Study II indeed produced evidence that less intense communication is the rule to a greater extent in families closer to the *zeitgeist* than in families distant from it. In the latter type of family, all members find life more interesting and offspring report a substantial say in family decisions.

There is only minimal direct influence of the *zeitgeist* on value transmission across all families. Only fathers seem to be influenced to some degree by the free-floating preference of HSI in the general public. Together with the finding on the role of closeness to and distance from the *zeitgeist*, and the finding that the influence of socioeconomic status on transmission is only marginal, this finding lends plausibility to the following more general model of *zeitgeist* influence on value transmission (Figure 19.3).

We now assume that the current general value climate of a society has only minimal direct influence per se on the formation of value-transmission processes in the family. As Boehnke (2004) showed, such a direct influence can only be assumed for values grossly rejected by the societal mainstream. Transmission of religious values in a generally nonreligious society (e.g., East Germany) may be such a case. The pure knowledge of the rejecting climate of the society may increase the transmission of traditional religious values in a family.

In general, however, knowledge about the societal preferences seems to elicit a specific reaction of the family, which either concurs with the societal mainstream or deviates from it. Only in the latter case is there an influence on transmission processes, in the way that parent–child communication is intensified and transmission processes are strengthened in the family.

Influences other than the *zeitgeist* could not be corroborated in the current studies; however, beyond a general measurement of the social class of a family, no other context variables were included; therefore, further research is needed in this field.

Two final puzzles remain with the findings of the current studies. Unlike in our earlier studies using the Schwartz Value Survey as the instrument to measure value preferences (Boehnke, 2001), fathers had more impact on their children's values than mothers, *and* same-sex cross-generational similarity was *not* higher than opposite-sex cross-generational similarity. At the same time, transmission to sons was higher than transmission to daughters. We assume that this finding is a result of the specific content of the transmitted-value syndrome. Values of power and achievement – and self-enhancement in general – are strongly "masculine" because males are socialized to show dominance, whereas females continue to be encouraged to show "caringness" (Hadjar, Baier, & Boehnke, 2003; Hagan, Gillis, & Simpson, 1979; Hagan, Rippl, Boehnke, & Merkens, 1999). Parents may deliberately not want their daughters to acquire the masculine HSI value orientation. This interpretation is also backed by the means: Boys and fathers show higher HSI values than the opposite-sex counterparts in their family. These differences are highly significant.

In summary, this study has once again shown that intrafamilial value transmission should not be studied without reference to the societal context of the family or without a clear statement as to which specific value orientations are under consideration. Value transmission differs for different societal contexts and for different values.

REFERENCES

Adorno, T. W., Frenkel-Brunswik, E., Levinson, D., & Sanford, R. N. (1950). *The Authoritarian Personality*. New York: Science Editions.

Akademie der pädagogischen Wissenschaften, Abt. Bildungssoziologie (1989). *Berufslaufbahnen, Lebenspläne und Wertorientierungen* [Professional careers, life plans, and value orientations]. Berlin: Akademie der Pädagogischen Wissenschaften der DDR, Research Report.

Baier, D., & Hadjar, A. (2004). Wie wird Leistungsorientierung von den Eltern auf die Kinder übertragen? Ergebnisse einer Längsschnittstudie [How is achievement orientation transmitted from parents to children? Results of a panel study]. *Zeitschrift für Familienforschung, 15*, 156–177.

Boehnke, K. (1988). *Prosoziale Motivation, Selbstkonzept und politische Orientierung: Entwicklungsbedingungen und Veränderungen im Jugendalter* [Prosocial motivation, self-concept, and political orientation: Development and change in adolescence]. Frankfurt am Main: Lang.

Boehnke, K. (2001). Parent–offspring value transmission in a societal context: Suggestions for a utopian research design – with empirical underpinnings. *Journal of Cross-Cultural Psychology, 32*, 241–255.

Boehnke, K. (2004). Do our children become as we are? Intergenerational value transmission and societal value change – two unlinked concepts in social research. In F. Hardt (Ed.), *Mapping the world* (pp. 99–118). Tübingen: Francke.

Boehnke, K., & Hadjar, A. (2004). Authoritarianism. In C. Spielberger (Ed.), *Encyclopedia of Applied Psychology* (pp. 251–255). San Diego, CA: Academic Press.

Boehnke, K., Ittel, A., & Baier, D. (2002). Value transmission and zeitgeist: An underresearched relationship. *Sociale Wetenschappen, 45*, 28–43.

Boehnke, K., Merkens, H., & Claßen, G. (1998). *Dominanzideologie, Geschlechtsrollen und Delinquenz bei Jugendlichen in Toronto und Berlin* [Dominance ideologies, gender roles, and delinquency among adolescents in Toronto and Berlin]. Chemnitz/Berlin: Proposal to the Deutsche Forschungsgemeinschaft.

Christie, R., & Geis, F. L. (1970). *Studies in Machiavellianism.* New York: Academic Press.

Festinger, L. (1954). A theory of social comparison processes. *Human Relations, 7*, 117–140.

Goodnow, J. J. (1997). Parenting and the "transmission" and "internalization" of values: From social-cultural perspectives to within-family analyses. In J. E. Grusec & L. Kuczynski (Eds.), *Handbook of parenting and the transmission of values* (pp. 333–361). New York: Wiley.

Grusec, J. E., & Goodnow, J. J. (1994). Impact of parental discipline methods on the child's internalization of values: A reconceptualization of current points of view. *Developmental Psychology, 30*, 4–19.

Hadjar, A. (2004). *Ellenbogenmentalität und Fremdenfeindlichkeit bei Jugendlichen: Die Rolle des Hierarchischen Selbstinteresses* [Elbow mentality and xenophobia among adolescents: The role of hierarchic self-interest]. Wiesbaden: Verlag für Sozialwissenschaften.

Hadjar, A., & Baier, D. (2003). Familiale Vererbung von Dominanzideologien in verschiedenen sozio-ökonomischen Kontexten [Familial heredity of dominance ideologies in different socioeconomic contexts]. *Zeitschrift für Politische Psychologie, 10*, 303–320.

Hadjar, A., Baier, D., & Boehnke, K. (2003). Geschlechtsspezifische Jugenddelinquenz: Eine Beurteilung der Power-Control Theory [Gender-specific juvenile delinquency: An evaluation of power-control theory]. In J. Mansel, H. Griese, & A. Scherr (Eds.), *Theoriedefizite der Jugendforschung* (pp. 174–193). Weinheim: Juventa.

Hagan, J., Gillis, A. R., & Simpson, J. (1979). The sexual stratification of social control: A gender-based perspective on crime and delinquency. *British Journal of Sociology, 30*, 25–38.

Hagan, J., Hefler, G., Claßen, G., Boehnke, K., & Merkens, H. (1998). Subterranean sources of subcultural delinquency beyond the American dream. *Criminology, 36*, 309–342.

Hagan, J., Rippl, S., Boehnke, K., & Merkens, H. (1999). Interest in evil: Hierarchic self-interest and right-wing extremism among East and West German youth. *Social Science Research, 28*, 162–183.

Henning, H. J., & Six, B. (1977). Konstruktion einer Machiavellismus-Skala [Construction of a Machiavellism scale]. *Zeitschrift für Sozialpsychologie, 8*, 185–198.

Hirsch, F. (1977). *Social limits to growth.* Cambridge, MA: Harvard University Press.

Inglehart, R. (1977). *The silent revolution.* Princeton, NJ: Princeton University Press.

Inglehart, R. (1997). *Modernization and postmodernization: Cultural, economic, and political change in 43 societies.* Princeton, NJ: Princeton University Press.

Jerusalem, M. (1984). *Selbstbezogene Kognitionen in schulischen Bezugsgruppen* [Self-related cognitions in school-based peer groups]. Berlin: Freie Universität Berlin.

Kagitcibasi, C. (1967). *Social norms and authoritarianism: A comparison of Turkish and American adolescents.* Berkeley: University of California, doctoral dissertation.

Knafo, A. (2003). Contexts, relationship quality, and family value socialization: The case of parent–school ideological fit in Israel. *Personal Relationships, 10,* 371–388.

Kohn, M. L. (1983). On the transmission of values in the family: A preliminary formulation. *Research in Sociology of Education and Socialization, 4,* 3–12.

Kohn, M. L., Slomczynski, K. M., & Schoenbach, C. (1986). Social stratification and the transmission of values in the family: A cross-national assessment. *Sociological Forum, 1,* 73–102.

Küpper, B., & Heitmeyer, W. (2004). Feindselige Frauen: Zwischen Angst, Zugehörigkeit und Durchsetzungsideologie [Hostile women: Between anxiety, affiliation, and dominance ideology]. In W. Heitmeyer (Ed.), *Deutsche Zustände,* Folge 3 (pp. 108–128). Frankfurt am Main: Suhrkamp.

Lederer, G. (1983). *Jugend und Autorität* [Youth and authority]. Opladen: Westdeutscher Verlag.

Machiavelli, N. (1984/1532). *The prince (Il principe).* Oxford: Oxford University Press.

MacPherson, C. B. (1962). *The political theory of possessive individualism: From Hobbes to Locke.* London: Oxford University Press.

Mead, G. H. (1934). *Mind, self, and society.* Chicago: University of Chicago Press.

Sagy, S., & Antonovsky, A. (1992). The family sense of coherence and the retirement transition. *Journal of Marriage and the Family, 54,* 983–993.

Schwartz, S. H. (1992). Universals in the content and structure of values: Theoretical advances and empirical tests in 20 countries. *Advances in Experimental Social Psychology, 25,* 1–65.

Simmel, G. (1978/1900). *The Philosophy of Money.* London/Boston: Routledge & Kegan Paul.

Smith, A. (1776). *An inquiry into the nature and causes of the wealth of nations.* London: W. Strahan and T. Cadell.

Troll, L., & Bengtson, V. (1979). Generations and the family. In W. R. Burr, R. Hill, F. I. Nye, & I. L. Reiss (Eds.), *Contemporary theories about the family, Vol. 1* (pp. 127–161). New York: The Free Press.

Urban, D., & Singelmann, J. (1998). Eltern-Kind-Transmissionen von ausländerablehnenden Einstellungen: Eine regionale Längsschnitt-Studie zur intra- und intergenerativen Herausbildung eines sozialen Orientierungsmusters [Parent–child transmission of xenophobic attitudes: A regional panel study on genesis of social orientation patterns within and across generations]. *Zeitschrift für Soziologie, 27,* 276–296.

Weber, M. (1930). *The Protestant ethic and the spirit of capitalism.* London: Unwin/Hyman.

Wegener, B. (1988). *Kritik des Prestiges* [Critique of prestige]. Opladen: Westdeutscher Verlag.

Zetterberg, H. L. (1992). *The sociology of values: The Swedish value space.* Paper presented at the 87th Annual Meeting of the American Sociological Association, August 20–24, Pittsburgh, PA.

Zetterberg, H. L. (1997). The study of values. In R. Swedberg & E. Uddhammar (Eds.), *Sociological endeavor: Selected writings* (pp. 191–219). Stockholm: City University Press.

Zetterberg, H. L. (1998). Cultural values in market and opinion research. In C. McDonald & P. Vangelder (Eds.), *Handbook of marketing and opinion research* (pp. 995–1013). Amsterdam: ESOMAR.

20

Epilogue: Toward a Model of Cultural Transmission

UTE SCHÖNPFLUG

INTRODUCTION

This epilogue provides some afterthoughts to the wealth of ideas in the chapters collected for this volume. It provides a summary of the main ideas, theoretical approaches, and results presented by putting together what is already in place and – to a greater extent – what is still needed to develop an integrated theoretical model of transmission. It may well be that this goal will not be reached, and research and theorizing is not sufficiently far advanced to decide whether the efforts invested were worth the time. Nevertheless, that which has been achieved in various disciplines to clarify the mechanisms and results of cultural transmission processes seems promising. We know some of the fundamental *transmission mechanisms* and *transmission belts*. However, there are more to discover and we have to clarify the conditions for the *transmission gap* (Fox, 1995) – that is, the lack of reproductive transfer of social orientations, skills, and knowledge across generations and peers.

1.0. THE CULTURAL EVOLUTIONARY PERSPECTIVE

1.1. Selectivity of Transmission

The most challenging issues for transmission research and theory to emerge from the framework of cultural evolution are certainly the following questions: What causes the differential transmission of cultural elements or traits? Which factors are responsible for the relatively high transmissibility of some elements and the relatively low transmissibility of others? The adaptiveness of a cultural form and, hence, the probability of being transmitted depend in part on who is transmitting (i.e., male parent, female parent, teacher, peer), to whom (i.e., male offspring, female offspring, student, peer), when (i.e., during childhood, adolescence, adulthood), and in what context (i.e., family, school, playground, work, society, cultural group). These factors might be referred to as the *conditions* of transmission. In addition, we have to consider the *content* of the transmission. The content can greatly influence its transmissibility. Theoretically, content may be expected to influence the transmissibility of any characteristic that demands considerable time, energy, resources, or risk taking. Therefore, it must be part of any general theory of cultural transmission. According to Mark (2002), there is no cultural trait or content as such; what makes a trait cultural is the way in which it is acquired through social or cultural transmission. In addition, a cultural trait is one that is widely distributed within a culture space.

Durham's (1982, 1990) main hypothesis in his evolutionary theoretical framework is that the content of cultural heritage influences the nature of human phenotypes, which in turn influence the transmissibility of the cultural heritage. During cultural evolution, cultural transmission became increasingly self-selecting through a transmissible set of values, ideas, and beliefs that reflect the trials and errors of hominid experience. According to Kamela and Nakanishi (2002), the cultural schemata and social orientations that endure over generations are intuitive concepts that in psychology are called "folk" concepts (e.g., "folk psychology," "folk biology") but also "intuitive" (e.g., "intuitive parenting") or "subjective" concepts (e.g., "subjective psychology"). Scientific knowledge and skills seldom reach the wide distribution of cultural traits.

The issue of contents of cultural transmission still needs further clarification. When looking for conceptual dimensions such as the one discussed herein, the question needs to be answered not only of which cultural contents have a higher probability of being transmitted but also the many possible interactions of type of contents with mode of transmission must be detected. There seems to be no systematic answer in terms of the mechanisms and success of transmission observed for such diverse contents as social orientations or attitudes and values, skills and knowledge, and behaviors. It seems plausible to assume that the transmission of knowledge and skills has to involve more explicit teaching than the transfer of social attitudes. The transmission of behaviors might also imply an explicit teaching component (e.g., in the case of folk dancing or songs) as well as a deliberate learning or imitation component. The transmission of attitudes presumably takes place through implicit channels. To find answers to these questions, we have to vary the type of contents more *systematically*.

1.2. Speed of Transmission

Cavalli-Sforza and Feldman (1981) claimed that if new members of a culture enter and leave the system slowly, the mechanisms of transmission can be slow and diffuse. If new members join and exit rapidly or in large numbers relative to those who stay, then culture must be transmitted quickly and intensively if it is to be maintained. The authors did not provide empirical evidence for this point, but it does have intriguing implications. The contemporaneous epochal trend toward mobility, migration, and globalization involves rapid exchange of members of a cultural group. The forms and results of transmission observed in migrant populations, for example, might be the result of such necessary increased efforts to maintain culture when confronted with rapid change. We have no systematic information on the speed of transmission either. So far, it is not conceivable how one could measure speed of transmission in vertical parent–offspring transmission. Parents try to influence their offspring through the life span. Measuring parent–offspring similarity at particular points in time might indicate speed of transmission, but this similarity also depends on the developmental state of the transmitter and the adopter and the associated openness for societal information, such as normative distributions of values in the social context. In horizontal or peer transmission, the number of individuals showing the cultural trait between two consecutive measurements is the usual way to assess speed of transmission. This requires fixing criteria when a cultural trait exists in an individual. In the case of quantitatively varying traits, criterion strength of the traits has to be given. As may be seen from these short elaborations, the speed of vertical transmission is difficult to compare to horizontal transmission.

1.3. Direction of Transmission

Vertical social transmission from the parent's generation to the offspring generation is less responsive to environmental variability (Laland, 1993) than other directions of transmission. However, the process of vertical cultural transmission does not lead to a constant replication of culture in successive generations; rather, it falls somewhere between an exact transmission (with hardly any difference between parents and offspring) and a complete failure of transmission (with hardly any similarity between the generations). Functionally, either extreme would be problematic for a society: Exact transmission would not allow for novelty and change and, hence, the ability to respond to new situations, whereas failure of transmission would not permit coordinated action between generations (Boyd & Richerson, 2005). In times of extreme reforms and revolution, this lack of coordinated action becomes highly visible. Only the interpreters of these social movements do not argue with a failure of transmission and the dangers thereof. It would be an interesting challenge for social scientists to elaborate on this line of argumentation from cultural evolutionary theory and reinterpret times of violent social change.

1.4. Quantitative Modeling of the Transmission Process

New research in biology with well-designed studies began by broaching the original issue of nongenetic inheritance. Cavalli-Sforza and Feldman (1981; Cavalli-Sforza, Feldman, Chen, & Dornbusch, 1982) had in mind the development of a quantitative theory of cultural evolution when they focused on cultural transmission as a critical mechanism that allows variation to be predicted between and within populations over time and space. In their 1982 paper, the authors provided prospects for analyzing vertical (i.e., parent–offspring) and horizontal (i.e., conjugal partners and offspring–peers) transmission. They claimed, "No statistical measure of association can indicate bona fide causation (transmission). Yet if an individual, at the end of a period of socialization and education resembles its mentors, some process of transmission (conscious or subconscious) must have been going on" (p. 26). The tentative measure they used is bivariate correlation or partial correlation. They found strong correlations hinting at vertical transmission as the appropriate path for political attitudes and religion along with forms of entertainment and sports, superstitions and beliefs, and customs and habits. Mother and father are differentially efficient transmitters with regard to various transmission content areas; however, among all the content areas looked at in their analyses, there was no evidence of an interaction between the two parental transmission components. The authors also suggested some age periods in ontogenesis that might be more sensitive to the reception of cultural transmission. These considerations, together with the fact that the mode of cultural transmission is presumably also culturally transmitted, suggest that variations between and within populations could be strongly influenced by specific circumstances of the given epoch. Potential applications of the Cavalli-Sforza et al. (1982) approach are found in linguistics, psychology, anthropology, sociology, and communication sciences. Perhaps the most exciting prospect is that of being able to use observations on transmission to predict variation between individuals and populations over space and time.

New formal models of cultural evolution analyze how cognitive processes combine with social interaction to generate the distributions and dynamics of cultural mental "representations." Recently, cognitive anthropologists have criticized such models, making three points: (1) mental representations are nondiscrete, (2) cultural transmission is highly inaccurate, and (3) mental representations are not replicated but rather "reconstructed" through an inferential process that is strongly affected by cognitive factors. They argue that from these three claims, it follows that (a) models assuming replication or replicators are inappropriate, (b) selective cultural learning cannot account for stable traditions, and (c) selective cultural learning cannot generate cumulative adaptation. Henrich and Boyd (2002) used formal models to show that even if the premise of these critiques is correct, the deductions that have been made from them are false. If there is no replication, then the discussion of transmission becomes meaningless.

1.5. The Conflict Model of Transmission

Lumsden's (1984) *conflict model of transmission* starts with the premise that a basic understanding of cultural norms, values, roles, and lore is achieved by the offspring because the parents are motivated to transmit those contents. However, the parents may have the opportunity to teach things that are more of value to themselves than to their offspring, engendering costly acts of conflict with the offspring. When taken together, costs to the parents of teaching or preparing learning situations are likely to increase as a function of offspring age and amount of cultural information already learned. The transmission model behind these thoughts is that the transfer of information is cumulative but also that accumulation is accompanied by the loss of receptiveness for new transmission contents. To state it in psychological terms: The working models built up during transmission in the past become more stable and fixed.

At some point, costs to the parents of enculturating the offspring with specific types and amounts of information may exceed the benefit. When the costs are equal to or greater than the benefits, a conflict constellation arises. The parents might stop transmission efforts either totally or regarding a specific topic. This does not mean that the offspring do not elicit cultural transmission behaviors from the parents. This model provides an explanation for the parents' transmission motivation in terms of rational payoff constellations. All the premises of the conflict model are still speculative; as Schönpflug and Bilz (Chapter 10, this volume) found, there do not seem to be any parents with no motivation to transmit even in situations with contextual discontinuity – and for the content area investigated (i.e., values). A lack of motivation in specific content areas seems to be more plausible. In addition, to a certain extent, the parents' motivation to transmit is driven by the children's search for information and orientation. Schönpflug and Bilz also found a cluster of families in which children feel strongly influenced by the parents, whereas the parents report medium motivation to transmit. Lumsden's (1984) cultural evolutionary conflict model thus finds some support in a psychological study with a developmental background. The factors for emergence of an increased strength of motivation were not explored in this study. Further investigations need to search for evidence for the payoff hypothesis of predicting *transmission conflict.*

An additional factor of the cost and benefit model of parental transmission efforts is the number of siblings toward which the transmission efforts have to be directed. The more children that parents have, the smaller the share of transmission efforts each offspring receives. The situation might occur in which the offspring favors more transmission efforts than the parents are able or willing to give. Parental transmission efforts are enforced by the coeducation of older siblings, as Cavalli-Sforza et al. (1982) and Schönpflug (2001) demonstrated.

In view of Lumsden's (1984) conflict model, the hypothetical case must be considered in which parents refrain from transmission efforts and the offspring still demands transmitted information. The child provokes the parents into transmitting more information than they wish to transmit. Also, if the parents continue to be reluctant to transmit, they discourage the child from learning. This extreme situation has not been reported in any empirical study, at least not within the frame of reference of transmission theory. However, perhaps clinical reports exist about parent–child constellations from which further conclusions might be drawn.

A comprehensive theory of transmission and behavior in general, of course, would incorporate both cultural and genetic evolution. The dynamics of cultural transmission, however, are complex, and a comprehensive theory is still beyond our grasp. For the present, all theories of transmission behavior rely on some form of simplification. We have to consider the merits of two such simplifications: (1) purely cultural models, which ignore genetic evolution; and (2) purely acultural models, which ignore cultural evolution. The first are justified only when biological constraints on culture are weak, the second only when they are strong (Rogers, 1988). Essentially, according to Rogers, there is no cultural transmission bias for the fittest individuals. Why should the fittest take over widely distributed cultural information when they are more competent than the transmitter? Also, there is no learning bias favoring transmission of behaviors that enhances fitness.

Therefore, Rogers (1988) concluded that the value of culturally transmitted information does not accumulate; it decays – but only if no new motivation for reviving of cultural information arises. Models of simultaneous genetic and cultural transmission and coevolution were developed to shed some light on the many unclear issues (Lumsden & Wilson, 1981).

2.0. CULTURE IS ONLY HUMAN: A DEVELOPMENTAL SCIENCE PERSPECTIVE OF TRANSMISSION

2.1. Animal and Human Transmission

Comparative animal studies suggest that many species live in complex social groups using techniques and rituals; only humans seem to live in cultures. Cultures are most clearly distinguished from other forms of social organization by the nature of their products – for example, material artifacts, social institutions, behavioral traditions, and languages. These cultural traditions share, among other things, the characteristic that they accumulate modifications over time. Once a practice has been initiated by some member or members of a culture, others acquire it relatively faithfully but then modify it from the need to deal with novel exigencies. The modified practice is then acquired by others, including progeny, who may in turn add their own modifications and so on across generations. This accumulation of modifications over time is called the *ratchet effect* because each modification stays firmly in place in the group until further modifications are made. No cultural products exhibiting anything like the ratchet effect have ever been observed in the ontogenetically acquired behaviors or products of nonhuman animals (Tomasello, 1990; Tomasello, Krüger, & Ratner, 1993a, 1993b). A recent study by White, Gros-Louis, King, Papakhian, and West (2007) points to an aspect of transmission similar to what Tomasello (Chapter 3, this volume) puts forward: They exposed cowbirds to different social experiences with adults in their first year. The authors then determined whether different social patterns could be transmitted to new generations of juvenile males. The juveniles never had the opportunity to observe some of the courtship and competition behavior that they came to replicate. The study revealed that the role of adults was to establish a social structure in the groups with the consequence of modifying juveniles' early social interactions. Juveniles were then "cultured" within these different learning environments, *constructing* social behavior similar to the adult males' behavior in the juveniles' first year. This interpretation suggests that further forms of assuring cultural continuity might be operating: Certain behavior patterns of the adult generation may elicit the development of *adequate* but not similar juvenile behavior patterns, in the same way as the adults' behavior to the same behavioral pattern was learned by their respective parental generation.

Large differences in products between animal and human societies may be most directly explained by a small but important difference in process. Simply stated, human beings learn from one another in ways that animals do not. In particular, human beings *transmit* ontogenetically acquired behavior and information, both within and across generations, with a much higher degree of fidelity than other animal species. Humans are able to teach by using such teaching strategies as slow and exact demonstration and repetition. The learning processes that ensure fidelity serve to prevent information loss (i.e., the ratchet effect) and, thus, in combination with individual and collaborative inventiveness, form the basis for cultural evolution. Human beings are also able to learn from each other in this way because they have powerful, perhaps uniquely powerful, forms of social cognition. Human beings understand and take the perspective of others in a manner and to a degree that allows them to participate more intimately than nonhuman animals in the knowledge and skills of conspecifics.

These particular capabilities emerge with the understanding of other people in terms of their intentions and beliefs, or even in terms of their *theory of mind*. Tomasello et al.'s (1993a, 1993b) main concept of cultural learning implies that human beings engage in a special form of social learning. In cultural learning, learners do not only direct their attention to the location of another individual's activity, they also actually attempt to see a situation the way the other sees it – from inside the other's perspective, as it were. An individual does not learn from another but through another. This is possible because human beings are able to take on the perspectives of others. Cultural learning is also social as far as the result is concerned: What is retained via social interaction is also social. In all cases of cultural learning, the learner has to keep the learning contents and the form of interaction (e.g., demonstration, instruction) by which he or she learned it. This *internalization* is a special manifestation of basic processes of learning. The important point for current purposes is that the cognitive representation resulting from cultural learning includes something of the perspective of the interactional partner. This perspective guides the learning and behaviors of the learner when the original learning experience is over. This internalization does not (by definition) occur in other forms of social learning. In that sense, the social learning of autistic children and chimpanzees is *acultural*. Thus, cultural learning plays a central role in the evolution of human culture and cognition.

The three basic forms of cultural learning are – in order of development – imitative learning, instructed learning, and collaborative learning. The direction of intentionality in the three forms of cultural learning are from learner to model (i.e., vertical imitative learning), predominantly from instructor to learner and weakly from learner to instructor (i.e., vertical instructed learning), and equally strong from collaborator to learner and vice versa (i.e., horizontal collaborative learning). True imitation is only possible if the imitator understands the goals and intentions of the model; that is, he or she uses the model's behavioral strategies in the appropriate functional context. Human infants are able to do this in the language domain from 8 to 9 months onward. They keep the words in mind and the intentions of the model inherent in the given speech act. Engaging in instructed learning implies understanding the perspective and intentions of the instructor; when these are internalized, only then can the instructions be understood as cultural learning. When the learning child has mastered the instructed behavior or knowledge, he or she will perform or transmit the instructed behavior with the same nonverbal directives of the instructor to guide his or her own performance because the child might also use the same words of the instruction on other occasions. Imitative learning and instructional learning are means of cultural transmission: By modeling or by instruction, the adult or an older child passes on valued elements of culture to the learning child. In collaborative learning, neither interactant is an expert; the intersubjectivity is symmetrical. Two peers work together to solve a common problem and, in arriving jointly at a solution, they coconstruct knowledge. They then individually internalize this coconstruction. Collaborative learning is thus distinct from the other two processes of cultural learning in that it is a process of cultural creation or coconstruction rather than transmission.

Although not all primate researchers would agree with these conclusions as they speak of primate culture and cultural transmission among primates (McGrew, 1992) (see also the discussion following Tomasello et al.'s 1993 article in *Behavioral and Brain Sciences*), evidence seems to exist that nonhuman animals maintain their traditions with social-learning processes other than those known from human beings. Furthermore, relying only on imitative learning would lead to a limited culture. Instruction and deliberate teaching and the internalization of the instructions are needed to learn most human cultural skills. In addition, a desire to teach has to increase the chances that more systematic and widespread distribution of a skill or trait will be the result of instructed learning. The ability and motivation to teach is clearly a necessary ingredient of the human evolutionary scenario, and it is dependent on understanding the other as mental agent. Chimpanzees do not seem to understand others in that way, which means that they can neither teach nor internalize the instructions of others – not to mention learning from one another collaboratively.

Following the suggestion by the zoologist Midford (1993), different kinds of transmission have to be considered, probably specific to a culture (including animal cultures) and age (Gopnik & Meltzoff, 1993; Lillard, 1993; Trevarthen, 1993) of the transmitter and the transmittee – for example, conditioned learning, interactive learning, or trial-and-error learning directed by enhancement. This suggestion is worth following up. Just as animal transmission is different from human transmission, the transmission process might be different in different cultures. The various chapters including cross-cultural research in this volume demonstrate that there are fundamental differences as far as the dominant transmitter, the receptivity of the transmittee, the selection of content, and the moderating and mediating variables are concerned. If we follow up this line of research, the universal components and conditions of the transmission process will be better known.

In addition, in this research, the samples are usually small and therefore biased. Larger datasets from various cultures and longitudinal data as well as single measurement data have to be used. A longitudinal sequential design allows the relative impact of many mechanisms of transmission to be compared. Longitudinal analyses are invaluable in assessing constancy and direction of influence, possibly age effects, and critical periods. Transmission research provides a good perspective from which to evaluate transgenerational comparisons and to make better predictions about cultural continuity and change.

3.0. TOWARD A MODEL OF CULTURAL TRANSMISSION

3.1. Prerequisites for a Model of Transmission

The approaches to cultural transmission presented throughout the chapters in this volume involve the most important components of the transmission process: the transmitter, the transmittee, the variety of contents of transmission, the selectivity concerning the type of content, the developmentally motivated, or situationally determined receptivity of the transmittee to type of contents, type of transmitter, and motivation to transmit at various stages of the life span, the (dis)continuous social context, and the support from the social environment for one's own views. Furthermore, numerous mechanisms and transmission belts have been identified: from explicit learning of single forms of behavior through imitation to complex identification processes. Yet, many facets that belong to a comprehensive model of transmission need clarification. The following issues are among the most urgent to be considered for further research leading toward a general model of the transmission process.

3.2. Working Models: The Role of Cognition in the Transmission Process

A *working model* is far from being an automatic endowment of an early set of cultural experiences. Social and cognitive acquisition of social orientations, including values and attitudes, skills, knowledge, and behaviors, accumulate and integrate in the individual working model. The working models of both parent and child may thus be regarded as functional units that regulate transmission. The working models also involve a cognitive representation of the perception of the normative pressure in the social context. However, working models are not only pure cognitive representations, they also imply motivations – in our case, motivation to transmit and to be ready for transmission. Preferences for certain transmission contents over others are also part of this motivational component. The parents' and the child's working models of taking over (i.e., internalization) and of expressing (i.e., externalization) values as conceptualized by Kuczynski, Marshall, and Schell (1997) execute cognitive functions such as interpreting, selecting, forgetting, and rejecting – in summary, manifesting or assimilating the contents of transmission. Note that the same cognitive mechanisms are claimed for internalization and externalization. The respective working models are the loci of change and development over the life span; they are open to constant challenge and reconstruction.

The postulated externalization and internalization mechanisms are still unquestioned and should be subject to further empirical exploration and testing. On the basis of individual differences or the social role, the working models might differ in terms of the four specific internalization or externalization mechanisms. The expressive component could be more emphasized in parents who may show a greater interest in transmitting than their child does, or when one parent is more receptive to a transfer initiated by the child, which may strengthen the internalization component. In addition, we cannot be sure whether interpreting, forgetting, selecting, and rejecting are the only mechanisms involved in the externalization and internalization functions associated with the working models. The processing mechanisms may account for information processing as well as for the processing of the motivational part of the working model; however, there are further mechanisms that should be considered. One important cognitive mechanism is learning. Observational learning, but also other modes of implicit or explicit learning, should be listed among the cognitive processing mechanisms. Thus, cognitive processing of cultural products transmitted during social interaction so far neither involves factors governing the accurate perception, processing, and learning of cultural messages nor factors concerning their acceptance.

Individual processing of the working models suggests that the active construction of difference in addition to potential similarity between transmitter and transmittee is a normative outcome of internalization. In a certain period of childhood and adolescence when negativism is paired with the exploration of options, the choice of the various agents of transmission is another source for a way of processing that interferes with the other modes. The lack of empirical evidence for the stimulating model of Kuczynski et al. (1997) should also be a challenge to cognitive psychologists without close ties to either social or developmental psychology.

The differentiation between a *cognitive route* and an *emotional route* to cultural transmission (Norenzayan & Atran, 2004) seems to be an interesting one, albeit gained in an area that is only of specific interest: the transmission of natural and unnatural beliefs. The cognitive route to cultural transmission is the path of transmission of "counterintuitive" or scientific concepts. Concepts that have no ontology-violating features at all are not interesting. They have to be taught and learned against the intuitive insight of people. They are difficult to memorize and, therefore, this cognitive route of transmission seems to be less successful. Ideas that achieve cultural success in the form of transmission are those that happen to be the most successful at exploiting the peculiarities of the human memory system. The concept of "ghost" is an example; superstitions are another. The transmission of minimally counterintuitive concepts is most successful because the authors claim that these concepts are cognitively "optimal." The minimally counterintuitive concepts are transmitted via an emotional route because emotions are attached to them (i.e., anxiety in the case of ghosts and superstitions). Boyer and Ramble (2001) tested the assumption of better transmissibility of minimally counterintuitive concepts in three cultures with varying exposure to supernatural beliefs. The memory advantage of the minimally counterintuitive concepts was observed in all three groups.

Both routes, the cognitive and the emotional, may occur independently in the way in which all kinds of cultural beliefs emerge. Moreover, even though the outcome they produce may look cognitively similar in terms of the way in which natural and nonnatural beliefs are combined, the origin, emergence, and underlying psychological processes that support these routes may be quite different.

3.3. The Role of Emotions in the Transmission Process

The assumption of an emotional route of transmission opens up new perspectives for future research in the transmission domain. The well-known finding from cognitive psychology that emotional items are better remembered than neutral items (Ellis & Hunt, 1993) has to be differentiated, however. Sad emotions attached to specific contents do not result in better memory of otherwise meaningless items. Moreover, a transfer to the transmission of contents associated with emotions does have some pitfalls: Whose emotions are relevant – the transmitter's and/or the transmittee's? Most likely, the transmitter's emotions will be of primary relevance; however, emotions might influence the motivation to transmit. Thus, the question arises of whether positive emotions attached to contents render that content more transmissible as compared to negative emotions attached to contents. If the transmittee is ready to accept the emotions attached to specific transmission content, the transmission will be more efficient than if the transmittee is not willing to share the emotion. All of these questions open up new research perspectives about the role of emotions in the transmission process.

4.0. CULTURAL TRANSMISSION AND CULTURAL REPLICATION: THE LIMITS OF TRANSMISSION

4.1. The Transmission Gap

From evolutionary theory, the question has been raised about whether cultural evolution requires replication of representations (Henrich & Boyd, 2002). Formal models of cultural evolution and transmission analyze how cognitive processes combine with social interaction to generate the distributions and dynamics of cognitive "representations." The authors insist that cultural transmission is inaccurate and that mental representations are not replicated but rather reconstructed through inferential processes that are strongly affected by cognitive factors. Sperber (1996) argued that because cultural replication is highly inaccurate, the social processes of cultural transmission cannot give rise to cultural inertia or cumulative cultural adaptation. Unlike genes, mental representations are not replicated during cultural transmission. Instead, mental representations give rise to behaviors (or "public representations") that are observed by others who must then infer the underlying mental representations that in turn give rise to the observed behavior. Because individuals differ and public representations provide incomplete information, this inferential process is highly inaccurate. If Sperber was correct, it follows that cultural transmission cannot give rise to cultural inertia for the same reasons as genetic transmission. When cultural learning occurs, naïve individuals (perhaps children) observe a sample of individuals from these distributions, make inferences, and then construct their own mental representation. This provides the basis for variation and modifications. On the other hand, there is conformist transmission – the trend in a population toward the common representations. Any transmission process that would lead to accurate replication – and the common representations tend to do so – lead at the population level to cultural inertia and allow cumulative adaptation.

Further limits of transmission lie in the transmissibility of the trait, in the consistency of the transmission process, and in the recipients' current conceptual and behavioral repertoires (Daly, 1982). In addition, social influence also involves negative modeling and failure of observation: The bad example of a "culture parent" does not hinder individuals to follow in his or her footsteps.

Daly's major misgivings about the transmission models are that (1) they treat people as passive recipients of social influence, and (2) cultural transmission is a misrepresentation of the strategic behavior of self-interested people. On the other hand, following up on processes of how "bad" cultural models transmit their "bad" content means exploring a transmission route that is highly relevant to society (see Uslucan and Fuhrer, Chapter 17, this volume).

Putallaz, Constanzo, Grimes, and Sherman (1998) concluded after reviewing the literature on the continuity of attachment status in three generations that the continuity, although well above chance levels, was certainly not perfect. Many identified a group of parents who did not repeat the pattern of unsupportive parenting and instead established secure relationships with their children. Furthermore, none of the basic work on continuity they looked at provides documented data that parent and child share a "working cognitive model" that implies similar representations and functioning.

Furthermore, fathers seem to exert less influence on their children than mothers in many content areas of transmission, as van Ijzendoorn (1995) found in several meta-analyses. He identified a weak mediating variable that has not been considered so far in the transmission analyses presented in this volume. Ijzendoorn labels the variable *sensitive responsiveness* on the part of the transmitter and the transmittee. The small effect of this variable indicates the existence of some unknown but important variable referred to in the transmission process as *generation gap*. The generation gap is explained by a *transmission gap*. Correlated measurement errors, genetic influences such as temperament, and interactive transmission mechanisms like parental harmony or concordance might account for the transmission gap. It is also quite possible that the translation of early experiences of proximity into mental models is conditioned on a wide array of variables, which bear a relationship to the development of social cognitive schemata. If individual differences in temperament or personality play a significant role in the development of relationships during the first years of life, then what van Ijzendoorn described as the transmission gap may involve the transmission of certain salient temperamental characteristics. The most likely characteristics, as Fox, Kimmerly, and Schafer (1991) proposed, might be reactivity and affective bias. Thus, in the case of attachment, the concordance between parent and child, other aspects of personality, or current psychological status rather than a state of mind or working model regarding early attachment experiences might determine the emergence of a transmission gap. However, assortative mating stabilizes the marital partnership and enforces transmission, although there are many instances in which partners do not share the same working model of a trait. Therefore, many chances for breaking the intergenerational cycle of transmission of a trait exist.

The focus on the generation gap and its many aspects has been widely neglected. Researchers were keen to find replicative transmission results. This focus has to be supplemented by a diversity of research approaches to provide more evidence for competing transmission influences and for ineffective and hindering transmission mechanisms. Furthermore, the chances in the transmission gap for change and creativity have to be perceived and evaluated.

4.2. Bidirectional Transmission

The role of the child in the intergenerational transmission process as an actively selecting agent should be stressed further. The role of the child in the transmission process was seen as a passive agent because transmission effects were usually smaller than the effects in the opposite direction from parent to child (Homer, 1993; Kohn, Slomczynski, & Schoenbach, 1986; Schönpflug & Silbereisen, 1992). The child's filter described in Schönpflug and Bilz (Chapter 10, this volume) and by Kuczynski et al. (1997) are two approaches to conceptualize retroactive transmission; Bengtson and Troll's (1978) forerunner model is another (see also Pinquart & Silbereisen, 2004). In addition to the varying strength of the effect in both directions, it is necessary to identify the mediating and moderating variables that differentiate between transmissions in both directions. Kuczynski et al. (1997) introduced in their bidirectional model of socialization the ecology of either working model of parent and child. The ecology involves the other parent, siblings, peers, school, and media; thus, Kuczynski et al. (1997) conceptualize all other directions of transmission – horizontal and oblique – as functioning simultaneously and bidirectionally. The bidirectional transmission process in directions other than the vertical is still widely unknown. Researchers take for granted that in horizontal transmission, both directions function alike. Retroactive transmission in the oblique direction is probably negligible, but this still has to be demonstrated.

4.3. Intergenerational Transformation of Values

As discussed in the previous section, the transmission process has its limitations. The replicative nature of the transmission process may be given up totally in certain content domains and/or in certain contextual or family situations. If parents extrapolate into the future of their children, they may recognize that their own working model of what should be transmitted is invalidated by contextual changes. The externalization process suggests that parents may evaluate and confront the adequacy of their own working models with reference to their adaptiveness in their own life, the future of their children, and their fit to the surrounding culture. In discontinuous social contexts, as given with migration or the fall of ideologically oriented regimes (e.g., in Eastern Europe), different social orientations, values, and skills are adaptive. The most important transmitters, the parents, were socialized in the old context, but they have to socialize their children for adaptation to the new environment. This requires a transformation of contents in the transmission process. The parents' working models have to be transformed before they even begin to attempt to influence their children in relevant spheres. Another possibility to think of is that the parents' working models will be inactivated and a new working model for transmission to the child will be constructed. The old model may be activated in specific interaction situations, such as parental peer interactions. Conceptualization of personal integrity and identity render such parallel working models highly problematic – especially if the new one is incompatible with the old. As Knafo and Schwartz (2001) reported, such inconsistent information externalized to the child is less effective than consistent information; the transmittee will show less internalization of the transmitted content than under conditions of working models and consistent modes of expression on the side of the transmitter.

Most of the issues raised in this section are highly speculative, but exploring the social and cognitive processing in the transmission process is an urgent task to accomplish. Experimental evidence in addition to interview or questionnaire data is probably needed for clarification of these issues.

5.0. CONCLUSIONS

There has been recent recognition of the need to broaden the factors, the conceptual models, and their guiding questions to further elucidate the mechanisms of transmission underlying the intergenerational cultural transfer of social orientations, attitudes, skills, and knowledge. Two research options may be learned from the afterthoughts presented in this epilogue. The first is a challenge to those who are interested in the elaboration of the transmission model: more factors that are part of the transmission process, more cross-cultural evidence, more developmental evidence of variations in the transmission mechanisms, and results for both transmitter and transmittee. One promising group of factors seems to be the emotions attached to the transmission content shared by transmitter and transmittee.

The second option is that researchers should try to account for the transmission gap; that is, they should study the mechanisms through which parental working models or representations affect children's working models or behaviors in such a way that internalization is minimized. Researchers might use analyses of discordant cases of adult–children pairs and make use of cross-cultural studies, in particular, to explore the contextual constraints of the transmission process. However, the phase in the individual life span of the transmitter and the transmittee might account for different extents of the transmission gap as well. Focusing the analysis on the role of other transmitters in interaction with the transmitter might help in clarifying forms of reduplicative transmission. Furthermore, the issue of multiple transmission paths has to be clarified. Will one integrated working model emerge from the multiple transmission influences to which a child is exposed, or can multiple working models be functional simultaneously?

The study of transmission will attract researchers' attention in the future just as it has elicited theorizing and empirical investigations for more than 150 years. It has the potential to answer questions regarding how genetics are supplemented by cultural transmission, and it may help to clarify how a given culture is maintained or transformed.

REFERENCES

Bengtson, V. L., & Troll, L. (1978). Youth and their parents: Feedback and intergenerational influence in socialization. In M. R. Lerner & G. B. Spanier (Eds.), *Child influences on marital and family interaction: A life span development* (pp. 215–240). New York: Academic Press.

Boyd, R., & Richerson, P. J. (2005). *Culture and the evolutionary process.* Chicago: University of Chicago Press.

Boyer, P., & Ramble, C. (2001). Cognitive templates for religious concepts: Cross-cultural evidence for recall of counter-intuitive representations. *Cognitive Science, 25,* 535–564.

Cavalli-Sforza, L. L., & Feldman, M. W. (1981). *Cultural transmission and evolution: A quantitative approach.* Princeton, NJ: Princeton University Press.

Cavalli-Sforza, L. L., Feldman, M. W., Chen, K. H., & Dornbusch, S. M. (1982). Theory and observation in cultural transmission. *Science, 218,* 19–27.

Daly, M. (1982). Some caveats about cultural transmission models. *Human Ecology, 10,* 401–408.

Durham, W. H. (1982). Interaction of genetic and cultural evolution: Models and examples. *Human Ecology, 10,* 289–323.

Durham, W. H. (1990). Advances in evolutionary culture theory. *Annual Review of Anthropology, 19,* 187–210.

Ellis, H. C., & Hunt, R. R. (1993). *Fundamentals of cognitive psychology* (5th ed.). Dubuque, IA: WCB Brown & Benchmark.

Fox, N. A. (1995). On the way we were: Adult memories about attachment experiences and their role in determining parent–infant relationships: A commentary on van Ijzendoorn. *Psychological Bulletin, 117,* 404–410.

Fox, N. A., Kimmerly, N. L., & Schafer, W. D. (1991). Attachment to mother/attachment to father: A meta-analysis. *Child Development, 62,* 210–225.

Gopnik, A., & Meltzoff, A. (1993). Imitation, cultural learning and the origins of "theory of mind." *Behavioral and Brain Sciences, 16,* 521–522.

Henrich, J., & Boyd, R. (2002). On modeling cognition and culture: Why cultural evolution does not require replication of representations. *Journal of Cognition and Culture, 2,* 87–112.

Homer, P. M. (1993). Transmission of human values: A cross-cultural investigation of general and reciprocal influence effects. *Genetic, Social and General Psychology Monographs, 119,* 343–367.

Kamela, T., & Nakanishi, D. (2002). Cost-benefit analysis of social/cultural learning in a stationary uncertain environment: An evolutionary simulation and an experiment with human subjects. *Evolution and Human Behavior, 23,* 373–393.

Knafo, A., & Schwartz, S. H. (2001). Value socialization in families of Israeli-born and Soviet-born adolescents in Israel. *Journal of Cross-Cultural Psychology, 32,* 213–228.

Kohn, M. I., Slomczynski, K. M., & Schoenbach, C. (1986). Social stratification and the transmission of values in the family: A cross-national assessment. *Sociological Forum, 1*, 73–102.

Kuczynski, L., Marshall, S., & Schell, K. (1997). Value socialization in a bidirectional context. In J. E. Grusec & L. Kuczynski (Eds.), *Parenting and children's internalization of values: A handbook of contemporary theory* (pp. 23–50). New York: John Wiley & Sons.

Laland, K. N. (1993). The mathematical modeling of human culture and its implications for psychology and the human sciences. *British Journal of Psychology, 84*, 145–169.

Lillard, A. S. (1993). Moving forward on cultural learning. *Behavioral and Brain Sciences, 16*, 528–529.

Lumsden, C. J. (1984). Parent–offspring conflict over the transmission of culture. *Ethology and Sociobiology, 5*, 111–136.

Lumsden, C. J., & Wilson, E. O. (1981). *Genes, mind and culture*. Cambridge, MA: Cambridge University Press.

Mark, N. P. (2002). Cultural transmission, disproportionate prior exposure, and the evolution of cooperation. *American Sociological Review, 67*, 323–344.

McGrew, W. C. (1992). *Chimpanzee material culture: Implications for human evolution.* Cambridge, MA: Cambridge University Press.

Midford, P. (1993). Cultural transmission is more than cultural learning. *Behavioral and Brain Sciences, 16*, 529–530.

Norenzayan, A., & Atran, S. (2004). Cognitive and emotional processes in the cultural transmission of natural and nonnatural beliefs. In M. Schaller & C. S. Crandall (Eds.), *The psychological foundations of culture* (pp. 149–169). Mahwah, NJ: Lawrence Erlbaum Associates.

Pinquart, M., & Silbereisen, R. K. (2004). Transmission of values from adolescents to their parents: The role of value content and authoritative parenting. *Adolescence, 39*, 83–100.

Putallaz, M., Constanzo, P. R., Grimes, C. L., & Sherman, D. M. (1998). Intergenerational continuities and their influences on children's social development. *Social Development, 7*, 389–427.

Rogers, A. R. (1988). Does biology constrain culture? *American Anthropologist, 90*, 819–831.

Schönpflug, U. (2001). Intergenerational transmission of values: The role of transmission belts. *Journal of Cross-Cultural Psychology, 32*, 174–185.

Schönpflug, U., & Silbereisen, R. K. (1992). Transmission of values between generations in the family regarding societal keynote issues: A cross-cultural longitudinal study on Polish and German families. In S. Iwawaki, Y. Kashima, & K. Leung (Eds.), *Innovations in cross-cultural psychology* (pp. 269–279). Lisse, the Netherlands: Swets & Zeitlinger.

Sperber, D. (1996). *Explaining culture: A naturalistic approach.* Cambridge, MA: Blackwell.

Tomasello, M. (1990). Cultural transmission in the tool use and communicatory signaling of chimpanzees? In S. Parker & K. Gibson (Eds.), *Language and intelligence in monkeys and apes* (pp. 274–311). Cambridge, MA: Cambridge University Press.

Tomasello, M., Krüger, A. C., & Ratner, H. H. (1993a). Cultural learning. *Behavioral and Brain Sciences, 16*, 495–552.

Tomasello, M., Krüger, A. C., & Ratner, H. H. (1993b). Culture, biology and human ontogeny. *Behavioral and Brain Sciences, 16,* 540–546.

Trevarthen, C. (1993). Predispositions to cultural learning in young infants. *Behavioral and Brain Sciences, 16,* 534–535.

van Ijzendoorn, M. H. (1995). On the way we are: On temperament, attachment, and the transmission gap: A rejoinder to Fox (1995). *Psychological Bulletin, 117,* 411–415.

White, D. J., Gros-Louis, J., King, A. P., Papakhian, M. A., & West, M. J. (2007). Constructing culture in cowbirds (*molothrus ater*). *Journal of Comparative Psychology, 121,* 113–122.

INDEX

abuse
  of child, 402
acculturation, 95, 97, 103, 104, 107, 111, 112,
    136, 165, 169, 171, 174, 175, 178, 179, 183,
    190, 195, 197, 198, 199, 200, 215, 226,
    227, 269, 280, 281, 282, 283, 284, 290,
    389
acculturation attitudes, 291
acculturation model, 182
acculturation strategies, 281
acculturative stressors, 193
achievement, 106, 223, 339
achievement goals, 223, 224
achievement values, 231, 236, 241, 253,
    259, 271, 376, 382, 383, 386, 444,
    456
adolescence, 23, 25, 148, 151, 185, 201, 214,
    222, 229, 267, 322, 323, 343, 362, 371,
    384, 423, 424, 435
adolescents, 23, 133, 135, 142, 143, 144, 194,
    251, 285, 297, 298, 301, 308, 360, 404, 419
  ethnic, 192
  role of, 421
adulthood, 23, 26, 103, 129, 134, 151, 201, 222,
    230, 300, 308, 322, 326, 397, 398, 423,
    424, 425
  middle, 134, 344
  violence in, 397
  young, 134
adults, 422
  middle-aged, 344
  older, 344
  young, 344, 419
affluence, 14, 100, 109, 112, 120, 121
  levels of, 115
Africa, 96, 99, 109

African American, 187, 201, 202
Africans, 187
Afro-Caribbeans, 187
aggression, 394
aggressive style, 412
Alaska, 186, 188
Alaska Native, 186
Algeria, 109
Allport, G., 11, 26
America, 206, 209
American, 75, 84, 191, 201, 275
American Indian, 186
Americanization, 193, 196
anthropology
  ecological, 96
anti-model, 340
anti-Semitism, 373
Arctic, 99
Asia, 102, 109, 141, 142, 143, 144, 155, 186,
    188, 194, 196, 205, 206, 274, 326
Asian, 186, 187
Asian American, 194, 202
Asian Indians, 187
Asians, 142, 188, 197
assimilation, 3, 15, 161, 169, 170, 173, 174,
    175, 178, 189, 191, 193, 199, 281, 284,
    288
  cognitive, 161, 163
  cultural, 195
  identification, 162, 180
  social, 162, 163, 180
  structural, 161, 200
assimilation model, 179
assimilation theory, 178, 180
assurance, 143
assurance vs. trust, 141

attachment, 25, 75, 130, 132, 141, 150, 338, 387, 472
  definition of, 397
  insecure-avoidant, 397
  secure, 397
attachment theory, 394, 397, 398
aunts/uncles, 110
Australia, 99, 261, 271
autonomy, 11, 24, 133, 134, 140, 141, 143, 216, 223, 292, 297, 298, 300, 304, 307, 308, 339, 340, 406
  emotional, 385
autonomy goals, 223, 224
autonomy support, 272, 280

Baldwin effect, 65, 66
Baltes, M. M., 133, 153
Baltes, P. B., 133, 153, 159
Bandura, A., 153, 237, 259, 339, 363, 396, 414
basic psychological needs, 339
Baumrind, D., 129, 154, 217, 237
Becker, G. S., 333, 420
Bedouin children, 289
behavioral genetics, 85
Benedict, R., 130, 136, 137, 154
benevolence values, 231, 241, 252, 254, 259, 374, 376, 386
Bengtson, V. L., 14, 22, 27, 135, 154, 214, 236, 237, 240, 242, 257, 258, 259, 264, 268, 322, 323, 327, 333, 335, 336, 338, 341, 342, 344, 346, 359, 361, 363, 364, 368, 423, 437, 438, 449, 458, 473, 475
Berry, J. W., 6, 95, 97, 99, 100, 103, 104, 107, 121, 122, 123, 124, 126, 154, 190, 207, 213, 237, 281, 293
bias function, 15
  assimilation (copy others), 15
  innate (genetic), 15
bicultural, 186, 189, 190, 191, 192, 194, 198, 200, 206
bicultural strategies, 207
biculturalism, 185, 189, 190, 191, 193, 196, 197, 198, 201, 202, 205, 206
bidirectionality of socialization, 132
bilingual, 193
bilingualism, 197
biracial, 202, 203, 206
biracial heritage, 206
birth order, 75, 76, 86

Bloom, P., 65
Boehnke, K., 4, 5, 243, 258, 265, 339, 341, 342, 359, 363, 368, 374, 388, 413, 415, 441, 442, 446, 451, 455, 456
Boesch, C., 37, 45
Bourdieu, P., 4, 7, 319, 334, 429, 437
Boyd, R., 3, 5, 7, 9, 16, 20, 45, 70, 87, 90, 96, 105, 123, 212, 215, 222, 231, 236, 237, 238, 462, 463, 471, 475
Boyer, P., 3, 7, 470, 475
Brazil, 109
Bretherton, I., 340, 364
Brewer, M. B., 377, 388
Britain, 109
Bronfenbrenner, U., 130, 140, 154, 271, 272, 273, 291, 293
Bulgaria, 109

California Longitudinal Study of Generations, 327
Canada, 109
Caribbean, 188
caringness, 456
Cavalli-Sforza, L. L., 2, 5, 7, 12, 15, 22, 27, 28, 95, 102, 123, 126, 154, 155, 212, 216, 221, 222, 229, 236, 237, 292, 293, 340, 364, 374, 388, 461, 462, 464, 475
Chicano, 191
child
  role of in transmission, 473
child abuse, 401, 402, 403
  effects of, 403
  physical, 400
child victim
  of abuse, 402
childhood, 23, 25, 75, 79, 104, 133, 143, 300, 422
  violence in, 391
children, 6, 11, 14, 19, 20, 23, 24, 25, 26, 35, 40, 43, 45, 76, 86, 105, 110, 112, 129, 138, 142, 143, 148, 166, 168, 185, 192, 194, 195, 196, 201, 206, 215, 223, 265, 305, 340, 431
  adult, 135, 143, 328, 347, 355, 363, 374
  biracial, 203
  difficult, 402
  influence on parents, 261
  number of, 12, 18, 102
  training of, 101
  values of, 249, 261

Chile, 109
chimpanzee, 19, 35, 37, 38, 467
chimpanzee culture, 34
China, 146, 152
Chinese, 102, 142, 187, 188, 194
Chomsky, N., 52, 58, 65, 67
Christiansen, M. H., 62, 67
closeness
  genetic, 85
closeness to parents, 284
co-biography, 339
co-evolution, 465
  gene-culture, 15
Cole, M., 136, 139, 154
collectivism, 99
competence, 339
competitiveness, 444, 445
conditioning, 2, 15
conflict
  parent-offspring, 86
conflict hypothesis, 77
conformism, 16
conformism values, 217, 218
conformist transmission. *See* transmission,
  conformist
conformity, 5, 13, 106, 133, 143, 152, 236, 246,
  319, 323, 382
  social, 99
conformity bias, 18
conformity goals, 223, 224, 236
conformity values, 14, 144, 231, 241, 249, 251,
  253, 260, 261, 341, 376, 383, 386
Conroy, S. J., 6, 317, 322, 336
conservation values, 231, 234
conservatism
  cultural, 423, 429, 430
  cultural, development of, 434
  economic, 423, 430
content
  of transmission, 461
context
  continuous, 25
  cultural, 5
  discontinuous, 25
  for acculturation, 291
  for development, 232, 345, 427,
    467
control, 141, 142, 150, 272, 298, 309,
  344
  of cultural transmission, 2
  external, 137, 292
  freedom from, 105

maternal, 149
of values, 347
over goal attainment, 350
parental, 142, 263, 323, 397
perceived, 341, 344, 345, 346, 349, 352, 353,
  363
perceived over goals, 356
personal, 339, 340, 342
social, 162, 175
conventionalization, 20
Cosmides, L., 3, 8, 70, 85, 91, 326, 334
critical period, 6
  in development, 422, 468
Cronk, L., 3, 7
Cubans, 187
cultural adoption. *See* transmission, cultural
cultural aids, 98
cultural awareness, 199
cultural capital, 4
cultural change, 185, 213, 468
cultural continuity, 25, 128, 185, 195, 466,
  468
cultural ecology, 96
cultural model, 86, 137, 138, 143, 465
cultural pattern, 137
cultural persistence, 2, 212, 213
cultural practices, 137, 138, 140, 193, 206,
  291
cultural relativism, 137
cultural resistance, 13
culture, 3, 7, 8, 9, 15, 27, 28, 29, 34, 36, 51,
  57, 61, 62, 65, 70, 95, 96, 103, 140,
  143, 158, 195, 204, 269, 271, 287, 291,
  334
  acquisition of, 3
  American, 196, 198, 206, 207
  biological basis of, 17
  chimpanzee, 20
  continuous, 26
  control of, 26
  definition of, 101
  discontinuous, 26
  dominant, 421
  dual, 189
  foreign, 423
  hierarchical, 289
  human, 45
  mainstream, 189, 298
  maintenance of, 2, 9, 13, 215, 223
  primate. *See* primate culture
  Russian, 289
  youth, 422

culture contact, 4, 181
culture differences, 277
culture learning, 97
culture of origin, 169, 190, 215, 281, 282, 287
culture, collectistic, 222
culture, transmitted, 3
culturegen, 15
Cyprus, 109
Czech Republic, 146, 148

D'Andrade, R. G., 137, 139, 154
Darwin, C., 10, 56, 67
de Lamarck, J., 10, 27
Denmark, 404
development, 51, 64, 66, 69, 129, 132, 133, 134, 137, 140, 142, 143, 146, 147, 148, 149, 150, 151, 152, 153, 206, 216, 223, 297, 298, 305, 306, 308, 343, 344, 345, 466, 467
  adolescent, 214, 220, 221, 421
  attachment, 397
  behavioral, 100, 121
  bicultural, 185, 186
  bidirectional approach to, 129
  children, 13, 50, 53
  cognitive, 5, 403
  human, 4, 21, 25, 48, 71
  identity, 203, 204
  infant, 130
  life-span, 469
  mid-life, 134
  of adolescent consciousness, 421
  of mental models, 138
  of self, 141
  perceptual-cognitive, 99
  social, 25, 403
developmental tasks, 133, 134, 144, 147, 343, 347, 356, 358, 360
discrimination, 162, 166, 167, 170, 171, 174, 175, 178, 180, 181, 200, 201, 204, 206, 207, 223, 276, 371
Dominicans, 187
Dunham, P., 39, 46
Durham, W. H., 15, 27, 461, 475
dynamic systems theory, 55, 65

East German, 377
ecocultural approach framework, 97, 98, 99, 100, 104, 107, 109, 111, 112, 121

ecological psychology. *See* psychology, ecological
ecosystem, 106, 119, 121
Ecuadorians, 187
education, 24, 51, 121, 463
egalitarianism, 292
Egeland, B., 392, 398, 402
Elder, G., 22, 26, 27, 134, 155, 342, 362, 364
emic, 137
emotional bond, 111, 121
empathy, 130, 143
emulation, 19, 20, 35
emulation learning, 36
enculturation, 17, 23, 25, 95, 97, 101, 103, 105, 107, 185, 196, 213, 464
entropy, 49, 66
environmental determinism, 96
Erikson, E. H., 133, 155, 191, 208, 292, 293, 364
ethnic loyalty, 199
ethnocentric bias, 129
ethnopsychology, 139
etic, 137
Euler, H. A., 2, 3, 70, 72, 75, 79, 88, 197
Euro-American, 195
Europe, 1, 109
European, 377
evolution, 4, 16, 19, 20, 28, 35, 68, 89, 201, 466
  biological, 43, 62
  cognitive, 42
  cultural, 15, 35, 36, 37, 43, 45, 460, 461, 463, 471
  genetic, 3, 465
  human, 42
  of cooperation, 213
  of language, 63
evolutionary theory, 83
exogamy, 206
expressive family role, 113, 115
extended family, 103, 111, 121, 134, 196, 198
externalization, 372, 469

family context, 423
family role, 110, 122
  child care, 111
  expressive, 110
  financial, 111, 113
  instrumental, 111
family types, 235, 453
  of transmission rate, 232
family values, 111, 112, 122, 149, 227, 455
  Turkish, 226
father–son dyad, 351

Feldman, M. W., 2, 5, 7, 12, 15, 27, 95, 102, 123, 126, 154, 212, 216, 229, 237, 374, 388, 461, 462, 475
Festinger, L., 444, 457
field independence, 99
Filipinos, 187, 188, 194
Fodor, J. A., 52, 68
France, 109, 146
French, 75
Fuhrer, U., 6, 389, 391, 413, 416, 472

gene-environment correlation, 263
generation gap, 217, 218, 422, 425, 426, 472
Georgas, J., 6, 99, 100, 107, 111, 121, 123, 213, 281, 293
Georgia, 109
German, 11, 73, 75, 78, 84, 142, 147, 158, 163, 170, 214, 218, 223, 258, 297, 301, 377
German immigrants, 299
German language, 304
German repatriate, 164
German youth, 421
Germany, 109, 142, 146, 148, 149, 163, 171, 184, 215, 219, 221, 222, 226, 229, 308, 368, 372, 376, 387, 392, 393, 398, 404, 443
Germany, East, 231, 373, 374, 375, 404, 445, 455
Ghana, 109, 187
Gilligan, C., 331, 334
goal
  achievement, 345
  education-related, 345
  extrinsic, 339, 356, 360
  family-related, 345
  importance of, 358
  intrinsic, 339
  perceived, 356
  property-related, 345
  self-focused, 347, 360
  self-related, 345
  societal, 360
goal importance, 349, 353
Golinkoff, R. M., 63, 65, 68
Goodnow, J. J., 131, 136, 148, 154, 155, 223, 238, 241, 249, 260, 261, 264, 265, 291, 293, 298, 311, 340, 362, 364, 365, 451, 457
grandchildren, 328, 340
grandparental solicitude, 73, 74, 75, 77, 79
grandparental uncertainty, 73
grandparent–grandchild relationship, 79
grandparent–grandchild similarity, 351
grandparenting, 25

grandparent–parent relationship, 72
grandparents, 25, 340
  role of, 134, 196
Greece, 74, 109
Greek, 74, 163, 170
Greenfield, P., 138, 141, 155, 156
Grob, A., 338, 339, 344, 360, 365
Grusec, J. E., 8, 28, 122, 129, 131, 147, 148, 155, 157, 216, 238, 241, 249, 260, 262, 264, 265, 266, 274, 289, 291, 293, 340, 364, 365, 389, 451, 457, 476
Guatemalans, 187
Guyana, 187

Haiti, 187
Hall, G. S., 421
Harkness, S., 139, 140, 155, 158
Hawaii, 188, 205
Hayes, K. J., 35, 46
hedonism values, 217, 218, 231, 241, 253, 341, 376, 382, 383, 386
Henrich, J., 9, 16, 17, 28, 231, 236, 238, 463, 471, 475
heritage culture, 186, 199, 200
Herskovits, M. J., 103, 124
Hewlett, B. S., 22, 28, 155
hierarchic self-interest, 443
Hirsh-Pasek, K., 63, 65, 68
Hispanics, 186, 187, 188, 191, 202, 205, 206
Hofstede, G., 292, 298, 299, 311
Hollich, G. J., 63, 65, 68
homogamy, 167
  ethnic, 167
Hondurans, 187
Hong Kong, 109, 271
host culture, 193, 195, 196, 215, 281, 287, 288, 298, 299
human capital, 24, 164, 197, 200, 318, 320, 323, 324, 325, 326, 330
humanism values, 217

identification
  ethnic, 163, 165, 166, 172, 173, 175, 178, 179, 183, 189, 191, 200, 201, 203
  with parents, 284
identity, 133, 191, 203, 204, 213, 262, 474
  cultural, 205
  development of, 191, 422
  dual, 203
  ethnic, 201, 290

identity (*cont.*)
  fragmented, 204
  generational, 343, 419
  Mexican, 192
  racial, 202, 204
  regional, 377
  social, 213, 386, 425
identity achievement, 202
identity conflict, 204
identity crisis, 192
identity formation, 292
imitation, 2, 15, 16, 19, 20, 26, 34, 35, 37, 85,
    129, 130, 138, 342, 396, 461, 467,
    468
learning, 467
immigrant heritage, 192
immigrants, 161, 170, 174, 186, 191, 200, 223,
    297, 303, 423
  adolescent, 288
imprinting, 2, 15
independence, 12, 24, 105, 106, 127, 140, 141,
    142, 143, 144, 146, 147, 152, 194, 224,
    298
  of adolescents, 424
  of children, 133
India, 99, 109, 146, 150
individualism, 99, 220, 224, 239, 292
Indochinese, 188
Indonesia, 109, 142, 146, 149
inheritance
  social, 429
inheritance of acquired traits, 10
innovation, 37
instrumental family role, 113
integration, 281, 284
interdependence, 127, 132, 134, 140, 141, 142,
    143, 144, 146, 147, 148, 149, 194
intergenerational, 26, 75, 76, 77
intergenerational contract, 323, 324
intergenerational relationship, 84, 133, 148,
    153, 223, 325
intergenerational transfer, 182, 319, 321, 323,
    325, 331
intermarriage, 206
internalization, 5, 13, 131, 150, 151, 152, 241,
    257, 372, 451, 466, 469, 474
  model of, 131
  of norms, 321
investment
  grandparental, 72
  in progeny, 71, 78
  intergenerational, 84

  maternal, 72
  nepotistic, 84
  of aunts and uncles, 72, 83
  paternal, 72
Iran, 109
Israel, 146, 164, 273, 280
Israeli, 269, 273, 277, 279
Italian, 163
Iterated Learning Model, 62

Jamaica, 187
Japan, 109, 142, 152, 321
Japanese, 138, 142, 143, 152, 188, 194, 201,
    205, 298
Jewish immigrants, 163
joint attention, 33, 39, 130

Kagitcibasi, C., 107, 124, 140, 141, 182, 183,
    238, 239, 293, 298, 311, 452, 458
Kaufman, J., 392, 394, 413, 416
Keller, H., 155
kin-keeper, 84, 342
kinship, 14, 71, 88, 110, 112, 141, 167, 172,
    182, 317, 318
kinship-centeredness, 167, 173
Kitayama, S., 141, 155, 156
Knafo, A., 3, 4, 5, 136, 148, 156, 240, 243, 266,
    269, 276, 288, 292, 389, 441, 447, 451,
    458, 474, 475
Kohlberg, L., 331, 335
Kohn, M. L., 14, 21, 28, 150, 156, 214, 238, 242,
    243, 254, 261, 263, 266, 292, 295, 300,
    301, 311, 341, 342, 347, 366, 441, 442,
    447, 458, 473, 476
Korea, 109, 146
Korean, 142, 147, 158, 187, 188, 193,
    194
Kroeber, A., 124, 137
Kuczynski, L., 5, 8, 26, 28, 132, 152, 155,
    159, 238, 241, 243, 261, 262, 266, 288,
    290, 293, 372, 389, 457, 469, 470, 473,
    476

Laland, K. N., 5, 8, 28, 212, 238, 462, 476
Lamarckism, 10
language, 3, 5, 6, 33, 36, 40, 41, 43, 51, 52, 53,
    58, 60, 61, 104, 165, 193, 195, 197, 198,
    200, 213, 284, 297, 467
  evolution of, 63
  transmission of, 52, 58
language acquisition, 61, 63, 64, 65, 66, 86, 161,
    163, 166, 167, 169, 178, 179, 180

language development, 58, 67
language evolution, 61, 66
language instruction, 203
language learning, 61, 62
language retention, 163, 166, 167, 169, 175,
    178, 180
language use, 173
Latin America, 186, 188, 196, 206
Latinos, 187, 191, 200
learned helplessness, 412
learning, 5, 6, 11, 15, 17, 18, 19, 20, 21, 26, 34,
    51, 57, 62, 63, 68, 72, 129, 175, 197, 421,
    464, 466
  chimpanzee, 35
  cognitive, 16
  collaborative, 19, 131, 467
  conditioned, 371, 468
  cultural, 6, 14, 19, 26, 35, 36, 38, 40, 41, 43,
    45, 130, 131, 193, 194, 463, 466, 467, 471,
    475
  deliberate, 461
  emulation. *See* emulation learning
  explicit, 468
  from sibling, 103
  imitative, 19, 35, 36, 37, 39, 40, 41, 131
  instructed, 19, 20, 131, 467
  mechanisms of, 102
  model of, 396
  observational, 16, 85, 138, 213, 396,
    469
  of language, 62
  operant, 52
  primate, 45
  social, 3, 6, 16, 17, 18, 19, 20, 35, 36, 38, 43,
    130, 212, 342, 396, 466, 467
  social–cultural, 18
  social-cognitive, 36
learning model
  iterated, 62, 64
learning theory, 394, 412
Lerner, R. M., 340, 366, 475
life goals, 362
  definition of, 338
life span, 1, 58, 59, 61, 128, 130, 132, 133, 140,
    143, 144, 146, 148, 151, 342, 343, 344,
    360, 363, 368, 468
life-span development, 104, 343, 345
life-span psychology, 127, 129, 133, 144
lifestyle, 101
looking-glass self, 204
love withdrawal, 272, 273, 276, 278, 280,
    284

Lumsden, C. J., 15, 17, 28, 463, 464, 476

Machiavellism, 445
MacWhinney, B., 64, 65, 68
Magdeburg Juvenile Violence Study (MJVS),
    403
majority culture, 201
Mannheim, K., 126, 156, 269, 295, 343, 361,
    366, 419, 422, 426
marginal person, 190
marginalism, 205
marginality, 190, 191, 400
marginalization, 169, 281, 284
marital harmony, 221
Markus, H., 141, 155, 156, 344, 345, 347, 360,
    364
marriage endogamy, 170, 171
Mead, M., 13, 25, 130, 136, 269, 295, 447, 458
Meeus, W. M. J., 4, 296, 419, 422, 423, 425, 437,
    438
Meltzoff, A., 40, 46, 130, 468, 475
Mendel, G., 68
mental model, 138, 472
mentifacts, 15
Mexican American, 191
Mexican identity, 192
Mexicans, 187, 191, 194, 201, 205
  three generations, 195
Mexico, 109, 188, 197
Middle East, 188
migration, 271, 287, 291
mixed heritage, 202, 205, 206
mixed marriage, 188, 205
moral capital, 318
moral development, 331
Moroccan, 228
motherese, 64
mother-in-law–daughter-in-law relationship,
    79, 80
motivation to transmit, 228, 229, 231, 232,
    233, 235, 236, 464, 468, 469, 471
multiracial, 188, 203

Native Hawaiian, 186
nature-nurture controversy, 129
Nauck, B., 4, 6, 24, 135, 146, 153, 157, 158, 160,
    161, 162, 164, 170, 173, 175, 178, 182,
    183, 184, 198, 223, 238, 301, 312, 386,
    389
Neo-Lamarckism, 10
neo-Marxists, 422, 427
Netherlands, 109, 226

network, 86, 100, 163, 171, 175, 200, 399
   intraethnic, 181
   multiplexity, 166
network density, 167
network size, 166, 171, 174
New Guinea, 99
Nicaraguans, 194
Nigeria, 109, 187
normative beliefs, 328
normatively appropriate behavior, 327
norms, 18, 71, 84, 370, 392
   definition of, 327
   social, 323
North America, 109, 142
   aboriginal, 96
Norway, 404
Nowak, M. A., 62, 63, 68
nuclear family, 100, 101, 102, 111, 112, 120,
   328

observational learning, 396
ontogeny, 6, 36. *See also* development
   chimpanzee, 20, 36
   human, 19, 33, 38, 39
openness to change values, 231, 234

Pacific Islanders, 186
Padilla, A. M., 185, 189, 193, 196, 199, 200,
   203, 204, 209, 210
Pakistan, 109
Palestine, 146
parental goals, 129, 147
parent–child
   authoritarian relationship, 430
   relationship, 441
   similarity, 433, 441, 442
parent–child conflict, 277
parent–child dyad, 80, 163, 165, 217, 226, 227,
   228, 253, 257, 258, 259, 271, 281, 291,
   341, 346, 350, 351, 352, 359, 361, 413, 430
parent–child relationship, 82, 127, 148, 271,
   279, 287, 289, 290, 321, 322, 399, 423, 431
parent–child similarity, 22, 301, 305, 342
parenting, 12, 14, 21, 24, 25, 51, 71, 72, 89, 129,
   131, 136, 142, 149, 150, 192, 194, 243,
   260, 263, 280, 301, 309, 338, 340, 342,
   361, 404, 413
   Asian, 195
   autocratic, 273
   autonomy-supportive, 274, 276, 277, 278,
      284, 289
   Chinese, 194

controlling, 274
empathetic, 215, 217, 219
grandparenting, 342
love-withdrawal, 288
nonviolent, 392
rigid-authoritarian, 217
unsupportive, 472
parenting style, 14, 25, 146, 150, 194, 214, 215,
   217, 219, 221, 271, 273, 275, 276, 277,
   278, 279, 282, 283, 284, 287, 289, 291,
   301, 374, 387, 392, 412
   Chinese, 194
   democratic, 442
parenting, Asian, 195
parenting, rigid-authoritarian, 219
parents, 11, 25
   abusive, 400
   middle-aged, 355
   nonabusive, 400
paternity uncertainty, 72, 73, 75, 79, 80, 81,
   83
perceived control, 349
perspective-taking, 19
Peruvians, 187
Pervin, L. A., 339, 364, 367
Phalet, K., 223, 238, 301, 312, 372, 386, 389
Phinney, J., 107, 191, 201, 209, 215, 239, 280,
   295
Piaget, J., 52, 68
Pinker, S., 58, 65, 68, 70, 86, 89
Plomin, R., 85, 86, 89, 129, 157, 259, 263, 266,
   267, 340, 367
Poland, 261
Polish, 214
polygyny, 80
Portes, A., 186, 195, 198, 200, 209
Portrait Values Questionnaire (PVQ), 244
Positive Parenting Program, 413
possibilism, 96
postmaterialism, 421
power, 42, 100, 110, 121, 142, 194, 339, 347,
   352, 353
power values, 217, 218, 231, 241, 244, 251, 253,
   254, 259, 376, 382, 383, 386, 442, 444, 456
power-distance, 292
prejudice, 11, 201, 204, 370, 376, 379
   ethnic, 384
press
   ecological, 111
pressure toward assertion, 106
pressure toward compliance, 105, 107
primate, 33, 45, 467

primate culture, 33, 38
psychology
 cross-cultural, 4, 95, 96, 97, 104
 ecological, 105
 environmental, 96
 evolutionary, 70
Puerto Ricans, 187
PVQ (Portrait Value Questionnaire), 244
pygmy, 23

Raaijmakers, Q. A. W., 419, 423, 430,
 439
race, 188, 202, 203, 204, 370, 385
 mixed, 206
racism, 373
ratchet effect, 36, 37, 43, 465
relatedness, 133, 140, 141, 143, 339
relationship
 father-in-law/daughter-in-law, 82
 father-in-law/daughter-in-law relationship,
 82
 intergenerational, 182, 346
 parent–child, 82, 86, 103, 130, 132, 133, 134,
 136, 139, 140, 141, 142, 143, 144, 146,
 320
 rejective, 83
 supportive, 83
repatriate, 163, 170, 372
replication
 genetic, 67, 85
representation
 cognitive, 42
 mental, 3, 15, 138, 386, 463, 471
reproductive potential, 82
resource utilization, 96
Reynolds, P. C., 9, 29, 47
Richerson, P. J., 3, 5, 7, 16, 20, 45, 70, 87, 90,
 96, 105, 123, 212, 215, 222, 237, 462,
 475
rightism, 373
Rokeach, M., 240, 267, 373, 389, 423,
 439
Rosen, B. C., 11, 29
Rowe, D. C., 90, 367
Rumbaut, R. G., 186, 195, 198, 200,
 209
Russia, 273
Russian, 275, 279, 288
Russian immigrants, 164, 275, 277, 280, 283,
 287, 288, 291
 to Israel, 263, 273
Russian Israeli, 165

Russian Jewish, 170
Russian youth, 277

Salvadorans, 187, 194
sandwich generation, 134
Saudi Arabia, 109
Savage-Rumbaugh, S., 35, 46, 47
Scarr, S., 262, 267
Schmitt-Rodermund, E., 297, 300, 309,
 312
Schneewind, K. A., 340, 367
Schönpflug, U., 1, 4, 6, 9, 12, 29, 84, 90, 136,
 158, 212, 213, 214, 217, 223, 229, 236,
 238, 239, 267, 271, 295, 300, 307, 308,
 312, 313, 341, 346, 368, 370, 372, 374,
 377, 386, 389, 412, 417, 460, 464, 473,
 476
Schwartz Value Survey (SVS), 244
Schwartz, S. H., 3, 4, 5, 136, 148, 156, 214, 215,
 217, 222, 231, 239, 240, 243, 244, 262, 266,
 267, 269, 276, 288, 292, 296, 339, 368,
 374, 389, 390, 442, 444, 456, 458, 474,
 475
second generation, 165, 169, 170, 175, 178,
 181, 195, 196, 198, 299
second-generation immigrants, 195
security, 141, 350, 354
 economic, 182
security values, 217, 231, 241, 245, 251, 254,
 263, 376, 382, 383, 386
segregation
 ethnic, 164
self, 339
self-acceptance, 355
self-determination
 occupational, 442
self-determination theory, 289
self-determination values, 14, 231, 376, 383,
 386
self-direction, 214
self-direction values, 217, 218, 241, 244, 253,
 260
self-enhancement values, 231, 234, 254, 259,
 444, 454, 456
self-organization, 48, 50, 51, 52, 53, 57, 58, 62,
 65, 66
self-reliance, 106
self-transcendence values, 231, 234, 259
Seligman, M. E. P., 412
separation, 281, 284
Shannon, C. E., 50, 56, 69
Sherif, M., 29

Shore, B., 137, 138, 140, 158
Shweder, R. A., 140, 158
sibling, 12, 77, 78, 105, 216, 330, 445,
    464
sibling competition, 86
sibling equity hypothesis, 77
sibling position, 219, 220, 221, 222, 235, 374,
    402
Silbereisen, R. K., 134, 154, 157, 159, 214, 239,
    297, 298, 300, 304, 309, 312, 313, 473,
    476
Silverstein, M., 6, 186, 196, 197, 210, 317, 322,
    324, 325, 327, 336
similarity
    intergenerational, 359
    parent–offspring, 2
Six, B., 4, 6, 12, 213, 231, 236, 370, 390, 445,
    457
Skinner, B. F., 52, 69
social capital, 6, 166, 174, 175, 180, 181, 182,
    183, 318, 322
    definition of, 319
    of children, 322
social cognition, 36
social comparison theory, 444
social exchange, 319
social inheritance, 10
social referencing, 39
social support, 392
socialization, 15, 86, 95, 97, 101, 103, 104,
    105, 106, 120, 126, 129, 139, 144, 149,
    151, 158, 185, 190, 192, 206, 241, 250,
    269, 271, 275, 318, 322, 370, 442, 463,
    473
    bidirectional approach to, 129
    broad, 106
    dual culture, 185
    ethnic, 186, 189, 191, 201, 202
    narrow, 106, 261
    parental, 249
    racial, 203
    theory of, 136
socialization goals, 223, 224
socialization practices, 98, 107
socialization values, 244
socializing agents, 11, 130, 185, 192
solicitude
    grandparental, 72
solicitude diffusion effect, 76
South Africa, 146
South America, 187
Soviet Union, 272

Spain, 109
Spencer, H., 10, 29
stereotype, 207, 370
stigma, 200, 201, 207
stigmatization, 207, 414
stimulation values, 217, 218, 231, 241, 253,
    254, 261, 341, 376, 383, 386
Stroufe, L. A., 392, 398
success orientation, 444, 445
Sulloway, F., 82, 86, 90
Super, C. M., 139, 140, 155, 158
Sweden, 261, 326, 404
Switzerland, 348

teaching, 2, 5, 15, 17, 464
    deliberate, 104
ter Bogt, T. F. M., 4, 288, 296, 420, 422,
    437
theory of mind, 130, 466
Thorndike, E. L., 10, 11, 29
three generations, 14, 25, 110, 112, 266,
    338, 340, 341, 342, 343, 347, 348, 358,
    472
Tomasello, M., 1, 2, 6, 16, 18, 29, 33, 35, 40, 45,
    46, 64, 65, 69, 97, 124, 130, 158, 228, 231,
    239, 465, 467, 476
Tooby, J., 3, 8, 70, 85, 91, 326,
    334
traditionalism
    family, 430
traditionalism values, 217, 218, 231, 241, 376,
    382, 383, 386
transmission, 51, 131
    absolute, 151
    biased, 212
    bicultural, 192
    cognitive route to, 470
    conflict model of, 463
    conflict of, 464
    conformist, 16, 17
    conformity, 23, 212
    content of, 236, 461, 464
    cultural, 1, 2, 5, 6, 9, 10, 11, 12, 14, 15, 16,
        18, 19, 20, 21, 22, 23, 26, 33, 35, 64, 70,
        72, 85, 86, 95, 97, 100, 101, 102, 104,
        105, 121, 126, 129, 130, 133, 134, 136,
        139, 140, 141, 143, 144, 146, 149, 151,
        186, 193, 194, 197, 201, 204, 205, 212,
        215, 223, 229, 231, 280, 287, 288, 289,
        290, 291, 460, 462, 463, 465, 467,
        471
    cultural, definition of, 15

cultural, limits of, 3
cultural, mechanisms of, 9
directions of, 462
dual culture, 191
emotional route to, 470
entropic model of, 53
exhaustive, 3
filter, 234
filter model of, 229
genetic, 2, 10, 22, 56, 57, 58, 59, 65, 86, 97,
    212, 229, 471
horizontal, 3, 5, 6, 14, 15, 19, 22, 23, 77, 95,
    102, 104, 107, 126, 128, 134, 135, 213,
    223, 385, 462, 463, 467, 473
intergenerational, 3, 4, 7, 11, 24, 62, 65, 71,
    84, 85, 126, 128, 129, 130, 131, 134, 135,
    143, 144, 146, 147, 161, 167, 169, 171, 174,
    175, 179, 181, 182, 186, 189, 204, 206,
    212, 221, 223, 224, 227, 228, 269, 271,
    317, 324, 328, 368, 376, 384, 393, 397,
    398, 403, 411, 413, 419, 441, 442, 448,
    454
mechanisms of, 5, 34
model of, 260
moderators of, 219
negative, 412
non-genetic, 462. *See* transmission, cultural;
    transmission, social
oblique, 5, 17, 95, 102, 104, 107, 126, 128,
    134, 223, 473
of collectivism, 224
of collectivistic values, 222
of information, 54
of language, 52, 58
of moral capital, 331
of values, 218, 236, 253, 257, 318, 340, 374,
    445
of violence, 397, 398, 411, 412
of xenophobia, 373, 380
relative, 22, 151
retroactive, 22, 214, 340, 467
selective, 151
social, 16, 18, 20, 22, 71, 84, 85, 86, 189,
    462
speed of, 461
teacher/mentor. *See* transmission, oblique
three generations, 350, 352
unbiased, 17, 212
vertical, 3, 5, 6, 7, 14, 15, 16, 17, 18, 19, 22,
    23, 26, 71, 95, 102, 104, 107, 126, 127,
    128, 134, 135, 212, 217, 223, 449, 452,
    462, 463, 467, 473

transmission advantage, 23
transmission belt, 4, 5, 24, 84, 127, 129, 130,
    131, 134, 138, 142, 149, 214, 221, 235,
    267, 301, 308, 361, 373, 374, 376, 382,
    386, 460, 468
transmission bias, 16
transmission gap, 25, 460
transmission mechanisms, 460
transmission network, 213
transmission rate
    of violence, 409
transmittee, 2, 7, 9, 16, 21, 214, 468, 470, 472,
    474
transmitter, 2, 4, 5, 7, 9, 14, 16, 21, 23, 24, 150,
    214, 216, 228, 231, 235, 236, 462, 465,
    468, 470, 472, 474
    qualities of, 222
    resources, 221
Triandis, H. C., 140, 158, 239, 298, 311
Triple P. *See* Positive Parenting Program
Trivers, R. L., 17, 30, 71, 86, 91
Trommsdorff, G., 6, 126, 127, 128, 129, 130,
    133, 134, 135, 137, 139, 140, 141, 142,
    143, 144, 146, 147, 148, 149, 153, 156,
    157, 158, 239, 298, 313
trust, 132, 141, 318
Turkey, 109, 146, 215, 218, 221, 404
Turkish, 163, 170, 218, 222, 223, 228,
    392
Tylor, E. B., 100, 124

U.S. *See* United States of America
Ukraine, 109
unbiased transmission. *See* transmission:
    unbiased
uncles/aunts, 110
United States of America, 1, 11, 84, 109,
    143, 186, 189, 198, 261, 271, 292, 298,
    331
Universal Grammar, 58, 64, 65
universalism values, 217, 218, 231, 241, 251,
    253, 259, 376, 386
Uslucan, H.-H., 6, 389, 391, 392, 404, 413, 416,
    417, 472
Utrecht Study on Adolescent Development
    (USAD), 429

Valsiner, J., 51, 69, 135, 152, 158, 160, 340,
    368
value acceptance, 276, 277
value congruence, 240, 241
    parent–child, 261, 271, 275

value discrepancy, 151
value of children (VOC), 144, 146
value orientations. *See* values
values, 3, 5, 9, 14, 15, 16, 18, 22, 26, 70, 71, 77,
    84, 100, 102, 104, 109, 113, 140, 148, 166,
    185, 195, 213, 215, 231, 267, 291, 301,
    304, 308, 310, 323, 338, 341, 342, 359,
    361, 370, 373, 392, 421, 438, 442,
    464
  acceptance of, 148, 254, 257, 284
  accurate perception of, 148, 253, 255
  adolescent, 244, 249
  basic, 140
  collectivistic, 147, 213, 217, 218, 219, 223,
    226, 387
  collectivistic, transmission of, 222
  continuity of, 133
  cultural, 143
  definition of, 269, 327, 339
  family, 318, 329, 330
  generalized, 328
  individualistic, 147, 151, 213, 217, 218, 223,
    236, 341, 343, 387
  of children, 261
  moral, 332
  parental, 131, 133, 147, 242, 243, 244,
    247, 260, 271, 275, 277, 280, 281, 292,
    340
  postmaterialism, 421
  socialization of, 269
  transmission of, 213, 218, 236
values, Schwartz, 244, 253
values, societal, 426
van Geert, P., 2, 3, 48, 51, 54, 69
van Ijzendoorn, M. H., 24, 215, 239, 472,
    477
Vermulst, A. A., 21, 30
victim career, 412
victimization, 403, 413
  higher risk of, 412
victims
  of domestic violence, 406

Vietnamese, 188, 194
violence, 394
  domestic, 409
  in adulthood, 397
  in childhood, 391, 393
  transmission of, 397
  transmission rate of, 409
violence acceptance, 413
violent act, 413
Völkerpsychologie, 138
Vollebergh, W. A. M., 301, 313, 419, 421, 423,
    424, 425, 429, 433, 440
Vygotsky, L. S., 38, 47, 51, 69, 138, 160

Wandervogel, 420
Weismann, A., 10
well-being, 291
  subjective, 276
Whiten, A., 35, 47
Whiting, B. B., 136
Whiting, J. W., 136
Wilson, E. O., 15, 28, 75, 465, 476
working model, 340, 397, 398, 469, 472, 473

xenophobia, 213, 236, 371, 376, 379, 443
  definition of, 373
  in adolescence, 381
  transmission of, 380

youth
  German, 421
youth centrism, 6, 426, 427, 430, 431, 433, 435
  definition of, 421, 424
youth culture, 420, 422, 426, 427

zeitgeist, 4, 7, 26, 70, 384, 442, 445, 447, 449,
    451, 452, 455
  and culture, 454
  definition of, 454
  operationalization of, 449
Zinnecker, J., 425, 437, 440
Zucker, L. G., 12

For EU product safety concerns, contact us at Calle de José Abascal, 56–1°,
28003 Madrid, Spain or eugpsr@cambridge.org.

www.ingramcontent.com/pod-product-compliance
Ingram Content Group UK Ltd.
Pitfield, Milton Keynes, MK11 3LW, UK
UKHW040411060825
461487UK00006B/463